ANNUAL REVIEW OF SOCIOLOGY

ANNUAL REVIEW
OF SOCIOLOGY

VOLUME 27, 2001

KAREN S. COOK, *Co-Editor*
Dake University

JOHN HAGAN, *Co-Editor*
Northwestern University

www.AnnualReviews.org   science@AnnualReviews.org   650-493-4400

ANNUAL REVIEWS
4139 El Camino Way • P.O. BOX 10139 • Palo Alto, California 94303-0139

ANNUAL REVIEWS
Palo Alto, California, USA

International Standard Serial Number: 0360-0572
International Standard Book Number: 0-8243-2227-4
Library of Congress Catalog Card Number: 75-648500

Typeset by TechBooks, Fairfax, VA
Printed and Bound in the United States of America

 *Annual Review of Sociology*
Volume 27, 2001

CONTENTS

ERRATA
An online log of corrections to *Annual Review of Sociology* chapters (if any have yet been occasioned, 1997 to the present) may be found at http://soc.AnnualReviews.org/errata.shtml.

Related Articles

Annu. Rev. Sociol. 2001. 27:1–22

VIOLENCE AND THE LIFE COURSE:
The Consequences of Victimization for Personal and Social Development

Ross Macmillan

Department of Sociology, University of Minnesota, 909 Social Sciences, 267 19th Ave S, Minneapolis, Minnesota 55455-0412; e-mail: macmilla@atlas.socsci.umn.edu

Key Words   development, crime, psychological well-being, education, status attainment

■ **Abstract**   Considerable research documents the consequences of criminal violence for victims. At the same time, a strong relationship exists between age and risk of violent victimization; risk is greatest in childhood and adolescence. This article joins these two issues by examining the implications of violent victimization for personal and social development. The discussion is divided into three sections. The first section situates violent victimization in the life course by examining age-differentiation in victimization risk. With high risk during adolescence, victimization is most likely to occur during a period of the life course in which a variety of life course trajectories are formed. The second section reviews research on the implications of victimization for life course development with respect to psychological distress and well-being, involvement in crime and deviance, and educational and socioeconomic attainment. Finally, the third section proposes a theoretical framework for understanding the myriad life course consequences of victimization and suggests directions for future research. In examining the role of violence in shaping individual life courses, this article links criminological and sociological inquiry to further understandings of the social factors that influence individual development.

INTRODUCTION

Researchers who study development and the life course often focus on the dark side of human relations. Macro-level conditions such as wars, recessions, and depressions, as well as more personal experiences such as divorce, unemployment, poverty, and dislocation have all been central aspects of life course inquiry. The objective of this work is to understand the role that such experiences play in shaping life fortunes. By linking together distinct events, experiences, and behaviors, researchers can map out developmental pathways from childhood to old age (Clausen 1991, Elder 1998, Rutter 1989). Issues of continuity and change are central as research seeks to identify links between disparate phenomena over the

0360-0572/01/0811-0001$14.00

life course and thus to describe the social processes that both produce and alter developmental trajectories. Such links are keys to understanding the continuity of status, experience, and behavior, as well as life course changes that produce new, perhaps unanticipated states and circumstances. Importantly, this concern with developmental processes encompasses a wide range of life outcomes, both conventional and deviant (Robins & Rutter 1990).

One of the more prominent themes in life course research is the identification of factors that put one at risk for adversity in later life. Studies of poverty and joblessness, for example, often focus on childhood and adolescent factors that inhibit the generation of human capital necessary for socioeconomic success (Duncan et al 1998, Caspi et al 1998). Likewise, research on psychological well-being pays close attention to the exposure to stress and trauma in early life that activate long-term trajectories of mental distress (Cherlin et al 1998, Turner et al 1995). Further work on interpersonal relationships, including dating, marriage, and child-rearing, also demonstrates the importance of early life for understanding relationship failure and parenting problems (Diekmann & Engelhardt 1999, Straus & Smith 1990). In all of this work, behaviors, experiences, and circumstances in early life have a profound impact on quality of life in later adulthood.

Research on criminal violence also emphasizes the issue of quality of life. In particular, considerable research documents the many costs and consequences of victimization. For some, this involves estimating the costs of crime in terms of loss of property, hospital bills, and lost wages (Cohen et al 1994). For others, it also involves a concern with the harm that crime and violence cause through injury and mental distress (Moore et al 1994). Finally, research often considers criminological outcomes, such as fear of crime and behavioral adaptations designed to reduce future risks (Skogan & Maxfield 1981). Importantly, this work shows crime and violence to be a detrimental experience, both personally and socially.

While both life course studies and research on the consequences of criminal violence are important areas of social science inquiry, there have been few attempts to integrate their tenets toward a developmental theory of victimization (Finkelhor 1995). Yet, two empirical facts suggest the importance of victimization in the life course. First, violent victimization is strongly concentrated early in the life cycle (Finkelhor 1997, Hindelang 1976, Laub 1997). Second, victimization, at least in the short term, has profound psychological consequences (Freedy et al 1994, Lurigio 1987, Norris et al 1997, Otis & Skinner, Resick 1987, Resick et al 1993). As salient events that occur during pivotal stages of the life course play a significant role in shaping life course trajectories (Elder 1994), violent victimization should have important implications for personal and social development.

To further understanding of experiences that shape life course fortunes and increase the likelihood of adversity in later life and as well our understanding of the costs and consequences of violence, this review examines violence and its consequences within a life course context. First, it reviews theory and research on victimization risk, paying particular attention to the age structure of violent victimization. Second, it considers research on the consequences of victimization for personal and social development. Three key areas of the life course are highlighted: psychological well-being, involvement in crime and deviance, and educational and socioeconomic attainment. After articulating the developmental consequences of violent victimization, the third section outlines a general theory of the life course consequences of victimization.

Victimization Risk over the Life Course

While life course research involves many different aspects, issues of age and aging occupy a prominent position (Elder 1998, 1994). Life course research is explicitly concerned with developmental issues and therefore focuses on the longitudinal or temporal progression of people's lives. In understanding life course progress, age is thus important in determining the types of experiences people have because it influences the normative environments, social institutions, and social networks to which they are exposed.

Life course concerns with environments, institutions, and networks have parallels with contemporary theories of victimization risk. Such theories typically begin from the common sense notion that people are differentially exposed to violence by virtue of their social location, their geographic or ecological circumstances, and their own actions. In an early statement, Hindelang and colleagues (1978) explained differences in victimization risk in terms of *lifestyle exposure*. From this perspective, sociodemographic characteristics give rise to lifestyle differences that manifest themselves in the types of activities engaged in, the time in which these activities occur, and the places where these activities occur. Individuals who spend more of their time in public spaces, particularly at night and amid strangers, have greater exposure to potential offenders and consequently are at greater risk of victimization.

Extensions of Hindelang and colleagues work led to *opportunity perspectives* on victimization risk (Cohen et al 1981, Meithe & Meier 1990). In particular, Cohen and colleagues (1981) argued that probability of victimization is influenced by four factors: exposure to potential offenders, proximity to potential offenders, guardianship against victimization, and attractiveness as a target. Exposure is often conceptualized as the degree to which one's activities influence contact with potential offenders. Proximity refers to the physical distance between the locus of one's activities (i.e., one's home or work) and pools of potential offenders. In the context of violence, guardianship and attractiveness typically refer to the particular actions of victims that limit their ability to defend against an attacker (i.e., alcohol and drug use) or increase their suitability for victimization (i.e., aggression against a potential attacker). Research in this tradition has focused on social differentiation (Cohen et al 1981, Miethe et al 1987), ecological dimensions of risk (Kennedy & Forde 1990, Sampson & Wooldredge 1987), and the role of both normative (Miethe & Meier 1990) and deviant behaviors (Sampson & Lauritsen 1990). This work provides the starting point for understanding the life course consequences of violent victimization by suggesting age as a key determinant of victimization risk.

Age and Victimization Risk

Social scientists have long recognized the importance of age for criminal activity. Data from the United States and other industrialized countries indicate that involvement in property and violent crime rise rapidly in adolescence, peak between the ages of 16 and 19, and then decline precipitously through the remainder of the life course (Hirschi & Gottfredson 1983). While researchers disagree as to theoretical implications, age differences in offending are shown in official statistics (Federal Bureau of Investigation 1998), self-report surveys (Rowe & Tittle 1977), and victimization surveys (Hindelang 1981).

From an opportunity perspective, robust age differences in offending should translate into significant age differences in victimization. As social activities in most societies are structured by age, younger people are more exposed to potential offenders, are more likely to live proximate to potential offenders, and are more likely to engage in activities that make them more suitable targets for victimization. Data from a wide array of sources indicate that violent victimization is strongly concentrated in the early life course.

A systematic link between age and victimization risk was first articulated in Hindelang's (1976) study of criminal victimization in eight American cities. Examining personal crime, rates of victimization increased from 87 per 1,000 people for respondents 12 to 15 years of age to 114 per 1,000 for persons 16 to 19 years of age and then declined with increasing age. By age 65, risk of personal victimization was only 29 per 1,000 persons, one fourth that of adolescents.

Recent data from the National Crime Victimization Survey show an even stronger relationship between age and violent victimization (Bureau of Justice Statistics 1999a: Table 3.4). For all crimes of violence in 1998, rates of victimization increased from 87.9 per 1,000 for adolescents 12 to 15 years of age to 96.2 for those 16 to 19 years of age, and then declined precipitously with advancing age. By age 65, the rate was 4.4 per 1,000 or one twentieth the rate for adolescents. When these data are disaggregated by offense type, all show a similar relationship with age. Robbery and sexual assault victimization were 10 times more likely in adolescence than in old age, while assault was 23 times more likely. From its inception in the early 1970s, data from the NCVS shows that risk of victimization peaks in late adolescence, remains relatively high in early adulthood, and then declines rapidly and consistently with advancing age (Bureau of Justice Statistics 1975, Bureau of Justice Statistics 1985, Bureau of Justice Statistics 1999b). Data from other nations show similar age-differentiation in victimization risk (Mirrlees-Black et al 1998, Sacco & Johnson 1990, van Dijk et al 1990).

Although the NCVS data and other national crime surveys show a strong pattern of age differentiation in violent victimization, specific studies of juvenile victimization suggest even greater prevalence. For example, Wells & Rankin's (1995) assessment of juvenile victimization in the National Youth Survey and the Monitoring the Future Survey showed that approximately 25% of adolescents experienced some form of violence. Boney-McCoy and Finkelhor's (1995) national survey of children between the ages of 10 and 16 found even higher rates of victimization. Examining prevalence for 9 types of violence, ranging in severity from simple assaults to attempted kidnappings and contact sexual assault and encompassing both familial and nonfamilial incidents, some 47 percent of males and 33 percent of females reported some form of violent victimization. Almost half of these reported multiple incidents.

As a final comment on the age structure of victimization risk, we consider the issue of family violence against children. While national crime surveys and their counterparts concerning adolescents typically yield poor accounts of within-family victimization (Skogan 1990), studies of violence among family members suggest a similar pattern of risk. While a full review of research on intra-family violence is beyond the scope of this article, a few points merit note. First, rates of violence between siblings are comparatively very high. Data from the 1975 National Family Violence Survey show that 80% of children report some form of sibling violence and almost half report severe forms (Straus & Gelles 1990). Second, data from the 1985 National Family Violence Survey indicates that almost half of all children experienced some form of physical punishment, while just over 2% experienced physical abuse (Straus & Gelles 1990). Finally, rates of parent-to-child violence are almost four times greater than rates of violence between spouses (Straus & Gelles 1990). Finkelhor (1997) suggests that the dependency relationship of children and adolescents make them uniquely vulnerable to violence from family members. They have comparatively little choice regarding whom they associate with, and they have the least access to resources that could allow them to negotiate changes in their treatment or change in their living circumstances.

Thus, data from a wide array of sources indicate that violent victimization is strongly concentrated in the early life course. Whether focusing on victimization within family or violence from strangers, children and adolescents have considerable risk of victimization. With victimization most prevalent early in the life course, it is most often experienced during the key stages of development and thus has the potential to influence developmental pathways and shape the character and content of later life.

The Personal and Social Consequences of Violence

As age influences the experiences that people have, it also shapes the consequences of these experiences for later life (Elder 1994). Experiences interact with stages of the life cycle to give them particular meaning and significance. Elder's (1974) classic study of children of the Great Depression, for example, showed that the age at which children experienced the depression had important implications for its long-term consequences. Likewise, Uggen's (2000) study of the effects of job creation programs on desistance from crime showed that employment was only effective in preventing crime among older offenders for whom work would be more salient. Such research demonstrates the important conditioning effects of age as the life course consequences of various events and behaviors are shaped by the life cycle stage in which they occur.

Against this backdrop, the age-structure of violent victimization has important implications for the life course. Violence is most common during the early life cycle, typically occurs before or during the transition to adulthood. While all stages of the life cycle are significant, the early life course is particularly important. Childhood and adolescence are the periods in which the personal and psychological resources that guide cognition and decision-making are developed (Caspi 1987, Clausen 1991, Elder 1994). It is also the period in which individuals accumulate the various "capitals," human, social, and cultural, that shape the content of later lives (Hagan 1998). Violence occurring during this critical period should have important developmental implications. Violence at other stages may ultimately have few life course consequences.

To examine this issue, this section focuses on the consequences of violent victimization in early life for personal and social development. Evidence of such consequences comes from a number of sources that made use of different research designs, and focused on a wide range of life domains and experience. Importantly, this work documents the personal and social consequences of victimization with respect to three key areas of child and adolescent development: mental health and psychological distress, involvement in crime and deviance, and educational and socioeconomic attainment.

MENTAL HEALTH AND PSYCHOLOGICAL DISTRESS   Life course research on mental health provides an important framework for identifying links between early experiences of violence and psychological distress in later life. This research shows that there are important continuities in psychological disorders from childhood, through adolescence, to adulthood (Harrington et al 1991, Kandel & Davies 1986). It also shows that much distress stems from the experience of stressful life events or traumas (Thoits 1983). As a consequence, research on psychological well-being attempts to identify events and experiences early in the life course that put people at risk for continuous or repetitive distress over the life course (Coyne & Downey 1991). Violent victimization is one such experience that influences psychological well-being over the life course.

The implications of victimization for psychological development begin by acknowledging the short-term consequences of victimization. Numerous studies document the prevalence of post-victimization distress (Freedy et al 1994, Lurigio 1987, Norris et al 1997, Otis & Skinner, Resick 1987, Resick et al 1993). Specific studies of children and adolescents reveal similar consequences. Victims of physical and sexual abuse before adolescence have increased prevalence of anxiety, depression, and post-traumatic stress disorder (PTSD) symptomology (Hjorth & Ostrov 1982, McLeer et al 1988, White et al 1988, Wolfe & Mosk 1983). Consistent with this, Boney-McCoy and Finkelhor (1995) found that victims of nonfamilial violence have higher risk of PTSD symptoms and were more likely to report feelings of sadness. Martinez & Richters' (1993) interviews with children and adolescents living in high crime neighborhoods also found that children victimized by violence showed significantly greater distress symptoms, while Bagley and colleagues (1997) found that sexual assault increased risk of emotional disorders among adolescent women.

With significant continuities in psychological well-being over the life course, it is not surprising that violence has long-term consequences on mental health. Research on abused children, in particular, shows higher rates of psychological distress in adulthood (Briere & Runtz 1988, Chu & Dill 1990, Kessler & Magee 1994). Bryer et al's (1987) study of female psychiatric inpatients, for example, found that victims of child abuse had both higher rates and more severe forms of mental distress, while Kessler & Magee (1994) found that childhood family victimization was associated with significantly higher rates of adult recurrence of depression.

Studies of nonfamilial violence also suggest long-term psychological consequences. Data from the Los Angeles Epidemiologic Catchment Area indicated that victims of sexual assault in childhood and adolescence were much more likely to suffer from depression, alcohol or drug dependence, or phobic disorders (Burnam et al 1988). Likewise, Kilpatrick et al's (1987) interviews with adult females found significant associations between victimization in early life and current PTSD symptoms. Duncan et al (1996) further found that physical assault in childhood dramatically increased the odds of current major depressive episodes and current PTSD symptoms, while the Arboleda-Flores & Wade (1999) examination of Canadian data found that childhood victimization doubled the odds of having a major depressive episode in adulthood. While these retrospective analyses are consistent in showing significant effects of victimization on psychological distress over the life course, a recent prospective study found few long-term effects (S Menard, forthcoming).

Thus, considerable research indicates that early experiences of violence influence long-term trajectories of psychological well-being. Research on violent victimization among children indicates considerable psychological distress. Research on abused and neglected children and research on female victims of rape indicate both short-term consequences and continued evidence of distress in later life, while retrospective analyses, particularly those involving female rape victims and victims of other serious violence, show significant long-term consequences. Overall, violent victimization in early life seems an important precursor to long-term or recurring psychological distress over the life course.

INVOLVEMENT IN CRIME AND DEVIANCE   In addition to studying psychological distress, research on child and adolescent development often focuses on involvement in crime and deviance. Whether in the context of juvenile delinquency (Thornberry 1997) or crime over the life course (Sampson & Laub 1993), research documents important continuities in offending. Offending tends to begin early in the life course; adult offenders have histories of juvenile delinquency and even patterns of misbehaving in early childhood (Sampson & Laub 1993, White et al 1990).

Moreover, longitudinal research shows that early onset of offending is associated with longer and more involved criminal careers (Wolfgang et al 1972). Such findings have encouraged research to identify factors that put people at risk for early involvement in crime and deviance. The role of violent victimization has been central to such inquiries (Widom 1989).

Research on links between early victimization and later involvement in crime and deviance has typically focused on the cycle-of-violence thesis. This thesis predicts that victims of violence in early life, usually victims of child abuse, will have greater involvement in crime and violence in later life (Lewis 1992, Widom 1989). Other work suggests connections between victimization and offending beyond the family, arguing that victimization, in general, plays an important role in the learning of definitions favorable to crime (Fagan et al 1987) or by suggesting that a subculture of violence can develop from victimization (Black 1983, Singer 1986).

Considerable research shows victimization to be a precursor to involvement in crime and deviance. Studies of abused children provide much of the initial evidence of the criminogenic consequences of victimization. For example, adolescents in both correctional (Lewis et al 1979, Sendi & Blomgren 1975) and mental health (Cavaiola & Schiff 1988, Kent 1976, Tartar et al 1984) facilities tend to have high rates of physical abuse. Consistent with this, Rivera & Widom (1990) further found that abused children had earlier involvement in violence. Other studies indicate that physical abuse in childhood increases dating violence in adolescence (Reuterman & Burcky 1989, Roscoe & Callahan 1985).

Further research indicates that nonviolent offending and substance use are also associated with child abuse. Cavaiola & Schiff's (1988) study of adolescents in a residential treatment facility found that victims of abuse had more legal problems, were more likely to act out sexually, more likely to run away, and even more likely to be involved in accidents (see also McCord 1983). More recently, Hagan & McCarthy's (1997) study of street kids in Toronto and Vancouver revealed that physical and sexual abuse were key precursors to widespread involvement in both violent and nonviolent crime, including prostitution, theft, and drug use.

While the volume of work is somewhat smaller, violence outside the family also appears to precipitate involvement in crime and deviance. Fagan et al's study (1987) of a sample of inner-city adolescents from six American cities found that violent victimization was associated with more serious involvement in crime. Lauritsen and colleagues (1991) further found that victimization influenced "delinquent lifestyles" in a sample of American adolescents. Interestingly, their measure of delinquent lifestyles included both self-report offending for a wide range of activities and measures of peer involvement in offending. Victimization thus may influence not only personal involvement in crime and deviance but also associations with delinquent peers. This is consistent with research showing that gang involvement and other delinquent associations are often responses to perceived threat of crime and violence (Hagedorn 1988).

Research on more long-term links between early victimization and adult involvement in crime and deviance also suggest important developmental consequences. Again, much of this work focuses on victims of child abuse. Widom (1989), for example, analyzed the arrest histories of adults who were victims of child abuse and a matched control group and found that victims were twice as likely to have an arrest for a violent offense. Numerous other studies indicate that abused children are more likely to be involved in physical (Briere & Runtz 1988, Kalmuss 1984, McCord 1983, Pollock et al 1990, Riggs et al 1990) and sexual violence (Groth 1979, Seghorn et al 1987, Widom & Ashley-Ames 1994) in adulthood. Family victimization also influences involvement in nonviolent offending and substance use. Studies of prostitution, particularly among females (Lake 1993, Maher & Curtis 1992, Richie 1996, Simons & Whitbeck 1991, Widom & Ashley-Ames 1994), property and driving offenses (Pollock et al 1990), and alcoholism and drug use (Brown & Anderson 1991, Kroll et al 1985) all show that victimization is an important precursor.

As a final issue, there also appear links between nonfamilial victimization in early life and offending in later adulthood. Two studies are of particular note. Singer (1986) used data from a 10% sample of the 1945 Philadelphia birth cohort and found that victims of violence in adolescence were more likely to be arrested in adulthood and were more likely to be involved in more serious offending. Consistent with this, S Menard (forthcoming) examined the effects of victimization on violent, property, and drug offenses in later adulthood and found wide ranging consequences. Controlling for earlier involvement and a host of sociodemographic characteristics, adolescent victimization almost tripled the odds of both violent and property offending in adulthood, doubled the odds of domestic violence, and increased the odds of problem drug use by almost 90%.

Overall, research indicates important effects of early victimization on trajectories of offending over the life course. Studies of both victims of child abuse and victims of nonfamilial violence indicate greater involvement in offending in both adolescence and adulthood. While early work anticipated such findings for violent offending, victimization has wide-ranging effects, influencing involvement in violence, property offending, and substance use. Victimization appears an important precursor to the development of long-term patterns of offending over the life course.

EDUCATIONAL AND SOCIOECONOMIC ATTAINMENTS   A third important area of child and adolescent development is educational and socioeconomic attainment. Educational and socioeconomic attainment are typically viewed as a developmental or life course process (Elder 1982). This process begins with the intergenerational transmission of aspirations and expectations and the cultivation of human, cultural, and social capital in early life that ultimately result in educational attainment, occupational status, and income indicative of socioeconomic standing (Sewell & Hauser 1975). In the context of this process, researchers are often interested in identifying salient life events that alter socioeconomic trajectories and produce continuity and discontinuity in attainment over time and across generations (see for example, Sampson & Laub 1996). Against this backdrop, early victimization has important implications for trajectories of educational and socioeconomic attainment.

Initial evidence of the educational and socioeconomic consequences of violent victimization also comes from studies of abused children. Sadeh et al (1994), for example, examined a sample of children between the ages of two and fourteen who had been admitted to a psychiatric unit and found that sexually abused children had lower IQ scores (see also Rogeness et al 1986). Further research shows that abused children have poorer school achievement (Kent, 1976, Rogeness et al 1986, Salzinger et al 1984, Tartar et al 1984, Wolfe & Mosk, 1983). Straus & Gelles (1990: Figure 24.4), for example, found that abused children were almost three times as likely to have failing grades in school.

Consistent with this, Eckenrode et al's examination (1993) of a matched sample of maltreated and nonmaltreated children in kindergarten to grade 12 found that maltreated children performed significantly worse on standardized tests, had lower grades, and were more likely to have repeated a grade. Also using a matched sample design, Perez & Widom's (1994) multivariate analyses revealed even longer-term consequences. Victims of abuse had lower IQ's, lower reading ability, lower intellectual ability, and lower educational attainment in adulthood. Victims were also more likely to have repeated a grade, more likely to be truant, more likely to have been expelled, and less likely to have graduated from highschool. One explanation for these findings may be that victims of abuse are less oriented to future educational and vocational goals (Hjorth & Ostrov 1982). While no research explicitly assesses the issue, the key role of education in the process of socioeconomic attainment suggests that the educational deficits stemming from child abuse likely translated into considerable socioeconomic disadvantage in later life.

Research on the educational and socioeconomic consequences of non-familial victimization demonstrates even more widespread effects. Macmillan (2000) used data from a national probability sample of American adolescents tracked into early adulthood to examine the educational and socioeconomic consequences of violent victimization in adolescence. These data showed that victimization initially undermined educational aspirations and effort. Both directly and through diminished educational investments, victimization had further negative effects on grade point average (see also Boney-McCoy & Finkelhor 1995).

From diminished educational performance, victimization had further implications for educational and occupational attainment (Macmillan 2000). Adolescent victims had lower overall educational attainment and lower occupational status in early adulthood. Finally, through lower educational and occupational attainment, adolescent victimization ultimately undermined income realization in early adulthood. Adolescent victims earned on average 14% less per hour than similarly situated nonvictims. Similar educational and socioeconomic consequences were also seen in data from a national sample of Canadians (Macmillan 2000). In these latter data, victims of violence in adolescence had annual incomes that were almost $6000 lower than those not victimized. Consistent with a sociogenic model, educational and occupational attainment substantially mediated the effects of adolescent victimization in both the Canadian and US data. Hence, research on both family and nonfamily victimization indicate wide-ranging educational and socioeconomic consequences.

Understanding the Life Course Consequences of Violent Victimization

A wide array of studies indicates the significant life course consequences of violent victimization. These include studies of the short- and long-term consequences of child physical and sexual abuse and studies of peer and stranger victimization. Importantly, this research draws upon data from a wide array of samples, makes use of different research designs, and considers life course outcomes across a number of domains and measures. In all this work, violence appears as a salient and powerful life experience that shapes developmental pathways and influences the character and content of later life.

While the evidence of such consequences is fairly clear, this work is largely empirical and fails to fully explore the life course context of violent victimization. In particular, comparatively little work explains *why* victimization has long-term consequences. This is particularly the case in studies of the effects of victimization on processes of educational and socioeconomic attainment. Moreover, where theories are proposed, they are typically organized around specific outcomes. Research on the psychological consequences of victimization typically focus on the idea of victimization as stressful life event. In contrast, research on the impact of victimization on involvement in crime and deviance typically adopt a learning model in which victimization promotes definitions and values favorable to offending. Missing from such work is a general model that would account for the myriad consequences of victimization and explain the role of victimization in life course development. Towards this end, this final section proposes a sociogenic model of the consequences of victimization.

Understanding the developmental consequences of victimization begins by identifying the meaning of experiences of victimization, particularly violent victimization. Victimization inherently implies a power relationship in which one party dominates another (Hagan 1989). Violent victimizations are interactions in which some people were simply unable to prevent themselves from being attacked, raped, or robbed. As a consequence, victimization has implications for an individual's sense of agency, self-efficacy, and perceptions of others in the social world.

Developing this understanding of victimization, Fischer (1984) conducted interviews with 50 crime victims to understand what it was like to be criminally victimized. She concluded that victimization challenges individual assumptions and perceptions about self and society. It represents a disruption of daily routine that calls into question issues of safety, freedom, sanctity, and future. It compels one to reassess their ability to act purposefully and shape one's destiny and alters one's sense of others in society by transforming others from potential resources to potential threats.

From this perspective, victimization undermines two basic sets of beliefs. First, it undermines individual perceptions of agency and self-efficacy. There are various arguments for why victimization undermines perceptions of agency and self-efficacy. For some, it stems from the loss of control over life course events (Burgess & Holstrom 1979, Frieze et al 1987). Others emphasize the diminished belief in personal invulnerability to harm that may follow from victimization (Bard & Sangrey 1979, Frieze et al 1987, Janoff-Bulman & Frieze 1983, LeJeune & Alex 1973). Still others suggest the victimization activates negative self-images as victims see themselves a weak or helpless (Janoff-Bulman & Frieze 1983, McCann et al 1988, Peterson & Seligman 1983) or as somehow deviant and deserving of their experience (Frieze et al 1987). Regardless of the specific psychological basis of the attribution, victimization has the potential to undermine individual perceptions of self as purposive and effective agents, as individuals who are able to determine future life experiences.

In addition to an undermined sense of self, victimization also changes one's perceptions of and beliefs about others in society. It does so by indicating others as sources of threat or harm rather than sources of support. Several studies of crime victims emphasize altered conceptions of community, society and others. Bard & Sangrey (1979), for example, argued that victimization undermines an individual sense of trust (see also McCann et al 1988). Janoff-Bulman & Frieze (1983, see also Frieze et al 1987) similarly suggest that victimization challenges perceptions of the world as meaningful and bound together by a shared sense of social order. As crime victimization represents a deliberate violation of self by another, it highlights the predatory potential of others. Ultimately, as victimization erodes cognitive ties to others, it has the potential to alter the way in which one interacts with others and makes use of them in the pursuit of individual goals.

This description of the phenomenology of victimization is a foundation for understanding the influence of victimization on life course development. Perceptions of agency and self-efficacy are key determinants of child and adolescent development (Gecas 1989). The degree to which individuals envision future states, plan courses of action, and invest themselves, psychologically and socially, in processes to achieve desired goals give life courses their distinctive shapes and forms (Clausen 1991, Elder 1994). Furthermore, child and adolescent development is shaped by the social relationships that one has. Elder (1994) uses the term "linked lives" to refer to both the positive and negative experiences that result from the character and quantity of social connections that people have. With the importance of perceptions of both agency and social relations, the negative effects of violent victimization on self-efficacy, trust, and social interactions should have wide-ranging developmental consequences.

In keeping with this, a theory of the developmental consequences of victimization must situate victimization within a life course context. This involves simultaneous attention to both the precursors of victimization, its implications for individual beliefs and actions, and its short-term and long-term consequences. Research on the precursors of victimization clearly highlights important effects of structural factors, including class, gender, and race, ecological context, and behavior on exposure to violence. In particular, young minority males, either from lower-class families or living in low-income, disadvantaged urban neighborhoods have dramatically higher risk of victimization (Sampson & Lauritsen 1994). Involvement in crime and deviance further increase exposure to violence (Jensen & Brownfield 1986, Lauritsen et al 1991, Sampson & Lauritsen 1990). As victimization risk is not distributed evenly across social groups, it is important to incorporate factors that influence differential exposure to violence. This would further illuminate the social structure surrounding the life course consequences of victimization and also reduce the possibility that victimization effects are spurious due to the presence of some unmeasured factor.

While focusing on the precursors of victimization, understanding the developmental consequences of victimization requires further study of the immediate psychological consequences of victimization. The implications of victimization for perceptions of agency and trust are well established (Fischer 1983, Janoff-Bulman & Frieze 1983, LeJeune & Alex 1973, McCann et al 1988). Yet, a theory of the life course consequences of victimization should link these short-term psychological consequences to the attitudes, beliefs, aspirations, expectations, and actions that ultimately shape life course trajectories. As previous work has focused more on documenting developmental outcomes, there is surprisingly little work incorporating the social psychological dimensions of victimization in explanations of the life course consequences of victimization. Fully understanding the life course implications of victimization requires a consideration of the immediate psychological consequences of victimization, its implications for perceptions of self, agency, efficacy, and trust, and how these influence the attitudes, beliefs, and actions that shape later life.

Understanding the life course consequences of victimization also requires consideration of a broad array of developmental outcomes. Contemporary research has been organized around a relatively narrow range of issues. Criminologists have typically studied either short-term consequences such as fear of crime, reporting behavior, and behavioral adaptations or the offending behaviors of abused and neglected children (for example, Lurigio 1987, Skogan 1987, Widom 1989). Psychologists, on the other hand, have concentrated largely on postvictimization distress and links between victimization and long-term psychological well-being (for example, Freedy et al 1994, Lurigio 1987, Norris et al 1997, Otis & Skinner, Resick 1987, Resick et al 1993). Missing from such work is a concern with the more social aspects of development that have been the cornerstone of sociological research. As agentic orientations exert profound effects on a wide range of social processes (Clausen 1991), the negative effects of victimization on such orientations should influence a wide array of life course trajectories that have not been considered in prior work. In addition to a continued focus on psychological well-being, involvement in crime and deviance, and educational and socioeconomic attainment over the life course, theory and research should also focus on the formation of ties to peers and family, the development of intimate relationships through dating, marriage, and child rearing. A consideration of such outcomes would broaden our understanding of how victimization shapes life fortunes.

As a final issue, understanding victimization in the life course also requires a consideration of contingencies in the consequences of victimization. There has been little attention to structural, psychological, experiential, and behavioral factors that may exacerbate or ameliorate the negative consequences of victimization. Two avenues of inquiry seem particularly important. While we recognize the propensity for victimization to afflict those already disadvantaged in society (Sampson & Lauritsen 1994), we know little about whether structural location, be it gender, race, or class, conditions the effects of victimization on child and adolescent development. From one perspective, the negative consequences of victimization may be compounded by the same disadvantage that makes it more likely to be experienced. Thus, social advantage may buffer the long-term costs of criminal violence. On the other hand, victimization may actually be less important to the life course adversity of disadvantaged groups because limited life chances may be more firmly established. From this perspective, victimization may be a turning point in the lives of advantaged children.

Related to this, the presence of psychological and social resources may also buffer the immediate psychological consequences. In one respect, this could involve the intimate networks that already surround victims. Research suggests that families are an important source of social capital and resilience for children (Furstenberg et al 1999, Hagan et al 1996) and may thus offset the developmental consequences of victimization. Additionally, victim services might also concentrate on children and adolescents and attempt to restore the sense of agency and trust that victimization undermines. While victim services are currently not organized in this manner (Elias 1986), a simple redirection of resources may go a long way to preventing the developmental deficits that victimization appears to produce. Fully understanding the life course consequences of victimization necessitates more consideration of factors that may condition the life course consequences of victimization.

CONCLUSIONS

Synthesizing contemporary work on both risk factors and consequences of violent victimization, this chapter examines the life course structure of violent victimization. Understanding this structure begins with two empirical facts. First, risk of violent victimization is age-graded with greatest risk occurring typically before the transition to adulthood. Second, violent victimization is an experience that undermines perceptions of individual agency, disrupts social networks, and increases negative ideation. As violence occurs during a key formative stage of the life course and undermines social and psychological orientations, it plays an important role in shaping life course trajectories. In research on victimization both within and beyond the family, victimization has profound effects on child and adolescent development and has consequences that extend deep into the life course. Early victimization increases psychological distress, both producing postvictimization distress and increasing the likelihood of recurring distress throughout adulthood. It also increases risks of long-term involvement in crime and deviance and undermines processes of educational achievement and socioeconomic attainment. Menard (forthcoming) provides a useful summary of the developmental consequences of adolescent victimization: Victimization undermines stable transitions to adulthood with effects on employment, normative beliefs, relational stability and support, and involvement in crime and deviance.

Recognition of the life course consequences of victimization has important implications for both sociological research on the life course and criminological research on the consequences of violence. First, the delineation of the life course consequences adds to emerging work on interconnections between deviance and conformity in life course progress. It does so by furthering our understanding of how exposure to and involvement with crime shapes both normative and deviant life course trajectories (Hagan 1991, Robins & Rutter 1990, Sampson & Laub 1993). Second, this work furthers our understanding of factors that shape the character and content of later life. In particular, it suggests that more ephemeral experiences also shape developmental pathways. Life course research typically focuses on sustained patterns of interaction, such as families and peer groups or on experiences that occur over long periods of time (Elder 1974, Hagan et al 1996, Sampson & Laub 1996). Yet, victimization, particularly when it involves strangers, is typically a rare and somewhat fleeting event. That it still has profound life course consequences suggests that the duration of events is only one consideration; salience and impact are also important. Furthermore, the profound effects of victimization suggest that other short-term experiences may also shape life course development.

Understanding these consequences of victimization has further relevance for two emerging bodies of research. First, there is increasing interest in the role of neighborhood context in child and adolescent development (Sampson et al 1999, Sampson et al 1997). In such work, neighborhood conditions facilitate or inhibit child development by fostering either collective efficacy that enables prosocial development or criminogenic conditions that undermine the ability of families effectively to supervise and socialize their children. A second body of work focuses on more general exposure to violence, both within and beyond the family, and its influence on child and adolescent well-being (Gabarino et al 1992, Rosenthal 2000, Schwab-Stone et al 1999). Importantly, recent work integrates and extends these two traditions by examining the impact of communities on exposure to violence and the negative consequences of such exposure for life course orientations (Swisher 2000). The life course dimiensions of victimization and development articulated in the current chapter add to this emerging field by suggesting further mechanisms by which neighborhoods and crime shape life course fortunes.

Recognition of the life course consequences of victimization also has direct implications for criminological work. Traditional research on the consequences of crime focuses on a relatively narrow range of outcomes over a relatively short period of time (Cohen et al 1994, Moore et al 1994). While such work is important, the recognition of the life course structure of victimization suggests the consequences of crime are considerably broader than previously imagined. It also suggests the need to consider the social processes, the experiential and behavioral links, which produce long-term developmental deficits. While victimization can produce the long-term psychological change that have been the focus of most prior work, it is also important to consider how victimization influences the attitudes, beliefs, and actions that determine the nature of later life. That victimization shapes life course fortunes across a number of realms illuminates the significant and far reaching costs of crime, both personally and socially.

As a final note, recognizing the life course structure of violent victimization further illuminates the problem of violence in society. Yet while much work suggests that the costs of crime are relatively short lived, a consideration of the developmental consequences of violence highlights the profound, long-term deficits that victimization incurs. Furthermore, the tendency of violence to proliferate early in the life cycle and afflict those already at risk for adversity further links violence to broader patterns of inequality that undermine quality of life. Thus, the myriad life course consequences of victimization serve to highlight the necessity and importance of efforts to protect children from violence.

ACKNOWLEDGMENTS

The author would like to thank Annette Nieronbisz and the *ARS* reviewer and editors for commenting on earlier drafts of this chapter. Further thanks to Jeylan Mortimer, Candace Kruttschnitt, Karen Lutfey, Scott Eliason, Chris Uggen, John Hagan, Rosemany Gartner, Scot Wortley, and Vince Sacco for providing invaluable commentary and advice on how to think about life course consequences of victimization.

Visit the Annual Reviews home page at www.AnnualReviews.org

LITERATURE CITED

Arboledal-Flores J, Wade T. 1999. *Childhood and adult victimization as risk factor for major depression.* Presented at Annu. Meet. Am. Psychiatric Assoc., Washington, DC

Bagley C, Bolitho F, Bertrand L. 1997. Sexual assault in school, mental health, and suicidal behaviors in adolescent women in Canada. *Adolescence* 32:341–66

Bard M, Sangrey D. 1979. *The Crime Victim's Book.* New York: Scribners

Black D. 1983. Crime as social control. *Am. Sociol. Rev.* 48:34–45

Boney-McCoy S, Finkelhor D. 1995. Psychosocial sequelae of violent victimization in a national youth sample. *J. Consult. Clin. Psychol.* 63:726–36

Briere J, Runtz M. 1988. Symptomatology associated with childhood sexual victimization in a non-clinical sample. *Child Abuse Neglect* 12:51–59

Brown G, Anderson B. 1991. Psychiatric morbidity in adult inpatients with childhood histories of sexual and physical abuse. *Am. J. Psychiatry* 148:55–61

Bryer J, Nelson B, Miller J, Krol P. 1987. Childhood sexual and physical abuse as factors in adult psychiatric illness. *Am. J. Psychiatry.* 144:1426–30

Bureau of Justice Statistics. 1975. *Sourcebook of Criminal Justice Statistics–1974.* Washington, DC: US Dep. Justice

Bureau of Justice Statistics. 1985. *Sourcebook of Criminal Justice Statistics–1984.* Washington, DC: US Dep. Justice

Bureau of Justice Statistics. 1999a. *Sourcebook of Criminal Justice Statistics–1998.* Washington, DC: US Dep. Justice

Bureau of Justice Statistics. 1999b. *Criminal Victimization 1998: Changes 1997–98 with trends 1993–98.* Washington, DC: US Dep. Justice

Burgess A, Holstrom L. 1979. Rape: sexual disruption and recovery. *Am. J. Orthopsychiatry* 49:658–69

Burnam A, Stein J, Golding J, Siegel J, Sorenson S, Forsythe A, Telles C. et al. 1988. Sexual assault and mental disorders in a community population. *J. Consult. Clin. Psychol.* 56:843–50

Carmen E, Rieker P, Mills T. 1984. Victims of violence and psychiatric illness. *Am. J. Psychiatry* 141:378–83

Caspi A. 1987. Personality in the life course. *J. Personality Soc. Psychol.* 53:1203–13

Caspi A, Wright B, Moffitt T, Silva P. 1998. Early failure in the labor market: childhood and adolescent predictors of unemployment in the transition to adulthood. *Am. Sociol. Rev.* 63:424–51

Cavaiola A, Schiff M. 1988. Behavioral sequelae of physical and/or sexual abuse in adolescents. *Child Abuse Neglect* 12:181–88

Cherlin A, Chase-Lansdale L, McRae C. 1998. Effects of parental divorce on mental health throughout the life course. *Am. Sociol. Rev.* 63:239–249

Chu J, Dill D. 1990. Dissociative symptoms in relation to childhood physical and sexual abuse. *Am. J. Psychiatry* 147:887–92

Clausen J. 1991. Adolescent competence and the shaping of the life course. *Am. J. Sociol.* 96:805–42

Cohen L, Kluegel J, Land K. 1981. Social inequality and predatory criminal victimization: an exposition and test of a formal theory. *Am. Sociol. Rev.* 46:505–24

Cohen M, Miller T, Rossman S. 1994. The costs and consequences of violent behavior in America. In *Understanding and Preventing Violence*, ed. A Reiss, J Roth. Washington, DC: Natl. Acad. Press

Coyne J, Downey G. 1991. Social factors and psychopathology: stress, social support, and coping processes. *Annu. Rev. Psychol.* 42:401–25

Diekmann A, Engelhardt H. 1999. The social inheritance of divorce: effects of parent's family type in postwar Germany. *Am. Sociol. Rev.* 64:783–93

Duncan G, Yeung W, Brooks-Gunn J, Smith J. 1998. How much does childhood poverty affect the life chances of children? *Am. Sociol. Rev.* 63:406–23

Duncan R, Saunders B, Kilpatrick D, Hanson R, Resnick H. 1996. Childhood physical assault as a risk factor for PTSD, depression and substance abuse: findings from a national survey. *Am. J. Orthopsychiatry* 66:437–48

Eckenrode J, Laird M, Doris J. 1993. School performance and disciplinary problems among abused and neglected children. *Dev. Psychol.* 29:53–62

Elder G. 1998. Life course as developmental theory. *Child Dev.* 69:1–12

Elder G. 1994. Time, human agency, and social change: perspectives on the life course. *Soc. Psychol. Q.* 57:4–15

Elder G. 1985. *Life Course Dynamics: Trajectories and Transitions, 1968–1980.* Ithaca, NY: Cornell Univ. Press

Elder G. 1992. Models of the life course. *Contemp. Sociol.* 21:632–36

Elder G. 1974. *Children of the Great Depression*. Chicago, IL: Univ. Chicago Press

Elias R. 1986. *The Politics of Victimization: Victims, Victimology, and Human Rights*. New York: Oxford Univ. Press

Fagan J, Piper E, Cheng Y. 1987. Contributions of victimization to delinquency in inner cities. *J. Crim. Law Criminol.* 78:586–613

Federal Bureau of Investigation. 1998. *Uniform Crime Reports for the United States, 1997*. Washington, DC: US Govt. Printing Off.

Finkelhor D. 1997. The victimization of children and youth: developmental victimology. In *Victims of Crime*, ed. R Davis, A Lurigio, W Skogan. Thousand Oaks, CA: Sage. 2nd ed.

Finkelhor D. 1995. The victimization of children: a developmental perspective. *Am. J. Orthopsychiatry* 65:177–93

Fischer C. 1984. A phenomenological study of being criminally victimized: contributions and constraints of qualitative research. *J. Soc. Issues*. 40:161–78

Freedy J, Resnick H, Kilpatrick D, Dansky B, Tidwell R. 1994. The psychological adjustment of recent crime victims in the criminal justice system. *J. Interpers. Violence* 9:450–68

Frieze I, Hymer S, Greenberg M. 1987. Describing the crime victim: psychological reactions to victimization. *Prof. Psychol.* 18:299–315

Furstenberg F, Cook T, Eccles J, Elder G, Sameroff A. 1999. *Managing to Make It: Urban Families and Adolescent Success*. Chicago, IL: Univ. Chicago Press

Garbarino J, Dubrow N, Kostelny K, Pardo C. 1992. *Children in Danger: Coping with the Consequences of Community Violence*. San Francisco, CA: Jossey-Bass

Gecas V. 1989. The social psychology of self-efficacy. *Annu. Rev. Sociol.* 15:291–316

Groth N. 1979. Sexual trauma in the life histories of rapists and child molesters. *Victimology* 4:10–16

Hagan J. 1998. Life course capitalization and adolescent behavioral development. In *New Perspectives on Adolescent Risk Behavior*, ed. R Jessor. New York: Cambridge Univ. Press

Hagan. 1991. Destiny and drift: subcultural preferences, status attainments, and the risks and rewards of youth. *Am. Sociol. Rev.* 56:567–82

Hagan J. 1989. *Structural Criminology*. New Brunswick, NJ: Rutgers Univ. Press

Hagan J, McCarthy B. 1997. *Mean Streets: Youth Crime and Homelessness*. New York: Cambridge Univ. Press

Hagan J, Macmillan R, Wheaton B. 1996. New kid in town: social capital and the life course effects of family migration on children. *Am. Sociol. Rev.* 61:368–87

Hagedorn J. 1988. *People and Folks: Gangs, Crime, and the Underclass in a Rust–Belt City*. Chicago, IL: Lake View Press

Harrington R, Fudge H, Rutter M, Pickles A. 1991. Adult outcomes of childhood and adolescent depression: II. Links with antisocial disorders. *J. Am. Acad. Child Adolescent Psychiatry* 30:434–39

Hindelang M. 1976. *Criminal Victimization in Eight American Cities*. Cambridge, MA: Ballinger

Hindelang M. 1981. Variations in sex-race-age-specific incidence rates of offending. *Am. Sociol. Rev.* 46:461–74

Hindelang M, Gottfredson M, Garofalo J. 1978. *Victims of Personal Crime: An Empirical Foundation for a Theory of Personal Victimization*. Cambridge, MA: Ballinger

Hirschi T, Gottfredson M. 1983. Age and the explanation of crime. *Am. J. Sociol.* 89:552–84

Hjorth C, Ostrov E. 1982. The self-image of physically abused adolescents. *J. Youth Adolescence* 11:71–76

Hodges E, Perry D. 1999. Personal and interpersonal antecedents and consequences of victimization by peers. *J. Personal. Soc. Psychol.* 76:677–85

Janoff-Bulman R, Frieze I. 1983. A theoretical perspective for understanding reactions to victimization. *J. Soc. Issues* 39:1–17

Jensen G, Brownfield D. 1986. Gender,

lifestyles, and victimization: beyond routine activity. *Violence Victims* 1:85–99

Kalmuss D. 1984. The intergenerational transmission of marital aggression. *J. Marriage Fam.* 46:11–19

Kandel D, Davies M. 1986. Adult sequelae of adolescent depressive symptoms. *Arch. Gen. Psychiatry* 43:255–62

Kennedy L, Forde D. 1990. Routine activities and crime: an analysis of victimization in Canada. *Criminology* 28:137–51

Kent J. 1976. A follow-up study of abused children. *J. Pediatric Psychology.* 1:25–31

Kessler R, Magee W. 1994. Childhood family violence and adult recurrent depression. *J. Health Soc. Behav.* 35:13–27

Kilpatrick D, Saunders B, Veronen L, Best C, Von J. 1987. Criminal victimization: lifetime prevalence, reporting to police, and psychological impact. *Crime Delinq.* 33:479–89

Kroll P, Stock D, James M. 1985. The behavior of adult alcoholic men abused as children. *J. Nervous Mental Dis.* 173:689–93

Lake E. 1993. An exploration of the violent victim experiences of female offenders. *Violence Victims* 8:41–50

Laub J. 1997. Patterns of criminal victimization in the United States. In *Victims of Crime*, ed. R Davis, A Lurigio, W Skogan. Thousand Oaks, CA:Sage. 2nd ed.

Lauritsen J, Sampson R, Laub J. 1991. The link between offending and victimization among adolescents. *Criminology* 29:265–92

LeJeune R, Alex N. 1973. On being mugged. *Urban Life Culture* 2:259–87

Lewis D. 1992. From abuse to violence: psychophysiological consequences of maltreatment. *J. Am. Acad. Child Adolescent Psychiatry* 31:383–91

Lewis D, Shanok S, Balla D. 1979. Perinatal difficulties, head and face trauma, and child abuse in the medical histories of seriously delinquent children. *Am. J. Psychiatry* 136:419–23

Lurigio A. 1987. Are all victims alike? The adverse, generalized, and differential impact of crime. *Crime Delinq.* 33:452–67

Macmillan R. 2000. Adolescent victimization and income deficits in adulthood: rethinking the costs of criminal violence from a life course perspective. *Criminology* 38:553–88

Maher L, Curtis R. 1992. Women on the edge of crime: crack cocaine and the changing contexts of street-level sex work in New York City. *Crime, Law, Soc. Change* 18:221–58

Martinez P, Richters J. 1993. The NIMH community violence project: II. Children's distress symptoms associated with violence exposure. *Psychiatry: Interpers. & Biol. Processes.* 56:22–35

McCann L, Sakheim D, Abrahamson D. 1988. Trauma and victimization: a model of psychological adaptation. *Couns. Psychologist* 16:531–94

McCord J. 1983. A forty year perspective on effects of child abuse and neglect. *Child Abuse Neglect* 7:265–70

McLeer S, Deblinger E, Atkins M, Foa E, Ralphe D. 1988. Post-traumatic stress disorder in sexually abused children. *J. Am. Acad. Child Adolescent Psychiatry* 27:650–54

Menard S. 2001. Short and long term consequences of criminal victimization. In *Violent Behavior in the Life Course*, ed. S Menard, D Huizinga, D Elliott. Thousand Oaks, CA: Sage. Forthcoming

Miethe T, Meier R. 1990. Opportunity, choice, and criminal victimization: a test of a theoretical model. *J. Res. Crime Delinq.* 27:243–66

Miethe T, Stafford M, Long J. 1987. Social differentiation in criminal victimization: a test of routine activities/lifestyle theories. *Am. Sociol. Rev.* 52:184–94

Mirrlees-Black C, Budd T, Partridge S, Mayhew P. 1998. *The 1998 British Crime Survey: England and Wales.* London, UK: Govt. Statist. Serv.

Moore M, Prothrow-Stith D, Guyer B, Spivak H. 1994. Violence and intentional injuries: criminal justice and public health perspectives on an urgent national problem. In *Understanding and Preventing Violence*, ed. A Reiss, J Roth. Washington, DC: Natl. Acad. Press

Norris F, Kaniasty K. 1991. The psychological experience of crime: a test of the mediating role of beliefs in explaining the distress of victims. *J. Soc. Clin. Psychol.* 10:239–61

Norris F, Kaniasty K, Thompson M. 1997. The psychological consequences of crime: findings from a longitudinal population-based study. In *Victims of Crime*, ed. R Davis, A Lurigio, W Skogan. Thousand Oaks, CA: Sage. 2nd ed.

Otis M, Skinner W. 1996. The prevalence of victimization and its effect on mental wellbeing among lesbian and gay people. *J. Homosexuality* 30:93–121

Perez C, Widom C. 1994. Childhood victimization and long-term intellectual and academic outcomes. *Child Abuse Neglect* 18:617–33

Peterson C, Seligman M. 1983. Learned helplessness and victimization. *J. Soc. Issues* 39:103–16

Pollock V, Briere J, Schneider L, Knop J, Mednick S, Goodwin D. 1990. Childhood antecedents of antisocial behavior: parental alcoholism and physical abusiveness. *Am. J. Psychiatry.* 147:1290–93

Resick P. 1987. Psychological effects of victimization: implications for the criminal justice system. *Crime Delinq.* 33:468–78

Resick P, Kilpatrick D, Dansky B, Saunders B, Best C. 1993. Prevalence of civilian trauma and posttraumatic stress disorder in a representative national sample of women. *J. Consult. Clin. Psychol.* 61:984–91

Reuterman N, Burcky W. 1989. Dating violence in high school:A profile of the victims. *Psychology: J. Hum. Behav.* 26:1–9

Richie B. 1996. *Compelled to Crime:The Gender Entrapment of Battered Black Women.* New York: Routledge

Riggs D, O'Leary K, Breslin F. 1990. Multiple correlates of physical aggression in dating couples. *J. Interpers. Violence* 5:61–73

Rivera B, Widom C. 1990. Childhood victimization and violent offending. *Violence Victims* 5:19–35

Robins L, Rutter M. 1990. *Straight and Devious Pathways from Childhood to Adulthood.* New York : Cambridge Univ. Press

Rogeness G, Amrung S, Macedo C, Harris W. 1986. Psychopathology in abused and neglected children. *J. Am. Acad. Child Psychiatry* 25:659–65

Roscoe B, Callahan J. 1985. Adolescent's self-report of violence in families and dating relations. *Adolescence* 20:545–53

Rosenthal B. 2000. Exposure to community violence in adolescence: trauma symptoms. *Adolescence* 35:271–84

Rowe A, Tittle C. 1977. Life cycle changes and criminal propensity. *Sociol. Q.* 18:223–36

Rutter M. 1989. Pathways from childhood to adult life. *J. Child Psychol. Psychiatry Allied Disc.* 30:23–51

Sacco V, Johnson H. 1990. *Patterns of Criminal Victimization.* Ottawa, Canada: Statistics Canada

Sadeh A, Hayden R, McGuire J, Sachs H, Civita R. 1994. Somatic, cognitive, and emotional characteristics of abused children in a psychiatric hospital. *Child Psychol. Hum. Dev.* 24:191–200

Salzinger S, Kaplan S, Pelcovitz D, Samit C, Krieger R. 1984. Parent and teacher assessment of children's behavior in child maltreating families. *J. Am. Acad. Child Psychiatry* 23:458–64

Sampson R, Laub J. 1996. Socioeconomic achievement in the life course of disadvantaged men: military service as a turning point, circa 1940–1965. *Am. Sociol. Rev.* 61:347–67

Sampson R, Laub J. 1993. *Crime in the Making:Pathways and Turning Points through Life.* Cambridge, MA: Harvard Univ. Press

Sampson R, Lauritsen J. 1994. Violent victimization and offending: individual-, situational-, and community-level risk factors. In *Understanding and Preventing Violence*, ed. A Reiss, J Roth. Washington, DC: Natl. Acad. Press

Sampson R, Lauritsen J. 1990. Deviant lifestyles, proximity to crime, and the offender-victim link in personal violence. *J. Res. Crime Delinq.* 27:110–39

Sampson R, Morenoff J, Earls F. 1999. Beyond social capital: spatial dynamics of collective efficacy for children. *Am. Sociol. Rev.* 64:633–60

Sampson R, Raudenbush S, Earls F. 1997.

Neighborhoods and violent crime—a multilevel study of collective efficacy. *Science* 277:918–24

Sampson R, Wooldredge J. 1987. Linking the micro- and macro-level dimensions of lifestyle–routine activity and opportunity models of predatory victimization. *J. Quant. Criminol.* 3:371–93

Schwab-Stone M, Chen C, Greenberger E, Silver D, Lichtman J, et al. 1999. No safe haven II: the effects of violence exposure on urban youth. *J. Am. Acad. Child. Adolescent Psych.* 38:359–67

Seghorn T, Prentky R, Boucher R. 1987. Childhood sexual abuse in the lives of sexually aggressive offenders. *J. Am. Acad. Child Adolescent Psychiatry* 26:262–67

Sendi I, Blomgren P. 1975. A comparative study of predictive criteria in the predisposition of homicidal adolescents. *Am. J. Psychiatry* 132:423–27

Sewell W, Hauser R. 1975. *Education, Occupation, and Earnings: Achievement in Early Career.* New York: Academic Press

Silbert M, Pines A. 1981. Sexual child abuse as an antecedent to prostitution. *Child Abuse Neglect.* 5:407–11

Simons R, Whitbeck L. 1991. Sexual abuse as a precursor to prostitution and victimization among adolescent and adult homeless women. *J. Family Issues* 12:361–79

Singer S. 1986. Victims of serious violence and their criminal behavior: subcultural theory and beyond. *Violence Victims* 1:61–70

Skogan W. 1990. The polls–a review: the national crime survey redesign. *Public Opinion Q.* 54:256–72

Skogan W. 1987. The impact of victimization on fear. *Crime Delinq.* 33:135–54

Skogan W, Maxfield M. 1981. *Coping with Crime: Individual and Neighborhood Reactions.* Beverly Hills, CA: Sage

Snyder H, Sickmund M. 1999. *Juvenile Offenders and Victims: 1999 National Report.* Washington, DC: Natl. Cent. Juvenile Justice

Straus M, Gelles R. 1990. How violent are American families? Estimates from the Na-

tional Family Violence Resurvey and other studies. In *Physical Violence in American Families: Risk Factors and Adaptations to Violence in 8,145 Families,* ed. M Straus, R Gelles. New Brunswick, NJ: Transaction

Straus M, Smith C. 1990. Family patterns and child abuse. In *Physical Violence in American Families: Risk Factors and Adaptations to Violence in 8,145 Families,* ed. M Straus, R Gelles. New Brunswick, NJ: Transaction

Swisher R. 2000. *Neighborhood effects on adolescent college expectations.* PhD diss. Univ. N Carolina, Chapel Hill

Tartar R, Hegedus A, Winsten N, Alterman A. 1984. Neuropsychological, personality, and familial characteristics of physically abused delinquents. *J. Am. Acad. Child Psychiatry* 23:668–74

Thoits P. 1983. Dimensions of life events that influence psychological distress: an evaluation and synthesis of the literature. In *Psychosocial Stress:Trends in Theory and Research,* ed. H Kaplan. New York: Academic press

Thornberry T. 1997. *Developmental Theories of Crime and Delinquency.* New Brunswick, NJ: Transaction

Turner R, Wheaton B, Lloyd D. 1995. The epidemiology of social stress. *Am. Sociol. Rev.* 60:104–25

Uggen C. 2000. Work as a turning point in the life course of criminals: a duration model of age, employment, and recidivism. *Am. Sociol. Rev.* 529–46

Van Dijk J, Mayhew P, Killias M. 1990. *Experiences of Crime Across the World:Key Findings from the 1989 International Crime Survey.* Boston, MA : Kluwer Law and Taxation Publ.

Wells E, Rankin J. 1995. Juvenile victimization: convergent validation of alternative measurements. *J. Res. in Crime Delinq.* 32:287–307

White S, Halpin B, Strom G, Santilli G. 1988. Behavioral comparisons of young sexually abused, neglected, and nonreferred children. *J. Clin. Child Psychol.* 17:53–61

White J, Moffitt T, Earls F, Robins L, Silva

P. 1990. How early can we tell? Predictors of childhood conduct disorder and adolescent delinquency. *Criminology* 28:507–33

Widom C. 1989. The cycle of violence. *Science* 244:160–66

Widom C, Ashley-Ames M. 1994. Criminal consequences of childhood sexual victimiza-tion. *Child Abuse Neglect* 18:303–18

Wolfe D, Mosk M. 1983. Behavioral compar-isons of children from abusive and distressed families. *J. Consult. Clin. Psychol.* 51:702–08

Wolfgang M, et al. 1972. *Delinquency in a Birth Cohort.* Chicago: Univ. Chicago Press

Annu. Rev. Sociol. 2001. 27:23–45

URBAN POVERTY AFTER *THE TRULY DISADVANTAGED* : The Rediscovery of the Family, the Neighborhood, and Culture

Mario Luis Small[1] and Katherine Newman[2]

[1]Department of Sociology, Harvard University, Cambridge, Massachusetts, 02138;
e-mail: Small@wjh.harvard.edu
[2]Kennedy School of Government, Harvard University, Cambridge, Massachusetts,
02138; e-mail: Katherine_Newman@harvard.edu

Key Words   inner city, neighborhood effects, underclass, culture, birthrates

■ **Abstract**   In what follows we critically assess a selection of the works on urban poverty that followed the publication of WJ Wilson's *The Truly Disadvantaged* (1987), with a particular focus on the family, the neighborhood, and culture. We frame our discussion by assessing the broad explanations of the increased concentration of poverty in urban neighborhoods characteristic of the 1970s and 1980s. Then, in the section on the family, we address the rising out-of-wedlock and disproportionately high teenage birthrates of poor urban women. Next, we critique the literature on neighborhood effects. Finally, in the discussion of culture, we examine critically the new efforts at complementing structural explanations with cultural accounts. We conclude by calling for more comparative, cross-regional, and historical studies, broader conceptions of urban poverty, and a greater focus on Latinos and other ethnic groups.

INTRODUCTION

The most important publication in urban poverty over the past twenty-five years has been WJ Wilson's *The Truly Disadvantaged* (1987; henceforth, *TTD*). The hundreds of books and articles on urban poverty that followed the book's publication all responded in some way to the hypotheses it advanced. In what follows, we examine critically a selection of this literature, focusing on three topics—the family, the neighborhood, and culture—that we find especially important. Indeed, researchers have recently examined critical questions on these three topics that either lay dormant during the 1970s and 1980s or had not been addressed systematically at all. Given space limitations, our coverage must be selective, emphasizing the issues we find to be most pressing. We must also ignore other important topics in urban poverty—such as immigration, ethnicity, and politics. The latter,

0360-0572/01/0811-0023$14.00

23

however, are covered extensively in several recent reviews (Waters & Eschbach 1995, Walton 1993, Marks 1991, Teitz & Chapple 1998).

THE NEW URBAN POVERTY

The Truly Disadvantaged argues that, since 1970, structural changes in the economy, such as the shift from manufacturing to service industries and the departure of low-skilled jobs from the urban centers, increased black joblessness in central city ghettos (Wilson 1987, 1991a, 1996). The inner cities also suffered from the flight of middle- and working-class blacks who took advantage of affirmative action and fair housing laws to relocate to higher-income urban neighborhoods and the suburbs. As working families departed and the nonworking families stayed behind, inner-city neighborhoods became mired in concentrated poverty. The result, Wilson argues, was a new "underclass" of single-parent families, welfare dependency, joblessness, and overall increased "social pathologies" (1987:viii).

Most sociologists agree that (*a*) urban poverty changed over the 1970s and 1980s and that (*b*) it became more concentrated. (What happened over the 1990s will be known when Census 2000 data become available.) But there are marked differences in how sociologists think about these two issues, reflecting conceptual arguments over the dynamics of urban poverty. We discuss these differences below to frame our discussion of the family, the neighborhood, and culture.

Recent Urban Poverty as a New Phenomenon

Wilson and others argue that changes in the inner city produced a new, distinct, and growing phenomenon: "the underclass" (Kasarda 1989, Wacquant & Wilson 1989, Wilson 1987, Massey & Denton 1993; see also Marks 1991, Lawson 1992, Mincy 1994, Jargowsky & Bane 1990). This class is characterized by its geographic concentration, its social isolation from the middle class, and its joblessness. Indeed, it is these characteristics, Wilson argues, that distinguish the underclass as a new entity.

Jencks (1991, 1992) counters that the idea of a new class contributes nothing to our understanding of the urban poor, and he suggests that "the underclass" is simply a new term for what was known in the 1960s as "the lower class." He believes, furthermore, that the term gives the mistaken impression that all urban problems are worsening, and he argues instead for a focus on the proportion of individuals experiencing specific social problems, such as joblessness and dropping out of school.[1]

---

[1]This is a version of the classic debate in stratification between the "class approach," which posits that society is composed of distinct classes, and the "gradational approach," which posits that society is composed not of classes but individuals who vary in terms of income, occupation, and status (Grusky 1994).

At the time of Jencks's writing, male joblessness had risen and out-of-wedlock births had increased (and still continue to increase), but dropout rates and reading and mathematics skills had improved (and continue to improve, though only slightly in the case of reading and math) (Jencks 1991, Jencks & Peterson 1991, US Census Bureau 1999). In addition, the rate of black male joblessness, high throughout the 1980s, declined over the 1990s as labor markets tightened (Freeman & Rodgers 1999). The notion of an underclass, Jencks argues, masks the diversity of these trends.

At the onset of this debate, several researchers grappled with whether the underclass was a separate class (Marks 1991, Lawson 1992, Mincy 1994, Jargowsky & Bane 1990), but over time both the term and that debate have gradually been abandoned. Given the negative implications of the term, Wilson officially abandoned it in favor of "the ghetto poor" (Wilson 1991b), a change that also represented a subtle shift from a designation of classes to one of individuals. The only component of the underclass still debated is the neighborhood, which we discuss at length later. Many sociologists were convinced by Jencks's (1991) argument for the individual-centered approach (an approach perfected over decades by status-attainment researchers) because it allows for a relatively parsimonious discernment of which urban problems are worsening and which are not. Yet some worried about the dangers of the approach; a too strict individual-centered perspective assumes unproblematically that other units of analysis such as classes, networks, or places are unimportant.

The result over the past few years has been a sort of amalgam of the two approaches. Most empirical studies now implicitly follow a model of society as a collective of individuals (not classes), but individuals whose neighborhood of residence is important. This middle ground provides the important benefit that individuals are much easier to measure than classes (see, e.g., Wright 1985) and that neighborhoods can be measured by means of the census tract. However, it has left sociologists with little motivation to think theoretically about the relationship between neighborhoods and people, pushing researchers instead to focus on the methodological problems of using neighborhoods to explain individual variation (see section on neighborhoods). It has also, finally, left unresolved the question of whether recent urban poverty constitutes a sociologically new phenomenon.

The Increased Concentration of Poverty

One of Wilson's arguments has provoked little disagreement, that urban poverty became more concentrated over the 1970s and 1980s. Jargowsky (1994, 1997), who defines a high-poverty neighborhood as one in which 40% of the population is poor, confirms that both neighborhood poverty (the number of such neighborhoods) and the concentration of the poor (the proportion of all poor people living in such neighborhoods) increased between 1970 and 1990. The question is, Why? Three principal explanations have been offered (Quillian 1999; see also Teitz & Chapple 1998).

One is the black middle-class flight model discussed above (Wilson 1987), which blames the departure of working blacks from the inner city (Wilson 1996, Jargowsky & Bane 1991, Jargowsky 1997). A second is the residential segregation model, which argues that fair housing laws were so poorly enforced that they did little to dismantle the racial divide in housing; this lack of enforcement, combined with the growth of black poverty in cities, led to the increase in neighborhoods with high concentrations of poor black people (Massey & Denton 1987, 1993, Denton & Massey 1988, Massey et al 1994). The third is the departure of low-skilled jobs model, which, borrowing from Kain's (1968) spatial mismatch thesis, argues that manufacturing jobs moved from inner-city neighborhoods, especially during the 1970s, increasing joblessness among black men and thus increasing the neighborhoods' concentration of poverty (Wilson 1987, Kasarda 1989, Weicher 1990, Kain 1992, Jencks & Mayer 1990a).

A great deal of the literature pits these explanations against one another as if they were mutually exclusive when in fact they are not. Quillian (1999) explains this cogently in a recent paper that ostensibly adjudicates between Wilson's black middle-class flight and Massey & Denton's segregation explanation. Relying on census-matched longitudinal evidence, Quillian shows that over the 1970s and 1980s nonpoor blacks were moving rapidly into white neighborhoods, as Wilson argued. But he also finds that racial segregation is a more important explanation than middle-class black out-migration of the present concentration of poverty, as Massey & Denton argued. Although segregation is a better account of contemporary concentrations of poverty, it cannot explain the increase in poverty concentration over the 1970s and 1980s because during that time the levels of segregation did not increase—in fact, they declined slightly (Massey & Denton 1993:64, Farley & Frey 1994). Quillian (1999) suggests, therefore, that middle-class flight correctly explains the movement of blacks over time; residential segregation strongly accounts for the concentration of poverty in a cross-section of neighborhoods. In general, however, few studies employ the requisite longitudinal data to assess these explanations; thus, although the three of them appear to contain a grain of truth, none of them has been overwhelmingly supported.

These accounts, along with much of the post-*TTD* work on urban poverty, are also weakened by several important limitations. Three are particularly salient: (*a*) their focus on dense cities in the midwest and northeast; (*b*) their almost exclusive focus on African-Americans; and (*c*) their relative neglect of the influx of new immigrants to the inner cities (see Weicher 1991, Jargowsky & Bane 1991, Waldinger & Bozorgmehr 1996, Moore & Pinderhughes 1993, Waters 1999, Waters & Eschbach 1995, Ong et al 1994). The major perspectives described above would be of little help in explaining the changes taking place over the past 30 years in Los Angeles, Houston, or Miami, cities not only outside the northeast-midwest belt but also populated by high proportions of nonblack poor people, many of whom are immigrants (see e.g., Waldinger & Bozorgmehr 1996). [In a recent review prepared for this journal, Waters & Eschbach (1995) cover the literature on immigration and other ethnic groups extensively.] During the discussions that follow, we note several points on which the literature is held back by this undue focus on African-Americans in the northeast and midwest.

FAMILY STRUCTURE

Recent studies of poor urban families have focused on family management and parenting practices (Furstenberg et al 1999) and the causes and consequences of teenage and out-of-wedlock births (McLanahan & Sandefur 1994, Geronimus 1991, Geronimus & Korenman 1992, 1993, Hoffman et al 1993a, 1993b, Cherlin 1992, Luker 1996, Kaplan 1997). Here we dwell on the debates over causal explanations, which we consider the most pressing.

Wilson (1987) argues that much of the increase in urban poverty reflects the sharp increase in the proportion of female-headed families among blacks. He correctly points out that black women are marrying at lower rates and never-married black women are having children at a higher rate than are married black women. The main concern of this literature has been to explain why, and several researchers either produced new explanations or revisited old ones.

We should note two issues. First, these are in fact two separate phenomena: the teen birthrate and the out-of-wedlock birthrate. Since most births to teenage mothers occur out of wedlock, many sociologists have addressed the two problems as one, but they are distinct. Only the out-of-wedlock birthrate is rising rapidly, though the teen birthrate is disproportionately higher among blacks and Latinas than among whites. Second, most of these researchers focus not on poor women in general but on black women (but see Luker 1996, Vega 1990, Dietrich 1996). This bias results in part from a legitimate demographic concern: the rate of births to unmarried mothers among blacks in 1997 was a disturbing 69.1%; their rate of births to teens was 22.5%, double that of whites (US Census Bureau 1999). But the out-of-wedlock and teen birthrates among Latinas were not far behind (40.9% and 17.3%, respectively), while the out-of-wedlock birthrate is growing faster among whites than any other race (US Census Bureau 1999). Thus, the literature we discuss below tends to present a skewed picture of the problem, a picture that should be corrected with more studies on Latinas and whites, to say nothing of other ethnic groups.

Out-of-Wedlock Births

The recent literature has produced three new (or revisited) explanations for the increasing proportion of out-of-wedlock births among poor urban (mostly black) women. One is the marriageable-male-pool explanation, which posits that declining economic opportunities in the inner cities reduced the pool of black men with steady jobs, leaving black women with fewer attractive mates (Wilson 1987). Another is the slavery explanation, revived recently by Patterson (1998), which contends that the institution of slavery produced lasting effects on relationships between black men and women, including the tendency of black women to bear children out of wedlock. A third explanation argues that widespread cultural changes throughout American society are to blame, since out-of-wedlock births have increased among women of all races (Jencks 1992, Cherlin 1992; see also Luker 1996).

None of the explanations has accumulated enough evidence to be overwhelmingly convincing. Proposed partly in response to Murray's (1984) argument that federal welfare policies were to blame, the marriageable-male-pool hypothesis is the most empirically substantiated, though support has been mixed (Rolison 1992, Stokes & Chevan 1996, Hess 1990, Lerman 1989, Mare & Winship 1991). Moreover, since the mid-1980s, when the hypothesis was advanced, the jobless rate among black men has plummeted; if the explanation is correct, this shift should have increased the marriage rates among poor urban blacks. But no one, as far as we can tell, has tested for this.

The other two explanations have received relatively little empirical attention, partly because good data to test them are more difficult to obtain. Patterson's revival of the slavery hypothesis is an attempt to counter the work of Gutman (1976), whose study of ante-bellum census records convinced many sociologists that the effects of slavery on the black family were negligible (see also Preston et al 1992). One of the main problems with the slavery explanation is the impossibility of calculating a metric that can associate slavery with a certain percent decline in blacks' likelihood of marriage. This tends to frustrate researchers who expect precise estimates, thus weakening the reception of the work. Most sociologists sympathetic to the theory support it partly, but suggest that other factors matter as well (Cherlin 1992). A proponent of the widespread cultural change argument, Jencks (1992:134) notes that "during the 1960s ... [society] moved from thinking that society ought to discourage extramarital sex, and especially out-of-wedlock births, to thinking that such efforts were an unwarranted infringement on personal liberty." Yet it is hard to ascertain whether the shift in cultural attitudes led to across-the-board changes in out-of-wedlock births, or whether the increase in those births led to changes in public attitudes. We know of no tests that ascertain which way the causal arrow points.

Teenage Births

Sociologists have produced three new (or revisited) explanations for the high rate of teenage births among the poor in urban centers. One is the inner-city culture explanation, which contends that "street" families in poor (usually black) urban neighborhoods share a cultural code whereby early sexual activity (despite its risks) improves girls' reputation among peers (Anderson 1994, 1991, 1999). Another is the "weathering" explanation, which posits that deterioration in the health of poor women leads to premature aging and therefore transforms early childbearing from a risky strategy to a rational response to objective conditions. Older black mothers have higher infant mortality rates; hence, the explanation goes, having children at an early age makes sense (Geronimus 1991, 1996, Geronimus & Bound 1990, Geronimus et al 1996, 1999a,b). Finally, a few researchers advance what Kaplan (1997) labels the "poverty of relationships" explanation, which states that women have children as teens to make up for the unsatisfying relationships they sustain with teachers, mothers, fathers, and boyfriends (also Dietrich 1998). In Kaplan's words (1997:181), the black teen mothers "had babies because they were isolated from society and unwanted by everyone around them."

The three explanations have been examined with mixed results. Elements of Anderson's thesis find some support (Luker 1996:138–39), but Dietrich (1998:47) finds that the Chicana girls she studies value virginity above all, and that it is virginity, not promiscuity, that assures them a favorable reputation. With respect to the weathering hypothesis, there was some debate early on over the quality of the data (Furstenberg 1991, 1992, Geronimus 1991), but recently Geronimus and her colleagues have accumulated convincing evidence that mortality rates are higher among African-Americans in general, the infants of older blacks, and the black urban poor (Geronimus et al 1996, 1999a,b). Yet it remains unclear whether black female teens are aware of the infant mortality differential between themselves and adult black women, and whether this knowledge motivates them to bear children early (see Furstenberg 1991). Thus, the weathering hypothesis is at a critical juncture where the demographic evidence must be complemented by interview data. Kaplan's explanation is a refinement of a general theory that links women's poverty to both their loneliness and a yearning for social status (see also Dietrich 1998, Stack 1974).

In her comprehensive treatment of the issue, Luker (1996:134–174) advances a multi-causal explanation that attributes disproportionately high birthrates of minority teens to their poverty, their limited life choices, their ineffectiveness (for various reasons) with respect to contraception, and the difficult negotiations around sex that take place with their male partners. She also presents enough evidence to suggest that each of these explanations is plausible. This multi-factor approach constructively avoids what we call the trap of false adjudication: the inclination to pit explanations against each other that are not necessarily contradictory.

In all, the new literature on both teen and out-of-wedlock birthrates shows some promising leads, but much more empirical work remains to be done, especially on other ethnic groups. This research is critical because the higher these birthrates are among a poor population, the higher the chances its members will experience long-term poverty.

THE NEIGHBORHOOD

Perhaps no single question in urban inequality has produced more research than whether neighborhood poverty affects the life chances of the poor. Wilson (1987) argues that the concentration of poverty results in the isolation of the poor from the middle class and its corresponding role models, resources, and job networks; more generally, he argues that being poor in a mixed-income neighborhood is less damaging than being poor in a high poverty neighborhood. Concentration effects increase the likelihood of being unemployed, dropping out of school, taking up crime, and becoming pregnant out of wedlock. A large body of empirical research has tested for neighborhood effects on unemployment (Vartanian 1999, Elliott 1999), dropping out of school (Crane 1991), crime (Sampson & Groves 1989), out-of-wedlock births (Crane 1991, Anderson 1991, 1999, South & Crowder 1999), and cognitive development (Brooks-Gunn et al 1997a, 1997b). The body of research is large enough to require its own separate review, and indeed, several of them exist (Jencks & Mayer 1990b, Gephart 1997). Instead of repeating the work of these reviewers, we (a) discuss the most important methodological problems with measuring whether neighborhoods have these hypothesized effects; (b) report the latest findings on whether neighborhood poverty affects life chances; and (c) examine what we argue is the most pressing unresolved question with respect to neighborhood effects: how they work.

Much of the literature on neighborhood effects has been methodological, and with good reason. It is extremely difficult to test the hypothesis that, everything else being equal, an individual living under any particular neighborhood condition is worse off than in the absence of that condition. Several problems are related to this difficulty, such as the need for longitudinal data, the challenge of disentangling neighborhood from school effects, and the possibility of nonlinear effects (for extended discussions, see Duncan et al 1997, Tienda 1991, Jencks & Mayer 1990b). But two problems are particularly important.

First, people are not randomly distributed across neighborhoods. People live in neighborhoods as a result of both observable and unobservable characteristics that may themselves, independently of neighborhoods, affect life outcomes. For example, parents with little education are more likely to live in poor neighborhoods, and they are also more likely to have children who drop out of high school. By neglecting to control for the parents' low educational attainment, researchers may overstate the impact of living in a poor neighborhood. Most published studies of neighborhood effects deal with this question in a perfunctory fashion, adding a small number of controls for parental education and income. There are exceptions, such as Duncan et al (1997), who control for a battery of typically unmeasured variables; Duncan et al (1997) and Cutler & Glaser (1997), who make use of instrumental variables; and Rosenbaum & Popkin (1991), who, via the Gautreaux program, approximate a randomized experiment (see also Spencer et al 1997). But the bottom line is that most neighborhood studies are unable to make causal links and can only point to strong associations.

Second, how do we define and measure neighborhoods? The problem involves three interrelated issues: conceptualizing neighborhoods, drawing their geographic boundaries, and determining which neighborhood characteristics should be used to measure disadvantage. Most sociologists conceptualize neighborhoods in terms of informal relationships or social networks among persons living in a geographic space; thus, when we use the term "neighborhood" we tend to mean "community" (Wellman 1988, Chaskin 1997, Sampson 1999). But geographic location and social networks are separate and distinct attributes that may have different effects on individuals. Failing to account for this and for the many possible ways neighborhoods may be defined will result in an increasingly muddled discourse on the effects of neighborhoods on people. A few recent scholars have proposed that we conceive of neighborhoods in terms of several separate and complementary dimensions, such as (a) a social space, (b) a set of relationships, (c) a set of institutions, and (d) a symbolic unit (Chaskin 1997); or that we think of neighborhoods alternatively as (a) sites, (b) perceptions, (c) networks, and (d) cultures (Burton et al 1997). These works, though still in their conceptual infancy, push us toward the important task of developing greater clarity over what is meant by neighborhoods.

Even if we sharpen our thinking about neighborhoods in terms of nongeographic concepts, we still have to determine their geographic boundaries if we want to test whether they matter for poverty outcomes. This task is not straightforward. Most sociologists resort to the census tract, but, depending on how we think neighborhoods matter, census tracts may be woefully inadequate proxies. For example, the perceptions of local residents regarding the boundaries of their neighborhoods may be important determinants of how the neighborhoods affect them; in that case, census-tract operationalizations will be of little use. Some scholars suggest replacing census tracts with the smaller block groups (a practice common in the fields of demography and public health), which allow for a narrower geographic area of socialization (C Jencks, personal communication). A few recent studies (Sampson et al 1997, Sampson & Groves 1989) employ "neighborhood clusters" or "localities," which are neighborhood boundaries drawn by researchers explicitly for the purpose of studying neighborhood effects. The advantage of these clusters is that they are often drawn with an eye to local perceptions about what constitutes the end of one neighborhood and the beginning of another. The disadvantage is that the more accurately they reflect local perceptions of neighborhood boundaries, the more costly and time-consuming it is to draw them.

Finally, what characteristics should we employ to measure disadvantage (Gephart 1997, Mincy 1994, Elliot et al 1996)? There are many possibilities: neighborhood poverty, segregation, the unemployment rate, and the level of educational attainment. Consequently, some researchers have combined these measures into composite "disadvantage" or "risk factor" indexes that encompass race, class, and other variables (e.g., Brooks-Gunn et al 1997a,b, Duncan & Aber 1997, South & Crowder 1999). These indexes have the advantage of statistical parsimony, especially since many of these variables tend to be correlated. Yet indexing makes replication cumbersome, especially when the index employs survey data. Furthermore, that solution does not help us discern which neighborhood characteristics affect people and which do not. The substantively important question is whether neighborhood unemployment or racial homogeneity or resource-deprivation affects life chances. A composite index that lumps all of these variables obscures which factors are creating the effect (see Massey 1998).

Methodological difficulties notwithstanding, several major recent studies have collected copious and increasingly sophisticated data that suggest neighborhoods matter with respect to certain variables. In an early release of the findings from the Gautreaux program, Rosenbaum & Popkin (1991) report that low-income black families who moved from public housing to the suburbs were more likely to be employed than similar families who remained in the inner city. Brooks-Gunn et al (1997a,b,c), employing data from the Working Group on Communities and Neighborhoods, Family Processes, and Individual Development, find that neighborhood conditions are often predictors of children's development, that the effect is strongest during early childhood and late adolescence, and that affluent or middle-class neighborhoods increase children's development and improve adolescents' achievement. After interviewing 500 families in Philadelphia, Furstenberg et al (1999) uncovered the fact that neighborhood conditions affect parents' family management practices (e.g., the more dangerous the neighborhood, the more restrictive the parents), but not achievement among early adolescents. Relying on data compiled in Chicago, Denver, and Philadelphia by the Neighborhood Project, Elliott et al (1996) find that neighborhood disadvantage affects successful behavioral development and delinquency among adolescents, but only via the mediating effect of informal social control (a concept encompassing many of the variables of social organization and collective efficacy, which we discuss below). Using data from the Multi-City Study of Urban Inequality, Tigges et al (1998) find that neighborhood poverty significantly increases social isolation and decreases access to resources. The ambitious Moving to Opportunity study is preparing early findings at the time of this writing. We should reiterate that most of these studies, though they may point to strong correlations, cannot make causal statements. Still, if these studies are any indication, future, more sophisticated work will probably show that (a) neighborhoods affect life chances during early childhood and late adolescence, that (b) most neighborhood effects are not as strong as family effects, and that (c) social networks, which sometimes are linked to neighborhoods but often transcend them, are critical.

The Mechanisms Behind Neighborhood Effects

How does neighborhood poverty produce its negative effect? Surprisingly few studies have tackled this question seriously, although many researchers have argued that we need to do so (Jencks & Mayer 1990b, Tienda 1991, Furstenberg & Hughes 1997). Based on the works that have addressed this question (Wilson 1987, 1996, Jencks & Mayer 1990b, Massey & Denton 1993), we identify two general categories of models: socialization mechanisms, which describe how neighborhoods socialize those who grow up in them, and instrumental mechanisms, which describe how individual agency is limited by neighborhood conditions.[2]

---

[2]Jencks & Mayer (1990a) propose a categorization based on whether advantaged or disadvantaged neighbors are beneficial or detrimental to a person's life chances. Our categorization is based on the type of effect the mechanism is purported to have.

Socialization mechanisms tend to conceive of individuals as (relatively passive) recipients of powerful socializing forces, suggesting that neighborhoods mold those who grow up in them into certain behavioral patterns. For this reason, these mechanisms tend to focus on children and adolescents. There are six socialization mechanisms. The epidemic model (Jencks & Mayer 1990b, Wilson 1987) argues that when many of a child's neighborhood peers engage in a certain type of behavior, the child will be socialized into engaging in such behavior. The collective socialization model (Jencks & Mayer 1990b, Wilson 1987) argues that having a scarcity of successful role models in their neighborhood makes children less likely to envision success for themselves (see also Cutler & Glaeser 1997, Newman 1999). The institutional model (Jencks & Mayer 1990b) argues that nonresident adults (such as teachers and police officers) attached to institutions in the neighborhood will treat young people worse if the neighborhood is poor (thus either teaching them poorly or treating them as criminals). A fourth, the linguistic isolation model, refers to the socialization of African-American children in poor, segregated neighborhoods (Massey & Denton 1993, also Labov & Harris 1986). It argues that black children under such circumstances become isolated from Standard American English, absorb only Black English Vernacular, and therefore do poorly in school and when interviewing for jobs. The fifth, relative deprivation, model argues that poor children will be worse off in rich than in poor neighborhoods (Jencks & Mayer 1990b). Because people judge their economic position by comparing themselves to those around them, poor children will develop more unfavorable opinions of themselves the richer the neighborhoods they live in, resorting (in many cases) to deviance as a maladaptive response. The sixth is the oppositional culture model (Massey & Denton 1993 and Jencks & Mayer 1990b call this the cultural conflict model), which argues that either segregation or neighborhood poverty causes residents to develop a culture opposed to mainstream norms and values.

Whereas socialization models explain how neighborhood environments socialize individuals, instrumental models focus on how individual agency is limited by neighborhood environment. Here, the mechanisms tend to focus on adults, rather than children and adolescents. The most prominent of these is the networks isolation model,[3] which argues that being in a poor, or extensively unemployed, neighborhood will disconnect individuals from social networks of employed people, making it difficult for them to obtain information about job opportunities (Wilson 1987, 1996, Elliott 1999, Tigges et al 1998). The resource model argues that poor neighborhoods, deprived of institutional resources such as schools, churches, recreational areas, and daycare centers, make it difficult for parents to raise their children effectively (Wilson 1987, Brooks-Gunn et al 1997a,b). (See Jencks & Mayer 1990b for a variant of this model.) The final one is the limitation of

---

[3] Wilson uses the term "social isolation" to encompass the combined effects of job network isolation, role models, peers, and resource deprivation. We believe that disentangling them into their separate components allows for more systematic future work.

political alliances model. Massey & Denton (1993), focusing not on neighborhood poverty but on neighborhood segregation, argue that blacks have a difficult time developing political alliances across racial lines because, in conditions of segregation, no neighborhood-specific benefits accrued to blacks will accrue to members of other races. Consequently, they are unable to attract the public resources that will undergird decent schools, playgrounds, and business investment.

Most of these models have received little or no theoretical or empirical attention (Newman 1992; but see Rankin & Quane 2000, Fernandez & Harris 1992, Huckfeldt 1983, Elliott 1999, Tigges et al 1998). Most of them require observational and interview data that students of urban poverty have not collected systematically. Students have also spent little time thinking through these explanations, some of which rely on tenuous assumptions about how much time people spend in their neighborhoods, how much they interact with their neighbors, and how attitudes and values develop (see Wellman 1988, 1999, Fischer 1982).

There is one more model of how neighborhood effects work, one that focuses on the effects not on individuals but on neighborhood crime. Building on the foundation laid by the works of Shaw & McKay (1942), Sampson and his colleagues argue that a major cause of delinquency is social disorganization or the lack of collective efficacy (Sampson 1988, 1999, Sampson & Groves 1989, Sampson & Raudenbush 1999, Sampson & Wilson 1995, Sampson et al 1997). In empirical papers, both terms have referred to (*a*) the density of social networks in a neighborhood, (*b*) the extent of neighbors' involvement in voluntary associations, and (*c*) the degree to which neighbors are willing to supervise the young and intervene in social situations for the collective good; the term collective efficacy has tended to refer in greater degree to the latter attribute. Sampson and his colleagues have collected a wide array of evidence to demonstrate that neighborhoods with a high level of social organization and collective efficacy have lower crime rates, regardless of their poverty level. Since poor neighborhoods tend to be lower on these factors, their crime rates tend to be high.

Yet like most neighborhood studies the work is unable to make strong causal statements. Furthermore, Patillo-McCoy (1998, 1999) finds in recent work that social organization does not always lead to lower crime. On the contrary, in the black middle-class neighborhood she studied, dense, organized internal networks between gang and nongang residents make for highly organized, powerful drug-dealers. Most of the dealers grew up in the neighborhood, so residents, reluctant to see their nephews, cousins, and grandchildren in jail, fail to seek the police enforcement the neighborhood could use. A more general problem with the social organization literature is that, despite its impressive cross-sectional evidence, it has produced little on how social organization is generated in a neighborhood and how it changes over time (but see Gregory 1998).

The literature on neighborhood effects has produced some of the most fruitful, and in some ways most sophisticated, recent work in urban poverty. Much of this work has been methodological of necessity. But this narrow focus has shifted attention away from the important questions of how we should think about neighborhoods and by what mechanisms they affect the people who live in them. This neglect makes many of the studies on neighborhood effects unsatisfying, both because they often fail to account for the methodological problems that make them unreliable and because often the most they can tell us is that census tracts are highly correlated with certain social problems. In the words of Tienda (1991:258), "[b]efore encouraging further statistical modeling to capture neighborhood effects, more conceptual groundwork is needed to specify . . . the exposure, selection, and feedback effects that define how neighborhoods shape the behavior of the poor."

CULTURE

The rigid distinction between structural and cultural explanations has begun to loosen, and many sociologists now employ both types of explanations in their accounts of urban poverty (Anderson 1999, Massey & Denton 1993). Wilson (1987, 1996), generally known as a structuralist, argues that, though the lack of jobs was the ultimate cause behind the inner-city destitution, cultural and behavioral patterns perpetuate the conditions of the poor. Because this resurgence is still in its infancy, much of the new work is a revision or revisiting of theories developed during the late 1960s and early 1970s. Below we cover this work, focusing on inner-city or underclass culture and on the approaches from the sociology of culture recently being applied to urban poverty.

Inner-City or Underclass Culture

An overarching issue in this new literature has been whether there is an inner-city or underclass culture that, whatever its cause, perpetuates inequality (see Marks 1991, Gould 1999, Lawson 1992, Mincy 1994, Wilson 1996). The issue requires sociologists to examine (*a*) how they define culture, (*b*) whether there is a relatively homogenous culture of the inner city, and (*c*) whether this inner-city culture, if it exists, is significantly different from other forms of American culture. The first question has tormented both sociologists and anthropologists for decades, and there is no reason to believe we will ever arrive at a consensus. The discourse, however, appears to have shifted away from the narrow definitions of culture as values or norms characteristic of conservative accounts. Most sociologists today who think about this issue follow (at least nominally) Swidler's (1986:273) definition of culture as a "'tool kit' of habits, skills, and lifestyles from which people construct 'strategies of action.'" Beyond this, however, students of urban poverty still treat culture somewhat simplistically.

Equally important are the questions of whether it is sensible to think of inner-city culture as internally homogeneous, and in what ways this culture differs from middle-class or mainstream culture. Most scholars do not view inner-city culture as completely homogeneous, but much of the literature, focused largely on African-Americans, ignores the diversity created by the influence of Latinos, Asians, and

West Indians living in inner cities and large metropolitan areas (see Waters & Eschbach 1995, Moore & Pinderhughes 1993, Bourgois 1995, Waters 1999). To the extent that contemporary scholars see inner-city culture as heterogeneous, they usually follow the lead of the seminal works of Hannerz (1969), Rainwater (1970), and Valentine (1968), who tended to describe inner-city culture as composed of both "ghetto-specific" and "mainstream" (in Hannerz' 1969 terms) forms of behavior. Anderson (1999), e.g., in a study of inter-personal relations in inner-city Philadelphia, finds what he calls both "street" and "decent" families living in the same urban neighborhoods.

Categorizations such as street culture, however, can easily slip into compendia of all undesirable cultural traits, leaving massive conceptual and empirical gaps. This issue is so critical that an example is worth discussing. Consider Massey & Denton's (1993) recent application of the oppositional culture thesis, which posits that black inner-city culture is not only different but also directly and self-consciously opposed to the norms and values of the white middle-class. The term originates in the work of Ogbu, who presented evidence that black adolescents in a predominantly black high school devalued schoolwork out of a fear of being called braniacs; Ogbu argued that this devaluation was the result of their rejection of white culture (Fordham & Ogbu 1986; Ogbu's thesis has been challenged recently).[4] Massey & Denton (1993), whose intent is to provide a mechanism for how neighborhood segregation affects life chances, argue that black people in segregated neighborhoods develop their culture as an oppositional stance against "white" cultural traits. Consider the following passage:

> [B]lack street culture . . . [legitimizes] certain behaviors . . . that . . . [are] held in contempt by white society. . . . If whites speak Standard American English, succeed in school, work hard at routine jobs, marry, and support their children, then to be "black" requires one to speak Black English, do poorly in school, denigrate conventional employment, shun marriage, and raise children outside of marriage. To do otherwise would be to "act white." (Massey & Denton 1993:167–68)

The implication of this passage is that poor urban blacks—not just the teens in Ogbu's schools but also adults—shun work because whites work; shun marriage because white women marry; and speak Black English vernacular because whites speak Standard English. No evidence is produced in support of what seems, on its face, an implausible set of conclusions. Indeed, there is ample empirical

---

[4]See Carter (1999), Cook & Ludwig (1998), and Ainsworth-Darnell & Downey (1998), most of whom find that black students are no more likely than white students to rebel against schoolwork. Indeed, the same phenomenon is widely acknowledged in ethnographic studies of white students (e.g., Willis 1977, Kinney 1993). The fact that most of us, regardless of race, can recall either rebelliousness or the fear of being called "braniacs" or "nerds" should raise suspicions about an obligatory link between race and opposition to school among teens. On the other hand, we should point out that the presence of "oppositional cultures" across racial groups does not mean that the consequences of adopting that stance is the same for teens of all races.

evidence that these characterizations are either misguided or incorrect (on work, see Newman 1999, Petterson 1997, Duneier 1992, 1999; on marital attitudes, see Wilson 1996:98–105, Anderson 1991, 1999:Ch. 5; on the historical origins of Black English Vernacular, see Dillard 1972; on attitudes toward achievement in education, see Carter 1999).[5] Massey & Denton (1993) have produced some of the most sophisticated and trenchant work in urban poverty, and their general arguments about the importance of persistent segregation (see above) are both cogent and well supported by the available evidence. Nonetheless, the application of the oppositional culture thesis to urban poverty is empirically unsubstantiated.

The overall literature on inner-city culture should address the specific ways this culture (or cultures) differs from mainstream or middle-class culture (or cultures). Any strict inner-city/mainstream or underclass/middle-class dichotomy faces the danger of degenerating into stereotypes. Indeed, several recent ethnographic works offer fresh perspectives and correctives on the differences, real or alleged, between inner-city and mainstream culture. Nightingale (1993) finds that the black boys he studies in inner-city Philadelphia not only receive a steady influx of American mainstream culture but in fact embody what the author considers its preeminent cultural values: violence, individualism, materialism, and consumerism. What is poignant about Nightingale's work is that it forces us to face not just sociology's stereotypes of the inner city, but also its romantic notions of what constitutes the mainstream. The perceptions of the middle-class we use to compare to the ghetto are generally impressionistic and selective ideals based on what we believe society should look like; these are poor heuristics for interpreting cultural practices in the inner city.

Pattillo-McCoy (1999) dismantles many of our perceptions of what constitutes the middle class in her study of a black middle-class neighborhood in Chicago. She finds that the black middle class is not isolated from the black lower class and that part of its daily struggle is to attain the crime-free character of many white middle-class neighborhoods. Another recent attack on stereotyping by sociologists is Duneier's (1992), which shows that many of the poorer black men of Chicago value work, responsibility, honesty, loyalty, and integrity as much as or more than the average middle-class person. Newman (1999), one of the authors of this review, finds that many of the poor residents of Harlem are not only willing but anxious to take no-benefit, minimum-wage jobs and that they believe in work, family, and

---

[5]We should also note a problem with the basic logic of the thesis. In order for individuals to reject a set of cultural attitudes, they must have some exposure to it. To reject schoolwork, they must have been in school; to rejects whites, they must have seen them, or at least heard about them. Thus, in order for Afro-Americans to develop an oppositional culture, they need to have come into contact with the culture they are trying to oppose. But the more segregated neighborhoods are, the *less* inter-racial contact there is, so the fewer the number of whites to associate with certain cultural traits and the fewer the cultural traits blacks would know to oppose. If a teenager sees almost no whites in her day-to-day life, then why should she associate any particular cultural traits with whites? In fact, the more logical proposition would be that blacks in predominantly white, not predominantly black, environments are likely to develop an oppositional identity.

responsibility. These works do not represent a coherent theory of how to think about inner-city culture, and they are limited in their generalizability because they often focus on one city or even one neighborhood. They provide important correctives to the predominant perceptions among sociologists and open the door to more nuanced and systematic theoretical work—work that may well uncover an inner-city culture that is not only heterogeneous but also contradictory and unsystematic.

There is a final issue in the inner-city culture literature with which new research must contend. Some cultural theorists argued that, though the original cause of inner-city cultural patterns was the (structural) absence of jobs, this culture was somewhat self-perpetuating, so that people would find it difficult to start working even if conditions did improve. Wilson (1996, 1987), for instance, rejects Lewis's (1968) culture-of-poverty theory but argues that long-term unemployment generates a low self-efficacy among urban dwellers, making it difficult for them to take advantage of economic opportunities if and when these arise. But labor markets have tightened and joblessness among black men has dropped precipitously (Freeman & Rodgers 1999). This does not automatically refute the self-efficacy thesis, but it forces scholars to assess how widespread self-efficacy (or any cultural trait) is and, most importantly, how resistant it is to change.

Cultural Approaches Recently Applied to Urban Poverty

A few approaches from the sociology of culture have been applied recently to issues in urban poverty. One of these is the boundary work approach (Lamont 1992, Lamont & Fournier 1992). The approach, with roots in the sociology of ethnicity (Barth 1969) and of science and knowledge (Gieryn 1995, Small 1999), is the topic of an important new collection of papers (Lamont 1999). Boundary-work, rather than a comprehensive theory, is a perspective by which sociologists examine relationships between individuals or groups not by studying their inherent characteristics but by analyzing the boundaries they draw between and among one another, such as when the working poor define themselves in opposition to the poor who do not work. The collection applies the perspective to the relationship among race, culture, and urban poverty; it examines boundary-work within the black community, black and white attitudes toward race, and attitudes among blacks toward urban street culture. Much research remains to be done to determine whether and how this boundary work has lasting effects on the perpetuation of urban poverty.

Finally, the work of Bourdieu (1977, Bourdieu & Wacquant 1992) has been touched by a number of students in urban poverty. Wilson (1996) hints at the notion of habitus and cites Bourdieu when he describes the disposition-forming effects of prolonged unemployment. McLeod (1995) employs it to analyze the differences between two groups of boys, one black, one white, who have different aspirations despite their similar structural conditions. Young (1999a, 1999b) finds that the young black men he studies have accumulated varieties of cultural capital, but not enough of it to ensure their upward mobility. Nevertheless, most applications of Bourdieu's work to urban poverty do not engage Bourdieu's deeper theoretical questions—particularly the relationship among the concepts of habitus, capital, and field—that applications do in other fields, such as political sociology, (see, e.g., Brubaker 1996). If they did, they would do much to improve the quality of our thinking about whether Bourdieu has something to offer to studies of urban inequality.

CONCLUSION

We have argued that some of the current work on the family, the neighborhood, and culture in urban poverty revisits ideas from the 1960s and early 1970s; some of it is empirically weak, and some of it is under-conceptualized. Yet we have also shown that much of it is provocative and promising. Throughout the paper we have signaled several important avenues for further study, but a few issues merit greater discussion. The most important is for mainstream work in urban poverty to take more seriously the greater and recent demographic changes taking place in cities, such as the growth of large metropolitan areas in the west and southwest (e.g., Los Angeles, Houston); the recent re-entry of the middle-class into certain cities (e.g., Boston, New York, San Francisco) and the accompanying tighter housing markets; the long-standing and rapidly increasing "digital divide" between the rich and poor; and the economic, cultural, and social dynamics generated by the increasing presence of Asian, Latino, and recent Eastern European immigrants. This work demands more comparative and historical research, studies that examine differences between nations, ethnic groups, cities, and geographic regions. Here, it is particularly pressing that students go beyond the easily available census data, which will always pull research toward its strengths: census tracts and black-white differences (the Latino data, e.g., are notoriously problematic).

Comparative work is also necessary on the work on birthrates. In particular, the quickly rising out-of-wedlock birthrate among white women and the rates among Latinas should be a greater preoccupation of mainstream urban poverty students, especially since Latinos are quickly becoming the largest minority (and already are in some cities). This work should also consider how the recent drop in unemployment affects marriage. Indeed, research on the working poor should come to the fore in light of recent welfare reform and the growth of the low-wage labor market. We noted many issues in the work on neighborhoods, but we should emphasize that the growing literature on social capital and networks, which we could not cover, should complement the neighborhood effects literature well (e.g., Wellman 1999). Finally, the cultural literature in urban poverty, still in its infancy (or early re-incarnation from the 1960s), is in dire need of conceptual work. In this vein, comparative and historical studies are particularly important to assess the origins and development of urban cultures. The existing ethnographies have provided critical insights, but because so few of them have been comparative, they have not taken us far enough on the cultural front. If anything, these ethnographies, and the new work in urban poverty as a whole, has laid the groundwork for the important work to come.

ACKNOWLEDGMENTS

Support for this paper was provided by a National Science Foundation Integrative Graduate Education and Research Traineeship Grant (NSF No. 9870661). In addition we thank Silvia Dominguez, Herbert Gans, Christopher Jencks, and James Quane for comments and criticisms.

Visit the Annual Reviews home page at www.AnnualReviews.org

LITERATURE CITED

Ainsworth-Darnell J, Downey D. 1998. Assessing the oppositional culture explanation for racial/ethnic differences in school performance. *Am. Sociol. Rev.* 63:536–53

Anderson E. 1991. Neighborhood effects on teenage pregnancy. See Jencks & Peterson 1991, pp. 375–98

Anderson E. 1994. The code of the streets. *Atlantic Monthly* (May)

Anderson E. 1999. *Code of the Street: Decency, Violence, and the Moral Life of the Inner City.* New York: Norton

Barth F. 1969. *Ethnic Groups and Boundaries.* London: George Allen & Unwin

Bourdieu P. 1977. *Outline of a Theory of Practice.* Cambridge, UK: Cambridge Univ. Press

Bourdieu P, Wacquant L. 1992. *An Invitation to Reflexive Sociology.* Chicago: Univ. Chicago Press

Bourgois PI. 1995. *In Search of Respect: Selling Crack in El Barrio.* Cambridge, UK: Cambridge Univ. Press

Brooks-Gunn J, Duncan GJ, Aber JA. 1997a. *Neighborhood Poverty:* Vol. I: *Context and Consequences for Children.* New York: Russell Sage Found.

Brooks-Gunn J, Duncan GJ, Aber JA. 1997b. *Neighborhood Poverty:* Vol II: *Policy Implications in Studying Neighborhoods.* New York: Russell Sage Found.

Brooks-Gunn J, Duncan GJ, Leventhal T,

Aber JL. 1997c. Lessons learned and future directions for research on the neighborhoods in which we live. See Brooks-Gunn et al 1997a, pp. 279–98

Brubaker R. 1996. *Nationalism Reframed: Nationhood and the National Question in the New Europe.* Cambridge, UK: Cambridge Univ. Press

Burton LM, Price-Spratlen T, Spencer MB. 1997. On ways of thinking about measuring neighborhoods: implications for studying context and developmental outcomes for children. See Brooks-Gunn et al 1997b, pp. 132–44

Carter PL. 1999. *Balancing "acts": issues of identity and cultural resistance in the social and educational behaviors of minority youth.* PhD dissertation. Columbia Univ., New York

Chaskin RJ. 1997. Perspectives on neighborhood and community: a review of the literature. *Soc. Serv. Rev.* 71(4):521–47

Cherlin AJ. 1992. *Marriage, Divorce, Remarriage: Revised and Enlarged Edition.* Cambridge, MA: Harvard Univ. Press

Cook P, Ludwig J. 1998. The burden of "acting white": Do black adolescents disparage academic achievement? In *The Black White Test Score Gap*, ed. C Jencks, M Phillips, pp. 375–401. Washington, DC: Brookings Inst.

Crane J. 1991. Effects of neighborhoods on

dropping out of school and teenage child-bearing. See Jencks & Peterson 1991, pp. 299–320

Cutler D, Glaeser E. 1997. Are ghettos good or bad? *Q. J. Econ.* 112:827–62

Denton NA, Massey DS. 1988. Residential seg-regation of blacks, Hispanics, and Asians by socioeconomic status and generation. *Soc. Sci. Q.* 69(4):797–817

Dietrich LC. 1998. *Chicana Adolescents: Bitches, 'Ho's, and Schoolgirls.* Westport, CT: Praeger

Dillard JL. 1972. *Black English: Its History and Usage in the United States.* New York: Ran-dom House

Duncan GJ, Aber JL. 1997. Neighborhood mo-dels and measures. See Brooks-Gunn et al 1997a, pp. 62–78

Duncan GJ, Connell JP, Klebanov PK. 1997. Conceptual and methodological issues in estimating causal effects of neighborhoods and family conditions on individual devel-opment. See Brooks-Gunn et al 1997a, pp. 219–50

Duneier M. 1992. *Slim's Table: Race, Res-pectability, and Masculinity.* Chicago: Univ. Chicago Press

Duneier M. 1999. *Sidewalk.* New York: Farrar, Straus, & Giroux

Elliott D, Wilson WJ, Huizinga D, Sampson R, Elliott S, Rankin B. 1996. The effects of neighborhood disadvantage on adolescent development. *J. Res. Crime & Delinquency* 33(4):389–426

Elliott JR. 1999. Social isolation and labor mar-ket insulation: network and neighborhood ef-fects on less-educated urban workers. *Sociol. Q.* 40(2):199–216

Farley R, Frey WH. 1994. Changes in the seg-regation of whites from blacks during the 1980s: small steps toward a more integrated society. *Am. Sociol. Rev.* 59:23–45

Fernandez R, Harris D. 1992. Social isolation and the underclass. In *Drugs, Crime, and Social Isolation*, ed. A Harrell, G Peterson, pp. 257–93. Washington, DC: Urban Inst. Press

Fischer C. 1982. *To Dwell Among Friends: Per-sonal Networks in Town and City.* Chicago: Univ. Chicago Press

Fordham S, Ogbu J. 1986. Black students' school success: coping with the burden of 'acting white.' *Urban Rev.* 18(3):176–206

Freeman RB, Rodgers WM. 1999. Area eco-nomic conditions and the labor market out-comes of young men in the 1990s expansion. *NBER Work. Pap. No. W7073*

Furstenberg FF. 1991. As the pendulum swings: teenage childbearing and social concern. *Fam. Relat.* 10:127–38

Furstenberg FF. 1992. Teenage childbearing and cultural rationality: a thesis in search of evidence. *Fam. Relat.* 41:239–43

Furstenberg FF, Cook TD, Eccles J, Elder GH, Sameroff A. 1999. *Managing to Make It: Urban Families and Adolescent Success.* Chicago: Univ. Chicago Press

Furstenberg FF, Hughes ME. 1997. The influ-ence of neighborhoods on children's devel-opment: a theoretical perspective and a re-search agenda. See Brooks-Gunn et al 1997b, pp. 23–47

Gephart MA. 1997. Neighborhoods and com-munities as contexts for development. See Brooks-Gunn et al 1997a, pp. 1–43

Geronimus AT. 1991. Teenage childbearing and social reproductive disadvantage: the evolu-tion of complex questions and the demise of simple answers. *Fam. Relat.* 40:463–71

Geronimus AT. 1996. Black/white differences in the relationship of maternal age to birth-weight: a population-based test of the weath-ering hypothesis. *Soc. Sci. Med.* 42(4):589–97

Geronimus AT, Bound J. 1990. Black/white differences in women's reproductive-related health status: evidence from vital statistics. *Demography* 27(3):457–66

Geronimus AT, Bound J, Waidman TA. 1999a. Poverty, time, and place: variation in ex-cess mortality across selected US popula-tions, 1980–1990. *J. Epidemiol. & Commu-nity Health* 43(6):325–24

Geronimus AT, Bound J, Waidman TA. 1999b.

Health inequality and population variation in fertility-timing. *Soc. Sci. & Med.* 49(12):163–36

Geronimus AT, Bound J, Waidman TA, Hillemeier MM, Burns PB. 1996. Excess mortality among blacks and whites in the United States. *N. Engl. J. Med.* 335(21):1552–8

Geronimus AT, Korenman S. 1992. The socioeconomic consequences of teen childbearing reconsidered. *Q. J. Econ.* 107:1187–214

Geronimus AT, Korenman S. 1993. The socioeconomic costs of teenage childbearing: evidence and interpretation. *Demography* 30(2):281–90

Gieryn T. 1995. Boundaries of science. In *Handbook of Science and Technology Studies*, ed. S Jasanoff, G Markle, JC Petersen, T Pinch, pp. 393–441. Thousand Oaks, CA: Sage

Gould M. 1999. Race and theory: culture, poverty, and adaptation to discrimination in Wilson and Ogbu. *Sociol. Theory* 17(2):171–200

Gregory S. 1998. *Black Corona: Race and the Politics of Place in an Urban Community.* Princeton, NJ: Princeton Univ. Press

Grusky DB. 1994. *Social Stratification: Class, Race, and Gender in Sociological Perspective.* Boulder, CO: Westview

Gutman HG. 1976. *The Black Family in Slavery and Freedom, 1750–1925.* New York: Pantheon

Hannerz U. 1969. *Soulside: Inquiries into Ghetto Culture and Community.* New York: Columbia Univ. Press

Hoffman SD, Foster EM, Furstenberg FF. 1993a. Reevaluating the costs of teenage childbearing. *Demography* 30(1):1–13

Hoffman SD, Foster EM, Furstenberg FF. 1993b. Reevaluating the costs of teenage childbearing: response to Geronimus and Korenman. *Demography* 30(2):291–96

Hess SC. 1990. The effect of employment and welfare on family structure: explaining the time-trend of female-headed families. *Am. Econ.* 34(1):76–82

Huckfeldt R. 1983. Social contexts, social networks, and urban neighborhoods: environ-

mental constraints on friendship choice. *Am. J. Sociol.* 89:651–69

Jargowsky PA. 1994. Ghetto poverty among blacks in the 1980s. *J. Policy Analysis & Manage.* 13:288–310

Jargowsky PA. 1997. *Poverty and Place: Ghettos, Barrios, and the American City.* New York: Russell Sage Found.

Jargowsky PA, Bane MJ. 1990. Ghetto poverty: basic questions. See Lynn & McGeary 1990, pp. 16–67

Jargowsky PA, Bane MJ. 1991. Ghetto poverty in the United States, 1970–1980. See Jencks & Peterson 1991, pp. 235–73

Jencks C. 1991. Is the American underclass growing? See Jencks & Peterson 1991, pp. 28–100

Jencks C. 1992. *Rethinking Social Policy: Race, Poverty, and the Underclass.* Cambridge, MA: Harvard Univ. Press

Jencks C, Mayer S. 1990a. Residential segregation, job proximity, and black job opportunities. See Lynn & McGeary 1990, pp. 187–222

Jencks C, Mayer S. 1990b. The social consequences of growing up in a poor neighborhood. See Lynn & McGeary 1990, pp. 111–86

Jencks C, Peterson P. 1991. *The Urban Underclass.* Washington, DC: Brookings Inst.

Kain JF. 1968. Housing segregation, Negro employment, and metropolitan decentralization. *Q. J. Econ.* 82(2):1975–97

Kain JF. 1992. The spatial mismatch hypothesis: three decades later. *Housing Policy Debate* 3(2):371–460

Kaplan EB. 1997. *Not Our Kind of Girl: Unraveling the Myths of Black Teenage Motherhood.* Berkeley: Univ. Calif. Press

Kasarda JD. 1989. Urban industrial transition and the underclass. *Annals, AAPSS* 501:26–47

Kinney DA. 1993. From nerds to normals: the recovery of identity among adolescents from middle school to high school. *Sociol. Ed.* 66:21–40

Labov W, Harris W. 1986. De facto segregation of black and white vernaculars. In *Current Issues in Linguistic Theory 53: Diversity and*

Dichotomy, ed. D. Sankoff, 1–24. Amsterdam: Benjamins

Lamont M. 1992. *Money, Morals, and Manners*. Chicago: Univ. Chicago Press

Lamont M. 1999. *The Cultural Territories of Race: Black and White Boundaries*. Chicago: Univ. Chicago Press & Russell Sage Found.

Lamont M, Fournier M. 1992. *Cultivating Differences: Symbolic Boundaries and the Making of Inequality*. Chicago: Univ. Chicago Press.

Lawson BE. 1992. *The Underclass Question*. Philadelphia, PA: Temple Univ. Press

Lerman RI. 1989. Employment opportunities of young men and family formation. *Am. Econ. Rev.* 79(02):62–67

Lewis O. 1968. The culture of poverty. In *On Understanding Poverty: Perspectives from the Social Sciences*, ed. DP Moynihan, pp. 187–220. New York: Basic Books

Luker K. 1996. *Dubious Conceptions: The Politics of Teenage Pregnancy*. Cambridge, MA: Harvard Univ. Press

Lynn L, McGreary M. 1990. *Inner-City Poverty in the United States*. Washington, DC: Natl. Academy Press

Marc RD, Winship C. 1991. Socioeconomic change and the decline of marriage for blacks and whites. See Jencks & Mayer 1991, pp. 175–202

Marks C. 1991. The urban underclass. *Annu. Rev. Sociol.* 17:445–66

Massey DS. 1998. Back to the future: the rediscovery of neighborhood context. *Contemp. Sociol.* 27(6):570–72

Massey DS, Denton NA. 1987. Trends in the residential segregation of blacks, Hispanics, and Asians: 1970–1980. *Am. Sociol. Rev.* 52:802–25

Massey DS, Denton NA. 1993. *American Apartheid: Segregation and the Making of the Underclass*. Cambridge, MA: Harvard Univ. Press

Massey DS, Gross AB, Shibuya K. 1994. Migration, segregation, and the geographic concentration of poverty. *Am. Sociol. Rev.* 59:425–45

McLanahan S, Sandefur G. 1994. *Growing Up With a Single Parent: What Hurts, What Helps*. Cambridge, MA: Harvard Univ. Press

McLeod J. 1995. *Ain't No Makin' It: Aspirations and Attainment in a Low-Income Neighborhood*. Boulder, CO: Westview

Mincy RB. 1994. The underclass: concept, theory, and evidence. In *Confronting Poverty: Prescriptions for Change*, ed. SH Danziger, GD Sandefur, DH Weinberg, pp. 109–46. New York: Russell Sage Found.

Moore JW, Pinderhughes R. 1993. *In the Barrios: Latinos and the Underclass Debate*. New York: Russell Sage Found.

Murray CA. 1984. *Losing Ground: American Social Policy, 1950–80*. New York: Basic Books

Newman KS. 1992. Culture and structure in *The Truly Disadvantaged*. *City & Soc.* 6(1):3–25

Newman KS. 1999. *No Shame in My Game: The Working Poor and the Inner City*. New York: Knopf & Russell Sage Found.

Nightingale C. 1993. *On the Edge: A History of Poor Black Children and Their American Dreams*. New York: Basic Books

Ong PM, Bonacich E, Cheng L. 1994. *The New Asian Immigration in Los Angeles and Global Restructuring*. Philadelphia, PA: Temple Univ. Press

Patterson O. 1998. *Rituals of Blood: Consequences of Slavery in Two American Centuries*. Washington, DC: Civitas/Counterpoint

Pattillo-McCoy M. 1998. Sweet mothers and gangbangers: managing crime in a black middle-class neighborhood. *Soc. Forces* 76(3):747–74

Pattillo-McCoy M. 1999. *Black Picket Fences: Privilege and Peril among the Black Middle Class*. Chicago: Univ. Chicago Press

Petterson S. 1997. Are young black men really less willing to work? *Am. Sociol. Rev.* 62(4):605–13

Preston SH, Lim S, Morgan SP. 1992. African-American marriage in 1910: beneath the surface of census data. *Demography* 29(1):1–15

Quillian L. 1999. Migration patterns and the growth or high-poverty neighborhoods, 1970–1990. *Am. J. Sociol.* 105(1):1–37

Rainwater L. 1970. *Behind Ghetto Walls: Black Families in a Federal Slum*. Chicago: Aldine

Rankin B, Quane J. 2000. Neighborhood poverty and the social isolation of inner-city African-American families. *Soc. Forces* 79(1):139–64

Rolison GL. 1992. Black, single female-headed family formation in large U.S. cities. *Sociol. Q.* 33(3):473–81

Rosenbaum JE, Popkin SJ. 1991. Employment and earnings of low-income blacks who move to middle-class suburbs. See Jencks & Peterson 1991, pp. 342–56

Sampson RJ. 1988. Local friendship ties and community attachment in mass society: a multi-systemic model. *Am. Sociol. Rev.* 53:766–79

Sampson RJ. 1999. What community supplies. In *Urban Problems and Community Development*, ed. R Ferguson, WT Dickens, pp. 241–92. Washington, DC: Brookings Inst.

Sampson RJ, Groves WB. 1989. Community structures and crime: testing social disorganization theory. *Am. J. Sociol.* 94:774–802

Sampson RJ, Raudenbush SW. 1999. Systematic social observation of public spaces: a new look at disorder in urban neighborhoods. *Am. J. Sociol.* 103:603–51

Sampson RJ, Raudenbush SW, Earls F. 1997. Neighborhoods and violent crime: a multilevel study of collective efficacy. *Science* 277:918–24

Sampson RJ, Wilson WJ. 1995. Toward a theory of race, crime, and urban inequality. In *Crime and Inequality*, ed. J Hagan, R Peterson, 37–55. Stanford, CA: Stanford Univ. Press

Shaw C, McKay H. 1942. *Juvenile Delinquency and Urban Areas*. Chicago: Univ. Chicago Press

Small ML. 1999. Departmental conditions and the emergence of new disciplines: two cases in the legitimation of African-American Studies. *Theory Soc.* 28:659–707

South SJ, Crowder KD. 1999. Neighborhood effects on family formation: concentrated poverty and beyond. *Am. Sociol. Rev.* 64(1):113–32

Spencer MB, McDermott PA, Burton LM, Kochman TJ. 1997. An alternative approach to assessing neighborhood effects on early adolescent achievement and problem behavior. See Brooks-Gunn et al 1997b, pp. 145–63

Stack C. 1974. *All Our Kin*. New York: Harper & Row.

Stokes RG, Chevan A. 1996. Female-headed families: social and economic context of racial differences. *J. Urban Affairs* 18(3): 245–68

Swidler A. 1986. Culture in action: symbols and strategies. *Am. Sociol. Rev.* 51:273–86

Teitz MB, Chapple K. 1998. The causes of inner-city poverty: eight hypotheses in search of reality. *Cityscape* 3(3):33–70

Tienda M. 1991. Poor people and poor places: deciphering neighborhood effects on poverty outcomes. In *Macro-Micro Linkages in Sociology*, ed. J Huber, pp. 244–63. Newbury Park, CA: Sage

Tigges LM, Browne I, Green GP. 1998. Social isolation of the urban poor: race, class, and neighborhood effects on social resources. *Sociol. Q.* 39(1):53–77

US Census Bureau. 1999. *Statistical Abstract of the United States: 1999*. Washington, DC: USGPO

Valentine CA. 1968. *Culture and Poverty: Critique and Counter-proposals*. Chicago: Univ. Chicago Press.

Vartanian TP. 1999. Adolescent neighborhood effects on labor market and economic outcomes. *Soc. Serv. Rev.* June:142–67

Vega WA. 1990. Hispanic families in the 1980s: a decade of research. *J. Marriage & Fam.* 52:1015–24

Wacquant LJ, Wilson WJ. 1989. The cost of racial and class exclusion in the inner city. *Annals, AAPSS* 501:8–25

Waldinger R, Bozorgmehr M. 1996. *Ethnic Los Angeles*. New York: Russell Sage Found.

Walton J. 1993. Urban sociology: the contribution and limits of political economy. *Annu. Rev. Sociol.* 19:301–20

Waters MC. 1999. *Black Identities: West Indian Immigrant Dreams and American Realities*. New York: Russell Sage Found.

Waters MC, Eschbach K. 1995. Immigration and ethnic and racial inequality in the United States. *Annu. Rev. Sociol.* 21:419–46

Weicher JC. 1990. How poverty neighborhoods are changing. See Lynn & McGeary 1990, pp. 68–110

Wellman B. 1988. The community question reevaluated. *Compar. Urban & Commun. Res.* 1:81–107

Wellman B. 1999. *Networks in the Global Village: Life in Contemporary Communities.* Boulder, CO: Westview

Willis P. 1977. *Learning to Labor: How Working Class Kids Get Working Class Jobs.* New York: Columbia Univ. Press

Wilson WJ. 1987. *The Truly Disadvantaged: The Inner City, the Underclass, and Public Policy.* Chicago: Univ. Chicago Press

Wilson WJ. 1991a. Public policy research and *The Truly Disadvantaged.* See Jencks & Peterson 1991, pp. 460–82

Wilson WJ. 1991b. Studying inner-city social dislocations: the challenge of public agenda research: 1990 presidential address. *Am. Sociol. Rev.* 56(1):1–14

Wilson WJ. 1996. *When Work Disappears: The World of the New Urban Poor.* New York: Knopf

Wright EO. 1985. *Classes.* New York:Verso

Young AA. 1999a. Navigating race: getting ahead in the lives of "rags to riches" young black men. See Lamont 1999, pp. 30–62

Young AA. 1999b. The (non)accumulation of capital: explicating the relationship of structure and agency in the lives of poor black men. *Sociol. Theory* 17(2):201–27

Annu. Rev. Sociol. 2001. 27:47–76

CASES AND BIOGRAPHIES: An Essay on Routinization and the Nature of Comparison

Carol A. Heimer

Northwestern University and American Bar Foundation, Evanston, Illinois 60208;
e-mail: c-heimer@northwestern.edu

Key Words cognition, institutions, markets, law, organizations

■ **Abstract** Routines, protocols, and organization charts focus attention, structure cognition, and shape decision making. Participants in organizations, legal systems, and markets compare *cases*, deciding which protocol governs the treatment of each case in a stream. But situations vary in the extent to which thought and action are effectively governed by routines and standard operating procedures. In less structured or more chaotic situations, *biography* is an alternative form of analysis that shapes cognition and helps people make sense of otherwise uninterpretable events. Biography and narrative do their work by constructing the causal unity of objects over time rather than by constructing causation from a comparison across similar cases. Using examples such as critically ill infants, animals, heirlooms, the penalty phase of capital trials, juvenile justice, the lower criminal courts, religious relics, and cloth, the paper compares case and biographical analysis in organizations, legal settings, and markets, asking how these different ways of thinking come about and what follows from them.

INTRODUCTION

"The tool kit of any culture can be described as a set of prosthetic devices by which human beings can exceed or even redefine the 'natural limits' of human functioning," writes Bruner (1990, p. 21). Using the example of the natural limits on short-term memory, Bruner discusses how the constraints of biology can be mitigated by cultural devices and effective memory expanded. Although these cultural prosthetic devices can be employed to expand our vision, they can also be used to restrict it; like horses' blinders, culture can restrict vision to enhance focus.

Bureaucracies, legal systems, and markets all are social forms that make a virtue of standardization. In bureaucracies, we gain efficiency by having routines that tell us how to think about and work with similar objects. By working with objects that are standardized and ignoring the features that make them different one from the other, we are able to streamline our work and eliminate the noise from differences that are not central to the tasks we are performing. In legal systems, universalism is held up as an ideal because only by treating like cases alike can we be fair. By focusing on the key features of cases and ignoring those that are not made relevant by the law, we artificially restrict our attention so that we will not base decisions or judgments about guilt and innocence on irrelevant differences. In markets, standardization facilitates the comparison of goods and services that brings prices down and gives producers an incentive to improve their production practices. When the core similarities of goods are obscured by too many functionally irrelevant differences, consumers may not be able to make appropriate comparisons.

Bureaucratic routines act on standard objects; legal systems abstract cases from the rest of life; standardized commodities with a single cost and price are bought and sold in markets. All of those acts are also done by people who are born, grow up, work, form families, sicken, and die. All acts in bureaucracies, legal processes, or markets are, then, both instances of general categories and pieces of people's biographies. This truism implies that, for some purposes, acts and their subjects and objects may be analyzed and treated as "cases" of general processes and may be compared to other cases. For other purposes, the actions, objects, and persons may be analyzed and treated as having "biographies" that makes them unique. This paper analyzes these alternative ways of organizing thought about actions, actors, and objects by looking at how people react differently to cases and biographies in bureaucracies, legal settings, and markets.

Structures stand outside the people using them, though of course they are ultimately constructed and reshaped by them, both purposefully or through accretion. Though thinking may be shaped by systems of categories and the routines in which they are employed, it is as much by continual rebellion against case analysis as by conformity. We produce singularity in a wide variety of ways, many of which depend on some of the infrastructure of category systems. The unique identity of proper names, for instance, depends on surnames, which convey membership in a group, as well as on first and middle names, which identify a distinct member of the group (though perhaps one linked sentimentally to others). Identity comes both from the category and from being a unique, distinguishable member of the category. Without the substratum of standardization (e.g., in professional education), the contrast of the distinct identifier carries less meaning (e.g., having been trained in a specific subdiscipline or in a particularly good institution).[1] Guidelines for action come from category membership, but breaking the schema, offering a new interpretation, makes a person or other entity a unique example. A musical script is a template for a performance; by identifying the genre it supplies a set of standards that make a new interpretation understandable and meaningful. Surprisingly little may be required to enlist others to collaborate in creating

---

[1] See, for instance, Larson's discussion of the cognitive conditions for professional monopoly (1977, pp. 31–39).

meaningful distinctions—the value of prints apparently depends on a number signifying their place in a printing sequence (Melot 1986).[2] And sometimes uniqueness arises less by rebellion against case analysis or elaboration of categories than by the accumulation of categorical identifiers, whose intersection (in Simmelian fashion) creates a distinctive identity. These minor rebellions and embellishments also are crucial in supporting our sense of ourselves as active social beings, as agents.

Because we learn, do our work, exchange goods, form social groups, and create our identities through comparison and simultaneously through singularization, we need to examine the places where categorical systems and singularity overlap and look for the places where categorical systems fail. Where is singularization especially likely? Are there particular types of objects, actions, or actors that especially resist attempts to treat them as cases? Are there particular social locations, for instance on the boundaries of organizations, where case analysis breaks down? Are there particular users who resist the disciplining effects of routines? Do particular tasks require different mixes of case and biographical analysis?

VARIATIONS IN ROUTINIZATION

All sorts of institutions create routines, though, as we shall see, they also encounter people, situations, and objects not easily managed by their routines. The forms, check-lists, routines, scripts, organization charts, procedural requirements, and face-to-face meetings of organizations all serve to focus the attention and activity of participants. Sociologists vary in their assessments of the efficacy of these organizational efforts. Participants sometimes seem to find routines helpful; Leidner's (1993) trainees found scripts a useful crutch as they learned how to sell insurance. At other times routines seem irksome or even counterproductive; Vaughan (1996) shows how the engineers working on the O-ring problem were hindered by the "bureaupathology" of the space shuttle program. Although there may be some consensus that routines, protocols, and scripts provide an important template for novices and increase the likelihood that key tasks will be performed, organizational participants can be overwhelmed by routines. When too many items are considered critical (for instance in NASA's Flight Readiness Review), the value of such a designation diminishes (Vaughan 1996). After a certain point routines cease to focus attention. Apparently only an intermediate level of scripting or routinization focuses attention, just as Goffman (1961) argued that only an intermediate level of uncertainty makes games fun. Too many rules and too little uncertainty make the game boringly predictable; too few rules and too much uncertainty decrease incentives for mastery. Likewise, too much routinization is mind-numbing and

---

[2]After 1860, prints bore only the sequence number and the autograph of the artist who made the original print; the names of craftsmen doing the engraving or printing no longer appeared (Melot 1986).

dulls attention, but with too little routinization participants receive too few cues about where to direct their attention. These unanalyzable "numerous inpouring currents" result in the "blooming buzzing Confusion" described by William James (1984, p. 21).

Sociologists suggest that routines, scripts, protocols, and institutions shape attention and structure thinking (see, e.g., Berger & Luckmann 1967 DiMaggio 1997, Giddens 1984, Meyer & Rowan 1977; papers in Powell & DiMaggio 1991, Scott 1995 Zucker 1983). But sociologists also argue that culture is not integrated and coherent but instead is more appropriately thought of as fragmented, more a toolkit that people draw on than a unified system that constrains them (Bourdieu 1990, Sewell 1992, Swidler 1986).[3] Less attention has been given to how these two observations fit together. If institutionalized practices and routines are some of the "stuff" in the cultural toolkits that people might draw on, shouldn't we be asking what about these practices and routines might contribute to the fragmentary nature of culture? An examination of situations that varied in levels of routinization may tell us something about when and how institutions shape cognition and behavior and about what happens when individuals, objects, or actions resist categorization and so disrupt routines.

Three such situations come to mind: situations so mind-numbingly over-institutionalized that participants ignore routines, situations so under-institutionalized that participants must act without much guidance, and situations in which the conflict among institutions requires participants to decide which rules and routines are most appropriate or most compelling. Elsewhere I have shown how institutional competition reduces constraints on the behavior of organizational participants and creates the space for strategic manipulation of organizational routines (Heimer 1996, 1999).[4] Here I instead explore variation in levels of routinization—the activities of one group highly routinized, those of another much less shaped by routine and protocol—to show how routine and biography function as alternative ways of organizing cognition and shaping behavior. I develop this argument through a series of examples, one analyzed in considerable detail, the others more briefly, that show these divergent styles of thought in several different settings. In essence, I take comparison itself as my subject, asking how the routines of organizations, law, and markets contribute to variations in the kinds of comparisons people commonly make.[5]

---

[3]Note the parallel between the idea of culture as a toolkit and Chomsky's (1966) idea that a generative grammar can be used to create an infinity of sentences.

[4]Other kinds of constraints on cognitive processes also may be lessened by the give and take of social life. For instance, the powerful framing effects observed by psychologists such as Kahneman, Slovic, and Tversky (1982) may be more important in the laboratory than in ordinary social life (Heimer 1988) where people may contest a received frame.

[5]Douglas (1986), Zerubavel (1991) and Espeland & Stevens (1998) share this interest in the nature of comparison, though perhaps with less interest in its relation to routinization.

ORGANIZATIONS: BUREAUCRATIC ROUTINES AND FAMILY TIES

The productive processes of organizations have mostly been analyzed as processes that transform raw materials into consumable products. Clearly, organizations work on animate as well as on inanimate objects, on people as well as on things (Hochschild 1983, Leidner 1993, Heimer & Stevens 1997). It may seem most natural to us to think of inanimate objects as the concern of bureaucratic routines, the raw materials for productive processes. We are not surprised to find organizational routines that direct the attention of those who have to process iron into steel or make cars from the steel. It seems natural to have classification systems that tell us how to sort inanimate objects, what to do with them. Neither are we surprised to find that human beings are dealt with biographically. We know that people have relationships, that they develop from infants to children to adults, that they are active participants who help shape their world. What I have tried to show here, though, is that the division of biography and case does not map well onto the division between animate and inanimate. Things have biographies and people can be treated as raw materials and cases. Here I show how bureaucratic routines tend to produce case analysis, whether the bureaucracies process people, animals, or objects. But not all organizations are bureaucracies. Some organizations do not much rely on routines even though they are sites where people regularly pool their efforts and employ resources to achieve some common purpose and to keep the organization going (Ahrne 1994). Some of these, such as families, rely more on an infrastructure of commitment than an infrastructure of routine.

Conceiving Children: One Object in Two Settings

We generally think of children as being mainly the concern of their families, with increasing involvement of other bodies, such as schools, as they mature. Unlike other newborns, critically ill infants begin their lives as the focus of attention of a team of medical experts in a neonatal intensive care unit (NICU) as well as of their parents.[6] Occasionally, when medical careproviders and parents disagree about treatment, they also receive scrutiny from the legal system. Critically ill infants are thus a good example of how a single object is thought about and acted upon in multiple settings. The same infant is conceived as a patient by the medical team; as a young citizen by attorneys, court-appointed guardians, and judges; and as a child by parents (Heimer & Staffen 1998, pp. 137–77). Further, these settings vary in the degree to which activity is governed by schemas and protocols: families are less routinized and scripted than courts or hospitals.

---

[6]Social science studies of NICUs include Frohock (1986), Guillemin & Holmstrom (1986), Anspach (1993), and Heimer & Staffen (1998).

Clearly the hospitalized infant and the infant who has gone home are not *identical* entities. Parents care for one at home; the other is so sick that hospitalization is essential. Nevertheless there is substantial continuity in the object (the infant), coupled with a sharp discontinuity in the way activities are organized and documented and the infant conceptualized; this is what merits investigation.

Physicians are sometimes accused of treating by the numbers. Poring over medical records and engrossed in discussions with colleagues, they may scarcely glance at the patient. In contrast, parents spend little time with the numbers and many hours with the baby. Not knowing the contents of the medical record and unable to interpret test results, their best hope is to develop a parallel analysis grounded in visual and other sensory information, structured less by a medical conceptual scheme than by an evolving understanding of the child. Staff and familial observations are clearly about the same events and the same child, but the uses they make of information may contribute to quite different understandings of the situation. For instance, medical staff and parents both make use of the images produced by ultrasonography. But while medical texts tell physicians how to detect abnormalities and use the biparietal diameter of the fetal skull or the fetal femur length to estimate gestational age, baby books and cards accompanying the ultrasound print instruct parents to treat the print as a first photograph of their baby. These contrasting uses of ultrasonography are emblematic of the patterns of activity, contact, and thought that differentiate case from biographical analysis. These core differences, summarized in Table 1, are here illustrated with examples from infant intensive care.

Medical staff and parents identify infants in different ways. Among themselves, medical staff are likely to refer to the child by symptom ("the 25 weeker" or "the gastroskesis"); parents refer to their baby by name. Noticing this difference, one mother repeatedly reminded staff to call her child by name because "I just wanted to make sure that he was a person." Staff and parents also differ in the comparison points they employ. Staff continually compare their infant patient with others with similar diagnoses ("that's common in kids with hypoplastic left heart"); parents make comparisons over time and talk about the pregnancy, the child's future, and its anticipated relationship with other family members.

As ethnoanalysts thinking about the baby, medical staff and parents differ in how they characterize their relation to the baby, the baby's role, and their own actions. In their conversation, records, and notes, medical staff tend to portray themselves as the ones who make decisions and take action in treating their patient; infants are depicted as quite passive, either responding or not to the treatment. An occasional infant is depicted as more active, sometimes, tellingly, as refusing to go along with treatment (e.g., "he tried to die"). Generally, though, this is a relation of a subject acting on an object, a worker manipulating materials. Parents much more often describe a relation of subject-to-subject, the infant as a creature with interpersonal competence, and portraying the baby as acting, as having a personality and intentions. Although parents, like staff, give medications and administer therapies, they much more often depict the baby as an active participant whose

TABLE 1 Logic of comparison in case and biographical analysis

	Case analysis	**Biographical analysis**
Identity of entity	Member of category	Unique individual often indentified by proper name
Point of comparison	Other similar objects	Same object over time
Relation of ethnoanalyst to entity	Worker to materials, subject to object	Subject to subject
Agency of entity	Passive, acted upon	Active, shapes outcome, interacts with ethnoanalyst
Prototypical actions	Processing, acting on, exchanging, selling	Working together, exploring, interacting with, developing intimacy
Emotional tone	Affectively neutral, universalistic	Affective involvement, particularistic
Specificity of role	Specific, limited responsibility	Diffuse, global responsibility
Infrastructure	Organizational routines, standard operating procedures, protocols, rules, regulations, laws, prices, files, documents	Less structured situation, infrastructure of personal ties and commitment
Origin of cognitive frame	Pre-existing (with respect to case)	Emergent

cooperation must be elicited. Parents may even give their babies motivational talks. One mother told the baby that she was her mother, described their home, and assured her that this wasn't what life was going to be like: "I figured that for her to survive we had to make it clear to her that she had to fight and stay with it and not think that this is what she was created for." A biography is about an entity that has a future, and so has possible lives outside its present category and its present situation.

Emotional tone and role specificity are other points of difference. After many years of treating critically ill babies, physicians and other medical staff are able to maintain some distance from their young charges, recognizing that they cannot expend all of their energy on a single infant. Parents worry that the staff see their child as "just another case" without noting the peculiarities of the baby's medical situation or the uniqueness of the child as a person. Parents are deeply involved, often describing their baby's hospitalization as a rollercoaster ride filled with uncertainty and emotional turmoil. With an elaborate division of labor, staff members may see themselves as having rather circumscribed responsibilities; parents feel that they are diffusely responsible, that it is their job to see that their baby gets what it needs.

These extensive differences between medical staff and parents in how they think about and relate to hospitalized infants are grounded in rather substantial differences in the levels of routinization of hospital units as compared to family life, as is discussed below. Routines are of course human creations, developed partly in response to the complexities of individual cases. But because the massive historical accretion dominates what is created anew by staff confronting a new case, the cognitive frame is for all practical purposes pre-existing. For parents the situation is quite different. With meager infrastructure to organize their activity and thought, they create a much larger portion of their conceptual framework as they go along.[7]

Routinized NICUs and Less Routinized Homes

NICU life is predictable and orderly—a surprising assessment given that the tiny patients receive around-the-clock monitoring precisely because their needs and responses are *unpredictable*. NICU life is not *naturally* predictable and orderly. Its orderliness and predictability are important social achievements, produced in part by a stunning array of careful routines to channel attention and labor efficiently, to standardize, regulate, coordinate, and ensure the appropriateness of the healthcare team's activities. Elaborate records and charts help people track what has been accomplished and what remains to be done.

The predictability of NICU life contrasts sharply with the unpredictability of the homes to which infants are discharged. Infants' homes are more variable than NICUs on three dimensions. Parents vary more than hospital staff in their preparation and willingness to care for a sick baby. NICU staff all have undergone rigorous training and chosen this work. Parents may or may not have chosen to have any baby, let alone a sick one, and certainly have received no training in how to care for a critically ill newborn. Some parents acquire new skills quickly and eagerly while others become only marginally competent at rudimentary medical tasks.

The social control system of a home is also more variable than that of an NICU. In NICUs a clear hierarchy governs and supervises the activity of staff and staff monitor each other. The social control infrastructure (including medical records, alarm systems, and timers) makes social control less obtrusive and less costly. The need for oversight is reduced because in conforming to scripts, workers discipline *themselves*.

Some households are characterized by intensive "supervision" of caregivers by other family members; very little supervision occurs in others. A few families post charts to help them track whether medications have been administered and temperatures taken. When an infant requires home nursing, routines that approximate those of a hospital unit incorporate nurses into the household and coordinate the team's work. In others there are few mechanisms for supervision and few

---

[7]Heimer (2001) discusses how these two different styles of analysis are grounded in the documents of NICUs and families.

incentives for doing a good job. Some families provide exceptionally careful monitoring on a wide variety of indicators. Others supply inadequate care with little monitoring and consequently little hope of corrective action. NICU social control systems ensure higher floors—minimum levels of attention and quality of care—than some parents can provide but are unable to duplicate the one-on-one attentiveness that raises the ceiling in other families.

Finally, there is less variability in the congruence of interests between NICU careproviders and infants than between parents and infants. NICU staff have only a brief, and even then intermittent, responsibility for their patients. Parents have a long-term stake in their own children. Parents and family also are more likely to find that their interests conflict with the child's. If they need special care, are unusually fussy, or become ill often, former NICU patients can cost their parents more than other babies while giving back less.

Although it wouldn't be fair to say that NICUs are identical and completely interchangeable, they are much more uniform than households. Such uniformity is built into the design of healthcare, and provides a foundation for the construction of hospital routines. In contrast, the households of NICU patients are very variable— in composition, resources, and even approaches to childrearing—and this variation makes it difficult to import pre-existing routines without reshaping the household in fundamental ways. Nurses are interchangeable in ways that parents are not.

As organizations focused on meeting the unpredictable needs of a precarious newborn, NICUs and homes employ quite different devices to direct attention and orchestrate activity. NICUs place a premium on responsibility—on thoughtful adaptation of pre-existing medical protocols and routines to the needs of individual patients. In contrast to responsible doctoring and nursing, responsible parenting depends much less on a foundation of routines and documentation. During the baby's hospitalization, parents are required to fit into hospital routines, their labor supplementing the work of hospital staff. Parental roles shift dramatically when the baby goes home. Without the hospital's carefully planned routines, parents often discover how hard it is to ensure that medications are given in the correct doses at the right times, therapies administered on a regular schedule, equipment checked and maintained, and supplies restocked. But what substitutes for this infrastructure? If responsible careproviding is not ensured by routines and protocols, screening and training of workers, supervision by co-workers and bosses, and is not so much organized around the production and use of records, how then does it come about? Without protocols to guide them and to make order out of the chaos, how do parents decide which things merit their attention?

Case and Biography as Alternative Ways to Organize Information

Medical protocols and medical routines focus on infants as *patients* appropriately compared with other patients. How organizational participants think about and treat "cases" depends on the other cases they have encountered (see, e.g., research on social control decision making by Emerson 1981, 1983, Gilboy 1991, 1992,

Sudnow 1965, Swigert & Farrell 1977, Waegel 1981). The processing of one case may set precedents for others deemed similar; the treatment of one case depends on which others compete with it for resources, since resources are allocated to categories. What seems normal or aberrant depends on how a case is classified. In NICUs, infants are seen predominantly as cases, and important aspects of care are determined by how cases are classified. Is the child a premie? Is it experiencing drug withdrawal? Does it have some genetically based syndrome?

At the most basic level, classification determines how much nursing attention an infant gets. An ECMO patient (whose blood is oxygenated by a machine) requires the full attention of a nurse and a technician; a "feeder and grower" may have to compete with several other infants for a nurse's time. If a unit can only treat two ECMO patients simultaneously, ECMO patients compete for a scarce resource. Which specialists and therapists consult on an infant's case also depends on classification. A baby suspected of having necrotizing enterocolitis will be examined by a gastroenterologist. One with a cleft palate will be evaluated by a speech therapist before decisions about bottlefeeding are made. And the advice given to parents about when and whether to expect their baby to come home depends on how the infant is classified.

Classification focuses attention on one or a few features of the case. Usually, this is a good thing because it leads careproviders to see the relation between symptoms and to deal with more serious problems first. Sometimes, though, cases are misclassified and attention is then inappropriately focused. Symptoms that are unexpected may be misinterpreted or overlooked. Roth (1972), for instance, discusses what happens when emergency room patients are perfunctorily classified as inebriated. A case orientation also tends to be associated with abstraction (so the infant is discussed as a diseased body part or congenital malformation), with merit accorded to some kinds of evidence (e.g., test results) and discounting of others (e.g, nurses' visual inspection), and with skepticism about the reports of some (patients themselves, family members) and respect for the opinions of others (physicians) (Anspach 1988, 1993).

But such case-based analysis depends on an infrastructure (forms and documents, medical protocols, trained personnel to sort, analyze, and act on cases) and a stream of cases to be classified and compared. Further, such analysis becomes increasingly possible as the situation becomes more routine. Case streams do not exist on the cutting edge of fields with rapid technological innovation (e.g., when ECMO was first used in neonatology), when an established technology is being extended to a new environment, or when something is being encountered for the first time. Rather than comparing quite similar cases, analysts then must work with partial precedents, reason by analogy, and splice together bits and pieces of relevant information. Social systems may not facilitate efficient use of fragmentary information; they may instead construct barriers, impose rules, or standardize information in ways that make it seem foreign in other settings.[8]

---

[8]Heimer (1985) and Vaughan (1996) comment on social barriers that inhibit the importation and use of "foreign" information. In analyzing the use of information for rate setting in a

Families do not typically think of their child as a "case."[9] Case-based decision making requires that one be able to draw on a case base. Typically only repeat players have access to such case bases. Parents are essentially always one shotters in these situations, with all of the disadvantages that implies, although they occasionally are able to draw on the aggregated experiences of other one shotters (e.g., through parent support groups).

To say that families do not analyze their child as a case does not mean that they do no analysis, however. Rather than comparing their infant with other infants, parents for the most part compare the infant with itself. Rather than comparing one case with another, they compare current experiences and observations with previous experiences and observations with the *same* case. Coherence is supplied, then, by biography rather than by categorization. But what does it mean to say that coherence comes from an analysis of biography rather than an analysis of similar cases? And how is the process of creating cognitive coherence different when biography is the source of coherence?

Three differences are important. Although both biographical and case analysis are supported by conceptual scaffolding, in biographical analysis, a larger proportion of the conceptual edifice is created by the person concerned, the ethnoanalyst, rather than being received from others. A basic understanding of childhood and childrearing practices is meager cognitive scaffolding compared with the system of categories, diagnoses, medical data and basic science, and supporting bureaucratic forms that undergird the medical care of a hospitalized infant. Although we can assume that all parents have some cultural tools for thinking about children, some have more elaborated and others more restricted conceptual schemes. Because they are more likely to be exposed to the middle class parenting "curriculum," more elaborate cognitive categorizations of infants' behavior are especially likely to occur in well-educated people and are more common among women than men. Women read more about pregnancy, child development, and their child's specific condition; they also were the family leaders in seeking out materials and highlighting the sections for men to read. Such differences, not surprisingly, shape what parents see when they spend time with their child.

Second, because much of the task is to understand the unique properties of the child and to interpret current events in the light of past and anticipated future events, first-hand contact is more important to biographical than to case analysis. A cognitive framework, however it is supplied and elaborated, may prime parents to notice things about the baby—to assemble the components for a biographical analysis. But a cognitive framework is insufficient by itself if the parent has little

---

new area of insurance (Norwegian North Sea oil fields), Heimer shows that information can be *technically* sufficient without being *socially* sufficient. Vaughan shows how "structural secrecy" made information unavailable for problem-solving (in the space shuttle O-ring case) even in an organization that was conscientious about circulating information.

[9]Schneider & Conrad (1983), Charmaz (1991), and Frank (1995) suggest that people who are ill or disabled tend not to identify themselves mainly as "patients."

opportunity to *use* that framework. Without observation of the child, a cognitive framework can only create an abstract understanding of the infant's situation. Conception and perception tend to reinforce one another here. Because different parents see different things when they look at infants, their conceptual schemes evolve differently, and this in turn influences what and how much they perceive later. At the most basic level, parents who visit are more likely to see things that reinforce their view of their baby as fully human. But those who already think of the baby as a person are more likely to visit.

Finally, because biographical meaning is about relations among (different) objects, often with proper names, rather than about comparisons of (similar) objects, analysis is more likely to focus on how the object acts on and shapes the world than on how external forces have acted on the object. In short, the object becomes a subject, an agent, in biographical analysis. Personalities are ascribed to infants. Some infants are described as "fighters," others "decide that it's time to go." Such attributions introduce continuity into observations of and interactions with the child, helping the parent to construct a unique relationship with the child and to sustain commitment in bleak circumstances. Biographical analysis produces empathy.

Although the ideologies, observations, emotional responses, and cognitions of parents may not arise from anything as concrete as prescribed organizational routines, they are rather clearly supported by the routinized practices of families or larger groups. When parents say that the mother reads the parenting books, discusses them with her husband, and highlights sections for him to read, they are reporting on a household routine that helps parents to refine their conceptual categories and so to increase the acuity of their observations of the child. Routines that bring the parents into contact with the child (e.g., visiting every evening after work), that require collection of information about the child (e.g., telephoning before going to bed, keeping the baby book), or that necessitate discussion of that information with others (e.g., transmitting telephoned news to the other parent), support attentiveness to the child's experience.[10] Although many of these routines for creating the child's personhood are especially common in couples, they can and do exist in other relationships.

The construction of the child as a person undergirds parental commitment to meeting the child's needs, and that this constructive process is no more automatic than the process of constructing a medical case. The construction of humanness, whether it be the humanness of women, people of color, or premature babies, is supported by props that emphasize relationships with others. As evidence of familial ties, names, family pictures, clothing, and other gifts from friends and relatives reconfirm precarious humanness. The humanness of NICU patients and the babies who go home is thus produced by uncertain and imperfect social technologies,

---

[10]See Layne (1996) on how the obligation to report on a baby's progress shapes parents' understanding of the situation.

precariously routinized, and adopted and supported by some but not others.[11] I have shown what characteristics of people themselves and what features of the ways they conduct their lives increase the chance that this particular social product—the humanness of a fragile child—will be produced. I also argue that this social construction takes the form of a biographical narrative of a unique person, a person already embedded in a family.

Biography is constructed in conversations with family and friends and in conferences with physicians, social workers, nurses, and discharge planners. It is in these conversations that the narrative of a child's life is worked out—parents talk of their desire for a child; of how this pregnancy compared with others; of siblings' sympathy, anger, or bewilderment; of the contributions of the child's unique personality to its medical course; of their hopes and plans for the child. And in these conversations, documents and artifacts bolster the construction of biography—not just by supplying evidence about the child's fragility or the nature of the illness, but also by offering a text from which glimmers of personality and relationship can be extracted. Some might see only tubes and machines in NICU photographs, but as constructors of their child's biography, parents guide naive observers to more subtle and sophisticated readings. The baby's eyes are always open in the photographs, they might point out. That's not the case with for all NICU babies, but *she* always had her eyes open; she was from the beginning so interested in the other people around her. Or they might note how the child's fingers entwine the naso-gastric tube. He always hated that tube, pulled it out whenever the nurse turned her back. That was characteristic of him from the beginning; always a fighter, he was, and that determination was probably what got him through. In such discussions and with such materials is the uniqueness of a child constructed.

Organizational Specialization: Interchangeable Animals or Individual Animals, But Not Both

Constructions of the uniqueness of nonhuman animals are more difficult to sustain. Bureaucracies may treat humans as mere cogs in the machinery, but they simultaneously honor claims of singularity, particularly at their boundaries. Organizations that work with animals are less often confronted by such boundary claims; animals are either individuals or interchangeable members of a species, but not both.

---

[11]See Heimer & Stevens' (1997) analysis of how variations in a hospital's financial dependence on patients makes some NICUs more attentive than others to symbolic proprieties such as affirming the humanness of infants hovering between life and death, between an existence as fetus and as baby. In effect, the willngness of hospitals to use boundary workers such as social workers to treat families more "biographically" depends on how much the hospital depends on families' goodwill.

Zelizer (1985), examining a very different institutional system, also shows the activities of families and other organizations jointly work out our cultural understandings of the meaning and value of children.

E.B. White's are among the most eloquent renditions of a classic dilemma: to others Stuart may be merely a mouse, but to Mr. and Mrs. Little, he is a son; to Fern (and of course Charlotte), Wilbur is not potential bacon, but "Some Pig"; to Sam Beaver, Louis is a talented trumpeter and friend, not just another swan (White 1973, 1952, 1970, respectively). In real life, people routinely recognize their relationships with animals by awarding their pets many of the privileges of family membership: a unique name, a place in the family photo album, regular medical and even dental care, gifts on holidays, and a funeral at the end of life.

Although the wrenching betrayal experienced by Jody in *The Yearling* (Rawlings 1966) is clearly atypical, children inevitably discover the limits of their parents' willingness to include the beloved animal as "one of us." But only rarely does anyone ask how we reconcile our genuine affection for the family pet with the routine appearance of other animals on the dinner table. What is sociologically interesting here is how we come to classify essentially identical creatures in different ways and how that shapes our treatment of them. Often we manage this by exaggerating the differences between near relatives (parakeets are pets, chickens are food), by physical segregation (pets live in our homes; food animals live on factory farms), by the use of euphemisms (we eat pork, not pigs, and certainly not Wilbur), and by packaging (we see cuts of meat, not dead animals).

We also very commonly offer distorted images of animals' lives, minimizing the brutality of human exploitation of other species. In most of the literary renditions, animals who are not family members are either barnyard animals living on old-fashioned farms or animals living in the wild. Without the intervention of Fern and Charlotte, Wilbur might end up as bacon, but he would nevertheless lead a fairly pleasant life before being sent to market. Less well depicted in literary accounts is the bureaucratic treatment of animals, which is so extreme that one could plausibly argue that Foucault could have written as productively about the henhouse as the prison. Totalitarianism reaches its peak in the modern henhouse, where chickens are confined to tiny cages, beaks clipped so they won't hurt themselves, lights dimmed to reduce aggression. Social life, lifespan, and even body shape are distorted by the feeding, medication, and breeding regimes of animal husbandry. Perhaps even more extreme is the production of lab animals, bred to develop tumors or to have other traits desirable for scientific experiments.

Literary silence makes it easy for us to imagine that the factory farm as a sunny barnyard. Organizational routines and governmental regulations shape our thinking and our behavior when we actually encounter animals of the corporation. Mice are an instructive example here. The full range of possibilities is laid out by Herzog (1988). Within a laboratory, mice can be classified as laboratory animals who will be the subjects of experiments, food for other experimental animals, or pests. A mouse intended for use in an experiment is protected by the regulations for the humane treatment of animals; if that same mouse escapes, it becomes a pest to be trapped and killed in whatever fashion is convenient. In a particularly macabre twist, a mouse intended as food for a laboratory snake would not be protected, but that same mouse would be protected if paired with the same snake in an experiment designed to study fear or evasion in prey. And of course, an identical mouse might be a family pet in the experimenter's household; as a pet it would be fed, cherished, and ultimately mourned at death.

Often when an animal is constructed biographically, as a being with a past, present, and future, its relation with a person or family is key to this reconceptualization. But some especially valuable animals, such as race horses or pure bred dogs, are accorded the dignity of a biography more or less independent of their relationships to human beings. In these cases, biography takes a stylized form—lineage, physical traits, and accomplishments are tracked by workers using templates and following organizational routines.[12] The documents produced to chart the animal's life bear only a remote resemblance to a family photo album.

Value need not lead to even stylized biography if it is the group rather than individuals who are valued. Members of endangered species, for instance, may be considered valuable, without being thought of biographically. Rules about the appropriate treatment of members of endangered species may actually inhibit biographical thinking, as is illustrated by the custody battle over Cookie, a Cercopithecus diana monkey (Feuer 2000). Valued as a family member by her current owners, Cookie goes for walks with her "parents" and "older sister" in the neighborhood and watches the news on TV with them; her birthday is celebrated and she is pictured in the family photo album. But private ownership of members of endangered species is illegal, so state wildlife authorities want to take Cookie from her "family" and reunite her with other diana monkeys in an appropriate facility. The state's reasoning takes little account of Cookie's peculiar biography. To the New York State Department of Environmental Conservation (a bureaucracy with routines for prescribing what should be done with members of endangered species), Cookie is a case. As a member of an endangered species, she should be treated as the law would require for any other member of an endangered species; as a diana monkey, she should be thought of as any other member of that species, and

---

[12]The case of race horses is instructive here. The treatment of horses varies dramatically with how they are categorized. Admired as wild creatures, horses are also domesticated and used as work animals or as entertainers on the race track or in the circus ring, and they may end up as ingredients in salamis or dogfood. Of the 450,000 horses in Poland, 420,000 are work animals and only 1000 are Arabians; 100,000 horses are exported annually from Eastern Europe for slaughter in the European Union. Describing the World War II efforts of grooms to preserve race horses, one journalist commented on how the fates of Arabians compared to those of horses destined for the slaughterhouse: "Janow's stud book, with the lineage of each new-born foal written in an exquisite hand, could not be more of a contrast. The names here stretch back 20 generations or more, until, at last, an empty box signifies that the sire or dam was a desert Arabian, unnamed, brought perhaps by Count Dzieduszycki himself. Poring over these stud books—stolen by the Nazis, disdained by the communists—brings a poignant reflection: far more is remembered of these horses, of their manners, bodies, and parentage, than of the brave grooms who attended them" (*Economist* 2000, p. 86). A true biographical treatment could not have omitted relations with grooms from a horse's biography.

wild animals need to be with their own kind. Cookie's family (a less bureaucratic organization) reasons from biography: Cookie has grown up with a human family and that has made her different than other diana monkeys. That biography, they contend, should be allowed to shape her future.

As a category falling between humans, whose agency is fully recognized and honored and inanimate objects over which human sovereignty is seen as completely unproblematic, animals challenge our sense of what it is just and proper for organizations to do. As long as they stay in their assigned category as simple members of species or as family pets, the problem is manageable. But creatures capable of independent action and relationship are difficult to govern. They may not be able to make the rules or create their own biographies, but they do sometimes break them and they even more often appeal to those applying the rules, in so doing stimulating others to create biographies for them. Because they had now become individuals with biographies, the Ginger Tamworth pigs (popularly referred to as Butch and Sundance) could not simply be returned to the British slaughterhouse from which they had escaped. "These pigs have stepped out of line. They have crossed over from being farm animals to companions. They have been given names. Once that happens you can't reverse the process," psychologist Julia N. Berryman explained (Vallely 1998, p. 16). As an individual with a biography, Cookie likewise cannot be made to fit comfortably into the valuable but still undifferentiated group of diana monkeys.

The Curatorial Sensibility: Using Heirlooms to Extend the Biography of a Lineage

Decisions about consumption have consequences for identity, a fact that has brought handsome profits to the producers of brand name sneakers, cars, and even multicolored iMacs. The use of such products to construct people's identities and biographies depends on the image of the product. Fully interchangeable sneakers are of little use in projecting an image, but too much differentiation also makes identification with others difficult. Constructing an appropriately differentiated and appealing image (or biography) for the consumer good is thus a delicate task. Decisions about purchases typically bolster identification with aggregates as much as with known others. Careful purchases allow a family to keep up with the Joneses but also make the family identifiable to others of their social group away from home; adolescents' attire marks symbolic boundaries in distant cities as well as at the local high school.

Singular goods with fully developed biographies serve mainly to cement local ties, as McCracken (1988) illustrates in his analysis of Lois Roget's remarkable use of family heirlooms to integrate new generations into the family lineage and to tie them to a locale. Each object (a cookie jar, a plate, a chair) is associated with the people who owned and used it, with important events in their lives, as well as with the local craftsmen who made the object from indigenous materials. A curatorial consumer such as Lois Roget uses family history to construct the biography of an heirloom and then in turn uses the heirloom to construct the lineage. Using "an object charged with historical family significance in the creation of an event charged with contemporary family significance" (p. 48) simultaneously extends the heirloom's biography into the present and fashions links between generations. Imbued with archival meaning, these objects become valuable as mnemonic devices and repositories of family history, but also artifacts without which rituals would seem incomplete. They then constrain family members in three ways. Those who inherit heirlooms have fewer opportunities to choose objects consistent with the identities they wish to develop. Because heirlooms are already laden with meaning, inheritors have less room to create fresh meanings of their own. Finally, in accepting an heirloom, a person becomes a steward, charged with protecting the object and transmitting and renewing its biography. Inanimate objects may need human agents to write their biographies, but they can in turn be powerful shapers of the collective biographies of whole lineages.

LEGAL CASES: TREATING LIKE CASES ALIKE, HONORING DIFFERENCE

When organizations standardize and routinize, they treat entities as cases for somewhat different reasons than do legal systems. In organizations, the objective is efficiency or perhaps a sensible allocation of resources. In the legal system, the stated objective is fairness: those who have committed the same crime should receive the same treatment under the law; those who have the same characteristics have the same rights under the law. But just as organizations only sometimes treat objects as cases, legal systems only sometimes treat people as cases. Biography is taken into account in some kinds of organizations, particularly those that are organized around commitment rather than efficiency, or where life cycles and developmental changes have to be taken into account. Likewise with variations in legal tasks, in entities being processed by the legal system, and in the needs and expectations of participants in legal processes within legal systems, case analysis is displaced or supplemented by biographical analyses. Other, sometimes unacknowledged, goals are pursued alongside the articulated, official goal of universalism.

The standardization assumed by the legal system runs into difficulties because the objects whose innocence or guilt it evaluates, whose agreements it monitors and enforces, and among whom it allocates the goods of a society are not the neat, uniform objects its procedures are designed to manage. Here three kinds of difficulties are examined, all in the sphere of criminal law, although the argument should apply equally well to other spheres. Legal systems are better equipped to manage assessments about events in the instant, particularly an instant in the past, than about events that are ongoing, unfolding, particularly those expected to continue unfolding into the uncertain future. Legal systems also tend to assume the constancy of the subject, the actor whose guilt or innocence is being questioned. Difficult as character is to establish in ordinary circumstances and difficult as it may be to say with any confidence how actions are related to persons, these assessments are even more difficult for children whose characters are not fully formed. Trauma, duress, mental illness, and old age may also create instabilities that render legal assumptions about the constancy of objects problematic if not absurd. Finally, legal systems work best when the technical core of law can be protected, when problems can be preprocessed, shorn of the extraneous mess of real life, and transformed into legal cases before legal experts do their work. Less insulated portions of the criminal justice system, with less savvy supplicants seeking the assistance of the courts and fewer subordinate workers to preprocess cases, may find themselves modifying court procedures at this messy, contested boundary between law and not-law.

Judging an Instant, Punishing over Time: Guilt and Penalty Phases in Capital Trials

The rules of procedure of the criminal law call for the comparison of real plaintiffs and defendants with abstract, stylized individuals who theoretically might come before the court and with real people whose cases have in fact come before the courts in the past. One key objective is the universalistic treatment of similarly situated individuals in similar ways. Indeed because the focus is on a single act or event, lawyers, judges, and jurors often are prohibited from considering anything that falls outside the spotlight. The universalism of the law calls for categorization of actions and comparison of people and their acts as *cases*, treating as relevant only the core questions about agency (could the act have been avoided?) and purpose (was the act intended?) that undergird our understandings of responsibility, morality, and justice (Lempert & Sanders 1986). Judging guilt or innocence, one of the law's most important tasks, does seem to require case analysis. But do other tasks require case analysis, or do legal actors adopt biographical analyses when they move beyond assessing culpability?

Universalistic case-style analysis is supplanted by biographical analysis in several protected areas of legal proceedings. According to the rules for the penalty phase of a capital trial, defendants cannot be precluded from offering any mitigating evidence that might support a more lenient sentence than death (*Eddings v. Oklahoma*, 1982; *Lockett v. Ohio*, 1978; *Penry v. Lynaugh*, 1989), and defense lawyers typically present information about the defendant as a person that has not been offered during the guilt phase. The defendant's life is examined less in comparison with the lives of other convicted murderers or in reference to the categories established by law and more as an interconnected past, present, and future constructed of relationships with other people.

From their research on the penalty phase of capital trials, Lynch and Haney conclude that the defense arguments "presented a unique life story of an individual" (n.d., p. 22). As in other biographical analyses, ties to other people were central. Defense attorneys stressed the relationships between defendants and their parents, siblings, spouses and children. These relationships were analyzed for varying purposes. Sometimes they supported a discussion of how formative childhood experiences of rejection, punishment, and violence had damaged and limited the defendant. But they also displayed defendants connected to others, human because they were tied to others as sons, lovers, parents, or even as clients to whom attorneys felt emotionally attached. The act that was the subject of the guilt phase of the trial continued to be an entity appropriately analyzed as a case. But the person, now separated from the act, was recast during the penalty phase as an entity more appropriately considered through a biographical analysis.

Inconstant Objects: Judging and Sentencing Malleable, Morally Immature Children

Elster (2000) writes about the difficulties of making decisions on behalf of our future selves, worrying about when we should require that a person be bound by precommitments he or she made as a different person in the past, one who could not know the situation, needs, or preferences of the future self. The notion of precommitment is not so troubling when we are asking the present self to make investments that will benefit the future self. The idea of a social security system is that our present (younger, employed) selves should be saving money on behalf of our future (older, retired) selves. But it becomes more problematic when there is more doubt about whether a future self would welcome the decisions made by the present self. For instance, should our present, healthy and mentally fit selves be able to express preferences about how future, unhealthy, mentally impaired selves should be treated?

These same questions about the continuity of the self plague the legal system, although here it is others making decisions about an inconstant object rather than a person making decisions about his or her own future self. The court decides on punishment at the termination of a trial, but decisions about punishment are reassessed episodically by parole boards, except in those cases where parole is specifically prohibited. As Hawkins notes, " Labels of deviance are at once plastic and persistent" (1983, p. 125). The court's original finding continues to shape the board's view, but evidence of rehabilitation and genuine remorse suggest that the person being punished is no longer really the same person as the one who committed the crime.

Biography is especially hard to ignore among children, whose identities are not thought to be fully formed. Indeed some discontinuity is desirable, because only then is it reasonable to hope that through normal maturational processes and rehabilitation a delinquent child will become a law-abiding adult. Although we may feel comfortable consigning a violent adult criminal to a long prison term, we may not believe such a sentence appropriate for a younger one whose understanding of the crime may not be sufficient to meet the most rigorous tests for agency and intention, and who may repent and reform long before the sentence has been served. But we also believe that serious crimes should receive serious punishments.

The legal system's ambivalence about child criminals is reflected in a tendency to broaden the kinds of information considered in its case analysis, in the nature of the judgment it renders and the style of argumentation employed, and in the division of labor between judging and imposing sentences (as occurs also in adults' trials). Before the first juvenile courts were established in the United States in 1899, children engaged in criminal activity were subjected to the same punishments as adults.[13] Regarded as a back-up to compensate for the failures of such primary institutions as the family and the schools, juvenile courts regarded as relevant "everything about the child and his situation" (Lempert & Sanders 1986, p. 261). Unlike other courts, the juvenile court aimed for a broad negotiated agreement between the parties rather than a winner-takes-all decision imposed by the court. This ideal has not been achieved. Court procedures tend to focus on single issues rather than on patterns of behavior or relationships among disputants. Moreover, inequality among the parties and the brief contacts between them limit investment and negotiation; compromises occur among state agents (police, probation officers, judges) but do not extend to families or the juvenile offenders. And the stark reality of violent crime has made courts less accepting of arguments that malleable children can be reformed.

Emerson's (1969) careful fieldwork in a juvenile court helps us see just how legal case analysis becomes more biographical. The task of juvenile courts is not so much to judge guilt or innocence as to locate "trouble." But, unlike in adult cases, the offense itself is not seen as a good guide for court response. Instead, what should be done depends on whether the child, over subsequent contacts with the court, is assessed as having normal, criminal-like, or disturbed character. Assessments of character are formed by two types of presentations, one focusing on the delinquent's acts, trying to construct a pattern from them to show whether or not they are "typical" delinquencies (like Sudnow's 1965 "normal crimes"), and the other focusing on biography, attempting to located the delinquent and his or her offenses in a developmental pattern (e.g., that might be outgrown). If a court's response depends on its assessment of the child's character, not just on the delinquent act, then the court necessarily must consider the child's past and future rather than simply applying the penalty appropriate to the act. When biographies are considered, one shoplifter is seen as a criminal-like youth headed for reform school while another is a normal child briefly led astray. Note, though, that the more contact a child has with the juvenile justice system, the less "biography" there is to be considered alongside the routine-based institutional accounts produced by courts, police, probation officers, and reform schools.

---

[13]Some of the distinctions between juvenile and adult courts were in fact the legal innovations of custodial institutions for juveniles, established in the 1820s in New York, Philadelphia, and Boston. These institutions recognized a difference between juvenile and adult offenders, used indeterminate sentences, and broadened their jurisdiction to include children who were neglected or incorrigible as well as those who had broken the law (Sutton 1988, p. 45).

Although the juvenile court, whose charge is to treat juvenile offenders with "care, custody, and discipline" (Emerson 1969, p. 6), may seem much more inclined to biographical analyses than are "regular" courts, Emerson argues that competing commitments to rule-based punishment and more discretionary rehabilitation are institutionalized by separating the finding of delinquency from disposition: " The child is given an impartial hearing in the facts of the case against him, and only after a finding of 'delinquent' has been made does the court begin to function as a social agency, now operating with a different set of rules and purposes" (1969, p. 14). When the work of the court, and especially of the probation officers and psychiatric clinic, requires more contact with the community, more circumscribed case analyses tend to be replaced by more biographical discussions. Police, schools, group homes, and youth correctional facilities do not frame the issues in quite the same way as the court. Each institution has a different case set, so what seems serious or trivial, normal or deviant varies with the cases with which any new case is compared (Emerson 1983, p. 429).

But the focus of case analysis also varies from one organization to another. The achievements and failings by which children are classified by teachers and social workers in schools do not overlap neatly with the offenses of interest to the police or courts. "In conducting collective work, people coming together from different social worlds frequently have the experience of addressing an object that has a different meaning for each of them. Each social world has partial jurisdiction over the resources represented by that object, and mismatches caused by the overlap become problems for negotiation," Star & Griesemer note (1989, p. 412). As they negotiate over how to share responsibility for this "boundary object," here a delinquent child, facts relevant to one body but not to the other inevitably enter the conversation; discussions take on a biographical character. The analyses, represented in conceptions of the object, "contain at every stage the traces of multiple viewpoints, translations, and incomplete battles" (Star & Griesemer 1989, p. 413). The legalistic shadow cast by the courthouse fades with distance as judging is replaced by treating and reforming, and as boundary workers such as probation officers take over management of the case.

But while a boundary worker may consider a broader range of facts, do more personal observation, and consider a longer period of time than is common in case analysis, the constraints of the job nevertheless mean that the probation officer (for instance) has only a limited capacity to think about the child over time, to compare behavior at age three with acts committed at age fifteen, or to establish the sort of personal tie that would lead to thinking about working with, rather than on, the child. Sutton's conclusion emphasizes the very limited nature of the juvenile court's movement toward biographical thinking. In his view, "The delinquent, alleged to be the subject of therapeutic intervention, in fact became an object bent to the conflicting needs of an ambivalent institution" (1988, p. 153). The division of labor between parole officers and judges and the institutionalization of a system of categories for thinking about delinquency really just formalized and legitimized moralizing about juvenile offenders. The main effect was not to get therapeutic intervention for delinquent children but to create a boundary object, a pawn in negotiations.

Boundaries Between the Legal System and Real Life: Problems and Cases

Even when they are thinking about legal problems, the interpretive schemas that people use are not exclusively legal (Ewick & Silbey 1998, p. 49). That means that it is not just people, such as the delinquents discussed in the last section, who have lifecyles to be analyzed biographically; the troubles that bring people to court have biographies as well. The ideal of law may be cases, but its practice has to be fashioned from biography because that is what people bring to the court.

Looking at the same situation, lay people see broader problems and legal actors see the narrower version that constitutes a legal case. The core of a problem, say a landlord/tenant dispute or a marital disagreement, and a case may be the same, but their boundaries are quite different, Merry (1990) notes. A problem tends to be ongoing, a series of disturbing incidents, often without a clear starting point. The associated legal case is constrained to be about a single event, an event which may well have been the last straw in an ongoing problem. Problems also have an emotional intensity that may be muted in the legal case.

The problems people bring to the courts often have a core legal issue (e.g., neighborhood problems often are about property). Despite this, the problems that seem serious to the plaintiffs may be seen by court personnel as legally trivial. Court personnel may then try to reframe the problems as something other than legal cases. Framing problems in moral or therapeutic terms, they often meet resistance from plaintiffs who correctly perceive these reframings as refusals to render legally binding decisions. The dilemma of the legal system is this then: to refuse to treat problems as cases is to deny their importance and to refuse to lend the authority of the court to people who may need its support. But to treat problems as cases is to ignore biography and to pretend to resolve problems that cannot adequately be captured within the constraints of legal rules. The court can resolve the case without doing much at all to resolve the problem (Merry 1990, p. 99).[14] The "remains" of these cases may then form the basis of a new set of problems. The legal system functions best when it can work with cases, but where the boundary between the legal system and the rest of society is porous, it will continue to get problems that demand some form of biographical analysis.

---

[14]Legal forms that aim for reintegrating offenders into the community and reconciling offenders and victims (Braithwaite 1989) use the case as a springboard for addressing the larger problem.

EXCHANGE AND MARKETS: STANDARDIZED COMMODITIES, QUALITY, AND SINGULARITY

The idea of markets depends on standardization, on the comparability of the objects being exchanged. Pricing depends on traders knowing that goods are essentially the same entity and then comparing them on quantity and quality. But of course some goods are appealing precisely because they are not fully comparable. A rare jewel, a painting by a recognized master rather than one that merely has the traits common to the pictures that people say they like (Wypijewski 1997), an authentic Persian carpet, not merely one that is high quality (Spooner 1986), a pot made by one of the acknowledged artists rather than by an unknown for the tourist trade (Dauber 1993), an article of clothing designed by a famous designer and fabricated in an approved factory all depend for their appeal on claims of noncomparability. But just as comparability is socially constructed, so is scarcity and uniqueness. Often singularity depends on the creation of an association with a person (the designer, artist, chef), but the biographies of objects can surely be created in other ways as well.

Agency and Authenticity: The Commoditization and Exchange of Religious Relics

Not all circulation of goods occurs through market exchange, Geary (1986) reminds us in his essay on medieval relics. Barter and sale are common modes by which goods circulate only when people have neutral relations with one another; friends bestow gifts and enemies plunder and steal. But it is especially in barter and sale that goods are treated as commodities, objects with known and uniform traits and so interchangeable with one another. In the language used above, interchangeability depends on items exchanged being "cases" of a commodity.

For some kinds of commodities, authenticity is important in creating value. Original paintings by masters are much more valuable than excellent copies. Beautiful museum replicas sell for much less than the originals excavated from Mayan ruins. The market for rare goods depends on an infrastructure to certify their authenticity, just as other markets depend on the standardization of weights and measures. Although certifications of authenticity now often come from investigations by neutral, established experts employed by museums or auction houses, during other periods the process of establishing value, like the circulation of goods, depended on personal ties. And in some cases, these ties were with the goods themselves.

For religious relics, value depends on authenticity, but in medieval times authenticity depended less on the tracing of a tie to the saint than on a demonstration of the relic's efficacy. One could tell that one truly had a fragment of a saint's body or a scrap of the saint's clothing when miracles occurred. When miracles were not forthcoming, this could be because the relic was not authentic or because the community had failed to establish an appropriate relationship with the saint, not honoring his or her memory, for instance. Divine intervention may seem to us a peculiar way to establish authenticity, even of relics, but we should keep in mind that divine intercession was likewise sought in establishing guilt or innocence and deciding whether to go into battle.

Besides being established by a biographical account and confirmed through miracles, authenticity was also corroborated through relationships. Relics belonged either to religious officials (bishops or the Pope) or to congregations; burial in a crypt in a church could be regarded as a guarantee that the body truly belonged to the saint. Relics were sometimes stolen during battle, and the fact that the saint allowed the sacking of a town and permitted the theft of his or her body was regarded as evidence that the saint was dissatisfied with his or her relationship with the community. But relics were also sometimes bestowed as gifts, and such gifts were less costly to the giver than one might expect because small portions of the body or property of the saint were expected to be just as efficacious as larger ones. It is a rare good indeed that can be subdivided without losing its value.

As congregations multiplied, though, the demand for relics grew, and with it a market. Because purchases of relics took place before miracles could be expected, and in any case merchants could not produce the miracles, biographies of relics became more important in establishing authenticity. Nevertheless, it is biographical analysis (and not case analysis) that supports claims that relics are something more than fragments of cloth or pieces of long-dead corpses and that the process of authentication is not really just an elaborate autopsy.

Establishing Quality: Known Producers or Known Production Processes

People buy brand name products because they believe they then know what they are getting. Much of the infrastructure that undergirds markets institutionalizes category systems for classifying and regulating objects to be traded and the media of exchange so that merchants and consumers can be confident that they are getting beef rather than pork, beef with a specified fat content, a sixteen ounce pound, and that the dollars they pay will be accepted as payment.

These guarantees of quality, so fundamental to markets, can take two different forms, though. Assurances about quality can take a quasi-biographical form when they are grounded in knowledge about, confidence in, or a relationship with the producer. Alternatively, quality can be assured through the standardization of production processes. By examining the market for cloth around the time of the French Revolution, Reddy (1986) shows the difficulties created for merchants and consumers by a change in how quality was guaranteed and therefore how knowledge of quality was understood and disseminated.

Under the *ancien régime*, understandings of different types and qualities of cloth were organized around guild rules and locales because it was they who regulated and standardized production; those who understood the quality of cloth and what it depended on were connoisseurs. Savary des Bruslons's *Dictionnaire Universel du Commerce*, a reference work for merchants first published between

1723 and 1730 and reissued at least six more times between 1741 and 1784, systematized this knowledge about cloth (and other commodities). After the Revolution, the productive process itself was much more standardized, and understandings of types and qualities of cloth came to depend on knowledge about production rather than about variations among guilds and geographical locations. As the *ancien régime* unraveled, Savary's *Dictionnaire* came to be regarded as unsatisfactory because it reflected neither the new philosophical thinking nor the social change taking place in the organization of production. Despite this dissatisfaction, attempts to prepare new reference works came to naught. Only in 1839 was a comprehensive work finally published. Reddy argues that this delay occurred because it took that long for the reorganization of production to gel: "Until knowledge was rebuilt on the firm foundation of the notion of a production process, it would be extremely difficult to categorize and evaluate goods in the absence of the old regulatory structure [of the guilds]" (p. 280). After this time, the quality guarantees on which the market for cloth depended were grounded in standardization of the routines of production rather than a biographical analysis of who was producing the cloth.

In combination, these discussions of relics and cloth illustrate what we already knew from Weber's (1950) *General Economic History*: that exchange depends on standardization of measures of quality and quantity and on institutions to guarantee those standards. But Geary (1986) also reminds us that for some types of goods, standardization is not the issue and guarantees may be beside the point. The authenticity of a relic is established not by a firm demonstration of the origins of a bone fragment or piece of clothing but instead by a biography telling us what the relic has done. And Reddy (1986) offers a salutary reminder that guarantees of standards and uniformity can come about through knowledge about producing groups, often disseminated by a named connoisseur, rather than by our knowing that producers have followed established routines.

CONCLUSION: DOES IT MATTER WHETHER COHERENCE IS CONSTRUCTED BY CASE ANALYSIS OR BIOGRAPHICAL ANALYSIS?

The contrast I have drawn between cognition and activity structured by an analysis of streams of cases versus streams of events in a biography is of course overdrawn. While physicians and nurses may think of a patient as "the product of a 28 week gestation" and so compare the infant with other premies or as "a hypoplastic left heart" appropriately compared with other heart patients, they of course also look at family medical histories, information about the pregnancy, and the infant's medical course. Similarly, although parents do not mainly think about how their baby compares with other 28 weekers or other heart patients, they do sometimes draw on such categorical schemes. "Parenting professionals" make their living reminding parents of the dangers of relying too heavily on biographical analysis.

The classification of children as infants, toddlers, pre-adolescents, adolescents, or young adults introduces some modicum of comparison into parental thinking. When biographies in schools consist of passing through age grade levels, the school's classification system strongly shapes how famlies think; graduation is a family event as well as a school event. Nevertheless, the dominant mode of thought is different in families than in schools or infant intensive care units. And subsequent uses of the archives constructed around cases are different than the uses of archives constructed with biographical materials. The archives of a hospital are usually opened only if the patient becomes a legal case, a "mistake" to be reviewed, or a "subject" in research. The archives of a biography are reopened for weddings, funerals, birthdays or other anniversaries, and holidays. They are props that support claims about identity and relationship and mark transitions. These archives are revisited because of people's commitments to each other.

I have argued that the effect of formal routines in social life decreases when people are so overloaded with routines that routines become noise rather than signal and cease to focus attention, when institutional competition undermines the capacity of institutions hegemonically to shape cognition or action, or when institutions are underdeveloped or absent, as often occurs on the fringes or beyond the boundaries of formal organizations. Critically ill infants are boundary objects (Bowker & Star 1999), seen simultaneously as patients by hospital staff working in carefully structured NICUs and as children by the parents who cross the boundary into the NICU and ultimately take the babies home. Although for both staff and parents the task is to create some sort of cognitive order from the disorder (as Star 1985 argues is the case for all scientific work), they proceed in different ways. Medical workers compare the infant patient to other infant patients, making causal arguments about what they know of human biology and the effects of medical and pharmacological interventions on "outcomes," a small part of the child's future. In contrast, parents construct the causal unity of the child over time, looking to the child's past and distant future for explanations.

Sociologists have shown how seeing a single case as one in a stream of cases shapes its treatment. Cases compete for resources. Attention is focused on some features rather than others, with some resulting tendency for analysts to overlook or misunderstand inconsistent information. When a case is seen in isolation, analysis must proceed by scrutinizing the case itself. Rather than being imposed, categories emerge in conversations and attempts to act. Lacking precedents, parents treat their child as an individual. The vaunted particularism of parents may thus arise as much from the absence of the universalizing pressures of a preexisting case base as from the tendency of parents to value the uniqueness of their child.

I have suggested that biographical analysis tends to be emergent, the result of an inductive process, while the analysis of case streams tends to be more deductive, arising from comparison of each new case with an imposed and pre-existing cognitive system embodied in routines and protocols. In biographical analyses, documents supply the analytic context by fashioning an account of a person's past and hinting at an extended future; in case analyses, in contrast, the function of documents is to structure comparisons across cases. In addition, though, in biographical analyses, the objects under scrutiny are more likely to be permitted to play an active role in the construction of the cognitive edifice. To some degree this observation is artifactual, arising from a study of cognitions about human beings. Nevertheless, because some parents expect that infants can give and not just "give off" information (to use Goffman's 1969 terms), they look for and attempt to interpret rudimentary communications from their child and give such data an important place. The causal continuity of biography requires a sentient human being to be meaningful, and part of a biographical analysis is to construct that being when it has only a precarious existence.

Finally, a brief note on the degree to which action is constrained or enabled. I have argued that people need some cognitive structure to give them the tools to make sensible observations. Without a conception of the child as a person, parents do not look for and see the child's human response to pain or comfort. Without some understanding of neural tube defects, physicians wouldn't know what they were seeing in a sonogram. But order is hard to impose on an unruly object, such as a child that can be expected to change over its life course. One could argue that a rudimentary cognitive structure that encourages people to continue to re-examine the evidence would encourage deliberative rather than schematic thinking (DiMaggio 1997, D'Andrade 1995) and a strategic rather than unthinking use of cultural tools. If parents think that there is "never a dull moment" and that their young children "keep them hopping," it may be because schema failure is so common in parenting that biographical analysis works better than a more constraining routine-based analysis of case streams of the sort that is supported by hospital documents and forms.

I have here summarized the main conclusions with reference to how critically ill children are thought about through biographical and case analyses; these conclusions apply with appropriate adjustments to what goes on in the legal system and markets as well as what goes on in organizations, and to inanimate objects and animals as well as to our thinking about people. What I have attempted here is to show that something like the Marxist existentialist goal, outlined by Sartre (1963), of understanding both individuals and history typically is accomplished by a division of labor in which the more routinized portions of markets, the legal system, and organizations understand history and the less routinized parts specialize in understanding individuals. If both objectives are ever accomplished, it is most likely at the interstices, where two or more systems of understanding confront one another.

ACKNOWLEDGMENTS

For stimulating discussions and insightful suggestions, I am grateful to Paul DiMaggio, Wendy Espeland, Magali Larson, Eviatar Zerubavel, and especially Arthur Stinchcombe. Barry Cohen and Rebecca Culyba were exemplary research assistants. I thank the Research School of the Social Sciences, Australian

National University, where I began the paper, and the American Bar Foundation, where I finished it, for supporting my work. Warm thanks as well to the Lochinvar Society.

Visit the Annual Reviews home page at www.AnnualReviews.org

LITERATURE CITED

Ahrne G. 1994. *Social Organizations: Interaction Inside, Outside and Between Organizations*. London: Sage

Anspach RR. 1988. Notes on the sociology of medical discourse. *J. Health Soc. Behav.* 29:357–75

Anspach RR. 1993. *Deciding Who Lives*. Berkeley: Univ. Calif. Press

Appadurai A, ed. 1986. *The Social Life of Things: Commodities in Cultural Perspective*. Cambridge, UK: Cambridge Univ. Press

Berger PL, Luckmann T. 1967. *The Social Construction of Reality*. New York: Doubleday

Bourdieu P. 1990. Structures, *habitus*, practices. In *The Logic of Practice*, pp. 52–65. Stanford, CA: Stanford Univ. Press

Bowker GC, Star SL. 1999. *Sorting Things Out*. Cambridge, MA: Mass. Inst. Technol. Press

Braithwaite J. 1989. *Crime, Shame, and Reintegration*. Cambridge, UK: Cambridge Univ. Press

Bruner JS. 1990. *Acts of Meaning*. Cambridge, MA: Harvard Univ. Press

Charmaz K. 1991. *Good Days, Bad Days*. New Brunswick, NJ: Rutgers Univ. Press

Chomsky N. 1966. *Topics in the Theory of Generative Grammar*. The Hague: Mouton

D'Andrade RG. 1995. *The Development of Cognitive Anthropology*. New York: Cambridge Univ. Press

Dauber KW. 1993. Shaping the clay: Pueblo pottery, cultural sponsorship and regional identity in New Mexico. Unpublished PhD dissertation, Univ. Arizona

DiMaggio P. 1997. Culture and cognition. *Annu. Rev. Sociol.* 23:263–87

Douglas M. 1986. *How Institutions Think*. Syracuse, NY: Syracuse Univ. Press

Economist. 2000. Horses with wings. *Economist,* July 1 2000:85–86

Elster J. 2000. *Ulysses Unbound: Studies in Rationality, Precommitment, and Constraints*. Cambridge, UK: Cambridge Univ. Press

Emerson RM. 1969. *Judging Delinquents: Context and Process in Juvenile Court*. Chicago: Aldine

Emerson RM. 1981. On last resorts. *Am. J. Sociol.* 87:1–22

Emerson RM. 1983. Holistic effects in social control decision-making. *Law Soc. Rev.* 17:425–55

Espeland WN, Stevens ML. 1998. Commensuration as a social process. *Annu. Rev. Sociol.* 24:313–43

Ewick P, Silbey SS. 1998. *The Common Place of Law: Stories from Everyday Life*. Chicago: Univ. Chicago Press

Feuer A. 2000. Family's monkey is rare, as is this custody battle. *New York Times*, July 19. A1, 27

Frank AW. 1995. *The Wounded Storyteller*. Chicago: Univ. Chicago Press

Frohock FM. 1986. *Special Care*. Chicago: Univ. Chicago Press

Geary P. 1986. Sacred commodities: the circulation of medieval relics. See Appadurai 1986, pp. 169–91

Giddens A. 1984. *The Constitution of Society*. Berkeley: Univ. Calif. Press

Gilboy JA. 1991. Deciding who gets in: decisionmaking by immigration inspectors. *Law Soc. Rev.* 25:571–99

Gilboy JA. 1992. Penetrability of administrative systems: political "casework" and immigration inspections. *Law Soc. Rev.* 26:273–314

Goffman E. 1961. Fun in games. In *Encounters*,

pp. 15–81. Indianapolis, IN: Bobbs-Merrill

Goffman E. 1969. *Strategic Interaction*. Philadelphia: Univ. Penn. Press

Guillemin JH, Holmstrom LL. 1986. *Mixed Blessings*. New York: Oxford Univ. Press

Hawkins K. 1983. Assessing evil. *British J. Criminol*. 23:101–27

Heimer CA. 1985. Allocating information costs in a negotiated information order: interorganizational constraints on decision making in Norwegian oil insurance. *Admin. Sci. Q.* 30:395–417

Heimer CA. 1988. Social structure, psychology, and the estimation of risk. *Annu. Rev. Sociol.* 14:491–519

Heimer CA. 1996. Explaining variation in the impact of law: organizations, institutions, and professions. *Stud. Law, Politics Soc.* 15:29–59

Heimer CA. 1999. Competing institutions: law, medicine, and family in neonatal intensive care. *Law Soc. Rev.* 33:17–66

Heimer CA. 2001. Conceiving children: how documents support case vs. biographical analyses. In *Documents: Artifacts of Modern Knowledge*, ed. A Riles. Durham, NC: Duke Univ. Press. In press

Heimer CA, Staffen LR. 1998. *For the Sake of the Children: The Social Organization of Responsibility in the Hospital and the Home*. Chicago: Univ. Chicago Press

Heimer CA, Stevens ML. 1997. Caring for the organization: social workers as frontline risk managers in neonatal intensive care units. *Work Occup.* 24:133–63

Herzog HA Jr. 1988. The moral status of mice. *Am. Psychol.* 43:473–74

Hochschild AR. 1983. *The Managed Heart*. Berkeley: Univ. Calif. Press

James W. 1984. *Psychology, Briefer Course*. Cambridge, MA: Harvard Univ. Press

Kahneman D, Slovic P, Tversky A, eds. 1982. *Judgment under Uncertainty*. Cambridge, UK: Cambridge Univ. Press

Larson MS. 1977. *The Rise of Professionalism*. Berkeley: Univ. Calif. Press

Layne LL. 1996. "How's the baby doing?" Struggling with narratives of progress in a neonatal intensive care unit. *Med. Anthropol. Q.* 10:624–56

Leidner RL. 1993. *Fast Food, Fast Talk*. Berkeley: Univ. Calif. Press

Lempert R, Sanders J. 1986. *An Introduction to Law and Social Science*. Philadelphia: Univ. Penn. Press

Lynch M, Haney C. n.d. Impelling/impeding the momentum toward death: an analysis of attorneys' final arguments in California capital penalty phase trials. Unpublished manuscript, San Jose State Univ.

McCracken G. 1988. *Culture and Consumption: New Approaches to the Symbolic Character of Consumer Goods*. Bloomington: Indiana Univ. Press

Melot M. 1986. La notion d'originalité et son importance dans la définition des objets d'art. In *Sociologie d'Art*, ed. R Moulin. Paris: La Documentation Française

Merry SE. 1990. *Getting Justice and Getting Even: Legal Consciousness among Working-Class Americans*. Chicago: Univ. Chicago Press

Meyer JW, Rowan B. 1977. Institutionalized organizations: formal structure as myth and ceremony. *Am. J. Sociol.* 83:340–63

Powell WW, DiMaggio PJ, eds. 1991. *The New Institutionalism in Organizational Analysis*. Chicago: Univ. Chicago Press

Rawlings MK. 1966 (1938). *The Yearling*. New York: Collier Macmillan

Reddy WM. 1986. The structure of a cultural crisis: thinking about cloth in France before and after the Revolution. See Appadurai 1986, pp. 261–84

Roth JA. 1972. Some contingencies of the moral evaluation and control of clientele: the case of the hospital emergency service. *Am. J. Sociol.* 77:836–49

Sartre J-P. 1963. *Search for a Method*. Trans. HE Barnes. New York: Knopf

Schneider JW, Conrad P. 1983. *Having Epilepsy*. Philadelphia, PA: Temple Univ. Press

Scott WR. 1995. *Institutions and Organizations*. Beverley Hills, CA: Sage

Sewell WH Jr. 1992. A theory of structure:

duality, agency, and transformation. *Am. J. Sociol.* 98:1–29

Spooner B. 1986. Weavers and dealers: the authenticity of an oriental carpet. See Appadurai 1986, pp. 195–235

Star SL. 1985. Scientific work and uncertainty. *Soc. Stud. Sci.* 15:391–427

Star SL, Griesemer JR. 1989. Institutional ecology, 'translations' and boundary objects: amateurs and professionals in Berkeley's Museum of Vertebrate Zoology, 1907–39. *Soc. Stud. Sci.* 19:387–420

Sudnow D. 1965. Normal crimes: sociological features of the penal code in a public defender office. *Soc. Problems* 12:255–76

Sutton JB. 1988. *Stubborn Children: Controlling Delinquency in the US 1640–1984.* Berkeley: Univ. Calif. Press

Swidler A. 1986. Culture in action: symbols and strategies. *Am. Sociol. Rev.* 51:273–86

Swigert V, Farrell R. 1977. Normal homicides and the law. *Am. Sociol. Rev.* 42:16–32

Vallely P. 1998. The Saturday Story: How flying pigs became a crackling good tale. *Independent* (London) Jan 17, 1998: Features, p. 16

Vaughan D. 1996. *The Challenger Launch Decision.* Chicago: Univ. Chicago Press

Waegel WB. 1981. Case routinization in investigative police work. *Soc. Problems* 28:263–75

Weber M. 1950 (1927). *General Economic History.* Trans. FH Knight. Glencoe, IL: Free Press

White EB. 1952. *Charlotte's Web.* New York: Harper

White EB. 1970. *The Trumpet of the Swan.* New York: Harper & Row

White EB. 1973 (1945). *Stuart Little.* New York: Harper & Row

Wypijewski J, ed. 1997. *Painting by Numbers: Komar and Melamid's Scientific Guide to Art.* New York: Farrar Straus Giroux

Zelizer VAR. 1985. *Pricing the Priceless Child.* New York: Basic Books

Zerubavel E. 1991. *The Fine Line: Making Distinctions in Everyday Life.* Chicago: Univ. Chicago Press

Zucker LG. 1983. Organizations as institutions. In *Research in the Sociology of Organizations,* ed. SB Bacharach, pp. 1–47. Greenwich, CT: JAI

CASES CITED

Eddings v. Oklahoma, 455 U.S. 104 (1982)
Lockett v. Ohio, 438 U.S. (1978)
Penry v. Lynaugh, 492 U.S. 302 (1989)

Annu. Rev. Sociol. 2001. 27:77–102

EDUCATION AND STRATIFICATION IN DEVELOPING COUNTRIES: A Review of Theories and Research

Claudia Buchmann[1] and Emily Hannum[2]

[1]Duke University, Department of Sociology, Durham, NC 27708;
e-mail: cbuch@soc.duke.edu
[2]Harvard University, Graduate School of Education, Cambridge, MA 02138;
e-mail: emily_hannum@harvard.edu

Key Words   comparative research, family background, school effects, industrialization, social mobility, international education

■ **Abstract**   This review examines research on education and inequality in developing regions. In tracing the progress of this field of inquiry, it focuses on empirical studies of educational inequality in four broad areas: macro-structural forces shaping education and stratification; the relationship between family background and educational outcomes; school effects; and education's impact on economic and social mobility. It assesses the contributions of research in Africa, Asia, and Latin America to the general study of education and social stratification and the theoretical leverage gained from examining stratification processes in developing regions of the world. Finally, the review discusses recent developments that hold promise for addressing the knowledge gaps that remain; these include utilizing relatively new data sources and methods in comparative, cross-national studies and greater collaboration between researchers who study strikingly similar questions but remain segregated due to their focus on either industrialized or developing societies.

INTRODUCTION

Research on education and social stratification in developing countries has a long history. Even before Blau & Duncan (1967) published their seminal work on educational and occupational attainment in the United States, researchers such as C. Arnold Anderson (1956), Philip Foster (1963), and Remi Clignet (Clignet & Foster 1966) were attempting to assess the "function of formal schooling as it relates to the emergence of new patterns of social differentiation or to processes of social mobility" in developing regions (Foster 1963:150). These early studies and nearly all those that followed are implicitly or explicitly comparative in scope: They extend major theoretical questions and concerns about stratification processes in industrialized contexts to developing regions.

0360-0572/01/0811-0077$14.00

Less-developed societies have long interested students of stratification for the very different conditions they present in contrast to more industrialized societies. These may include class structures that are less differentiated, educational systems that vary in the extent to which they have been institutionalized, and occupational structures that are shaped by low levels of economic development and a weak position in the world system. Research in such social contexts can be useful for developing new theories. More commonly, however, these societal differences have provided opportunities for testing, refining, and extending theoretical perspectives that have emerged from research on industrialized countries.

In this paper, we review the literature on educational stratification in developing countries. We assess the empirical and theoretical contributions of this research to the general study of education and stratification and so illuminate areas where research has been notably limited. To keep the review manageable, we limit our geographic scope to developing regions that have been sites of the most research—countries in Latin America, sub-Saharan Africa, and South and East Asia. We include studies of rapidly industrializing East Asian countries such as Taiwan, Hong Kong, and South Korea, but exclude research on Eastern European and former Soviet-bloc nations. Also noticeably absent is the Middle East region, where, with the exception of Israel, research on education and stratification has been very limited. While our main focus is on the work of sociologists, we also cover relevant studies by demographers, economists, educational researchers, and anthropologists.

Figure 1 provides a conceptual framework for this broad field of study. As indicated by the figure, educational inequality is shaped by a wide range of factors on multiple levels. It is a consequence of dynamic interrelationships between family decisions about education (commonly referred to as demand) and the provision of educational opportunities (commonly referred to as supply).[1]

A significant body of research has examined how macro-structural elements, including state policies and global forces, shape educational stratification through their effects on the demand for education or the structure and supply of schooling. There has also been substantial research on how aspects of family background, such as socioeconomic status, family structure, and material resources, influence children's educational outcomes in developing countries. Perhaps as a result of the preoccupation with the "family versus schools" debate discussed below, few studies have considered how family and school factors interact to produce educational stratification. Instead, research on school-based determinants of educational strati-fication has developed relatively independently from research on family factors, and such research examines school processes or material inputs as they relate to

---

[1]The terms demand and supply are frequently used in education research because they help distinguish the provision of educational opportunities from the decisions to take advantage of such opportunities. But is it also important to acknowledge that this terminology simplifies the interrelated nature of supply and demand processes and neglects the point that some forces simultaneously impact educational supply and demand.

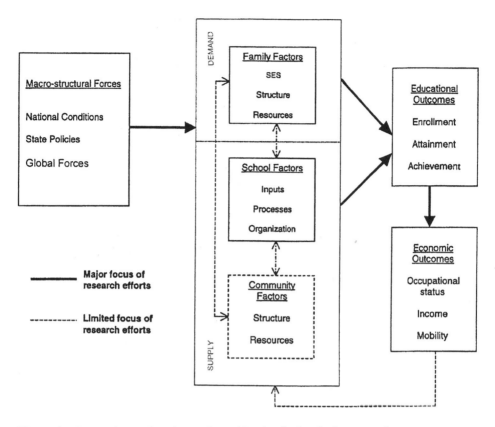

Figure 1   Research on education and stratification in developing countries.

attainment and achievement differences. There is also a notable lack of research on how community factors, operating independently or in conjunction with schools and families, shape educational outcomes in less-industrialized contexts. Finally, following the tradition of status attainment research in the United States, some researchers have addressed questions regarding the role of education in determining occupational mobility and other economic outcomes as well as changing patterns of social mobility in developing countries.

In the sections that follow, we discuss research in four broad areas, represented by the bold arrows in Figure 1: (*a*) macro-structural forces shaping educational stratification, (*b*) the impact of family background on educational attainment and achievement, (*c*) school factors as they relate to educational outcomes, and (*d*) the impact of education on social mobility in developing regions. Where applicable, we highlight key studies conducted in industrialized settings that have served as a foundation or stimulus for research in less-industrialized contexts. Rather than provide an exhaustive review of the work in each area, we focus on studies that illustrate the theoretical and empirical contributions of research in developing countries. The paper concludes with a summary of the contributions of research on educational stratification in developing countries to broader concerns, and we offer specific strategies for overcoming the gaps in knowledge that remain.

MACRO-STRUCTURAL FORCES SHAPING EDUCATIONAL STRATIFICATION

Whether they view the state as a bearer of functional modernity, an agent of economic elites, or a mediator of class conflict, most theorists acknowledge a central role for the state in education. The nation-state may shape the provision of educational opportunities and determine the structure of the educational system through its educational policies. It can also spark demand for education by improving school quality, passing laws on compulsory schooling, or emphasizing the benefits of education (Fuller & Rubinson 1992).

Case studies of developing countries highlight the varied nature and efficacy of state educational policies. For example, in the rapidly industrializing city-state of Hong Kong, when the government mandated free and compulsory primary school and provided substantial funding for this mandate, it appeared that educational opportunities for children from all socioeconomic backgrounds increased (Post 1994). Educational policies in Malaysia (Lillard & Willis 1994) and the Philippines (King & Lillard 1987) had similar impacts, although Smith & Cheung (1986) demonstrate that, despite educational expansion in the Philippines, the association between social origins and educational transitions remained relatively stable over time. Strong authoritarian states, such as communist China and South Africa under apartheid, dramatically altered stratification processes in their societies through educational policies. In China, major shifts in state policy directly affected the life chances of individuals from different social groups (Zhou et al 1996). Most strikingly, during the Cultural Revolution, a radical egalitarian agenda dominated education policies. As a result, well-educated and upper-class individuals lost mobility, but regained advantages in the post-Mao era (Deng & Treiman 1997, Zhou et al 1998). Rural residents and women gained greater access to education during the Cultural Revolution, but the trends toward equality in education slowed for women and reversed for rural dwellers thereafter (Hannum & Xie 1994, Hannum 1999). In South Africa, during apartheid's long reign, the state used the educational system and other institutions to thoroughly block the social mobility of the black majority while ensuring promotion of the white minority (Seidman 1999, Treiman et al 1996). It remains to be seen whether deeply entrenched racial inequalities can be reduced in the post-apartheid era.

Such examples of state strength are relatively rare in the developing world. Usually governments face substantial barriers–severely limited economic and organizational resources, a lack of legitimacy, and peripheral status in the world system—in their attempts to shape educational opportunities or to boost school demand. In these cases, Third World states may be able to signal mass educational opportunity by devising national exam systems or expounding the benefits of education, but may be too weak to create stable and effective educational institutions (Fuller 1991). Several studies have examined the deleterious effects of state weakness in the education sector, including excessive demand for higher education, extreme regional disparities in school supply, and poor school quality (Buchmann 1999, Parrado 1998, Fuller 1991, Post 1990). Others have noted that, in the absence of strong states, non-state actors such as local community groups and national and international nongovernmental organizations (NGOs) can facilitate the development and expansion of educational systems (Bradshaw 1993, Schafer 1999). These studies illuminate the capabilities and limitations of states as they try to expand and improve education in less-industrialized world regions.

Beyond the state, global forces, such as the policies and preferences of international organizations or the spread of Western ideology and organizational forms (including modern education) throughout the world, influence education and stratification processes within developing countries. World institution theory views worldwide educational expansion as the result of a social movement that has spread across national boundaries, regardless of economic and political particularities of nation states (Meyer & Hannan 1979, Boli et al 1985). Thus, the Third World state's drive to construct and expand education comes, in part, from the external pressures of a global political culture related to modern ideals of individual and national development (Inkeles & Sirowy 1983, Meyer et al 1992). The result is the convergence of educational systems throughout the world, in terms of both school organization (Ramirez & Boli 1987) and curricular content (Benavot et al 1991). In emphasizing the institutional effects of education, these scholars note that educational expansion alters allocation patterns in society to impact both schooled and nonschooled populations (Meyer 1977). For example, as the ideology of formal schooling constructs new rights and duties for women, even uneducated women may become integrated into the economic and political arenas of society (Ramirez & Weiss 1979). International institutions, such as UNICEF, UNESCO, and the World Bank, further propagate a worldview supportive of gender equity in education (Bradley & Ramirez 1996, Boli & Thomas 1997).

Other scholars have been more critical of the role of global forces and international organizations. Drawing on dependency theories, they argue that educational opportunities in developing countries are severely constrained by structural inequalities in the global economy and these countries' dependence on multinational corporations and international organizations. Clark (1992) maintains that multinational corporations' strategies, such as the mass hiring of women for unskilled labor, undermine women's entry to higher education in developing countries. Some research links educational declines in developing countries to the structural adjustment policies (SAPs) mandated by the International Monetary Fund (IMF) and other international financial organizations. These policies, which facilitate debt servicing through fiscal austerity and reduced government intervention in indebted nations, have been traced to declines in educational spending, teacher quality, and educational demand (Reimers 1991). Other evidence indicates that

SAPs disproportionately affect female participation in education, likely through their detrimental impact on survival strategies in poor households (Buchmann 1996). Finally, the pressures from the IMF and donor agencies on indebted governments to privatize and decentralize their educational systems may lead to greater inequities and declining educational participation (Arnove 1997). In sum, research on macro-structural determinants of education and inequality demonstrates that the efficacy of state actors in expanding education and shaping stratification patterns is highly variable over time and place and is enhanced or constrained by global institutions and forces.

FAMILIES, SCHOOLS, AND EDUCATIONAL OUTCOMES

In the past three decades, a great deal of research has focused on the role of family background and school effects on educational attainment and achievement. The stimuli for much of this research were two major projects, the Coleman Report (Coleman et al 1966) in the United States and the Plowden Report (Peaker 1971) in Great Britain, which generally concluded that family background was more important than school factors in determining children's educational achievement. These studies sparked a great deal of interest in assessing the determinants of educational attainment and achievement and set off a lively debate regarding the roles of family and school factors.

This debate was largely limited to industrialized countries until Stephen Heyneman published the results of his "Coleman Report for a developing country" (1976) in which he found family background to be less important than school factors in determining academic achievement in Uganda. In subsequent research, Heyneman & Loxley (1983) generalized these findings to other developing countries and found that the portion of the variance in achievement attributable to family background was generally much smaller, and that attributable to school quality generally much larger, in developing versus industrialized countries. They concluded that, "the poorer the country, the greater the impact of school and teacher quality on achievement" (1180). In the years that followed, many studies sought to assess the role of family background and school factors on educational attainment and achievement in a wide range of developing countries.

Family Background

Heyneman's findings of weak effects of family background notwithstanding, there is significant evidence that family factors are important for educational outcomes in the developing world. Research has examined the role of socioeconomic status, family size and structure, and family decision-making processes in an attempt to explain how they relate to educational inequalities in developing countries. Of course, the relationship between family socioeconomic status and school achievement is complicated in contexts where enrollment and attainment themselves are conditional on family economic circumstances. Case studies using culturally specific measures of class have found significant effects of family class status on students' mathematics and language achievement (Lockheed et al 1989, Niles 1981). Moreover, numerous studies indicate marked disparities in enrollment and attainment associated with socioeconomic status (Sathar & Lloyd 1993 for Pakistan, Stash & Hannum 2001 for Nepal, Hannum 2000 for rural China, Patrinos & Psacharopoulos 1996 for Bolivia and Guatemala). In a recent systematic cross-national analysis of this relationship, Filmer & Pritchett (1999) analyzed the "wealth gap" in education in 35 countries in Africa, the Middle East, South Asia and East Asia. Their results revealed substantial cross-country variation in the differences between median years of school obtained by students in the top 20% compared to the bottom 40% of the wealth distribution. All countries (except Kazakhstan) displayed a difference between rich and poor children's attainment; the largest wealth gaps emerged in the countries of South Asia.

In addition to socioeconomic status, research has examined how family structure and size influence educational outcomes in developing regions. Importantly, much of this research questions the universality of findings from the United States and other industrialized countries. For example, in the United States the well-documented negative effects of single parenthood on children's educational outcomes range from a greater probability of school drop-out to lower achievement. These effects have been attributed in part to economic stress associated with female headship, and in part to the lack of human or social capital in the household (see Seltzer 1994 for a review).

Interestingly, in some African contexts female headship appears to be associated with greater, not fewer, educational opportunities for children. For example, in a study of adolescent girls in South Africa, Fuller & Liang (1999) reported that father absence served to *decrease* girls' risk of leaving school. Lloyd & Blanc (1996) analyzed the effects of female headship on children's schooling in seven sub-Saharan African countries. Female-headed households tended to be poorer than other households, but children in female-headed households were consistently more likely to be enrolled in school and to have completed grade four than were children in households headed by men. They maintain that "female household heads are more likely to invest resources, including time, money and emotional support, in facilitating the education of children living in their household" (288). The different effects of family structure in Africa and other regions may also be linked to the nuclear family's embeddedness in larger kinship networks. For example, Lloyd & Blanc (1996) noted that extended family networks in sub-Saharan Africa enable children with academic promise to move to households of "patron" family members, who help them gain access to higher quality schools. Pong (1996) similarly illustrated the importance of extended kinship systems in moderating the effects of family structure on children's schooling in Malaysia. Children of divorced mothers, but not of widowed mothers, have lower school participation rates than do children of two-parent families. Pong attributed these results to the buffering role of large kinship systems: in Malaysia, widows receive more material support from family members than do divorced mothers (248).

Studies on sibship size and schooling in developing countries similarly cast doubt on the generalizability of patterns found in industrialized countries. Research in the United States consistently documents an inverse relationship between number of siblings and educational attainment (Blake 1989, Steelman & Powell 1989). A prominent explanation for this relationship is the "resource dilution hypothesis" which stresses that material resources and parental attention are diluted with additional children in the household. Negative associations between sibship size and educational outcomes have been replicated in some developing countries, including Thailand (Knodel et al 1990), Malaysia (Pong 1997, Shreeniwas 1997, Parish & Willis 1993), the Dominican Republic and the Philippines (Montgomery & Lloyd 1997).

Yet the negative association between sibship size and schooling is not consistently observed. For example, Anh and associates (1998) demonstrated that the negative relationship between sibship size and enrollment in Vietnam disappeared when controls for socioeconomic status were added. In Kenya, Buchmann (2000) found no effect of sibship size on children's probability of enrollment, and Montgomery & Lloyd (1997) found no impact of excess fertility (fertility departing from stated family-size preferences) on educational attainment. Earlier research in Africa reported that siblings may even contribute to household resources in some contexts. In rural Botswana, the number of seven- to fourteen-year-old children in the household was positively related to educational enrollment and attainment (Chernichovsky 1985), and sibship size was positively associated with years of schooling in Kenya (Gomes 1984). These studies suggest an important caveat to the resource dilution hypothesis by demonstrating that effects of sibship size are not consistent across societies. The extended family systems common in Africa can provide resources that moderate the effects of sibship size and actually facilitate children's schooling.

A second caveat relates to the point that a child's position within the sibship structure may determine whether siblings contribute or dilute resources for education. For example, in addition to documenting positive effects of older siblings in Botswana, Chernichovsky (1985) found that the presence of very young siblings was detrimental to children's schooling. Similarly, Parish & Willis (1993) found that in Taiwan, early-born siblings receive less education while later-born siblings receive more; having older sisters is helpful to male and female children alike. Echoing Gomes' (1984) findings from Kenya, Lloyd & Gage-Brandon (1994) noted that some of the costs of high fertility in Ghana are borne by older siblings rather than by parents; thus later-born children may benefit from the economic resources provided by older siblings.

A final caveat to the resource dilution interpretation highlighted by research in developing countries lies in evidence for what economists call the quality-quantity trade-off. This term refers to the idea that parents may anticipate educational costs and modify fertility decisions in order to have fewer but better-educated children. Caldwell's (1980) influential work explicitly identified the direct costs of schooling and the increased pressures on parents to invest in their children as important factors for bringing about fertility decline. Micro-demographic research in Nepal (Axinn 1993) found that children's schooling exerted a strong influence on parents' fertility preferences and behavior. Studies in Taiwan (Hermalin et al 1982, Parish & Willis 1993) and Malaysia (Shreeniwas 1997) showed that the negative relationship between sibship size and education began to emerge only after the onset of fertility limitation. Taken together, these findings suggest that observed negative effects of larger sibships might reflect not the dilution of resources per se, but rather prior decisions and preferences that determine both numbers of children in the household and investments in their education. In sum, the literature on family structure and schooling in developing countries illustrates the potential buffering effect of larger kinship structures and the often-significant impact of order and gender composition of siblings. More generally, the research highlights the importance of focusing critically on the social and economic contexts in which family effects operate.

In addition to the research on family structure, a growing body of research on family decision-making investigates conventional notions regarding parental values and preferences, cultural beliefs, and the allocation of children to work or school. For example, while early research attributed gender inequalities in education to patriarchy (Csapo 1981, Greenhalgh 1985), recent research emphasizes the context-specific nature of family decisions regarding education for sons and daughters. Some studies have demonstrated how multiple factors–labor market conditions, the family economy, parental beliefs and preferences–inform educational decisions (Parish & Willis 1993, Fuller et al 1995, Buchmann 2000). Similarly, researchers have begun to examine relationships between gender and poverty in household decisions about schooling (Knodel & Jones 1996, World Bank 2000).[2]

The allocation of children to productive activities in the home or the labor market is thought to be a common survival strategy for poor families, but more research is needed to determine whether and how child labor interferes with schooling. Studies have found detrimental effects of child household labor on schooling in Botswana (Chernichovsky 1985), Malawi (Lockheed et al 1989), Colombia, Bolivia, and the Philippines (Grootaert & Patrinos 1999). But in other contexts, where school has been effectively legitimated as the proper place for children or where employment opportunities for children are scarce, child labor is less likely to interfere with schooling. In a recent study of Botswana, Fuller and his associates (1995) found no effect of household labor tasks on girls' probability of leaving school. In Kenya, Buchmann (2000) found little evidence that wage labor or housework competes with school enrollment. These studies underscore that child labor and schooling need not be mutually exclusive activities. The varied results of the research on child labor strongly suggest that the relationship between schooling and working depends on social structural factors that determine the range of options available to families as they make decisions. Cross-national comparative research is needed

---

[2]A thorough review of gender inequality in education in developing countries is beyond the scope of this paper. For a comprehensive review, see King & Hill (1993).

to determine whether there are patterns underlying what appears to be a myriad of results from single-country case studies.

School Factors and Processes

The literature on the impact of school factors and processes on academic achievement in developing countries has developed largely independently from that on family background and educational outcomes. Much of the research in the former tradition can be traced to Heyneman's (1976) study of seventh grade students from 67 primary schools in Uganda. Replicating the design of the Coleman Report, Heyneman found significant effects of school facilities and weak effects of family background on academic achievement. He believed these results to be due to the greater variance in physical facilities of schools and the smaller variance of social class in Uganda. Following Heyneman's lead, more than 60 studies of school effects had been conducted by 1989 in a wide range of developing countries, the majority of which found significant effects of school factors, net of family background, on achievement [see Fuller (1987) and Fuller & Clarke (1994) for reviews]. Most of these studies utilized the production function approach[3] and regression analysis to identify the specific determinants of achievement and make inferences about the relative importance of the various inputs to student performance.

From these studies, some generalizations can be made regarding which school inputs increase student achievement in less-developed countries. While much US-based research suggests that per-pupil expenditure and quality of school facilities have little impact on student achievement,[4] studies in developing countries have found that basic material inputs such as textbooks, libraries, and teacher training strongly determine achievement (Heyneman & Jamison 1980, Heyneman & Loxley 1983, Lockheed et al 1986, Behrman & Birdsall 1983). More expensive inputs such as science laboratories, increased teachers' salaries, and reduced class size appear to have little effect (Cohn & Rossmiller 1987). The general conclusion is that basic material inputs are most important in contexts that have inadequate or very unequally distributed educational resources (developing countries) but are less important in contexts that have achieved a minimum level of basic resources (industrialized countries).

Importantly, some researchers questioned the rationale and methodology of school effects research. Indeed, one shortcoming of most studies of the impact of school effects versus family effects was their reliance on OLS regression analysis

---

[3]This approach focuses on the relationship between school outcomes and measurable educational inputs and is derived from the notion that the output of the educational process, namely individual student achievement, is related directly to a series of inputs (Hanushek 1995:228–9). Family inputs are commonly measured by parental education, income, wealth, and family size. School inputs are typically conceptualized as teachers' characteristics, school organization, and community factors.

[4]Although some recent research demonstrates clear advantages of small class size and other educational resources in the United States; see Arum (2000).

and the total variance in achievement (R^2) to measure the impact of family and school effects on student achievement. As Riddell (1989) noted, "Criticism of such arbitrary use of the proportion of variance as a measure of importance is at least as old as the criticism of the Plowden report. Yet such criticism does not seem to have prevented its continued misuse" (487). Another methodological caveat of the school effects research involved the "misapplication of a single-level model to a reality that is clearly hierarchical" (Riddell 1989:484). This problem was likely exacerbated by the use of aggregate data, which inflates estimated effects of family background relative to classroom and school effects (Bidwell & Kasarda 1980).

In the late 1980s, a new generation of research on effective schools in the United States revisited long-standing questions regarding school and family effects on achievement with multi-level modeling techniques (Aitkin & Longford 1986, Goldstein 1987, Raudenbush & Bryk 1986). These analytical strategies allow researchers to take account of the hierarchical nature of most educational data, thereby addressing some of the methodological shortcomings of prior work. While only a few studies have utilized multi-level models to examine school effects in developing countries, their results are quite interesting. In contrast to previous research utilizing the production function approach, these studies found greater effects of family background than of school factors on educational achievement in Zimbabwe (Riddell 1989) and Thailand (Lockheed & Longford 1991). For example, in their analysis of Thai data, Lockheed & Longford (1991) found that school-level differences contributed 32% of the explained variance while family and individual factors contributed 68% of the explained variance in student mathematics achievement. More recently, with cross-national data from the Third International Math and Science Study (TIMSS), Baker and colleagues (1999) examine whether the relationship between national wealth and large school effects found by Heyneman and Loxley in the early 1980s persists in the 1990s. They replicate Heyneman and Loxley's OLS method of analysis but also utilize hierarchical linear modeling procedures to examine the explained variance in achievement attributable to school and family factors in a wide range of countries. They find no association between national wealth and the size of school effects. Regardless of national levels of wealth, family factors are more important predictors of educational achievement than are school factors in most countries. They attribute this finding to continued educational expansion and greater standardization of school quality at minimal levels in less-developed nations. Baker and colleagues appropriately acknowledge the possibility that large school effects on educational achievement persist in very poor developing countries, which did not participate in the TIMSS.

These studies raise questions about past generalizations regarding the differential effects of family background and school factors in developing versus developed countries. Moreover, they have reinvigorated debates over the proper way to measure and study school effects (for a recent exchange, see Hanushek 1995 and Kremer 1995). Clearly, the long debate regarding school effects is far from resolved, and more research is needed before definitive conclusions can be made.

In its concern with assessing the impact of school material inputs versus family background factors, the school effects literature has also neglected important questions regarding *how* schools impact achievement in developing countries (Fuller & Clarke 1994). Largely due to data limitations and a lack of qualitative school-based research in developing regions, our knowledge of how school organization and classroom processes influence children's educational experiences in these contexts is limited. The very few studies that have examined the role of teachers and administrators as managers of student learning find significant effects of teacher quality (Lockheed & Komenan 1989), classroom management and hours of instruction (Saha 1983, Fuller & Snyder 1991, Fuller et al 1994), and classroom dynamics (Lloyd et al 2000) on student achievement. These results are generally consistent with those found in the United States and other developed countries (Barr & Dreeben 1983). Thus, comments made by Bruce Fuller (1987:288) many years ago are still relevant today:

> Few observational studies within Third World classrooms have occurred. To date this work tends to be atheoretical and rarely involves quantitative analysis . . . the school effects literature from the U. S. and Europe suggests a variety of research avenues related to the social organization of schools and classrooms. But these roads have yet to be traveled by investigators working in developing countries.

The few studies that have traveled such roads demonstrate how research on school organization in contexts quite different from the United States can advance our understanding of educational stratification more generally. One example is Broaded's (1997) research on tracking in Taiwan. In an investigation of the effects of tracking on the educational aspirations and attainments of Taiwanese junior high school students, Broaded found school achievement variables (placement in high ability track, grade-point average) to be stronger predictors of educational aspirations and senior high school placement than were family background factors. Based on these results, and in contrast with much of the United States–based research that finds that tracking reinforces social-class inequalities (Oakes et al 1992), Broaded maintained that ability grouping as it is practiced in Taiwan contributes to greater equality of educational opportunity. This difference is likely due to institutional aspects of Taiwan's educational system, such as uniform elementary education and a nationally standardized curriculum, as well as smaller racial, ethnic, and income inequalities in Taiwan. As one of the few studies of tracking in less-industrialized contexts, this study demonstrates how research on school processes in developing countries can illuminate the ways in which societal differences condition stratification processes.

THE EFFECTS OF EDUCATION ON ECONOMIC OUTCOMES AND SOCIAL MOBILITY

The literature on the longer-term effects of schooling is quite broad. It encompasses research on education's impact on society (i.e., its role in fostering economic development and democracy) as well as its impact on a wide range of individual behaviors (i.e., fertility practices, child rearing, perceptions and attitudes, labor market participation, occupational status, social mobility). This section reviews research on the effects of schooling only as they relate to changes in occupational status, labor market participation, and social mobility.

Much of the research on education and social mobility in developing countries has been grounded in the work of Blau & Duncan (1967) and the Wisconsin model of status attainment (Sewell et al 1969, Sewell & Hauser 1975). For example, Hansen & Haller (1973) replicated the Wisconsin model with longitudinal data for a sample of male Costa Rican high school students in order to examine the relationship between family background, education, and occupational attainment. The Costa Rica model differed from the Wisconsin model in that there was no strong association between family background and educational attainment. The authors attributed this finding to the relative homogeneity of occupational status among fathers in rural Costa Rica. As in the Wisconsin model, educational attainment and occupational aspirations had direct effects on the occupational attainment of Costa Rican males. In a study of occupational attainment in Chile, Farrell & Schiefelbein (1985) used longitudinal data for students interviewed in eighth grade and re-interviewed eight years later. The study found that the degree of respondents' occupational mobility depended, in part, on their class status. For the middle class, education was significant in determining occupational attainment; for respondents with either upper-class or very poor parents, intergenerational status inheritance was much more likely. Finally, Strudwick & Foster (1991) investigated intergenerational mobility in Jamaica, a lower-middle income country with a rigid class structure, and concluded that massive expansion of educational opportunities at the secondary level did little to increase the permeability of the Jamaican social structure.

The diverse foci and findings of even these few studies reflect a lack of cohesion in the limited research on status attainment in developing societies. In contrast to several major efforts to compare status attainment and intergenerational mobility processes across industrialized countries (Erikson & Goldthorpe 1992, Ganzeboom et al 1989, Shavit & Blossfeld 1993, Shavit & Mueller 1998), the research on less-developed regions is far more sparse and disjointed.

A somewhat different, but related, area of research is concerned with how industrialization alters the processes by which individuals are sorted into status hierarchies. The idea that the level of intergenerational occupational mobility in a society depends on its level of industrialization was first put forth by Lipset & Bendix (1959). In a study of nine industrialized nations, they found little variation in rates of mobility and concluded that this was due to the uniform level of industrialization across the countries. In a widely cited publication, Treiman (1970) expanded upon these ideas to provide a detailed explanation of the mechanisms by which industrialization should promote greater mobility. As societies develop, urbanization, mass communication, and industrialization should lead to greater social openness and a shift from particularistic to universalistic bases of achievement. As a result, the direct influence of father's occupational status on son's occupational status, as well as father's educational and occupational status on son's educational attainment, should decline, while the direct influence of son's educational attainment on his occupational status should increase (Treiman 1970:221).

During the 1970s and 1980s, researchers set out to test these propositions. Most studies examined historical or regional differences within a single society, and few found support for the industrialism thesis. For example, in a study of occupational mobility in Toro, Uganda, Kelley & Perlman (1971) found a high degree of occupational mobility in pre-industrial Toro; mobility actually declined as Toro industrialized. Holsinger (1975) compared the effects of father's occupational status on son's education across four Brazilian cities with different levels of development and found no evidence of smaller effects of parental status on son's education in more developed areas. A decade later, Bills & Haller (1984, Bills et al 1985) reassessed Holsinger's conclusions with nationally representative data. They also found little evidence that patterns of status attainment vary by level of industrialization in Brazil. Finally, a study of occupational mobility in pre- and post-independence Zaire similarly challenged the thesis of industrialism (Mukweso et al 1984). Rather than finding an increasing impact of education on occupational attainment over time, results indicated that educational attainment was important for occupational attainment in both periods. After independence, ascribed characteristics such as religion and ethnicity declined in importance, but socioeconomic status became more important in determining occupational attainment.

Despite the obvious need for cross-national studies to inform questions regarding the industrialism thesis, to the best of our knowledge, only two such published studies exist. In a cross-sectional comparison of Haiti, Costa Rica, Great Britain, and the United States, Lin & Yeager (1975) concluded that at middle levels of industrialization, the direct influence of education on occupational status is suppressed by the influence of father's occupational status. Only at higher levels of industrialization does the influence of father's occupational status decline and the influence of son's educational attainment for his own occupational status increase. These findings provide some support for the industrialism thesis, but the authors acknowledged the need to test the results for a wider range of countries.

In 1989, Treiman & Yip set out to examine the industrialism thesis with cross-national data for 21 countries, including four developing countries (Brazil, India, the Philippines, and Taiwan). Like Lin & Yeager (1975), they found that the impact of social origins on educational and occupational attainment declines with industrialization, but they concluded that this is primarily due to a decline in the level of status inequality in industrialized societies and is not a result of industrialization per se: "Both industrialization and status equality promote achievement at the expense of ascription . . . The strongest effect on the achievement-ascription mix is the level of inequality of father's education" (Treiman & Yip 1989:393). Given the reliance on data from a single country in most studies on the issue,

Treiman & Yip's study is the most comprehensive assessment of the industrialism thesis to date. Yet, we are far from a definitive answer regarding how educational-occupational linkages vary by level of industrialization. This situation may soon be rectified. In a recent paper, Treiman & Ganzeboom (1997) discussed plans to use 250 sample surveys from 40 nations to test the industrialism thesis as well as other hypotheses regarding the impact of social change on stratification processes, in the hope of producing a comprehensive understanding on these issues.

A variant of the industrialization hypothesis exists in recent debates about education's effects in countries undergoing the transition from socialism to capitalism. Although much of the literature on this topic has focused on Eastern Europe and the former Soviet Union, and thus is beyond the scope of this paper, a significant part of the debate has focused on China. The onset of rapid market transition in China has presented an unusual opportunity to test basic tenets related to the industrialization hypothesis. One strand of market transition theory postulates that the shift from a planned to market-based economic system should increase the returns to human capital and decrease the returns to political capital (for a recent review, see Nee & Matthews 1996). Empirical results have been mixed. For example, Xie & Hannum's (1996) analysis of city- and individual-level data indicated that economic growth depressed the returns to education and did not affect the net differences between party members and nonmembers. Zhou's (2000) analysis of urban retrospective panel data found increasing returns to education, but no decline in the returns to political capital. Although a consensus has yet to be reached, ongoing research about China's transition to a market economy carries the potential to illuminate broader debates about the relationship between education and mobility over the course of industrialization.

Finally, in contrast to a well-developed literature on ethnic and gender stratification in labor markets in industrialized countries, very few studies of developing countries have examined educational inequalities as they related to ethnic and gender inequalities in labor force participation or occupational status. Telles (1994) examined the relationship between industrialization and race-based occupational stratification in Brazil to conclude that industrialization and educational expansion were associated with decreased racial inequality across the full occupational distribution, but with greater racial inequality in professional and white-collar sectors. Hannum & Xie (1998) found similarly ambiguous implications of educational expansion in Northwest China for ethnic differences in occupational attainment. Over an eight-year period, increased ethnic inequality in occupational status could be explained by increased ethnic differences in education. In South Africa, Treiman and coworkers (1996) found that educational disparities played an important role in maintaining race-based differences in occupational status, but explained a much smaller fraction of race-based income inequalities.

Brinton and associates (1995) investigated the relationship between education and women's employment in the rapidly industrializing societies of Taiwan and Korea. Interestingly, they found very different education-employment relationships for women in the two societies. In Taiwan, higher levels of education increased women's probability of employment (see also Tsai 1998), while in Korea, highly educated women were less likely to be employed. The authors attribute this finding to differences in labor market conditions. An adequate supply of educated males offered Korean employers few incentives to reduce barriers to employment of married women; in Taiwan "an inadequate supply of males has forced employers to alter their patriarchal preferences" (Brinton et al 1995:1111). Gender differences in labor market opportunities can, in turn, influence male and female enrollment rates. For example, Buchmann & Brakewood (2000) found that differences in the labor structures of Kenya and Thailand were related to gender differences in enrollment rates in the two societies. In Thailand, a "feminization" of the manufacturing sector appeared to be related to demand for female secondary education; in Kenya, where the manufacturing sector is dominated by males, the size of local manufacturing sectors had no impact on female secondary enrollment rates. These studies push forward our understanding of the complex ways in which educational and occupational linkages are complicated by notions of gender and ethnic hierarchies within particular societies, which are shaped by contextual factors such as state policies and institutionalized discrimination.

In conclusion, the literature on the effects of education on occupational and social mobility in developing countries, with a few notable exceptions, has been dominated by single-country studies often utilizing less-than-ideal data and methods. In part, the dearth of studies has been due to data constraints. Collecting longitudinal data of the kind generally needed for status attainment research is especially time consuming in less-developed countries and "not to be commended to academics concerned with high publication rates and consequent tenure" (Strudwick & Foster 1991:153). Moreover, the development of reliable and valid, yet comparable, measures of class status, income, and occupational mobility is made especially challenging in developing societies, in part because the common constructs of these processes used in industrialized countries may be inappropriate in less-industrialized contexts.

SUMMARY AND CONCLUSION

Research on education and stratification in developing countries is as diverse as it is extensive. For the most part, the questions that have been the focus of this research—on the relationship between family background and educational outcomes, on the effects of schools on learning and achievement, and on the role of education in determining occupational status and social mobility—are the same central concerns that have guided research on education and stratification in industrialized contexts. In precisely the instances where answers to these central questions appear most different, the theoretical leverage to be gained from research on developing contexts is most readily apparent.

For example, research on aspects of family structure, such as female-headship and sibship size, indicates the need to refine the common definition of family to include broader kinship structures. Empirical evidence of the buffering effects of strong kinship networks in developing countries also suggests fruitful lines of exploration in more industrialized contexts. Indeed, good examples are Shavit & Pierce's (1991) finding that sibship size is not significantly related to educational attainment among Israeli Arab groups with strong kinship networks and Blake's (1989) conclusion that the negative educational effects of large families in the United States could be somewhat offset by an exceptionally strong kin cohesion. Research on the codetermined nature of fertility and schooling decisions in less-industrialized societies also urges scholars to use caution in making causal interpretations of sibship size on educational attainment. Finally, this research highlights the importance of understanding the social and economic contexts in which families make educational decisions for their children.

The study of school factors and educational outcomes similarly highlights the importance of the social and economic contexts of schools. By offering counterpoints to the common notions (usually based on US research) regarding how school factors affect student achievement, studies in less-developed contexts clearly demonstrate that the impacts of specific policy initiatives depend on the environment in which schools function. Finally, the mixed results of research on economic outcomes and social mobility highlight the need to revisit theories about the impact of industrialization on social inequality. These examples illustrate how educational and stratification processes and outcomes are affected by the institutional variations between developing and industrialized contexts. Thus, as students of stratification increasingly are interested in understanding how institutional arrangements shape educational and stratification processes (Kerckhoff 1995), they would do well to look to developing countries and the variability in social context such cases offer.[5]

Focused research on less-industrialized societies may also provide answers to longstanding questions regarding the changing nature of stratification processes over the course of broad societal transformations. For example, early research attributed weak effects of family background on educational achievement to a smaller variance in social class and larger variance in quality of school facilities in developing countries. Recent research reports findings of strong family background effects and weak school effects on achievement that are more in line with those from industrialized countries. If these findings are real and can be documented across a broad range of developing countries, they may be indicative of increasing heterogeneity in family background and increasing homogeneity in educational institutions. Such findings would be in line with world institution theorists' claims of the global isomorphism of educational institutions and so could invigorate theorizing in the broad area of social change.

Other large gaps in knowledge remain to be addressed. In Figure 1, dashed lines indicate areas for which research is notably limited or weak. For example,

---

[5]At the same time, research on developing contexts could draw inspiration from the growing literature on the role of institutional arrangements for educational processes in industrialized countries (Shavit & Mueller 1998, Kerckhoff 2001), and research could focus more explicitly on the structural similarities and differences of developing countries' educational systems.

a growing interest among researchers in the United States relates to the role of community forces as they operate independently or in concert with family factors to affect educational attainment and achievement (for a review, see Arum 2000). Some research finds that community factors such as the concentration of poverty and the racial composition of neighborhoods are significantly related to unequal educational outcomes (Garner & Raudenbush 1991, Duncan 1994, Halpern-Felsher et al 1997). These studies are important in that they recognize that children develop within a set of embedded contexts and tap into the multifaceted nature of determinants of educational inequality. Indeed, poor societies often display enormous community-level variations in wealth and schools provided, and community groups are often actively involved in funding, building, and managing local schools. However, virtually no research has examined such community variations and processes in education. Thus, the neglect of community factors in most research to this point indicates a serious gap in the study of education and stratification in less-developed contexts.

Moreover, only a handful of studies explicitly examine family background and school factors as simultaneous and interactive forces in determining educational inequality, although research from the United States has found these interactions to have important consequences for children's educational experiences (Lareau 1989, Schneider & Coleman 1993). Finally, it is striking that, despite having been the focus of much empirical research in recent decades, the major debates regarding school versus family effects or the impact of industrialization on social mobility remain largely unresolved.

Recent developments in both data collection and analytical methods suggest that great progress can be made in overcoming these knowledge gaps. Many current data sources contain extensive information of the type needed to advance the study of education and stratification in developing countries. Appendix A lists several data sets that are well suited to such analysis and, with some exceptions, have been underutilized by researchers in this area. Especially exciting about these data sets is that most of them are cross-national, longitudinal, or multilevel in scope. By utilizing these data in conjunction with relatively new analytic strategies, such as multilevel statistical methods, researchers could make great strides toward resolving some of the longstanding questions central to this field. For example, by using hierarchical-linear modeling (HLM) strategies to analyze surveys containing nested data on individuals, families, and schools for a wide range of countries, researchers should be able to come to some definitive conclusions regarding the relative impact of family and school effects on educational outcomes in developing regions. The investigation of community factors, an area of research that has proven fruitful in industrialized contexts, is also possible with such data and could go far in advancing our understanding of the ways families, schools, and communities interact to determine unequal school outcomes. Alternatively, some of the gaps illuminated above might best be addressed with in-depth, qualitative research. Our limited knowledge of the impact of school processes and organization on children's achievement in the developing world stands to be richly informed by careful, detailed research in schools and classrooms.

Just as the 1990s was marked by the increasingly comparative study of stratification in industrialized societies (Treiman & Ganzeboom 1997), the next few decades could bring a parallel development in the research on developing countries. This would require a shift from the past focus on single-country studies to explicitly comparative, multiple-country studies using secondary data, as well as new data collection projects. We believe that the time is ripe for such a shift, but it will require efforts on several fronts.

First, research in the broad field of education and stratification in developing countries is relatively fragmented by the disciplinary divisions between sociology, economics, demography, and education, all of which have made contributions to the field. This fragmentation must be overcome; only through greater cross-fertilization and the sharing of research strategies and findings can our knowledge cumulate in this interdisciplinary area of study. Strategies that have been used in the last decade by comparative researchers of stratification processes in industrialized countries are readily applicable to building a more comparative literature on developing countries. For example, collaborative efforts that utilize comparable data and methods to analyze specific stratification processes in a range of countries (thus following the lead of Shavit & Blossfeld 1993, Shavit & Mueller 1998) would help to produce a more generalized understanding of patterns of educational stratification in the developing world.

Second, in order to ensure that contemporary data gathering efforts can address the longstanding concerns in this field, sociologists must play a greater role in large-scale international data collection efforts of the type outlined in Appendix A. For example, the Third International Math and Science Study (TIMSS) contains an impressive array of data for primary, middle-school and secondary-school students in 42 countries. The survey includes items on student achievement in math and science, their perceptions and expectations regarding education, as well as data on students' schools and families. Notably absent in the realm of family background, however, are data on family income, parent's occupational status, family structure, race and ethnicity.[6] Such gaps limit the study's usefulness for addressing questions that are of central concern to sociologists of education and stratification.

Finally, we must acknowledge that the developed/developing country distinction, while useful in some cases, is a greatly simplified dichotomy. In reality, the world is composed of a wide range of countries that differ in countless ways. We now know that the variability among industrialized countries and among developing countries is just as great as the variability between—and also within—them. Our research strategies need to reflect this reality. Thus, we encourage greater collaboration between researchers who study similar questions but often remain

---

[6]The Third International Math and Science Study includes some data on family size and structure, but they are of limited use to analysts interested in assessing aspects of family structure across a range of contexts because the question format is incomplete. Thus, it is not possible to know the total number of siblings or the birth order of siblings in the household. Despite these limitations, TIMSS offers an impressive array of comparable data on several developing countries that should be of great use to researchers.

segregated due to their focus on either industrialized or developing societies. Working collaboratively, these researchers may make the greatest cumulative advances in knowledge on education and stratification processes across a broad range of contexts.

ACKNOWLEDGMENTS

We are grateful to members of the ISA Research Committee (28) on Stratification, especially Richard Arum, Marlis Buchmann, Adam Gamoran and Michael Hout, for thoughtful comments on early drafts of this paper. Daniel Bekele, Sandra Clavero, and Ben Dalton provided valuable research assistance.

APPENDIX A: DATA SOURCES FOR ANALYSES OF EDUCATION AND INEQUALITY IN DEVELOPING COUNTRIES

Living Standards Measurement Study (LSMS) of the World Bank. Household surveys for 21 developing countries, some with repeated cross-sections. Generally include data on education, employment, income, and health data for all household members, but which varies by country. Some countries have community and school data that can be linked to households. http://www.worldbank.org/html/prdph/lsms

Third International Math and Science Study (TIMSS) of the International Association for the Evaluation of Educational Achievement (IEA). Data on student achievement in math and science, family background, teacher, classroom, and school data for primary, middle, and upper secondary populations of students in 42 countries, 8 of which are developing countries. Also includes a wide range of data on student perceptions and aspirations. http://timss.bc.edu

World Fertility Surveys (WFS). Internationally comparable surveys on fertility in 41 developing countries from the late 1970s and early 1980s. Data on demographic characteristics and fertility histories as well as education, employment, and health data for representative sample of women ages 15–50 and their household members. http://opr.princeton.edu/archive

Demographic Health Surveys (DHS). The successors to the World Fertility Surveys that contain additional runs of surveys during the 1990s, including an extended module on education and community level data for some countries. Many countries have data for multiple years. http://opr.princeton.edu/archive and http://www.measuredhs.com

Family Life Surveys (FLS), conducted by RAND, for Malaysia, Indonesia, Guatemala, and Bangladesh. Surveys contain detailed current and retrospective data on family structure, economic status, education/training, transfers, migration, and other topics, as well as community and school data. Upon completion of the third wave of the Malaysia Family Life Survey, the three Malaysian surveys will enable researchers to examine the effects of family background on educational outcomes over half a century. Surveys for Malaysia and Indonesia are two of the few longitudinal surveys for developing countries. http://www.rand.org/FLS

International Stratification and Mobility File. A collection of standardized sample surveys with information on social stratification and social mobility created and maintained by Professor Harry Ganzeboom at Utrecht University in the Netherlands in collaboration with Professor Donald J. Treiman at the University of California, Los Angeles. Some resources are open for public access. http://www.fss.uu.nl/soc/hg/ismf/index.htm

Program for Student Assessment (PISA) of the Organization for Economic Cooperation and Development (OECD). An internationally standardized assessment of the skills and knowledge of 15-year-olds in 32 countries, 28 of which are members of the OECD, and 4 of which are developing countries (China, Brazil, Korea, Mexico). First round of surveys completed in 2000 contain data on student achievement in reading, math and science, family background, teacher, classroom, and school data, as well as student perceptions and aspirations. http://www.oecd.org/els/pisa/

African Census Analysis Project at The University of Pennsylvania. An archive of census data for over 20 African countries, many containing multiple years. Resources are generally only available to project members, but inquiries can be directed to the project director, Professor Tukufu Zuberi. http://www.acap.upenn.edu

Visit the Annual Reviews home page at www.AnnualReviews.org

LITERATURE CITED

Aitkin M, Longford N. 1986. Statistical modeling issues in school effectiveness studies (with discussion). *J. R. Stat. Soc., Ser. B* 149: 1–43

Anderson CA. 1956. The social status of university students in relation to type of economy: an international comparison. *Trans. Third World Congr. Sociol.* 5:51–63

Anh TS, Knodel J, Lam D, Friedman J. 1998. Family size and children's education in Vietnam. *Demography* 35:57–70

Arnove R. 1997. Neoliberal education policies in Latin America: arguments in favor and against. In *Latin American Education: Comparative Perspectives*, ed. CA Torres, A Puiggros, pp 79–100. Boulder: Westview

Arum R. 2000. Schools and communities: ecological and institutional dimensions. *Annu. Rev. Sociol.* 26:395–418

Axinn WG. 1993. The effects of children's schooling on fertility limitation. *Popul. Stud.* 47:481–93

Baker DP, Goesling B, LeTendre GK. 1999. *Social class, school quality, and national economic development: a cross-national analysis of the "Heyneman-Loxley" effect.* Presented at Annu. Meet. Am. Sociol. Assoc., 94th, Chicago

Barr R, Dreeben R. 1983. *How Schools Work.* Chicago: Univ. Chicago Press

Behrman JR, Birdsall N. 1983. The quality of schooling: quantity alone is misleading. *Am. Econ. Rev.* 73:928–46

Benavot A, Cha Y, Kamens D, Meyer JW, Wong S. 1991. Knowledge for the masses: world models and national curricula 1920–1986. *Am. Sociol. Rev.* 56:85–100

Bidwell CE, Kasarda JD. 1980. Conceptualizing and measuring the effects of school and schooling. *Am. J. Educ.* 88:401–30

Bills DB, Haller AO. 1984. Socio-economic development and social stratification: reassessing the Brazilian case. *J. Dev. Areas* 19:59–70

Bills DB, Haller AO, Kelley J, Olson MB, Pastore J. 1985. Class, class origins, regional socioeconomic development and the status attainment of Brazilian men. *Res. Soc. Strat. Mobil.* 4:89–127

Blake J. 1989. *Family Size and Achievement.* Berkeley: Univ. Calif. Press

Blau PM, Duncan OD. 1967. *The American Occupational Structure.* New York: Wiley

Boli J, Ramirez FO, Meyer JW. 1985. Explaining the origins and expansion of mass education. *Comp. Educ. Rev.* 29:145–70

Boli J, Thomas GM. 1997. World culture in the world polity: a century of international nongovernmental organization. *Am. Sociol. Rev.* 62:171–90

Bradley K, Ramirez FO. 1996. World polity and gender parity: women's share of higher education, 1965–1985. *Res. Sociol. Educ. Socialization* 11:63–91

Bradshaw YW. 1993. State limitations, self help secondary schooling and development in Kenya. *Soc. Forces* 72:347–78

Brinton MC, Lee YJ, Parish WL. 1995. Married women's employment in rapidly industrializing societies: examples from East Asia. *Am. J. Sociol.* 100:1099–1130

Broaded CM. 1997. The limits and possibilities of tracking: some evidence from Taiwan. *Sociol. Educ.* 70:36–53

Buchmann C. 1996. The debt crisis, structural adjustment and women's education: implications for status and social development. *Int. J. Comp. Sociol.* 37:5–30

Buchmann C. 1999. The state and schooling in Kenya: historical developments and current challenges. *Africa Today* 46:95–117

Buchmann C. 2000. Family structure, parental perceptions and child labor in Kenya: What factors determine who is enrolled in school? *Soc. Forces* 78:1349–79

Buchmann C, Brakewood D. 2000. Labor structures and school enrollments in developing societies: Thailand and Kenya compared. *Comp. Educ. Rev.* 44:175–204

Caldwell JC. 1980. Mass education as a determinant of the timing of fertility decline. *Popul. Dev. Rev.* 6:225–55

Chernichovsky D. 1985. Socioeconomic and demographic aspects of school enrollment and attendance in rural Botswana. *Econ. Dev. Cult. Change* 33:319–32

Clark R. 1992. Multinational corporate investment and women's participation in higher education in non-core nations. *Sociol. Educ.* 65:37–47

Clignet R, Foster PJ. 1966. *The Fortunate Few: A Study of Secondary Schools and Students in the Ivory Coast.* Evanston, IL: Northwestern Univ. Press

Cohn E, Rossmiller RA. 1987. Research on effective schools: implications for less developed countries. *Comp. Educ. Rev.* 31:377–99

Coleman JS, Campbell E, Hobson C, McPartland J, Mood A, et al. 1966. *Equality of Educational Opportunity.* Washington, DC: Dep. Health, Educ., Welfare

Csapo M. 1981. Religious, social and economic factors hindering the education of girls in northern Nigeria. *Comp. Educ.* 17:311–19

Deng Z, Treiman DJ. 1997. The impact of the cultural revolution on trends in educational attainment in the People's Republic of China. *Am. J. Sociol.* 103:391–428

Duncan GJ. 1994. Families and neighbors as sources of disadvantage in the schooling decisions of black and white adolescents. *Am. J. Educ.* 103:20–53

Erikson R, Goldthorpe JH. 1992. *The Constant Flux: A Study of Class Mobility in Industrial Societies.* Oxford, UK: Clarendon

Farrell JP, Schiefelbein E. 1985. Education and status attainment in Chile: a comparative challenge to the Wisconsin model of status attainment. *Comp. Educ. Rev.* 29:490–560

Filmer D, Pritchett L. 1999. The effect of household wealth on educational attainment: evidence from 35 countries. *Popul. Dev. Rev.* 25:85–120

Foster PJ. 1963. Secondary schooling and social mobility in a West African nation. *Sociol. Educ.* 37:150–71

Fuller B. 1987. What school factors raise achievement in the developing world? *Rev. Educ. Res.* 57:255–92

Fuller B. 1991. *Growing Up Modern: The Western State Builds Third World Schools.* New York: Routledge

Fuller B, Clarke P. 1994. Raising school effects while ignoring culture? *Rev. Educ. Res.* 64:119–57

Fuller B, Hua HY, Snyder CW. 1994. When girls learn more than boys: the influence of time in school and pedagogy in Botswana. *Comp. Educ. Rev.* 38:347–76

Fuller B, Liang X. 1999. Which girls stay in school? The influence of family economy, social demands, and ethnicity in South Africa. In *Critical Perspectives on Schooling and Fertility in the Developing World*, ed. CH Bledsoe, J Casterline, J Johnson-Kuhn, J Haaga, pp. 181–215. Washington DC: Natl. Acad. Press

Fuller B, Rubinson R. 1992. *The Political Construction of Education.* New York: Praeger

Fuller B, Singer J, Keiley M. 1995. Why do daughters leave school in southern Africa? Family economy and mothers' commitments. *Soc. Forces* 74:657–80

Fuller B, Snyder CW. 1991. Vocal teachers, silent pupils? Life in Botswana classrooms. *Comp. Educ. Rev.* 35:274–94

Ganzeboom HBG, Luijkx R, Treiman DJ. 1989. Intergenerational class mobility in comparative perspective. *Res. Soc. Strat. Mobil.* 8:3–84

Garner CL, Raudenbush SW. 1991. Neighborhood effects of educational attainment: a multilevel analysis. *Sociol. Educ.* 64:251–62

Goldstein H. 1987. *Multilevel Models in Educational and Social Research.* New York: Oxford Univ. Press

Gomes M. 1984. Family size and educational attainment in Kenya. *Popul. Dev. Rev.* 10:647–60

Greenhalgh S. 1985. Sexual stratification: the other side of 'growth with equity' in East Asia. *Popul. Dev. Rev.* 11:265–314

Grootaert C, Patrinos HA. 1999. *The Policy Analysis of Child Labor: A Comparative Study.* New York: St. Martin's

Halpern-Felsher BL, Connell JP, Spencer MB, Aber JL, Duncan GJ, et al. 1997. Neighborhood and family factors predicting educational risk and attainment in African American and white children and adolescents. In *Neighborhood Poverty: Contexts and Consequences for Children*, Vol. 1. ed. J Brooks-Gunn, GJ Duncan, JL Aber, pp. 146–73. New York: Russell Sage

Hannum E. 1999. Political change and the urban-rural gap in basic education in China, 1949–1990. *Comp. Educ. Rev.* 43:193–211

Hannum E. 2000. *Opportunity lost: rural children and educational opportunity in reform-era China.* Harvard Univ., Mimeo

Hannum E, Xie Y. 1994. Trends in educational gender inequality in China: 1949-1985. *Res. Soc. Strat. Mobil.* 13:73–98

Hannum E, Xie Y. 1998. Ethnic stratification in northwest China: occupational differences between Han Chinese and national minorities in Xinjiang, 1982–1990. *Demography* 35:323–33

Hansen DO, Haller AO. 1973. Status attainment of Costa Rican males: a cross-cultural test of a model. *Rur. Sociol.* 38:269–82

Hanushek E. 1995. Interpreting recent research on schooling in developing countries. *World Bank Res. Observ.* 10:247–54

Hermalin AI, Seltzer JA, Lin CH. 1982. Transitions in the effect of family size on female education and educational attainment: the case of Taiwan. *Comp. Educ. Rev.* 26:245–70

Heyneman SP. 1976. Influences on academic achievement: a comparison of results from Uganda and more industrialized societies. *Sociol. Educ.* 49:200–11

Heyneman SP, Jamison DT. 1980. Student learning in Uganda: textbook availability and other factors. *Comp. Educ. Rev.* 24:206–20

Heyneman SP, Loxley WA. 1983. The effect of primary school quality on academic achievement across twenty-nine high- and low-income countries. *Am. J. Sociol.* 88:1162–94

Holsinger DB. 1975. Education and the occupational attainment process in Brazil. *Comp. Educ. Rev.* 19:267–75

Inkeles A, Sirowy L. 1983. Convergent and divergent trends in national educational systems. *Soc. Forces* 62:303–33

Kelley J, Perlman ML. 1971. Social mobility in Toro: some preliminary results from western Uganda. *Econ. Dev. Cult. Change* 19:204–21

Kerckhoff AC. 1995. Institutional arrangements and stratification processes in industrial societies. *Annu. Rev. Sociol.* 15:323–47

Kerckhoff AC. 2001. Education and social stratification processes in comparative perspective. *Sociol. Educ.* 74 In press

King EM, Hill A. 1993. *Women's Education in Developing Countries: Barriers, Benefits and Policies.* Baltimore: Johns Hopkins Univ. Press

King EM, Lillard LA. 1987. Education policy and school attainment in Malaysia and the Philippines. *Econ. Educ. Rev.* 6:167–81

Knodel J, Havanon N, Sittitrai W. 1990. Family size and the education of children in the context of rapid fertility decline. *Popul. Dev. Rev.* 16:31–62

Knodel J, Jones GW. 1996. Post-Cairo population policy: Does promoting girls' schooling miss the mark? *Popul. Dev. Rev.* 22:683–702

Kremer M. 1995. Research on schooling: what we know and what we don't (a comment on Hanushek). *World Bank Res. Observ.* 10:247–54

Lareau A. 1989. *Home Advantage: Social Class and Parental Intervention in Elementary Education.* Philadelphia: Falmer

Lillard LA, Willis RJ. 1994. Intergenerational educational mobility: effects of family and state in Malaysia. *J. Hum. Resour.* 29:1126–66

Lin N, Yeager D. 1975. The process of occupational status attainment: a preliminary cross-national comparison. *Am. J. Sociol.* 81:543–62

Lipset SM, Bendix R. 1959. *Social Mobility in Industrial Society.* Berkeley: Univ. Calif. Press

Lloyd CB, Blanc AK. 1996. Children's schooling in sub-Saharan Africa: the role of fathers, mothers and others. *Popul. Dev. Rev.* 22:265–98

Lloyd CB, Gage-Brandon AJ. 1994. High fertility and children's schooling in Ghana: sex differences in parental contributions and educational outcomes. *Popul. Stud.* 48:293–306

Lloyd CB, Mensch BS, Clark WH. 2000. The effects of primary school quality on school dropout among Kenyan girls and boys. *Comp. Educ. Rev.* 44:113–47

Lockheed ME, Fuller B, Nyirongo R. 1989. Family effects on students' achievement in Thailand and Malawi. *Sociol. Educ.* 62:239–55

Lockheed ME, Komenan A. 1989. Teaching quality and student achievement in Africa: the case of Nigeria and Swaziland. *Teach. Teach. Educ.* 5:93–113

Lockheed ME, Longford NT. 1991. School effects on mathematics achievement gain in Thailand. In *Schools, Classrooms and Pupils: International Studies of Schooling From a Multi-level Perspective*, ed. SW Raudenbush, JD Willms, pp. 131–48. San Diego: Academic

Lockheed ME, Vail S, Fuller B. 1986. How textbooks affect achievement in developing countries: evidence from Thailand. *Educ. Eval. Policy Anal.* 8:379–92

Meyer JW. 1977. The effects of education as an institution. *Am. J. Sociol.* 83:55–77

Meyer JW, Hannan M, eds. 1979. *National Development and the World System.* Chicago, IL: Univ. Chicago Press

Meyer JW, Ramirez FO, Soysal YN. 1992. World expansion of mass education, 1870-1980. *Sociol. Educ.* 65:128–49

Montgomery MR, Lloyd CB. 1997. Excess fertility, unintended births and children's schooling. *Policy Res. Div. Work. Pap. No. 100.* New York: Popul. Council

Mukweso M, Papagiannis GJ, Milton S. 1984. Education and occupational attainment from generation to generation: the case of Zaire. *Comp. Educ. Rev.* 28:52–68

Nee V, Matthews R. 1996. Market transition and societal transformation in reforming state socialism. *Annu. Rev. Sociol.* 22:401–35

Niles FS. 1981. Social class and academic achievement: a third world reinterpretation. *Comp. Educ. Rev.* 25:419–30

Oakes J, Gamoran A, Page RN. 1992. Curriculum differentiation: opportunities, outcomes, and meanings. In *Handbook of Research on Curriculum*, ed. PW Jackson, pp. 570–608. New York: Macmillan

Parish WL, Willis RJ. 1993. Daughters, education, and family budgets: Taiwan experiences. *J. Hum. Resour.* 28:863–98

Parrado EA. 1998. Expansion of schooling, economic growth, and regional inequalities in Argentina. *Comp. Educ. Rev.* 42:338–64

Patrinos HA, Psacharopoulos G. 1996. Socioeconomic and ethnic determinants of age grade distortion in Bolivian and Guatemalan primary schools. *Int. J. Educ. Dev.* 16:3–14

Peaker G. 1971. *The Plowden Children Four Years Later*. London: Natl. Found. for Educ. Res. in England and Wales

Pong SL. 1996. School participation of children from single-mother families in Malaysia. *Comp. Educ. Rev.* 40:231–49

Pong SL. 1997. Sibship size and educational attainment in Peninsular Malaysia: Do policies matter? *Sociol. Perspect.* 40:227–42

Post D. 1990. The social demand for education in Peru: students' choices and state autonomy. *Sociol. Educ.* 63:258–71

Post D. 1994. Educational stratification, school expansion, and public policy in Hong Kong. *Sociol. Educ.* 67:121–38

Ramirez FO, Boli J. 1987. The political construction of mass schooling: European origins and worldwide institutionalization. *Sociol. Educ.* 60:2–17

Ramirez FO, Weis J. 1979. The political incorporation of women. In *National Development and the World System*, ed. JW Meyer, M Hannan, pp. 238–49. Chicago: Univ. Chicago Press

Raudenbush SW, Bryk AS. 1986. A hierarchical model for studying school effects. *Sociol. Educ.* 59:1–7

Reimers F. 1991. The impact of economic stabilization and adjustment on education in Latin America. *Comp. Educ. Rev.* 35:319–53

Riddell AR. 1989. An alternative approach to the study of school effectiveness in third world countries. *Comp. Educ. Rev.* 33:481–97

Saha LJ. 1983. Social structure and teacher effects on academic achievement: a comparative analysis. *Comp. Educ. Rev.* 27:69–88

Sathar Z, Lloyd C. 1993. Who gets primary schooling in Pakistan: inequalities among and within families. *Popul. Council Work. Pap.* 52:1–40

Schafer M. 1999. International nongovernmental organizations and third world education in 1990: a cross-national study. *Sociol. Educ.* 72:69–88

Schneider B, Coleman JS, eds. 1993. *Parents, Their Children, and Schools*. Boulder, CO: Westview

Seidman G. 1999. Is South Africa different? Sociological comparisons and theoretical contributions from the land of apartheid. *Annu. Rev. Sociol.* 25:419–40

Seltzer JA. 1994. Consequences of marital dissolution for children. *Annu. Rev. Sociol.* 20:235–66

Sewell WH, Haller AO, Portes A. 1969. The educational and early occupational attainment process. *Am. Sociol. Rev.* 34:82–92

Sewell WH, Hauser RM. 1975. *Education, Occupation and Earnings: Achievement in the Early Career*. New York: Academic

Shavit Y, Blossfeld HP, eds. 1993. *Persistent Inequality: Changing Educational Attainment in Thirteen Countries*. Boulder, CO: Westview

Shavit Y, Mueller W, eds. 1998. *From School to Work: A Comparative Study of Educational Qualifications and Occupational Destinations*. Oxford, UK: Oxford Univ. Press

Shavit Y, Pierce JL. 1991. Sibship size and educational attainment in nuclear and extended families: Arabs and Jews in Israel. *Am. Sociol. Rev.* 56:321–30

Shreeniwas S. 1997. Family size, sex composition and children's education: ethnic differentials over development in Peninsular Malaysia. *Popul. Stud.* 51:139–51

Smith HL, Cheung PL. 1986. Trends in the

effects of family background on educational attainment in the Philippines. *Am. J. Sociol.* 9:1387–1408

Stash S, Hannum E. 2001. Who goes to school? Educational stratification by gender, caste and ethnicity in Nepal. *Comp. Educ. Rev.* 45 In press

Steelman LC, Powell B. 1989. Acquiring capital for college: the constraints of family configuration. *Am. Sociol. Rev.* 54:844–55

Strudwick J, Foster PJ. 1991. Origins and destinations in Jamaica. *Int. J. Educ. Dev.* 11:149–59

Telles EE. 1994. Industrialization and racial inequality in employment: the Brazilian example. *Am. Sociol. Rev.* 59:46–63

Treiman DJ. 1970. Industrialization and social stratification. In *Social Stratification: Research and Theory for the 1970s*, ed. EO Laumann, pp. 207–34. Indianapolis, IN: Bobbs-Merrill

Treiman DJ, Ganzeboom HBG. 1997. *The fourth generation of comparative stratification research.* Presented at Int. Sociol. Assoc. Res. Counc. 28 Meet. Montreal, Canada

Treiman DJ, McKeever M, Fodor E. 1996. Racial differences in occupational status and income in South Africa, 1980 and 1991. *Demography* 33:111–32

Treiman DJ, Yip K. 1989. Educational and occupational attainment in 21 countries. In *Cross-National Research in Sociology*, ed. ML Kohn, pp. 373–94. Beverly Hills, CA: Sage

Tsai SL. 1998. The transition from school to work in Taiwan. See Shavit & Mueller 1998, pp. 443–70

World Bank. 2001. *Engendering Development Enhancing Development Through Attention to Gender.* Washington DC: World Bank and Oxford Univ. Press. In press

Xie Y, Hannum E. 1996. Regional variations in earnings inequality in reform-era urban China. *Am. J. Sociol.* 101:950–92

Zhou X. 2000. Economic transformation and income inequality in urban China: evidence from panel data. *Am. J. Sociol.* 105:1135–74

Zhou X, Moen P, Tuma NB. 1998. Educational stratification in urban China, 1949–94. *Sociol. Educ.* 71:199–222

Zhou X, Tuma NB, Moen P. 1996. Stratification dynamics under state socialism: the case of urban China, 1949–1993. *Soc. Forces* 74:759–96

Annu. Rev. Sociol. 2001. 27:103–24

THE GREAT AGRICULTURAL TRANSITION: Crisis, Change, and Social Consequences of Twentieth Century US Farming

Linda Lobao[1] and Katherine Meyer[2]

[1]Rural Sociology Program, Department of Human and Community Resource Development, Ohio State University, Columbus, Ohio 43210; e-mail: Lobao.1@osu.edu
[2]Department of Sociology, Ohio State University, Ohio State University, Columbus, Ohio 43210; e-mail: Meyer.23@osu.edu

Key Words   agriculture, economic development, farm population, family farming, farm women

■ **Abstract**   One of the most profound changes in the United States in the past century is the national abandonment of farming as a livelihood strategy. This change is evident both in the exodus of Americans from farming and in the conditions faced by the farmers remaining, most of whom are marginal producers in an increasingly concentrated industry. In this article, we provide a retrospective account of the empirical and sociological fate of family farmers. While sociologists have had longstanding interest in agrarian change, research on contemporary farmers is largely confined to speciality publications, with a loss to the discipline at large. We examine three distinct research traditions that continue to document farm transformation: research on macro-level transformation, community impacts, and household response. While these traditions evolved separately, we describe how they overlap and inform each other. Most notably, research on household and community responses delineates meso- and micro-level institutional factors that extend macro-level theory. Research on the contemporary farm population offers an alternative context in which to interrogate conventional accounts of economic development; such research yields insights about aspects of social life being rediscovered as part of the new economy and continues to pull sociologists into politically charged public policy debates.

INTRODUCTION

The exodus of Americans from farming is one of the most dramatic changes in the US economy and society in the past century. In the early 1900s, more than one of every three Americans lived on farms, a number greater than that at any other point in our country's history. At the century's end, the farm population stood at under 2%, and even for those who remained in farming, almost 90% of

0360-0572/01/0811-0103$14.00

household income came from nonfarm sources. By and large the magnitude of this transition and its social consequences have been missed in the general sociological literature. Subfields, particularly rural sociology, have a rich legacy of addressing agrarian change. The literature, however, tends to be fragmented, visible mainly in specialty journals, and its significance for the general sociological discipline remains underestimated. This article examines the epic transition from farming, the theoretical explanations for this transition, and the social consequences for farm communities and households.

By the agricultural transition, we refer to the abandonment of farming as a household livelihood strategy. This transition is evident both in the mass decline of the farm population and in the structural transformation of agriculture, whereby most remaining farms are marginal units incapable of fully employing and sustaining families. While a number of literatures span this topic, we limit our focus to research concerned foremost with the fate of the independent farm population, family farmers or those who provide most of the labor, management, and capital in operating their farms.[1] Our goal is to provide a retrospective account of the changes experienced by family farmers by taking stock of this population at the twentieth century's end.

We examine three research traditions that address changes experienced by the independent farm population. First is the large literature on the structural transformation of farming, which tends to be macro-level theorizing about national trends. This literature provides conceptual explanations for the empirical contours of the agricultural transition, such as the decline in the number of farms and growth of inequality in the existing system. The consequences of these macro-level transformations are manifest at lower analytical levels across communities and households. The second research tradition incorporates a longstanding, often politically charged, literature on the impacts of farm change on communities. As family farming declines, analysts generally hypothesize that community class polarization increases and local well-being deteriorates, even in a postindustrial society. The third research tradition addresses the effects of farm change on households, much of this centering on the gender division of labor and on social-psychological well-being. Considering these three traditions allows us to examine the major paths by which sociologists have sought to understand farm transformation, capturing heuristically the changes experienced by farmers at the national, community, and household levels.

---

[1]Family farmers hold class positions that approach the petite-bourgeois ideal. Empirically, today's family farmers range on a continuum from this ideal. Most are semi-proletarianized through family members' off-farm work; others are closer to the capitalist class in depending on wage labor. Family farms are often contrasted to non-family units, where labor, capital, and management functions are provided by different entities. Terms often used synonymously for the latter are industrialized, corporate, capitalist; scale references are also made. We do not focus on non-owner farm workers nor on production networks beyond the farm gate, such as global commodity chains and local food systems. These are important topics, meriting separate reviews.

The next section provides an overview of sociological attention to farm change. We then describe the agricultural transition and turn to each of the three research traditions above, describing research themes and conceptual bases. To provide a synopsis of these large literatures, we necessarily present a selective and schematic account.

THE SIGNIFICANCE OF RESEARCH ON
THE FARM POPULATION IN SOCIOLOGY

Sociologists have long looked to the farm population to understand major issues of the discipline, but the visibility of this research varies historically. The agrarian sector was the starting point for Marx, Weber, and Durkheim, who saw changes in agriculture as reinforcing capitalist expansion. Early US sociology took a social problems orientation with two strands, a focus on urban social organization epitomized by the Chicago School, and a rural counterpart consisting of rural and regional sociology. Rural sociology developed in large part from federal concern with the farm population (Summers 1986). Political unrest in the countryside from widespread economic hardship as well as concern that farmers would out-migrate en masse to urban areas led to federal creation of the Country-Life Commission in 1908 and, in turn, to rural sociology's institutionalization in land-grant universities. Regional sociology gained prominence from the work of southern regionalists, who shared the Chicago School's human ecology paradigm but focused largely on the rural farm population (Odum & Moore 1938). The significance of the farm population for most sociologists today comes mainly through its historical role in US society. Farmers serve to illuminate key historical issues about state transformation (Gilbert & Howe 1991, Hooks 1990, Moore 1996, Skocpol & Finegold 1982), social movements (Mooney & Majka 1995), and African American's northern exodus (Mandle 1978, Tolnay 1999).

Despite the centrality of the farm population to early and historical sociology, one is hard pressed to find any articles on contemporary farmers published in major, general sociological journals. While the *Annual Review of Sociology* has featured some articles on the rural population, the last one devoted to farming was published nearly twenty years ago (Newby 1983). Sociologists tend to take a modernist view of US economy and society, which privileges formal sector, paid work, manufacturing and services, and urban locations. This prevailing account of work renders invisible populations engaged in alternative livelihood strategies and industries such as farming, whose organization does not fit neatly into frameworks purporting to explain contemporary economic structure. Modernist, mass society assumptions center urban social relationships as topics of sociological investigation and discount diversity based on rurality (Falk 1996, Lobao 1996, Lichter & McLaughlin 1995, Tickamyer 1996). By neglecting farming, sociologists miss significant aspects of national social change, an opportunity to interrogate conventional conceptualizations of work and economic development, and a key policy sector.

Despite the decline of the farm population, farming remains essential for charting national social change. Farming, direct production of food and fiber, is the cornerstone of agriculture, which includes inputs, processing, and distribution and employs nearly 20% of Americans (USDA 1999:27). Farming itself is important both as an export sector in global commodity chains and as a source of income in rural communities. Some of today's most serious social issues, such as use of genetically modified organisms, environmental conservation, land use preservation, and food safety, arise from farming. Farmers also retain a significant ideological role, evidenced in global free-trade debates and World Trade Organization protests over preservation of family-farming, as well as in media attention in films and Farm Aid events.

Second, as a business dependent on unpaid household labor, farming always possessed distinct characteristics now being rediscovered as part of an emerging post-Fordist economy. Farming provides a fertile empirical example for studying the informal sector and household livelihood strategies; conceptually, this example raises the questions of why family businesses still characterize this industry amidst their failure elsewhere. More than 98% of the nation's 2.07 million farms are classified as family operations. Only 3% are incorporated, and of these, nearly 90% are closely held by the operators' families rather than external shareholders (Sommer et al 1998:iv).

Third, farming presents a unique case for interrogating conventional sociological views about the economy. Farming has not followed a linear development path, and its organization does not fit neatly into industrial sociology's categorizations. Partly due to the biological basis of farming, direct corporate involvement has lagged, and the family, which can adjust labor to match seasonal production cycles and consumption to match income flows, remains the typical operating entity (Mann & Dickinson 1978). Farming also reflects vestiges of different capitalist eras. As with early simple commodity production, it is typified by home-base production. Postwar industrial segmentation theory recognizes farming as a peripheral industry, composed of small firms producing bulk commodities, sandwiched between oligopoly input and output industries. Some also see evidence of post-Fordist trends. Rising inequality in US society has created a segment of affluent consumers driving demand for speciality commodities. New technologies and flexible production methods are tailoring output toward these high value, shifting, niche markets (Kenney et al 1989).

Uneven development also is evident as marginal units are reproduced in the midst of growing concentration. Farming is often described as a dualistic system, composed of a large number of small farms that cannot sustain families and a few large farms with expanding market shares. In 1997, small farms (defined here by annual gross sales under $50,000) made up nearly three-fourths of the nation's farms but accounted for only about 7% of sales, while the top 3.6% percent of farms (those with sales over a half million dollars) accounted for more than half of sales nationally (US Bureau of the Census 1999:676). Moderate-sized farms that support a family through farming alone and require little hired labor are edged out of this system. Inequality among farmers is thus high. In 1990, the Gini coefficient for income inequality for farm households was 0.64, nearly 50% percent higher than that for all US households (Ahearn et al 1993).

Finally, the farm population is significant from a state-policy standpoint. Farmers are subject to a legacy of interventions from land grant college research, extension service outreach, farm bill legislation, export promotion programs, and numerous USDA programs. Unrecognized by most sociologists is that there is probably no other workforce over which our discipline has such extensive policy influence, mainly through rural sociologists' long history of work with federal and state officials on farm and rural development policy (Jahr et al 1986, Swanson 1988b).

Though the sociological significance of the existing farm population is underestimated, one would expect greater disciplinary visibility on the basis of its large literature alone. For most of twentieth century rural sociology, "rural" was equated with "farm" and hence, there was intrinsic concern with farm families and communities. However, the economic development of farming was neglected, a topic left to agricultural economics. Emerging in the 1970s, the sociology of agriculture centered on agricultural development and drew largely from Marxian theory (Friedland et al 1981, Newby 1983). This literature long focused on domestic farm organization and more recently on global commodity chains (McMichael 1994, 1996, Bonnano et al 1994), local food systems (Kloppenburg et al 1996, Olson & Lyson 1999), and women in farming (Sachs 1996, Whatmore 1991). The farm population also is of intrinsic interest to rural demographers (Brown et al 1993, Brown & Wardwell 1981, Fuguitt & Beale 1989). For other researchers, farmers serve more as a rich empirical case to inform a specific disciplinary concern. Studies addressing life course and family (Elder & Conger 2000), gender divisions of labor (Rosenfeld 1985, Lobao & Meyer 1995), spatial inequality (Lobao 1990), and civic society (Tolbert et al 1998) see farmers as providing useful insights for these literatures.

THE AGRICULTURAL TRANSITION

Structural changes in farming over the past century (Table 1) show a decline in the number of farms and in farm population, growth of larger farms in terms of acreage, sales, and real estate capitalization, and gradual replacement of family with hired labor.[2] The post-World War II period ushered in the most rapid transformation, brought about by New Deal interventions and diffusion of new technologies (Goss et al 1980). From 1940 to 1980, the farm population declined tenfold, the number

---

[2]The Census definition of a farm has changed ten times since 1850. Prior to 1974, definitions were based on acreage and sales criteria. From 1974 to 1992, a farm was any establishment that generated $1000 or more of agricultural sales in the past year. This farm definition was expanded in 1993 to include several new categories of commodities.

TABLE 1   Structural changes in U.S. farming in the twentieth century[a]

Year	Farm[b] numbers (1,000)	Farm population[c] as % of total	Land in farms (100,000 acres)	Average farm size (acres)	Gross sales per farm (constant $1982)	Value of land & buildings per farm (constant $1982)	Family or unpaid workers/ hired workers
1900	5,737	—	839	146	—	—	—
1910	6,361	34.7	879	138	10,817	63,651	3.00
1920	6,447	30.0	956	148	10,341	54,060	2.96
1930	6,288	24.8	987	157	10,141	51,408	2.92
1940	6,096	23.1	1,061	174	10,577	40,769	3.10
1950	5,648	15.2	1,202	213	21,084	57,322	3.26
1960	3,955	8.7	1,171	296	27,831	111,974	2.74
1970	2,944	4.7	1,098	373	40,849	173,810	2.85
1980	2,428	2.7	1,036	427	67,167	366,861	1.84
1985	2,327	2.2	1,016	437	55,655	266,528	1.84
1990	2,146	1.9	987	460	59,122	242,880	2.24
1995	2,196	1.8	963	438	52,681	244,404	2.26
1999	2,191	—	956	436	55,238	255,496	2.27

[a]Figures from 1900–1985 and their sources are reported in Lobao (1990: Table 2.1). Figures for 1990–1997 are updated from comparable recent sources: farm numbers, average farm size, and value of land and buildings, USDA, Economic Research, Service, *Agricultural Outlook*; land in farms, gross sales per farm, and unpaid workers per farm (reported as family workers through 1970), USDA, National Agricultural Statistics Service.

[b]The definition of a farm was most recently changed in 1993 to include several new categories of commodities, slightly inflating the number of small farms.

[c]The farm population was not estimated by the Bureau of the Census prior to 1910. The figure for 1995 is from the most recent (1992) estimate and is reported by USDA, National Agricultural Statistics Service.

of farms declined by more than half, average acreage more than doubled, and real average sales increased sixfold. In addition to long-term structural changes, farmers experience periodic crises. The 1980–1990 decade includes the most recent farm crisis, illustrated in Table 1 in declining real estate values and farm sales relative to their 1980 peak.

The increase in both size and number of large farms and decrease in number of smaller farms is accompanied by production polarization (Buttel & LaRamee 1991). The market share of sales by the largest 5% of producers has steadily increased from 38.3% in 1939 to 54.5% by 1987 (Browne et al 1992:22). Agribusiness firms have expanded through vertical integration but more typically by production contracts through which farmers become the equivalent of factory-homeworkers, raising commodities to be turned over to agribusiness that they generally do not own. While only about 3% of farms operate under production contracts, they produce almost all poultry, half of all hogs, and a quarter of cattle (USDA 2000:51,54). At the same time, most farms have become marginal production units that cannot fully employ or sustain families. To survive in farming, families take off-farm jobs. Almost 90% of farmers' household income now comes from non-farm sources (Sommer et al 1998:48). A USDA commission recently determined that annual gross sales below $250,000 cannot adequately support a family, and that survival of farms below that size "is most endangered" (Sommer et al 1998:69). About 94% of US farms fall into this category.

Within the agricultural transition, there is much ethnic, regional, and gender diversity. African Americans were virtually entirely uprooted from farming. The number of African-American farmers peaked in 1920 when they accounted for 14.3% of farm operators compared to 1% today (Sommer et al 1998:40). This uprooting is attributed to the general decline of small farms, land erosion and boll weevil infestations of cotton, New Deal farm programs benefitting white landowners, postwar cotton mechanization, repressive ethnic relations, and the lure of northern jobs (Fligstein 1981, Mandle 1978, Seavoy 1998, Tolnay 1999). Remaining African-American farmers faced institutional discrimination and are older and poorer than others (Beauford 1986, Brown et al 1994, Jones 1994). Research on other ethnic groups as farm operators, rather than laborers, is limited. Hispanic and Native American farmers are usually considered in light of non-farm changes contributing to high rural poverty among these groups (Foley 1997, Snipp 1989, Snipp et al 1993). Whites now comprise 97.5% of farm operators, Hispanics 1.5%, African Americans, 1%, and Native Americans, 0.5% (US Bureau of the Census 1999:675). The agricultural transition also introduced regional change (Molnar 1986). As small farms have declined, the farm population has shifted from the South to the Midwest (Beale 1993).

Finally, the agricultural transition was experienced differently by gender as a large literature on farm women indicates. Women's role in farming, however, tends to be invisible, in part because it is difficult to document through the Census of Agriculture that allows for only one self-defined operator per farm. Census data show women increased from 6.3% of operators in 1987 to 8.6% a decade later.

Women's role is significant because farming involves orchestrating family work strategies, whether on- or off-farm. Surveys of farm women nationally (Rosenfeld 1985) and regionally (Barlett et al 1999, Lasley et al 1995) find a distinct gender division of labor in farm tasks. Midwestern women also are more likely to work off-farm than men, their proletarianization making possible the survival of family farming.

CONCEPTUAL EXPLANATIONS FOR AGRICULTURAL TRANSFORMATION

What social forces have displaced family farmers and led to the present system with its increasing concentration and reproduction of marginal units? Several perspectives address how farming in advanced nations evolves. It is worthwhile to note the neoclassical economic perspective because of its ideological dominance in the agricultural establishment and because it serves as a foil of sociological critique. The neoclassical perspective rests on several assumptions: the present farming system is socially desirable; individuals' behavior is guided by rational-choice decision-making; and human capital factors and life-style choices explain why families remain on nonviable units. The historical trend of larger and fewer farms results from natural market competition in an industry where domestic demand is inelastic. Farmers are on a technological treadmill to expand production (Cochrane 1979). Some farmers outperform others by using more advanced technologies and achieving economies of scale. Displacement of farmers from farming, in effect, is an indicator of the system's success.

Though its recent influence is less pervasive, the major sociological paradigm for analyzing domestic agricultural development remains Marxian political economy. Like the neoclassical perspective, the political economy paradigm acknowledges market competition and the technological treadmill as reasons why farms have grown larger and fewer. The major difference between the two perspectives lies in who controls and benefits from agricultural development. The political economy framework sees market competition as socially produced and regulated in ways that benefit large capital in and outside farming. The result is a food system detrimental to most farmers, consumers, and the environment. At least two volumes (Buttel & Newby 1980, Friedland et al 1991) and numerous articles summarize the political economy view of domestic farm organization.

The political economy paradigm draws from Kautsky's and Lenin's classical agrarian analyses of the early 1900s, which suggested that the ideal-type "family farmers" whose farms sustain the family and depend on its labor might persist for an extended time but would gradually become differentiated into large capitalist farmers and semi-proletarianized producers. Most focus has been on capitalist enterprises and persistence of family farming rather than on semi-proletarianization. A large literature explains why family farming persists. Capital still encounters barriers to profit-making in farming (Mann 1990), avoids low-profit production niches occupied by family farmers (Mottura & Pugliese 1980), and gains from exploiting farmers through agribusiness exchange (Davis 1980). Families remain an optimal farm workforce (Friedmann 1978), and family farms provide a legitimation function that presents the illusion that large capital does not colonize farming (Bonanno 1987). While political economy theory traditionally emphasized private market forces, greater attention is now given to the central state. Building from French regulation theory, analysts argue that federal programs and policies raised productive capacity, integrated farmers into global markets, and promoted low-cost food, all of which contribute to larger and fewer farms (Goodman & Watts 1994, Kenney et al 1989).

Taking stock of the political economy paradigm since Newby (1983) heralded its promise reveals the following issues. Research explicitly building from political economy principles has tended to move from focus on domestic farmers to the global agricultural system (Bonanno et al 1994, Marsden & Arce 1995). Sociologists who analyze US farming still widely use political economy theory to understand its macro-level development. However, when concern is with lower conceptual levels, such as farm households and communities, political economy theory is invoked more implicitly. While it may be used to set the structural context of change, analysts usually muster causal elements beyond the conventional paradigm. This disjuncture in employing theory is not only an artifact of moving to lower conceptual levels, but it also reflects the limitations of political economy theory, even for understanding macro-level development. First, as a structural approach, the political economy paradigm tends to ignore human agency and culture. It says little about how farmers' choices, beliefs, and political actions shape farm transformation. Second, as with neoclassical economic theory, there is a productionist bias: production exigencies promoting the growth of capitalist farming are emphasized over household or consumption-related factors that reproduce marginal units. Third, feminists note that when farm households are considered, they are often treated in a way similar to that of neoclassical economics, as a unit of consensus. Finally, the macro-level focus of political economy theory inherently downplays the role of subnational territorial units, such as communities and regions, in sustaining farm inequality.

Taken as a whole, the previous limitations reflect the neglect of institutional sources of farm system change "created by the sustained social practices of farmers themselves and their interaction with other actors," particularly as these involve gender, the household, state, farmers' political organizations, and community (Lobao & Meyer 2000:30). As researchers invoke ever-more eclectic elements to explain farm change, a coherent body of work is emerging that not so much challenges as extends the political economy paradigm toward consideration of meso- and micro-level institutional forces. First, farm households have customary social practices, values, and beliefs that make them exit or adapt to a farming system that disadvantages all but the largest producers. Cutting back on consumption and taking off-farm employment are well-known adaptive strategies. Values about the desirability of farming as an occupation and life-style and the desire to pass down land to children are incentives to remain in farming (Brown et al 1998, Garkovich et al 1995, Hinrichs 1998, Mooney 1988, Salamon 1992). Jackson-Smith (1999) concludes that survival in farming depends as much on such micro-level household dynamics as it does on strategic business behavior.

Second, feminists see institutionalized gender relationships as affecting farm change. Women underwrite farm survival through their household work, on-farm work, and off-farm work.

Third, the institutional legacy of the state at various levels affects farm change. While large farms reap greater government benefits, small and moderate-size farms also draw from various commodity, insurance, environmental, and disaster relief programs. In the 1996 Farm Bill, the Republican-controlled Congress attempted to deregulate farming, overhauling much remaining New Deal legislation. But declining prices and other problems in the interim have resulted in hefty federal farm aid packages, over $15 billion in year 2000 alone. Clinton's Agriculture Secretary Dan Glickman recently pronounced the 1996 Farm Bill a failure (*New York Times* 2000:A20). The importance of subnational state institutions is also recognized (DuPuis 1993). The decline of African-American farms provides a poignant example. A class action suit won in 1999 found that African-American farmers were denied federal loans and other aid given white farmers, with most documented discrimination due to county administrators (Sack 2000).

Fourth, farm households are embedded in local and regional contexts that affect farm survival (Pfeffer 1983, Schwarzweller & Davidson 1997). Ecological factors affect farm size and structure. Labor market conditions affect the ability to combine farm with off-farm employment. Urban proximity presents opportunities for niche marketing and local food system development.

Finally, farm transformation is a function of farmers' political actions. Farmers' mass-based political action has declined over time. A corporatist model has emerged in which most major farm organizations represent the interests of large producers. Farmers in marginal social positions appear to withdraw politically, excluding cases usually involving far right influences (Meyer & Lobao 1994). Inequality in the farm sector is maintained in part because most farmers are disengaged from political action and the organizations that might represent them.

In summary, while not necessarily a stated purpose, much recent sociological work provides an institutional response to the limitations of political economy theory. It remains to be seen if a more coherent approach that combines macro-level theory with meso- and micro-level insights might be worked out under the broader political economy banner.

Other approaches to farm change have received less attention. Human ecology traces the evolution of farming systems as individuals and organizations adapt to changing environmental resources, technologies, and population density (Albrecht 1997, Albrecht & Murdock 1990). Friedland (1991) argues that Jeffersonian populism characterizes some approaches that identify agribusiness corporations as responsible for the endangerment of family farms (e.g., Goldschmidt 1978, Rodefeld 1974). Populist approaches long have been contrasted with political economy theory that gives primary attention to the structural exigencies of capitalism over specific corporate behavior. Over the past decade, market concentration proceeded rapidly in hog and beef processing and expanded in grain processing and inputs, giving rise to a new round of social science concerns with corporate agribusiness. Though political economy theorists share this concern, to some extent the traditional divide persists; they take a systemic approach, viewing corporate behavior in light of broader capitalist development. In contrast, populist approaches are intrinsically concerned with creating competitive markets and preserving small farm businesses.

AGRICULTURAL TRANSFORMATION
AND ITS EFFECTS ON COMMUNITIES

Sociologists have produced extensive research on the community impacts of the agricultural transition (Berardi 1981). This research is usually concerned with three interrelated trends: farm population decline; the relative growth of large, hired-labor–dependent, "industrialized" farms; and the relative decline of moderate-size farms. The first trend, decline in farm population overall, a demographic change, was of foremost interest in the pre-1970s period of rapid farm decline. Concern was that small rural communities would decline as families left farming. For most places, however, farm population loss resulted in only short-term or negligible decline because of urban industrial influences (Swanson 1982). Present concern with farm population decline centers mainly on parts of the rural Midwest and metropolitan areas affected by urban-rural–interface land use issues (Pfeffer & Lapping 1994). The bulk of sociological literature is on the second two trends, which are structural in nature—growth of industrialized farms and the declining middle sector. Semantic reference may be to either or both changes, because they are treated as opposite sides of the same social problem, rising inequality. Four generations of research address this inequality.

The detrimental consequences of inequality in farming were recognized by sociologists in the 1930s (Tetreau 1938, 1940). Catapulting interest in the topic during the 1940s was a USDA report by anthropologist Walter Goldschmidt which presented a case-study of two California towns: Dinuba, a family farming community, and Arvin, a community dominated by large farms. Goldschmidt (see 1978 reference) found poorer conditions in Arvin: a smaller middle class, lower family incomes, poorer public services, and less civic participation. He argued that the scale of farming affected farm and local stratification patterns and, in turn, other community outcomes. Angry over the findings, owners of large farms staged burnings of Goldschmidt's report and Steinbeck's *Grapes of Wrath*, and they launched attacks that closed Goldschmidt's USDA department.

Controversy surrounding Goldschmidt's study contributed to the neglect of research on industrialized farms for over thirty years. With the advent of the sociology of agriculture, a flurry of studies emerged on the topic in the 1970s.

This second generation "Goldschmidt literature" involved updating that focused on postwar farm concentration and tested relationships quantitatively, typically using territorial units such as counties. Sociologists examined the relationship between indicators of farm scale and structure and indicators of local socioeconomic well-being, such as income and population change. Lobao's (1990) review of 18 studies conducted from 1972 to 1985 shows that half reported support for the hypothesis that growth of large farms and/or decline of moderate-sized farms adversely affects communities, while 7 noted mixed support and 2, no support. Critiques of this second generation research emerged in the 1980s. Methodologically, studies were cross-sectional, usually regionally specific, and often omitted pertinent, non-farm control variables. Conceptually, analysts were unclear whether farm scale (e.g., sales, acreage) or structure (e.g., use of hired workers, incorporation) was the significant causal force, and non-farm intervening factors were given little attention.

A third generation of Goldschmidt-type studies continues the quantitative tradition. This research attempts to address the issues above (Buttel et al 1988, Flora & Flora 1988, Gilles & Dalecki 1988, Lobao & Schulman 1991, MacCannell 1988, Skees & Swanson 1988, van Es et al 1988) and also to extend the topic to new theoretical questions. Examples of theoretical extensions include spatial inequality, how the fortunes of regional and local populations vary due to economic structure, the state, and other factors (Crowley 1999, Lobao 1990), and civic society, how vibrant local society is enhanced by small, locally owned business such as family farming (Irwin et al 1999, Tolbert et al 1998).

Third-generation findings about industrialized farms are more mixed. Of the studies above, MacCannell, Crowley, Tolbert et al, and Irwin et al report detrimental impacts; Buttel et al and van Es et al report no detrimental impacts; and the remainder are mixed. Some analysts find a curvilinear relationship between scale and well-being, with small units also related to poorer conditions (Skees & Swanson 1988). Impacts of moderate-sized farms, when significant, are usually beneficial. Regional differences suggest that institutional context, such as state regulatory efforts, citizen activism, and labor market conditions, may buffer adverse effects of industrialized farms. However, these institutional factors are yet to be fully elaborated. A lack of clarity remains as to whether farm size or structure is the relevant causal concept, though empirically both are related (Wimberley 1987). More broadly, the causal mechanisms by which farming affects communities remain under-conceptualized, and their empirical assessment is inherently limited by existing data and methodologies. Sociology has no equivalent of economic's input-out modeling, which, however problematic, is concerned with empirically disentangling how shifts in enterprises filter down to communities. Finally, it is noteworthy that most third-generation studies report some significant impacts of farm structure. These persist nationally, across varying levels of rurality and farming dependence, and over time. Even in a post-industrial society, farming affects communities, though obviously not to the degree of services and manufacturing.

Concurrent with third-generation studies is an emerging, new fourth generation focus on agribusiness expansion, mainly in livestock, where production is more easily rationalized. The most recent research involves case-studies of communities with hog confinement operations (NCRCRD 1999, Seipel et al 1999, Thu & Durrenberger 1998). These studies indicate that large confinement operations further erode family farmers' share of production. Communities receiving large operations may increase total income and employment but are also likely to experience increased social polarization and environmental problems.

To further carve out the rich sociological legacy regarding the community consequences of farming, the following issues remain. First, systematic comparisons across place and time are limited. Quantitative, longitudinal, and comparative case studies beyond 1990 are needed. Greater attention should be given both to conceptualizing the causal paths by which farm changes filter down to communities and to overcoming methodological barriers of assessing these paths. Research is still rather insular in terms of informing broader sociological theory. Institutional factors that mediate farm impacts require more attention. Some analysts suggest that maintenance of family farming itself is a marker of institutional context, signaling a healthy civic society (Tolbert et al 1998). Finally, this research tradition continues to pull sociologists into public controversy. An example is a recent lawsuit by agribusiness interests seeking to overturn a widely supported South Dakota law regulating industrialized farms. The suit pits sociologists whose research supports the public's vote for the law against economists whose position supports agribusiness.

AGRICULTURAL TRANSFORMATION AND HOUSEHOLDS

Research on the consequences of agricultural change for households is voluminous but less systematic than that on communities. Since enterprises and households are inextricably linked, farm transformation is reflected in family work and well-being. Even so, the farm economy and household were treated as separate spheres for much of the past century. Hence, most research explicitly linking farm economic and household change is of contemporary origin. While the 1970s brought political economy theory to the farm enterprise, the household continued to be treated as a unit of shared interests, much in the vein of functionalist and neoclassical economic theory. Though some researchers (Wilkening 1968, 1981) examined gender divisions of labor earlier, not until the 1980s, largely due to feminist influences, was the farm household widely subject to critical scrutiny. Farm economic and household dynamics of the past are revisited in critical, feminist historical studies (Adams 1994, Fink 1986, 1992). The sociological literature largely centers on the effects of the contemporary farm economy on households' labor strategies and well-being. It has the following characteristics.

First, the literature proceeds from two starting points, one from rural sociology's intrinsic concern with farm household survival, the second from other disciplinary-based concerns such as work, family, life course, and mental health. Second, research is conceptually eclectic, drawing from political economy, feminist, and general family, labor market, and social-psychological theories. As noted previously, these conceptually eclectic elements help to provide an institutionalist extension of political economy theory: farm households' customary labor and consumption strategies enable family farmers to survive and compete with larger-scale units, although often with social costs. Third, concern is with two types of farm transformation—long-term, macro-structural change, usually treated as manifest in present enterprise characteristics, and shorter-term financial stress from the 1980s crisis. With the exception of farm crisis case studies, almost all research draws from cross-sectional inferences. In some sense, this problem is irremediable unless small area studies are employed, as national longitudinal surveys do not adequately capture farmers. Finally, analysts recognize various survival strategies (e.g., Moen & Wethington 1992), including consumption adjustments (Brooks et al 1986, Bultena et al 1986), and political strategies (Meyer & Lobao 1997) that merit attention. However, for only two types of responses—labor strategies and social-psychological—have sustained research traditions developed.

Sociologists have examined the consequences of farm structural change and shorter-term financial hardship for both on- and off-farm labor strategies. The gendered nature of these labor strategies is well documented. Farm women participate in production tasks, are typically responsible for bookkeeping, and nearly entirely responsible for household tasks. Men participate more in direct farm production, and their work, whether on- or off-farm, is more closely tied to enterprise scale and structure than is that of women (Simpson et al 1988, Wilson et al 1994)—relationships that appear to hold even in the more progressive sustainable agriculture community (Meares 1997). Structural changes in farming affect off-farm work of both men and women. As farms become smaller, both men and women expand off-farm work. Researchers also question whether the gender division of labor in farming is altered by structural change (Haney & Knowles 1988). Some studies find that women's involvement in production tasks increases when farm units are smaller and less profitable (Buttel & Gillespie 1984, Coughenour & Swanson 1983, Sachs 1983).

The farm crisis period shows how shorter-term financial downturn affected work strategies. With regard to on-farm work, Gladwin's (1991) research in Florida and anecdotal evidence suggested that women increased their time and scope in farm work during the crisis. In contrast, research across twelve midwestern states (Lasley et al 1995) and case studies (Barlett 1993, Salamon 1992) found that the division of labor on the farm itself changed little during the crisis. Both men and women moved away from farming by taking off-farm work during the crisis, but the change was greater for women. Nationally, in the 1980s, farm women increased their labor force participation relative to earlier years, to farm men, and to other rural women (McDonald and Peters 1991, Ollenburger et al 1989). Over one third of Midwestern farm women and one quarter of men reported taking employment due to financial need during the crisis (Lasley et al 1995).

The social-psychological costs of farm change have received considerable attention. While some studies have focused on how farm structural position influences mental health outcomes (Martinson et al 1976), most contemporary attention is on shorter-term financial hardship from the farm crisis. At first, analysts were concerned with negative mental health outcomes of the crisis, often drawing from research on workers displaced by industrial restructuring. Later attention was given to intervening variables that lessen the effects of economic hardship, such as supportive networks and coping strategies, typical of mental health research. There is a need to broaden focus to other factors that mitigate stressors in the farm context, such as church membership and belief systems. Political activism also can be a useful crisis response, supplanting or supplementing other social-psychological coping mechanisms (Meyer & Lobao 1997). Finally, there is recent interest in the resiliency of farm households, reflecting social psychologists' concerns with emotional hardiness and happiness.

Research on stress and depression in the farm crisis replicates both findings from social psychology and extended sociological understanding of the interplay between economic hardship and mental health in contexts where economic problems are community-wide, not individualized, such as disaster settings and plant closings. Findings demonstrated the association between economic hardship, characteristics of farming as an occupation, and farmers demographic attributes with negative mental health outcomes (Armstrong & Schulman 1990, Belyea & Lobao 1990, Davis-Brown & Salamon 1987, Heffernan & Heffernan 1986, Lorenz et al 2000, Rosenblatt & Anderson 1981, Walker & Walker 1987). Gender comparisons found women bore disproportionate stress (Berkowitz & Perkins 1984). Findings from research on non-farm populations were often confirmed with a few exceptions: more educated and younger farmers had greater mental health problems because this group was more likely to have overcapitalized during the crisis. Conversely, older farmers had few mental health problems, provided their physical health was good. Other research centered on the impact of the crisis on paths of successive farm generations. The longitudinal studies of Iowa rural families, particularly their youth (Conger & Elder 1994, Elder & Conger 2000, Lorenz et al 2000) examined the ways in which family bonds and community supports counter the effects of agricultural downturn. In one of the few panel designs, Lorenz et al (2000) provide cross-time evidence that farm economic hardship results in depression, but that families who lost farms were resilient in recovering emotional health as financial stress abetted.

In summary, we have noted limitations with the literature on farm households, including its reliance on cross-sectional data and the need to more fully explore other adaptive strategies, particularly political activism. Research on farm households is important because it extends sociological generalizations to contexts overlooked by conventional research, places where work and household intertwine. It also raises new questions for sociology. For example, why are gender boundaries so inflexible in business labor allocation, even where the household itself, rather than an external entity, controls these decisions? What is special about a childhood embedded in the land and family work that confers resiliency in the face of hardship?

CONCLUSIONS

In this paper, we provided a retrospective and necessarily schematic account of the empirical and sociological fate of the independent farm population. In the course of the twentieth century, the farm population effectively disappeared from the national and general sociology landscape. Americans at large were expelled from farming, and most participating in this production sector were subject to material deprivation alleviated only by further withdrawal from farm work and reliance on the state. We caution against romanticizing the loss of this population, which represents a landed elite when compared to the mass of rural poor and landless Americans. However, farm decline does reflect the incursion of capital into possibly the last domestic economic sector dominated, at least numerically, by family businesses. And there has been a loss to sociology. The discipline as a whole missed one of the greatest sociological stories of the twentieth century as research on farm transformation became evermore confined to speciality journals. Examining farming can extend sociological inquiry beyond conventional contexts where household and enterprise are distinct. Unique industries such as farming allow interrogation of prevailing conceptualizations about domestic economic organization. More broadly, the farm sector provides an alternative social context that helps refine, revise, or challenge longstanding sociological generalizations presumed to hold across mass society.

We outlined three research traditions, those dealing with macro-level farm transformations, community impacts of farming, and household responses. While the three traditions developed as relatively distinct bodies of work, we noted their overlap. First, taken together they capture the major changes experienced by the farm population. Farming as a production system continues to undergo rapid transformation. The farm enterprise is inextricably connected to the household, so that production changes become reflected in work roles, hardship, stress, and resilience. As farms decline in number and grow in size, their effects reverberate across communities. Second, the three traditions recognize similar transformations, long-term structural and shorter-term changes. However, the causal paths by which these macro-level changes filter down to lower analytical units of household and communities tend to be assumed rather than explicitly explored. Although we noted methodological limitations for doing so, this topic merits more serious attention. Third, research on households and communities provides evidence of institutional mechanisms behind national farm transformation, in addition to private market and central state forces denoted by political economy theory. Attention to household and community institutions can extend current theory. Finally, research on communities and households needs to develop stronger theoretical underpinnings and links to sociological theory. While all three traditions speak to central issues of the discipline, there is a lack of effort in addressing broader audiences, compounded by general sociology's reluctance to be informed by peripheral places and the people who study them.

What lies ahead for the remaining farm population and for sociologists studying agriculture? In addition to continued interest in contemporary family farmers, research is becoming segmented along two different topical areas, reflecting global and local issues, noted earlier. The first is concerned with global production chains in which family farmers themselves play a relatively small part of the sociological story which centers largely on the actions of agribusiness, the state, and increasingly, non-governmental organizations concerned with trade and environment. The second area centers on farming and its embeddedness in local landscape and food systems. A growing literature on the urban-rural interface deals with farmland preservation in the context of metropolitan growth. Because farms are smaller closer to urban areas, such efforts may enhance family operations as well as local eco-systems. A related literature examines local food systems, which provide emerging opportunities for smaller, niche-oriented producers, often engaged in more sustainable agricultural practices. Some argue that the entire agricultural system itself is undergoing bifurcation, whereby remaining producers are moving towards operating in virtually separate, global or local oriented markets, the latter far more amenable to family farmers. In sum, as the classical agrarian political economists argued at the turn of the last century, the fate of the farm population is not yet sealed.

ACKNOWLEDGMENTS

We thank Glen Elder, Rachel Rosenfeld, Jeff Sharp, and Louis Swanson for their comments in developing this manuscript.

Visit the Annual Reviews home page at www.AnnualReviews.org

LITERATURE CITED

Adams J. 1994. *The Transformation of Rural Life: Southern Illinois, 1890–1990*. Chapel Hill: Univ. N Carolina Press

Ahearn MC, Perry JE, El-Osta HS. 1993. *The Economic Well-being of Farm Operator Households, 1988–1990, Agric. Econ. Rep. No. 666*, Econ. Res. Svc., US Dep. Agric.

Albrecht DE. 1997. The changing structure of agriculture: dualism out, industrialism in. *Rur. Sociol.* 62(4):474–90

Albrecht DE, Murdock SH. 1990. *The Sociology of U.S. Agriculture: An Ecological Perspective*. Ames, IA: Iowa State Univ. Press

Armstrong PS, Schulman MD. 1990. Financial strain and depression among farm operators: the role of perceived economic hardship and personal control. *Rur. Sociol.* 55:475–43

Barlett PF. 1993. *American Dreams, Rural Realities: Family Farms in Crisis*. Chapel Hill: Univ. N Carolina Press

Barlett P, Lobao LM, Meyer K. 1999. Diversity in attitudes toward farming and patterns of work among farm women: a regional comparison. *Agric. Hum. Values* 16:343–54

Beale C. 1993. Salient features of the demography of American agriculture. In *The Demography of Rural Life*, ed. D Brown, D Field,

J Zuiches, pp. 108–27. University Park, PA: NE Reg. Ctr. for Rur. Dev.

Beauford EY. 1986. Dilemmas facing minority farm operators in agricultural crisis. In *Agricultural Change: Consequences for Southern Farms and Communities*, ed. JJ Molnar, pp. 27–37. Boulder, CO: Westview

Belyea M, Lobao L. 1990. Psychosocial consequences of agricultural transformation: the farm crisis and depression. *Rur. Sociol.* 41 (1):391–405

Berardi G. 1986. Socioeconomic consequences of agricultural mechanization in the United States. In *The Social Consequences of New Agricultural Technologies*, ed. GM Berardi, pp. 9–22. Boulder, CO: Westview

Berkowitz AD, Perkins HW. 1984. Stress among farm women: work and family as interacting systems. *J. Marriage Fam.* 46:161–66

Bonanno A. 1987. *Small Farms: Persistence with Legitimation*. Boulder CO: Westview

Bonanno A, Busch L, Friedland WH, Gouveia L, Mingione E, eds. 1994. *From Columbus to CongAgra: The Globalization of Agriculture and Food*. Lawrence: Univ. Press of Kansas

Brooks NL, Stucker TA, Bailey JA. 1986. Income and well-being of farmers and the farm financial crisis. *Rur. Sociol.* 51:391–405

Brown A, Christy R, Gebremedhin T. 1994. Structural changes in US agriculture: implications for African American farmers. *Rev. Black Polit. Econ.* 22(4):51–72

Brown BB, Xu X, Toth JF. 1998. Lifestyle options and economic strategies: subsistence activities in the Mississippi Delta. *Rur. Sociol.* 63(4):599–623

Brown D, Wardwell J, eds. 1981. *New Directions in Urban-Rural Migration*. New York: Academic Press

Brown D, Field D, Zuiches J, eds. 1993. *The Demography of Rural Life*. University Park, PA: NE Reg. Ctr. for Rur. Dev.

Browne WP, Skees JR, Swanson LE, Thompson PB, Unnevehr LJ. 1992. *Sacred Cows and Hot Potatoes: Agrarian Myths in Agricultural Policy*. Boulder, CO: Westview

Bultena G, Lasley P, Geller J. 1986. The farm crisis: patterns and impacts of financial distress among Iowa farm families. *Rur. Sociol.* 41(4):391–405

Buttell FH, Gillespie GW. 1984. The sexual division of farm household labor: an exploratory study of the structure of on-farm and off-farm labor allocation among farm men and women. *Rur. Sociol.* 49:182–209

Buttel FH, LaRamee. 1991. The 'disappearing middle': a sociological perspective. In *Towards a New Political Economy of Agriculture*, ed. W Friedland, L Busch, FH Buttel, A Rudy, pp. 151–69. Boulder, CO: Westview

Buttel FH, Newby H, eds. 1980. *The Rural Sociology of Advanced Societies*. Montclair, NJ: Allanheld Osmun

Buttel FH, Lancelle M, Lee DR. 1988. Farm structure and rural communities in the Northeast. See Swanson 1988b, pp. 181–237

Cochrane WW. 1979. *The Development of American Agriculture: A Historical Analysis*. Minneapolis: Univ. Minn. Press

Conger RD, Elder GH Jr. 1994. *Families in Troubled Times: Adapting to Change in Rural America*. Hawthorne, NY: Aldine de Gruyter

Coughenour CM, Swanson LE. 1983. Working statuses and occupations of men and women in farm families and the structure of farms. *Rur. Sociol.* 48:23–43

Crowley M. 1999. *The impact of farm sector concentration on poverty and inequality: an analysis of North Central U.S. counties*. MA thesis. Ohio State Univ., Columbus

Davis JE. 1980. Capitalist agricultural development and the exploitation of the propertied laborer. In *The Rural Sociology of Advanced Societies*, ed. F Buttel, H Newby, pp. 133–54. Montclair, NJ: Allanheld Osmun

Davis-Brown K, Salamon S. 1987. Farm families in crisis: an application of stress theory to farm family research. *Fam. Relat.* 36:4

DuPuis EM. 1993. Sub-national state institutions and the organization of agricultural resources use: the case of the dairy industry. *Rur. Sociol.* 58(3):440–60

Elder GW, Conger RD. 2000. *Children of the*

Land: Adversity and Success in Rural America. Chicago, IL: Univ. Chicago Press

Falk W. 1996. The assertion of identity in rural sociology. *Rur. Sociol.* 61(1):159–74

Fink D. 1986. *Open Country, Iowa: Rural Women, Tradition and Change*. Albany, NY: Albany State Univ., NY Press

Fink D. 1992. *Agrarian Women: Wives and Mothers in Rural Nebraska, 1880–1940*. Chapel Hill: Univ. N Carolina Press

Fligstein N. 1981. *Going North: Migration of Blacks and Whites from the South, 1900–1950*. New York: Academic Press

Flora CB, Flora JL. 1988. Public policy, farm size, and community well-being in farming dependent counties of the plains. See Swanson 1988b, pp. 76–129

Foley N. 1997. *The White Scourge: Mexicans, Blacks, and Poor Whites in Texas Cotton Culture*. Berkeley: Univ. Calif. Press

Friedland WH. 1991. Introduction: shaping the new political economy of advanced capitalist agriculture. In *Towards a New Political Economy of Agriculture*, ed. W Friedland, L Busch, FH Buttel, A Rudy, pp. 1–34. Boulder, CO: Westview

Friedland WH, Barton AE, Thomas RJ. 1981. *Manufacturing Green Gold*. Cambridge, UK: Cambridge Univ. Press

Friedland WH, Busch L, Buttel FH, Rudy A, eds. 1991. *Towards a New Political Economy of Agriculture*. Boulder, CO: Westview

Friedmann H. 1978. World market, state and family farm: social bases of household production in an era of wage labor. *Comp. Stud. in Soc. Hist.* 20:545–86

Fuguitt G, Beale C. 1989. *Rural and Small Town America*. New York: Russell Sage

Garkovich L, Bokemeier J, Foote B. 1995. *Harvest of Hope: Family Farming/Farming Families*. Lexington: Univ. Kentucky

Gilbert J, Howe C. 1991. Beyond 'state vs. society': theories of the state and New Deal agricultural policies. *Am. Sociol. Rev.* 56:204–20

Gilles JL, Dalecki M. 1988. Rural well-being and agricultural change in two farming regions. *Rur. Sociol.* 53:40–55

Gladwin C. 1991. Multiple job-holding among farm families and the increase in women's farming. *Multiple Job-Holding among Farm Families*, ed. MC Hallberg, JL Findeis, D Lass, pp. 213–35. Ames: Iowa State Univ. Press

Goldschmidt W. 1978. *As You Sow: Three Studies in the Social Consequences of Agribusiness*. Montclair, NJ: Allanheld, Osmun

Goodman D, Watts M. 1994. Reconfiguring the rural or fording the divide? Capitalist restructuring and the global agro-food system. *J. Peasant. Stud.* 22(1):1–49

Goss K, Rodefeld R, Buttel F. 1980. The political economy of class structure in U.S. agriculture. In *The Rural Sociology of Advanced Societies*, ed. F Buttel, H Newby, pp. 83–132. Montclair, NJ: Allanheld Osmun

Haney WG, Knowles JB, eds. 1988. *Women and Farming: Changing Roles and Changing Structures*. Boulder, CO: Westview

Heffernan WD, Heffernan JB. 1986. Impact of the farm crisis on rural families and communities. *Rur. Sociol.* 6:160–70

Hinrichs CC. 1998. Sideline and lifeline: the cultural economy of maple syrup production. *Rur. Sociologist* 63(4):507–32

Hooks G. 1990. From an autonomous to a capture state agency: the decline of the New Deal in agriculture. *Am. Sociol. Rev.* 55:29–43

Irwin M, Tolbert C, Lyson T. 1999. There's no place like home: non-migration and civic engagement. *Envir. Plann. A* 31:223–38

Jackson-Smith DB. 1999. Understanding the microdynamics of farm structural change: entry, exit, and restructuring among Wisconsin family farmers in the 1980s. *Rur. Sociol.* 64(1):66–91

Jahr D, Johnson JW, Wimberley RC, eds. 1986. *New Dimensions in Rural Policy: Building Upon Our Heritage*. Washington, DC: US Gov. Print. Off.

Jones H. 1994. Federal agricultural policies: do black farm operators benefit? *Rev. Black Polit. Econ.* 22(4):25–50

Kenney M, Lobao L, Curry J, Goe WR. 1989. Midwestern agriculture in U.S. Fordism:

from New Deal to economic restructuring. *Soc. Ruralis.* 29(2):130–48

Kloppenburg J, Hendrickson J, Stevenson GW. 1996. Coming into the foodshed. *Agric. Hum. Values* 13(3):1–10

Lasley P, Leistritz FL, Lobao LM, Meyer K. 1995. *Beyond the Amber Waves of Grain: An Examination of Social and Economic Restructuring in the Heartland.* Boulder, CA: Westview

Lichter D, McLaughlin D. 1995. Changing economic opportunities, family structure, and poverty in rural areas. *Rur. Sociol.* 60:688–706

Lobao L. 1990. *Locality and Inequality: Farm and Industry Structure and Socioeconomic Conditions.* Albany: State Univ. NY Press

Lobao L. 1996. A sociology of the periphery versus a peripheral sociology: rural sociology and the dimension of space. *Rur. Sociol.* 61:77–102

Lobao LM, Meyer K. 2000. Institutional sources of marginality: midwestern family farming in a period of economic decline. *Res. Sociol. Work* 9:23–49

Lobao LM, Meyer K. 1995. Economic decline, gender, and labor flexibility in family-based enterprises: the case of Midwestern farming. *Soc. Forces* 74:575–608

Lobao LM, Schulman MD. 1991. Farming patterns, rural restructuring and poverty: a comparative regional analysis. *Rur. Sociol.* 56(4):565–602

Lorenz FO, Elder GH, Bao WN, Wickrama KAS, Conger RD. 2000. After farming: emotional health trajectories of farm, nonfarm, and displaced farm couples. *Rur. Sociol.* 65 (1):50–71

MacCannell D. 1988. Industrial agriculture and rural community degradation. See Swanson 1988b, pp. 15–75

Mandle J. 1978. *The Roots of Black Poverty: The Southern Plantation Economy after the Civil War.* Durham, NC: Duke Univ. Press

Mann SA. 1990. *Agrarian Capitalism in Theory and Practice.* Chapel Hill: Univ. N Carolina Press

Mann SA, Dickinson JM. 1978. Obstacles to the development of a capitalist agriculture. *J. Peasant Stud.* 5:466–81

Marsden TK, Arce A. 1995. Constructing quality: emerging food networks in the rural transition. *Environ. Plan. A* 27:1261–79

Martinson OB, Wilkening EA, Rodefeld RD. 1976. Feelings of powerlessness and social isolation among "large-scale" farm personnel. *Rur. Sociol.* 41(4):452–72

McDonald H, Peters A. 1991. Farm women in the new rural labor markets of the West North Central Region. In *Proc. 1991 Regional Conf. on the Rural Family, The Rural Community, and Economic Restructuring,* ed. K Root, J Heffernan, G Summers, J Stewart, pp. 51–73. Ames, IA: N. Central Reg. Ctr. for Rur. Dev.

McMichael P, ed. 1994. *The Global Restructuring of Agro-Food Systems.* Ithaca, NY: Cornell Univ. Press

McMichael P. 1996. *Development and Social Change: A Global Perspective.* Thousand Oaks CA: Sage

Meares AC. 1997. Making the transition from conventional to sustainable agriculture: gender, social movement participation, and quality of life on the family farm. *Rur. Sociol.* 62:21–47

Meyer K, Lobao L. 1994. Engendering the farm crisis: women's political response in the USA. In *Gender and Rurality,* ed. S Whatmore, T Marsden, P Lowe, pp. 69–86. London: David Fulton

Meyer K, Lobao L. 1997. Farm couples and crisis politics: the importance of household, spouse, and gender in responding to economic decline. *J. Marriage Fam.* 59:204–18

Moen P, Wethington E. 1992. The concept of family adaptive strategies. *Annu. Rev. Sociol.* 18:233–51

Molnar JJ, ed. 1986. *Agricultural Change: Consequences for Southern Farms and Communities.* Boulder, CO: Westview

Mooney P. 1988. *My Own Boss? Class, Rationality, and the Family Farm.* Boulder CO: Westview

Mooney P, Majka T. 1995. *Farmers' and Farm*

Workers' Movement: Social Protest in American Agriculture. New York: Twayne

Moore B. 1996. Social Origins of Democracy and Dictatorship. Boston, MA: Beacon

Mottura G, Pugliese E. 1980. Capitalism in agriculture and capitalist agriculture. In The Rural Sociology of Advanced Societies, ed. F Buttel, H Newby, pp. 171–199. Montclair, NJ: Allanheld Osmun

NCRCRD (North Central Regional Center for Rural Development). 1999. The Impact of Recruiting Vertically Integrated Hog Production in Agriculturally-Based Counties of Oklahoma. Ames: Iowa State Univ.

New York Times. 2000. President signs a $15 billion bailout for farmers. New York Times, June 21, 2000:A20

Newby H. 1983. The sociology of agriculture: toward a new rural sociology. Annu. Rev. Sociol. 9:67–81

Odum HW, Moore HE. 1938. American Regionalism: A Cultural-Historical Approach to National Integration. New York: Henry Holt

Ollenburger JC, Grana SJ, Moore HA. 1989. Labor force participation of rural farm, rural nonfarm, and urban women. Rur. Sociol. 54:533–50

Olson RK, Lyson TA, eds. 1999. Under the Blade: The Conversion of Agricultural Landscapes. Boulder, CO: Westview

Pfeffer MJ. 1983. Social origins of three systems of farm production in the United States. Rur. Sociol. 48(4):540–62

Pfeffer MJ, Lapping M. 1994. Farmland preservation, development rights, and the theory of the growth machine. J. Rur. Stud. 10(3):233–48

Rodefeld RD. 1974. The changing organization and occupational structure of farming and the implications for farm workforces, individuals, families, and communities. Ph.D. dissertation. Univ. Wisc., Madison

Rosenblatt PC, Anderson RM. 1981. Interaction in farm families: tension and stress. In The Family in Rural Society, ed. RT Coward, WM Smith, pp. 147–66. Boulder, CO: Westview

Rosenfeld RA. 1985. Farm Women: Work, Farm, and Family in the United States. Chapel Hill: Univ. N Carolina Press

Sachs CE. 1983. The Invisible Farmers: Women in Agricultural Production. Totowa, NJ: Rowman & Allanheld

Sachs CE. 1996. Gendered Fields: Rural Women, Agriculture, and the Environment. Boulder, CO: Westview

Sack K. 2000. To vestige of black farmers, bias settlement is too late. New York Times, January 6, 2000: A1, A12

Salamon S. 1992. Prairie Patrimony: Family, Farming, and Community in the Midwest. Chapel Hill: Univ. N Carolina Press

Schwarzweller H, Davidson A. 1997. Perspectives on regional and enterprise marginality: dairying in Michigan's north country. Rur. Sociol. 62(2):157–79

Seavoy R. 1998. The American Peasantry: Southern Agricultural Labor and Its Legacy, 1850–1995. Westport, CT: Greenwood

Seipel M, Dallman K, Kleiner A, Rikoon JS. 1999. Rural residents attitudes toward increased regulation of large-scale swine production. Presented at Annu. Meet. Rur. Sociol. Soc, Chicago

Simpson IH, Wilson J, Young K. 1988. The sexual division of farm household labor: a replication and extension. Rur. Sociol. 53:145–65

Skees JR, Swanson LE. 1988. Farm structure and well-being in the south. See Swanson 1988b, pp. 238–321

Skocpol T, Finegold K. 1982. State capacity and economic intervention in the early New Deal. Pol. Sci. Q. 97(2):255–78

Snipp CM. 1989. American Indians: The First of this Land. New York: Russell Sage

Snipp CM, Horton H, Jensen L, Nagel J, Rochin. 1993. Persistent rural poverty and racial and ethnic minorities. In Persistent Poverty in Rural America, ed. G. Summers. Boulder, CO: Westview

Sommer J, Hoppe RA, Greene RC, Korb PJ. 1998. Structural and Financial Characteristics of U.S. Farms, 1995: 20th Annual Family Farm Report to the Congress. USDA: Res.

Econ. Div., Econ. Res. Serv. Agric. Info. Bull. No. 746

Summers G. 1986. Rural community development. *Annu. Rev. Sociol.* 12:347–71

Swanson LE. 1982. *Farm and trade center transition in an industrial society: Pennsylvania 1930–1960.* Ph.D. diss. University Park: Penn. State Univ. Press

Swanson LE. 1988a. Farm and community change: a brief introduction to the regional studies. See Swanson 1988b, pp. 1–14

Swanson LE. 1988b. *Agriculture and Community Change in the US: The Congressional Research Reports.* Boulder, CO: Westview

Tetreau ED. 1938. The people of Arizona's irrigated areas. *Rur. Sociol.* 3:177–87

Tetreau ED. 1940. Social organization in Arizona's irrigated areas. *Rur. Sociol.* 5:192–205

Thu KM, Durrenberger EP, eds. 1998. *Pigs, Profits, and Rural Communities.* Albany, NY: State Univ. NY Press

Tickamyer A. 1996. Sex, lies, and statistics: Can rural sociology survive restructuring? *Rur. Sociol.* 61:5–24

Tolbert CM, Lyson TA, Irwin MD. 1998. Local capitalism, civic engagement and socioeconomic well-being. *Soc. Forc.* 77:401–28

Tolnay SE. 1999. *The Bottom Rung: African American Family Life on Southern Farms.* Urbana: Univ. Ill. Press

US Bureau of the Census. 1999. *Statistical Abstract of the United States: 1999.* Washington, DC: US Gov. Print. Off.

US Department of Agriculture. 1999. *Agricultural Outlook.* Washington, DC: Econ. Res. Serv. Dec 1999, p. 50, Table 31

US Department of Agriculture. 2000. *Rural Conditions and Trends, Rural Industry,* 10:2. Washington, DC: Econ. Res. Serv.

van Es JC, Chicoine DL, Flotow MA. 1988. Agricultural technologies, farm structure and rural communities in the Corn Belt: policies and implications for 2000. See Swanson 1988b, pp. 130–80

Walker LS, Walker JL. 1987. Stressors and symptoms predictive of distress in farmers. *Fam. Relat.* 36:374–78

Whatmore S. 1991. *Farming Women: Gender, Work, and Family Enterprise.* Macmillan

Wilkening EA. 1968. Aspirations and task involvement as related to decision-making among farm husbands and wives. *Rur. Sociol.* 33(1):30–45

Wilkening EA. 1981. Farm families and family farming. In *The Family in Rural Society,* ed. RT Coward, WM Smith, pp. 27–38. Boulder, CO: Westview

Wilson J, Simpson IH, Landerman R. 1994. Status variation on family farms: effects of crop, machinery, and off-farm work. *Rur. Sociol.* 59:136–53

Wimberley RC. 1987. Dimensions of US agriculture: 1969–1982. *Rur. Sociol.* 52(4):445–61

Annu. Rev. Sociol. 2001. 27:125–52

RELIGIOUS NATIONALISM AND THE PROBLEM OF COLLECTIVE REPRESENTATION

Roger Friedland

Departments of Religious Studies and Sociology, University of California, Santa Barbara, Santa Barbara, California 93106-9430; e-mail: res028tp@gte.net

Key Words institutional heterology, field, civil society

■ **Abstract** I first argue that religion partakes of the symbolic order of the nation-state and that contemporary nationalisms are suffused with the religious. I then suggest that religious nationalism calls into question the theoretical duality of the social and the cultural, a divide variously identified with the material and the symbolic, class and status, economy and civil society. Religious nationalism, I suggest, requires an institutional approach to the project of collective representation. Religious nationalism offers a particular ontology of power, an ontology revealed and affirmed through its politicized practices and the central object of its political concern, practices that locate collective solidarity in religious faith shared by embodied families, not in contract and consent enacted by abstract individual citizens. Understanding the institutional basis of religious nationalist discourse allows us to understand its affinities with socialist politics. If religious nationalism derives from religion's institutional heterology with the capitalist market and the democratic state, then it suggests the limits of a social theory that occludes that heterology. In the remainder of the paper, I argue that religious nationalism cannot be adequately understood either through Pierre Bourdieu's theory of habitus and field, nor through Jeffrey Alexander's theory of civil society. Bourdieu's theory of fields imports the logic of dominant institutions and thereby culturally homogenizes the institutional diversity of contemporary society, making the stake of politics a culturally empty space of domination. Alexander's theory of civil society, while rich in cultural substance, identifies civil society with democratic political culture and thereby makes unnecessarily restrictive assumptions about the institutional sources of collective representation in modern society.

INTRODUCTION

Once again God walks in history. As a century organized around the fear of a godless state comes to a close, we wake to a new terror: states armed with powers of the divine. We today confront the apparently premodern specter of religious nationalism. The territoriality and the historicity of the nation-state are being transformed into vessels of divine purpose, mechanisms by which to materialize a monist world.

0360-0572/01/0811-0125$14.00   **125**

Religious nationalism not only shatters the presumptions of geopolitics, it reveals the limits of sociological theory. Religious nationalism is a particular form of collective representation. In this essay I first argue that religion partakes of the symbolic order of the nation-state and that contemporary nationalisms are suffused with the religious. I then suggest that religious nationalism calls into question the theoretical duality of the social and the cultural, a divide variously identified with the material and the symbolic, class and status, economy and civil society. Religious nationalism, I suggest, requires an institutional approach to the project of collective representation. Religious nationalism offers a particular ontology of power, an ontology revealed and affirmed through its politicized practices and the central object of its political concern, practices that locate collective solidarity in religious faith shared by embodied families, not in contract and consent enacted by abstract individual citizens. Understanding the institutional basis of religious nationalist discourse allows us to understand its affinities with socialist politics. If religious nationalism derives from religion's institutional heterology with the capitalist market and the democratic state, then it suggests the limits of a social theory that occludes that heterology.

In the remainder of the paper, I argue that religious nationalism cannot be adequately understood either through Pierre Bourdieu's theory of habitus and field, nor through Jeffrey Alexander's theory of civil society. Bourdieu's theory of fields imports the logic of dominant institutions and thereby culturally homogenizes the institutional diversity of contemporary society, making the stake of politics a culturally empty space of domination. Alexander's theory of civil society, while rich in cultural substance, identifies civil society with democratic political culture and thereby makes unnecessarily restrictive assumptions about the institutional sources of collective representation in modern society.

RELIGION'S SOVEREIGN POWERS

Cleric, rabbi, sadhu, and mullah mount the rostrum, occupy the public place, seeking to ordinate society according to a text originating outside of it. Religious nationalists make politics into a religious obligation. We are wont to view the religious nationalist project as a retreat from modernity. The Enlightenment philosophers made the separation of state authority from religion an essential condition for freedom, for "mankind's exit from its self-imposed maturity" as Kant (1996) put it. In place of religion, the person and the polity would now assume sacred status in the modern western world, nationalism donning the trappings of a religion. These are modernity's terms for the satanization of public religion. In the resulting formation, which for so long seemed modernity's necessary terminus, religion was to set up shop in the interior of the believer's soul, within the walls of the family, not in the public square and the state house. Religion, whose transcendence and absoluteness used to bolster the rule of state, to set states into conquest and war, to spark civil wars, and to establish the ethical habits conditioning the accumulation of productive wealth, was sequestered, made safe and platitudinous. We have come to equate secularity, the disengagement and differentiation of the public sphere from religion, with modernity. This has led to its analytic neglect. Habermas, for example, who wants to construct a clean divide between citizenship and national identity, between the rights of man and the right to protect a particular national culture, neglects religion's role in establishing the cultural ground of that citizenship (Weiss 1999).

That religious groups, here religious nationalists, would want to seize the state is not unexpected. Both state and religion are models of authority, imaginations of an ordering power, and understandings of how one should relate to those who control forces upon which one depends, but over which one does not exercise control. Riesebrodt (2000) characterizes the distinctiveness of religious practices as those involving "superhuman or extraordinary personal or impersonal powers" that control human life and to which one can gain access.

Whereas secularization involves the breakdown of a religious cosmology in which all things, including the state, are subordinate to a divine order (Casanova 1994), religion can also be understood as immanent in the state itself. Derrida (1998) has argued that the state, like all forms of authority, indeed, of collectivity, depends on a faith that cannot be reduced to knowledge, on an unproducible and unnamable "other," an absolute, present-absent witness that guarantees all testimony, all witness, all nomination. Faith, beyond reason and proof, thus undergirds the performativity of authority, the saying so that makes it so.

God is a sovereign personality. It is difficult to recapture that understanding in our world where the institutional separation of church and state has transformed religion into a faith, a substance found in, and a regulatory principle operating on, an interior territory, a secret housed inside individual bodies, a basis for being good, sane, or secure. It is useful to look back at the moment when the modern state was stripped of its religious meaning, when this new discursive formation was put in place. Those who supported the *ancien regime* reacted as though it were a threat both to state and to religion. When the French Revolution ushered in the first European republic, its Catholic opponents understood the writings of the *philosophes* as its moral mandate and foundational ontology (McMahon 2001). Indeed, they understood *la philosophie* as Protestantism without God, leading inexorably to heretical division, a fissiparous force that would naturally issue in a chaos of sects. The two absolutisms were understood to be of a piece. It was no wonder that these abstract ideas, breaking with religious faith and historical experience, really illusionist's tricks, conjointly indicted religion and absolutist authority. The first European republic was understood as a usurpation of God's sovereignty.

Religions other than Christianity, which began as a stateless faith, have even greater political claim. Hinduism, Judaism, and Islam—to take a few examples—provide images and precepts for a society, indeed the foundations for a state, and thus presume that religion can and should have a role in the regulation of all of social life. They imagine political communities whose physical survival, territorial control, and material prosperity are all contingent upon their obedience to the revealed laws of God. The Torah, for instance, is understood as a covenant between a people and a God, a people whose capacity to occupy *eretz yisrael*, the Land of Israel, is dependent on following its laws (Friedland & Hecht 2000). The Qur'an, likewise, is not just about the relationship of the individual to God, but about a politically organized community of believers, the *umma*, called by their sovereign. The Qur'an spells out a political religion (Humphreys 1999).

The divine, as Durkheim (1995 [1912]) long ago pointed out, provides an image of the governing principle of our collective body. For us moderns, the house of state is our sacred place, our machinery for collective representation. Collective political claims are immanent in the divine, in a society's imagination of supra-human powers and the practices that relate to them. We can see this, for example, by examining how Protestant colonialists related to the Africans whose lands they colonized. As Chidester (1996) has shown, the colonials who took possession of South Africa insisted that the Africans—Zulu, Bechuana, Xhosa— they confronted on the colonial frontiers had no religion so long as European rule of these Africans was uncertain and the Africans were able to maintain their polities and resist subjugation. Africans without religion, who were therefore considered not fully human, childlike and superstitious, had no right to rule, no inherent right to territorial possession. Once each African population was conquered and sequestered, they could be granted a religion, a degenerated version of a religion from elsewhere (hence without rights to possession), a fetishism, an animism, or even a primitive "theism" from which the world's monotheisms had moved on. Denying a collectivity's right to polity was of a piece with the original denial of their possession of something recognized as a religion. Without God, African territory could be understood as a blank, empty space.

Religion provides what Juergensmeyer (1993, 1999) calls a "language of ultimate order." Religious discourse is replete with martial metaphor, of battles and enemies, of position and siege. Religions' originary histories are filled with military conquest whether, for example, of the ancient Jewish kings; of Muhammad's warriors and the tradition of *jihad*; of Lord Krishna's sermon, the Bhagavad Gita, delivered on a battlefield; of the final Sikh master, Guru Gobind Singh, commander of a huge army facing the Mughal invaders in the Punjab in the sixteenth and seventeenth centuries. Religion, a cosmology accomplished through violence, its cosmic war vicariously experienced and domesticated by rite, is thus inherently a natural competitor to the nationalism of the secular state. Juergensmeyer's comparative hermeneutics of religious terrorism (1999) follows politicized faith into the mayhem and pain imposed on innocent people. There are those who would argue that such vile conjunctions of spirit and cruelty, of religious belief and political violence, belie the religiosity of the terrorists, that religion is a mere wrapper. Authority rests on a metaphysics, an ontology of order, a moral and categorical system constituting the thinkable and actionable, and on an organization of violence that controls those who fail to think and act within its limits. Juergensmeyer argues that the desacralization of the modern nation-state, the return of religion to the public sphere, and the explosion of religious terror are a linked set. Religious terrorists are almost all religious nationalists, those seeking an alternative order on which to ground state authority. Religious terrorism is only the most extreme form of this general movement, this reclaiming of religion's inherent political powers, its final judgments.

Religious terrorism is not primarily an instrument to transform government policy as much as it is a ritual drama designed to be noticed, typically targeted at symbolically charged sites, usually public places—nodes in the exchange of goods, the movement of people, sites of authority. Religious terrorism represents a symbolic order more than it produces a profanely practical result. It is a theatre of war. While its religious opponents and the larger public declare terrorism to be antithetical to religion's peaceful purposes, religion, Juergensmeyer argues, gravitates naturally to the language and the postures of war. For warfare is an occasion for the display and adjudication of absolute, non-negotiable differences, for the performance of the incommensurable divide Emile Durkheim located between the sacred and the profane. War affords a distinctive moral architecture, an absolute partitioning into good and evil mapped onto us and them, a narration of empowerment stitched into the nature of things. Terror signals the immorality of one's foe, a sign of the absoluteness, the essentialness, of the other's evil. Terror is not here normal politics by scandalous means but a declaration that normal politics are not possible. It is perhaps the capacity for violence that ultimately marks the sacred, the disordering element that stands as the exterior guarantor of order, of division and partition. To violently broach the public sphere is to declare the absence of state guarantee, a state without God being a profane state, a profanity demonstrated by violence against the state.

Religious nationalism is not alien to the formation of the modern nation-state. Even a cursory look suggests that the formation of many non-Western modern national identities and nationalist movements was suffused with religious narrative and myth, symbolism and ritual—Iran, Sri Lanka, India, Pakistan, Saudi Arabia, Israel, and Palestine, to take just a few examples. Given religion's centrality to nation-formation, it is not surprising that religion is a ready reservoir for nationalist critique. Within these cosmologies, secular nationalism is easily perceived as a form of Christian political culture, one many now perceive as a failure. Juergensmeyer (1993), who has heralded the birth of a "new cold war," argues that there has been a "loss of faith in secular nationalism," such that many political leaders in the world increasingly see the secularism of Western nationalism as the reason for the moral failures of their own societies in the midst of modernization.

The emergence and form of the Western secular nation-state has itself everything do with Christianity, and Protestantism in particular (Bendix 1978, Harrison 1998, McLoughlin 1978, Rokkan 1975, Tilly 1998). The American Revolution, for example, was prepared by a diffuse transformation in Protestant belief, known as "the Great Awakening" (1730–1760), that located the basis of religious authority in personal faith, not in ordination, the profession of doctrine, or a church hierarchy. This "new light," an emotional, indeed physical knowing, as opposed to a disembodied intellectual knowing, of God, was open to all, to those without formal education, to the poor, even to women and slaves. This postmillennial religious transformation, in fact, helped create the inter-colonial unity, the solidarity and the democratic moral order that would forge the American nation-state (Heimert 1966, McLoughlin 1978, Walzer 1965). The French Revolution, which constituted the nation without respect to, indeed in opposition to, religion, has been the world historical exception.

RELIGIOUS NATIONALISM AND THE AUTONOMY OF CULTURE

Religious nationalism as discourse and social movement is often understood as an instance of culture's autonomy as a source of identity and critique, an autonomy manifested in the formation of politicized religious groups. It is a mistake to begin an analysis of religious nationalism through the social groups composing it, through the ascendant particularity of persons. From this vantage point, religious nationalism becomes a movement to defend a particular form of group identity, difference considered as attributes of persons, not unlike that of racial, gender, sexual or linguistic groups who launch movements to affirm or defend their particularity before or from the society's dominant group, here an instrument by which religious people secure membership in the political community or recognition in the public sphere.

Religious nationalism can be understood as one among the panoply of the apparently new social movements, defending identity as opposed to pursuing interest, a substitute or a stand-in for the redistributive material politics of class. Or it can be understood as a cultural refraction, or mediation, of underlying social grievances. These castings of politicized religion are both premised on distinguishing the social as an instrumental distributional system of things from the cultural as an expressive system of signs, on understanding the economy as a material institutional order, the paragon of the social, while civil society is a symbolic institutional order, the paragon of the cultural (see also Bonnell & Hunt 1999).

This duality of the social and the cultural suffuses interpretations of the rise of politicized religion. Barber's "Jihad vs. McWorld," particularistic tribalism as a reaction to universalistic globalism, is a good example (1992). The forces of globalism all issue from an economic hardscape—transnational markets, dependencies on foreign resources, technological revolution, and ecological process. In contrast, those of "Jihad," forces that fragment even modernity's nation-states, are about the soft stuff of symbol and myth. Religious nationalism has no political-economic import; it is an end in itself.

Others see politicized religion as an expression or medium of material interest. Lawrence (1998), for example, argues that it is brute matter, the stuff of existence, distributed ever more inequitably in the world, that not only exercises most Muslims but also explains Islamic politics. In the case of Islamic revivalism, as for instance in the cases of the Wahhabis or the Fulani-Qadiris in Nigeria, Islam was "an emblem of protest" against the contraction of trade caused by European mercantilism. The struggle between Asad's Baath regime and the Muslim Brothers in Syria was "not a religious struggle but a struggle for power in which religion was used by both sides as a mask for deeper grievances and more palpable stakes" (1998:73). The "real" reason, he argues, that Islamic traditionalists today exclude women from the public sphere is the job shortage for men (1998:39). Islam is here a medium through which other struggles find expression: group contests over power and income, national resistance to marginality and powerlessness in the world order.

In Foran's historical sociological analysis of Iran, Shiite Islam mediates between economic structure and oppositional, and particularly revolutionary, political action. Foran politicized Wallerstein's structuralist world systems theory by showing the ways in which the strategic political actions of domestic groups drawn from historically layered modes of production shape the development of a dependent nation (Foran 1993). In Foran's theory, the distinctive inequities and hardships—like displacement of the artisans and the bazaar merchants—generated by dependent development require a repressive personalistic state, the experience of whose exclusion generated a series of "political cultures of opposition"—Islam, republicanism, nationalism, Marxism, as well as their various syntheses. These oppositional cultures are the basis upon which urban multi-class coalitions repeatedly form as in the Constitutional revolution of 1905–1911, Mussadiq's nationalization of oil in the early 1950s, and the Islamic revolution of 1979. The distinctive quality of the 1979 revolution, as opposed to earlier junctures, was the simultaneous mobilization of both republican and Islamic discursive elements and the social bases who carried them, both the ulama and the organized white- and blue-collar workers. Foran argues that a social revolution can occur where there is a multi-class or populist oppositional culture, conditions of economic decline, or a world-system opening—generally an American failure to intervene decisively in the internal politics of the country.

Political cultures mediate between "structural determinants of grievances" and regime critique (Foran 1997a). Political culture, not ideology, is the medium through which economic interests are given political form, through which objective economic conditions are lived and interpreted (Foran 1992). The question is whether political culture mediates or constructs the revolutionary project. Given the lack of class specificity in these oppositional political cultures, that it is the particularism of the state, not economic conditions per se, that galvanizes oppositional mobilization, that in the Boolean analyses Foran has conducted across many nation-states, neither economic downturn nor dependent development discriminate between revolutionary and nonrevolutionary action (1997b), it is as arguable that oppositional movements form not out of economics politically understood, but out of politics itself. Foran here understands religion as autonomous cultural materials, a frame deployed in reaction to societal conditions, subjective meanings constructed in response to objective conditions.

Foran's neo-Marxist insistence on culture's autonomy from the economy as a basis for agency is shared by Alexander's post-Durkheimian school, which has grounded the autonomy of the cultural in the linguistic order of signs and symbols, in semiotic structure. Alexander and his students have looked on culture as a code or language with its own internal logic, insisting on its autonomy from the materiality of the social world (Alexander 1998, Alexander & Smith 1993, Kane 1991). As for Foran, more is at stake in culture's autonomy than just good social theory. Alexander analytically distinguishes between three "environments of action": the social, the cultural, and the personality. The analytic autonomy of the cultural realm enables generalizable significations—both typifications and inventions—independent of the social conditions of their use. In Alexander's view, culture's analytic, as opposed to its empirical, autonomy establishes a presuppositional warrant not only for its study but, as for Foran, for individual human freedom itself, for the formation of collective will. Autonomous, structured cultural codes provide the tools through and by which actors can recode themselves and the world and thereby create new worlds.

If Alexander grounds the autonomy of culture in semiotic order, he identifies the social system with an order of distribution. Reviewing Touraine's theorization of new postindustrial social movements, Alexander describes Parsons' distinction between values and norms, the latter involving "historically specific forms of organization that focus, not on general values, but on the distribution of rewards and sanctions" (1996). Alexander approves of how Touraine, unlike Parsons, does not idealistically conflate "existing forms of social organization with the cultural ideals that informed them." It is the gap between value and norm, between the cultural and the social, between cultural ideals and social norms, in which Alexander locates the possibility for reflexive agency and hence for social movements.

In their work on public sphere crises, Alexander & Smith (1993) marry Durkheim's religious sociology to the dualities of structuralist linguistics, making the dominant cultural codes into instances of the binary of sacred and profane—honest, independent, and universal all lining up naturally with the sacred pole of this duality. The analytic autonomy of the cultural code derives from its systematically structured homologies, its internal associations. The code's referentiality, its application to the social world—what, after all, is made to count as just or democratic—is the contingent political domain where groups can seek to position one another on different sides of the multiple binaries. In this approach politics is cultural, but there is little politics of culture, that is, few struggles over the codes themselves.

In analyzing social movements' two moments, Alexander rests the social on the cultural, distribution on value. "Vis a vis potential supporters, social movements in civil societies must present themselves as typifying sacred values . . . as cultural innovators who can create new norms and new institutions that will allow resources to be channeled in different ways." Because the code itself is not at stake, this makes the telos of the social movement into a culturally contentless redistribution of resources, not a transformation of culture. In that the ideals themselves are not at stake, the material world stands outside as an objective landscape in which and for which symbolic warfare periodically rages.

This same identification of the social with an order of distribution characterizes the work of Fraser, the Marxist political philosopher. Seeking to wend a way between the new politics and the oid, class and identity, Fraser (2001) argues that we need to distinguish analytically between the politics of redistribution rooted in the social relations of class and a politics of recognition rooted in the cultural relations of status. These politics are distinguished by the nature of the collectivities that carry them—classes and status groups, respectively. Fraser proposes a "bivalent" conception of justice drawing on both independent domains. For Fraser, "class is an artifact of an unjust political economy, which creates, and exploits a proletariat. The core injustice is exploitation, an especially deep form of maldistribution, as the proletariat shoulders an undue share of the system's burdens, while being denied its fair share of the system's rewards" (2001:7). By deriving class from distribution, Fraser instrumentalizes the economy, making its politics into a conflictual problem of group share. She thereby eviscerates the specificity of capitalism's institutional logic.

Exploitation does not, in Marxist theory and hence in much socialist ideology, derive from maldistribution but from the cultural materiality of property relations and the commodification of labor it makes possible. Marx's theory of exploitation is a cultural theory, a theory of valuation, the labor theory of value asserting a specific regime of temporality through which value is produced, expanded, and reproduced. Not only Marxists, but institutional theorists as well, have shown that property is not an objective material condition but a legal performative, a transrational substance known by how it is performed. Distributional conflicts drew their transformative possibilities from their origin in capitalism's contradictory logic of production. The institutional specificity of capitalism does not afford a culturally empty power contest between the dominant and the dominated but a struggle over commodification, over the production of capital. In Marxist theory, this is the source, the meaning, and the transformative end of distributional conflict.

In deculturalizing capitalism, making it about distribution, Fraser thereby empties working class interest of cultural meaning. Eyerman & Jamison (1991), for example, have shown the ways in which successful social movements—from environmentalism to socialism—create new public spaces in which new identities, new knowledges, and new organizational forms conjointly emerge. The socialist movement, not unlike the new social movements, sought to create a collective identity—the worker, the proletariat, a form of personhood that was sacralized, and whose value and inviolability were integral to mobilization. Socialist working class politics were premised on the assertion of an interested difference.

THE SOCIOLOGICAL FORCE OF LOVE: THE FAMILY POLITICS OF RELIGIOUS NATIONALISM

The historicist division between old, class-based materialist and new, identity-based cultural social movements cannot be sustained either theoretically or historically. Religious nationalism is both cultural and social. It is cultural in its

promotion of a particular cosmology, a codex of values, a program of comport-
ment, a way of life. But it is social in that its agents seek control over material
resources, the machinery of state, territory, reproductive bodies, the law courts and
the police, the schools. Religious nationalism is about both values and things, the
one through the other. It is about both recognition of a new collective subjectivity
and the redistribution of resources.

Religious nationalisms are animated by a family drama; they all center their
fierce energies on the family, its erotic energies, its gendered order. This is because
the institutional logic of religion centers on the order of creation, locating humanness in the cosmos, replicating cosmology through ritual, a practical metaphysics
that necessarily points before life and after death.[1]

Because the family is an order of creation, not merely an order of production
or governance (Foucault 1990), religions all seek to stitch its transitions, its relations, into religious rite and discourse, as a template through which their transrational order is given concrete form. Modern religion has ceded its territories, its
soldiers, its courts and sovereign powers; but everywhere it has held fiercely to
birth and burial, marriage and divorce. Religious nationalism, unlike the capitalist market or the democratic state, has the organization of sexuality at its center.
Religious nationalists give primacy to the family, not to democracy or the market,
as the social space through which society should be conceived and composed.
Familial discourse, with its particularistic and sexual logic of love and loyalty, is
pervasive.

Comparing the United States and Iran, Riesebrodt (1993) has argued that
the defense of the patriarchal family is the core of fundamentalism (see also
Apostolidis 2000). The American "fundamentalist" embrace of the family is a
post–World War II phenomenon. As Bendroth (1993, 1999) has shown, during
the nineteenth and early twentieth centuries concern with the family was at the
center of mainline Protestantism, a preoccupation that earlier Christian fundamentalists understood as feminized and sentimental. The fundamentalists then viewed
the veneration of the family as a diversion from the redemptive tasks at hand. It
was only with the rise of middle class divorce that defense of the family became
the central issue for the Christian right and the primal medium through which
they sought to reconstruct the social order. The polemical series that today constitutes American fundamentalist discourse is organized almost completely around
familial issues: divorce, birth control, abortion, feminism, homosexuality, and sex
education.

Algeria's Islamic Salvation Front, which won national elections in 1991 but was
prevented from taking power, has made the elimination of female employment part
of its program. Since it was banned, fundamentalists have murdered hundreds of
Algerian women for wearing Western clothes, for not wearing a headscarf, for

---

[1]Becker (1999) is quite right to reject Friedland & Alford's (1991) position that the institutional logic of religion, like science, is about truth.

working side by side with men. The Islamic Salvation Front promises to impose the death penalty on those who engage in sexual relations outside of marriage (Afary 1997).

The very first national religious mobilization of the Iranian Islamic forces took place in 1961 after Khomeini spoke at Qum on Ashura, the day of atonement, attacking the Shah for having transformed the legal status of women, allowing women into the army, the police, and the judiciary, giving them the vote, and over-riding Islamic law such that divorce required mutual consent (Lawrence 1998, Riesebrodt 1993). Iran's 1979 Islamic Revolution forbade co-education, closed down the childcare centers, and made the veil obligatory first in government offices and then in every public place. Women, of whatever age, had to obtain the permission of their fathers when they married for the first time (Nafisi 1999).

The Egyptian case suggests it was not the failures of secular nationalism that led to Islamic entry into the public sphere so much as the modern nationalists' commitments, incomplete as they were, to gender equality (Lawrence 1998). In 1952, Gamal Nasser, who had just come to power as a result of a coup by the Free Officers, vowed to mobilize women as full participants in the project to modernize the country. This decision led the Islamicists to break with him, eventuating in their repression. In 1954, Nasser supplanted the *shari'a* courts with a unitary secular state court, thereby expanding women's legal recourse, the immediate response to which was the first assassination attempt by the Muslim Brothers. Sadat's commitment to improving the legal, economic, and political status of women likewise galvanized massive Islamic opposition.

If one looks at the political programs of Islamic movements, there is no consistent economic policy nor form of government. The two pillars of contemporary Islamic politics involve, on the one side, a restrictive regulation of sexuality, eliminating it as a public presence and containing it within the family, and on the other side, the promotion of a welfare state that enables families to survive physically and to care for those—orphans and widows in particular as enjoined in the Qur'an—who cannot rely on families for support (Humphreys 1999). Although it might not be the kind we find compelling, Islamic politics is a politics of love.

Some analysts argue that religious regimes, like that of Iran or Pakistan, because they have failed to reduce unemployment or redistribute wealth, center their attention on familial relations, as though family politics were a substitute for, or sideshow from, the real business of state (Moghadam 1993). It is also tempting to interpret religious nationalism as sexist reaction, animated by interests in masculine privilege. In accounting for the rise of Islamic fundamentalism in North Africa, Mernissi (1992, 1987) has pointed to the rapidly increasing number of educated and employed women who not only compete with men for limited employment opportunities, but are able to choose when they will marry and to exert more influence within their families on account of the monies they bring home. For men, fundamentalism is then understood as a way to win back money and power; for potential rulers, to reduce unemployment. Reisebrodt (1993) interprets the emergence of fundamentalism in Iran and the United States as a defense of patriarchalism in a world where women have encroached steadily on male prerogatives, an encroachment whose weight falls forcefully on the father inside the family, particularly the sexual regulation of his daughters.

The evidence indicates, however, that women, too, find fundamentalism compelling. In the United States, for instance, both evangelicalism and fundamentalism draw disproportionately from women, not from men (Smith 1998). Women are attracted by the primacy that religious nationalists give to the family, its affirmation of male familial obligations as a religious duty, to the language of love. Although it is resolutely patriarchal, the religious nationalist community also offers a mechanism of social control of men, which becomes increasingly important as the eyes, the invitations, and the opprobrium that circulate in extended families and long-lived neighborhoods attenuate with geographic migration, the rising incidence of divorce, and the investment of social energy in friendship networks having nothing to do with kinship. Religious nationalists seek a return not to the pre-modern familial structure, with its extended networks of kin loyalties, but to the bourgeois nuclear family. As Abu-Lughod (1998) notes in the case of Egyptian Islamicists, it is their idealization of a nuclear family grounded in love, an imported Western middle class notion, which attracts so many Egyptian women to the movement. Women turn to fundamentalism in hopes of finding men who will be good fathers and good husbands, men who will provide for their families, remain with their wives, and contain their sexuality within the family (Enloe 1989, Ong 1990). In the United States, while fundamentalist Christians typically endorse the wife's submission to her husband, they also sacralize women's role as mothers who have the time to care for and the will to discipline their children, as well as the passion to keep their husbands. As Kintz (1997) discovered in her sojourn among America's fundamentalist women, the chance to occupy the sacred status of motherhood was, for many, a refuge from the uncertainty and constant threat of worthlessness they faced in the market. While men from the Christian right dominate the leadership of the anti-abortion movement in the United States, women have provided the bulk of its popular support. These women look to the movement as an integral part of their affirmation of a sexuality domesticated by monogamous marriage and gendered family roles (Luker 1984).

To make masculine interest the explanation of religious nationalism is to give primacy to an attribute of persons rather than the practices around which its discourse is organized or the institutional site in which it originates. Not only does it not distinguish religious nationalism from other social movements that are equally masculinist, it misses religious nationalism's distinct ontology of power, both its derivation of authority from divine sources and its constitution of society as a familial order. The elemental agents of religious nationalism are gendered and fleshy men and women, not the abstract individuals ordered through exchange and contract. Its space is the place of family, governed by relations of consubstantiality and caring, not the external, instrumental space of geopolitics, the public sphere, or the market. Religious nationalism is about home.

Religious nationalism thus has a kinship with socialism. Socialist politics were premised on the assertion of an interested difference, not just a redistribution of income, power, or respect. Marx theorized that difference as a contest between use value and exchange value, the former providing the cultural ground upon which resistance to the regime of the latter must proceed. Use value speaks of a specific institutional location; it refers to an individual's membership in human families, into which one is born and gives birth, has obligations not only to be fed but to feed and to care. While working class politics are typically fought on a distributional plane, as the share of wages versus the share of profits, they are animated by forces outside the economy.

The formation of the working class as a collective subject had to do not only with the extension of citizenship but with the defense of the family, not only with the demand for a "living wage," one that would support human life, but with protecting the family against capitalism, to put children—upon which the early stages of industrial capitalism massively depended, hence the fear of giving women the vote—outside the labor force, to protect the time upon which domesticity depended, to establish a wage upon which a family could survive not only when its members worked but when they no longer could. The assertion of human need, a term banished (as is power) both in the capitalist market and its theorization, is a familial discourse. The family's central institutional tendency involves the materiality of love, which, like property, is known by how it is practiced, by the conditions of access to fingers, nipples, milk, eggs and semen, mouths and eyes, beds and bowls of hot cereal, to the warmth and work of bodies.

There is then a way in which the institutional sources of religious nationalism parallel those of working class socialism, which had its own "fundamentalist" forms. Just as working class socialist politics can be understood as an effort to defend the family—its children, its time, its capacity to care—from the capitalist economy, so religious nationalists seek to defend the materiality of the family, not only its sexual codes but its capacity to cohere across time, from the logic of the capitalist market, which has commodified sexuality, transformed love into a consumption good, and made mothering materially impossible for an increasing proportion of women. By investing it with transcendent status, religious nationalists seek to restore the loving family, not the autonomous individual, as the elemental unit of which the social is composed. If socialism works the institutional logic of democracy and family against the capitalist market, religious nationalism constructs its oppositional cosmology from the codes of religion and family.

THE INSTITUTIONAL LOGIC OF COLLECTIVE REPRESENTATION

To interpret religious nationalism, we must specify the meaning of nationalism. Nationalism is a state-centered form of collective subject formation, a form of state representation, one grounding the identity and legitimacy of the state in a population of individuals who inhabit a territory bounded by that state. The cultural commonalities of that population do not, in themselves, constitute the basis for the formation of a nation. Nationality is a contingent and contested claim, not a social fact (Brubaker 2000, Smith 1991). Nationalism, the political processes organized through the state in the name of the nation, creates the nation, not the reverse (Calhoun 1998). Nationalism is a program for the co-constitution of the state and the territorially bounded population in whose name it speaks.

Nationalism is not ideology. It is a discursive practice by which the territorial identity of a state and the cultural identity of the people whose collective representation it claims are constituted as a singular institutional fact. The state is central in the process in that it is the direct relation between the state and individual through the organization of markets, armies, schools, and families that composes this national identity (Rokkan 1975). The abstract citizen is then a prerequisite to the formation of a culturally specific national subject. That abstract citizen is institutionally premised on an abstract collective subject, the nation-state, which relates as an equivalent "actor" to other states, relations organized through a variety of inter-state institutions (Giddens 1984).

Nationalism offers a form of representation—the joining of state, territoriality, and culture. It has nothing to say about the content of representation, the identity of that collective subject, or its values. Religion offers an institutionally specific way to organize this modern form of collective representation, how a collectivity represents itself to itself, the symbols, signs, and practices through which it is and knows itself to be. Religious nationalism is only a viable option when the collectivity has a religious basis in common. Thus, religious nationalism was possible in India, Israel, Iran, Turkey, and the United States, in part, because of the existence of a hegemonic religion—Hinduism, Judaism, Shiite Islam, Sunni Islam, and Protestantism, respectively. Religious nationalism has not developed very far in those countries, such as Iraq and Syria, which are divided between Shi'ite and Sunni branches of Islam. Where it does develop among nonhegemonic religious communities, it develops as a form of territorial separatism—the Sikhs in the Punjab, Tamils in Sri Lanka.

Religious nationalism does not change the form of collective representation, only its content, privileging a basis of identity and a criterion of judgment which cannot not be chosen. The religious criterion of judgment is, like human rights, racial purity, or technical rationality, beyond the reach of popular voice or the compelling interests of the state. Religion, with its universal claims, is not inherently inconsistent with nationalism; religious nationalism is not, as Lawrence (1998) argues, an oxymoron. Religious nationalists always center their energies on the nation-states in which they live. Even militant Islamicists, who have a historic transnational territorial ambit, indeed a universal ideal, and the actual tradition of the caliphate upon which to draw, almost all seek to create an Islamic order within the existent nation-states (Humphreys 1999). Extending the institutional logic of religion does not necessarily mean a reversal of the differentiation of religion and state, a theocratic installation. In his comparative analysis of Spain, the United States, Brazil, and Poland, Casanova (1994) has pointed out that the de-privatization of religion, its entry into civil society, does not imply a de-differentiation of religion and the state. Religious nationalism simply makes religion the basis for the nation's collective identity and the source of its ultimate values and purpose on this earth. Religious nationalism fills existent state forms with new cultural contents, new sources of authority; it does not displace them.

If nationalism does not provide a determinate basis of collective identity, neither do particular forms of religion provide a determinate basis of politics. Religious nationalism is a form of politicized religion, one in which religion is the basis of political judgment and identity, indeed in which politics take on the quality of a religious obligation. Religious nationalism is sometimes called "fundamentalist," an identification of which I have also made use above. The term refers back to those American Christians who proclaimed early in this century the inerrancy of the Biblical text, the "fundamentals." The term has now, of course, taken on general analytic significance. Martin Marty, for example, in his worldwide project to track the rise of "fundamentalism," identifies it with its absolutism and a Manichean world-view (Marty 1988). Arguing from early twentieth century American fundamentalism and the Iranian Shi'ite movement in Iran from 1961–1979, Riesebrodt argues that these fundamentalisms engage in a "traditionalistic literalism" in that they cleave to a mythical ideal order as identified in the sacred text or that they have "rationalistic, literalist-orthodox interpretations of religion" (1993:15–17, 31).

Religious nationalists all read religious texts politically. While it is decidedly textual, religious nationalism is not inherently more literalist in its application of its sacred texts, nor more absolutist in its ontologies and moral imperatives, that is, than its secular equivalents—socialism, democracy, nationalism, and modern science, to take four examples—each of which produce their own sacred texts, their own inviolable values. To speak of religion's entry into the public sphere simply as a form of "fundamentalism" is to deflect attention from the cultural specificity of its institutional commitments. In the American Protestant context, for example, Roof (1999) has recently studied the first post–World War II generation of Christians. He distinguishes between those who cleave to an evangelicalism oriented toward the spiritual needs of the self and those who are religiously drawn to fundamentalism with its paternal and monarchical sovereign God who sets down strict moral codes. While one might expect religious nationalists to derive overwhelmingly from the second as opposed to the first community, the Christian right, those who believe that America was founded as a Christian nation and should, by law, remain that way, draws from both evangelicals and traditionally pre-millenarian fundamentalists. A majority of both communities actively participate in conservative Christian politics (Roof 1999, Smith 1998).

Some analysts seek to distance religious nationalism from this vexed category of fundamentalism. Keddie has distinguished between two types of what she calls "new religious politics," one, the "fundamentalists," who seek to make the government conform to religious dictates and the other, which she terms "religious nationalism," which is targeted against some minoritarian religious group and has a communitarian and territorial logic at its core (1999). Keddie includes Gush Emunim and the Hindu nationalists, for example, in this second grouping. Keddie wants to distinguish the religious use of government authority from the religious control of territory. Keddie writes: "Religionationalist movements usually do not stress scripture or particular religious practices, while movements that want to increase religion in government do." This polarity will not hold. The territorial practices of religious Zionist Gush Emunim in Israel and the Hindu nationalist BJP and RSS in India are both understood and justified in terms of religious narratives (Friedland & Hecht 1998). Both make politicized use of ritual spaces and religious ritual practices as devices for mobilization. Every religious community, not just politicized ones, makes selective use of their textual tradition, tailor their interpretations to the tasks at hand. It is not possible to distinguish politicized religious movements from non-politicized ones based on the extent to which they follow the "fundamentals," themselves just a selective construction. The religious difference between attempts by Hindus or Jews to control particular pieces of contested territory and equivalent attempts by Muslims or American Christians, whom she includes in the fundamentalist category, to control the territories they already inhabit eludes me. Both of these "fundamentalists" seek to use state power to control elements of territorial choreography—work hours, cinema, food consumption, dress—basing their rights to do so in religious cosmology. Keddie's distinction is, I suspect, a crypto-Christian classification that makes individual orthopraxis the basis of a textually inspired politics and collective organization the basis of a territorially inspired politics.

RELIGIOUS NATIONALISM AS INSTITUTIONAL POLITICS

To understand religious nationalism we must begin not with groups but with an institutional architecture of the social, not with cultural, but with institutional, autonomy. An institutional approach not only necessarily creates an analytic space for the subject, it refuses the dualities of social theory. Modern society is composed of distinct, culturally laden institutional fields, each of which operates as if it were organized around transrational substances—power, love, faith, property, knowledge—ontologies whose reality is performed as much as revealed through routinized procedures enacted by culturally specific agents whose agency and interest are tied to those substances and the real relations which they make possible and which conjure them into existence.

Institutions are at once social and cultural. They are transrational ways of organizing bodies and objects in space and time (Friedland & Alford 1991). And they are themselves spaces and times, locations in which those bodies and objects carry particular meanings. Institutions form both values, in the sense of stakes, and the means by which such values are signified. Institutions constitute both ends and means. Ends are known, made accountable and actionable, through the techniques, the procedures, through which they are produced and distributed. One "makes" love through practices of kinship and its sensuous solidarities and exclusions; democracy through electoral practices, regular plebiscites understood as democratic practices; profit through monetized networks of exchange between holders of different properties, themselves known only through the rights regulating these exchanges. Love, democratic representation, and profit are ontological substances, constructed things, never truly had, but done.

The organizations of bodies and things in space and time become material signifiers for categories and values (see also Mohr & Duquenne 1997). This choreography of practice is not properly speaking a form of social signage. The material practices through which those categories and values, as well as the subjects they imply—voting, democracy and citizen, for example—are symbolizations, in that they have an inherent and nonarbitrary relation to the signified, democracy or representation in this case. Institutional analysis, with its profusion of performatives, requires us to move beyond the linguistic model in which the referent does not signify. Social practice is both referent and signifier; it is an ontological performance. Institutions have logics that must be made material in order to signify.

Moral cartography is produced by the distribution of material practices. Resources—guns or butter, bodies or things, territory or time—have little efficacy independent of the institutional codes that are a condition of their deployment. This is as true for the investment banker as it is for the mullah, each of whom must neutralize the efficacy of resources freighted with other institutional meanings. Things don't matter without meaning. And meanings—symbols and signs, narratives and metaphors—do not signify independently of their reference, and the history of that reference, in material practices. Institutional theory is not about the leftovers of rational action, the ways in which cultural conventions rush in where means-ends relations are opaque. Rather, institutional logics constitute the cosmology within which means are meaningful, where means-ends couplets make sense, are thought appropriate, and become the naturalized, unthought conditions of social action, performing the substance of the interests that are at stake within them. Resources are referents that signify; materiality is always meaningful.

If resources are bound to institutions, useful because meaningful, then interests in resources cannot be dissociated from the institutional conditions that establish their value. There is no political economy that is not simultaneously a cultural sociology, and vice versa. Every resource allocation is a process of signification, in which the categories, instruments, and agencies through which some object is produced or distributed are made real. Struggles over resources always contain the possibility of struggle over discourse/classification because they expand the materiality, the efficacy of those agents and languages that thereby organize those resources.

Religion, then, is not just a doctrine, a set of myths, a culture; it is an institutional space according to whose logic religious nationalists wish to remake the world. Religion is a network of sacred sites and ritual spaces, as well as community centers, associations, schools, hospitals, courts, and charities. In the face of failures, limits, and retrenchments of the welfare state, for instance, religious communities seek to fill the gap. Religious nationalist movements not only provide an alternative welfare-state to their members, its services are offered and consumed as a condition of and within a context of community, unlike the distant, bureaucratic, and often officious state. Islamic, Jewish, and Hindu nationalists all built their movements by offering things as simple as cooking oil and well-water, places to sleep and learn, as community acts of care, not the governmental management of a social problem. Religion offers a concrete cosmos within which an alternative vision of the social can be imagined and prefigured.

Religious nationalism grows out of modernity's institutional heterologies. Religious nationalism extends the institutional logic of religion into the domain of the democratic nation-state, deriving authority from an absolute divine writ, not the subjective aggregations of the demos; pushing toward redemption, not progress; locating agency in a disciplined self bound to God, not a sacralized, self-interested monad; constituting society not through the abstract, disembodied individual of the market but through the erotic and gendered flesh of the family. Religious nationalism posits an institutionally specific substance of the social, neither the procedures of reason nor the play of self-interest, but rather the communal solidarities of faith.

Religious nationalism can be understood as a heterologous project to promote a particular logic of collective representation. Institutional logic and collective representation are linked phenomena because groups form through particular institutional configurations and because institutions defend and extend themselves through group conflicts. Groups know themselves through their institutional projects, and through those projects they reshape the logic of collective representation, not just who is represented but the nature of the representation. Social movements are not just about inclusion and exclusion, domination and subordination, of social groups. The empirical question is the extent to which groups derive from and target particular institutional sites, and to which they draw on different institutional languages, and their success in making those particular languages primary. The invocation of a particular institutional logic is a political act, a performative claim that the institution to which it has most reference should have primacy, and hence that the groups/agents who politically intervene from it should have power.

RELIGIOUS NATIONALISM AND THE HOMOLOGOUS WORLDS OF PIERRE BOURDIEU

Religious nationalism requires a cultural sociological approach. In this and the following section, I examine the adequacy of Pierre Bourdieu's theory of the field and Jeffrey Alexander's theory of civil society, for the project of understanding contemporary religious nationalism.

Although I have been influenced by Pierre Bourdieu's insistence on the materiality and embodied quality of categorical knowledge, religious nationalism is difficult to apprehend within his habitus/field theory. Bourdieu conceives of society as a structure of domination, a structure for which one is prepared from birth through the inculcation of knowledges that are predominantly acquired not by design, but by living, a disciplining of the body through the choreography of life. Bourdieu calls this knowledge *habitus*, a knowledge that goes without saying because it came without saying. Habitus, the foundation stone of Bourdieu's theory, is an embodied categorical structure that simultaneously structures the object world and the subject's orientation within that world. One's position in the structure of domination is given by the resources to which one has access—money, power, cultural knowledge, technical expertise, social connections. Habitus translates this position into disposition. One knows one's place, one's chances, the moves and investments and their likely pay-offs.

Habitus is the tacit knowledge that is the condition of possibility of institutional life. Bourdieu looks upon institutional "fields" as relatively autonomous games, arenas each with its own gravitational logic, zones in which particular forms of capital have efficacy in the pursuit of that which is at stake in the game (Bourdieu & Wacquant 1992:97–101). Bourdieu derives the invariant laws of modernity's multiple fields from their homologous logics (Bourdieu & Wacquant 1992). Habitus binds unconsciously and efficiently because of the homologous distributions of resources across distinct institutional fields. Each field is polarized between those few who control its most important resources and those who have very few, if any, of those resources.

Homology, however, depends on a cultural homogenization. In Bourdieu's early work, every resource—economic, social, cultural, information—became another form of capital, every field another "market." Bourdieu economized all realms of social life in which one invests, develops credit, and reaps profits. Through the concept of several capitals, Bourdieu sought to convert Weber's distinct spheres of class, status, and power to a common conceptual metric. Thus, for example, the contest over control of legitimate violence—Weber's criterion for state power—became the "struggle to accumulate symbolic capital" (Bourdieu 1977:41, 60–61), that is, the capacity to impose one's categorical order on the social world, a monopoly on the violence of legitimation. More recently, Bourdieu has become indifferent in using the term power or capital (Bourdieu & Wacquant 1992:97).

Although Bourdieu has alerted us to the dangers of reproducing *doxa* by relying on folk categories in the construction of our theoretical objects, he himself imports the dominant fields—capitalism and the bureaucratic state—into the analytic categories—capital and power—by which we understand all fields. Bourdieu thus reproduces the dominance of the dominant institutions. To homologize institutionally, Bourdieu reduces all field relations to the power binary of dominant and dominated. It is only because Bourdieu has homogenized the principle of practice across fields—the binary of domination—that he can so easily homologize groups across fields (Bourdieu 1990). The several capitals are ultimately convertible in the "division in the labor of domination" (Bourdieu 1996, Bourdieu & Wacquant 1992). Accumulation of capital is a trans-historical mode of reproducing domination within a field, this "will to power" being the cultural content of interest within every field. The "field of power" is the "gaming space" in which holders of these diverse forms of power, the dominant groups within each field, struggle over which will be the dominant form of power, the exchange rate between them, and hence the "dominant principle of domination" (Bourdieu 1996). By making economic practice a trans-institutional instrument in the service of domination, Bourdieu makes the social into a general political economy, a significant theoretical achievement, but he thereby undercuts the transformative possibilities inherent in classificatory systems, both in their singularity and their plurality. The cultural constitution of groups is derived from this political economy, the stakes of the game are homogenized, and the group structure is homologized.

Religious nationalism is a break in modern *doxa*, our common sense of things, a failure in the modern state's capacity to produce a habitus that makes submission not into choice, but common sense, a natural attitude. Bourdieu writes that it is the modern state:

> ... which possesses the means of imposition and inculcation of the durable principles of vision and division that conform to its own structure, is the site par excellence of the concentration of symbolic power. (1998:47)

Because he locates the origin of the dominant vision in the political victories of dominant groups, whose domination rests on their constitution of the state, the modern state becomes an instrument for the institution of categorical knowledge, a monopoly medium for universalizing and naturalizing knowledge, a cognitive machine that plays a particular role in the "division of labor of domination" (Bourdieu 1998:58). Here, the substantive content of the universal is not of sociological import.

Bourdieu's theoretical apparatus does apply to religious nationalism in that it is a classification struggle over the dominant principle of domination, a struggle animated by a principle which could be defined by its distance from that of the liberal capitalist state. Religious nationalism, like the modern state itself, originates as a symbolic disordering out of the interested plays of agents who are particularly positioned. The position of religious agents is important in explaining the rise of religious nationalism. Specifically, religion's institutional autonomy from the state is a critical variable in accounting for the ability of its agents to promote their state vision. Religious nationalism developed earliest in those places where religion was not controlled by the state: in Iran, where the Sh'ite clergy, with their tradition of the *imam*, a non-political religious authority, had been able to maintain their autonomy from the Shahs; in Israel, where the rabbinate, although partially incorporated within the state was not subordinate to it; in the United States where the state was constitutionally prevented from controlling the religious domain; and in India where the state did not regulate Hindu religious institutions. Religious nationalism has not developed in those countries where religion is not allowed an independent institutional space such as China, Japan, and Korea, all places where the state actually controls religious finances and appointments (Rudolph 1997a).

However, even states that have sought to control religious institutions have not necessarily been able to prevent the politicization of religion as the cases of Turkey, Algeria, and Egypt all make clear (Humphreys 1999).

One could also point to the distinctive social composition of religious nationalism's carriers—its urban support, and specifically the way clerics marginalized by the modernized institutes of religious training often play such a critical role, making religious nationalism into a medium for distributional struggles for those lacking in symbolic capital or political power (Arjomand 1995, Riesebrodt 1993). Religious nationalism draws overwhelmingly from the middle class, precisely that class to which political sociologists have always looked as a bastion of support for democracy. However, there is no consistent pattern of support within that vast and variegated urban middle class. The adherents of religious nationalism come from declining sectors like the bazaar merchants, as well as from rising sectors like the professionals and state bureaucrats (Lawrence 1998, Riesebrodt 1993, Humphreys 1992). In the United States, the Christian right, those who believe that America was founded as a Christian nation and should, by law, remain that way, draws from both evangelicals and traditionally premillenarian fundamentalists. A majority of both communities actively participate in conservative Christian politics. American evangelicals and fundamentalists are smack dab in the middle class, less likely to be poor than the nonreligious (Hunter 1987, Roof 1999, Smith 1998). Indeed, a majority of the Christian right base communities report that their economic situation has improved over the last decade (Smith 1998).

Islamic radicalism likewise appeals to the urban middle class, not to the poor, the working class, or the rural peasantry. However, this still leaves a lot of social space and there is no consistent pattern across the cases. In Pakistan, it appeals to state employees and not to urban, under-employed young professionals. In Egypt and Tunisia, in contrast, it appeals predominantly to upwardly mobile middle classes, particularly the professionals. In Syria the merchants and landlords are key (Lawrence 1998). The only thing these disparate groups have in common is that they can read, which is no small thing.

Religious nationalism represents the return to text, to the fixity of signs, the renarrativization of the nation in a cosmic context. It returns us to bodies and souls, a zone to be defended against things on the one side and beasts on the other. Religious nationalism is literally about reading, the collective plumbing of a text for its timeless truths, as a basis for the narration of contemporary history. Islamic fundamentalists look to the Quranic history of the community founded by Prophet Muhammad in the seventh century as a template by which to gauge and goad the present order. Their Jewish counterparts locate their foundation and telos in the ancient Temple-centered kingdom that was the culmination of God's territorial promise to Abraham, Moses, and David documented in the Torah. Christian fundamentalists read the prophetic books of the Bible as a road-map by which they interpret contemporary social realities. Hindu nationalists derive their reading of the Indian state from the Hindi Ramayana, a narration of the foundational kingship of Ram, the avatar of Vishnu.

Religious nationalists read these books and commentaries on them together. This collective reading is the core of their *communitas*. The middle class is a class of the word. It owes its life, its earnings, to its ability to read books, to words and numbers that have a clear meaning and a certain use. That those who live off the book should seek to live by the book as a foundation for a new social trust, is, as Bourdieu might say, part of the middle class *habitus*, an unconscious disposition, an autonomic routine. In the Islamic world, the newly educated youth read and discuss a popular Islamic literature written in colloquial Arabic rather than the classical Arabic of the traditional scholarly Islamic elites. Protestant evangelicals and fundamentalists understand how God wants them to live by their reading of the Bible, not by what the Church teaches them (Smith 1998). Latin American Catholicism moved into Liberation Theory, not only because of the message of social justice contained in Vatican Council II, but also because of the post-WWII translation of the liturgy into local languages and the encouragement of lay Bible reading (Levine & Stoll 1997). In a pattern that replicates Protestantism's birth process, this collective interpretation of words by the people themselves feeds a diffuse associational network, a popular religious civil society, that is very difficult for the state or organized religious hierarchies to control (Rudolph 1997b).

While Bourdieu's schema captures part of its process, it misses the institutional substances at stake that make those struggles possible. Religious nationalism does not derive from the dominated groups within the dominant institutions—capitalism and state, but from an alternative institutional space altogether. By stripping means of their institutional meaning, by homogenizing the logic of practice as a generalized political economy, Bourdieu eliminates the institutional zones upon which alternative projects can be mounted. It is institutional heterology, not conflicts over the distributions of several capitals so central in Bourdieu's theory, nor an unspeakable outside as in some poststructuralist accounts, that is the critical source of human freedom.

RELIGIOUS NATIONALISM AND THE CIVIL CENTER

If religious nationalism is difficult to theorize within Pierre Bourdieu's culturally homogenous instrumentalized world, it is no less easy within the sacralized, normative world of Jeffrey Alexander. If that of Bourdieu is animated by instrumental, misrecognized struggles for power and capital mediated through the state, in Alexander, these struggles are not only refracted but constituted through the democratic culture of civil society, powered by struggles over membership and recognition. If the meaning of Bourdieu's universal is reduced to the bleak binary logic of domination, categories driven by distribution, in Alexander, its meanings are polysemous and efflorescent, moral dualities charged with sacrality (Alexander 1995).

Alexander, who pioneered the cultural sociological agenda and whose insistence on cultural constitution I share, locates the cultural in a specific institutional field—civil society, a sphere separated from both the economy and the state, as well as from religion, family, science, and primordial communities. Civil society is roughly equivalent to the public sphere, a zone where individual rights are protected, political participation organized, and societal membership defined. He writes:

> Such an independent civil sphere can exist only insofar as the privacy of individual interaction is protected, institutional independence is guaranteed for the creation of law and public opinion, and normative symbolic patterns make honesty, rationality, individual autonomy, cooperation and impersonal trust the basic criteria for membership in the binding community that defines 'society'. (Alexander 1996:225)

In contrast to Bourdieu's "field of power" as modern society's institutional center, Alexander accords this role to civil society, the source of the symbols out of which we define our collective identity and its terms of membership. Alexander derives the possibility of modern social movements from "an imagined community" whose content derives from this civil society's codes—honesty, rationality, individual autonomy, cooperation, and impersonal trust. It is these codes, this culture, of civil society that defines the "criteria for membership in the binding community that defines 'society.'"

Civil society, and civil society alone, provides the platform for collective and individual agency. Alexander writes:

> ... the most significant idioms, codes and narratives employed by strong social movements, new and old, positive and negative, are independent of their structural position in particular spheres. Indeed, when one examines these tropes, one can plainly see that it is their very distance from particular institutional arenas that allows them to offer social movements leverage, that creates the possibility of an escape from immediate institutional demands, that encourages the very exercise of agency vis a vis institutional constraints that the very existence of a social movement implies. (1996:226)

Social movements pose their demands, derive their possibility from, and depend for their success upon the "utopian notion of community" immanent in civil society, "according to which rational actors spontaneously forge ties that are at once self-regulating, solidaristic, and emancipatory, which are independent of market rewards, religious faith, family love, state coercion and scientific truth" (1996:227, 229). Agency depends on difference from every other institutional domain.

Alexander makes civil society, which he equates with the universalistic rights of democracy—not science, religion, economy, or family—into culture's central domain, the sacred's modern locus. Here Alexander follows Talcott Parsons' notion of "societal community," a zone of universalistic solidarity through which the social system is integrated (Mouzelis 1999). To equate society with its universalistic, rational civil zone deprives us of the absolute unreason, the erotic, ecstatic, kinetic "effervescence" of the social upon which Emile Durkheim insisted, an unreason taken up in the 1930s by the College de Sociologie. Alexander also, by fiat, negates the Marxist civil society tradition that understood civil society as a bourgeois order standing outside the state. If Bourdieu capitalizes the social, eliminating by concept the contradiction between institutional spheres, Alexander hives off the capitalist economy altogether, reducing the place modern society is defined to the public sphere and the content of its identity to democracy's moral codes. Alexander's civil society is suffused with political substance, but devoid of economic content, even though our categories of the person and his rights are historically suffused with property and its exchange. Alexander is, of course, correct to argue that democratic civil society is the most important medium through which groups reach for power not only within the polity, but within other particular institutional spheres. That, however, does not exhaust the sociological significance of many social movements, nor is the civil society the only site through which society is imagined, its values redistributed and/or reconstituted. While civil society may be a critical locus of will formation, it is not the only source of its content. Alexander mistakes a medium of political participation for the meaning of membership. And he reduces the meaning of political participation to membership in the demos, social movements being understood as media for groups carrying particular "social problems" into the public arena. T. H. Marshall has been mated with Emile Durkheim.

The problem was not that Parsons concretely conflated the cultural and the social, as a problem of observability, but that he analytically separated them, failing to articulate the cultural mediations by which production and distribution were systematically linked, and that he assumes a unitary cultural order, not just in the sense that differently positioned individuals have different interests in that order, [the dominant distributional critique of Parsons (Alexander & Colomy 1990)], but that different institutions, more than serving different systemic functions, produce and distribute different potentially contradictory values.

Alexander has relocated the sacred to the public sphere, distilled its ideal voice, the tropes of reasoned consensus. But each institutional sphere has its own sacrality, a capacity to organize social life and the collectivity in its own language, linked to its own techniques of production and distribution. Each provides its own distinctive collective imaginary, its own universals which movements and organizations try to socially concretize. Democracy's institutional distinctiveness lies not in its universality, but in the sacrality with which it invests the person, the primacy it accords the individual's voice. Capitalist markets, bureaucratic states, domestic families, scientific fields, religion—each generates a heterologous language, each produces and distributes specific values—money, rationality, love, truth, faith. While there are symmetries and interdependencies between institutional codes, there are also critical gaps and contradictions, incommensurabilities that provide politics' passionate energies, that afford the space for social movements like those of socialist workers, ecologists, feminists, or religious nationalists. It is these contradictions— not, as Alexander insists, the gap between value and norm that Talcott Parsons left unproblematic between the cultural and the social—that are also critical in making space for agency. It is the contradiction between democracy and society's two dominant institutions—capitalism and the state—that gives civil society much of its energizing power, and that between religion and the capitalist state that makes religious nationalism possible and provides its hermeneutic codes.

Alexander assumes what needs to be treated as historically variable, that successful social movements must convert their claims into the democratic language of civil society. Religious nationalisms are strong social movements, yet they violate civil society's codes, counterposing transrational belief to rationality, the communal solidarities of faith to impersonal trust, the revealed text to a compact founded on reasoned consent, involuntary subordination to divine dictates as opposed to individual autonomy. Religious nationalism, like socialism, indicates not only that civil society's moral codes need not have primacy in the formation of successful social movements, but that democracy cannot easily manage the heterologous logics of rationality, scientific truth, allocative efficiency, familial need, or religious faith.

CONCLUSION

Religious nationalism challenges the sociological imagination. It requires that we think anew. It forces us to rethink the duality of social and cultural, to move away from the group as the elemental constituent of social organization, to recognize the heterology of institutions as the basis of politics and collective agency, and through the institution to make the cultural content of power part of our understanding of the politics of culture.

ACKNOWLEDGMENTS

I would like to thank an anonymous reviewer for his comments and Karen Cook for her editorial suggestions.

Visit the Annual Reviews home page at www.AnnualReviews.org

LITERATURE CITED

Abu-Lughod L. 1998. The marriage of Islamism and feminism in Egypt: selective repudiation as a dynamic of postcolonial cultural politics. In *Remaking Women: Feminism and Modernity in the Middle East*, ed. L Abu-Lughod. Princeton, NJ: Princeton Univ. Press

Afary J. 1997. The war against feminism in the name of the Almighty: making sense of gender and Muslim fundamentalism. *New Left Rev.* 224:89–110

Alexander J. 1998. *Neo-Functionalism and After*. Oxford, UK: Blackwell

Alexander J. 1995. The reality of reduction: the failed synthesis of Pierre Bourdieu. In *Fin de Siecle Social Theory: Relativism, Reduction, and the Problem of Reason*, ed. J. Alexander, pp. 128–217. London: Verso

Alexander J. 1996. Collective action, culture and civil society: secularizing, updating, inverting, revising and displacing the classical model of social movements. In *Alain Touraine*, ed. M Blane, J Clark. Falmer, UK: Falmer

Alexander J, Colomy P. 1990. *Differentiation Theory and Social Change*. New York: Columbia Univ. Press

Alexander J, Smith P. 1993. The discourse of civil society: a new proposal for cultural studies. *Theory and Society*, 22(2):151–207

Apostolidis P. 2000. *Stations of the Cross: Adorno and Christian Right Radio*. Durham: Duke Univ. Press

Arjomand S. 1995. Unity and diversity in Islamic fundamentalism. In *Fundamentalisms Comprehended*, ed. ME Marty, RS Appleby, pp. 179– 98. Chicago: Univ. Chicago Press

Barber BR. 1992. Jihad vs. McWorld. *Atl. Mon.* Mar:25–33, 30

Becker P. 1999. *Congregations in Conflict: Cultural Models of Local Religious Life*. Cambridge: Cambridge Univ. Press

Bendix R. 1978. *Kings or People: Power and the Mandate to Rule*. Berkeley: Univ. Calif. Press

Bendroth ML. 1993. *Fundamentalism and Gender, 1875 to the Present*. New Haven: Yale Univ. Press

Bendroth ML. 1999. Fundamentalism and the family: gender, culture, and the American pro-family movement. *J. Women's Hist*, 10(4):35–53

Bonnell VA, Hunt L. 1999. Introduction. In *Beyond the Cultural Turn*, ed. VA Bonnell, L Hunt, pp. 1–32. Berkeley: Univ. Calif. Press

Bourdieu P. 1977 [1972]. *Outline of a Theory of Practice*, (transl. R Nice), Cambridge, UK: Cambridge Univ. Press

Bourdieu P. 1990. *The Logic of Practice*. (transl. R Nice). Stanford, CA: Stanford Univ. Press

Bourdieu P. 1996. *The State Nobility*. Stanford, CA: Stanford Univ. Press

Bourdieu P. 1998. *Practical Reason: On the theory of Action*. Stanford, CA: Stanford Univ. Press

Bourdieu P, Wacquant LJD. 1992. *An Invitation to Reflexive Sociology*. Chicago: Univ. Chicago Press

Brubaker R. 2000. Myths and misconceptions in the study of nationalism. In *Ernest Gellner and the Theory of Nationalism*, ed. J Hall. Cambridge: Cambridge Univ. In press

Calhoun C. 1998. *Nationalism*. Minneapolis: Univ. Minn. Press

Casanova J. 1994. *Public Religions in the Modern World*. Chicago: Univ. Chicago Press

Chidester D. 1996. *Savage Systems: Colonialism and Comparative Religion in Southern Africa*. Charlottesville/London: Univ. Press Virginia

Derrida J. 1998. Faith and knowledge: the two sources of 'religion' at the limits of reason alone. In *Religion: Cultural Memory in the Present*, ed. J Derrida, G Vattimo, pp. 1–78. Stanford, CA: Stanford Univ. Press

Durkheim E. 1995 [1912]. *The Elementary Forms of Religious Life*. (Transl. KE Fields) New York: Free Press

Enloe C. 1989. *Making Feminist Sense of International Politics: Bananas, Beaches, and Bases*. Berkeley: Univ. Calif. Press.

Eyerman R, Jamison A. 1991. *Social Movements: A Cognitive Approach*. University Park: Penn. State Univ. Press

Foran J. 1993. *Fragile Resistance: Social Transformation in Iran from 1500 to the Revolution*. Boulder, CO: Westview

Foran J. 1992. A theory of third world social revolutions: Iran, Nicaragua, and El Salvador compared. *Crit. Sociol.* 19(2):3–27

Foran J. 1997a. The future of revolutions at the fin-de-siècle. *Third World Q*. 18(5):791–820 London/New York: Routledge

Foran J. 1997b. The comparative-historical sociology of third world social revolutions: why a few succeed, why most fail. In *Theorizing Revolutions*, ed. J. Foran, pp. 227–67. London/New York: Routledge

Foucault M. 1990. *The Use of Pleasure*, Vol. 2. *The History of Sexuality*. New York: Vintage

Fraser N. 2001. Social justice in the age of identity politics: redistribution, recognition, and participation. In *The Cultural Turn*, ed. R Friedland, J Mohr. Cambridge, UK: Cambridge Univ. Press. In press

Friedland R, Alford R. 1991. Bringing society

back in: symbols, practices, and institutional contradictions. In *Institutionalism in Organization Analysis*, ed. W Powell, P DiMaggio, pp. 232–63. Chicago: Univ. Chicago Press

Friedland R, Hecht R. 1998. The bodies of nations: a comparative study of religious violence in Jerusalem and Ayodhya. *History of Religions*, 38(2):101–49

Friedland R, Hecht R. 2000. *To Rule Jerusalem.* Berkeley: Univ. Calif. Press

Giddens A. 1984. *The Nation-State and Violence.* Berkeley: Univ. Calif. Press

Harrison P. 1998. *The Bible, Protestantism and the Rise of Natural Science.* Cambridge, UK: Cambridge Univ. Press

Heimert A. 1966. *Religion and the American Mind.* Cambridge, MA: Harvard Univ. Press

Humphreys RS. 1982. The contemporary resurgence in the context of modern Islam. In *Islamic Resurgence in the Arab World*, ed. AEH Dessouki, pp. 67–83. New York: Praeger

Humphreys RS. 1999. *Between Memory and Desire.* Berkeley: Univ. Calif. Press

Hunter JD. 1987. *Evangelicalism: The Coming Generation.* Chicago: Univ. Chicago Press

Juergensmeyer M. 1993. *The New Cold War?: Religious Nationalism Confronts the Secular State.* Berkeley: Univ. Calif. Press

Juergensmeyer M. 1999. *Terror in the Mind of God: The Global Rise of Religious Violence.* Berkeley: Univ. Calif. Press

Kane A. 1991. Cultural analysis in historical sociology: the analytic and concrete forms of the autonomy of culture. *Sociol. Theory* 9(1):53–69

Kant I. 1996. An answer to the question: what is enlightenment? *What is Enlightenment: Eighteenth-Century Answers and Twentieth-Century Questions*, ed. J Schmidt, pp. 58–64. Berkeley: Univ. Calif. Press

Keddie NR. 1999. The new religious politics and women worldwide: a comparative study. *J. Women's Hist.* 10(4):11–33

Kintz L. 1997. *Between Jesus and the Market: The Emotions That Matter in Right-Wing America.* Durham, NC: Duke Univ. Press

Lawrence B. 1998. *Shattering the Myth: Islam*

Beyond Violence. Princeton, NJ: Princeton Univ. Press

Levine D, Stoll D. 1997. Bridging the gap between empowerment and power in Latin America, pp. 63–103. In *Transnational Religion and Fading States*, ed. SH Rudolph, J Piscatori. Boulder, CO: Westview

Luker K. 1984. *Abortion and the Politics of Motherhood.* Berkeley: Univ. Calif. Press

Marty M. 1988. Fundamentalism as a social phenomenon. *Bull. Am. Acad. Arts Sci.* 42(2):15–29

McLoughlin WG. 1978. *Revivals, Awakening, and Reform: An Essay on Religion and Social Change in America, 1607–1977.* Chicago: Univ. Chicago Press

McMahon DM. 2001. *Enemies of Enlightenment: The French Counter-Enlightenment and the Making of Modernity, 1778–1830.* New York: Oxford Univ. Press

Mernissi F. 1987. *Beyond the Veil: Male-Female Dynamics in Modern Muslim Society.* Bloomington: Indiana Univ. Press

Mernissi F. 1993. *Islam and Democracy: Fear of the Modern World.* Reading, MA: Addison-Wesley

Moghadam VM. 1993. *Modernizing Women: Gender and Social Change in the Middle East.* Boulder, CO: Westview

Mohr J, Duquenne V. 1997. The duality of culture and practice: poverty relief in New York City, 1888–1917. *Theory Soc.* 26:305–56

Mouzelis N. 1999. Post-Parsonian theory. *Sociol. Forum* 14(4):721–33

Nafisi A. 1999. The "veiled threat" *New Republic.* Feb. 22, 1999

Ong A. 1990. State vs. Islam: Malay families, women's bodies, and the body politic in Malaysia. *Am. Ethnol.* 17(2):250–76

Riesebrodt M. 1993. *Pious Passion: The Emergence of Modern Fundamentalism in the United States and Iran.* (transl. Don Reneau) Berkeley: Univ. Calif. Press

Riesebrodt M. 2000. Religion in global perspective. In *Global Religions: A Handbook*, ed. Mark Juergensmeyer. Oxford/New York: Oxford Univ. Press. In press

Rokkan S. 1975. Dimensions of state formation

and nation building: a possible paradigm for research in variations within Europe. In *The Formation of National States in Western Europe*, ed. C Tilly, pp. 562–600. Princeton, NJ: Princeton Univ. Press

Roof WC. 1999. *Spiritual Marketplace: Baby Boomers and the Remaking of American Religion*. Princeton, NJ: Princeton Univ. Press

Rudolph SH. 1997a. Dehomogenizing religious formations. pp. 243–263. In *Transnational Religion and Fading States*, ed. SH Rudolph, J Piscatori. Boulder, CO: Westview

Rudolph SH. 1997b. Introduction: religion, states, and transnational civil society. In *Transnational Religion and Fading States*, ed. SH Rudolph, J Piscatori, pp. 1–24. Boulder, CO: Westview

Smith A. 1991. *National Identity*. London: Penguin

Smith C. 1998. *American Evangelicalism Embattled and Thriving*. Chicago: Univ. Chicago Press

Tilly C. 1998. Social movements and (all sorts of) other political interactions—local, national, and international—including identities: Several divagations from a common path, beginning with British Struggles over Catholic Emancipation, 1780-1829, and ending with contemporary nationalism, *Theory Soc.* 27:453–80

Walzer M. 1965. *The Revolution of the Saints*. Cambridge, MA: Harvard Univ. Press

Weiss J. 1999. Dell'identita nazionale all'identita europea. Dal nazionalismo all'eurocentrismo. In *Proc. Identita Nazionali e Leadership in Europa*, Facolta di Scienze Politche. Rome: Univ. Rome, "La Sapienza"

Annu. Rev. Sociol. 2001. 27:153–85

SOCIOECONOMIC STATUS AND CLASS IN STUDIES OF FERTILITY AND HEALTH IN DEVELOPING COUNTRIES

Kenneth A. Bollen[1], Jennifer L. Glanville[2], and Guy Stecklov[3]

[1]Department of Sociology, University of North Carolina, Chapel Hill, North Carolina 27599-3210; e-mail: bollen@unc.edu
[2]Department of Sociology, University of Iowa, Iowa City, Iowa 52242-1401; e-mail: j_glanville@unc.edu
[3]Department of Sociology, Mount Scopus Campus, Hebrew University, Jerusalem 91905, Israel; e-mail: stecklov@mscc.huji.ac.il

Key Words measurement of socioeconomic status, dimensions of socioeconomic status, socioeconomic status and demography, socioeconomic status and population studies, permanent income, class, fertility, health

■ **Abstract** The concepts of socioeconomic status (SES) and class are pervasive in sociological studies, yet an examination of the sociological and social science literature suggests a lack of consensus on their conceptual meaning and measurement. Our review focuses on the use of SES and class in a specific substantive field, studies of child health and fertility in developing countries. We discuss the mechanisms that underlie the relationship between SES and fertility and child health and the divergent results found in this field. We then provide a brief review of the theoretical literature on SES and class, contrasting unitary and component views. Following this is a section on the use of SES and class in empirical studies of child health and fertility in developing countries. We investigate the relationship between the conceptual and empirical literature, highlighting the inconsistencies we find. In addition, we discuss the variety of meanings and measures of SES that researchers use in these studies. Next, we address a series of methodological issues that arise from the review. Finally, we make recommendations for the treatment of SES and class in these and related areas.

INTRODUCTION

Few concepts are as central to sociology as those of socioeconomic status (SES) and class. Whether in theories of the class structures conducive to democratic development at the macro level (e.g., Therborn 1977) or micro studies of social capital (e.g., Parcel & Menaghan 1994) or depression (e.g., Link et al 1993), SES or class is sure to play a key role in the analysis. Given the saliency of the concepts and the intensity of their examination over time, we might expect that a consensus has formed around their conceptual meaning and optimal operationalizations. Yet an examination of the sociological and social science literature suggests otherwise and the need to investigate their usage. Essentially, everyone knows that SES matters, but we do not know how it matters.

The literature employing class or SES measures is vast, and an attempt at reviewing all such works is futile. However, an examination of SES and class in a specific substantive area is both feasible and desirable, in that it grounds the research in a concrete problem rather than trying to generalize to numerous, quite different areas. At the same time, some of the findings about the typical ways that SES and class are defined, their measures, and their use represent practices that extend far beyond the specific substantive area. So in addition to providing information on the use of SES and class in a specific field, the review holds lessons for researchers who apply these concepts in other areas. With this in mind, our review concentrates on the use of SES and class in studies of child health and fertility in developing countries. These topics are key in sociology, public health, demography, economics, and related social science disciplines. Our choice of outcomes has the advantage not only of enabling us to understand how sociologists are using SES and class, but also of revealing the practices in neighboring disciplines that share our interests and both influence and are influenced by the use of these concepts in sociology.

More generally, measures of SES and class vary widely within and between disciplines regardless of the outcome. This is problematic for a number of reasons. First, it leads to ambiguity in interpreting model results. For instance, it is often difficult to determine whether SES or class operates as a unitary or a multidimensional construct. Moreover, we do not know if different conclusions would be drawn if different measures were employed. Second, a series of methodological problems emerge. Imperfect measurement of SES or class can bias coefficients for the SES variables as well as all other explanatory variables. This is true regardless of whether SES is used as a central or a control variable. These problems are exacerbated because we have little guidance on how to treat SES in empirical work. In fact, empirical implementations of SES and class are often driven by data availability and the empirical performance of indicators as much as they are by theoretical groundwork.

Our review of the literature seeks to shed light on current practices on several levels: Is SES unidimensional or multidimensional conceptually? If SES consists of components, then what are the key components? How often is the conceptual meaning of SES/class missing from or mismatched with the empirical implementation? Our approach differs from other recent reviews of the literature that have highlighted the tremendous diversity in the reported role and effect of SES variables in demographic and health studies and sought to explain the variation in findings (Behrman & Deolalikar 1988, Strauss & Thomas 1995, Strauss & Thomas 1998). In contrast we review the theoretical origins of SES and class, discuss their dimensionality and measurement, highlight the gap between theory and practice, and pay particular attention to the methodological issues that surround these approaches.

The paper is organized as follows. We first highlight key theoretical mechanisms and discrepancies in findings in research on the relationship between SES and child health and fertility. The next section provides a brief conceptual review of SES and class. We then turn to a review of how SES and class are conceptualized and measured in empirical studies of child health and fertility in developing countries. As part of this review, we examine the relationship between the conceptual and empirical literature, highlighting the inconsistencies we find. Following this is a section on methodological issues that arise in the use of SES and class. We conclude with recommendations for the treatment of SES in these and related areas.

CLASS AND SES EFFECTS: MECHANISMS AND DIVERGENT RESULTS

Studies of child health and fertility have benefited from conceptual frameworks that propose that all influences on these outcomes must operate through a set of intermediate or proximate determinants.[1] Exposure and susceptibility to disease are examples of two proximate determinants that affect a child's health (see Mosley & Chen 1984). The proximate determinants of fertility include factors such as age at marriage, contraceptive use, involuntary infecundity, and postpartum amenorrhea—factors that directly determine exposure to intercourse, conception, or gestation (Davis & Blake 1956, Bongaarts & Potter 1983). The only ways in which SES or class can influence child health or fertility are through their impact on these mediating variables. For instance, a child coming from a low-SES household may be more exposed to disease due to cramped housing conditions and poor sanitation than one from a higher-SES household; this in turn will create an inverse relation between SES and child health. Of course, SES and class may have contradictory effects on the proximate determinants. For example, we often find that more educated women tend to cease exclusive breastfeeding sooner than less educated women—a factor that contributes to higher fertility levels. However, more educated women are also more likely to use contraception and delay marriage—two factors that contribute to lower fertility and tend to overshadow the effects of reduced breastfeeding.

There are two common approaches to modeling SES effects on child health and fertility. One is to not include any of the proximate determinants—limiting the researcher to an analysis of exogenous total effects of the SES and class variables. A more demanding approach attempts to include the proximate determinants in

---

[1]The household production function approach in economics is closely related to the proximate determinants framework (Strauss & Thomas 1995).

order to estimate the mechanisms by which exogenous variables work through the proximate determinants. However, difficulties in measuring proximate determinants of child health and fertility typically prevent their inclusion. In fact, if all the proximate determinants are accurately measured and included in the model, the coefficients of the SES variables should be within sampling fluctuations of zero. But in practice the omission of the proximate determinants means that SES or class variables might well have nonzero coefficients. These coefficients represent indirect effects through omitted intermediate variables. Thus, when we interpret SES or class variable effects in empirical models, we must remember that any effects they have operate through one or more proximate determinants.

Despite some underlying agreement about the basic models for analysis of child health and fertility, there is growing disagreement about the estimated impact of SES or class. For example, in an influential study of mortality decline in Nigeria, Caldwell (1979) finds that lack of maternal education is a powerful predictor of child mortality and that its effect remains after controlling for occupational status and place of residence. In a comparative study, Cleland & Rodriguez (1988) use World Fertility Survey data from 38 countries and find that increased female education has an important negative effect on marital fertility rates after controlling for other household socioeconomic factors. Yet, as Strauss & Thomas (1995) and Schultz (1997) note, more recent studies reveal less consistency regarding SES or class effect on child health and fertility. In their analysis of household survey data from 17 developing countries, Bicego & Boerma (1993) find that the children of more educated mothers experience higher survival rates during the first two years of life. However, they note that the significance of the maternal education effect disappeared in all but 5 of the 17 countries once a coarse measure of household economic status was controlled. Similarly, Desai & Alva (1998) analyze household-level survey data from 22 developing countries and find that part of the effect on child health previously attributed to maternal education may be due to inadequate controls for other SES factors as well as correlations of households within sampling clusters.

Similar discrepancies appear in the estimated effects of income. Casterline et al (1989) observe that income, measured as income from all sources, influences child but not infant mortality in Egypt. This study also controls for education, occupation, and place of residence. Similarly, in their analysis of famine mortality in Bangladesh, Razzaque et al (1990) find that increased numbers of consumer durable goods owned by a household, a proxy for economic resources, significantly reduce child mortality but have no significant effect on infant mortality. In contrast, Waxler et al (1985) find that a similar proxy for economic resources, a sum of the number of consumer durable goods owned, has a negative effect on infant mortality in Sri Lanka, even after controlling for maternal education and more proximate determinants including nutrition and sanitation.

Though we could tally which SES or class variables are significant in which studies, this would not further our understanding of the impact of SES or class on health and fertility. We believe that there are more fundamental conceptual and methodological problems in these analyses and that these problems are at least partially responsible for the divergence in results that are found. The conceptual problems are the lack of theoretical definitions of SES or class in many empirical analyses and the differences in the implicit definitions of these concepts. We require an understanding of the definitions of SES or class to guide us as to the number of distinct dimensions that these concepts include. And it is the number of dimensions that helps us determine the nature of the indicators we require and how they should enter the model. Without clarifying the use of these terms, it is nearly impossible to assess the quality of the measures or the omission of variables. As Strauss & Thomas (1995) note, omitted variable bias and unobserved heterogeneity from factors such as "family background" are at least partially responsible for the divergent findings on the effects of socioeconomic variables. Since family background is related to SES, this suggests the need to consider the dimensionality of the measures. Closely related methodological problems are the failure to take account of the measurement error in indicators of SES or class and the ambiguity in the treatment of multiple indicators of the dimensions of these concepts. Our review focuses on these theoretical and methodological problems. Before we turn to the actual empirical studies of child health and fertility, we explore the primary meanings associated with SES or class.

CONCEPTS AND MEASURES OF SES AND CLASS

No one theory has a monopoly on the meaning of SES or class. Socioeconomic status refers to the position of individuals, families, households, or other aggregates on one or more dimensions of stratification. These dimensions include income, education, prestige, wealth, or other aspects of standing that members of society deem salient. There are different ideas about what class is, but it is generally defined relationally, referring to groups of people who share a similar position such as the relationship to the means of production. All too often SES and class are ambiguous terms that serve as shorthand expressions to refer to social and economic characteristics that are believed to be important, but the rationale or meaning of which is not always made clear.

There are nearly as many concepts of socioeconomic status and class as there are authors writing on them. However, distancing ourselves from the particulars of each work, it is possible to discern two broad approaches. The first sees class or SES as essentially a unitary concept. From this perspective, a fundamental dimension underlies class (or SES), and it is this dimension that is the primary driving force of some class analyses. The second viewpoint focuses on the components of SES or class and treats them as having distinct effects. This conceptualization disputes the unidimensionality of class or SES. It highlights the separate dimensions of stratification and predicts that different dimensions can have different consequences. We briefly describe each of these conceptualizations and typical ways in which they are operationalized below. Before detailing these distinctions, we note that having a unidimensional concept of class does not deny the possibility of including other components of inequality in an analysis. Many scholars who use class in their analyses do not assert primacy of class in determining all social phenomena (Wright 1996).

Unitary Concepts and Measures

The unitary concept of class is closely associated with the work of Marx. The key axis to his theory is a group's relationship to the means of production. The primary class actors in industrial capitalist societies were the owners of the means of production, the bourgeoisie, and the workers, the proletariat (Marx & Engels [1848] 1978). Key to Marx's analysis of class is the idea of exploitation (Marx [1894] 1978). The position of the owners of the means of production depends on their ability to appropriate the labor of the workers. The work of Wright (1997, Wright et al 1982) is the most thorough contemporary attempt to measure class positions empirically from a Marxist perspective, and these measures enable the examination of the effects of class on microlevel outcomes such as health and fertility. Wright's categorization of class emphasizes the exploitation inherent in the social relations of production. Specifically, he categorizes workers according to: (*a*) ownership, (*b*) authority, and (*c*) expertise (Wright 1985). All three axes represent a type of exploitation. Workers can occupy "contradictory locations" by being high on one axis and low on another.

A unitary measure of class not associated with relationship to the means of production is that of Warner (1949), who developed a measure by summing ratings on occupation, source of income, dwelling type, and neighborhood and then assigning scores to "classes." Yet another measure of social class, the British Registrar General's scale, has been the measure of status most widely used in studies of health and mortality in the United Kingdom (see, for example, Marmot et al 1991). The occupation of the head of the household is placed in one of five social classes: I, professional; II, intermediate; III, skilled (non-manual and manual); IV, partly skilled; and V, unskilled.[2] As commonly used as a single measure, this measure reflects a unitary construct. A comparable scale for the United States is the Edwards Social-Economic Grouping of Occupations (Liberatos et al 1988). Here, occupations are compiled into major groups based on the average income and the education required by the occupation.

Shared among these approaches is the idea of class being distinguished by categories rather than by continuums. The SES traditions represent an emphasis on continuous variables. For example, Duncan's (1961) socioeconomic index (SEI) is a common continuous measure of occupational standing in US studies. This index is based on the average educational attainment and income in an occupation. A

---

[2]Though occupation is often used interchangeably with class, Wright et al (1982) insist that a Marxist operationalization of class should not be based on occupation. A great deal of variation across the axes of exploitation can exist within an occupation.

large proportion of the US research in social stratification has used SEI to evaluate the extent of intergenerational mobility, but SEI scores have also been included in predicting numerous other outcomes. While the SEI scale itself reflects a unitary construct at the level of occupations, because it is often used as a component of the SES of individuals, we return to this scale in the next section. Another common index often used as a unitary measure of SES is Hollingshead's Two Factor Index of Social Position, published in Hollingshead & Redlich (1958), which combines education and occupation.[3]

There has also been limited exploration of general SES indexes for developing countries. Employing Warner's measure as a model to develop a scale for Bangladesh, Karim (1990) used characteristics of the dwelling, educational attainment of household members, occupation of household head, possession of a number of household items, membership in a cooperative, self-perception of class, amount of land owned, and food self-sufficiency. From these variables he constructed a scale based on all the variables whose correlations with the other SES variables were statistically significant. Cortinovis et al (1993) used multiple correspondence analyses to develop a SES index for Uganda. With the aim of developing an index for a survey of nutrition and health, they constructed this from a host of variables representing housing quality, literacy, cultural factors, demographic conditions, and economic conditions. In an exploration of the consequences of maternal education for fertility and child survival in Mexico, Levine et al (1991) employed an index of SES that includes husband's education, husband's occupational status, basic household services, and appliances owned. Despite these few cases of an index of SES being created for use in analyses of developing countries, this type of index is not common, as our review of such studies demonstrates.

Economists have not been as likely as sociologists to view SES as a unitary construct. However, a strange bedfellow who shares Marx's emphasis on a unitary concept, though from quite a different perspective, is economist Milton Friedman. We refer to Friedman's permanent income hypothesis, one of the most influential economic ideas of the twentieth century. Friedman offers a model to explain the relationship between consumption and income for individuals and aggregates. Essentially, Friedman states that income is composed of two components: permanent and transitory. "The permanent component is to be interpreted as reflecting the effect of those factors that the unit regards as determining its capital value or wealth: the nonhuman wealth it owns; the personal attributes of the earners in the unit, such as their training, ability, personality; the attributes of the economic activity of the earners, such as the occupation followed, the location of the economic activity, and so on" (Friedman 1957:21). Friedman suggests that consumption behavior is primarily determined by permanent income, a conceptual notion of income that differs from measured income and is never actually observed. According to Friedman, part of the reason that the correlation between consumption and income is not strong is that income is a poor measure for permanent income.

---

[3]See Hauser & Warren (1997) for a critique of the Hollingshead index.

Permanent income is a theoretical concept and is not readily measurable. Enormous effort has been undertaken over the years to develop proxy measures of permanent income. Since expenditures are generally considered to be less variable than income, annual household expenditures are often used to proxy permanent income (Deaton 1992). While researchers employ a permanent income proxy when studying longer-term outcomes, they often use transitory income and measures of uncertainty when they focus on shorter-term outcomes. For example, permanent income may be related to child stunting, which is an outcome that takes a longer period of time to develop, whereas transitory income may have a stronger relationship with child wasting, which is a more severe, short-term measure of child health (Strauss & Thomas 1995). In many ways, permanent income or its proxy is assumed to operate very much like a class or SES variable by capturing consumption behavior based on the attributes of the earner, not simply on last period's income.

Proxies for permanent income can also be found beyond the more traditional income estimates. Occupation is particularly popular as a proxy for permanent income. Friedman (1957) highlighted the importance of occupational categories in the permanent income hypothesis, and occupation is also tested as a proxy in Houthakker (1957) and Mayer (1963). In addition, Zimmerman (1992) demonstrated that occupation is a better predictor of generational immobility than is income measured at one point in time. Sociologists have also suggested that occupation is a good proxy for permanent income (Hauser & Warren 1997). Nevertheless, recent economic studies are more likely to use asset measures and lagged income variables to capture permanent income (see Deaton 1992). At the same time, innovative studies attempt to use measures such as adult height in historical studies when income is unavailable (Steckel 1995) or to capture unobserved family background (Thomas et al 1990).

Component Concepts and Measures

The second major formulation of class and SES is what we label the component approach. In contrast to the unitary view, the component perspective treats SES as having a number of distinct dimensions. Though some authors highlight one dimension over the others, most scholars who share this outlook suggest that each component is capable of exerting separate effects. Weber is the sociological theorist most often associated with this outlook. Weber's (1946) classic essay, "Class, Status, and Party," is one of his most concise statements on this issue. In it he argues that class (economic position), status (prestige), and party (political power) represent interrelated yet distinct dimensions of stratification, providing a corrective to Marx's economic determinism. While economic position can affect prestige and power, prestige and power can influence both one another and economic position.

Typically, sociologists who hold a component perspective on the measurement of SES employ a series of measures, most commonly some measure of education, income, and occupational standing and occasionally class. For example, research in the status attainment tradition reflects attention to the distinct effects of the various aspects of stratification (e.g., Hauser 1972). Models from the Wisconsin school often examine the effects of parental education, income, and occupation on the subsequent socioeconomic outcomes of their children separately. Several studies have found that the direct effect of father's occupational status on son's occupational standing is larger than its effect on son's earnings, and similarly, father's earnings have a larger effect on son's earnings than father's occupation does (Hauser 1972, Hauser et al 1983).

Though there are many occupation-based measures of status, the measure of occupational standing often used in status attainment and other American stratification research is the SEI scale introduced by Duncan (1961). However, we must ask if it is reasonable to combine income and education at the aggregate level of occupations (as is done with the SEI) when their unidimensionality at the individual level has been called into question. Indeed, recent research on the SEI index cautions against its use in predicting diverse outcomes and argues in favor of examining the effects of disaggregated occupational characteristics. Hauser & Warren (1997) find that the weights attributed to occupational education and income are model-dependent (which they show in structural equation models predicting prestige and other socioeconomic outcomes). The relative weights of occupation and education might differ for other outcomes as well, including health.

Occupational status has received relatively little attention in studies of population and health outcomes in developing countries, primarily due to somewhat constrained labor market conditions. However, Treiman (1977) developed an international scale for occupational prestige that could be used in developing country studies. Bills et al (1985), who developed a scale of occupations for Brazil based on occupational income and education, are another exception, but this approach has not been widely adopted. Given the importance this component of SES has in industrialized societies, it is worth further consideration in developing country settings, especially as they become increasingly urban and industrialized. In addition, we can refine agricultural status indicators to reflect the variation between capital and labor buyers and sellers, and such distinctions may prove fruitful in more fully capturing SES.

Economists have played an important role in developing many of the concepts and measures of SES and its various components. While it is true that economists are less likely to use the terms SES or class, they nonetheless use many of the same variables, such as various forms of income, education, and less frequently, occupation. Of course, economists have generally emphasized the role and measurement of economic resources. However, other aspects of SES are no longer considered to be outside the domain of economics. In most cases, the dimensions of SES are clearly incorporated as separate components rather than multiple aspects of a single, unitary concept. The transparency of this approach follows from the tendency toward presenting hypotheses as mathematical conjectures and requiring authors to define the exact role of socioeconomic and other exogenous and endogenous variables in the model.

In its basic form, the standard neoclassical model posits a representative agent (usually a household or individual) seeking to maximize a utility function in the face of a resource constraint. When the utility function includes factors such as child education and health, which are produced in the home as well as in markets, production functions are used to describe the relationship between the inputs and outcomes. The utility function generally includes those variables to be chosen by the household or individual. Despite the recognition that preferences may be shaped by SES, economists do not often attempt to model different preferences within the population. However, they do tend to include SES controls in their statistical models. In addition, many econometric methods have been developed for controlling unobserved factors that may be correlated with choice variables, such as child health or fertility. While there are many less traditional approaches, SES and its various components are typically incorporated through various income and endowment measures that are included in the resource constraint, the production technology, or both (see Strauss & Thomas 1995).

The simplest approach is when the utility function does not include SES factors, and the various sources of income implied in the resource constraint are the only aspects of SES included in the model. When income is defined as permanent income, as discussed earlier in terms of Friedman's work, the treatment of SES is best defined as unitary. When income captures various distinct elements, then it may be better labeled as component. Empirical studies normally resort to multiple measures, even when intending to capture the unitary permanent income concept. In contrast to many non-economists who typically include a single measure for household or individual income, economists prefer to divide income categories into specific groups according to their source, including wage income, rental income, transfer income, and other potential sources. Research by economists has demonstrated that these various sources of income have different effects on household behavior. For example, Hoddinott & Haddad (1995) use data from Côte d'Ivoire to show that when women bring in a greater share of the household income, the household budget is shifted toward food and away from alcohol and cigarettes.

The simple model we described above where SES is only incorporated through the resource constraint is less common today, particularly in models focusing on health or fertility outcomes. In such models, one often finds household utility functions that include some non-market-produced outcome such as child health or education. In their classic article, Becker & Lewis (1974) introduce terms for child quality in the utility function that are implicitly the result of household production decisions and depend on household endowments that allow households to produce quality more efficiently. Following Becker (1965, 1981) and Willis (1973), economists have increasingly turned toward incorporating explicit production functions to describe the process for generating nonmarket outcomes in the utility function. These production functions normally depend on individual and household endowments—many of which are unobserved—as well as community characteristics (Schultz 1997).

The econometric literature generated by this conceptual approach has shed important light on the potential effect of SES variables, not all of which support a component perspective. In their informative review of the literature on health and fertility in developing countries, Strauss & Thomas (1995) suggest that much of the variation in fertility and health behavior and outcomes can be attributed to unobserved background variables specific to individuals, families, and communities, and not to specific socioeconomic factors.

Ambiguous or Mixed Concepts and Measures

The preceding discussion portrays the distinction between the unitary and component concepts of SES as cleaner than it is in practice. In reality, SES and class are too often used ambiguously and casually, referring to education or income in one study or to an index based on only occupation in another. It is not uncommon for researchers to refer to the impact of SES in a general sense as something that "needs to be controlled," but in the empirical analysis to merely include a single component (e.g., education) to control for SES. We give some examples in our review of the studies that follows. In practice, often indicators of SES are used interchangeably as functional equivalents based on the availability of measures. Using income and education in one study and education and occupation in another, both as controls for SES, suggests that both sets of variables tap the same underlying concept. Alternatively, another hybrid approach is to hold a component view of SES, but to highlight only one or two components as the key ones to analyze. Finally, class theorists often recognize that distinct aspects of stratification such as education may have unique effects separate from those of class. Thus, it is possible that a unitary concept of class might operate in conjunction with more specific SES variables in influencing an outcome.

REVIEW OF SES AND CLASS IN CHILD-HEALTH AND FERTILITY STUDIES

Our objective is to examine articles representative of current practice in the use of SES in studies of developing countries related to fertility and child health.[4] To obtain a comprehensive perspective on current uses in this area, we selected the main demography journals, as well as the top journals of sociology and related disciplines. The journals included *Demography, Population Studies, Population and Development Review, American Sociological Review, American Journal of Sociology, Social Forces, Journal of Political Economy, American Economic Review, Econometrica, American Journal of Public Health*, and *Social Science and Medicine*. Then, we searched the citation database of the Institute for Scientific

---

[4]Montgomery et al (2000) provide a brief review of recent demographic studies that is more focused on indicators of economic resources.

Information for articles in the selected journals that contained any of the following terms: *fertility, contraceptive use, contraceptive choice, infant health, child health, infant mortality,* or *child mortality* in their title, abstract, or list of keywords.[5]

From this list of articles, we conducted cursory reviews and selected all of the articles that met our criteria. We focused only on articles that included multivariate analyses at the micro level for developing countries. Our exclusion of qualitative analyses means that we are unable to comment on an important body of literature. However, including such articles would introduce a much higher degree of subjectivity into our categorization process. Our review covered articles between 1990 and 1998. Our search generated a total of 69 articles that met our selection criteria. There were two articles that did not include a conceptual discussion of SES or any measures related to SES in their models, so our discussion below is based on 67 articles.

To reflect the split in the theoretical literature between a component and unitary conceptualization of SES or class, we first classified articles according to their conceptual approach along those lines.[6] The component approach was characterized by explicit hypotheses stated about the distinct ways in which the components of SES would affect the outcomes of interest. Articles that employed a unitary approach hypothesized about the effects of their various measures of SES in terms of a general notion of SES. We found that several articles could not be classified as conceptually unitary or component either because there was a lack of discussion or because the discussion was ambiguous. Rather than force an interpretation on the conceptual approach of these articles, we created another category, "ambiguous."

We also classified each article according to whether SES was measured with one variable or more than one variable in the empirical models. For this we included variables related to education, income, consumption, wealth, ownership of consumer durable goods, dwelling characteristics, occupation, and class. Some of these variables have potential roles in fertility and child health studies in addition to a socioeconomic role, and authors did not always discuss all of them as explicitly socioeconomic. To maintain consistency in the variables that were recorded across the studies, we included the variables that we considered to reflect SES, rather than relying on the authors' classifications. We anticipated that a unitary conceptualization implies the use of a single measure for SES. This might be a single measure such as income or education, or it might be an index that combines

---

[5]The search strategy should provide us with a complete list of all articles that use the preceding keywords. However, it is possible that there are other papers that are tied to the topic but failed to use the keywords. As such we cannot claim to have a census of all papers in the topic area, yet the sample should give us a broadly representative portrait of studies with this focus.

[6]Two of us coded the articles. Initially both coded the same subset of articles and then we compared our assessments to insure consistency in our coding. We found that we were not in disagreement about any of the articles that we coded, but there were some that neither of us could place initially. The three of us then discussed these articles to insure that they were placed correctly.

TABLE 1   Summary of conceptual and empirical approaches

	Conceptual Approach		
	Unitary	**Component**	**Ambiguous**
Single measure	0	5	9
Multiple measure	6	37	9

variables that others would consider to capture different dimensions. Further, we expected multiple variables to be used when the authors held a component conceptualization. This did not always turn out to be the case. The number of articles that fell into each category can be seen in Table 1. Below Table 1 we describe each cell in greater detail, discussing typical articles within each cell.

Unitary conceptually, single measure: Surprisingly, there were no articles that fit into this category.

Unitary conceptually, multiple measures: The six articles within this category expressed a global conception of SES but used more than one measure to capture its effects. Several articles within this category investigated a key SES variable in an effort to establish if its effect on fertility or child health was due to a unitary SES or if it had a separate effect. For example, Sandiford et al (1995) and Desai & Alva (1998) seek to establish whether maternal education has an effect on child health above and beyond its association with socioeconomic status. Sandiford et al (1995) ask, ". . . if statistical control by imperfectly measured socioeconomic status removes about half the apparent advantage of education, how much would be left if it were perfectly measured?" (p. 6). Their research context was unique in that they were able to take advantage of an adult literacy program in Nicaragua, which they argue allowed them to completely disentangle maternal literacy from SES without concern for measurement error. By grouping the women in their sample according to whether they were illiterate, educated by traditional means, or literate by the adult literacy program, and by including several measures of SES as controls, they claim to distill the separate effect of maternal literacy. In their analysis, literacy did have positive consequences for child health. In contrast, the findings of Desai & Alva (1998) that we noted previously cast doubt on the robustness of maternal education. Das Gupta (1997) offers some parallel results for income from the Punjab. Her article examines the relationship between child mortality and household SES and income. She finds that income plays no role once other SES factors are included in her model. In her words, the results " . . . suggest that familial risk is affected by household care practices, and by socio-economic status rather than by income level alone" (p. 199).

Conceptual component, single measure: Articles in this category were explicit about a conceptualization of SES that allowed different components to have distinct impacts. However, they only included one measure related to SES in their analyses. In most of the articles in this category, maternal education was the component of

SES featured by the authors, apparently because the authors considered it to be the most important or only important component of SES in the context of their analyses. For instance, Defo (1996) reviews the findings on maternal education and argues that it is the most important status variable. In the remaining article from this category, the author explained that education was the only measure available and thus had to suffice as a proxy for other components as well. "... [W]omen's employment and the socioeconomic level of the household could not be included in the analysis because they were measured at the time of survey, not at the time of pregnancy. Education is included in the model as a proxy for SES and as a measure of the awareness of the value of prenatal care" (Gage 1998:25).

Conceptual component, multiple measures: This category was clearly the dominant category and included more than half of the articles in our review. We placed articles in this category if they contained an explicitly stated hypothesis about at least one component and they used multiple measures of SES. Wood & Lovell (1992) investigate racial inequality in Brazil and determine that race remains an important factor in explaining mortality differences even after controlling for SES differences. To control for SES, they include a measure of monthly household income but they also note that "... income alone does not adequately control for socioeconomic status ... " (p. 713). Therefore, they also introduce controls for the education of both parents and indicate the specific channels through which each of these variables may affect child mortality. In another example, Bankole (1995) includes measures of wife's education and husband's occupation in his analysis of the effects of fertility desires of marital partners in Nigeria on their subsequent fertility. He does not include husband's education and wife's occupation due to their collinearity with wife's education and husband's occupation, respectively. That wife's education and husband's occupation are not considered to be collinear indicates a conceptualization of education and occupation as separate dimensions of SES. In yet another example, DeGraff et al (1997) explore community and individual-level determinants of contraceptive use in the Philippines. They find strong support for the importance of community-level effects on the decision to use modern contraception. In addition to a wide variety of community-level socioeconomic variables, they include individual and household-level variables such as wife's education and husband's occupation, as well as husband's education and the value of their land. Their specification of the separate effects of each of these variables clearly points to a component approach. The approach of these articles is typical of the many articles within this cell. Nevertheless, there is substantial variation in the actual SES components used, and we examine this issue in more detail below.

Ambiguous: There were 18 articles that contained little or no discussion of their conceptualization of SES or the reasoning underlying their measures. It is important to note that the objectives of many of the articles in our review, particularly several in this category, did not include an interest in the effects of SES on the fertility or child health outcome being studied. Often SES variables were used as controls, and in fairness one would not expect an extensive discussion of SES in these articles. In one example, Curtis et al (1993) examine demographic and familial effects on post-neonatal mortality in Brazil. They explain their use of maternal education " . . . as a general control for SES and for knowledge of health-related matters" (p. 36). We could not infer if this reflected a unitary conceptualization or if it simply meant that education was used as a proxy for SES because of its correlation with other dimensions of SES. In another example, Razzaque et al (1990) only include an indicator for wealth (an index of consumer durables) in their examination of the effects of famine on neonatal and postnatal mortality in Bangladesh. In some places in the article they refer to this as "economic status" while in other places they refer to it as "socioeconomic status." It was impossible to place these ambiguous articles in either the unitary or component categories.

Measures of SES Used in the Studies

In addition to considering the conceptual approaches and how they relate to the empirical strategies of the articles, we examined the actual measures in the analyses. We found that there is little consensus on the issues of which components of SES should be included and how they should be measured, outside of the widespread agreement that maternal education should be incorporated (Table 2). lists the number of articles in which the main variables appeared. The variables listed in Table 2 represent broad categories within which there was a good deal of variation across the studies. Initially, we compiled a detailed list of all the different ways in which each of these variables was measured. This list was too vast to represent in the table, but we describe some of the various ways in which each was measured and the meanings that authors assigned to them below.

Clearly, maternal education is the most frequently used socioeconomic variable in these studies. It was included in every study except one for which SES was incorporated in the empirical analyses. In contrast, husband's or paternal education was included in only about a third of the articles. Education was sometimes measured

TABLE 2   Frequencies of SES variables appearing in the 67 studies

Variable	Frequency
Female/maternal education or literacy	66
Durable goods, agricultural assets, and/or housing quality	35
Husband/paternal education or literacy	23
Husband/paternal occupation	15
Female/maternal occupation	13
Income or consumption	11
Pays social security (indicator of access to health care)	1
Received remittances	1
High-caste household	1

in years, but more commonly it was measured as a series of dichotomous variables indicating salient cutoffs for the educational system of the particular country being studied. The hypothesized role of maternal education in the outcome of interest also differed. For Gage (1998) maternal education is a proxy for SES, but maternal education has also been hypothesized to enhance child health by producing changes in individual behavior such as utilization of modern health services and a host of other health-related behaviors (Desai & Alva 1998; Defo 1996). It also improves women's status, which can have consequences both for child health and for fertility and contraception (Balk 1994). When included, paternal or husband's education is usually taken as a more straightforward representation of household SES. For example, in a study of the fertility decline of Iran, Raftery et al (1995) found that the decline was greater for women whose husbands were more educated (controlling for wives' education). They attribute this to husband's education being a "reliable proxy for husband's occupational status and hence the socioeconomic status of the household" (p. 177).

Over half of the studies employed a measure of ownership of consumer durable goods or agricultural assets and/or housing quality. In this category we included any indicator of housing quality, landholdings, and assets, both consumer durables and agricultural, and as such it is the most diverse category. However, the researchers' measurement strategies also contributed quite a bit to the heterogeneity in this category. The asset or housing characteristics considered varied substantially across studies. Some authors combined several characteristics into an index while others entered one or more as single variables. More rarely, the total value of household assets was used (e.g., Dargent-Molina et al 1994). Often, this type of variable is taken to represent wealth or is used as a proxy for permanent income. Common variables within this category, however, are not strictly socioeconomic. Direct determinants of mortality such as access to sanitary drinking water and toilet facilities have effects on child health that exceed their association with SES. One difficulty is that these types of variables are often included in composite measures of durable goods and housing quality.

The use of ownership of consumer durable goods as an indicator of economic status is a noteworthy difference in how researchers measure SES in developing countries compared with measures in developed countries. Income measures are used less frequently, which at least partially reflects the difficulty of obtaining accurate income data. It also reflects the widespread use of Demographic and Health Surveys (DHS), which collect durable good and housing quality information but no information on income or consumption. Consumption as measured by total household expenditures was used in only one study.

In comparison to other aspects of SES, occupation is included relatively infrequently, with maternal and paternal occupation each being used about equally as often. For males, occupation was generally coded into two or more occupational groups. The groups differed among studies, but a distinction between agricultural work and nonagricultural work was prevalent. Hirschman & Guest (1990), who classify husband's occupation into agriculture, production, sales/service, clerical, professional/administrative, and other, suggest that husband's occupation can be taken as a "crude measure of social class" (p. 374). However, generally when occupation is included, authors do not refer to it as a measure of class. More rarely authors made a distinction between working in agriculture for oneself and working for wages, which could be viewed as an indicator of class position. For women the same types of occupational categories were used, but an indicator of female employment outside of the home was also occasionally used.

We have also analyzed the frequency in the patterns of usage of the different combinations of SES and class variables. The degree of heterogeneity in the types of measures used—outside of the almost universal inclusion of maternal education— is quite striking. Out of the 67 studies, 13 include maternal education as their only SES variable. In addition, eight other articles include maternal education with household asset measures. Overall, we see that a measure of maternal education alone or in combination with some type of measure of economic resource such as assets, income, or occupation is most typical.

Levels of Measurement

Consideration of the different levels at which SES is measured identifies other complications in its treatment. Our review focuses on micro-level SES variables, but there is often ambiguity about whether the appropriate unit of analysis at this level is the individual or the household. In addition, the increasing use of aggregate-level variables in micro-level analyses requires us to briefly discuss their role.

The ambiguity in determining the appropriate unit of analysis at the micro level is particularly marked in the case of fertility studies where the unit of analysis is typically the woman, although it could be the household. In many contexts the benefits of high SES enjoyed by the male household head are not necessarily extended to other members of the household. For instance, Balk (1994) shows that in Bangladesh, women's status, as well as household SES factors, have strong influences on fertility. As we discussed above, several studies in the review included indicators of only maternal or female status. However, because in some studies maternal education serves as a proxy for household SES, we cannot infer that these articles assumed the individual woman to be the unit of analysis.

Turning to aggregate-level measures of SES, of the 67 articles we reviewed, 36 included at least one variable that can be viewed as an aggregate-level indicator of SES. The increased interest in aggregate-level measures is partly due to recognition of the importance of contextual effects on individual behavior as well as the development of statistical techniques, such as multi-level modeling, that allow these analyses (Robert 1999).

The relationship between SES and class variables on the individual and aggregate levels is complex, and researchers in this area attribute several different, yet interrelated, roles to aggregate socioeconomic variables. One role relates to the use of aggregate information as a proxy variable for SES, but at a community level. A number of articles suggested that urban households were better off than rural households, for example, and used this as an explanation of their findings. An important question is whether urban residence is merely a proxy for individual-level differences in status, or if it also captures an effect of community characteristics. In other words, will the consistently observed rural/urban differential in child health be eliminated with adequate controls for household SES? The evidence on this has been mixed. In a study of child mortality in Brazil, Sastry (1997) finds that specific community infrastructure factors play important roles in child mortality above and beyond the effect of household SES. In addition, Desai & Alva (1998) use a fixed-effects model to control for unobserved community-level factors and find that this greatly diminishes the effect of maternal education on child health.

A related function of aggregate variables is to shape the effects of SES variables measured at the individual level. A number of studies emphasized that the effects of individual-level SES indicators varied by the socioeconomic context of the community. In a recent study based on data from Ecuadorean Amazon, Lobao & Brown (1998) show that the effect of individual SES factors on fertility is greatly moderated by the existing development context and class structure. Dargent-Molina et al (1994) examine how the effect of maternal education on infant diarrhea in the Philippines differs between advantaged and disadvantaged communities. Durkin et al (1994) find that different SES measures are statistically significant in their four research populations, rural and urban Bangladesh and rural and urban Pakistan. The finding that various socioeconomic components operate differently in different contexts leads them to suggest the inclusion of a wide range of SES measures in studies of child health in developing countries. Residential information is a particularly important dimension and may alter the role of individual-level SES variables. However, many authors do not attempt to disentangle the separate effects of residence as a community proxy for SES and residence as a proxy for other factors.

Summary of Literature Review Findings

Several things stand out from our review of these articles. First, our findings highlight important gaps between the conceptual treatments and empirical implementations of SES and class. Despite the prominence of the unitary conceptual framework in the theoretical literature, a large majority of the empirical studies use a component perspective. The implicit assumption in the empirical implementation is that the component approach has won the debate. Explicit testing of a unitary versus component construct of SES is rare in this empirical work (see Durkin et al 1994 for an exception). On a related note, we found that the concept of class was very rarely used. We were also surprised by the number of studies that were ambiguous about their conceptualizations of SES.

Another observation is the centrality of maternal education in these analyses. It was included in all the studies that incorporated SES but one. When a single measure of SES or class is used, it is almost invariably maternal education. [One study, Razzaque et al (1990) used only an assets measure instead.] And several of the studies focused on the importance of maternal education in comparison with other SES variables or as a reflection of SES. But there have been conflicting results across these studies, and the exact role of maternal education in health and fertility outcomes is not fully understood.

Finally, it is clear that data availability influences the ways in which SES can be measured. In some cases this can account for the inconsistency between conceptualization and measurement that we found in some studies. Collecting socioeconomic data is costly, so often surveys do not include information on all of its components. The absence of consumption measures in the studies in this analysis is surprising in light of their theoretical relevance as measures of permanent income. The widespread use of DHS surveys accounts for a large number of the studies that employed indexes of consumer durable goods and housing quality. Eighteen of the studies in our literature review used one or more DHS surveys, and two used a World Fertility Study, the predecessor to DHS. Some data sets do collect income and extensive consumption data, such as the World Bank's Living Standards Measurement Studies (LSMS), which are available in several developing countries, and RAND's Family Life Surveys (FLS), which are available in four developing countries. Surprisingly, none of the studies in our analysis used an LSMS data set, and only three used an FLS data set (see Appendix for possible data sources). The remaining studies employed national or local surveys that were not part of these larger comparative efforts. More effort should be directed to developing surveys that reflect conceptual meanings and to investigating empirically the degree to which widely available measures reflect these meanings of SES.

METHODOLOGICAL ISSUES IN USING SES/CLASS

The literature review highlighted several methodological issues that arise in incorporating SES or class in analyses of fertility and child health outcomes. In this section we crystallize these issues in the abstract, but our analysis is driven by the concrete literature that makes up our review. A fundamental distinction that organizes this section is whether a researcher conceptualizes SES or class as unitary or as components. We treat the methodological issues surrounding the unitary concept first and then turn to the components.

Unitary Concept

Our literature review revealed that only a minority of the empirical studies treat SES or class as a single dimension. However, given that some do and given the strong theoretical traditions in sociology that do, it is important to consider the treatment of such unitary concepts. At the operational level there are two aspects to consider. One is whether the researcher measures the unitary concept with a single or with multiple indicators. A second aspect is whether the measures are *causal* or *effect* indicators. This latter distinction describes the relation of the latent concept to the measures. Causal indicators are measures that have a direct influence on the latent variable to which they are tied. Effect indicators are measures directly affected by the latent variable.

Some notation will facilitate our discussion. We refer to the fertility or child health outcomes by y, the SES or class measures by $x_1, x_2, \ldots, x_q$, and all the other substantive determinants of y by z. The ς_1 is the disturbance for y, and it is uncorrelated with all explanatory variables and has a mean of zero. It is an equation disturbance that incorporates all of the other determinants of y that are not explicitly included in the model. Figure 1a illustrates the case where SES or class is a unitary concept that we measure with a single variable, x_1, that is correlated with the other variables contained in z. The single-headed, straight arrows signify that the variable at the base of the arrow has a direct effect on the variable at the head of the arrow. The curved two-headed arrows indicate that the two connected variables covary, but the source of their association is not part of the analysis. The SES or class variable, x_1, could be an index or a single critical measure. For example, child health might be the outcome variable (y); maternal education might be our only measure of SES (x_1); and z might be composed of other individual characteristics such as maternal age, marital status, etc., and community characteristics such as urban/rural residence and proximity to health clinics. Regardless of its make-up, an implicit assumption in such a structure is that the x_1 variable is free or nearly free of any random or systematic measurement error. That is, we are assuming that the measure is a perfect representation of SES or class.

Stated so boldly, this assumption will arouse doubt as to its plausibility in most readers. If we do not treat x_1 as a perfect measure of SES, then we must distinguish whether x_1 is a causal or effect indicator of the latent variable SES or class. Figures 1b and c illustrate these two cases. In Figure 1b, x_1 is an effect indicator of the latent SES or class variable. The δ_1 is the error of measurement in x_1. It is the discrepancy between the true but unobserved SES variable and the observed variable we use to measure it. The δ_1 is uncorrelated with SES, z, and ς_1. In the above example, maternal education reflects the SES concept plus random measurement error. The major obstacle to estimating such a model is that without further information, it is not identified, and therefore it will not be possible to find unique values for the effects.[7]

One solution would be to have knowledge of the measurement error variance that could be incorporated into the estimation. This is frequently unavailable. Another possibility is to use multiple indicators of SES or class. We consider this possibility shortly.

But suppose that Figure 1b is the true model, yet we follow typical practice and ignore measurement error in the SES or class measure and estimate an incorrect model that looks like Figure 1a. In our example, this would mean that we would treat maternal education as a perfect representation of SES. As is well known, both our estimates of SES or class's impact on y and those of any elements of z that

---

[7]For a discussion of identification of these models see Chapters 7 and 8 in Bollen (1989).

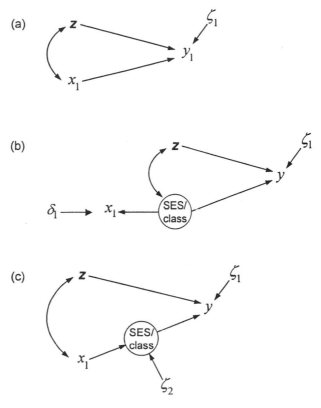

Figure 1 Unidimensional, single-indicator models of SES/class. Variables and symbols are defined in the text.

are correlated with x_1 will be biased (Theil 1957). This means that even if SES or class is a control variable, it can frustrate attempts to get a consistent estimator of the other variables' effects that are of more central concern.

Suppose now that Figure 1c is correct with x_1 being a causal indicator. In this case maternal education would still be an indicator of SES, but it influences SES rather than SES influencing it. Here too we have an identification problem. Without knowing the error variance of ς_2 for the latent SES or class variable, the model as a whole is underidentified. But the consequences of estimating Figure 1a when Figure 1c is true are different from what we found when Figure 1b was the true model. More specifically, the coefficient for the x_1 variable in the analysis of Figure 1a is a consistent estimator of the impact of SES or class on y, the fertility or child health outcome (see Bollen & Davis 1993). We need to qualify this by saying that the model assumes that x_1 directly affects SES or class and that x_1 is not a proxy or error-containing measure of some other construct. Furthermore, this model assumes that x_1 is the only causal indicator of SES. If these conditions hold, then surprisingly we get a consistent estimator of the effect of the latent SES or class variable on y using x_1 instead of the latent variable, and coefficients for the elements in z will not be asymptotically biased (Bollen & Davis 1993).

Maintaining the unitary concept view of SES or class, we now move to the case where multiple measures are available. Figure 2a is a path diagram that represents the model where each of the SES or class measures $(x_1, x_2, \ldots, x_q)$ enters separately. This corresponds to the few studies we discussed where a unitary concept was accompanied by multiple measures as individual SES variables in an equation (see Table 1). Returning to our earlier example, suppose maternal education was accompanied by household income and husband's occupation as additional SES indicators. This approach raises some complications. First, if SES or class is unidimensional, then the rationale for including several separate explanatory variables to measure it is hard to understand. If each is a perfect measure of SES or class then the measures should be perfectly correlated. If each is a nearly perfect measure, then near perfect collinearity between these variables will follow (Gordon 1968).

One way to resolve this issue is to acknowledge that measurement error is present and to view the SES or class measures $(x_1, x_2, \ldots, x_q)$ not as distinct variables but as a collection of effect indicators, each partially reflecting the unitary SES or class concept. Figure 2b captures these relations. Here the latent SES or class variable is in a circle. It underlies all of the measures $(x_1, x_2, \ldots, x_q)$, and it also affects the fertility or child health outcomes (y). For our hypothetical example, maternal education, household income, and husband's occupation would be the x variables reflecting the latent SES variable. This model is identical to the one represented in Figure 1b except that now we have multiple indicators whereas before we had a single measure. The multiple indicators are sufficient to overcome the identification problems that we faced with a single measure. Therefore, we can have a consistent estimator of all of the parameters in the model in Figure 2b.

What happens if Figure 2b is true but we estimate the model in Figure 2a instead? Unfortunately, inconsistent coefficient estimators of the SES or class effect as well as the effects of the variables in z are the likely result. The reason is that such a model includes a number of imperfect indicators of the same concept. As in the case of estimating the model in Figure 1a when the model in Figure 1b is correct, ignoring measurement error can result in inconsistent coefficient estimators for SES and the elements in z, including any aggregate measures that might be a part of it. To make matters worse, the SES or class part that is common to them could create collinearity problems. In brief if Figure 2b is the true model, estimating Figure 2a is a bad choice.

Suppose that the indicators $x_1, x_2, \ldots, x_q$ are causal indicators of the unitary SES or class concept. In this case we have the model in Figure 2c. The model matches that in Figure 1c except that now we have multiple causal indicators whereas before we had a single one. A good case could be made that maternal education, household income, and husband's occupation are causal indicators for

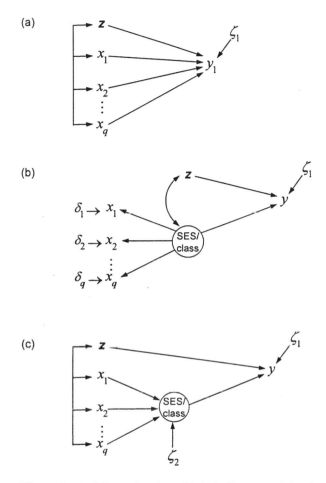

Figure 2   Unidimensional, multiple-indicator models of SES/class.

SES. Another example is to treat education and occupation as causal indicators of permanent income. Unfortunately, the additional causal indicators do not help to identify the model, and more specifically the error variances of ς_1 and ς_2 remain unidentified. Though if we use the model in Figure 2*a* in place of the model in Figure 2*c*, we can estimate the coefficients of the latter model consistently (Bollen & Davis 1993). This implies that we can separately enter multiple indicators of a unitary SES or class variable as explanatory variables, if these are causal indicators and the model corresponds to Figure 2*c*. As we saw above, with multiple effect indicators and a model that corresponds to Figure 2*b*, we will not have a consistent estimator of effects if we estimate a model like Figure 2*a*. So whether the indicators are causal or effect indicators matters. This points to the importance of reflecting on the nature of the indicators (Edwards & Bagozzi 2000).

Component Concepts

The premise of the discussion in the previous section was that SES or class was a unitary concept. A far more common assumption in the literature that we reviewed was that SES or class is composed of distinct components, each capable of exerting separate effects on fertility or child health. In this section we examine the issues that emerge under the component conceptualization of SES or class. As in the prior section, it is useful to draw a distinction between the number of SES or class variables used, the allowance for measurement error or not, and if there is error, whether there are causal or effect indicators.

Our starting point is the most typical model type that treats SES or class as several components with single variables representing each component. Figure 3a is the path diagram that corresponds to this situation. In it $x_1, x_2, \ldots, x_q$ are the components of SES or class measured without error, and they affect the fertility or child health outcome. Interestingly, this path diagram matches Figure 2a, in which there were multiple measures of a unitary concept of SES or class. The distinction is more analytical than a difference in diagrams. Here we are assuming that each SES or class variable represents a different component, whereas in the previous case we assumed that SES or class was a unitary concept but that the researcher employed multiple measures of it.

In contrast with our example in the above unitary section, we now assume that maternal education, household income, and husband's occupation are separate components with distinct effects on child health. Suppose that a researcher holds a component concept of SES but uses only maternal education. This implies that Figure 3a is the true model, but that the researcher estimated the model in Figure 1a. A classic case of omitted variable bias would accompany this strategy (Theil 1957). If x_1 is the included SES or class variable, its estimated effect would be contaminated by the omission of the $x_2, \ldots, x_q$ variables. Furthermore, the remaining determinants that compose z also would generally have biased and inconsistent coefficient estimators. The direction of bias would be difficult if not impossible to say without additional information about the impact of the omitted variables on y and the relation between the omitted and included explanatory variables.

Measurement error adds another layer of complexity. Consider first the case where we properly include measures of all components of SES or class, but each is an effect indicator of its respective component and contains random measurement error. Figure 3b is the path diagram that captures these relations, where the circles are the latent SES or class components and the x's are their corresponding measures. In our example, measures for maternal education, household income, and husband's occupation would not be perfect measures of the underlying three latent components. This is quite likely since both domestic and international studies have documented the measurement error in seemingly straightforward variables such as education (Bielby et al 1977, Strauss & Thomas 1996). If we ignore the measurement error in the x's and estimate a model that looks like Figure 3a when Figure 3a is true, then inconsistent estimators are the likely result, where the direction of bias would be difficult to determine. Recognition of the measurement error in the x's

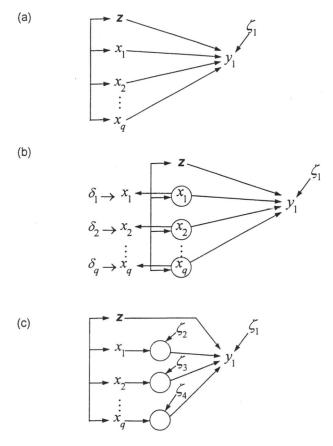

Figure 3 Multidimensional, multiple indicators for SES/class.

would only help if we knew its magnitude so that we could incorporate it into the estimation. Alternatively, we could vary the levels of measurement error variance to perform a type of sensitivity analysis (see Bollen 1989:Ch. 5).

Staying with the presence of measurement error in our SES or class variables, we move to the case where the measures are causal indicators of their respective latent component variables. Figure 3c is a path diagram of this situation. In a situation that is analogous to Figure 1a and Figure 2c, the model is not identified because unique values for the variances of the ζ's are unavailable. But remarkably, if we estimate the model in Figure 3a when Figure 3c is true, we will get consistent estimators of the regression coefficients.

Section Summary

The methodological problems in treating SES or class in studies of fertility or child health critically depend on whether (a) SES or class is unitary or has multiple components; (b) we have single or multiple measures; (c) variables contain measurement error or not; and (d) causal or effect indicators are present. Upon consideration of these methodological issues, the news is mixed.

On a positive note, in some of the cases we have described, failure to account for measurement error will not result in substantial problems. That is, in correctly specified models that have latent variables constructed by causal indicators, estimates of the coefficients for explanatory variables will be consistent even if the models are estimated without allowing measurement error. In contrast, this is not the case if the true model requires effect indicators. However, theory should guide decisions on the treatment of indicators as effect or causal.

Another encouraging conclusion is that sometimes we will be able to empirically distinguish between different models. For instance, a test of whether the coefficients of $x_2, \ldots, x_q$ are nonzero can distinguish the unitary concept and single-measure case in Figure 1a from the component multiple-variable SES or class model of Figure 3a. Yet in other cases we will not be able to differentiate models. An illustration is that the model in Figure 3a cannot be distinguished from the component model with causal indicators in Figure 3c or the unitary SES or class model in Figure 2c. This is an interesting case because the model in Figure 3a is a common one in the studies that we reviewed. This situation could be overcome by introducing additional dependent variables into the model. If, for instance, we had a second y variable that was directly influenced by SES or class but not the x's, we could form a MIMIC-type model (e.g., Hauser & Goldberger 1971). The unitary concept MIMIC model would imply proportionality constraints that would not be implied by the multicomponent SES or class construct so we could compare structures. Thus, the plausibility of SES as a unitary construct can be evaluated empirically (Hauser & Carr 1995).

In actuality, the situation is not necessarily as simple as that we have depicted. It is possible to have a model that combines the various scenarios we have described. For example, some of the SES components could have effect indicators, others could have causal indicators, and others could be relatively free of measurement error. The same consequences occur, however, in that failing to take measurement error into account in situations where the true model contains effect indicators or omitting a component can result in biased estimates. By formalizing these models we have been able to clarify important issues that arise in the treatment of SES. More attention should be devoted to evaluating the ways in which SES is empirically implemented. But interplay between theory and empirical analysis is also warranted.

CONCLUSIONS

From a sociological perspective, social class and socioeconomic status determine life chances. Prime representations of life chances are control over child mortality and control of fertility. Our literature review concentrated on the impact of SES or class on these variables in the context of micro, quantitative analyses in developing countries. Our framework organized studies according to whether they had a unitary, component, or ambiguous conceptualization of SES or class and whether they used single or multiple measures of these constructs. The pairing of a component concept of SES with multiple measures is the most common study type in our review. Though this is not surprising, it is surprising to find that in a significant proportion of studies we cannot determine whether the authors hold a unidimensional or multidimensional conception of SES. In addition, we did not expect to find, but did find, works that have component SES concepts but rely on a single measure to capture all components. We also did not expect the absence of papers that had a unidimensional concept for SES or class and a single measure or index for it. Overall, there was greater inconsistency in the dimensionality of concepts and the number of measures than we expected. Furthermore, with the exception of maternal education, there was considerable diversity in the measures of SES in these works.[8] So the literature is far from a consensus on either the definition or the measurement of SES or class. SES is often used as a control variable, and yet we do not fully understand how it operates and therefore how it should be measured.

One of the most glaring gaps we discovered is between the theoretical literature on class or SES and the manner in which these concepts appear in empirical work. Particularly striking is the absence of direct reference to measures of class. It is not infrequent to see social science arguments discuss the working class, middle class, landowning class, etc. as key players in societal development or as class positions that determine individual behavior. Yet the concept of class is barely mentioned in these papers, and instead many focus on the components of SES. One line of research that could bear fruit is to construct child health and fertility studies models that include variables to measure class, or the relation to the means of production. We mentioned Wright's (1985, 1997) approach to defining class. Including measures that capture this and other definitions of class in surveys and seeing how these perform compared to the typical SES measures would help to address this neglect. Miech & Hauser (1998) have investigated this issue with a Wisconsin data set, but we are unaware of research that addresses this issue for developing countries. Limited work on class is possible with the DHS and LSMS surveys. Some of the questions on these surveys provide information on the relation of the individual or the household to the means of production. These variables could be used to construct measures of class. A comparison of such measures to the more typical SES measures could reveal whether class has justifiably been ignored in these works. If SES has performance superior to class, then it will raise serious questions about the meaningfulness of sociological arguments suggesting an impact of class membership on individual behavior. Alternatively, if class has greater explanatory power than SES, we will need to reevaluate the effects that we have typically attributed to SES. So a high-priority item should be serious empirical comparisons of class vs. SES impacts on child health and fertility. Furthermore, if the results for class look promising, this would argue for incorporating better survey measures of class.

---

[8]A cursory look at articles from earlier years indicated that the patterns were not very different from those we discuss here.

An alternative to seeing SES and class as competing concepts is to better integrate them. One idea is to view class in the Marxian sense as the source of the other components of stratification. From this perspective, educational attainment, occupational prestige, income, and power have a common origin in class. Whether these specific parts mediate all of class's impact on other outcomes such as health and fertility is unknown. Furthermore, these specific components that derive from class could merge to form the SES construct.

Another conclusion we have reached is that sociologists and economists would do well to look beyond the domains of their own disciplines. Economists, for example, have focused enormous efforts on measuring and evaluating permanent income. While permanent income has received attention from some sociologists (see Hauser & Warren 1997 for example), it has not received the attention it deserves within sociology. There are some particularly intriguing parallels between permanent income and class. In a similar fashion, those economists interested in permanent income might benefit from examining the sociological literature on class.

Permanent income and class are both very general concepts. Moving in the opposite direction, the trend in the economic literature is toward disaggregating the various components of income, which may have quite different behavioral implications. Thus, combining all income sources into a total income measure and using this single measure in their empirical analysis may not be the most fruitful approach within a scenario of component explanatory variables. Sociologists might benefit from differentiating the components of income and including multiple sources when appropriate.

Another challenge to researchers is to determine the dimensionality of SES or class. Does each act as a single dimension, or is each made up of subparts that have distinct influences? A closely related issue is how best to measure SES or class and to specify the relation between the indicator variables and the constructs. Some of these issues were illustrated in the methodological section. The statistical technology that would enable us to address these and other questions exists, so this is not an obstacle to their investigation.

A response to the call for an examination of the unidimensionality of SES or class might be that this issue has already been resolved. For instance, Hauser (1972) demonstrated that variables such as parent's income, education, and occupational prestige have separate effects on status attainment, and Hodge (1970) showed that different components of SES have different effects on various social and political integration indicators. However, the behavior of these variables could depend on the outcome, and we are unaware of explicit tests in the context of child health and fertility. As Strauss & Thomas (1995) argue, some of the divergences in the findings on socioeconomic variables in the field of child health could reflect the failure to adequately account for unobservable factors such as family background. This is consistent with a unidimensional SES background type of effect. Furthermore, most of the attention in this area has been to SES to the neglect of class. Even if SES is best thought of as a collection of components, this does not address the standing of class as a unidimensional or multidimensional concept. In addition, there continues to be a gap between more qualitative literature, particularly in sociology where class plays a central role, and the quantitative empirical literature, where class barely appears in models. There is a need to confront these differences and to resolve the role of class.

Our focus in this review has been the relation of SES and class to child health and fertility in developing countries. But many of our findings and recommendations for the study of SES and class extend beyond these outcomes to research in developed as well as developing countries. Domestic stratification research shows some promising signs, but our impression is that many of our findings on the treatment of SES and class would hold for most such studies. Given the centrality of SES and class, we would all benefit from further attempts to answer the questions posed in our review.

ACKNOWLEDGMENTS

All authors contributed equally. This study was funded by a grant from the MEASURE Evaluation Project (USAID Grant Number HRN-A-00-97-0018-00). We thank Barbara Entwisle, David Guilkey, Rinku Murgai, Rachel Rosenfeld, and an anonymous reviewer for helpful comments. Direct correspondence to Kenneth Bollen, CB #3210, Dept. of Sociology, University of North Carolina, Chapel Hill, NC 27599-3210. E-mail: *bollen@email.unc.edu*. Fax: 919-962-7568.

APPENDIX A: DATA SOURCES FOR ANALYSES OF EDUCATION AND INEQUALITY IN DEVELOPING COUNTRIES

Living Standards Measurement Study (LSMS) of the World Bank. Household surveys for 21 developing countries, some with repeated cross-sections. Generally include data on education, employment, income, expenditures, and health data for all household members, but this varies by country. Some countries have community and school data that can be linked to households. http://www.worldbank.org/html/prdph/lsms

Third International Math and Science Study (TIMSS) of the International Association for the Evaluation of Educational Achievement (IEA). Data on student achievement in math and science, family background, teachers, classrooms, and schools for primary, middle, and upper secondary populations of students in 42 countries, eight of which are developing countries. Also includes a wide range of data on student perceptions and aspirations. http://timss.bc.edu

World Fertility Surveys (WFS). Internationally comparable surveys on fertility in 41 developing countries from the late 1970s and early 1980s. Data on demographic characteristics and fertility histories as well as education, employment, and health data for representative sample of women ages 15–50 and their household members. http://opr.princeton.edu/archive

Demographic Health Surveys (DHS). The successors to the World Fertility Surveys that contain additional runs of surveys during the 1990s, including an extended module on education and community-level data for some countries. Many countries have data for multiple years. http://opr.princeton.edu/archive and http://www.measuredhs.com

Family Life Surveys (FLS), conducted by RAND, for Malaysia, Indonesia, Guatemala, and Bangladesh. Surveys contain detailed current and retrospective data on family structure, economic status, education/training, transfers, migration, and other topics, as well as community and school data. Upon completion of the third wave of the Malaysia Family Life Survey, the three Malaysian surveys will enable researchers to examine the effects of family background on educational outcomes over half a century. Surveys for Malaysia and Indonesia are two of the few longitudinal surveys for developing countries. http://www.rand.org/FLS

International Stratification and Mobility File. A collection of standardized sample surveys with information on social stratification and social mobility created and maintained by Professor Harry Ganzeboom at Utrecht University in the Netherlands in collaboration with Professor Donald J. Treiman at the University of California, Los Angeles. Some resources are open for public access. http://www.fss.uu.nl/soc/hg/ismf/index.htm

Program for Student Assessment (PISA) of the Organization for Economic Co-operation and Development (OECD). An internationally standardized assessment of the skills and knowledge of 15-year-olds in 32 countries, 28 of which are members of the OECD, and four of which are developing countries (China, Brazil, Korea, Mexico). First round of surveys completed in 2000 contain data on student achievement in reading, math, and science, family background, teachers, classrooms, and schools, as well as student perceptions and aspirations. http://www.oecd.org/els/pisa/

African Census Analysis Project at The University of Pennsylvania. An archive of census data for over 20 African countries, many containing multiple years. Resources are generally only available to project members, but direct inquiries to the project director, Professor Tukufu Zuberi. http://www.acap.upenn.edu

Visit the Annual Reviews home page at www.AnnualReviews.org

LITERATURE CITED

Balk D. 1994. Individual and community aspects of women's status and fertility in rural Bangladesh. *Popul. Stud.* 48(1):21–45

Bankole A. 1995. Desired fertility and fertility behavior among the Yoruba of Nigeria: a study of couple preferences and subsequent fertility. *Popul. Stud.* 49:317–28

Becker GS. 1965. A theory of the allocation of time. *Econ. J.* 75:493–517

Becker GS. 1981. *A Treatise on the Family.* Cambridge, MA: Harvard Univ. Press

Becker GS, Lewis HG. 1974. On the interaction between the quantity and quality of children. *J. Polit. Econ.* 81(2):S279–88

Behrman JR, Deolalikar AB. 1988. Health and nutrition. In *Handbook of Development Economics*, ed. H Chenery, TN Srinivasan, 1:631–711. Amsterdam: North Holland Press

Bicego GT, Boerma JT. 1993. Maternal education and child survival: a comparative study of survey data from 17 countries. *Soc. Sci. Med.* 36(9):1207–27

Bielby WT, Hauser RM, Featherman DL. 1977. Response errors of black and non-black males in models of intergenerational transmission of social status. *Am. J. Sociol.* 82:1242–88

Bills DB, Godfrey DS, Haller AO. 1985. A scale to measure the socioeconomic status of occupations in Brazil. *Rural Sociol.* 50(2):225–50

Bollen KA. 1989. *Structural Equations with Latent Variables.* New York: Wiley

Bollen KA, Davis W. 1993. *Causal indicator models: identification, estimation, and testing.* Unpublished manuscript, Dep. Sociol., Univ. N Carolina, Chapel Hill

Bongaarts J, Potter RG. 1983. *Fertility, Biology and Behavior: An Analysis of the Proximate Determinants.* New York: Academic Press

Caldwell JC. 1979. Education as a factor in mortality decline: an examination of Nigerian data. *Popul. Stud.* 33(3):395–413

Casterline J, Cooksey E, Ismail AF. 1989. Household income and child survival in Egypt. *Demography* 26(1):15–36

Cleland J, Rodriguez G. 1988. The effect of parental education on marital fertility in developing countries. *Popul. Stud.* 42(3):419–42

Cortinovis I, Vella V, Ndiku J. 1993. Construction of a socio-economic index to facilitate analysis of health data in developing countries. *Soc. Sci. Med.* 36(8):1087–97

Curtis SL, Diamond I, McDonald JW. 1993. Birth interval and family effects on postneonatal mortality in Brazil. *Demography* 30:33–43

Dargent-Molina PS, James A, Strpoatz DS, Savitz DA. 1994. Association between maternal education and infant diarrhea in different household and community environments. *Soc. Sci. Med.* 38(2):343–50

Das Gupta M. 1997. Socio-economic status and clustering of child deaths in rural Punjab. *Popul. Stud.* 51(2):191–202

Davis K, Blake J. 1956. Social structure and fertility: an analytic framework. *Econ. Dev. Cult. Change* 4(3):211–35

Deaton A. 1992. *Understanding Consumption.* New York: Oxford Univ. Press

Defo BK. 1996. Areal and socioeconomic differentials in infant and child mortality in Cameroon. *Soc. Sci. Med.* 42(3):399–420

DeGraff DS, Bilsborrow RE, Guilkey DK. 1997. Community-level determinants of contraceptive use in the Philippines: a structural analysis. *Demography* 34:385–98

Desai S, Alva S. 1998. Maternal education and child health: Is there a strong causal relationship? *Demography* 35(1):71–82

Duncan OD. 1961. A socioeconomic index for all occupations. In *Occupations and Social Status,* ed. AJ Reiss, Jr, pp. 109–38. New York: Free Press

Durkin MS, Islam S, Hasan ZM, Zaman SS. 1994. Measures of socioeconomic-status for child health research—comparative results from Bangladesh and Pakistan. *Soc. Sci. Med.* 38(9):1289–97

Edwards JR, Bagozzi RP. 2000. On the nature and direction of relationships between constructs and measures. *Psychol. Methods* 5:155–74

Friedman M. 1957. *A Theory of the Consumption Function.* Princeton: Princeton Univ. Press

Gage AJ. 1998. Premarital childbearing, unwanted fertility, and maternity care in Kenya and Namibia. *Popul. Stud.* 52(1):21–34

Gordon RA. 1968. Issues in multiple regression. *Am. J. Sociol.* 73:592–616

Hauser RM. 1972. Disaggregating a social-psychological model of educational attainment. *Soc. Sci. Res.* 1:159–88

Hauser RM, Carr D. 1995. Measuring poverty and socioeconomic status in studies of health and well-being. Unpubl. ms., Dep. Sociol., Univ. Wisc. Madison

Hauser RM, Goldberger AS. 1971. The treatment of unobservable variables in path analysis. In *Sociological Methodology 1971,* ed. HL Costner, pp. 81–117. San Francisco: Jossey-Bass, Inc

Hauser RM, Tsai S, Sewell WH. 1983. A model of stratification with response error in social and psychological variables. *Sociol. Educ.* 56(1):20–46

Hauser RM, Warren JR. 1997. Socioeconomic indexes for occupations: a review, update, and critique. In *Sociological Methodology*, ed. AE Raftery, pp. 177–298. Cambridge, UK: Blackwell

Hirschman C, Guest P. 1990. Multilevel models of fertility determination in four southeast Asian countries: 1970 and 1980. *Demography* 27(3):369–96

Hoddinott J, Haddad L. 1995. Does female income share influence household expenditures? Evidence from the Cote D'Ivoire. *Oxford B. Econ. Stat.* 57(1):77–96

Hodge RW. 1970. Social integration, psychological well-being, and their socioeconomic correlates. In *Social Stratification: Research and Theory for the 1970s*, ed. EO Laumann. New York: Bobbs-Merrill Company, Inc

Hollingshead AB, Redlich FC. 1958. *Social Class and Mental Illness*, pp. 387–97. New York: Wiley

Houthakker HS. 1957. The permanent income hypothesis: a review article. *Am. Econ. Rev.* 47(2):396–404

Karim MB. 1990. Measuring socio-economic status of rural households in third world countries. *Int. J. Compar. Sociol.* 27:183–207

Levine RA, Levine SE, Richman A, Uribe FMT, Correa CS, Miller PM. 1991. Women's schooling and child-care in the demographic-transition—a Mexican case-study. *Popul. Dev. Rev.* 17(3):459–96

Liberatos P, Link BG, Kelsey JL. 1988. The measurement of social class in epidemiology. *Epidemiol. Rev.* 10:87–121

Link BG, Lennon MC, Dohrenwend BP. 1993. Socioeconomic-status and depression—the role of occupations involving direction, control, and planning. *Am. J. Sociol.* 98(6):1351–87

Lobao LM, Brown LA. 1998. Development context, regional differences among young women, and fertility: the Ecuadorean Amazon. *Soc. Forces* 76(3):819–49

Marmot MG, Smith GD, Stansfeld S, Patel C, North F, et al. 1991. Health inequalities among British civil servants: the Whitehall II Study. *Lancet* 337:1387–93

Marx K. [1894] 1978. *Capital*, Vol. 3. In *The Marx-Engels Reader*, ed. RC Tucker. New York: Norton. 2nd ed,

Marx K, Engels F, [1848] 1978. The Communist Manifesto. In *The Marx-Engels Reader*, ed. RC Tucker. New York: Norton. 2nd ed.

Mayer T. 1963. The permanent income theory and occupational groups. *Rev. Econ. Stat.* 45(1):16–22.

Miech RA, Hauser RM. 1998. *Social class indicators and health at midlife*. Unpublished manuscript. Dep. Sociol., Univ. Wisconsin-Madison

Montgomery MR, Gragnolati M, Burke KA, Paredes E. 2000. Measuring living standards with proxy variables. *Demography* 37(2):155–74

Mosley WH, Chen LC. 1984. An analytical framework for the study of child survival in developing countries. *Popul. Dev. Rev.* 10 (Suppl.):24–45

Parcel TL, Menaghan EG. 1994. Early parental work, family social capital, and early-childhood outcomes. *Am. J. Sociol.* 99(4):972–1009

Raftery AE, Lewis SM, Aghajanian A. 1995. Demand or ideation? Evidence from the Iranian marital fertility decline. *Demography* 32(2):159–82

Razzaque A, Alam N, Wai L, Foster A. 1990. Sustained effects of the 1974–75 famine on infant and child mortality in a rural area of Bangladesh. *Popul. Stud.* 44(1):145–54

Robert SA. 1999. Socioeconomic position and health: the independent contribution of community socioeconomic context. *Annu. Rev. Sociol.* 25:489–516

Sandiford P, Cassel J, Montenegro M, Sanchez G. 1995. The impact of women's literacy on child health and its interaction with access to health services. *Popul. Stud.* 49:5–17

Sastry N. 1997. Family-level clustering of

childhood mortality risk in northeast Brazil. *Popul. Stud.* 51:245–61

Schultz TP. 1997. Demand for children in low income countries. In *Handbook in Population and Family Economics, Vol. 1A*, ed. MR Rosenzweig, O Stark, pp. 349–430. Amsterdam: Elsevier Press

Steckel RH. 1995. Stature and standard of living. *J. Econ. Lit.* 33(4):1903–40

Strauss J, Thomas D. 1995. Human resources: empirical modeling of household and family decisions. In *Handbook of Development Economics*, Vol. 3A, ed. J Behrman, TN Srinivasan, pp. 1883–2023. Amsterdam: Elsevier

Strauss J, Thomas D. 1996. Measurement and mismeasurement of social indicators. *Am. Econ. Rev.* 86(2):30–34

Strauss J, Thomas D. 1998. Health, nutrition and economic development. *J. Econ. Lit.* 36:766–817

Theil H. 1957. Specification errors and the estimation of economic relationships. *Rev. Int. Statist. Inst.* 25:41–51

Therborn G. 1977. The rule of capital and the rise of democracy. *New Left Rev.* 103:3–42

Thomas D, Strauss J, Henriques M. 1990. Child survival, height for age and household characteristics in Brazil. *J. Dev. Econ.* 33(2):197–234

Treiman DJ. 1977. *Occupational Prestige in Comparative Perspective*. New York: Academic Press

Warner WL. 1949. *Social Class in America.* Chicago: Sci. Res. Assoc.

Waxler NE, Morrison BM, Sirisena WM, Pinnaduwage S. 1985. Infant mortality in Sri Lankan households—a causal model. *Soc. Sci. Med.* 20(4):381–92

Weber M. 1946. Class, status, and party. In *From Max Weber: Essays in Sociology*, trans. HH Gerth, CW Mills, pp. 180–95. New York: Oxford Univ. Press

Willis RJ. 1973. New economic approaches to fertility. *J. Polit. Econ.* 81(2):S14–S64

Wood CH, Lovell PA. 1992. Racial inequality and child mortality in Brazil. *Soc. Forces* 70(3):703–24

Wright EO. 1985. *Classes*. London, UK: New Left Books

Wright EO. 1996. The continuing relevance of class analysis—comments. *Theor. Soc.* 25(5):693–716

Wright EO. 1997. *Class Counts: Comparative Studies in Class Analysis*. Cambridge, UK: Cambridge Univ. Press

Wright EO, Costello C, Hachen D, Sprague J. 1982. The American class structure. *Am. Sociol. Rev.* 47:709–26

Zimmerman DJ. 1992. Regression toward mediocrity in economic stature. *Am. Econ. Rev.* 82:409–29

Annu. Rev. Sociol. 2001. 27:187–212

SPORT AND SOCIETY

Robert E. Washington and David Karen

Bryn Mawr College, Bryn Mawr, Pennsylvania 19010-2899;
e-mail: rwashing@brynmawr.edu, dkaren@brynmawr.edu

Key Words class, race, gender, media

■ **Abstract** Despite its economic and cultural centrality, sport is a relatively neglected and undertheorized area of sociological research. In this review, we examine sports' articulation with stratification issues, especially race, class, and gender. In addition, we look at how the media and processes of globalization have affected sports. We suggest that sports and cultural sociologists need to attend more closely to how leisure products and practices are produced and distributed and how they intersect with educational, political, and cultural institutions. We propose the work of Bourdieu and the new institutionalism to undergird future research.

INTRODUCTION

In "Program for a Sociology of Sport, " Bourdieu (1988:153) referred to the "special difficulties that the sociology of sport encounters: scorned by sociologists, it is despised by sportspersons." A few years ago, a member of the Bryn Mawr College curriculum committee responded to our request to teach a course on "Sport and Society" with an incredulous "why don't people just read the daily sports page?" The American Sociological Association not only lacks a Sociology of Sports section, its 2000 Annual Meeting lists only 5 of its 577 sessions under the designation "Leisure/Sports/Recreation."[1]

Yet, sports, indeed, constitute a major part of the US economy: the expenditures in 1998 for commercial sports totaled $17.7 billion and an additional $21.4 billion was spent on physical fitness, golf, bowling, and sports and recreation clubs (US Census Bureau 1999:46). These numbers don't even include the payments made by television to air sporting events. The pervasive interest in sports is revealed in

---

[1]An external reviewer commented that, in arguing that sport studies ought to be more central in sociology, we "overstate the underdevelopment of sport sociology as a working network of scholars who have been at it for 20–30 years." The reviewer goes on to point out that there is a free-standing association—North American Society for the Sociology of Sport, an annual meeting, a journal, and a sports book series by SUNY Press. Our work, very obviously, owes a lot to the work of these scholars. Our point, however, is precisely that they have been marginalized by the ASA and have had to go elsewhere to do their work.

varied forms. Sports get a separate section in every major daily newspaper; they fill stadiums and arenas around the world on a regular basis as people root, often maniacally, for their home teams; they spawned thousands of rotisserie leagues (i.e., sports leagues composed of fan-chosen teams) along with debates about the best players, teams, etc.; they occupy the weekends and evenings of parents and children; they receive massive expenditures of funds by schools and colleges in the United States; they occupy hours and hours of weekly commercial radio and television air time with accompanying astronomical advertising revenues; and they are increasingly the object of public policy as they engage the concerns of voters and politicians at the local, state, and federal levels. For all these reasons, we need a deeper understanding of this industry/activity/market/field.

The last review of sport and society in *Annual Review of Sociology* (Frey & Eitzen 1991) lamented the lack of theoretical development in the field. Though the field is still relatively underdeveloped, our review discovered an increased number of studies that are theoretically driven by two concerns: social stratification (especially with respect to race/ethnicity, gender, and, to a much lesser extent, class) and the institutional/organizational context of sports. Much of this new work draws on two fields *related* to sociology—cultural studies and social history. Though we do not attempt to cover all the work published by our disciplinary cousins, we do incorporate their insights into our discussion of stratification and social context. Briefly stated, this review article both explicates the new theoretical directions and summarizes the relevant literature pertaining to sports sociology.

Our cultural studies cousins have engaged various themes, such as hegemony and the body, in their attempt to understand the role of sports in the larger US culture. Drawing on the work of Raymond Williams (1977), students of sport began to use the concept of hegemony in their examination of media coverage of sport, sports fans' behavior (e.g. soccer hooliganism), and "hegemonic masculinity" (e.g., Connell 1990, 1995). In addition, various developments in sport have been studied as aspects of popular culture (Andrews & Loy 1993) and examined as residual or emergent phenomena (Williams 1977), constituting various forms of resistance (or challenges for incorporation) to the dominant hegemonic patterns. This approach suggests that sports and popular culture "be viewed as a site of ideological struggle where individual lives and experiences are involved in a process of interpretive negotiation with the surrounding social structures" (Andrews & Loy 1993:269, McDonald & Birrell 1999). Here, too, we must stress that we wish to link individual experience and meaning with the larger structural patterns in the society.

The cultural studies focus on the body and sport is often associated with issues of gender, sexuality, and feminism. There is an attempt to deal with how the body is presented and marketed, incorporated and marginalized. There are many examples of cultural studies' attention to the social constructions of the body and the ways in which these articulate with hegemonic notions of maleness, femaleness, homosexuality, and heterosexuality as well as race/ethnicity. Though many of these studies are focused on one or another specific "text" and thus have limited generalizability, there is an abiding attention to power and its contestation or reinforcement.

We have generally restricted ourselves to writings published since 1989. In a few cases, we cite earlier studies to contextualize a given argument or to highlight a portion of the field not covered in the previous review. Also, though we refer to some studies in other societies and the topic of "globalization of sport," this review emphasizes sport/society relations in the United States.

SOCIAL CLASS AND SPORT

As is true of its linkage to many institutions in the United States, social class is perceived as being only marginally relevant to sports. In fact, the sports sphere–with its obvious meritocratic orientation–prides itself on the degree to which one's social origins are of no import on the field, court, or course. The Williams sisters in tennis, African-Americans from modest social origins, have succeeded in a sport that caters primarily to those who are white and upper middle class or above. Indeed, there are many examples of athletes who have ascended from working class backgrounds into wealth and fame via sports. Hoberman (1997) has suggested that the astronomical social mobility of many black athletes, who represent, obviously, only a small percentage of the population, distort public perceptions of the opportunity structure for blacks, causing many whites to assume that blacks no longer face discrimination. But as a number of recent reviews have pointed out, the notion that sport is a readily accessible avenue to upward social mobility is a myth that continues to fuel the American Dream (Eitzen 1999, Coakley 1998, Reiss 1990a). The only studies that show statistically significant positive effects on mobility are those that focus on the collegiate experience (see, e.g. Sack & Thiel 1979).

Other studies of the link between social class and athletics have been produced primarily by historians (for an overview, see Pope 1997 and Reiss 1990b), who generally include class, race, and ethnicity in their discussions of sports. Steven Riess, in a rich, highly contextualized study (1989), has examined how different social classes related to sports as the urban landscape changed from the late nineteenth through the twentieth century. Gorn (1997) focuses on the articulation of boxing with working class culture after the Civil War. Markovits & Hellerman (2001 and see below) discuss the role of social classes in helping to cement the sports space of a country during the period of industrialization. Foley (1990) discusses the ways the rituals that surround football in a small Texas town help to reproduce patterns of race, gender, and class inequality. E. Digby Baltzell (1995), known for his studies of the upper class, studied the transformation of tennis from an aristocratic sport of amateur gentlemen, playing under the rule of a class authority that emphasized duty, to a democratic and bureaucratized game of professionals that recognizes only rights. This transformation, Baltzell argues, is part and parcel of the decline of civility in sports and in society more generally.

As noted above, Gramsci's notion of hegemony—especially as interpreted by Raymond Williams—has become an important concept in sports studies, especially in relation to discussions of social class. Gruneau & Whitson's *Hockey Night in Canada* (1993) and Eric Dunning's *Sport Matters* (1999), for example, discuss the ways in which class variations in emotions and notions of decorum lead to different patterns of behavior for both players and fans. Indeed, current discussions of violence in sport and among fans (especially soccer hooliganism) owe much to the figurational sociology of Norbert Elias and his students (see, e.g. Elias and Dunning 1986).

From our perspective, social class is a key component of our understanding of sports. It is important to understand what connects particular groups of people to particular sports activities and what role these play in the reproduction of inequality in a given society. Bourdieu's major statement on "Sports and Social Class" (1991; originally published in 1978; see, also, Bourdieu 1988) makes a number of key points: (*a*) sports must be considered a "field" which has its own dynamics, history, and chronology and is relatively autonomous from the society of which it is a part; (*b*) "sport, like any other practice, is an object of struggles between the fractions of the dominant class and between the social classes" (1991:361); (*c*) we must understand both what led to the "shift whereby sport as an elite practice reserved for amateurs became sport as a spectacle produced by professionals for consumption by the masses" (1991:364) and the political economy of all the accompanying personnel and industries involved with equipment, production, administration, etc.; and (*d*) the relationship between a social class and its sports participation will depend on spare time, economic and cultural capital, and the meanings and functions attributed to the sports practices by the various social classes. The latter, according to Bourdieu, might have to do with whether, for example, one wants to produce a strong body with protruding muscles, as in the working class, or a strong, healthy body, "properly" toned, as for the dominant class. Finally, along with any intrinsic benefits that might go to the body, Bourdieu wishes to add an appreciation of the "social value accruing from the pursuit of certain sports by virtue of the distinctive rarity they derive from their class distribution" (1991:369). The golf and polo practiced at exclusive clubs, Bourdieu suggests, for example, "enable the accumulation of social capital" and are a "pretext for select encounters . . . a technique of sociability" (1991:372). Part and parcel, then, of an understanding of sports participation is the conscious and unconscious orientations of different groups toward engaging in distinctive (as conceived by their social group), potentially rewarding (economically, culturally, and socially), and reinforcing (especially their positions in their local community) practices.

Bourdieu's sociology of taste, elaborated in *Distinction* (1984), attempts to link specific classes or class fractions to a particular orientation to the future (which he calls the *habitus*). These dispositions are related to these groups' relations to their bodies and to the adoption of specific lifestyles. Thus, Bourdieu elaborates the links between the locations of people in social space and their patterns of participation in and attention to different sports as a key aspect of the sociology of sports. This is revealed by the relatively autonomous space of sporting practices and its relation to leisure practices in general. Further, Bourdieu argues that class fractions not only engage in different sports but even when they engage in the same one, they often attach different intrinsic or extrinsic meanings to it. Critical to this approach is an historical or contextual grounding: hence this approach, for example, would analyze college football in 1900 by emphasizing its links to elite colleges, while in 2000 it would perhaps analyze college football by highlighting its links to television contracts and the professional game.

We believe that Bourdieu's emphasis on both the body and the relation of a group's social origin to its sports space provides a more theoretically grounded approach to the sociology of sports than those previously offered. Bourdieu's notion of habitus, which links one's social origins to one's likely destination through a set of dispositions toward the future, manifests itself in the body, which in turn is the "materialization of class taste" (Bourdieu 1984: 190). In addition, Bourdieu argues that each class and class fraction has a different instrumental relation to the body and that this is associated with its most common sports preferences: the working classes preferring contact sports; the middle classes (especially the upwardly mobile) orienting toward activities that lead to an attractive "body-for-others"; and the dominant classes engaging in sports activities that are played in exclusive clubs with little, if any, bodily contact between the competitors (1984: 212–217). Bourdieu hypothesizes "a general law that a sport is most likely to be adopted by a social class if it does not contradict that social class's relation to the body at its deepest and most unconscious level, i.e. the body schema, which is the depository of a whole world view and a whole philosophy of the person and the body" (1984: 217–18).[2]

With this perspective in mind, we can see how Wacquant's ethnographic account of a boxing gym on the South Side of Chicago not only allows us to understand the attraction of a violent sport insofar as it provides respite from the unplanned violence of the city (1992) (as well as a vague possibility of economic advance) but "the promise of social difference and even transcendence: the professional ethic of sacrifice enables boxers to tear themselves away from the everyday world and create a moral and sensual universe *sui generis* wherein a transcendent masculine self may be constructed" (1998:325).

Though Bourdieu's work focuses primarily on social class, a broader notion of social origin, which would include race/ethnicity and gender, would be appropriate for the United States. Along these lines, then, we might think of using biographies of athletes to understand the links between their social origin, habitus, and ultimate sport destination. Similarly, we think that comparative studies of cultural consumption and participation would help us delineate more clearly the complex links between background, habitus, and sport participation.

RACE AND SPORT

As in the larger society, patterns of race discrimination in sport are rampant. These patterns, including evidence of institutional racism, receive far more attention than any other topic in the area of race relations and sport. In addition, however,

---

[2]Bourdieu's work includes empirical research on France; his approach needs to be tested in cross-cultural context.

sociologists have attended to the effect of sports participation for racial and ethnic minorities on social mobility, self-esteem, and group identity. The role of the media in creating and reinforcing racialized representations of athletes has also been discussed. Finally, there have been exchanges about sport and race as contested terrain (see, below, gender as well) along with the issue of race and differential sports performance.

Though some of the studies about race and sport concern past discrimination, most focus on current practices. The key issues addressed are: racial disparity in the payment of professional athletes, stacking (discrimination in allocating players' positions in team sports), retention barriers (discrimination in retaining sub-star minority athletes), and continuing practices of racial exclusion or tokenism.

Several recent studies have pointed to unequal pay for equal ability in the National Basketball Association (NBA). One suggests that the NBA's black players are paid from $17,000 to $26,000 less than white players (Koch & VanderHill 1988). Another study, focusing only on sub-star starters, indicates that whites are paid 18% more than blacks, but it goes on to suggest that white sub-star starters are preferred because they increase fan attendance (Leonhardt 1997). In the case of major league baseball (MLB), it has been suggested that analyses of racially based pay disparities are confounded by the fact that many more sub-star whites are likely to be retained on team rosters, such that the remaining pool of blacks have clearly superior statistics (Eitzen 1999:22). Similar racial disparities have been found in the salaries of coaches. One study, for example, comparing coaches at the same hierarchical level, found that white coaches were paid as much as 14% more than their black counterparts (Pattnayak & Leonard 1994).

Stacking, or allocating minorities to playing positions that have less central-ity and control, has been documented in such sports as college and professional football, professional baseball, and women's volleyball (Smith & Leonard 1997, Margolis & Piliavin 1999, Eitzen 1999). During the 1998 National Football League (NFL) season, stacking was evidenced in the following positions: quarterback (91% white), center (83% white), wide receiver (92% black), running back (87% black), cornerback (99% black) and safety (91% black) (Lapchick 1999a). Preference for whites in certain playing positions has also been evidenced in high school football, sometimes with corrosive effects on a community's race relations (Hersch 1989).

In reference to the issues of racial group exclusion and tokenism in sports, recent works consist of both retrospective and current accounts that assess oppor-tunities for participation. One source of retrospective accounts of racial exclusion is journalistic, specifically recent biographical profiles and biographies of pioneer black American athletes: e.g., Jackie Robinson in baseball (Kahn 1997, Tygiel 1983), Arthur Ashe in tennis (Ashe & Rampersad 1993), and Tiger Woods in golf (Feinstein 1998). Each discusses the earlier practices of segregation and the cur-rent state of progress in the sport. Other accounts present historical studies of racism and racial exclusion focused on, among other topics, African-American golfers, sports in the late-nineteenth-century Philadelphia black community, and British rugby (Dawkins & Kinlock 2000, Jable 1994, Eisen & Wiggins 1994). An excellent critical historical overview is provided by Sammons (1994).

Studies of current opportunities for participation in sports document persisting patterns of institutional racism in sports organizations. For example, professional team contrasts between percentages of white owners and black players: (NFL 100% vs. 67%); (NBA 100% vs. 80%); (MLB 97% vs. 18%). Similar predominance of whites can be seen among professional team head coaches/managers, directors of player personnel or general managers, and assistant coaches (Lapchick 1999a, Kravitz 1998, Weiberg 1998). In the four major professional sports leagues, for example, the NBA shows the greatest representation of head coaches/managers of color with only 17% (5 of 29) at the beginning of the 1997–1998 season. College sports organizations also exhibit strong patterns of institutional racism (Lapchick 1999a, Eitzen 1999). For example, in 1997–1998, excluding historically black institutions, Divisions I, II, and III colleges employed white head coaches in over 87% of basketball programs and approximately 97% of football and baseball programs. Similarly, over 95% of the Athletic Directors in each of the three divisions were white (Lapchick 1999a). There has also been some discussion of strategies for remedying institutional racism in sports (Shropshire 1996, Magdalinski 1997, Eitzen 1999).

While the topic of discrimination attracted the most scholarly interest, there has been increasing interest in sports as a contested terrain where racial meanings "are not only made but struggled over" (Hartmann 2000). South Africa has been a major object of studies that demonstrated the influential role of sports in the struggle against racial apartheid (Rees 1996, Booth 1998, Jarvie 1985). Also, several studies of British sports have focused on sports contests and sport stadiums as settings where white working class fans routinely harass racial minorities both on the playing fields and in the surrounding neighborhoods. One study notes that, while Britain had a strong and effective anti-apartheid movement in the 1970s and 1980s advocating sanctions against white South African sports teams, recent Parliamentary legislation has weakened protests against racism in British sports (Greenfield & Osborn 1997). A related set of recent studies have focused on the ways in which racial minorities use sports to manifest resistance to racial subordination: the black American athletes' revolt at the 1968 Olympics as a courageous stand that threatened to disrupt the link "between sport culture and liberal democratic ideology that legitimizes individualist, assimilationist visions of racial justice in the United States" (Hartman 1996, Moore 1991); black American expressiveness on the playing field as defiance of white control (Andrews 1996); black cricket clubs in Britain as both assertions of black masculinity and symbolic markers of black community (Carrington 1998); and Native American protests against sports teams' use of Native American mascots as challenges to traditional notions of white American masculinity (Davis 1993). Taking a different direction with interesting implications for these conflicts, several studies present social policy perspectives suggesting that sports sociology should operate not only as an intellectual enterprise but also as a vehicle for promoting universal norms of democratization and social justice (Donnelly 1993, Rowe 1998).

Contrasted to these studies of sports as a site of conflict and resistance are studies that emphasize the effects of sports for minority group members' social mobility, group identity, and self-esteem. While many individual minority group members have experienced upward social mobility as a result of their achievements in sports, most studies agree that actual mobility outcomes for minority group communities have been exaggerated. For instance, the odds facing a high school graduate who aspires to a professional sports career is a prohibitive 10,000 to 1 (Eitzen 1999). Moreover, such opportunities for racial minorities have been provided by only a few sports (baseball, basketball, football, and boxing). Nevertheless, despite the prohibitive odds, aspirations for upward social mobility through sports can sometimes affect the culture of an entire society as in case of the Dominican Republic (Klein 1991). This theme also appears in works focused on basketball and boxing in inner city black American communities (Frey 1994; Wacquant 1992).

Most studies dealing with sports and social mobility in minority group communities emphasize the negative effects. These studies stress such things as the exaggerated expectations the sports success of a Julius Erving or a Michael Jordan can encourage in minority youths (Lashley 1995); the enormous time demands on college student-athletes that cause them to disengage from their student roles (Adler & Adler 1991); the exploitation of black student athletes by colleges resulting in low academic performance and reinforcement of the American racial hierarchy (Spigner 1993, Zimbalist 1999); and the abysmally low graduation rates of black student-athletes in many top level Division I basketball and football programs (Eitzen 1999). While these rates approximate the overall poor graduation rates for college students, there is little evidence that college athletic departments care about improving the academic skills of the black student athletes they recruit (Eitzen 1999, Zimbalist 1999).

The NCAA passed Proposition 48, a measure raising admission standards for college athletes, which most black NCAA coaches opposed because they felt it unfairly deprived underprivileged black athletes of an opportunity to attend college (Reed & Chaney 1989). With specific reference to female athletes, studies of the effects of sports participation indicate there were benefits for white and Hispanic women; no equivalent academic benefits were found for black females (Kraus & Hanson 1999). More studies of the academic experiences of black college female athletes are needed to clarify the actual dynamics of their student-athlete roles. In contrast to the apparent negative impact of sports participation on minorities' academic performance, several studies have found that it enhances their self-esteem—through allowing them to display a more individualistic style (Sailes 1996); acquire more social capital (Miller, et al. 1999); or develop a positive identity that eases the struggle to assimilate into the United States from an immigrant culture (Lord 1984). The benefit derived from sports most highlighted in recent studies is that of community or subcultural identity: through playing basketball in Brooklyn, NY (Frey 1994); through playing football for Black Americans and

Native Americans (Gems 1998); through boxing in a black Chicago inner city gym (Wacquant 1992); through segregated sports in black Pittsburgh (Ruck 1993); through an Irish football club in twentieth century Scotland (Bradley 1996).

These studies of mobility, identity, and self-esteem are directly relevant to the theoretical conceptions of sports as contested terrain and the Bourdieu-an approach. Just as individuals struggle to enhance their personal status/distinction within their sport and community, they also struggle to enhance their sport's status in the larger community and society. Focusing on those sports, we must study the layered relationships of the individual sports participants to the community's and society's reward structure as well as to the larger opportunity structure.

Studies of media representations of racial minority athletes and their sports achievements have increased sharply over the past decade—in part reflecting the expanded role of media in big-time college and professional sports. Most of these studies share the assumption that "race is constructed largely in media culture . . . ," which serves the interests of the dominant white community (Kellner 1996). This is reflected in the predominance of white radio and television announcers for professional sports—NBA 77%; NFL 82%; and MLB 78% (Lapchick 1999a). Lapchick also reports that 90% of the 1600 daily newspapers in the United States have no African-American sports writers. Many of these studies regard the media as the source of negative racial stereotypes of black athletes that stress their physical rather than intellectual abilities (Curry 1997, McCarthy & Jones 1997, Rada 1996). Also, it has been suggested that the media disproportionately emphasize black athletes' social deviance (Albom 1993, Lapchick 1999b). In an interesting departure from these static conceptions of the media's representations of black athletes, a recent biography of Joe Louis revealed a dynamic process of media racial representation as it showed how Joe Louis' image was transformed from racist stereotype to heroic figure after he defeated the German champion (Mead 1985).

Another important area of investigation focused on media representation of minority athletes in advertising. Here, too, most studies suggest that the media has played a negative role. One study based on a content analysis of ads in *Sports Illustrated* from 1985 to 1995 indicated that black athletes were more likely to be depicted as succeeding because of their innate ability, whereas white athletes were more often depicted as succeeding because of hard work, intelligence, or leadership skills. Black athletes were also depicted in these ads as being angry, violent, and hypersexual (Dufur 1997). Similar views were presented by other studies suggesting, for example, that a Nike advertising campaign stereotyped black athletes as belonging to either athletic groups or gangs (Cole 1996) and that the media routinely indulges in "enlightened racism" or token racism to mask the society's class, sexual, and racial inequalities (McKay 1995; see also Jamieson 1998 on Nancy Lopez).

A more neutral assessment of the effects of advertising on black athletes is presented in a *Sports Illustrated* article that concludes that some black superstars (e.g. Michael Jordan, David Robinson) have achieved cross-over status, which allows them to shed their racial identity and cash in on their celebrity (Swift

1991). Going even further, another study sees the effects of advertised images of black superstars as positive because they transcend the historical stereotypes of black men as being erotic or dangerous (McDonald 1996). These few positive accounts of the media's role notwithstanding, most studies indicate that the media representations are damaging because they have a large hand in projecting negative public images of black American males.

Closely related and perhaps the most emotionally charged debate pertaining to sports and race relations focuses on the disproportionate black American presence in certain professional and big time collegiate sports. This debate was ignited most recently by John Hoberman, who argues in *Darwin's Athletes*, that black sports achievements are sustaining the traditional stereotypes of blacks as physically primitive. Hoberman also argues that the current cultural fixation on black athletes has negatively impacted black intellectual achievement (1997). The book encountered a groundswell of critical reviews. Most targeted his argument alleging a black community fixation on sports. Among their counterarguments were suggestions that the overrepresentation of black Americans in major sports was due to the failure of the American political economy to provide adequate opportunities for black Americans (Curtis 1998) and that the fixation on sports derived not from the black community but American society (Sigelman 1998). Others argued that Hoberman's book reinforced ideas about black inferiority and contributed to preserving the mythical concept of race (Myers 1998). Several black scholars argued that Hoberman's book not only insulted black intellectuals and black athletes but also exhibited white intellectual arrogance by suggesting that the alleged black fixation on sport had resulted in the underdevelopment of the black intellectual commmunity (Shropshire & Smith 1998).

Hoberman's book was hardly written in an intellectual vacuum. Several earlier articles in *Sports Illustrated* had drawn attention to the way black athletes in the 1960s transformed racially restrictive or segregated college and professional sports (Fimrite 1987, Kirkpatrick 1991, Price 1997). Such articles and the Hoberman book led to a new book that pushed the debate about black athletic dominance beyond cultural arguments to a genetic explanation. This view was presented in the provocatively titled book—*Taboo: Why Black Athletes Dominate Sports and Why We Are Afraid To Talk About It* (Entine 2000). Despite its controversial thesis, this book has attracted much less serious scholarly attention than Hoberman's book. No doubt this was influenced by the fact that the author lacked training in biology. Genetic explanations of black athletic achievements have been countered by both social constructionist arguments and physical anthropological research (Harrison 1998, Gladwell 1997, Goldsmith 2000).

GENDER AND SPORT

The work in the field of gender and sport ranges from the very concrete, empirical reports of the *Racial and Gender Report Card* (Lapchick 1999a) and marketing studies (Lopiano 1998, Millman 1997) to the more ethereal cultural studies that include references to Baudrillard and Foucault (e.g. Andrews 1998, Eskes et al 1998). The two primary foci in this area concern constructions of masculinity and femininity and Title IX. Scholars have begun to ask questions about how gender articulates with race, class, and sexuality in determining patterns of sports partic- ipation and experience (e.g. Festle 1996, Carrington 1998, McKay et al. 2000, Gruneau & Whitson 1993, Messner 1992, Davis 1997). The literature on Title IX, primarily journalistic, focuses on the struggles for athletic resources among contending groups, the various court cases that have arisen, and the successes and failures of its implementation. The work that deals with femininity and masculinity recognizes that many contradictions lurk beneath the assumed positive outcome of increased female sports participation such as homophobia, "emphasized feminin- ity" (Connell 1990), etc. This area of research also touches on issues involving the media (especially, lack of coverage of women's sports'), the body, and language.

At a very basic level, there is the question of gender equity in sports: Are equivalent resources available to men and women? The answer, despite an enor- mous start to closing the gap, is NO. A number of new opportunities for women have emerged in the US sports world. Perhaps, most notably, the relatively new Women's National Basketball Association (WNBA) has provided unprecedented opportunities for women to play professional basketball.[3] Women's soccer has quickly established itself as world class. Similarly, an explosion has occurred in women's sports participation in schools and colleges. In the first 25 years after Title IX's enactment in 1972, the number of girls playing interscholastic sports increased eightfold. At the college level, even two years after Title IX was passed, the ratio of male to female athletic scholarships was 1,000 to 1; in 1998, it was 1.38 to 1 (US Department of Education 1997, Lapchick 1999a). At the same time, women's participation in professional and college sports–at all levels (manage- ment, coaching, playing)–pales in comparison to men's (for an extensive review, see Lapchick 1999a). Perhaps the most disappointing effect of Title IX has been with respect to the coaches of women's teams: In 1972, more than 90% of women's teams were coached by females, whereas in 1998 men held the majority of head coaching positions of women's teams.[4]

The most recent data (Suggs 2000) reveal that in 1998–1999 women made up 42% of Division I athletes, received 42% of scholarship monies, 31% of recruiting budgets, 34% of coaching-salary budgets, and 33% of total operating expenses. According to Andrew Zimbalist (2000:B9), women "still play in inferior facilities, stay in lower-caliber hotels on the road, eat in cheaper restaurants, benefit from smaller promotional budgets, and have fewer assistant coaches." Bhonslay (1997) notes women athletes' major advances in getting product endorsement deals but

---

[3] Banet-Weiser (1999) suggests, in fact, that the emergence of the WNBA, especially in comparison to the male NBA, makes possible as well new representations of masculinity and femininity.
[4] For a longitudinal overview of women's participation in intercollegiate sport, see Acosta & Carpenter (2000).

laments that their attempts to commodify themselves lag behind men's [see also Lopiano (1998), Millman (1997)].

The research on masculinity and femininity in sports encompasses a diverse range of topics—from male/female participation and media studies to studies of resistance and transformation of gendered power relations. The most impressive works attempt to relate sports participation to theories of gender identity and inequality and to examine the links among gender, race, class, and the larger political economy. Carrington (1998), for example, argues that the assertion of a masculine identity through sports allows black men to assert their racial identity in a more unified way, one that protects them from the ideologies and practices of white racism. He goes on to point out, however, how this excludes black women from this construction of racial identity.

The starting point for much of this work on gender construction and sport is Messner's (1988) claim that female athletes' identities are *contested ideological terrain*. Messner's and others' (e.g. McKay et al 2000, Klein 1993) work on masculinities also focuses on the contested nature of this gender construction. A number of historical studies of women athletes recognize this and attempt to describe the nature and social construction of that contested terrain (e.g., Griffin 1998, Festle 1996, Cahn 1994, Nelson 1994, Guttman 1991).

Research on masculine identities and sports often focuses on the relationship between sports and violence. Nixon (1997), in a very exploratory study, found that for men, a belief in the value of toughness in sport, an experience of having hurt other athletes, and participation in team and contact sport were related to physical aggression outside of sport; whereas for women only participation in contact sport was related to physical aggression outside of sport. In a study of the relationship between gender, athletic participation, and attitudes toward violence, Nixon (1996) found that both general socialization of males and specific socialization of males in sport engender attitudes of toughness and perceptions of pressure to play hurt, which, in turn, could cause them to engage in risky or violent behavior. McKay and associates' (2000) *Masculinities, Gender Relations, and Sport* devotes an entire section to "men's violence and sport," with specific studies on such phenomena as televised sports and domestic violence, bar fights and college athletics, and the violence of boxing.

Many of these analyses on the social construction of gender suggest that males and females are pressured to help maintain the appearances of "hegemonic masculinity" (Connell 1987), in which men appear to be well-muscled, strong, unemotional, and extremely oriented to a win-at-all-costs code of athletics, and women appear uninterested in sports. If they do engage in athletic endeavors, women must "emphasize their femininity" (Connell 1987) by wearing their hair long and their dresses frilly; if possible, they should sport a husband. Jane O'Hara (1997) reports that her mom told her that if she was going to be an athlete, she should "walk softly and carry a big lipstick." The dominant constructions of masculinity and femininity hover menacingly above athletes' behavior. For example, in women's sports, homophobic concerns are especially troubling (Greendorfer &

Rubinson 1997, Griffin 1998). Pointing to one major source of these hegemonic constructions, Messner and associates (1993) argue that televised sports commentary tends to reinforce gender and racial hierarchies by considering women athletes and activities as "other," by infantilizing them, and by framing women athletes' accomplishments ambivalently. Another series of studies focuses on the way dominant gender relations are structured and reinforced among adolescents. Eder & Parker (1987), in an analysis of a peer-group culture at a working class middle school, found that athletic-related activities–especially the male athletic events that were the main social activities of the school—tended to reinforce dominant notions of gender because sports usually gave the male athletes and female cheerleaders high visibility and social status. The boys' involvement in competitive, achievement-oriented activities and the girls' involvement in appearance and emotion-management activities helped further cement the hegemonic notions of gender.

Shifting to a related but different emphasis, Miller and colleagues (1998) focus on the relationship between sports participation and sexual behavior. They note that athletic participation, while enhancing each gender's social status, has opposite effects on boys' and girls' sexual activity: boys gain greater resources to get sex and the girls greater resources to resist it. Similarly, Holland & Andre's (1994) analysis of high school and college students also suggests that higher social status is associated with athletic participation and that this is even more the case for athletes in "sex appropriate" sports. Investigating the links between sports, gender construction, and status, two studies of elementary school—one low-income, primarily black (Hasbrook & Harris 2000) and the other upper middle-class white (Adler et al 1992)–found very similar constructions of hegemonic masculinity with physically dominant, sports-oriented boys enjoying relatively high status.

Many of the analyses of masculinity and femininity look for contradictions, revealing how current sporting practices may in some ways resist or subvert the hegemonic influences while in other ways they reinforce it. Kane (1995), Theberge (1997, 1998), and, in a more anecdotal vein, Nelson (1994) present both theoretical and empirical analyses that suggest how sport may transform the assumed female/male "oppositional binary." Kane argues that sport should be seen as a continuum on which, simply, *athletes* (of different levels) compete; the male/female dichotomy is dropped and the possibilities for, e.g., co-ed competition become real. The social construction of mixed-sex cheerleading as a sport suggests both that sport is not an exclusive male preserve and that it is not only women athletes who struggle with assumptions of gender-inappropriate behavior (Grindstaff & West 2000). In a series of interesting analyses of women's ice hockey, Theberge (1997, 1998, 2000) argues that even as women's hockey contests dominant notions of gender construction, it still reinforces them in that the men's game is considered the norm against which all else is measured. Andrews' (1998) study of "feminizing Olympic reality" similarly showed that even as women's sports and female athletes got increased coverage in the 1996 Olympics, NBC consciously tried (successfully!) to seduce female viewers into watching sports in a way that reinforced essentialist notions of women and femininity.

Eskes and colleagues (1998) argue that women's fitness texts use a feminist label—empowerment—to draw women into the exercise and fitness regimens, only to resurrect and reinforce ideals of physical beauty and conventional notions of femininity, rather than focusing on "true" empowerment: health and equality in the larger society. As Judith Butler says, "you only have permission to be this strong if you can also look this beautiful" (quoted in Wheaton & Tomlinson 1998). In their study of windsurfing subcultures, Wheaton & Tomlinson (1998) provide a trenchant analysis of an attempt by women to construct a new cultural identity in the context of a new subculture. Their work suggests both the possibilities of engaging in oppositional activity—e.g., constructing identities as female athletes, developing muscles and bodily skills—and the difficulties of undermining dominant power relations. In an interesting but methodologically flawed analysis, Snyder & Ammons (1993) report on patterns of male-female play on the field in a coed softball league that is dedicated through its rules to equalizing men's and women's participation. It turns out that as the level of skill of the league increases, competition increases, and men increasingly attempt to exclude women from key plays. Thing (1998), in a study of Danish female elite athletes, found that the women tended to maintain a dual gender notion but enjoyed the emotions associated with sport even (especially?) as they deviated from traditional notions of femininity. Thing asks how the emotions that are associated with sport play out differently in men and women outside of sport.

Though the range of issues that we have subsumed under the label of masculinity and femininity is quite broad, all can be linked to issues of power, status, and social construction. While this broader focus has become more common in studies of gender and sport, we urge scholars to incorporate this focus in studies of race/ethnicity and social class (as some already have) and to contextualize their studies in reference to the political, economic, and organizational dynamics of cultural consumption and participation in the larger society.

MEDIA AND SPORTS

Scholars have explored the relations of various media to sports but have focused chiefly on television, which most think has fundamentally altered sports. In the words of one, "television does not present us with a sports event but with a sports event (already highly structured by the commodity-logic) that is mediated by television" (Jhally 1989). A variety of analytical models and theoretical perspectives have been used to explore the role and significance of mediated sports. Among the most prominent are the critical approaches, the transactional model, and the circuit of capital model. The critical approaches stress the negative ideological effects of mediated sports on political consciousness and political mobilization. While highlighting important issues, these critical approaches too often are based on simplistic explanations that reduce sports to their presumed political significance. The transactional model presents a more complex approach that consists primarily of a research agenda on mediated sports, which focuses on: (*a*) the audience experience—how it differs from the stadium experience, its unique grat-ifications, and its socialization effects; (b) the nature of mediated sports content—the different languages presented (spoken, written, visual), value motifs, and links to dominant American values; and (c) the dynamics of the mediated sports pro-duction complex comprised of sports and media organizations that exert pressures on sports journalism—issues of ownership, organizational control, and internal decision making (Wenner 1989). In contrast, the circuit-of-capital model is based on an adaptation of Marxian theory that focuses on four moments: (a) the pro-duction of cultural products; (b) the texts that are produced; (c) how these texts are read by ordinary people; and (d) 'lived cultures' and social relations—the use made of reading texts and their potential as materials for new cultural production (Jhally 1989). These more complex analytical approaches to understanding the relationship of media and sports (which may include concern with the ideological implications) focus primarily on *process.*

It is now generally acknowledged that mediated sports are a highly profitable commodity. The increased importance of media in sports is revealed in the scale of finances involved. In the NBA, the 1999 regular season 30-second commercial cost $75,000 rising to $400,000 for the championship (Heisler 1999). For the 1999 World Series, NBC initially charged $300,000 for a 30 second commercial, about 20% more than Fox charged in 1998. The demand, however, was so strong that NBC increased its rate to $320,000 per 30 seconds (Freeman et al. 1999). For the Super Bowl, in 1998, the cost for a 30-second spot averaged $1.6 million, which was up from $1.3 million two years before; and in 1999, the average price increased by 25% with one advertiser paying $3 million for a 30-second ad (McClellan 1999).

The increased financial leverage of mediated sports has augmented its influence and power. This can be seen in both big time Division I college sports and profes-sional sports (Eitzen 1999). Some scholars suggest that this media involvement has resulted in the increased commodification of sports, which has ruined sports for the fans (Klatell & Marcus 1988). One study predicts, based on current trends, that economic forces will remove the most important sports events from broadcasting to pay-per-view unless Congress intervenes to constrain them (Eastman & Meyer 1989). This rampant commercialization has already occurred in boxing. Noting that the balance of power has tilted in favor of television, another study suggests a model of government intervention based on the experience of Australia where the government imposed controls over media imperialism to protect citizens' cultural rights (Rowe 1996). This may not, however, be feasible in some nations.

Looking at the media-sports linkage from the other end, one study found that commercial sports had greater influence over the daily press than did noncom-mercial sports because sports writers, under the pressure of deadlines, depend on routine news sources (e.g. athletes, spokespersons, team officials). Commercial sports teams easily provided these news sources, thus making the sports writ-ers' alliance with them a practical necessity (Lowes 1997). This is yet another illustration of the impact of commodification.

Also attracting a good deal of recent scholarly attention is the topic of media influence on images of race and gender in society (Duncan & Messner 2000). While there have been some notable examples of positive racial images, for example in the representations of such black sports superstars as Michael Jordan and Tiger Woods, the media has often used its enormous power to represent black athletes as poster boys for various social transgressions and taboos (Kellner 1996, Lapchick 1999b). An example of this is revealed in a recent *Sports Illustrated* article on out-of-wedlock fathers, which highlighted mostly black NBA players (Wahl & Wertheim 1998). Numerous studies have also documented skewed representations of gender in everything from coverage of women's sports and descriptions of women's sports in media guides to comments about non-athletic aspects of the women's lives (Eitzen 1999). Sports media also influence governmental perceptions of social problems as evidenced, for example, in the influence of *Sports Illustrated* reports that prompted Congress to hold hearings on steroid use (Denham 1997).

One of the most frequently discussed topics in sports sociology concerns the meaning of sports for social identity. "The identities forged in sport which may be multiple or overlapping, include gendered, local, ethnic, national, or supernational" (MacClancy 1996). While studies of the impact of sports on social identity initially focused on this topic without regard to the media, a number of recent studies have explored directly the effects of mediated sports on social identity, particularly national identity. One study, finding pervasive national stereotypes in newspaper and television sports reporting, concluded that the media has the ability both to unify a nation with pride and to create hostile feelings toward opponents or outsiders (Blain et al. 1993). Coming to similar conclusions, another study, investigating the role of media in constructing images of several nations (England, Ireland, Scotland, and Wales) during the 1995 Rugby World Cup match in South Africa, found that the media contributed significantly to the "I/we and us/them identities" of those national groups (Tuck 1998). What if the sport and the sports media hail from different countries? A study based on a content analysis of *Sports Illustrated Canada* suggests that national identity may be weakened if the sport and media are foreign (Vallentine 1997). *Sports Illustrated Canada* was forced to close after three years because it failed to meet the 80% Canadian content level required by Canadian law. Sometimes these issues of national identity may be complicated by having to choose between cultural protection of national identity and consumer freedom of choice (Boyle & Haynes 1996).

One of the most important and complex topics pertaining to mediated sports concerns the quality of the television viewers' experience. While it is generally agreed that the television experience differs fundamentally from the stadium experience, there is much debate about its nature. An earlier 1984 study argued that television altered the relationship between fan and athlete, causing irreparable damage to the traditional spectator experience (Rader 1984). Relating the development of television sports to broader social changes, it argued that this development corresponded to the increasing suburbanization of the population and the privatization of leisure. Moreover, it argued that as the teams with television contracts became more professionalized and commercialized, amateur sports declined. Expressing a similar view, a more recent study has argued that the mediated sport has several consequences: it creates a pseudo-social relationship between viewer and athlete; it nurtures symbolic identification with dominant societal values and norms; and—perhaps most important—it reduces life's complexities to simple competition within the framework of rules, making sport a central, if not entirely artificial, source of life motivation and social gratification (Weiss 1996). With the proliferation of rotisserie leagues, a fan's interest in individual players supersedes that in the team or the game; the rotisserie team owner's relationship to sport is through a box score or, in some leagues, through email and web reports.

Most of these negative assessments of mediated sports are based on theoretical arguments rather than empirical data. One earlier study offering a more empirically grounded analysis compared the effects of media on national sports in Britain (cricket and soccer) and the United States (football and baseball) and tennis in both countries. Among its findings, this study suggested that British sports are centered around live attendance, whereas sport in the United States is centered around television viewing. And following from the more important role of televised sports viewing in the United States, it noted, television announcers in the US were expected to entertain and attract large audiences. In contrast, it suggested Britain lacked a similar level of mediated, commercialized sports (Chandler 1988).

Recent studies of televised sports viewing have evidenced a stronger emphasis on determining empirical patterns (Wenner & Gratz 1989). Among some of the more interesting empirical findings: (*a*) men gravitate to contact and fast paced sports, and women to more slow-paced and less violent sports; (*b*) the strongest affective involvement in sports viewing came in "feeling happy" when fan favorites did well. As expected, viewers of contact or fast paced sports felt greater amounts of both happiness and sadness in responding to the fates of their teams. Perhaps the most important finding—that different kinds of people (e.g. casual fans vs. serious fans, men vs. women, tennis vs. pro football fans) have different experiences of watching TV sports—underscores the complexity of the viewing experience and the need for more empirical studies.

Increasing concentration and centralization of sports team ownership by media conglomerates may radically change the mediated nature of sports presentation. Future studies must focus on the ways that the changing nature of ownership affects the control of team and league policy, the relations to players, and the quality of the sports experience for fans. This has been recently evidenced in the "feminized Olympic reality" (Andrews 1998) foisted upon fans in 1996 and the "TV time-outs" (rather than a coach's time-out or even an "official" time-out) experienced by viewers of March madness. Equally important, we must study how the increasingly mediated field of sport is affected by patterns of power in the larger political economy.

GLOBALIZATION AND SPORT

Intimately connected with our discussion of the media, the globalization of sport—some argue that it should be termed "Americanization" (e.g. Whannel 1992, McKay & Miller 1991)—seems to follow patterns associated with the political economy of the world system. Indeed, at a basic level, US corporate sport—at the core of the world economy—appears to have a dominant position. There are football teams owned by the National Football League that play in Europe, regular season National Basketball Association games are played in Japan, and the National Hockey League draws a large percentage of its players from Europe. Student athletes (raw materials?) in US colleges and universities increasingly are recruited from the economic periphery abroad and increasingly are the winners in NCAA events—especially track and field. Without much of a soccer presence, the United States was still able to host the 1994 World Cup. And, in a twelve-year period, the US was able to be home to two Summer Olympics games.[5]

Despite claims of the impending globalization of everything, which would involve, among other processes, integration, diffusion, emulation, homogenization, and interdependence of economic, political, and cultural forces around the world (see, e.g., Friedman 1999), many scholars have correctly pointed to the continued role of multinational corporations, transnational organizations [e.g., Fédération Internationale de Football Association (FIFA)], national states, and local and regional cultural patterns, especially the peculiarities of individual sports' developments in given countries, to understand the international situation (Maguire 1994, Rowe et al. 1994, Sugden & Tomlinson 1998, Markovits & Hellerman 2001, Guttmann 1994). Indeed, it is only at the very general level of what Guttmann calls "ludic diffusion" that we see true globalization. Under closer examination, we always see specific, differentially resourced interests struggling at the local level to incorporate, resist, or transform the sport(s) that is being "offered." Whether it is basketball in Trinidad and Tobago (see Mandle & Mandle 1988, 1994) or golf in Japan (see Horne 1998), most authors argue that one needs to take into account local culture, organization, and economic and political power to understand the expansion and incorporation of a particular form of sports. Horne, for example, reminds us that for every corporation that attempts to build another golf course in Japan, there are many environmental activists and advocates for the poor who oppose the diverting of waters from rice paddies to golf courses or the increased use of grass fertilizers.

Klein (1997), as well, contributes to our understanding of the expansion of sports across national borders by offering a fascinating ethnographic account of one minor league baseball team—the *Tecolotes de los Dos Laredos*—which considered its hometown both Laredo, Texas, US and Nuevo Laredo, Tamaulipas, Mexico. Klein examines closely issues of nationalism and identity in this bi-national context.

One of the most interesting attempts to understand the spread of sports internationally is Markovits & Hellerman's *Offside* (2001). Not only do they question the seemingly teleological globalization thesis, but they assert that we need to

---

[5]Lenskyj (2000), in an expose/political economy of the Olympics industry, argues that the Olympics should be examined as a transnational corporation that has and should call forth local resistance movements to its almost inevitable economic exploitation, stifling of democracy, and media collaboration.

understand a given country's history and even more so its sports history to grasp how its sports space is configured. Thus, in attempting to explain "why there is no soccer in the US," they discuss the role that powerful organizations have played in cementing baseball, basketball, and football (and to a lesser extent, hockey) into the US sports space during the key 1870–1930 industrialization period and how difficult it has been for other endeavors to gain a strong foothold. Markovits & Hellerman's integration of media, political, and economic factors into this analysis and their complex comparative design (comparisons of sports, countries, time periods) provide us with an excellent model to follow and engage in our further studies of the internationalization (or not!) of sports.

CONCLUSION

Our review of sport and society has focused on inequality by race/ethnicity, class, and gender as well as the changing social context of sports, especially as revealed by the expanded role of the media and globalization. We have stressed the need for studies that clarify how sports articulate with other patterns of cultural consumption and participation by different social groups. Cultural and sports sociologists need to attend more closely to how leisure products and practices are produced and distributed, and how they intersect with educational, political, and cultural institutions.

As Bourdieu suggests, one must build into the analysis of sport an explanation of its institutional context. Though Bourdieu's discussions of "fields of power" and "social spaces" are useful, we believe it is more straightforward to use the notion of organizational field (DiMaggio & Powell 1983) to situate our understanding of sports. This notion highlights the degree to which sport constitutes its own relatively autonomous field (and thus cannot simply be seen as a reflection of society[6]) as well as the necessity of seeing it in relation to its relevant markets (e.g. for audiences, products, advertisers, suppliers, etc.), regulators, competitors for entertainment dollars, etc. The "new institutionalism" (Powell & DiMaggio 1991), in fact, provides an excellent lens through which to view developments in sports, especially as they engulf and are engulfed by other organizations and social spaces (e.g. government, media, education, etc.). In addition, we must understand historically the social composition of the contemporary sports space and the limits of relative autonomy from other organizational fields. From this perspective, it behooves us, for example, to think about the relative explosion of "new" Olympic sports in the last few decades. We would not be able to understand the change in women's track and field from the pentathlon to the heptathlon or the inclusion of a

---

[6]As we hope we have made clear in our discussions of various forms of inequality, the study of sports also provides a window into other societal processes that are more apparent in the field of sports than they are in other domains. The unassailably meritocratic character of sports provides clear evidence when deviations from the meritocratic standard occur.

women's marathon and pole vault without understanding the role of the worldwide women's movement and the implementation of Title IX in the United States. Indeed, it would be interesting to try to understand the logic and patterns of new sports' inclusion into the Olympic pantheon. Why, for instance, was tennis—a sport with upper-class origins—included in the Olympics only in 1988[7] while weightlifting—a working class sport—has been part of the Games for decades. Obviously, the class origins of a given sport are not the key variable: the relationships among nations, other sports organizations, the composition of the Olympic committee, etc. all have important effects. An institutional analysis of the development of sport implores us to include in our explanations the roles of urbanization, immigration, industrialization, and government's role in the development of these processes. To understand fully the social composition of today's soccer teams in the United States, for example, we must understand how the forces of industrial development and the government's role in transport and housing markets after World War II stimulated the growth of the suburbs. These emergent patterns, along with immigration, played a major contextual role in determining the disproportionately white and middle class character of today's US-born soccer playing youth.

Finally, we must mention the increasing concentration and centralization of capital, especially as it manifests itself through the media, that is fueling the dynamics of change and stasis in the field of big time sports. As media conglomerates involve themselves not only in broadcasting sports but in owning franchises, they obviously become bigger players on the sports stage. Similarly, through various sorts of mimetic organizational processes (DiMaggio & Powell 1983), the powerful actors involved in sports production enact scripts that increasingly lead to the costs of sports being socialized (e.g., through the state's use of taxes in funding new stadiums) while the benefits remain privatized. Though this is not an entirely new phenomenon, the competition among cities, states, and regions within the United States to attract professional sports teams has magnified the degree to which the sports field is an object of public policy and a potential cause of fiscal struggle and crisis (Noll & Zimbalist 1997, Eitzen 1999). Indeed, a neo-institutional analysis would predict a similar set of processes to occur throughout the United States in all the sports leagues. Though we have not reviewed the field of sports and public policy, we hope that this field continues to develop, especially insofar as it incorporates an emphasis on inter-institutional relations.

We end this review with a call to sociologists to make sports more central to our analysis of society. After all, as a number of media critics have noted, there are many cities about whose newspapers it could be written: If the president were assassinated yesterday, today's City Press headline would read Hometown 3, Visitors 2. Sociologists, most of whom, we suspect, did not play starring roles on their high school sports teams, have ignored this object of mass attention. While the upper classes have made attendance at other cultural events and institutions (theater,

---

[7]It *had* been included in the Olympics from 1896 until 1924.

opera, museums, etc.) a component of elite status–and an object of sociologists' attention (!), sport seems to have escaped such appreciation. An institutional and reflexive analysis of sociology would suggest that, in ignoring sport, we have been following the scripts set by the powerful forces both in our discipline and in the larger society. It is time to give sport its due.

ACKNOWLEDGMENTS

The authors gratefully acknowledge the research assistance of Liza Meltzer, Alissa Anderson, Jake Rosenfeld, Tara Ghei, and Emily Adams. Lorraine Kirschner helped with manuscript preparation. Order of authorship was determined by a coin flip.

Visit the Annual Reviews home page at www.AnnualReviews.org

LITERATURE CITED

Acosta RV, Carpenter LJ. 2000. Women in intercollegiate sports: a longitudinal study; twenty-three year update, 1977–2000. Brooklyn College-CUNY Dep. Phys. Ed. and Exercise Sci, and Smith Coll. Project on Women and Social Change

Adler PA, Adler P. 1991. *Backboards and Blackboards: College Athletes and Role Engulfment.* New York: Columbia Univ. Press

Adler P, Kless SJ, Adler P. 1992. Socialization to gender roles: popularity among elementary school boys and girls. *Sociol. Educ.* 65:169–87

Albom M. 1993. *The Fab Five.* New York: Warner Books

Andrews DL. 1998. Feminizing Olympic reality: preliminary dispatches from Baudrillard's Atlanta. *Int. Rev. Sociol. Sport.* 33(1):5–18

Andrews DL, Loy JW. 1993. British cultural studies and sport. *Quest* 45(2):255–76

Andrews V. 1996. Black bodies, white control: the contested terrain of sportsmanlike conduct. *J. Afr. Am. Men* 2(1):33–59

Ashe A, Rampersad A. 1993. *Days of Grace.* New York: Knopf

Baltzell ED. 1995. *Sporting Gentlemen: Men's Tennis from the Age of Honor to the Cult of the Superstar.* New York: Free Press

Bhonslay M. 1997. Women for sale. *Women's Sports Fitness,* 19 (Sept):60–62

Blain N, Boyle R, O'Donnell H. 1993. *Sport and National Identity In The European Media.* New York: Leicester Univ. Press (Distrib. St. Martin's Press)

Booth D. 1998. *The Race Game: Sport and Politics in South Africa.* London, UK: Portland

Bourdieu P. 1984. *Distinction: A Social Critique of the Judgment of Taste.* Cambridge, MA: Harvard Univ. Press

Bourdieu P. 1988. Program for a sociology of sport. *Sociol. Sport J.* 5:153–61

Bourdieu P. 1991. Sport and social class. In *Rethinking Popular Culture: Contemporary Perspectives in Cultural Studies,* ed. C Mukerji, M Schudson, pp. 357–73. Berkeley/Los Angeles: Univ. Calif. Press

Boyle R, Haynes R. 1996. The Grand Old Game: football, media, and identity in Scotland. *Media, Culture Soc.* 18(4 Oct):549–64

Bradley JM. 1996. Facets of the Irish diaspora: Irishness in 20th century Scotland. *Irish J. Sociol.* 6:79–100

Cahn SK. 1994. *Coming on Strong: Gender and Sexuality in Twentieth-Century Women's Sport.* New York: Free Press

Carrington B. 1998. Sport, masculinity, and

black cultural resistance. *J. Sport Soc. Iss.* 22:275–98

Chandler J. 1988. *Television and The National Sports: The United States and Britain.* Urbana: Univ. Ill. Press

Coakley J. 1998. *Sport in Society: Issues and Controversies.* New York: McGraw Hill. 6th ed.

Cole C. 1996. American Jordan: P.L.A.Y., consensus and punishment. *Sociol. Sport J.* 13(4):366–97

Connell RW. 1987. *Gender and Power: Society, the Person, and Sexual Politics.* Stanford, CA: Stanford Univ. Press

Connell RW. 1990. An iron man: The Body and some contradictions of hegemonic masculinity. In *Sport, Men, and the Gender Order: Critical Feminist Perspectives,* ed. M. Messner, D. Sabo, pp. 83–96. Champaign, IL: Human Kinetics

Connell RW. 1995. *Masculinities.* Berkeley, CA: Univ. Calif. Press

Curry TM. 1997. The cultural significance of Jackie Robinson. *Soc. Forces* 30(4):307–9

Curtis RL. 1998. Racism and rationales: a frame analysis of John Hoberman's *Darwin's Athletes. Soc. Sci. Q.* 79(4 Dec):885–91

Davis LR. 1993. Protest against the use of Native American mascots: a challenge to traditional American identity. *J. Sport Soc. Iss.* 17:9–22

Dawkins MP, Kinlock GC. 2000. *African American Golfers During the Jim Crow Era.* Westport, CT: Praeger

Denham BE. 1997. *Sports Illustrated,* the 'War on drugs,' and the Anabolic Steroid Control Act of 1990: a study in agenda building and political timing. *J. Sport Soc. Issues* 21(3):260–73

DiMaggio PJ, Powell WW. 1983. The iron cage revisited: institutional isomorphism and collective rationality in organizational fields. *Am. Sociol. Rev.* 48:147–60

DiMaggio PJ, Powell WW. 1991. Introduction. In *The New Institutionalism in Organizational Analysis,* ed. WW Powell, PJ DiMaggio, pp. 1–38. Chicago: Univ. Chicago Press

Donnelly P. 1993. Democratization revisited: seven theses on the democratization of sport and active leisure. *Soc. Leisure* 16(2):413–34

Dufur M. 1997. Race logic and 'being like Mike' representations of athletes in advertising, 1985-1994. *Soc. Forces* 30(4):345–56

Duncan MC, Messner MA. 2000. Gender in televised sports: 1989, 1993, and 1999. W. Wilson, ed. Sept. http://www.aafla.org.

Dunning E. 1999. *Sport Matters: Sociological Studies of Sport, Violence, and Civilization.* London/New York: Routledge

Eastman S, Meyer T. 1989. Sports programming: scheduling, costs, and competition. See: L. Wenner 1989, pp. 97–119

Eder D, Parker S. 1987. The cultural production and reproduction of gender: the effect of extracurricular activities on peer-group culture. *Sociol. Educ.* 60:200–13

Eisen G, Wiggins DK, eds. 1994. *Ethnicity and Sport in North American History and Culture.* Westport CT: Greenwood

Eitzen DS. 1999. *Fair and Foul: Beyond the Myths and Paradoxes of Sport.* Lanham, MD: Rowman & Littlefield

Elias N, Dunning E. 1986. *Quest for Excitement: Sport and Leisure in the Civilizing Process.* Oxford: Blackwell

Entine J. 2000. *Taboo: Why Black Athletes Dominate Sports and Why We Are Afraid to Talk About It.* New York: Public Affairs

Eskes TB, Duncan MC, Miller EM. 1998. The discourse of empowerment: Foucalt, Marcuse, and women's fitness texts. *J. Sport Soc. Iss.,* 22:317–44

Feinstein J. 1998. *The First Coming: Tiger Woods–Master or Martyr.* New York: Ballantine Books

Festle MJ. 1996. *Playing Nice: Politics and Apologies in Women's Sports.* New York: Columbia Univ. Press

Fimrite R. 1987. It was more than just a game. *Sports Illus.* 67 (Nov 18):106–15

Foley D. 1990. The great American football ritual: reproducing race, class, and gender inequality. *Sociol. Sport J.* 7:111–34

Freeman M, Frotkin A, Cooper J, Consoli J.

1999. Fox nets puts squeeze on broadcasters. *MediaWeek* 9(28):8

Frey D. 1994. *The Last Shot: City Streets, Basketball Dreams.* New York: Touchstone

Frey JH, Eitzen DS. 1991. Sport and society. *Annu. Rev. Sociol.* 17:503–22

Friedman T. 1999. *The Lexus and the Olive Tree.* New York: Farrar Strauss & Giroux

Gems GR. 1998. The construction, negotiation, and transformation of racial identity in American football: a study of Native and African Americans. *Am. Ind. Cult. Res. J.* 22

Gladwell M. 1997. The sports taboo: why blacks are like boys and whites are like girls. *The New Yorker* (Sept 19):50–55

Goldsmith PA. 2000. *The social production of racial differences in high school sports participation.* Paper pres. at Annu. Meet. Am. Sociol. Assoc. Washington, DC

Gorn EJ. 1997. The meanings of prizefighting. See Pope 1997, pp. 225–50

Greendorfer SL, Rubinson L. 1997. Homophobia and heterosexism in women's sport and physical education. *Women Sport Phys. Act. J.* 6(2):189–202

Greenfield S, Osborn G. 1997. Enough is enough: race and cricket. *Soc. Forces* 30 (4 Oct):373–83

Griffin P. 1998. *Strong Women, Deep Closets: Lesbians and Homophobia in Sport.* Champaign, IL: Human Kinetics

Grindstaff L, West E. 2000. *Gender, sport, and spectacle: cheerleading and the bid for cultural legitimacy.* Presented at Annu. Meet. Am. Sociol. Assoc., Washington DC

Gruneau R, Whitson D. 1993. *Hockey Night in Canada: Sport, Identities, and Cultural Politics.* Toronto: Garamond

Guttmann A. 1991. *Women's Sports: A History.* New York: Columbia Univ. Press

Guttmann A. 1994. *Games and Empires: Modern Sports and Cultural Imperialism.* New York: Columbia Univ. Press

Harrison CK. 1998. Themes that thread through society: racism and athletic manifestation in the African-American community. *Race, Ethnic., Educ.* 1:63–74

Hartmann D. 1996. The politics of race and sport: resistance and domination in the 1968 African American Olympic protest movement. *Ethnic Rac. Stud.* 19(3):548–66

Hartmann D. 2000. Rethinking the relationships between sport and race in American culture: golden ghettos and contested terrain. *Sociol. Sport J.* 17:229–53

Hasbrook CA, Harris O. 2000. Wrestling with gender: physicality and masculinities among inner-city first and second graders. See McKay, Messner, Sabo. 2000, pp. 13–30

Heisler M. 1999. NBA-At this rate, NBC is hoping Knicks extend their run. *Los Angeles Times* (June 16):D1

Hersch H. 1989. Choosing sides. *Sports Illus.* 71 (Nov 27):42–47

Hoberman J. 1997. *Darwin's Athletes: How Sport Has Damaged Black America and Preserved the Myth of Race.* Boston: Houghton Mifflin

Holland A, Andre T. 1994. Athletic participation and the social status of adolescent males and females. *Youth Soc.* 25(3):388–407

Horne J. 1998. The politics of sport and leisure in Japan. *Int. Rev. Sociol. Sport* 33(2):171–82

Jable TJ. 1994. Sport in Philadelphia's African-American community, 1865-1900. See Eisen & Wiggins 1994, pp. 157–76

Jamieson KM. 1998. Reading Nancy Lopez: decoding representations of race, class, and sexuality. *Sociol. Sport J.* 15(4 Dec):343–58

Jarvie G. 1985. *Class, Race and Sport in South Africa's Political Economy.* Boston: Routledge, Kegan Paul

Jhally S. 1989 Cultural studies and the sports/media complex. See LA Wenner, ed. 1989, pp.70–93

Kahn R. 1997. Box score: Has baseball fulfilled Jackie Robinson's promise? *New Yorker* (14 April):5–6

Kane MJ. 1995. Resistance/transformation of the oppositional binary: exposing sport as a continuum. *J. Sport Soc. Iss.* 19:191–218

Kellner D. 1996. Sports, media culture, and

race–some reflections on Michael Jordan. *Sociol. Sport. J.* 13(4):458–67

Kirkpatrick C. 1991. The night they drove old Dixie down. *Sports Illus.* 74 (Apr 1):70–81

Klatell DA, Marcus N. 1988. *Sports for Sale: Television, Money, and the Fans.* New York: Oxford Univ. Press

Klein AM. 1991. *Sugarball: The American Game, The Dominican Dream.* New Haven: Yale Univ. Press

Klein AM. 1993. *Little Big Men: Bodybuilding Subculture and Gender Construction.* Albany, NY: State Univ. NY Press

Klein AM. 1997. *Baseball on the Border: A Tale of Two Laredos.* Princeton, NJ: Princeton Univ. Press

Koch JV, VanderHill CW. 1988. Is there discrimination in the 'black man's game'? *Soc. Sci. Q.* 69:83–94

Kraus R, Hanson S. 1999. *The benefits of sports and science for young women: race makes a difference.* Pap. pres. Annu. Meet. Am. Sociol. Assoc. Chicago

Kravitz B. 1998. NFL practices look like racism. *Denver Rocky Mountain News* (January 21):3N

Lapchick RE. 1999a. *Racial And Gender Report Card.* Ctr. for Study Sport Soc., Northeastern Univ. http://www.sportinsociety.org

Lapchick RE. 1999b. *Crime and Athletes: The New Racial Sterotypes of the 1990s.* Ctr. for Study Sport Soc, Northeastern Univ. http://www.sportinsociety.org

Lashley H. 1995. Race, sport, and black youth: an historical perspective. *Youth Policy* 49:73–86

Lenskyj HJ. 2000. *Inside the Olympic Industry: Power, Politics, and Activism.* Albany, NY: SUNY Press

Leonard WM II. 1995. Economic disparity in major league baseball: marginal revenue products of majority and minority group members. *J. Sport Soc. Iss.* 19:180–90

Leonhardt D. 1997. Color line on the court? *Bus. Week* (December 22):6

Lopiano D. 1998. "The strong fem side of women's sports." *Brandweek* 39 (Feb 2): 14

Lord B. 1984. *In the Year of the Boar and Jackie Robinson.* New York: Harper & Row

Lowes MD. 1997. Sports page: a case study in the manufacture of sports news for the new press. *Sociol. Sport J.* 14(2):143–59

MacClancy J. ed. 1996. *Sport, Identity, and Ethnicity.* UK: WBC Book

Magdalinski T. 1997. International perspectives on race, ethnicity, identity, and sports. *Int. Rev. Sociol. Sport* 32(3):311–14

Maguire J. 1994. Sport, identity politics, and globalization: diminishing contrasts and increasing varieties. *Sociol. Sport. J.* 11(4):398–427

Mandle JR, Mandle JD. 1988. *Grass Roots Commitment: Basketball and Society in Trinidad and Tobago.* Parkersburg, IA: Caribbean Books

Mandle JR, Mandle JD. 1994. *Caribbean Hoops: The Development of West Indian Basketball.* Langhorne, PA: Gordon & Breach

Margolis B, Piliavin JA. 1999. 'Stacking' in major league baseball: a multivariate analysis. *Sociol. Sport J.* 16:16–34

Markovits AS, Hellerman SL. 2001. *Offside: Soccer and American Exceptionalism in Sports.* Princeton NJ: Princeton Univ. Press

McCarthy D, Jones RL. 1997. Speed, aggression, strength, tactical naiveté: the portrayal of the black soccer player on television. *J. Sport Soc. Iss.* 21(4):348–62

McClellan S. 1999. Super Bowl close to sold out. *Broadcast. Cable* 129(45):10

McDonald MG. 1996. Michael Jordan's family values: marketing, meaning and post-Reagan America. *Sociol. Sport J.* 13(4):344–65

McDonald MG, Birrell S. 1999. Reading sport critically: a methodology for interrogating power. *Sociol. Sport J.* 16:283–300

McKay J. 1995. 'Just Do It': corporate slogans and the political economy of 'enlightened racism.' *Discourse: Stud. in Cult. Polit. Educ.* 16(2):191–201

McKay J, Messner MA, Sabo D. 2000. *Masculinities, Gender Relations, and Sport.* Thousand Oaks CA: Sage

McKay J, Miller T. 1991. From old boys to men and women of the corporation: the Americanization and commodification of Australian sport. *Sociol. Sport J.* 8(1):89–91

Mead C. 1985. *Champion: Joe Louis, Black Hero in White America.* New York: Penguin

Messner MA. 1988. Sports and male domination: the female athlete as contested ideological terrain. *Sociol. Sport J.* 5:197–211

Messner MA. 1992. *Power at Play: Sports and the Problem of Masculinity.* Boston: Beacon

Messner MA, Duncan MC, Jensen K. 1993. Separating the men from the girls: the gendered language of televised sports. *Gender Soc.* 7:121–37

Miller KE, Sabo D, Farrell MP, Barnes GM, Melnick MJ. 1998. Athletic participation and sexual behavior in adolescents: the different worlds of boys and girls. *J. Health Soc. Behav.* 39:108–23

Miller KE, Sabo D, Farrell M, Barnes G, Melnick M. 1999. *Athletic participation and adolescent sexual behavior: where race and gender intersect.* Pap. pres. Annu. Meet. Am. Sociol. Assoc. Chicago

Millman J. 1997. Women's sports play in unique arena. *Brandweek* 38(Dec 15):12

Moore K. 1991. A courageous stand. *Sports Illus.* 75(Aug 5):60–73

Myers SL Jr. 1998. Hoberman's fantasy: how neoconservative writing on sport reinforces perceptions of black inferiority and preserves the myth of race *Soc. Sci. Q.* 79(4):878–97

Nelson MB. 1994. *The Stronger Women Get, The More Men Love Football: Sexism and the American Culture of Sports.* Orlando, FL: Harcourt Brace

Nixon HL II. 1996. Explaining the pain and injury attitudes and experiences in sport in terms of gender, race, and sports status factors. *J. Sport Soc. Iss.* 20:33–44

Nixon HL II. 1997. Gender, sport, and aggressive behavior outside sport. *J. Sport Soc. Iss.* 21:379–91

Noll RG, Zimbalist A, eds. 1997. *Sports, Jobs, and Taxes: The Economic Impact of Sports Teams and Stadiums.* Washington, DC: Brookings Inst. Press

O Hara J. 1997. Better? Yes. Equal? Not by a long shot. *Maclean's,* 110(Apr 7):70

Pattnayak SR, Leonard JE. 1994. Explaining discrimination in the National Football League: a study of coaches' salaries. *Sociol. Viewpoints* 10:35–44

Pope SW. 1997. *The New American Sport History: Recent Approaches and Perspectives.* Urbana, IL: Univ. Ill. Press

Price SL. 1997. Whatever happened to the white athlete? *Sports Illus.* (Dec 7):31–51

Rader B. 1984. *In Its Own Image: How Television Has Transformed Sports.* New York: Free Press

Rada JA. 1996. Color blind sided: racial bias in network television coverage of football games. *Howard J. Commun.* 7(3):231–39

Reed W, Chaney J. 1989. A new proposition. *Sports Illus.* 4(3) (Jan 23):16ff.

Rees RC. 1996. Race and sport in global perspective: lessons from post-apartheid South Africa. *J. Sport Soc. Iss* 20:22–32

Riess S. 1989. *City Games: The Evolution of American Urban Society and the Rise of Sports.* Urbana, IL: Univ. Ill. Press

Riess S. 1990a. Professional sports as an avenue of social mobility in America: some myths and realities. In *Essays on Sport History and Sport Mythology,* ed. DG Kyle, GD Stark, pp. 83–117. College Station, TX: Texas A&M Univ. Press

Riess S. 1990b. The new sport history. *Rev. in Am. Hist.* 18:311–25

Rowe D. 1996. The global love-match: sport and television. *Media, Culture Soc.* 18:(4 Oct):565–82

Rowe D. 1998. Rethinking power and resistance in sport *J. Sport Soc. Iss.* 22(3):241–51

Rowe D, Lawrence G, Miller T, McKay J. 1994. Global sport? Core concern and peripheral vision. *Media Cult. Soc.* 16:661–75

Ruck R. 1993. *Sandlot Seasons: Sport in Black Pittsburgh.* Urbana, IL: Univ. Ill. Press

Sack AL, Thiel R. 1979. College football and social mobility: a case study of Notre Dame football players. *Sociol. Educ.* 52:60–66

Sailes G. 1996. An examination of basketball performance orientation among African American males. *J. Afr. Am. Men* 1 (4, Spring):37–46

Sammons J. 1994. Race and sport: a critical historical examination. *J. Soc. Hist,* 21(3):203–78

Shropshire K. 1996. *In Black and White–Race and Sports in America.* New York: NY Univ. Press

Shropshire K, Smith E. 1998. The Tarzan syndrome. John Hoberman and his quarrels with African American intellectuals. *J. Sport Soc. Iss:* 22:103–12

Sigelman L. 1998. The African American athletic fixation. *Soc. Sci. Q.* 79(4):892–97

Smith E, Leonard WM II. 1997. Twenty five years of stacking research in major league baseball: an attempt at explaining this re-occurring phenomenon. *Sociol. Focus* 30:321–31

Snyder EE, Ammons R. 1993. Adult participation in coed softball: relations in a gender integrated sport. *J. Sport Behav.* 16:3–15

Spigner C. 1993. African American student athletes: academic support or institutionalized racism? *Education* 114(1):144–49

Sugden J, Tomlinson A. 1998. Power and resistance in the governance of world football. *J. Sport Soc. Iss.* 22(3):299–16

Suggs W. 2000. Uneven progress for women's sports. *Chron. High. Educ.* (Apr 7):A52

Swift EM. 1991. Reach out and touch someone. *Sports Illus.* 75(Aug 5):54–59

Theberge N. 1997. It's part of the game: physicality and the production of gender in women's hockey. *Gender & Soc.* 11:69–87

Theberge N. 1998. Same sport, different gender. *J. Sport Soc. Iss.* 22:183–98

Theberge N. 2000. *Higher Goals: Women's Ice Hockey and the Politics of Gender.* Albany, NY: SUNY Press

Thing LF. 1998. Emotions and gender in sport. Paper pres. ISSA Conf., Montreal

Tuck J. 1998. *Rugby Union, national identity politics and the media at play.* Pap. pres. Annu. Meet. Int. Sociol. Assoc.

Tygiel J. 1983. *Baseball's Great Experiment: Jackie Robinson and His Legacy.* New York: Vintage Books

US Census Bureau. 1999. *Current Business Reports BS/98, Service Annual Survey: 1998.* Washington, DC: USGPO

US Department of Education. 1997. Title IX: 25 Years of Progress. http://www.ed.gov/pubs/TitleIX

Vallentine J. 1997. Global sport and Canadian content: the *Sports Illustrated Canada* controversy *J. Sport Soc. Iss.* 21(3):239–59

Wacquant LJD. 1992. The social logic of boxing in black Chicago: toward a sociology of pugilism. *Sociol. Sport J.* 9:221–54

Wacquant LJD. 1998. The prizefighter's three bodies. *Ethnos* 63(3):325–52

Wahl G, Wertheim LJ. 1998. Paternity. *Sports Illus.* (4 May):64–71

Weiss O. 1996. Media sports as a social substitution. *Int. Rev. Sociol. Sport* 31(1):109–18

Wenner LA. 1989. Media, sports, and society: the research agenda. See LA Wenner 1989, pp. 13–48

Wenner LA, ed. 1989. *Media, Sports, and Society.* Newbury Park, CA: Sage

Wenner LA, Gratz W. 1989. Experience with sports on television. See Wenner 1989, pp. 241–69

Whannel G. 1992. *Fields in Vision: Television Sport and Cultural Transformation.* London: Routledge

Wheaton B, Tomlinson A. 1998. The changing gender order in sport? The case of windsurfing subcultures. *J. Sport Soc. Iss.* 22:252–74

Wieberg S. 1998. Black coaches still snubbed in football. *USA Today* (Jan 9):1C

Williams R. 1977. *Marxism and Literature.* New York: Oxford Univ. Press

Zimbalist A. 1999. *Unpaid Professionals: Commercialism and Conflict in Big-Time College Sports.* Princeton, NJ: Princeton Univ. Press

Zimbalist A. 2000. Backlash against Title IX: an end run around female athletes. *Chron. High. Educ.* (Mar 3):B9

Annu. Rev. Sociol. 2001. 27:213–34

US Social Policy in Comparative and Historical Perspective: Concepts, Images, Arguments, and Research Strategies

Edwin Amenta, Chris Bonastia, and Neal Caren

Department of Sociology, New York University, New York, NY 10003;
e-mail: amenta@mail.soc.nyu.edu

Key Words   political sociology, welfare state, states

■ **Abstract**   In this article we review theory and comparative and historical research on US social policy. We discuss first the conceptual frameworks used to think about social policy, the changing images of American social policy implied by these different frameworks, and the questions they raise. From there we examine the arguments offered to answer questions about US social policy as well as the research strategies and evidence used to appraise the arguments. We address work that situates US social policy in comparative perspective as well as work that examines the development of American social policy historically or across states. Although many lines of argumentation have some empirical support, we find that some lines of political and institutional analyses provide the best supported answers to the questions and the greatest potential for wide usage in comparative and historical studies. We conclude that scholars would do well not to treat American social policy as so exceptional as to require separate images, explanations, and approaches. We suggest promising new lines of empirical inquiry prompted by new conceptualizations of social policy and other developments in this literature.

INTRODUCTION

When scholars discuss welfare states or social policy, they typically refer to the efforts of states to address economic insecurity and inequality due to risks to regular income. Modern social policy and other social services have transformed the character of states. Many states, including the American one, now devote themselves mainly to the maintenance of incomes, the treating of the ill, and the provision of services to citizens rather than the traditional pursuits of warfare and coercive control over subject populations. In short, they have become welfare states.

Comparative and historical scholarship suggests that the US state and social policy has been transformed reluctantly and partially, often treating American social policy as aberrant. Comparative scholars want to know why American social

0360-0572/01/0811-0213$14.00

insurance programs were relatively late in coming and patchy in character as compared to those of Western Europe, why the United States spends less on social policy, why the United States resembles the residual "liberal" welfare state type, or why US social policy has undergone relatively severe retrenchment over the last two decades. US historical scholars ask why the United States developed the mix of policies that it did, focusing often on the 1930s and 1960s, when gains were made. Other scholars address differences in social policy across US states, which vary widely on programs in which they share governmental authority. Often the American-centered investigations appraise different sets of explanatory arguments, as if US social policy developments were so exceptional that they required their own explanations. (For reviews of comparative research, see Skocpol & Amenta 1986, Quadagno 1987, Piven & Cloward 1993; specific arguments, Shalev 1983, Esping-Andersen & van Kersbergen 1992, Burstein 1998, Thelen 1999; specific aspects of US social policy, Howard 1999, Manza 2000; feminist research, Gordon 1990, Orloff 1996, Haney 2000).

In reviewing the comparative and historical literature on American social policy, we find that treating US social policy as so exceptional is unwarranted. US policy is not always and has not always been backward relative to other rich capitalist countries. This is true even in respect to the standard conceptualization of social policy, and a more nuanced US image is coming into view as scholars develop new conceptualizations. Partly for that reason, the most fruitful lines of research are those in which scholars develop or appraise arguments that can be applied in different settings, rather than trying to focus solely on exceptionalism. Comparative scholars do best when their arguments are constructed in such a way as to be able to address the development of US social policy over time, instead of treating the American case as forever a residual category. Scholars focused on US developments are most compelling when they devise or assess arguments that are not conceptualized so narrowly as to have few implications for other settings. In the most telling research, scholars situate developments in US social policy in cross-national and historical contexts, employ claims that have implications comparatively, across states, and over time, and appraise these claims through analyses of historical sequences or against the experiences of similarly situated countries or states. Lines of research combining portable argumentation and cross-national and historical perspective are likely to be the most productive ones in the future, as scholars develop new conceptualizations and images of social policy and devise new questions about it.

CONCEPTUALIZATIONS OF SOCIAL POLICY AND IMAGES OF US SOCIAL POLICY

Modern social policy is usually understood as state programs and services that address economic inequality resulting from risks to income and are bureaucratically administered to specified groups of citizens in specified circumstances. In conceptualizing modern social policy in this way (Heclo 1974), scholars placed social insurance programs at the center of social policy (Flora & Heidenheimer 1981), with means-tested social assistance and social service programs taking a secondary role. In comparing across countries, states, and over time, scholars have often addressed the amounts expended on these programs and services as a percentage of national income or product, an operationalization known as spending effort (Wilensky 1975), and the timing of adoption of major programs and their development (Flora & Alber 1981). According to this conceptualization, the image of American social policy is one of stinginess and backwardness. The United States has spent less effort on social policy than major capitalist democracies in the postwar era. In 1993, according to OECD statistics on "social security" efforts, for instance, only Japan and Australia spent less than the United States among 17 long-standing members (Castles 1998a:151; see also Huber & Stephens 2000a). Of the five major social insurance programs. America had adopted only workmen's compensation before 1935, late among industrialized countries (Collier & Messick 1975, Hicks et al 1995). Old-age and unemployment insurance were added in 1935, but health insurance was added only for the aged in 1965, along with health benefits for the poor, and family allowances were never adopted (Weir et al 1988).

Over the past decade scholars have conceptualized social policy more holistically, with Esping-Andersen's (1990) "welfare state regimes" notably addressing social policy's influence on labor-market relations. According to this scheme, the "social democratic" regime is best for workers and is based on the principles of universalism and "decommodification." The latter term means that workers are freed from inequality based on being wholly reliant on labor markets for income. The second-best, "conservative corporatist" regime is also universal but does not smooth status distinctions between groups and upholds the traditional family. The "liberal-type" welfare regime is designed to make labor markets run smoothly—at the expense of people by forcing them to take what these markets offer. In the liberal type, public social policy has a small presence and a large means-tested component, and it is augmented by private control over social policy areas elsewhere often handled by the state (see also Castles & Mitchell 1993). According to regime models, postwar American policy is deemed to approximate the liberal type, because of its relatively low expenditures, its large share of private benefits for retirement and health, and its relatively large component of means-tested expenditures.

These understandings of social policy have come into question, however. One set of challenges involves considering state programs other than the major social insurance programs and allied assistance programs that address modern societal risks to employment, income, and economic security (Weir et al 1988). Scholars have considered, among others, education (Heidenheimer 1981, Katznelson & Weir 1985, de Swaan 1988), taxation policy (Steinmo 1993; Howard 1997, Myles & Pierson 1997), veterans' benefits (Skocpol 1992), housing policy (Castles 1998b, Conley 2000), economic policy (Weir 1992, Leicht & Jenkins 1998), and work programs (Amenta 1998). Other scholars argue that social relations in the modern capitalist and democratic world produce perils to income beyond the standard ones and programs to address them, such as drug policies (Benoit 2000), anti-discrimination policies (Burstein 1985, Orloff 1996, Skrentny 1996, Bonastia 2000), abortion policies (Halfmann 1999), and imprisonment policies (Western & Beckett 1999).

Works that address a wider view of social policy have altered the standard images of and stories about American social policy and provide new empirical puzzles to solve. As Skocpol (1992) has shown, veterans' benefits for the Civil War provided retirement and disability benefits for a significant segment of the northern population in the late nineteenth century and early twentieth century. These Civil War pensions were often more generous than old-age insurance for industrial workers in Germany and means-tested old-age pensions in Britain. In addition, the United States was also briefly a leader in modern social spending policy in the 1930s (Amenta 1998). Spending for relief programs, especially government-provided work programs (Amenta et al 1998), resulted in US social spending efforts rising from less than one half of a percentage point of GNP in 1929 to more than six percent in 1939, ahead of other capitalist countries. Research also suggests that the distinction between "social security" and "welfare" was not intended or an initial result of 1930s legislation (Derthick 1979, Amenta 1998, Tynes 1996), but developed over time and may be overstated (Howard 1999). The United States has also been a leader in taxation expenditures for social purposes (Steinmo 1993, Howard 1997), though it has not made comparatively great strides in tax relief for the working poor (Myles & Pierson 1997). The United States is also among the leaders in home ownership, although research has not indicated how much this is due to housing policy (Castles 1998b, Conley 2000). And the United States has traditionally been a leader in public education policy (Heidenheimer 1981), a policy that applies more to equality of opportunity than of incomes, and such US spending efforts have slowed in recent decades (Castles 1998a).

Research on social policy and gender inequality has also provided new conceptualizations of social policy and corresponding new images of US policy (reviews in Orloff 1996, Haney 2000). Orloff (1993b) adopts Esping-Andersen's types, but transforms them by adding new dimensions, including the ability to establish an autonomous household and access to paid labor, because commodifying women often promotes their financial autonomy from men (see also O'Connor 1993). Within the liberal type, America is not always laggard and has shown some commitment to gender equality, particularly in occupational integration and protection from sexual assault and harassment (O'Connor et al. 1999). By contrast Sainsbury (1996) replaces Esping-Andersen's types with two based on unequal gender relations—the breadwinner and individual models (see also Lewis 1992, Fraser 1994). Sainsbury (1996) finds that women who lived in countries such as the United States and the United Kingdom where claims were based on need and marital status fare less well than in countries with other bases for claims. Conservative corporatist countries are often closer to the breadwinner model, however, with benefits transferred primarily to the head of household. In the Netherlands, for example, wives making less money than their husbands are ineligible for unemployment benefits (Sainsbury 1996). Historically speaking, Skocpol (1992) shows that although many US social policy proposals failed in the first decades of the twentieth century, some successes were in a "maternalist" direction.

Other scholars focus specifically on the process of retrenchment of social policy, bids to cut back social policy that were common in the last two decades of the twentieth century (Mishra 1990). Pierson (1994) distinguishes between programmatic retrenchment—the cutting back of programs—and systemic retrenchment—institutional reforms that weaken the state's revenue base and pro-welfare state interest groups. He argues that the United States suffered more from systemic than programmatic retrenchment in the 1980s. Huber & Stephens (2000b, 2001) find that in most cases retrenchment efforts served only to reduce the rate of growth of social policy expenditures (cf. Clayton & Pontusson 1998). Pierson (2000b) suggests that scholars analyze changes along new dimensions. Among liberal welfare states, where recommodification or the dismantling of worker protections has been the most visible goal, the United States stands as an intermediate case between the severe retrenchment of New Zealand and the United Kingdom and the "compensated restructuring" in Australia and Canada.

THEORETICAL ARGUMENTS AND RESEARCH ON US SOCIAL POLICY IN COMPARATIVE PERSPECTIVE

To explain the differences across countries in social policy, scholars have put forward many theoretical arguments, sometimes couched as theories of public policy and sometimes as theories of the state. Three main arguments currently dominate thinking about comparative social policy. The most empirically successful of these arguments, however, have little to say about the development of American public policy, as they tend to focus on causes that are absent or negligible in the American setting. And so they need to be revised at least in part to make sense of positive developments in American social policy and great variations in policy across states.

Modernization and Economic Development

One important argument focuses on economic development and the changing needs of populations as they industrialize (Wilensky 1975). Based in Durkheimian and modernization theoretical traditions, the argument is that economic development brings the need for extensive social policy for a number of reasons. More people work for wages or salaries and thus rely on incomes. But risks to incomes increase notably as the population ages, leaving older workers unnecessary and placing burdens on increasingly nuclear families. Industrialization also provides economic means to pay for social policy. According to this argument, as industrialization proceeds all countries have reason and means to adopt modern social programs, especially social insurance, and increase their spending for them, more or less regardless of political conditions.

When operationalized by the level of economic development and similar measures, this argument does well to explain differences between the social policies of the richest and poorest countries, and the richest and poorest states (see review in Skocpol & Amenta 1986). It is true as well that countries have converged on similar social programs (Stinchcombe 1985) that can be considered modern. It also seems possible that modified aspects of the industrialization thesis, such as the degree to which women work in the labor force, may influence the character of social policy (Huber & Stephens 2000a). All the same, the modernization argument has not done well in explaining great differences in the adoption of major social insurance programs among richer countries (Collier & Messick 1975, Hicks et al 1995). And although some economic measures have remained important in regression models, they do not mainly explain differences in spending efforts among capitalist democracies in the postwar period (Hicks & Misra 1993, Huber et al 1993, Pampel 1994). Yet another limitation on this line of thinking is that countries vary greatly in the degree to which they rely on social insurance programs (Esping-Andersen 1990). From this perspective, the United States is an anomaly in that it has been a relatively rich country that has lagged in social spending efforts. Also, this line of argumentation does not help to explain differences among states with different social policies, but at largely similar economic levels, and the uneven development of US social policy over time.

Social Democratic and Partisanship Models, Catholic Parties, and Political Coalitions

Another major line of argumentation holds that democratic political action influences social policy most after a certain level of economic development is reached. One set of explanations holds that partisan politics and political action most strongly influence the fate of social policy. Of these arguments the most prominent is the social democratic or power resources model (Stephens 1979, Korpi 1983), rooted in Marx's theory of class struggle. It holds that class divisions are fought out at the political level, with differences in the form and structure of their political organizations influencing who wins out in public policy. The social democratic thesis holds specifically that social democratic parties tied to strong and centralized labor movements provide the greatest impetus to the adoption and expansion of redistributive social policy and services (see reviews in Shalev 1983, Esping-Andersen & van Kersbergen 1992). This thesis has been amended slightly by others who focus on the discouraging effects on social policy of unified right-wing parties (Castles & Mair 1984) or the moderating influence of center parties on social policy (Hicks & Swank 1992). An additional line of argumentation somewhat more on Weberian lines holds that Christian democratic parties promote social spending of most standard sorts, but not state employment, many social services, or education. A further set of theoretical claims focuses on the policy impact of coalitions of worker organizations with wider groups of political actors, including farmer's organizations and movements (Esping-Andersen 1990, Sanders 1999) and expert advocacy organizations and civic associations (Orloff 1993a).

The social democratic thesis has done very well in helping to explain differences among capitalist democracies since World War II (see review in Huber et al 1993, Huber & Stephens 2000a). There is also a rough alignment between social democratic rule and Christian democratic rule and the social democratic and conservative corporatist regime types. However, specific analyses of retrenchment show a pronounced decline in partisan effects with the exception of public social service employment (Huber & Stephens 2000b). More important, the argument has failed to explain the adoption of social policy in the years before the war, as social democratic parties rarely gained power during this period and most adoptions came during the other types of political regimes (Orloff & Skocpol 1984, cf. Hicks 1999). The arguments about coalitions have greater plausibility in this period, though Esping-Andersen (1990) does not engage in the kind of historical study needed to appraise his arguments. In addition, it is not clear why such coalitions would emerge in some places and times and not others.

In the US setting, arguments about partisanship have had more mixed results. The social democratic model is not strictly applicable, given America's lack of a centralized labor movement and a social democratic party; also inapplicable are arguments about Christian parties. More applicable is the argument about unified right-wing parties, but that does little to explain advances in social policy. A coalition among workers and policy officials may have been necessary to gains in the United States, but not sufficient. Partisanship arguments suggest that advances in US social policy, to the extent they would happen, would result from the taking of power by the Democrats after its turn to the left in the 1930s. The Democratic party, however, has been greatly divided among its pro-social policy and anti–social policy wings, and Democratic rule has only sometimes resulted in gains at the national level (Amenta 1998) and in states of the Union (Amenta & Poulsen 1996, Brown 1995, Soule & Zylan 1997). The research suggests that only really large Democratic majorities at the national level have led to gains and that Democratic rule at the state level leads to social spending gains only in structurally conducive situations or where the party's base of support was along cleavages dating from the New Deal. That said, these partisan situations have not been able to explain the nature and character of these policy gains.

Institutional Theory: Polity Structure, Domestic Bureaucracies, Policy Feedbacks

The other main argument to explain empirical patterns in social policy has been institutional. Based in the tradition of Weber and Tocqueville, institutional theory holds that the structure of political institutions and organizations strongly influence the possibilities of social policy (reviews in Immergut 1998, Thelen 1999). Specifically, institutional arguments hold that the adoption and expansion of social spending policies is encouraged by centralized political institutions and states with greater bureaucratic and financial capacities and frustrated by fragmented political institutions and incapable states. Institutional arguments also claim that the initial structure of social policies influences or has "feedback" on their fate.

Following Tocqueville, many social scientists argue that the centralization of the polity promotes social policy and fragmentation hinders it because the latter facilitates the ability of opponents to deflect social policy initiatives. These claims have received some support in cross-national studies of overall spending across capitalist democracies (Huber et al 1993) as well as small-N studies explaining differences in the development of social policy and taxation policy (Immergut 1992, Steinmo 1993, Maoini 1998). This argument holds that the checks and balances in US government and its historically weak executive institutions limit what is possible in social policy. The US polity is fragmented in ways more multifaceted than that found in other democracies (Huntington 1968). Political authority in the United States has never been horizontally or vertically integrated. At the national level of government, the United States has a presidential and nonparliamentary system that allows intramural conflict. Members of Congress from the same party can defect from the president's legislative program without risking loss of office and can initiate competing programs. There are two legislative bodies, and legislators represent geographical districts, not parties. Any laws that make it through this maze can be declared unconstitutional by the US Supreme Court. A strong candidate to explain the general backwardness of US social policy and difficulties in adopting new social programs, this argument refers to an unchanging, systemic aspect of the US polity, however, and thus cannot easily explain changes in US social policy. Nor can this argument help to explain long-standing differences in social policy among states of the Union—whose polities are each similarly fragmented. Research has not yet sorted out which of these forms of fragmentation matter most and how with regard to social policy-making.

A second argument concerns state bureaucracies. Skocpol (1985, 1992) argues that state bureaucracies are potentially capable of autonomous action. In democratic and capitalist societies, states can be considered autonomous when they create strategies of action independently of capitalists and organized business groups, political parties, interest groups, movement organizations, and public opinion. Autonomy in turn depends on money, which states have gained through dependable modern taxes on sales, payrolls, and incomes (Steinmo 1993; see also Carruthers 1994), and a civil service not captured by political or social groups through selection or prospective employment. According to this argument, state autonomy in social spending bureaucracies aids the development of modern public spending programs. Scholars have also focused on organizational and intellectual capabilities in policymaking agencies (Heclo 1974, Rueschemeyer & Skocpol 1996).

Historical research has indicated that the structure and abilities of bureaucracies are important in various aspects of social policymaking. Skocpol (1980) argues that limited state capacities can rule out certain lines of action, showing that because of limited abilities to plan public works programs the United States could not turn dramatically to them to fight the Great Depression. Orloff (1993a) argues that the general public may refuse to support social spending programs if the agencies administering them are not staffed professionally and finds that US old-age policy was slowed by this. In a comparison across programs, Amenta (1998) finds that having a national social bureaucracy was an important determinant of an issue reaching the policy agenda of the social security legislation and that the purview of the agencies influenced the proposals. Nevertheless, agencies themselves were not powerful enough to get their proposals passed. Skrentny (1996, 1998) argues that despite many obstacles US employment bureaucracies developed affirmative action to fulfill agency objectives after a case-by-case approach to employment discrimination proved ineffective. State capacities of different sorts have been found to spur social policy across states of the Union (Amenta & Poulsen 1996, Cauthen & Amenta 1996, Howard 1999) as well as in cross-national studies (Hicks & Misra 1993), though this argument is often difficult to quantify because of the lack of readily available comparative data.

Scholars have also argued in a similar way that social policies make their own politics through their initial character and engender specific policy feedbacks (Skocpol 1992). These scholars thus argue that the process of social spending policy is path-dependent. The initial form a program assumes may influence its political future by determining whether groups will mobilize around it in support. In comparing the fates of different American programs, for example, Lowi (1972) finds that distributive programs engender greater interest group support than do redistributive programs, including most social spending, because the latter impose costs on specific people (see also Wilensky 1981). More generally, programs whose recipients are confined to the poor tend to gain little support (Weir et al 1988). Pierson (1994) argues further that mature programs have lock-in effects that counter bids to cut them. Dividing welfare states into Esping-Andersen's types helps to explain cross-national differences in retrenchment efforts (Pierson 2000b; see also Swank 2001).

All the same, policy feedback arguments have not always received empirical support. For instance, the corruption in Civil War pensions from the nineteenth century did not prevent tremendous social spending in the Depression era, and a lack of public employment programs then did not prevent the construction of extensive ones. Groups sometimes form in support of programs, sometimes not. Those groups that supported the adoption of mothers' pensions programs in 1910, for instance, had lost interest in them by 1930 (Cauthen & Amenta 1996). Moreover, need-based programs can have generous standards and be politically popular, as they were during the New Deal (Amenta 1998). There were competing policy legacies in housing bureaucracies and in education and employment civil rights bureaucracies when the Civil Rights Act of 1968 called for fighting housing discrimination (Bonastia 2000). We now know more about the nature of policy feedback arguments (Pierson 2000a, Mahoney 2000), and scholars making these promising claims need to provide more specific expectations linking aspects of policy to the processes that influence their fate.

AMERICA-CENTERED THEORY AND RESEARCH

The literature on social policy in America has employed the arguments above but has often gone in its own direction and developed its own theoretical arguments. This is partly because analyses of US social policy were undertaken before most of the breakthroughs in comparative research in the last generation (review in Howard 1999), but also because cross-national arguments often do not have many implications for American social policy. The economic arguments employed in comparative research do not help much in explaining developments in US social policy, partly because with its high income and relatively low spending the United States is an anomaly and partly because developments in US social spending have not followed historically along with economic growth. The political theories invoke actors that are not present in the American scene, such as social democratic or Christian democratic political parties. The institutional arguments highlight the influence of political structures, such as a centralized polity or strong domestic bureaucracies that are more characteristic of some European states than of the American one. These arguments provide not only pessimistic expectations, but little leverage to explain the types of gains that have been made and the great variations across time and space in a century in which the American state, too, became a welfare state. The alternative American arguments typically specify forces behind policy changes that seem to stimulate social policy in the US setting, but sometimes they try to explain American exceptionalism in social policy.

Race and US Social Policy

In recent years, many scholars have examined the role of race in the incomplete development of American social policies (Quadagno 1990, 1994, Lieberman 1998, Skocpol 1995, Davies & Derthick 1997, Brown 1999, Alston & Ferrie 1999). Lieberman (1998) argues, for instance, that race inhibited the development of a strong and centralized welfare state in America. Other scholars argue similarly and specifically that the Roosevelt administration bowed to political pressure from southern members of Congress to alter old-age insurance and unemployment compensation to exclude agricultural and domestic workers, effectively denying most African-Americans these benefits (Quadagno 1994, L Gordon 1994). Davies & Derthick (1997) maintain that there are plausible reasons other than race for the specific shape of the Social Security Act, notably that every other nation initially excluded domestic and agricultural workers from social insurance coverage and that members of Congress might have opposed public assistance legislation because poorer states sought to maximize their gains from the program, and because of animosity toward central administrators and practical difficulties in creating national standards. More generally, Skocpol (1995) cautions against analyses that point to racial division as an overarching explanation for the belated US welfare state and the stigmatization of policies directed at the poor.

Other analyses have examined the interplay between race and social policy in employment policy (Weir 1992) and the War on Poverty (Quadagno 1994). A growing body of work attempts to understand the unusual set of circumstances that resulted in the development of affirmative action policies in employment (Skrentny 1996, 1998, Pedriana & Stryker 1997, Sugrue 1998). Other work explains why various policies meant to address racial inequalities in employment, education, and housing differ markedly in their approaches and strength (Bonastia 2000). Although these arguments need to be worked out further, especially with regard to cross-national implications, this work on race and social policy offers interesting empirical challenges to previous perspectives.

Social Movements and Interest Groups

Partly because of a lack of centralized labor unions and a social democratic political party, an American version of the power resources thesis has focused on social movements and some interest groups as serving as something like functional equivalents to social democratic parties. Piven & Cloward (1977) argue that mass turbulence by poor people's movements in times of electoral instability would produce social spending concessions. Skocpol (1992) argues more generally that widespread federated interests, whether movements or interest groups, are likely to be most successful in America's fragmented polity. The list of potentially effective groups has included among others—the unemployed (Piven & Cloward 1977), women's organizations (Skocpol et al 1993, Clemens 1997), farmers (Sanders 1999), and the aged (Amenta et al 1992, 1999).

Although there is agreement that social movements have had some influence on American social policy, the extent and nature of the effects are still contested. Demonstrating a causal chain between specific social movements and specific policy outcomes has often been difficult (see reviews in Skocpol & Amenta 1986, Giugni 1998), partly because political theories to explain social movements often are similar to those that explain social policy (Amenta et al 1992). Research in this vein has often used individual states as cases and has been able to control for a number of factors that might cause both social movements and social spending outcomes. This research often finds that the effects of the movements are mediated by political (Fording 1997) and institutional factors (Amenta et al 1992, 1994, 1999). This line of argumentation has been considered at the cross-national level (Hicks & Misra 1993), but beyond strike activity it is difficult to do so in a systematic way because of a lack of data on social movements and their activities.

Capitalists and the Development of Social Policy

Rooted in the theoretical traditions of Marx and C. Wright Mills, other social scientists have argued for the causal role of individual capitalists, capitalist organizations, and factions of capitalists in the making of American social policy. These claims have produced vigorous contention about the role of US capitalists in policy-making, especially during the 1930s (see review in Manza 2000:301–3).

Most participants tend to agree at least that a sizeable fraction of capitalists—ultra conservatives (Domhoff 1990, 1996) or small businessmen (Quadagno 1984)—in the American setting have vigorously opposed the development of social policy in the United States, with this fraction perhaps being more powerful than similar ones in other countries (Vogel 1989), that business associations have often fought social policy (Orloff & Parker 1990, Amenta & Parikh 1991), and that businessmen tend to have more negative views of social policy than the US public as a whole (Amenta 1998). There also seems to be agreement that in important instances business organizations and representatives have been able to reduce benefits in social policy proposals (Amenta 1998, Swenson 1996) that were eventually adopted. There is greater disagreement on whether businessmen have generally formulated or devised the character of social policy breakthroughs when they happen in the US setting and whether some groups of far-sighted businessmen generally provide or did provide key support for social policy breakthroughs.

Sometimes, however, the arguments degenerate into unedifying debates about whether state officials are always autonomous, whether businessmen always dominate in (American) politics or who "really" influenced whom in some specific instance. Those who argue that businessmen decisively influenced the content of US social insurance proposals need to contend with the fact that by the 1930s, when the US adopted two social insurance programs, there was already great cross-national experience with and knowledge of these programs. More important, scholars who argue that businessmen have a stimulant role in public policy need to devise more systematic explanations for variations in public policy across time and place and research designs to appraise these arguments. One option might be to make explanatory links between variations in the way that businesses are organized, in the structure of business political organizations, or in the lines of political action taken by them to specific policy outcomes. Vogel (1989), for instance, maps out historically when business influence was at its strongest or weakest across recent American history, and argues that the state of the economy helps to account for these differences. Comparative work addressing the political action of capitalists along the lines of that done for workers (Swenson nd) seems promising and likely to alter the standard line from the social democratic model that capitalists uniformly oppose social policy (cf. Huber & Stephens 2001). Berkowitz & McQuaid's (1992 [1984]) argument that welfare capitalists were influential because the models that they developed in the private sector filled a void created by America's underdeveloped bureaucracy might be developed cross-nationally and over time. The reciprocal influence of the private and public social policy (Dobbin 1992, Shalev 1996) is also worth studying further. It seems possible that the presence of private policies influences the political predispositions of different groups of capitalists.

The Role of Public Opinion

A more recent line of thinking employed to explain American social policy suggests that organized interests do not directly matter in democracies. Burstein (1998) argues that public opinion instead mainly determines social policy outcomes, particularly when the public's level of concern is high; by ignoring public opinion scholars may overestimate the impact of parties, interest groups, and movements (Burstein & Eaton 2000; see also Page & Shapiro 1983). Burstein's (1985) study of equal employment opportunity legislation finds that congressional support for EEO legislation was a function of public opinion. In a comparison of the creation of the American Medicare system and the British National Health Service, Jacobs (1993) finds that the public socially constructs the conditions for public policies and creates the conditions for politicians to overcome interest group competition. Stimson et al (1995) find that policy responsiveness varies across branches of the US government but that government generally responds to public opinion through rational anticipation of elections and compositional change due to electoral outcomes (see also Erikson ct al 1993). This research suggests that if the public is decisive about a specific issue that is narrowly understood, politicians seem highly likely to heed these views.

Other studies suggest that public opinion formation is a complex process and the process by which politicians gain and understand that information is also complex, with uncertain effects on policy. Opinion and policies are often coupled loosely, as numerous policies can be compatible with a particular opinion, and there is often a disjuncture between citizens' specific policy preferences and more general, abstract values (Weir 1992). Public opinion is often vaguely formed on many issues and can change rapidly. Work on policies involving affirmative action has shown that public opinion can shift substantially according to the wording of questions (see Schuman et al 1997; see also Kahneman et al 1982). What is more, politicians can lead public opinion and often interpret public opinion differently and systematically along party or ideological lines (Grogan 1994). Politicians also have various ways of concealing their actions to avoid electoral fallout from public opinion (Pierson 1994). It may be sensible for politicians in many instances to vote with their financial backers rather than with public opinion. One study finds that public opinion is consistent with welfare policy only half the time (Monroe 1998). Also, it is not clear that US politicians had the means to ascertain public opinion in the formative years of social policy in the 1930s or paid much attention to it when they did (Amenta et al 1994). To achieve its promise this line of thinking needs to address more fully the connections between the actions of organized groups, political leaders, public opinion, and policy-making.

Patronage-Oriented Political Parties

Another candidate to explain the relative underdevelopment of American social policy is the dominance of patronage-oriented political parties: hierarchical organizations that seek to win elections and maintain their organizations through individualized benefits to party workers and other supporters (see Mayhew 1986:19–20, Banfield & Wilson 1963, Shefter 1994, Katznelson 1981). The leaders of such patronage-oriented parties are concerned with the survival of the organization, which depends in turn on contesting and winning elections, using the spoils of office to reward party workers and contributors. Mayhew (1986:292−94) claims that patronage-oriented parties avoid programmatic social policy because they find professional bureaucracies threatening: the kind of person attracted to patronage parties is unlikely to want to build programs; pro-spending groups like the labor movement cannot easily exercise influence in them; and these parties promote issue-less politics and a political culture of pessimism about government. Leaders of patronage-oriented parties have other important motives to oppose modern social spending programs (Amenta 1998: ch. 1). Social spending programs rarely provide the often remunerative opportunities provided by soliciting contracts for public business. Automatic social spending, moreover, potentially drains resources from programs that might be deployed in an individualistic way and implies higher taxes, reducing the ability of politicians to lower taxes in a selective way for contributors. Finally, patronage-oriented political parties have reason to discourage social movements seeking to promote modern social spending policies. Shefter (1994) has argued that because democratic practices preceded state bureaucracies in America, political parties, especially in the Northeast and Midwest, oriented themselves toward patronage.

This line of argument has been borne out in some American research. In a study of the formative decades of US taxation policy at the state level, Mayhew (1986) finds that a measure of "traditional party organization" significantly lowers taxation efforts. Amenta & Poulsen (1996) find similarly that the measure reduces the generosity of means-tested assistance programs under the Social Security Act. Amenta & Halfmann (2000) find that patronage-oriented parties provided more support for social programs characterized by greater discretion in the provision of benefits. Although the arguments refer to long-standing aspects of political parties and probably cannot account for changes over time, these arguments seem applicable in broadly comparative research. Shefter (1994) argues that the US political party system resembled Italy's and stood in contrast to the programmatic parties of Germany, with the British party system somewhere in between. It seems worth attempting to assess this argument systematically outside the US context.

Democratic Polities and Practices

Another line of explanation derived from American research concerns the nature and the degree to which a polity is democratized. Based on the early arguments of Key (1949), who studied the polities of the US South, it has been argued that a central obstacle to social spending policy is an underdemocratized polity—in which political leaders are chosen by way of elections, but in which there are great restrictions on political participation, political assembly and discussion, voting, and choices among leadership groups (Dahl 1971). In an underdemocratized political system, there is little electoral reason for politicians to promote policies to aid the less well off, according to the argument, and politicians will do more to seek the support of those in privileged economic positions—whose preferences generally stand opposed to social spending (Amenta 1998: ch. 1). Also, pro-spending mass movements have less reason and ability to organize themselves in an underdemocratized polity and are more likely to be repressed.

Most of the evidence for this argument has concerned the timing of adoption of policies and the formative years of policy-making. Flora & Alber (1981), for instance, find that the extension of the suffrage encouraged program adoptions between 1880 and 1920 in European parliamentary democracies, and Schneider (1982) finds that per capita votes in national elections encouraged earlier adoptions of all types of programs in 18 Western nations between 1919 and 1975. Amenta & Poulsen (1996) find that a measure tapping the ability to vote strongly influenced the initial construction of social programs at the US state level in the 1930s, and thus it likely had a profound effect on their development in the postwar period. Amenta & Halfmann (2000) find that a similar measure had a strong impact on the voting records of senators on the issue of generosity of wages for work programs in the same era.

This argument stands as a strong candidate for explaining American exceptionalism in social policy. It helps to explain American spending in the late nineteenth century, when the United States was a leader in democratic practices, and American backwardness in the twentieth century, two thirds of which was characterized by restricted voting rights in a substantial part of the polity (Kousser 1974, Piven & Cloward 1989). It also does well in explaining some long-standing differences across states in social policy. The argument is highly structural, however, and the evidence is mixed regarding whether the less blatant obstructions to voting in the past 30 years have had as great an impact on the expansion and retrenchment of social policy (see Skocpol & Amenta 1986, Huber et al 1993).

DISCUSSION AND CONCLUSION: PROMISING LINES OF THINKING AND RESEARCH

Comparative and historical scholars have made great strides in studying the causes of US social policy, but there are many ways in which this thinking and research might be advanced, and we start by discussing conceptualizations of social policy. Although regime types are intriguing ways of conceptualizing social policy, they are not as flexible and useful as previous understandings. For instance, it is difficult to address the question of why the United States developed a liberal welfare state regime, because the model implies that it has always been liberal. It would be useful in historical research for scholars to devise conceptual categories falling somewhere between policy regimes and individual programs, perhaps based on concepts such as decommodification, commodification, and autonomy.

It may be useful to think of states holistically in different ways, however. Scholars studying the state have focused almost exclusively on social policy. It seems to be an assumption that as social policy predominates in state's budgets and administration that the punishing and disciplining aspects of states will diminish. This is not necessarily true, however. Recent US experience has indicated that increased social spending has gone along, not only with reduced military spending, but also with increased efforts toward imprisonment. State conceptualizations and theories may need to address the character of entire states, not merely focusing on the aspects of the state that provide services and income protection from risks, while treating the rest as residual.

Divergences from the standard conception of social policy, especially those that address programs as social policy outside the traditional mode, are highly flexible, but offer challenges as well as opportunities. For instance, the point is well taken that scholars of social policy need to take into account tax expenditures for social purposes (Steinmo 1993, Howard 1997). It is not clear, however, how to classify some tax expenditures, many of which are probably not redistributive. Similarly, in considering home ownership policy as an alternative form of income maintenance and possibly economic redistribution (Castles 1998b, Conley 2000), scholars need to separate out what is due explicitly to state policy. From here, it should be possible to indicate how much these policies matter as compared to the standard transfer programs and services on issues such as the reduction of poverty. Perhaps most of all, the feminist conceptualizations of social policy have opened up many new opportunities for research and similar challenges. There is great benefit in probing policy outside the standard understanding of it, and these new understandings may help to deepen the concept. But in each case the relationship between these additional policies and social policy previously understood needs to be thought through and made clear.

On the theoretical side, the most promising lines of argumentation are those that are portable, with empirical implications for different settings. Scholars devising arguments to explain variation across nations in social policy would do well to think through the implications for variations in policy over time in the United States or across states of the Union. Similarly, those who have developed explanations from American policies alone should think through and elaborate implications cross-nationally or in other time periods. That said, scholars need to go beyond theoretical claims along the lines that one or another factor or process matters in every instance or that a previously unidentified feature of the American polity explains it all. We need neither the grand explanations of social policy of the sort that economic modernization theory provided, nor additional one-of-a-kind interpretations of American exceptionalism.

Although the theoretical perspectives have been arrayed above as if scholars were proponents of one or another theory alone, some of the more promising theorizing combines lines of argumentation, especially regarding institutional situations and the political actors that work within them (Skocpol 1992, Huber et al 1993, Hicks & Misra 1993, Amenta 1998). Comparative and historical work suggests more generally that some explanatory claims may be appropriate for different phases of welfare state development. Partisanship may have its greatest effect in the phases of adoption and consolidation; policy feedback effects, in the phases of expansion and retrenchment, and more systemic influences of the state likely have mediating effects all the way through. Path-dependent lines of argumentation also promise to advance these varieties of middle-range theorizing.

A number of research strategies seem promising for the future for the comparative and historical study of US social policy. Examining policy differences across the states of the Union for a number of policies related to the wider conceptualizations of social policy seem well worthwhile, especially to assess long-standing and new theoretical arguments. Relatively untapped sources of information, such as voting for social policy, also would be helpful in appraising arguments. Although there have been many good studies of individual programs, comparisons among social programs developed around the same time will help to hold relatively constant political situations, but can address why programs turned out differently than others. Also, studies would do well to go further and take full advantage of the possibilities of historical study by comparing the development of successful programs with ones that failed. These studies help to get around the biases of the tendency in the literature to study successful programs only. In each case historical scholars working mainly on the United States would do well to situate their claims in a cross-national perspective. This would go far in illuminating what is exceptional in US policies and what is not. And whenever possible scholars should appraise their claims against evidence in similar polities, whether countries or other states, as the best small-N studies do.

American social policy has come a long way in the last century, and the study of it has made great strides in the last generation. By exploiting the newer conceptualizations of social policy, extending theoretical arguments in ways that address US and cross-national developments, and employing imaginative and multifaceted research strategies, scholars can go further in an area that is likely to draw more and more attention.

ACKNOWLEDGMENTS

We thank Vanessa Barker, Drew Halfmann, Francesca Polletta, Karen S. Cook, and an anonymous referee for their comments on a previous version of this article and Denise Krassner for editorial assistance. This work was supported in part by National Science Foundation grant SBR-9709618.

Visit the Annual Reviews home page at www.AnnualReviews.org

LITERATURE CITED

Alston L, Ferrie J. 1999. *Southern Paternalism and the American Welfare State*. New York: Cambridge Univ. Press

Amenta E. 1998. *Bold Relief: Institutional Politics and the Origins of Modern American Social Policy*. Princeton, NJ: Princeton Univ. Press

Amenta E, Benoit E, Bonastia C, Cauthen NK, Halfmann D. 1998. Bring back the WPA: work, relief, and the origins of American social policy in welfare reform. *Stud. Am. Polit. Dev.* 12:1–56

Amenta E, Carruthers BG, Zylan Y. 1992. A hero for the aged? The Townsend movement, The political mediation model, and U.S. old-age policy, 1934–1950. *Am. J. Sociol.* 98:308–39

Amenta E, Dunleavy K, Bernstein M. 1994.

Stolen thunder? Huey Long's share our wealth, political mediation, and the Second New Deal. *Am. Sociol. Rev.* 59:678–702

Amenta E, Halfmann D, Young MP. 1999. The strategies and contexts of social protest: political mediation and the impact of the Townsend Movement in California. *Mobilization* 4:1–24

Amenta E, Halfmann D. 2000. Wage wars: institutional politics, the WPA, and the struggle for U.S. social policy. *Am. Sociol. Rev.* 64:506–28

Amenta E, Parikh S. 1991. Capitalists did not want the social reform: a political struggle interpretation of the origins of the American welfare state. *Am. Sociol. Rev.* 56:124–29

Amenta E, Poulsen JD. 1996. Social politics in context: the institutional politics theory and social spending at the end of the New Deal. *Soc. Forces* 75(1):33–60

Banfield EC, Wilson JQ. 1963. *City Politics.* Cambridge, MA: Harvard Univ. Press

Benoit E. 2000. *Controlling Drugs in the Welfare State: American Policy in Comparative, Historical Perspective.* PhD thesis. New York Univ.

Berkowitz E, McQuaid K. 1992 [1988]. *Creating the Welfare State: The Political Economy of Twentieth-Century Reform.* Lawrence: Univ. Press of Kans.

Bonastia C. 2000. Why did affirmative action in housing fail during the Nixon era?: Exploring the "institutional homes" of social policies. *Soc. Probl.* 47 forthcoming

Brown MK. 1999. *Race, Money, and the American Welfare State.* Ithaca, NY: Cornell Univ. Press

Brown RD. 1995. Party cleavages and welfare effort in the American states. *Am. Polit. Sci. Rev.* 89:23–33

Burstein P. 1985. *Discrimination, Jobs, and Politics: The Struggle for Equal Employment Opportunity in the United States since the New Deal.* Chicago: Univ. Chicago Press

Burstein P. 1998. Bringing the public back in: Should sociologists consider the impact of public opinion on public Policy? *Social Forces* 77:27–62

Burstein P, Eaton AL. 2000. *The Impact of Political Parties, Interest Groups, and Social Movement Organizations on Public Policy: Some Recent Evidence and Theoretical Concerns.* Presented at Annu. Meet. of the Am. Sociol. Assoc., Washington, DC

Carruthers BG. 1994. When is the state autonomous? Culture, organization theory, and the political sociology of the state. *Soc. Theory* 12:19–44

Castles FG. 1998a. *Comparative Public Policy: Patterns of Post-war Transformation.* Cheltenham, UK: Edward Elgar

Castles FG. 1998b. The really big trade-off: home ownership and the welfare state in the new world and the old. *Acta Politica* 33(1):5–19

Castles FG, Mitchell D. 1993. Worlds of welfare and families of nations. In *Families of Nations: Patterns of Public Policy in Western Democracies,* ed. FG Castles. Aldershot: Dartmouth

Cauthen NK, Amenta E. 1996. Not for widows only: institutional politics and the formative years of Aid to Dependent Children. *Am. Sociol. Rev.* 61:427–48

Clayton R, Pontusson J. 1998, Welfare-state retrenchment revisited: entitlement cuts, public sector restructuring, and inegalitarian trends in advanced capitalist societies. *World Polit.* 51(1):67–98

Clemens ES. 1997. *The People's Lobby: Organizational Innovation and the Rise of Interest Group Politics in the United States, 1890–1925.* Chicago: Univ. Chicago Press

Collier D, Messick R. 1975. Prerequisites versus diffusion: testing alternative explanations of Social Security adoption. *Am. Polit. Sci. Rev.* 69:1299–1315

Conley D. 2000. *Home ownership, the welfare state and cross-national poverty Comparisons. conference on saving, intergenerational transfers, and the distribution of wealth.* Presented at Jerome Levy Economics Instit. of Bard College

Dahl R. 1971. *Polyarchy: Participation and Oppostion.* New Haven, CT: Yale Univ. Press

Davies G, Derthick M. 1997. Race and social

welfare policy: the Social Security Act of 1935. *Polit. Sci. Q.* 112(2):217–35

de Swaan A. 1988. *In Care of the State: Health Care, Education and Welfare in Europe and the USA in the Modern Era.* New York: Oxford Univ. Press

Derthick M. 1979. *Policymaking for Social Security.* Washington DC: Brookings Inst.

Dobbin FR. 1992. The origins of private social insurance: public policy and fringe benefits in America, 1920–1950. *Am. J. Sociol.* 97:1416–50

Domhoff GW. 1990. *The Power Elite and the State: How Policy is Made in America,* Ch. 3. New York: Aldine de Gruyter

Domhoff GW. 1996. *State Autonomy or Class Dominance? Case Studies on Policymaking in America.* New York: Aldine de Gruyter

Erikson RS, Wright GC, McIver JP. 1993. *Statehouse Democracy: Public Opinion and Policy in the American States.* New York: Cambridge Univ. Press

Esping-Andersen G. 1990. *The Three Worlds of Welfare Capitalism.* Princeton, NJ: Princeton Univ. Press

Esping-Andersen G, van Kersbergen K. 1992. Contemporary research on social democracy. *Annu. Rev. Sociol.* 18:187–208

Flora P, Alber J. 1981. Modernization, democratization and the development of welfare states in Western Europe. In *The Development of Welfare States in Europe and America,* ed. P Flora, AJ Heidenheimer, pp. 37–80. New Brunswick, NJ: Transaction Books

Flora P, Heidenheimer AJ, eds. 1981. *The Development of Welfare States in Europe and America.* New Brunswick, NJ: Transaction Books

Fording RC. 1997. The conditional effect of violence as a political tactic: mass insurgency, welfare generosity, and electoral context in the American states. *Am. J. Polit. Sci.* 41:1–29

Fraser N. 1994. After the family wage: gender equity and the welfare state. *Polit. Theory* 22:591–618

Giugni MG. 1998. Was it worth the effort? The outcomes and consequences of social movements. *Annu. Rev. Sociol.* 24:371–93

Gordon C. 1994. *New Deals: Business, Labor and Politics in America, 1920–1935.* New York: Cambridge Univ. Press

Gordon L, ed. 1990. *Women, the State and Welfare.* Madison, WI: Univ. Wisc. Press

Gordon L. 1994. *Pitied But Not Entitled: Single Mothers and the History of Welfare, 1890–1935.* New York: Free Press

Grogan CM. 1994. Politico-economic factors influencing state Medicaid policy. *Polit. Res. Q.* 47:589–622

Halfmann D. 1999. *Institutional and Policy Influences on the Form of National Abortion Policy Reforms in the United States and Great Britain, 1966-1973.* Presented at Annu. Meet. Am. Sociol. Assoc., Chicago

Haney L. 2000. Feminist state theory: comparing gender regimes across apparatuses. *Annu. Rev. Sociol.* 26:641–66

Heclo H. 1974. *Modern Social Politics in Britain and Sweden.* New Haven, CT: Yale Univ. Press

Heidenheimer AJ. 1981. Education and social security entitlements in Europe and America. In *The Development of Welfare States in Europe and America,* ed. P Flora, AJ Heidenheimer, pp. 269–305. New Brunswick, NJ: Transaction Books

Hicks A. 1999. *Social Democracy and Welfare Capitalism: a Century of Income Security Politics.* Ithaca: Cornell Univ. Press

Hicks A, Misra J. 1993. Political resources and the growth of welfare in affluent capitalist democracies, 1960–1982. *Am. J. Sociol.* 99:668–710

Hicks A, Misra J, Ng TN. 1995. The programmatic emergence of the Social Security state. *Am. Sociol. Rev.* 60:329–49

Hicks A, Swank DH. 1992. Politics, institutions, and welfare spending. *Am. Polit. Sci. Rev.* 86:658–74

Howard C. 1997. *The Hidden Welfare State: Tax Expenditures and Social Policy in the United States.* Princeton, NJ: Princeton Univ. Press

Howard C. 1999. The American welfare state, or states? *Polit. Res. Q.* 52:421–42

Huber E, Ragin C, Stephens JD. 1993.

Social democracy, Christian democracy, constitutional structure, and the welfare state. *Am. J. Sociol.* 99(3):711–49

Huber E, Stephens JD. 2000a. Partisan governance, women's employment, and the social democratic service state. *Am. Sociol. Rev.* 65:323–42

Huber E, Stephens JD. 2000b. Welfare state and production regimes in the era of retrenchment. In *The New Politics of the Welfare State*, ed. P Pierson. New York: Oxford Univ. Press

Huber E, Stephens JD. 2001. *Political Choice in Global Markets: Development and Crisis of the Welfare States.* Chicago: Univ. Chicago Press

Huntington SP. 1968. *Political Order in Changing Societies.* New Haven, CT: Yale Univ. Press

Immergut EM. 1992. *Health Politics: Interests and Institutions in Western Europe.* New York: Cambridge Univ. Press

Immergut EM. 1998. The theoretical core of the new institutionalism. *Polit. Soc.* 26:5–34

Jacobs LR. 1993. *The Health of Nations: Public Opinion and the Making of American and British Health Policy.* Ithaca, NY: Cornell Univ. Press

Kahneman D, Slovic P, Tversky A. eds. 1982. *Judgment and Uncertainty: Heuristics and Biases.* New York: Cambridge Univ. Press

Katznelson I. 1981. *City Trenches: Urban Politics and the Patterning of Class in the United States.* New York: Pantheon

Katznelson I, Weir M. 1985. *Schooling For All: Class, Race, and the Decline of the Democratic Ideal.* New York: Basic Books

Key VO. 1949. *Southern Politics in State and Nation*, Ch. 14. New York: Knopf

Korpi W. 1983. *The Democratic Class Struggle.* London: Routledge

Kousser JM. 1974. *The Shaping of Southern Politics: Suffrage Restriction and the Establishment of the One-Party South, 1880–1910.* New Haven, CT: Yale Univ. Press

Leicht KT, Jenkins JC. 1998. Political resources and direct state intervention: the adoption of public venture capital programs in the American States, 1974–1990. *Soc. Forces* 76:1323–45

Lewis J. 1992. Gender and the development of welfare regimes. *J. Eur. Soc. Policy* 3:159–73

Lieberman RC. 1998. *Shifting the Color Line: Race and the American Welfare State.* Cambridge, MA/London: Harvard Univ. Press

Lowi TJ. 1972. Four systems of policy, politics, and choice. *Public Admin. Rev.* 32:298–310

Mahoney J. 2000. Path dependence in historical sociology. *Theory Soc.* Forthcoming

Manza J. 2000. Political sociological models of the U.S. New Deal. *Annu. Rev. Sociol.* 26:297–322

Maoini A. 1998. *Parting at the Crossroads: The Emergence of Health Insurance in the United States and Canada.* Princeton, NJ: Princeton Univ. Press

Mayhew D. 1986. *Placing Parties in American Politics*, pp. 19–20. Princeton, NJ: Princeton Univ. Press

Mishra R. 1990. *The Welfare State in Capitalist Society: Policies of Retrenchment and Maintenance in Europe, North America, and Australia.* Buffalo, NY: Univ. Toronto Press

Monroe AD. 1998. Public opinion and public policy. *Public Opin. Q.* 62(1):6–28

Myles J, Pierson P. 1997. Friedman's revenge: the reform of "Liberal" welfare states in Canada and the United States. *Polit. Soc:* 25:443–72

O'Connor JS. 1993. Gender, class and citizenship in the comparative analysis of welfare state regimes: theoretical and methodological issues. *Br. J. Sociol.* 44:501–18

O'Connor JS, Orloff AS, Shaver S. 1999. *States, Markets, Families: Gender, Liberalism and Social Policy in Australia, Canada, Great Britain and the United States.* Cambridge, MA: Cambridge Univ. Press

Orloff AS. 1993a. *The Politics of Pensions: A Comparative Analysis of Britain, Canada, and the United States, 1880–1940.* Madison, WI: Univ. Wisc. Press

Orloff AS. 1993b. Gender and the social rights of citizenship: the comparative analysis of gender relations and welfare states. *Am. Sociol. Rev.* 58:303–28

Orloff AS. 1996. Gender in the welfare state. *Annu. Rev. Sociol.* 22:51–78

Orloff AS, Parker E. 1990. Business and social policy in Canada and the United States, 1920–1940. *Compar. Soc. Res.* 12:295–339

Orloff AS, Skocpol T. 1984. Why not equal protection? Explaining the politics of public social welfare in Britain and the United States, 1880s–1920s. *Am. Sociol. Rev.* 49:726–50

Page B, Shapiro RY. 1983. Effects of public opinion on policy. *Am. Polit. Sci. Rev.* 77:175–90

Pampel FC. 1994. Population aging, class context, and age inequality in public spending. *Am. J. Sociol.* 100:153–95

Pedriana N, Stryker R. 1997. Political culture wars 1960s style: equal employment opportunity-affirmative action law and the Philadelphia Plan. *Am. J. Sociol.* 103(3): 633–91

Pierson P. 1994. *Dismantling the Welfare State? Reagan, Thatcher, and the Politics of Retrenchment.* Cambridge, UK: Cambridge Univ. Press

Pierson P. 2000a. Path dependence, increasing returns, and the study of politics. *Am. Polit. Sci. Rev.* 94:251–67

Pierson P. 2000b. Coping with permanent austerity: welfare state restructuring in affluent democracies. In *The New Politics of the Welfare State*, ed. Pierson P. New York: Oxford Univ. Press

Piven FF, Cloward RA. 1993 (1971). *Regulating the Poor: The Functions of Public Welfare.* New York: Vintage. 2nd ed.

Piven FF, Cloward RA. 1989. *Why Americans Don't Vote.* New York: Pantheon

Piven FF, Cloward RA. 1977. *Poor People's Movements: Why They Succeed, How They Fail.* New York: Pantheon.

Quadagno JS. 1984. Welfare capitalism and the Social Security Act of 1935. *Am. Sociol. Rev.* 49:632–47

Quadagno JS. 1987. Theories of the welfare state. *Annu. Rev. Sociol.* 13:109–28

Quadagno J. 1990. Race, class, and gender in the U.S. welfare state: Nixon's failed family assistance plan. *Am. Sociol. Rev.* 55:11–28

Quadagno J. 1994. *The Color of Welfare: How Racism Undermined the War on Poverty.* New York: Oxford Univ. Press

Rueschemeyer D, Skocpol T. 1996. *States, Social Knowledge and the Origins of Modern Social Policies.* Princeton, NJ: Princeton Univ. Press

Sainsbury D. 1996. *Gender, Equality and Welfare States.* Cambridge, UK: Cambridge Univ. Press

Sanders E. 1999. *Roots of Reform: Farmers, Workers, and the American State, 1877–1917.* Princeton, NJ: Princeton Univ. Press

Schneider SK. 1982. The sequential development of social programs in eighteen welfare states. *Compar. Soc. Res.* 5:195–219

Schuman H, Steeh C, Bobo L, Krysan M. 1997. *Racial Attitudes in America: Trends and Interpretations.* Cambridge, MA: Harvard Univ. Press

Shalev M. 1983. The social democratic model and beyond: two 'generations' of comparative research on the welfare state. *Compar. Soc. Res.* 6:315–51

Shalev M, ed. 1996. *The Privatization of Social Policy? Occupational Welfare and the Welfare State in America, Scandinavia and Japan.* New York: St. Martin's Press

Shefter M. 1994. *Political Parties and the State: the American Historical Experience.* Princeton, NJ: Princeton Univ. Press

Skocpol T. 1980. Political response to capitalist crisis: neo-Marxist theories of the state and the case of the New Deal. *Polit. Soc.* 10:155–201

Skocpol T. 1985. Bringing the state back in: strategies of analysis in current research. In *Bringing the State Back In*, ed. PB Evans, D Rueschmeyer, T Skocpol, pp. 3–37. Cambridge, UK: Cambridge Univ. Press

Skocpol T. 1992. *Protecting Soldiers and Mothers: the Political Origins of Social Policy in the United States.* Cambridge, MA: Belknap Press of Harvard Univ. Press

Skocpol T. 1995. African Americans in U.S. social policy. In *Classifying By Race*, ed. PE Peterson, pp. 129–51. Princeton, NJ: Princeton Univ. Press

Skocpol T, Abend-Wein M, Howard C, Lehmann SG. 1993. Women's associations and the enactment of mothers' pensions in the United States. *Am. Polit. Sci. Rev.* 87:686–701

Skocpol T, Amenta E. 1986. States and social policies. *Annu. Rev. Sociol.* 12:131–57

Skrentny JD. 1996. *The Ironies of Affirmative Action: Politics, Culture, and Justice in America.* Chicago: Univ. Chicago Press

Skrentny JD. 1998. State capacity, policy feedbacks and affirmative action for blacks, women and Latinos. *Res. Polit. Sociol.* 8:279–310

Soule SA, Zylan Y. 1997. Runaway train? the diffusion of state-level reform in ADC/AFDC eligibility requirements, 1950–1967. *Am. J. Sociol.* 103:733–62

Steinmo S. 1993. *Taxation and Democracy: Swedish, British and American Approaches to Financing the Modern State.* New Haven, CT: Yale Univ. Press

Stephens JD. 1979. *The Transition from Capitalism to Socialism.* London: Macmillan

Stimson JA, MacKuen MB, Erikson RS. 1995. Dynamic representation. *Am. Polit. Sci. Rev.* 89:543–65

Stinchcombe AL. 1985. The functional theory of social insurance. *Polit. Soc.* 14:411–30

Sugrue TJ. 1998. The tangled roots of affimative action. *Am. Behav. Sci.* 41(7):886–97

Swank D. 2001. *Diminished Democracy? Globalization, Political Institutions, and the Welfare State in Advanced Market Economies.* New York: Cambridge Univ. Press

Swenson P. 1996. Arranged alliance: business interests in the New Deal. *Polit. Soc.* 25:66–116

Swenson P. n.d. *Labor Markets and Welfare States: Employers in the Making of the American and Swedish Systems.* Unpub. Ms., Dept. Polit. Sci., Northwestern Univ., Evanston, IL

Thelen K. 1999. Historical institutionalism in comparative politics. *Annu. Rev. Polit. Sci.* 2:369–404

Tynes SR. 1996. *Turning Points in Social Security: from 'Cruel Hoax' to 'Sacred Entitlement'.* Stanford, CA: Stanford Univ. Press

Vogel D. 1989. *Fluctuating Fortunes: The Political Power of Business in America.* New York: Basic Books

Weir M. 1992. *Politics and Jobs: The Boundaries of Employment Policy in the United States.* Princeton, NJ: Princeton Univ. Press

Weir M, Orloff AS, Skocpol T. 1988. Understanding American social politics. In *The Politics of Social Policy in the United States* ed. M Weir, AS Orloff, T Skocpol, pp. 3–27. Princeton, NJ: Princeton Univ. Press

Western B, Beckett K. 1999. How unregulated is the U.S. labor market? The penal system as a labor market institution. *Am. J. Sociol.* 104:1030–60

Wilensky H. 1975. *The Welfare State and Equality: Structural and Ideological Roots of Public Expenditures.* Berkeley/Los Angeles: Univ. Calif. Press

Wilensky H. 1981. Leftism, Catholicism, and democratic corporatism: the role of political parties in recent welfare state development. In *The Development of Welfare States in Europe and America*, ed. P Flora, AJ Heidenheimer, pp. 345–82. New Brunswick, NJ: Transaction Books

Annu. Rev. Sociol. 2001. 27:235–60

IS GLOBALIZATION CIVILIZING, DESTRUCTIVE OR FEEBLE? A CRITIQUE OF FIVE KEY DEBATES IN THE SOCIAL SCIENCE LITERATURE

Mauro F. Guillén

*The Wharton School and Department of Sociology, University of Pennsylvania,
Philadelphia, Pennsylvania 19104; e-mail: guillen@wharton.upenn.edu*

Key Words convergence, nation-state, modernity, global culture

■ **Abstract** The sociological, economic, political, and anthropological literatures
are devoting increasing attention to globalization. This chapter discusses the various
connotations of the term and puts it in historical perspective. Existing theoretical and
empirical research on globalization is organized around five key issues or questions:
Is it really happening? Does it produce convergence? Does it undermine the authority
of nation-states? Is globality different from modernity? Is a global culture in the making? A plea is made for a comparative sociology of globalization that is sensitive to
local variations and to how agency, interest, and resistance mediate in the relationship
between globalization causes and outcomes.

> The bulk of the earth must not only be spherical, but not large in comparison
> with the size of other stars.
> —Aristotle (384–322 BC), as quoted by Dreyer (1953, p. 118)

INTRODUCTION

Globalization is one of the most contested topics in the social sciences. Observers
and theorists of globalization have variously argued that the rapid increase in
cross-border economic, social, technological, and cultural exchange is civilizing,
destructive, or feeble, to borrow Albert Hirschman's (1982) celebrated metaphors.
Harold Levitt's "Globalization of Markets" (1983) or Kenichi Ohmae's *Borderless
World* (1990) promise boundless prosperity and consumer joy as a result of globalization, i.e. the global as civilizing. In sharp contrast to this view, the historian Paul
Kennedy warns in *Preparing for the Twenty-First Century* (1993) against our lack
of structures to deal with a global world, while political economist Dani Rodrik
rings a similar bell of alarm in *Has Globalization Gone Too Far?* (1997) concerning
the increasingly free international economic and financial flows (see also Gilpin
2000, Mittelman 2000). As in the civilizing view, the destructive interpretation

0360-0572/01/0811-0235$14.00

regards globalization as leading to convergence, albeit predicting harmful rather than beneficial consequences. Unlike the adherents to either the civilizing or the destructive views of globalization, other scholars, namely, Paul Hirst and Grahame Thompson in *Globalization in Question* (1996), and Robert Wade in "Globalization and Its Limits" (1996), see it as a feeble process that has not yet challenged the nation-state and other fundamental features of the modern world.

In this chapter I first define globalization and its timing. Then, I review the main contributions of the various social sciences to research on globalization, with an emphasis on sociological perspectives. I organize the discussion and critique around five key debates or questions: Is globalization really happening? Does it produce convergence? Does it undermine the authority of nation-states? Is globality different from modernity? Is a global culture in the making?

WHAT IS GLOBALIZATION?

Intuitively, globalization is a process fueled by, and resulting in, increasing cross-border flows of goods, services, money, people, information, and culture (Held et al 1999, p. 16). Sociologist Anthony Giddens (1990, p. 64, 1991, p. 21) proposes to regard globalization as a decoupling or "distanciation" between space and time, while geographer David Harvey (1989) and political scientist James Mittelman (1996) observe that globalization entails a "compression" of space and time, a shrinking of the world. Sociologist Manuel Castells (1996, p. 92) emphasizes the informational aspects of the global economy when he defines it as "an economy with the capacity to work as a unit in real time on a planetary scale." In a similar vein, sociologist Gary Gereffi (1994) writes about global "commodity chains," whereby production is coordinated on a global scale. Management scholar Stephen Kobrin (1997, pp. 147–148) describes globalization as driven not by foreign trade and investment but by increasing technological scale and information flows. Political scientist Robert Gilpin (1987, p. 389) defines globalization as the "increasing interdependence of national economies in trade, finance, and macroeconomic policy." Sociologist Roland Robertson (1992, p. 8) argues that globalization "refers both to the compression of the world and the intensification of consciousness of the world as a whole." Also sociologist Martin Albrow (1997, p. 88) defines globalization as the "diffusion of practices, values and technology that have an influence on people's lives worldwide." I propose to combine the perspectives of Robertson and Albrow, and so define globalization as a process leading to greater interdependence and mutual awareness (reflexivity) among economic, political, and social units in the world, and among actors in general (Guillén 2001, Held et al 1999, pp. 429–31, Petrella 1996, pp. 63–66, Waters 1995, p. 63).

Globalization, however, is also an ideology with multiple meanings and lineages. As Cox (1996) has observed, sometimes it appears loosely associated with neoliberalism and with technocratic solutions to economic development and reform (Evans 1997, McMichael 1996, p. 177). The term also appears linked to cross-border advocacy networks and organizations defending human rights, the environment, women's rights, or world peace (Guidry et al 1999, Keck & Sikkink 1998). The environmental movement, in particular, has raised the banner of globalism in its struggle for a clean planet, as in its "Think Global, Act Local" slogan (Held et al 1999, pp. 376–413). Thus, globalization is often constructed as an impersonal and inevitable force in order to justify certain policies or behaviors, however praiseworthy some of them might be. In a broader historical sense, Mazlish (1993, pp. 6–7) and Robertson (1992, pp. 68–71) cogently argue that not only capitalism or advocacy movements but also Christianity, Islam, and Marxism have made global claims and harbored global pretensions. Hirsch & Fiss (2000) document that use of the term "globalization" in the press appears associated with multiple ideological frames of reference, including "financial market," "economic efficiency," "negative effect," and "culture."

The start of globalization is also a contested issue (Held et al 1999). One could argue that globalization begins with the dawn of history. The literature, however, has tended to date the start of globalization more recently in the experience of the West. At one end of the spectrum, historians have noted the importance of the first circumnavigation of the Earth in 1519–1521 (Mazlish 1993). World-system theorists maintain that the expansion of European capitalism in the sixteenth century marks the start of globalization (Wallerstein 1974; see also Waters 1995, pp. 2–4). Some economic historians point to the turn of the twentieth century as the heyday of international trade and investment before the convulsions of World War I and the Great Depression threw the world into spiraling protectionism (Williamson 1996). Robertson (1992, p. 179) argues that globalization "took off" between 1875 and 1925 with the "time-zoning of the world and the establishment of the international dateline; the near-global adoption of the Gregorian calendar and the adjustable seven-day week; and the establishment of international telegraphic and signaling codes." Murphy (1994) recounts the history of international organizations to foster transportation and communication since 1850. Students of social movements for the abolition of slavery, woman suffrage, or the prohibition of female circumcision argue that the emergence of contemporary transnational advocacy networks can be traced back to the second half of the nineteenth century (Keck & Sikkink 1998, pp. 41–72).

A third group of scholars starts the analysis of globalization at the end of World War II, with the coming of the nuclear age, the emancipation of colonies, the renewed expansion of trade and investment, and the economic rise of Northeast Asia (Gilpin 1987, pp. 341–44, 2000, Guillén 2001, Kennedy 1993, pp. 47, 50, McMichael 1996). There is also justification for telling the story of globalization beginning with the unraveling of *pax americana* in the early 1970s or with the rise of neoliberal ideology in the late 1970s and early 1980s. In a more conceptually informed way, Kobrin (1997, pp. 147–148) distinguishes between the trade and investment linkages of nineteenth-century internationalization and the network and information ties of late twentieth-century globalization (see also Baldwin & Martin 1999, Held et al 1999). Thus, there is no agreement as to whether it was with Magellan and Mercator, James Watt and Captain Cook, Nixon and Kissinger, or Thatcher and Reagan that globalization started or, to be more precise, that the narrative of globalization ought to begin. Lastly, it should be noted that the English term "globalization" was first used around 1960 in its world-wide sense as opposed to its much older meanings of the global as something spherical, total, or universal (Waters 1995, p. 2).

Definitions and timing aside, one of the persistent problems afflicting the study of globalization is that it is far from a uniform, irreversible, and inexorable trend. Rather, globalization is a fragmented, incomplete, discontinuous, contingent, and in many ways contradictory and puzzling process (Giddens 2000, Gilpin 2000, p. 294, Guidry et al 1999, Held et al 1999, p. 431). Table 1 presents economic, financial, social, political, and bibliographical indicators of globalization. The measures are presented for the 1980–1998 period not because globalization started in 1980 but rather because of data limitations. Foreign direct (excluding portfolio) investment as a percentage of GDP is 2.5 times greater today than twenty years ago—and nearly four times greater in the developing world. Trade has also grown, although not as fast as foreign investment. Financial globalization has grown fastest: Foreign exchange turnover increased tenfold between 1979 and 1997 relative to world GDP, and both cross-border bank credit and assets have increased more than twofold as a percentage of world GDP.

Some key indicators of social exchange across borders are also increasing rapidly, including tourism and international telephone calls (see Table 1). International migration, though on the rise, has not reached important levels relative to world population. Also bucking the globalization trend is the growing number of nation-states—from 157 United Nations members in 1980 to 184 by 1998. And more ethnic groups than ever seem to be reasserting their identities and yearning

TABLE 1   Indicators of Globalization, 1980–1998

Indicators	1980	1985	1990	1995	1998
A. Economic					
Inward foreign direct investment stock, % world GDP	4.6	6.5	8.0	10.1	11.7[h]
Developed countries, % GDP	3.8	4.9	6.6	9.1	10.5[h]
Developing countries, % GDP	4.3	8.2	8.5	15.4	16.6[h]
Gross value added of foreign affiliates, % world GDP	—	5.2	6.4	6.3	7.8[h]
Exports of foreign affiliates, % total world exports	—	31.9	27.5	32.3	35.6
Exports + imports of goods, % world non-service GDP	72.7	68.1	76.0	87.5	92.1[h]
Developed countries, % non-service GDP	76.6	72.1	81.8	90.1	95.1[h]
Developing countries, % non-service GDP	60.9	54.6	55.0	77.3	83.2[h]

TABLE 1   (*Continued*)

Indicators	1980	1985	1990	1995	1998
Exports + imports of goods & services, % world GDP	40.0	38.8	38.9	42.9	45.2[h]
Developed countries, % GDP	40.2	39.4	38.3	41.2	43.8[h]
Developing countries, % GDP	39.1	36.6	41.0	49.5	50.6[h]
B. Financial					
Daily currency exchange turnover, % world GDP[a]	0.7	1.3	3.8	5.6	6.8
Cross-border bank credit stock, % world GDP[b]	13.9	19.9	34.3	33.1	—
Cross-border banking assets, % world GDP[b]	13.7	19.9	28.1	28.5	—
C. Social & Political					
International tourist arrivals, % world population	3.5	6.7	8.6	9.9	—
Stock of international migrants, % world population[c]	1.5	1.8	2.0	2.2	—
International calls, minutes per million $ world GDP[d]	—	1354	1600	2174	—
Internet hosts, number (thousands)[e]	—	5	617	12881	19459[h]
Nation-states with membership in the United Nations	157	157	159	184	184
International organizations, number	14273[g]	24180	26656	41722	48350
D. Bibliographical					
Literature on globalization, annual entries[f]:					
Sociological Abstracts	89	142	301	1068	1009
Econlit	19	269	608	1044	924
PAIS (Politics & International Relations)	64	101	309	366	698
Historical Abstracts	69	81	103	166	157
Anthropological Literature	6	2	6	1	34
Books in Print	48	92	328	689	589

[a]Data are for 1979, 1984, 1989, 1995, and 1998.

[b]Data are for 1981, 1986, 1991 and 1995.

[c]Estimates.

[d]Excludes international calls using cellular phones or private networks.

[e]Data are for 1986, 1991, 1996, and 1997.

[f]Articles or books with the words "global" or "globalization" in the title, subject heading or abstract.

[g]1981.

[h]1997.

Sources: *World Investment Report*; *International Trade Statistics Yearbook*; *UN Statistical Yearbook*; Baldwin and Martin (1999:12); Tschoegl (1998); Vernon (1998:198); Miguel Centeno, Department of Sociology, Princeton University; *Yearbook of International Organizations*; Penn Library Databases.

to create their own state—Palestinians and Kurds, Basques and Catalans, Scots and Welsh, Tibetans and Kashmiris, Corsicans and Quebecois (Friedman 1994, Geertz 1998, Robertson 1992, p. 98–108; for the dissenting view, see Rapoport 1996). Meanwhile, the number of international organizations has more than trebled. Among international advocacy groups, those concerned with human rights, the environment, Esperanto, women's rights, and world peace have grown fastest (Keck & Sikkink 1998, p. 11; see also Meyer et al 1997, Murphy 1994). And the internet has accelerated cross-border exchange during the 1990s, although less than two or three percent of the population has access to it in most countries except the very rich ones (Guillén & Suárez 2001).

It is perhaps ironic to observe that the fastest increase among the indicators included in Table 1 does not refer to globalization itself, but to the literature on globalization. As shown in Figure 1, there has been an explosion in the number of articles on globalization published in the economic, sociological, and political literatures. The number of books on globalization has also increased steeply. The historical and anthropological literatures, by contrast, have lagged behind. Among the social sciences, sociology was the first to pay attention to globalization. Sociology journals started to carry large numbers of articles on globalization during the early and mid 1970s, primarily induced by world-system theorizing (Wallerstein 1974). Some authors have attempted to summarize the literature (e.g. Held et al 1999, Sklair 1991, Waters 1995), and several edited volumes have been compiled (Dunning 1997, Featherstone 1990, Hargittai & Centeno 2001, Mittelman 1996, Sakamoto 1994, Mander & Goldsmith 1996). Perhaps the most bewildering feature of the literature is not its sheer size but the remarkable diversity of authors that have contributed to it, ranging from postmodernist scholars or social theorists who rarely, if ever, engage in empirical research to number-crunching empiricists, politicians, and management consultants.

FIVE KEY DEBATES

The five key debates that I identify in this chapter are not an exhaustive list of issues in the vast and rich literature on globalization. They capture, however, a broad spectrum of social, political, and cultural themes of interest to sociologists and other social scientists. Table 2 shows how different authors position themselves in the five key debates. One should not assume those on the same side of the fence regarding a particular question actually agree with each other on other issues or that they approach the issue from exactly the same perspective.

Is It Really Happening?

Most of the books and articles discussed in this chapter simply assume that the world is becoming more global, that is, more interrelated. Myriad policymakers, publicists, and academics take it as axiomatic that globalization is in fact happening without supporting their claim with data (e.g. Ohmae 1990, Naisbitt & Aburdene

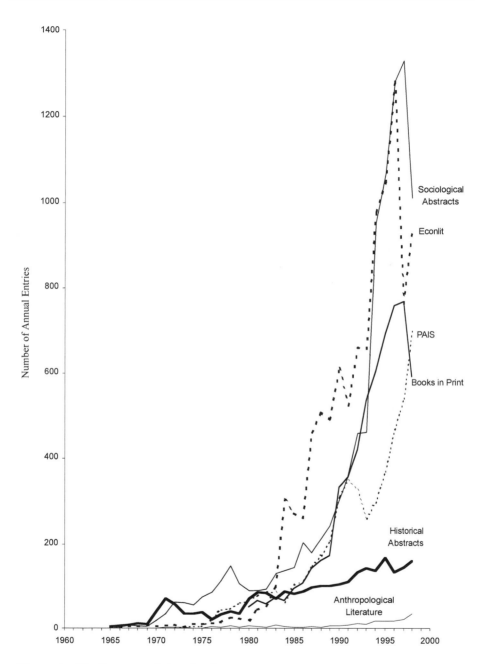

Figure 1   The literature of globalization.

TABLE 2   Five key debates about globalization

Debate	Answers in the Literature	
	Yes	**No**
1. Is It Really Happening?	Naisbitt and Aburdene 1990 Ohmae 1990 Castells 1996:66–147 Rodrik 1997:9 Held et al 1999 Gilpin 2000	Krugman 1994:146–148, 256–267 Berger 1996:7–8, 11, 19–21 Hirst and Thompson 1996:1–3, 18–98 Wade 1996:66–84 Doremus et al 1998 Fligstein 2001

2. Does It Produce Convergence?	Bell [1973]
	Meyer and Hannan 1979:
	  13–15
	Levitt 1983
	Williamson 1996
	Meyer et al 1997:145, 148,
	  152–154, 161
		Giddens 1990:63–64, 1991:21–22
		Stopford and Strange 1991:1–2
		Robertson 1992:27, 145
		Friedman 1994:210–211
		Berger 1996:2–7, 19–21
		Boyer 1996:33, 58
		Cox 1996:28, 30 n. 1
		Albrow 1997:86, 144, 149, 189
		Garrett 1998:1–11, 34–37, 51, 74,
		  1999
		Held et al 1999:431, 441
		Guillén 2001

3. Does It Undermine the Authority of Nation-States?	Vernon 1971:249–258, 1998:
	  172–175
	Kennedy 1993:53–64,
	  122–134, 330
	Mazlish 1994:4
	Sakamoto 1994:19, 36
	Waters 1995:96–123
	Cox 1996:26–27
	McMichael 1996:197–207
	Mander & Goldsmith eds.
	  1996
	Strange 1996:4–6, 189,
	  196–198
	Evans 1997:82–87
	Kobrin 1997:155–163
	Rodrik 1997: 1–6, 46–67, 85
	Stryker 1998:7–8, 14–15, 17,
	  32–33
	Vernon 1998:172–175
	Mosher 1999:25, 35
		Vernon 1971:265–270
		Cox 1987:254–259, 1992:30–31
		Gilpin 1987:389–406, 2000:315–319
		Stopford and Strange 1991:1–2,
		  97–136
		Hirst and Thompson 1996:143–194
		Panitch 1996:84–86
		Pierson 1994:1–9
		Sassen 1996:25–30
		Wade 1996
		Albrow 1997:164, 168
		Meyer et al 1997:153, 157
		Garrett 1998:1–2, 11, 107, 157–158,
		  1999
		Huber and Stephens 1999
		Held et al 1999:440
		O Riain 2000
		Fligstein 2001

TABLE 2   (*Continued*)

Debate:	Answers in the Literature:	
	Yes	**No**
4. Is Globality Different from Modernity?	Sklair 1991:75–81 Robertson 1992:27, 138– 145, 1995 Waters 1995 Castells 1996 Albrow 1997:4, 33, 95–101, 144 Kobrin 1997:147–154 Held et al 1999:429–431	Giddens 1990:63–64, 1991:21–22 Mittelman 1996 Meyer et al 1997:150, 164
5. Is a Global Culture in the Making?	McLuhan 1964 McLuhan and Fiore 1967 Levitt 1983 Sklair 1991:75–81 Waters 1995:124–157 Meyer et al 1997:162	Smith 1990 Mazlish 1993:14, 16 Friedman 1994 Appadurai 1996:4, 12, 32–43 Cox 1996:27 Portes 1997 Geertz 1998:107–110 Keck and Sikkink 1998:32–34, 210–211 Held et al 1999:374 Zelizer 1999 Inglehart and Baker 2000

1990). Political economist and policymaker Robert Reich (1991), for example, proclaims that "national economies" are disappearing and companies no longer have a nationality; only people do. There are, however, many skeptics.

Perhaps the best-documented case for the feeble argument against globalization has been made by Paul Hirst, an Oxford political scientist with ties to the Labour Party. In a recent book, Hirst & Thompson (1996, pp. 1–3, 18–98) argue that the globalization trend of the last twenty years has been overstated as a process: It is not unprecedented in world history, they say, and foreign investment and trade are concentrated in the so-called triad—Western Europe, North America, and Japan. In sum, they argue that the economy is becoming more international but not more global. Political scientist Robert Wade (1996, pp. 66–84) echoes these criticisms: The volume of trade is small relative to the size of most economies (see also Krugman 1994, pp. 146–48, 256–67); domestic investment is greater than foreign investment; multinationals locate most of their assets, owners, top managers, and R&D activities in their home countries (see also Doremus et al 1998); and vast areas of the world have not been affected by globalization, namely, South and Central Asia, and the bulk of Africa.

The argument for the feebleness of globalization is useful in that it provides an important corrective to visions and myths of globalization assuming its inevitability and irreversibility. There are, however, two key counterarguments. Regarding the issue of the heterogeneous spread of globalization across the world, Castells (1996, p. 102) correctly observes that the global economy is not meant to encompass the entire Earth. Rather, it comprises only certain segments of activity in both developed and developing countries (see also Kobrin 1997). The second counterargument is that proponents of the feeble thesis focus almost exclusively on the economic and financial aspects of globalization to the detriment of political, social, and cultural ones. The literature offers and discusses evidence in support of political and cultural globalization that is, on the whole, quite persuasive (Castells 1996, pp. 66–147, Meyer & Hannan 1979, Louch et al 1998, Petrella 1996, pp. 63–66). In addition, global warming, the AIDS pandemic, and the globalization of the media have heightened our awareness of living in an increasingly interconnected world (Held et al 1999). In sum, scholars arguing the feebleness of globalization have made a contribution in debunking certain myths and assumptions about a process that has all too often been uncritically reified. However, they are perhaps too wedded to a "monolithic" concept of globalization and oblivious to the notion that globality is a network of relationships that creates mutual awareness.

Does It Produce Convergence?

A second contested issue in the literature on globalization has to do with its consequences as to the convergence of societies toward a uniform pattern of economic, political, and even cultural organization. Most famously expressed in modernization theory, the spread of markets and technology is predicted to cause societies to converge from their preindustrial past, although total homogeneity is deemed unlikely. This line of thinking was advanced during the 1950s and 1960s by both economists and sociologists (Guillén 2001, Waters 1995, pp. 13–15, Albrow 1997, p. 49). Economic historians such as Jeffrey Williamson (1996) have documented convergence in income and labor markets during the nineteenth century and first decades of the twentieth. Sociologist Daniel Bell (1973) argued for a technologically driven convergence of postindustrial societies.

Further support for the convergence thesis comes from the world-society approach in sociology. In their summaries of an extensive empirical research program on the worldwide spread of educational systems and other forms of state activity, John Meyer and his associates and students argue that the expansion of rationalized state activities has acquired a momentum of its own, largely unaffected by cross-national differences in political structure or economic growth rates. Rather, the diffusion of rationalized systems follows the "exigencies of global social organization whose logic and purposes are built into almost all states." The result is that "the world as a whole shows increasing structural *similarities of form* among societies without, however, showing increasing *equalities of outcomes* among societies" (Meyer & Hannan 1979, pp. 3, 13–15). Nation-states are seen as exhibiting convergent structural similarity, although there is a "decoupling between purposes and structure, intentions and results." World-society researchers argue that conformity comes both from the world-culture of rationalized modernity and from domestic groups that make claims on the state following the "consensus" over the formal acceptance of "matters such as citizen and human rights, the natural world and its scientific investigation, socioeconomic development, and education." They even present evidence to the effect that nationalism and religious fundamentalism "intensify isomorphism more than they resist it" (Meyer et al 1997, pp. 145, 148, 152–154, 161).

Social and political theorists as well as historians have elaborated a comprehensive critique of the presumed convergent consequences of globalization. Political historian Robert Cox (1996, p. 28, 30 n. 1) writes that "the social and ethical content of the economy" may be organized differently in various parts of the world." Historian Bruce Mazlish (1993, p. 4) argues that "no *single* global history is anticipated." Sociologist Anthony Giddens (1990, pp. 64, 175) adds an interesting twist when asserting that globalization "is a process of uneven development that fragments as it coordinates. [. . .] The outcome is not necessarily, or even usually, a generalized set of changes acting in a uniform direction, but consists in mutually opposed tendencies." In another book (1991, pp. 21–22), Giddens elaborates: "Globalization has to be understood as a dialectical phenomenon, in which events at one pole of a distanciated relation often produce divergent or even contrary occurrences at another" (see also Giddens 2000, pp. 30–31, Held et al 1999, pp. 431, 441). In a similar vein, anthropologist Jonathan Friedman (1994, pp. 210–11) asserts that globalization is the product of cultural fragmentation as much as it is the result of modernist homogeneity, and that "what appears as disorganization and often real disorder is not any the less systemic and systematic."

These social and political theorists, however, have neither engaged in empirical testing of their propositions nor bothered to look for support in the existing literature. There is, though, a considerable body of empirical research backing the antithesis that globalization produces divergence and diversity or at least does not undermine national policies and institutions. Management scholar John Stopford and political economist Susan Strange (1991, pp. 1–2) document that the increasingly complex interaction between multinationals and states has produced a divergence in outcomes, while Doremus et al (1998) show that differentiated national systems of innovation, trade, and investment remain firmly in place.

Political scientist Geoffrey Garrett (1998, pp. 1–4, 10–11, 34–37, 51, 74) has perhaps contributed the most extensive and solid body of empirical evidence, though it refers mostly to the experience of the advanced industrial democracies. He argues and demonstrates empirically that in the context of a global economy at least two paths are possible for national economic and social policymakers: adherence either to neoclassical economics or to social democratic corporatism. Garrett's analysis refutes simplistic views about convergence, proposing instead to view the balance of left-right political power and labor market institutions as the two key variables in a contingent analysis of economic performance. The best macroeconomic performance is obtained when the two variables are aligned with each other. For example, redistributive and interventionist policies combine with encompassing labor market institutions to produce macroeconomic performance in terms of growth and unemployment that matches or even surpasses the achievements of laissez-faire policies combined with weak labor market institutions. He concludes that there are "enduring cross-national differences" in economic policy-making and engagement of the global economy. In a broader study encompassing over one hundred countries during the 1985–1995 period, Garrett (1999) finds no convergence in government expenditure patterns as a result of globalization. What has happened over the last decade is that many governments have pursued policies that buffer their citizens from the vagaries of global markets and, in the presence of free capital mobility, willingly and knowingly accepted higher interest rates to keep capital at home.

Students of the varieties of capitalism, mostly political scientists, have long argued that firms and countries pursue different paths of incorporation into the global economy. Thus, German, French, Japanese, and American firms are competitive in the global economy, but rarely in the same industry and market segment. German firms excel at high-quality, engineering-intensive industries such as advanced machine tools, luxury automobiles, and specialty chemicals (Soskice 1998, Streeck 1991); French firms at large-scale technical undertakings such as high-speed trains, satellite-launching rockets, or nuclear power (Storper & Salais 1997, pp. 131–48); Japanese firms at most categories of assembled goods, namely, household appliances, consumer electronics, and automobiles (Gerlach 1992); and American firms at software, financial services, or biotechnology (Storper & Salais 1997, pp. 174–88).

Comparative organizational sociologists have also presented qualitative and quantitative evidence to the effect that firms pursue different modes of economic action and adopt different organizational forms depending on the institutional and social structures of their home countries even as globalization increases. Moreover, they have collected data on newly industrialized countries in addition to the most advanced ones. Orrù et al (1997) draw a number of systematic comparisons among East Asian and Western European countries, demonstrating that unique national patterns of organization not only persist over time but also contribute to the international competitiveness of firms. Guillén (2001) presents systematic case-study and quantitative evidence demonstrating that firms and labor unions in Argentina, South Korea, and Spain diverged in their patterns of behavior, organizational form, and growth even as their home countries became more integrated with the global economy during the post–World War II period.

Taken together, the empirical evidence provided by sociologists and political scientists supports well the case for diversity, or at least resilience, in cross-national patterns in the midst of globalization. It must be admitted, however, that world-society researchers also have a point, and one that is well supported by empirical evidence. The reason behind these seemingly irreconcilable empirical results might be that world-society research has made measurements at levels of analysis and abstraction higher than the finer-grained analysis of comparative sociologists and political scientists.

It should be noted that some sociologists reject the very terms of the convergence debate by arguing that globalization homogenizes without destroying the local and the particularistic. For example, Viviana Zelizer (1999) argues that "the economy . . . differentiates and proliferates culturally in much the same way as other spheres of social life do, without losing national and even international connectedness." Thus, globalization is not seen as precluding or contradicting diversity. Like Zelizer, Robertson (1995, pp. 34–35) sees the global as the "linking of localities."

Perhaps the most controversial aspect of the convergence debate has to do with the impact of globalization on inequality across and within countries. The evidence unambiguously indicates that there is today *more* inequality across countries than ten, twenty, fifty or even one hundred years ago. Stunningly, the gap in per capita income between rich and developing countries has grown five-fold between 1870 and 1990 (Pritchett 1997, Temple 1999). There are, however, several noteworthy developing countries that have managed to close half or more of the gap since 1960, e.g. South Korea, Taiwan, and Ireland. Very few developing countries, though, have consistently grown faster than the most advanced ones since 1980. Thus, development levels across countries appear not to be converging as a result of globalization.

By contrast to cross-national inequality, it is not clear whether increased foreign trade and investment during the last twenty years have resulted in substantially higher wage inequality or unemployment *within* countries. Wage inequality has risen in most advanced countries during the last three decades. In a review essay, Kapstein (2000) presents several counterarguments to the claim that globalization has been the major cause of increased wage polarization, including that trade is too small a percentage of GDP to have a large impact, and that technological change is the ultimate cause of wage polarization. In agreement with Kapstein's reading of the evidence, Baldwin & Martin (1999, p. 21) summarize the empirical literature as follows: "Virtually all studies find some impact of trade on the labor market in both the United States and Europe. The range of findings, however, is wide. Some find that trade accounted for virtually none of the wage gap, while others assigned 100 percent of the gap to trade. The consensus range is perhaps 10–20 percent." As opposed to wage disparities, overall indicators of income inequality within countries have not increased during the last thirty years, and there is evidence indicating that when countries grow economically and become incorporated into the global economy poverty rates fall (Deininger & Squire 1996). Discussions and calculations of the impact of globalization on wage and income inequality within countries should take into account that while foreign trade and investment are powerful forces, domestic politics and processes still matter.

In sum, globalization does not seem to compel governments, firms, and individuals to converge in their patterns of behavior. While this may be regarded as a welcome aspect, it is important to bear in mind that increasing globalization has coincided in time with an exacerbation of income disparities across countries, and that at least part of the greater degree of income and wage inequality within countries is due to increased foreign trade and investment.

Does It Undermine the Authority of Nation-States?

A third key issue surrounding the topic of globalization is whether this process has outgrown the governance structures of the international system of states and undermined the authority of the nation-state. For example, economist Raymond Vernon (1971, pp. 249, 265–70, 284) has long argued that the spread of multinational corporations creates "destructive political tensions," and that there is a "need to reestablish balance" between political and economic institutions. Historian Paul Kennedy (1993, pp. 53–64, 122–34) asserts that governments are losing control, and that globalization erodes the position of labor and developing countries, and degrades the environment. "Today's global society," he writes, "confronts the task of reconciling technological change and economic integration with traditional political structures, national consciousness, social needs, institutional arrangements, and habitual ways of doing things" (Kennedy 1993, p. 330). In a similar vein, Kobrin (1997, pp. 157, 159) argues that globalization both challenges the autonomy or independent decision-making of the state and "raises questions about the meaning of sovereignty in its external sense of a system ordered in terms of mutually exclusive territoriality." And Mazlish (1993, p. 4) argues that global history is an attempt to "transcend the nation-state as the focus of history."

International relations scholar Yoshikazu Sakamoto (1994, p. 19, 36) and political scientist Robert Cox (1996, p. 26–27) concur in arguing that globalization generates problems of international governance and reduce the regulatory power of states. For Rodrik (1997, p. 1–6), globalization creates social and political tensions within and across nation-states. And political theorist Michael Mosher (1999, p. 35) asks, "is there a successful way of reconciling the boundary transgressing character of markets with the boundary maintaining activities of nation-states?" He further notes that globalization has placed two liberal practices—the liberalism of the market and the liberalism of democratic citizenship—on a collision course, raising the dilemma of whether "moral concerns stop at the national border" (Mosher 1999, p. 25).

Sociologists have also joined the chorus of state doomsayers. For Waters (1995, pp. 96–123), there is an "attenuation of the state," a rise of international organizations, and a trend toward more "fluid" international relations. McMichael (1996, pp. 197–207) also sees a decline of the state. For Albrow (1997, p. 164), "the nation-state has failed to confine sociality within its boundaries, both territorial and categorical. The sheer increase in cross-national ties, the diversification of modes of personal relationships and the multiplication of forms of social organization demonstrate the autogenic nature of the social and reveal the nation-state as just another timebound form." In a more empirically grounded way, Evans (1997, pp. 82–87) points out that globalization undermines the state because its associated neoliberal ideology is against the state and not because globalization is inextricably against the state. He further argues that the state may stage a comeback if there is a "return of the ideological pendulum," or a transformation of the state and a development of new elements of state-society synergy.

The analysis by British political economist Susan Strange is perhaps the most sophisticated articulation of the position that the international system of nation-states and the nation-state itself are coming under fire in a global world. She writes about the "declining authority of states" and preempts several possible criticisms. First, she notes that state interventionism is on the rise, although in relatively marginal matters. Second, she argues that there are more states in the world, especially after 1989, but that most of the new ones are weak and lack control. Third, she points out that the effectiveness of the East Asian state in orchestrating economic growth was only possible in a post–World War II order in which protectionism of the domestic market was acceptable and mature technologies were available (Strange 1996, pp. 4–6). She further observes three power shifts in the global world, namely, from weak to strong states, from states to markets, and from labor markets to financial markets, with some power evaporating or dispersing (Strange 1996, p. 189).

Not surprisingly, those who argue that globalization is a feeble process also maintain that it can be easily handled by nation-states. For example, Hirst & Thompson (1996, pp. 143–49, 170–94) and Wade (1996) assert that states can cope with globalization, although they have lost some freedom of action, especially concerning financial flows. Feeble proponents, however, are not alone challenging the notion that globalization undermines the nation-state.

Macrosociology has long maintained that the global arena is a "playground" for states, where they compete for economic, military, and political supremacy and survival. Thus, the world-system or the international arena, far from threatening states, actually fosters them (Wallerstein 1974, Tilly 1992). Neorealist international relations scholar Robert Gilpin (1987, pp. 389–406, 2000, pp. 51, 319–23) points out that globalization reinforces the importance of domestic policies, as countries engage in regionalization, sectoral protectionism, and mercantilistic competition in response to changes in the international location of economic activities, resulting in a "mixed system," increasingly globalized and at the same time fragmented (see also Berger 1996, pp. 7–21). A related, though distinct, argument against the presumed loss of state power in the wake of globalization comes from political scientist Leo Panitch (1996, p. 84–86). He rightly argues that "today's globalization is authored by states and is primarily about reorganizing rather than bypassing them" (see also O Riain 2000, Poulantzas 1974, p. 73). Moreover, as Cox (1992, pp. 30–31) observes, "power has shifted not away from the state but *within* the state, i.e. from industry or labor ministries towards economy ministries and central banks." And sociologist Seán O Riain (2000, p. 205) sees states not as passive pawns but rather as "adapting, whether out of necessity or desire."

Another influential social scientist, Saskia Sassen (1996, pp. 25–30), maintains that the state does not lose significance. Rather, there is a redefinition of the modern features of sovereignty and territoriality, a "denationalizing of national territory." Cox (1987, pp. 254–59) argues that globalization induces a transformation of the state, not its diminution. Stopford & Strange (1991, pp. 1–2, 97–136) examine the new possibilities for state action in the global economy and conclude that its role has actually become magnified and more complex (see also Held et al 1999, pp. 436–44). According to most political scientists, therefore, the nation-state is alive and well, and the Westphalian order is unlikely to be replaced by a fragmented, medieval one. A key effect of globalization, however, has been the rise of global cities—New York, London, Miami, Singapore—whose role and stature transcend the nation-state in which they happen to be located (Choi et al 1996, Sassen 1991).

Finally, the world-society view also rejects the claim that globalization undermines nation-states. Noting the expansion of state bureaucracies since World War II, Meyer et al (1997, p. 157) write that "globalization certainly poses new problems for states, but it also strengthens the world-cultural principle that nation-states are the primary actors charged with identifying and managing those problems on behalf of their societies." This argument is strikingly similar to the one offered by Panitch (1996, pp. 84–86) and Poulantzas (1974, p. 73). The modern nation-state, world-society scholars conclude, "may have less autonomy than earlier but it clearly has more to do" (Meyer et al 1997, p. 157).

The question of whether globalization undermines the authority of the nation-state comes best to life when examining the impact of globalization on the viability of the welfare state. Rodrik (1997, pp. 49–67) argues that globalization puts downward pressure on government spending for redistribution and welfare, and that the interaction of trade risk and openness calls for more welfare spending, but governments have trouble finding the money, an argument that Vernon (1998, pp. 172–175) finds persuasive. Stryker (1998, pp. 7–8, 14–15, 17, 32–33) summarizes her assessment of the evidence in that globalization places limits on expansionary policies, represents a loss of power for the working class, and causes welfare state retrenchment. According to these social scientists, the challenge is "to engineer a new balance between market and society, one that will continue to unleash the creative energies of private entrepreneurship without eroding the social basis of cooperation" (Rodrik 1997, p. 85). These arguments have become conventional wisdom among neoliberal policymakers and journalists. Gloomy, often unsubstantiated, forecasts about the inability of European welfare states to pay for generous social benefits have become commonplace since the early 1980s.

Other political scientists and sociologists, however, see things utterly differently. Political scientist Paul Pierson (1994, p. 1–9) argues that the welfare state has declined not so much as a result of globalization but because of such indirect actions of conservative governments as reductions in the revenue base of the state and attacks on the strength of interest groups, especially labor. This is an argument that Fligstein (2001) and Gilpin (2000, pp. 312–15) endorse. Garrett (1998, pp. 1–2, 11, 107, 132–33, 157–58) empirically demonstrates the viability of social democratic corporatism even with increasing exposure to globalization in the forms of cross-border trade and capital mobility. He also proves that it is possible to win elections with redistributive and interventionist policies, and that better economic performance in terms of GDP growth and unemployment obtains, though with higher inflation than in the laissez-faire countries (United States, Britain). Garrett (1998, p. 157) concludes that "big government is compatible with strong macroeconomic performance" and that markets do not dominate politics. In a direct rebuttal of Rodrik (1997), Garrett (1999) analyzes data on more than 100 countries during the 1985–1995 period to find that increasing exposure to globalization does not reduce government spending. Political scientist Evelyne Huber and sociologist John Stephens (1999) echo Garrett's conclusion that the welfare state is compatible with global capitalism, although they do admit that social democratic policies are today more constrained than in the so-called "golden age" of the 1950s and 1960s (see also Western 1997).

For Garrett, Huber, and Stephens and for Fligstein the welfare state is perfectly viable under conditions of globalization. Moreover, it may be able simultaneously to deliver social well-being and enhance national competitiveness. Thus, they reject the tradeoff that neoliberals see between welfare expenditures and economic competitiveness under conditions of globalization. In spite of the excellent, well-supported research by these authors, however, the debate in the media and among politicians throughout the world remains heavily tilted in favor of those blaming the welfare state for declining competitiveness and various social ills.

Is Globality Different from Modernity?

Perhaps the most difficult debate surrounding globalization has to do with whether it is merely a continuation of the trend toward modernity or the beginning of a new era. On one side of the fence, Giddens (1990, pp. 63, 64) argues that "modernity is inherently globalizing," and that "globalization [makes] the modes of connection between different social contexts or regions become networked across the earth's surface as a whole." This view follows directly from the concept of "disembedding" or "the lifting out" of social relations from local contexts of interaction and their restructuring across time and space," which Giddens (1990, p. 21) considers a prerequisite for modernization. World-society scholarship takes sides with Giddens on this point: Globalization results in a "sharing" of modernity across the world (Meyer et al 1997, pp. 150, 164).

On the other side of the fence, British social theorist Martin Albrow (1997, pp. 4, 33, 95–101, 144) argues that globalization is a "transformation, not a culmination," and the "transition to a new era rather than the apogee of the old." He proposes a stark distinction between modernity as the imposition of practical rationality upon the rest of the world through the agency of the state and the mechanism of the market, the generation of universal ideas to encompass the diversity of the world," and globality as it restored "the boundlessness of culture and promotes the endless renewability and diversification of cultural expression rather than homogenization or hybridization." Other noted social theorists of globalization also support the same distinction (Robertson 1992, pp. 27, 138–145), especially insofar as the modern-nation state is concerned: "The politics of identity substitutes for the politics of nation-building" (McMichael 1996, p. 234).

The debate over the relationship between modernity and globality is a central one for sociologists. If globality is merely the result of an intensification of modernizing trends, then the recent surge in the number of books and articles on this subject can hardly be justified. There is, however, a key theoretical argument to be made in favor of the view that globality is different from modernity. Modernity—like the distorting Mercator projection—is an outgrowth of the Western worldview. For reasons of theoretical consistency, one should reserve the terms "globalization," "global," and "globality" to denote, respectively, processes, qualities, and conditions that are not set into motion or dominated by any one model, paradigm, or worldview. In its broadest sense, globality is about a multiplicity of conceptions, not about cultural or paradigmatic hegemony; it is about the proliferation of cross-national network ties of an economic, political, social, and cultural nature (Guillén 2001, Held et al 1999). This criticism is especially germane in the case of authors who consider globalization to be an inevitable and sweeping process—neoliberals and Marxists in particular—as Fligstein (2001) has aptly pointed out.

Finally, Kobrin (1997, pp. 147–48) has proposed a distinction between global-ization in the late twentieth century and the previous period of modern expansion of the world economy that is useful empirically. The international economy of the nineteenth century "*links* discrete, mutually exclusive, geographical national markets through cross-border flows of trade and investment." By contrast, the global economy of the late twentieth century is driven by the increasing scale of technology, the surge in cross-border collaboration of firms along the value-added chain, and the cross-border integration of information flows. Thus, globalization has "substantive meaning" because, this time around, "national markets are *fused* transnationally rather than linked across borders" (Kobrin 1997, p. 148, see also Held et al 1999, pp. 429–31).

Is a Global Culture in the Making?

Perhaps the most popular and controversial of the debates about globalization has to do with the rise of a global culture. Actually, there are only a few scholars who maintain that a global culture is in the making. The idea goes back to Marshall McLuhan's slippery concept of the "global village" (McLuhan 1964, McLuhan & Fiore 1967), later picked up by some influential marketing researchers (Levitt 1983) who argued that the world was becoming increasingly populated by cosmopolitan consumers. Sociologist Leslie Sklair (1991, pp. 75–81) writes that a "culture-ideology of consumerism"—driven by symbols, images, and the aesthetic of the lifestyle and the self-image—has spread throughout the world and is having some momentous effects, including the standardization of tastes and desires, and even the fall of the Soviet order.

Other sociologists, however, argue against the homogenizing effects of mass consumerism. Zelizer (1999) writes that consumer differentiation should not be confused with segregation and posits that in the US economy differentia-tion is combined with connection: "the same consumer product can have at the same moment universal and local meaning." Zelizer urges sociologists to distin-guish between the phenomenon of worldwide diffusion and the experience at the receiving end, which seems to be growing more diverse even as globalization intensifies (see also Held et al 1999, p. 374). Similarly, anthropologist Arjun Ap-padurai (1996, pp. 4, 21) argues that "individuals and groups seek to annex the global into their own practices of the modern," and that "consumption of the mass media worldwide provokes resistance, irony, selectivity, and, in general, *agency*." Using cross-national attitudinal data over the 1981–1998 period, Inglehart & Baker

(2000) find that national cultures and values change over time, though in "path-dependent" rather than convergent ways. Even world-society arguments about the "world culture of educated individual choice and responsibility" (Meyer & Hannan 1979, p. 3) stop short of announcing a global culture à la McLuhan. However, they do describe world-culture as binding society and individuals together "by rationalized systems of (imperfectly) egalitarian justice and participatory representation, in the economy, polity, culture, and social interaction" (Meyer et al 1997, p. 162). Other researchers have found that the spread of the mass media is not enough to account for the rise of cross-border advocacy groups (Keck & Sikkink 1998, pp. 32–34, 210–11), although "global governance" of major aspects of cross-border communication has been on the rise since 1850 (Murphy 1994).

Political and social theorists and historians have noted the rise of what modernists would call "particularistic" identities as evidence against the rise of a global culture. Cox (1996, p. 27) writes about globalization producing a "resurgent affirmation of identities," whereas Waters (1995, pp. 124–57) contrasts a cultural and "religious mosaic" with global cultural production and consumption of music, images, and information. Mazlish (1993, p. 14) notes that "ethnic feeling is a powerful bond," and skeptically asks, "What counterpart can there be on the global level?" Political scientist Deborah Yashar (1999) rejects "global culture" and "global citizenship" concepts but also finds fault with the argument that globalization has induced the proliferation of ethnic movements. In her comparison of indigenous movements in Latin America, Yashar clearly demonstrates that no aspect of globalization—economic, political, social, or normative—can account for the rise of ethnic-based activism since the 1960s. Rather, globalization changes the characteristics of the state structures that activists face when making their claims.

Cross-border migration creates an unusually rich laboratory for assessing the rise of a global culture. Sociologist Alejandro Portes (1997, p. 3) proposes the term "transnational communities" to refer to cross-border networks of immigrants that are "'neither here nor there' but in both places simultaneously" (see also Portes et al 1999). Different transnational communities, however, exhibit different origins, features, and problems, and they certainly do not form a monolithic global class of cosmopolitan citizens. Similarly to Portes, Friedman (1994) accepts the basic notion of cultural fragmentation proposed by Appadurai, Smith, and Zelizer but argues that in today's world the existence of tribal societies cannot be correctly understood without explaining how they are embedded in global networks. In his view, cultural diversity must be seen in a global context.

Some of the most persuasive arguments against the idea of the emergence of a global culture come from anthropologist Clifford Geertz. He observes that the world is "growing both more global and more divided, more thoroughly interconnected and more intricately partitioned at the same time [...] Whatever it is that defines identity in borderless capitalism and the global village it is not deep going agreements on deep going matters, but something more like the recurrence of familiar divisions, persisting arguments, standing threats, the notion that whatever else may happen, the order of difference must be somehow maintained" (Geertz 1998, pp. 107–110). Like Geertz, sociologist Anthony Smith is skeptical and notes an interesting "initial problem" with the concept of "global culture": "Can we speak of 'culture' in the singular? If by 'culture' is meant a collective mode of life, or a repertoire of beliefs, styles, values and symbols, then we can only speak of cultures, never just culture; for a collective mode of life [. . .] presupposes different modes and repertoires in a universe of modes and repertoires. Hence, the idea of a 'global culture' is a practical impossibility, except in interplanetary terms" (Smith 1990, p. 171).

The ultimate question about the alleged rise of a global culture has to do with whether a global language is emerging. The diffusion of Esperanto has certainly not delivered on early expectations, and the "English-as-global-language" argument seems equally far-fetched and indefensible. As Mazlish (1993, p. 16) observes, English "is becoming a sort of lingua franca [but] there are serious limitations to the use of English as the daily language of a global culture." Moreover, English is being challenged as the dominant language in parts of the United States and the United Kingdom. Even on the Internet, fewer than 50 percent of world users know English as a first language, and the proportion is dropping steadily as the new medium diffuses throughout the world. It is also instructive to recall that the most successful world language ever, Latin, evolved into a mosaic of Romance languages after spreading in its various vulgarized forms throughout the territory of the Roman Empire. Smith (1990, pp. 185–86) notes that, rather than the emergence of a "global" culture held together by the English language, what we are witnessing is the emergence of "culture areas"—not necessarily at odds or in conflict with each other, as Huntington (1996) would have it. Thus, Spanish, Russian, Arabic, French, Kiswahili, and Chinese have become the shared languages of certain groups, communities or population strata across countries located in specific regions of the world, namely, Latin America, the CIS, the Arab world, Subsaharan Africa, East Africa, and South East Asia, respectively.

TOWARD A COMPARATIVE SOCIOLOGY OF GLOBALIZATION

The social science literature on globalization contains important theoretical and empirical disagreements. Scholars have provided very different answers to the five key debates discussed in this chapter. The balance of opinion appears to be tilted, however. Most research either assumes or documents that globalization is indeed happening, and most empirical studies—with the notable exception of the world-society approach—do not find convergence in political, social, or organizational patterns as a result of globalization. The most persuasive empirical work to date indicates that globalization per se neither undermines the nation-state nor erodes the viability of the welfare state. Some empirical evidence also documents that globality is different from modernity. Finally, it seems that no such thing as a global culture is emerging.

Relative to the other social sciences, sociology has contributed to the debate over globalization in three important ways. First, social theorists have developed an understanding of the nature and epochal implications of globalization. Although there is no agreement as to whether globalization is a continuation of modernity or not, there is an incipient body of work that outlines in detail what are the main theoretical perspectives and problems. Moreover, sociologists have called attention to the cultural, reflexive, and aesthetic aspects of globalization in addition to its economic and political dimensions (Albrow 1997, Castells 1996, Giddens 1990, 1991, Guillén 2001, Robertson 1992, Sklair 1991, Waters 1995). Second, world-society scholars have developed a macrophenomenological approach to globalization and the nation-state based on a sound institutional theoretical foundation, and they have supported their view with systematic empirical evidence encompassing the entire world (Meyer & Hannan 1979, Meyer et al 1997). Third, comparative sociologists have theorized about globalization's effects on cross-national difference and similarity. They have also offered empirical evidence in the forms of both rich case studies and quantitative analyses (Guillén 2001, Orrù et al 1997). Sociologists, however, need to continue reading the important contributions that economic historians, management scholars, political scientists, and anthropologists are making to the theoretical and empirical study of such a complex and multifaceted phenomenon as globalization.

The analysis and critique presented in this chapter indicate that globalization, far from being a feeble phenomenon, is changing the nature of the world. However, it is neither an invariably civilizing force nor a destructive one. Although further empirical investigation is warranted, there is already enough evidence available to reject either extreme (Held et al 1999). Globalization is neither a monolithic nor an inevitable phenomenon. Its impact varies across countries, societal sectors, and time. It is contradictory, discontinuous, even haphazard. Therefore, one needs to be open-minded about its unexpected and unintended consequences. One also needs to take into account the role that agency, interest, and resistance play in shaping it. As Pieterse (1996, p. 556) has pointed out, globalization does not necessarily pose a choice between condemnation and celebration. Rather, it begs to be engaged, comprised, given form (Geertz 1998).

The complexity of globalization certainly invites additional research. We are in great need of further theoretical work to clarify the economic, political, cultural, and aesthetic dimensions of globalization and how they interact with each other. We also lack theoretical perspectives that bridge the micro-macro gap, i.e. that move across levels of analysis from the world-system to the nation-state, the industry, sector, community, organization, and group. Many of the empirical disagreements in the literature are primarily due to the various levels of analysis at which different researchers operate. Understanding globalization will require us to gather more and better data about its myriad manifestations, causes, and effects. We still know very little about what exactly causes it and what are its consequences on such key sociological variables as organizational patterns, authority structures, social inequality, and social movements, to name but a few. And sociologists need to work hard on government agencies and other data-gathering organizations so that they pay more attention in their surveys and censuses to relationships at various levels of aggregation.

Given the infancy of our efforts to understand globalization and the complexity of the phenomenon, it seems sensible to ask not only for an intensification of our interdisciplinary awareness but also for a comparative approach to the sociology of globalization. Comparing lies at the heart of the sociological enterprise (Smelser 1976, Tilly 1984). We need to engage in comparative work in the dual sense of using multiple methods of data collection and analysis, and of applying our theoretical and empirical tools to a variety of research settings defined at various levels of analysis. The differences and similarities across such settings ought to give us a handle on the patterns according to which the causes and effects of globalization change from one setting to another. Without a comparative approach, the literature on globalization promises to remain as puzzling and contradictory as the phenomenon itself.

ACKNOWLEDGMENTS

This research was funded by a grant from the Jones Center at the Wharton School and a fellowship from the John Simon Guggenheim Memorial Foundation. I thank Howard Aldrich, Miguel Ángel Centeno, Randall Collins, Paul DiMaggio, Geoffrey Garrett, Clifford Geertz, Eszter Hargittai, Vit Henisz, Albert Hirschman, Evelyne Huber, John Kimberly, Steve Kobrin, Bruce Kogut, John Meyer, Marshall Meyer, James Mittelman, Walter Powell, John Stephens, Sandra Suárez, Gabriel Szulanski, Adrian Tschoegl, and Viviana Zelizer for helpful comments and/or for providing me with various references, information, and sources. I am also grateful to my work-study research assistants Anne Chun, Yi Jun, and Gina Mok.

Visit the Annual Reviews home page at www.AnnualReviews.org

LITERATURE CITED

Albrow M. 1997. *The Global Age*. Stanford, CA: Stanford Univ. Press

Appadurai A. 1996. *Modernity at Large: Cultural Dimensions of Globalization*. Minneapolis: Univ. Minn. Press

Baldwin RE, Martin P. 1999. Two waves of globalization: superficial similarities, fundamental differences. NBER Work. Pap. Ser. 6904. Cambridge, MA: Natl. Bur Econ. Res.

Bell D. [1973] 1976. *The Coming of Post-Industrial Society*. New York: Basic Books

Berger S. 1996. Introduction. In *National Diversity and Global Capitalism*, ed. S Berger, R Dore, pp. 1–25. Ithaca, NY: Cornell Univ. Press

Boyer R. 1996. The convergence hypothesis revisited: globalization but still the century of nations? In *National Diversity and Global Capitalism*, ed. S Berger and R Dore, pp. 29–59. Ithaca, NY: Cornell Univ. Press

Castells M. 1996. *The Rise of the Network Society*. Cambridge, MA: Blackwell

Choi SR, Park D, Tschoegl AE. 1996. Banks and the world's major banking centers, 1990. *Weltwirtsch. Arch.* 132(4): 774–93

Cox RW. 1987. *Production, Power and World Order: Social Forces in the Making of History.* New York: Columbia Univ. Press

Cox RW. 1992. Global Perestroika. In *New World Order? The Socialist Register 1992,* ed. R Miliband, L Panitch, pp. 26–43. London: Merlin

Cox RW. 1996. A perspective on globalization. In *Globalization: Critical Reflections,* ed. JH Mittelman, pp. 21–30. Boulder, CO: Lynne Rienner Publ.

Deininger K, Squire L. 1996. A new data set measuring income inequality. *World Bank Econ. Rev.* 10:565–91

Doremus PN, Keller WW, Pauly LW, Reich S. 1998. *The Myth of the Global Corporation.* Princeton, NJ: Princeton Univ. Press

Dreyer JLE. 1953. *A History of Astronomy from Thales to Kepler.* New York: Dover

Dunning JH, ed. 1997. *Governments, Globalization, and International Business.* New York: Oxford Univ. Press

Evans P. 1997. The eclipse of the state? *World Polit.* 50:62–87

Featherstone M, ed. 1990. *Global Culture.* London: Sage

Fligstein N. 2001. Is globalization the cause of the crises of welfare states? In *The Architecture of Markets.* Princeton, NJ: Princeton Univ. Press

Friedman J. 1994. *Cultural Identity and Global Process.* London: Sage

Garrett G. 1998. *Partisan Politics in the Global Economy.* New York: Cambridge Univ. Press

Garrett G. 1999. Trade, capital mobility and government spending around the world. Work. Pap., Dep. Polit. Sci., Yale Univ.

Geertz C. 1973. *The Interpretation of Cultures: Selected Essays.* New York: Basic

Geertz C. 1998. The world in pieces: culture and politics at the end of the century. *Focaal: Tijdschr. Antropol.* 32:91–117

Gereffi G. 1994. The organization of buyer-driven global commodity chains. In *Commodity Chains and Global Capitalism,* ed. G

Gereffi, M Korzeniewicz, pp. 95–122. Westport, CT: Greenwood

Gerlach ML. 1992. *Alliance Capitalism: The Social Organization of Japanese Business.* Berkeley, CA: Univ. Calif. Press

Giddens A. 1990. *The Consequences of Modernity.* Stanford, CA: Stanford Univ. Press

Giddens A. 1991. *Modernity and Self-Identity.* Cambridge, MA: Polity

Giddens A. 2000. *Runaway World: How Globalization is Reshaping our Lives.* New York: Routledge

Gilpin R. 1987. *The Political Economy of International Relations.* Princeton, NJ: Princeton Univ. Press

Gilpin R. 2000. *The Challenge of Global Capitalism.* Princeton, NJ: Princeton Univ. Press

Guidry JA, Kennedy MD, Zald MN. 1999. Globalizations and social movements. In *Globalizations and Social Movements: Culture, Power, and the Transnational Public Sphere,* ed. JA Guidry, MD Kennedy, MN Zald, pp. 1–32. Ann Arbor: Univ. Mich. Press

Guillén MF. 2001. *The Limits of Convergence: Globalization and Organizational Change in Argentina, South Korea, and Spain.* Princeton, NJ: Princeton Univ. Press

Guillén M, Suárez S. 2001. Developing the Internet: entrepreneurship and public policy in Ireland, Singapore, Argentina, and Spain. *Telecommun. Policy 25.* Forthcoming

Hargittai E, Centeno MA, eds. 2001. Mapping globalization. *Am. Behav. Sci.* In press

Harvey D. 1989. *The Condition of Postmodernity.* Oxford: Blackwell

Held D, McGrew A, Goldblatt D, Perraton J. 1999. *Global Transformations.* Stanford, CA: Stanford Univ. Press

Hirsch PM, Fiss PC. 2000. Framing globalization: the battle for definitions of a contested issue. Work. Pap. Kellogg Sch., Northwestern Univ.

Hirschman AO. 1982. Rival interpretations of market society: civilizing, destructive, or feeble? *J. Econ. Lit.* 20:1463–84

Hirst P, Thompson G. 1996. *Globalization in Question.* London: Polity

Huber E, Stephens JD. 1999. Welfare state and production regimes in the era of retrenchment. *Occas. Pap. No. 1, Sch. Soc. Sci.*, Inst. Adv. Stud., Princeton, NJ

Huntington SP. 1996. *The Clash of Civilizations and the Remaking of World Order.* New York: Simon & Schuster

Inglehart R, Baker WE. 2000. Modernization, cultural change, and the persistence of traditional values. *Am. Sociol. Rev.* 65:19–51

Kapstein EB. 2000. Winners and losers in the global economy. *Int. Organ.* 54:359–84

Keck ME, Sikkink K. 1998. *Activists Beyond Borders: Advocacy Networks in International Politics.* Ithaca, NY: Cornell Univ. Press

Kennedy P. 1993. *Preparing for the Twenty-First Century.* New York: Random House

Kobrin SJ. 1997. The architecture of globalization: state sovereignty in a networked global economy. In *Governments, Globalization, and International Business*, ed. JH Dunning, pp. 146–71. New York: Oxford Univ. Press

Krugman P. 1994. *Peddling Prosperity.* New York: Norton

Levitt T. 1983. The globalization of markets. *Harvard Bus. Rev.* 61(3):92–102

Louch H, Hargittai E, Centeno MA. 1998. *Who calls whom? Networks and globalization.* Pap. pres. Annu. Meet. Am. Sociol. Assoc., San Francisco

Mander J, Goldsmith E, eds. 1996. *The Case Against the Global Economy.* San Francisco: Sierra Club

Mazlish B. 1993. An introduction to global history. In *Conceptualizing Global History*, ed. B Mazlish, R Buultjens, pp. 1–24. Boulder, CO: Westview

McLuhan M. 1964. *Understanding Media.* London: Routledge

McLuhan M, Fiore Q. 1967. *The Medium is the Message.* London: Allen Lane

McMichael P. 1996. *Development and Social Change: A Global Perspective.* Thousand Oaks, CA: Pine Forge

Meyer JW, Boli J, Thomas GM, Ramirez FO. 1997. World society and the nation-state. *Am. J. Sociol.* 103(1):144–81

Meyer JW, Hannan MT. 1979. National development in a changing world system: an overview. In *National Development and the World System: Educational, Economic, and Political Change, 1950-1970*, ed. JW Meyer, MT Hannan, pp. 3–16. Chicago: Univ. Chicago Press

Mittelman JH. 1996. The dynamics of globalization. In *Globalization: Critical Reflections*, ed. JH Mittelman, pp. 1–19. Boulder, CO: Lynne Rienner

Mittelman JH, ed. 1996. *Globalization: Critical Reflections.* Boulder, CO: Lynne Rienner

Mittelman JH. 2000. *The Globalization Syndrome: Transformation and Resistance.* Princeton, NJ: Princeton Univ. Press

Mosher M. 1999. *Border Patrols and Border Crossings: The Seductions of Globalization.* Manuscript

Murphy CN. 1994. *International Organization and Industrial Change: Global Governance since 1850.* New York: Oxford Univ. Press

Naisbitt J, Aburdene P. 1990. *Megatrends 2000.* New York: Morrow

Ohmae K. 1990. *The Borderless World.* New York: Harper Business

O Riain S. 2000. States and markets in an era of globalization. *Annu. Rev. Sociol.* 26:187–213

Orrù M, Biggart NW, Hamilton GG. 1997. *The Economic Organization of East Asian Capitalism.* Thousand Oaks, CA: Sage

Panitch L. 1996. Rethinking the role of the state. In *Globalization: Critical Reflections*, ed. JH Mittelman, pp. 83–113. Boulder, CO: Lynne Rienner

Petrella R. 1996. Globalization and internationalization. In *States against Markets: The Limits of Globalization*, ed. R Boyer, D Drache, pp. 62–83. London: Routledge

Pierson P. 1994. *Dismantling the Welfare State? Reagan, Thatcher, and the Politics of Retrenchment.* New York: Cambridge Univ. Press

Pieterse JN. 1996. The development of development theory: towards critical globalism. *Rev. Int. Polit. Econ.* 3(4):541–64

Portes A. 1997. *Globalization from below: the rise of transnational communities. Work. Pap. 98-08.* Princeton, NJ: Cent. Migr. Dev.

Portes A, Guarnizo LE, Landolt P. 1999. The study of transnationalism: pitfalls and promise of an emergent research field. *Ethn. Racial Stud.* 22(2):217–37

Poulantzas N. 1974. *Classes in Contemporary Capitalism.* London: New Left Books

Pritchett L. 1997. Divergence, big time. *J. Econ. Perspect.* 11(3):3–17

Rapoport DC. 1996. The importance of space in violent ethno-religious strife. *Nationalism Ethn. Polit.* 2(2):258–85

Reich RB. 1991. *The Work of Nations.* New York: Knopf

Robertson R. 1992. *Globalization: Social Theory and Global Culture.* London: Sage

Robertson R. 1995. Globalization: time-space and homogeneity-heterogeneity. In *Global Modernities*, ed. M Featherstone, S Lash, R Robertson, pp. 25–44. London: Sage

Rodrik D. 1997. *Has Globalization Gone Too Far?* Washington, DC: Inst. Int. Econ.

Sakamoto Y. 1994. A perspective on the changing world order: a conceptual prelude. In *Global Transformation*, ed. Y Sakamoto, pp. 15–54. New York: UN Univ. Press

Sakamoto Y, ed. 1994. *Global Transformation.* New York: UN Univ. Press

Sassen S. 1991. *The Global City.* Princeton, NJ: Princeton Univ. Press

Sassen S. 1996. *Losing Control? Sovereignty in an Age of Globalization.* New York: Columbia Univ. Press

Sklair L. 1991. *Sociology of the Global System.* New York: Harvester Wheatsheaf

Smelser NJ. 1976. *Comparative Methods in the Social Sciences.* Englewood Cliffs, NJ: Prentice-Hall

Smith AD. 1990. Towards a global culture? *Theory, Cult. Soc.* 7:171–91

Soskice D. 1998. Divergent production regimes: coordinated and uncoordinated market economies in the 1980s and 1990s. In *Continuity and Change in Contemporary Capitalism*, ed. H Kitschelt, pp. 101–34. New York: Cambridge Univ. Press

Stopford JM, Strange S. 1991. *Rival States, Rival Firms.* New York: Cambridge Univ. Press

Storper M, Salais R. 1997. *Worlds of Production: The Action Frameworks of the Economy.* Cambridge, MA: Harvard Univ. Press

Strange S. 1996. *The Retreat of the State: The Diffusion of Power in the World Economy.* New York: Cambridge Univ. Press

Streeck W. 1991. On the institutional conditions of diversified quality production. In *Beyond Keynesianism: The Socio-Economics of Production and Full Employment*, ed. E Matzner, W Streeck, pp. 12–61. Hants, UK: Edward Elgar

Stryker R. 1998. Globalization and the welfare state. *Int. J. Sociol. Soc. Policy* 18(2-4):1–49

Temple J. 1999. The new growth evidence. *J. Econ. Lit.* 37:112–56

Tilly C. 1984. *Big Structures, Large Processes, Huge Comparisons.* New York: Russell Sage Found.

Tilly C. 1992. *Coercion, Capital, and European States, A.D. 990-1992.* Cambridge: Basil Blackwell

Tschoegl AE. 1998. Country and bank sources of international competitiveness: the case of the foreign exchange market. Work. Pap, Wharton School, Univ. Penn.

Vernon R. 1971. *Sovereignty at Bay: The Multinational Spread of U.S. Enterprises.* New York: Basic Books

Vernon R. 1998. *In the Hurricane's Eye: The Troubled Prospects of Multinational Enterprises.* Cambridge, MA: Harvard Univ. Press

Wade R. 1996. Globalization and its limits: reports of the death of the national economy are greatly exaggerated. In *National Diversity and Global Capitalism*, ed. S Berger, R Dore, pp. 60–88. Ithaca, NY: Cornell Univ. Press

Wallerstein I. 1974. *The Modern World-System.* New York: Academic Press

Waters M. 1995. *Globalization.* New York: Routledge

Western B. 1997. *Between Class and Market: Postwar Unionization in the Capitalist Democracies.* Princeton, NJ: Princeton Univ. Press

Williamson JG. 1996. Globalization, convergence, history. *J. Econ. Hist.* 56(2):277–306

Yashar DJ. 1999. *Citizenship claims and indigenous movements: contentious politics in an age of globalization.* Work. Pap. Dep. Polit., Princeton Univ.

Zelizer VA. 1999. Multiple markets: multiple cultures. In *Diversity and Its Discontents: Cultural Conflict and Common Ground in Contemporary American Society*, ed. NJ Smelser, J Alexander, pp. 193–212. Princeton, NJ: Princeton Univ. Press

Annu. Rev. Sociol. 2001. 27:261–81

RELIGIOUS PLURALISM AND RELIGIOUS PARTICIPATION

Mark Chaves[1] and Philip S. Gorski[2]

[1]Department of Sociology, University of Arizona, Tucson, Arizona 85721;
e-mail: mchaves@u.arizona.edu
[2]Department of Sociology, University of Wisconsin-Madison, Madison, Wisconsin 53706;
e-mail: pgorski@ssc.wisc.edu

Key Words   sociology of religion, rational choice, religious diversity, organizational competition, secularization

■ **Abstract**   For more than a decade, sociologists of religion have been debating the answer to a basic question: What is the relationship between religious pluralism and religious vitality? The old wisdom was that the relationship was negative, that pluralism undermines vitality. This view has been challenged by advocates of a supply-side model of religious vitality. They argue that the relationship is positive—that pluralism increases vitality—and this empirical claim has become foundational to the larger project of applying economic theory to religion. We review the relevant evidence and reach a straightforward conclusion: The empirical evidence does not support the claim that religious pluralism is positively associated with religious participation in any general sense. We discuss this conclusion's theoretical implications, and we identify potentially productive directions for future research on religious pluralism, church-state relations, and religious competition.

> It appears that North Americans are religious in spite of, not because of, religious pluralism. (Olson 1998a:761).

> [R]eligious practice is strongly and positively associated with pluralism. (Finke & Stark 1998:762)

INTRODUCTION

These two diametrically opposed statements indicate the conflicted state of the literature on a basic question in the sociology of religion: What is the relationship between religious pluralism and religious participation? For years sociologists of religion agreed that the relationship was negative—that pluralism undermined participation. The best-known version of this theory was advanced by Peter Berger (1969). He argued that religious pluralism reduces religious vitality through its effect on plausibility: The more worldviews there are, the less plausible each seems, and the less religious belief and activity there will be. Over the last decade this

0360-0572/01/0811-0261$14.00

wisdom has been challenged by advocates of a "religious economies" or a "supply-side" model of religious activity. Led by Roger Finke and Rodney Stark, the challengers have argued that the traditional view is backwards—that religious pluralism is *positively* associated with religious participation. For them, the key mechanism is not plausibility but competition. Starting from the assumption that "religious economies are like commercial economies," they argue that competition among religious groups increases the quantity and quality of religious products available to consumers and, consequently, the total amount of religion that is consumed (Finke & Stark 1988, p. 42).

This argument has drawn scholarly attention to the important phenomenon of competition among religious groups and to the possibility that such competition is a source of religious vitality. Although religious pluralism is not identical with religious competition, pluralism has commonly been treated as an indicator of competition, and analyses of the relationship between religious pluralism and religious participation have been the primary source of evidence in favor of the idea that religious competition leads to increased religious vitality. Furthermore, the empirical claim that pluralism and participation are positively associated has come to be considered the central discovery of a larger market model or rational choice approach to religion (Hechter & Kanazawa 1997, p. 198).

In this article we review existing evidence on the relationship between religious pluralism and religious participation. We begin with a comprehensive review of the large-N studies and a discussion of some of the methodological issues they raise. We then consider some of the relevant historical and comparative evidence and certain empirical and theoretical issues it raises. Our conclusion is simple: The empirical evidence does not support the claim that religious pluralism is positively associated with religious participation in any general sense. There may be times and places where increased religious pluralism produces increased levels of overall religious participation. But as Stark et al (1995, p. 436, emphasis in original) remind us, "the theory [including the proposition that pluralism increases overall levels of religious mobilization] is not about today, nor is it about the United States—it purports to be *general*." This aspiration to generality is not sustained by a comprehensive and dispassionate review of the empirical evidence. In the conclusion we discuss several theoretical implications of this fact, and we identify potentially productive directions for future research on religious pluralism, church-state relations, and religious competition.

THE LARGE-N QUANTITATIVE EVIDENCE

Our focus is on the empirical relationship between religious pluralism and religious participation, and we begin by specifying the boundaries of the relevant research. Several studies cited in the literature on pluralism and participation speak only indirectly, if at all, to the issue at hand. These include (*a*) two studies that use the number of congregations as the key independent variable (Finke & Stark 1992, p. 215; Welch 1993, p. 333); (*b*) one that uses religious switching as the dependent variable (Duke et al 1993); and (*c*) a set of studies that examine the relationship between a religious group's relative size—its market share—and involvement in that particular religion (Stark & McCann 1993, Zaleski & Zech 1995, Phillips 1998, Perl & Olson 2000). But the number of congregations does not indicate religious pluralism; religious switching is not a measure of religious participation levels; and a minority-religion effect should not be confused with a pluralism effect. Very few extant studies—three in all—use either the number of congregations as the independent variable or religious switching as the dependent variable. Additional comment is warranted, however, about the relevance of studies focused on a minority-religion effect.

There is evidence that religious groups evoke more commitment from their people when they are a smaller proportion of the population (Stark & McCann 1993, Zaleski & Zech 1995, Perl & Olson 2000, but cf. Phillips 1998). Although there may be conceptualizations of religious competition under which this subliterature would be relevant to an assessment of a broader relationship between religious *competition* and religious participation, the fact that a religion is a minority group in a particular region says little about how much religious *diversity* that area contains. A religion that has 10% of the population, for example, might be one of 10 religions, each with 10% of the population, or one of two religions, one of which has 90% of the population. Minority religions may or may not exist in highly pluralistic settings. We will return in the conclusion to the implications of our review of research on religious pluralism for more general claims about the consequences of religious competition. For now, the important point is that the subliterature on market share effects is not relevant to debate about the relationship between religious pluralism and religious participation because the market share held by a particular religion in a given area is not equivalent to the extent to which that area is religiously pluralistic.

Because studies of these sorts do not speak directly to the issue at hand—the empirical relationship between religious pluralism and religious participation—we limit our focus to those studies that use measures of religious pluralism and religious participation as their independent and dependent variables. We find 26 published articles or chapters of this sort, and we believe these 26 constitute the entire universe, at this writing, of published articles and chapters containing quantitative analyses of the pluralism-participation relationship. Ten of these articles find mainly a positive relationship (Finke & Stark 1988, 1989, Iannaccone 1991, Finke 1992, Stark et al 1995, Finke et al 1996, Hamberg & Pettersson 1994, 1997, Johnson 1995, Pettersson & Hamberg 1997). Eleven find mainly a negative relationship (Breault 1989a,b, Land et al 1991, Blau et al 1992, Bruce 1992, Blau et al 1993, Blau et al 1997, Hull & Bold 1998, Phillips 1998, Olson 1999, Olson & Hadaway 1999). Five find mainly null effects (Christiano 1987, Chaves & Cann 1992, Zaleski & Zech 1995, Verweij et al 1997, Perl & Olson 2000).

More informative than counting articles, however, is an examination of the individual analyses *within* these articles and chapters. We found 193 analyses reporting bivariate or partial correlations between religious pluralism and religious participation. We entered these analyses into a database (available from the first author upon request), noting for each the unit of analysis, the year and location of the data, and the dependent variable. For reasons that become apparent below, we also noted certain features of model specification and data analysis, especially whether or not the analysis includes a control for any specific religious group (or groups) constituting a large proportion of the population in at least some of the units. Most of the relevant analyses are regressions of some measure of religious participation on some measure of religious pluralism and selected control variables. We count each result presented in a table, ignoring for the sake of clarity the very few additional analyses mentioned in the text but not reported in a table. We do not double count identical analyses reported in two different articles. Our finding: Sixty-nine percent (133) of the published analyses report either a significant negative (86) or a null (47) relationship between religious pluralism and religious participation, while only 31% (60) report a significant positive relationship. The null findings were about evenly split between nonsignificant positive (26) and nonsignificant negative (21) coefficients.

These 193 analyses are not, of course, independent of each other. Many use the same datasets, and many are offered by the same authors. We know of no reasonable way to adjust our summary percentages to take this nonindependence into account, but we also see no reason that the links among these analyses created by common datasets or authors would favor one side or the other in the relevant debates. Scholars using the same datasets have reached opposite conclusions about the relationship between pluralism and participation. Furthermore, as we will see, the key issues involve model specification rather than any particular feature of the data, such as level of analysis or year in which the data were collected.

The relatively weak prima facie support for the supply-side prediction—only 31% of analyses find the expected positive relationship between pluralism and participation—is weaker than it initially appears. Of the 60 analyses reporting a significant positive relationship, only 23 use overall religious participation as the dependent variable. The other 37 analyses are of two sorts. Thirty-four of them use as their dependent variable participation in some specific religious group, examining, for example, only Baptist and Presbyterian growth (Johnson 1995), or finding that Methodists have increased in pluralistic settings in the United States but Catholics have not (Blau et al 1997). Studies of this sort do not address the general thesis about positive effects of pluralism, which predicts that increased pluralism will raise the *overall* market penetration of religion and thus raise *overall* levels of religious participation in an area. These studies suggest that some religious groups might do better than others in pluralistic situations, but this finding is not inconsistent with the old wisdom regarding religious pluralism. If in pluralistic settings small groups thrive and large groups decline, then the relationship between pluralism and overall participation could still, on balance, be negative.

Another three analyses obtaining positive results are from a cross-national analysis of religious participation, and the positive relationship between pluralism and participation holds only for a subset of units: It is present for predominantly

Protestant countries, but is null for predominantly Catholic countries (Iannaccone 1991). Moreover, Chaves & Cann (1992) use these same data to show that, once variation in the institutional arrangements between church and state are taken into account, the relationship between pluralism and participation is null even for Protestant countries. Other cross-national research also finds no general relationship between religious pluralism and religious participation (Verweij et al 1997).

If we discount these 37 analyses, only 23 published analyses (12%) yield results that appear to support the religious-economies claim regarding the positive effects of religious pluralism. Of the 133 negative or null analyses, 40 use participation in some specific subgroup as the dependent variable. If we ignore these analyses as well and look exclusively at the 116 analyses using overall religious participation as the dependent variable, only 20% (23/116) of these are positive; 80% are negative (52%) or null (28%).

Methodological Issues in the Large-N Evidence

Contributors to this literature have, of course, noticed the conflicting results, and much of the debate has turned on arguments about why we should place more confidence in one set of results than in another. Three methodological issues have emerged from this debate: whether to control for the presence of large religious groups, especially Roman Catholics; which unit of analysis is the proper one; and whether to use datasets that do not contain complete membership information on all religious groups.

Since the first of these issues is the most important, we consider it the most extensively. It emerged in the seminal analysis by Finke & Stark (1988) that used American cities in 1906 as the unit of analysis. In these data, the bivariate correlation between religious pluralism and religious participation (the percentage of religious adherents in each city, based on reports from each denomination about their membership) was moderately negative (−0.40), and the relationship became positive only when Finke & Stark added a control for the percent Roman Catholic in each city.

This finding was quickly challenged on both substantive and methodological grounds. Using data from US counties in 1980, Breault (1989a,b) found a negative correlation between religious pluralism and religious participation. Noting that the correlation between the two key "independent" variables used by Finke & Stark—percentage of a city population that is Catholic and the pluralism measure—was highly negative (−0.88), Breault argued that the positive effect of pluralism was obtained only because including this control for percent Catholic destabilized the equation, making it illegitimate to interpret that effect as a true causal relationship between pluralism and participation.

In their reply to Breault, Finke & Stark conceded that their result depended on the control for percent Catholic in each city, but they argued that the very high correlation between two independent variables was unproblematic (Finke & Stark 1989, p. 1055). The main reason it should be considered unproblematic, as they later put it, is that "the capacity of the Catholics to dominate many urban markets was due, in part, to their ability to sustain internal diversity" (Finke et al 1996, p. 206). In other words, they argued that the apparent homogeneity of Catholic-dominated areas conceals a great deal of de facto pluralism (within the Church), and that this internal diversity explains the relatively high levels of religious adherence within Catholic-dominated areas of the United States. They also objected to Breault's unit of analysis (counties rather than cities), arguing that it was too large, and they impugned the factual correctness of one of his key results, implying that his work was not credible, an implication they would later state explicitly (Finke et al 1996, p. 206 n).

The foregoing exchange inspired a steady stream of articles and chapters that employed various units of analysis, used data from various time periods and locations, and specified models in different ways. Evidence mounted on both sides, and it seemed that the debate was a stalemate, turning on a technical specification issue about which reasonable people could disagree.

The stalemate was decisively broken by Daniel Olson (1999). Olson did three things. First, he pointed out that, because the standard measure of religious pluralism uses the sum of the squared proportions of each religious group in an ecological unit (such as a city), the proportion Catholic in each unit is an arithmetic component of that measure, as is the proportion of every other group. Consequently, as any small religious group grows in size, pluralism necessarily increases—up to a point. Once a group reaches a certain proportion of the population, further increases in group size mean that the group is coming to be one of the largest in the area, and increasing its size necessarily decreases religious pluralism. Thus, for any group that varies across units from being a religious minority in some places to a religious majority in other places, there is a mathematically necessary strong curvilinear relationship between the proportion of the population belonging to that group and the standard measure of religious pluralism. If one limits analysis to units in which the proportion Catholic, for example, is large enough to be beyond the inflection point in this curve—as it is when analysis is limited to cities or urban counties in the United States—then a strong negative correlation between proportion Catholic and the usual pluralism measure is the automatic result.

Second, Olson observed that when the dependent variable is the overall proportion of religious adherents—the proportion of the population identified with *any* religious group—then the proportion of the population belonging to *each* religious group is also an arithmetic component of the dependent variable. This means that there is a mathematically necessary positive relationship between the proportion Catholic (or the proportion of any other group) in an area and the value of the usual dependent variable. If the group varies from very small to very large across units of analysis, that positive relationship will be strong.

The problematic situation, then, arises when percent Catholic is an arithmetic component of the other two variables *and* enough of the units have a Catholic population large enough to make the relationship between percent Catholic and pluralism strongly linearly negative rather than curvilinear. The combination of these features produces a strong negative correlation between the pluralism index (X1) and percent Catholic (X2), and a strong positive correlation between percent Catholic (X2) and the dependent variable (Y). This guarantees that controlling for percent Catholic will produce a positive relationship between pluralism and religious involvement. When X2 is a large enough component of both X1 and Y, this result will emerge no matter what the substantive variables involved.

The third part of Olson's demonstration drives home the point that it is not legitimate to defend controlling for percent Catholic in these models on the grounds that there is something substantively different about Catholics that warrants the control. He constructs an artificial pseudo-denomination—an aggregation of moderate Protestants, Jews, and Mormons—that makes no substantive sense but where the percent belonging to this bizarre denomination is statistically analogous to the percent Roman Catholic in the United States: It is negatively correlated with pluralism and positively correlated with religious participation. Both of these correlations, like correlations involving the percent Catholic, emerge as a matter of mathematical necessity because the percentage belonging to the pseudo-denomination (X2) is an arithmetic component of the other two variables, pluralism (X1) and the percentage of the population that are religious adherents (Y). Under these conditions, the pluralism relationship flips from negative to positive when this variable is controlled, just as it does when percent Catholic is controlled.

Olson (1999) clarified the most puzzling issue in this literature. He definitively showed that Breault was correct about the specification problem underlying Finke & Stark's original results, and his analysis undermined the defense that something substantively different about Catholics justifies the specification favored by Finke & Stark. Controlling for percent Catholic may give the impression of distinguishing between pluralism's effect and the separate effect of domination by a religious group that is somehow substantively different from the other religious groups that are present. But this impression is an illusion. In fact, when Roman Catholics are a large enough group in most of the units being analyzed, adding a statistical control for percent Catholic forces the pluralism effect to be positive because the percentage of Roman Catholics in an area is a major component both of the pluralism measure and of the usual dependent variable. Statistically controlling for the presence of any large religious group, whatever its internal substantive characteristics, would have the same effect on the model. In other words: Under these conditions the positive pluralism effect is a mathematical artifact without any substantive meaning. As of this writing, advocates of the supply-side arguments have not responded to this line of criticism in Olson (1999).

With hindsight sharpened by Olson, it is easier to see that debate about the basic question of whether, in general, pluralism enhances religious participation should have been settled with Breault's 1989 critique. The debate continued, however, fueled in part by a calculation error in Finke & Stark's (1989) attempt to replicate Breault's results. This error—the pluralism index was incorrectly calculated in a way that reversed the sign attached to it in regression models—was unrelated to the specification problem and had the unfortunate consequence of leading

Finke & Stark to assert (falsely) that a negative relationship between pluralism and participation reported by Breault was in fact positive (Finke & Stark 1989, p. 1054). Relying on this error, Finke & Stark successfully undermined Breault's critique by creating the false impression that his analyses were untrustworthy. The error was not discovered for another decade (Olson 1998a), and it is reasonable to wonder how research on this subject might have proceeded, and been received, had this error not been taken as fact.

Be that as it may, it now is clear that arithmetic relationships among the key variables compromise many of the analyses yielding a positive relationship between pluralism and participation. Of the 23 published analyses that yield a positive relationship between pluralism and participation, 12 obtain this result by controlling for a variable—usually the percent Catholic in each unit—under the problematic conditions described above. Since these results must be dismissed as artifactual, only 11 good positive results remain, less than 6% of the total.

About half of the analyses producing negative or null results also contain controls for percent Catholic or a similarly large group. But recall that the mere presence of such a control is not sufficient to create problems. That control is a problem only if it is an arithmetic component of both the pluralism measure and the dependent variable, and if the units under study are such that the first correlation is linearly negative rather than curvilinear. There are several ways to avoid this set of conditions, including using a more expansive set of units (such as all US counties rather than simply urban US counties) or operationalizing percent Catholic in a way that breaks the mathematical relationship between it and the dependent variable. Olson (1999), for example, recommends operationalizing percent Catholic as the percent of all religious adherents that are Catholic rather than as the percent of the total population that is Catholic. For us, the key point is that, although about half the analyses producing negative or null results contain controls for percent Catholic or a similarly large group, none of the negative results and only 5 of the 33 null results use this control under the full set of conditions that would make it problematic.

The bottom line: If we limit attention to the 93 analyses that use overall religious participation as the dependent variable, and for which the published articles contain enough information for us to be certain that the analysis is not compromised by problematic arithmetic dependencies among the key variables, only 12% yield a positive result and almost 90% yield negative (60%) or null (28%) results.

The second point of contention in this debate concerns the appropriate unit of analysis. Proponents of the market model argue that religious markets are local in scale, and that studies employing larger units of analysis (such as counties) may misrepresent the actual degree of pluralism faced by religious consumers insofar as the larger units aggregate a number of different local markets. There is one dataset, from New York State in 1865, in which the pluralism effect is positive when the unit is towns and null when the unit is counties (Finke et al 1996). But this pattern is not evident anywhere else in the literature. In an analysis of Canadian data, for example, Olson & Hadaway (1999) find a negative pluralism effect whether the unit is counties or cities. And in an analysis of data from England and Wales in 1851, Stark et al (1995) find that the pluralism effect is positive when the unit is counties but negative or null when the unit is cities—a pattern opposite that in the New York data and therefore unhelpful to their argument that smaller units are more appropriate.

Nor does increasing the level of magnification shift the general balance of evidence. Of the analyses in our database that focus on smaller units of analysis (such as cities or towns) and use overall religious participation as their dependent variable, only 41% yield a positive correlation between pluralism and vitality (37% are negative, 22% are null). And if we focus only on analyses that are not compromised by the specification problem described above, the figure drops to 27% positive (with 46% negative and 27% null). In sum, null or negative results occur more often than positive results even among analyses using the smaller units preferred by Finke & Stark (as in, for example, Christiano 1987, Stark et al 1995, or Olson & Hadaway 1999).

Olson & Hadaway (1999, p. 499) also point out that improved transportation makes larger units less problematic, even in theory, in more contemporary data. In addition, the potential aggregation problems when the pluralism index is applied to larger units cannot produce a negative relationship between religious pluralism and religious participation among larger units when the true relationship among smaller units is positive. Thus, for both empirical and theoretical reasons, criticizing negative or null results on the grounds that the unit of analysis is too big proves untenable.

This brings us to the third and final methodological issue in this debate. Finke & Stark (1989, p. 1054) have criticized one of the datasets commonly used in this literature—a 1980 county-level dataset of religious adherents in various denominations—on the grounds that it does not include congregations in many denominations. In particular, this dataset does not include congregations within several large African-American denominations and therefore yields a pluralism index that is too low in some settings. Breault (1989b, p. 1058) and Olson (1999, p. 159) have shown that this criticism is a red herring. Limiting analysis to units with few or no African Americans, rendering irrelevant the absence of black denominations from the dataset, changes nothing in the results. And even when all units are used, results would not be significantly altered if the dataset were more denominationally inclusive. Since the value of the pluralism measure is overwhelmingly determined by the largest few denominations in an area, the exclusion of many small groups, or even a few relatively large groups, has little effect on the pluralism index for a particular unit. And, in any event, there are many null or negative results for datasets not affected by this problem.

Excluding analyses that do not use overall religious participation as the dependent variable and those that we know to be compromised by arithmetical problems, we are left, then, with 82 nonpositive results and only 11 positive results. These 11 results are from four specific settings: New York State in 1865 (Finke et al 1996), Wales in 1851 (Stark et al 1995), contemporary Sweden (Hamberg & Pettersson

1994), and the 300 most unpopulated counties in the contemporary United States (Breault 1989b). While this body of evidence suggests that pluralism may stimulate participation in some times and places, it clearly does not support the proposition that pluralism and participation are positively associated in any general way.

We return in the conclusion to the question of how this evidence connects to the claim that religious competition (as opposed to religious pluralism) promotes higher levels of religious participation. We turn first, however, to historical and comparative evidence concerning the relationship between religious pluralism and religious participation.

THE HISTORICAL EVIDENCE

Most of the large-N studies in this literature have focused on nineteenth or twentieth century America, or have employed cross-sectional evidence from a single case such as Sweden or Wales. Only a few have attempted to assess the relationship between pluralism and participation from a cross-national or longitudinal perspective (Iannaccone 1991, Chaves & Cann 1992, Stark & Iannaccone 1994). Obviously, we cannot fill this gap in the literature here. We can, however, review existing comparative and historical evidence to see whether or not it supports the claim that pluralism and participation are, in general, positively related.

Let us begin by considering the survey evidence from post–World War II Europe and Canada (for example, Höllinger 1996, Dekker et al 1997, Cesareo et al 1995, Michelat et al 1991). It consistently and unequivocally shows two things: Orthodox religious beliefs and involvement in institutionalized religion (*a*) vary considerably from one country to another and (*b*) have steadily declined throughout Europe (and Canada), particularly since the 1960s. Are these variations associated with variations in religious pluralism? Relatedly, are they associated with variations in religious regulation—state intervention in the religious economy by means of legal repression of unwanted competitors or financial subsidy to official churches, either of which, by supply-side logic, will suppress religious pluralism and thereby decrease religious participation?

If one focused only on the Protestant-dominated polities of Northern and Western Europe, one might be tempted to support the religious economies proposition that pluralism and participation are positively related, since the lowest levels of religious vitality are to be found in the confessionally homogeneous and state-dominated religious economies of Scandinavia, with the more pluralistic and unregulated economies of Britain, the Netherlands, and Germany exhibiting higher levels of participation. When one turns to the Catholic-dominated countries of Southern and Eastern Europe, however, the picture is different. Despite their homogeneity, these countries display levels of religious belief and church attendance that are consistently higher than those found in the Protestant countries. Nor can these divergences be attributed solely to the intertwining of religious and political conflict, for they obtain not only in Ireland and Poland, where Catholicism and national liberation are historically connected, but also in Italy and Austria, where they are not. In Europe, as in the United States, the religious vitality of Catholic regions represents a troubling anomaly for the supply-side explanations.

What about longitudinal variations? Surveys show a steady decline of religious participation in postwar Europe and Canada, and other sources (religious censuses, church records) suggest that the decline began (or at least accelerated) during the late nineteenth century. Can this decline in vitality be traced either to a decline in pluralism or to an increase in regulation? That is not what the historical record suggests. Generally speaking, relations between church and state were becoming looser, rather than tighter, during this period, and new religious movements and denominations were emerging and expanding. Thus, the decline in vitality seems to have coincided with a growth in pluralism and a decrease in regulation, a picture confirmed in longitudinal studies of Canada, the Netherlands, England, Scotland, and Sweden (Beyer 1997, Gorski & Wilson 1998, Lechner 1996, Bruce 1999, Petterson & Hamberg 1997, p. 68). These trends in religious pluralism, regulation, and participation seem to have been general in Europe (Mola 1993, Helmreich 1979).

Nor do recent religious trends in post-Soviet societies provide much support for the supply-side approach, which would lead one to expect a major upswing in religious vitality following the demise of Communism. Although increases in religious affiliation occurred in Russia during the 1990s, declines occurred in other post-Soviet countries, such as Hungary and Slovenia. Still others, such as Poland, have been stable. The picture is similarly mixed with regard to church attendance. Like the longer-term pattern in the rest of Europe (and Canada), the recent trends in the post-Soviet countries for which we have data cannot be construed as showing a positive relationship between either deregulation or pluralism, on the one hand, and participation, on the other. At best, the relationship here is null (Inglehart & Baker 2000, Greeley 2000).

Market model advocates recognize that some of the cases mentioned above are problematic for their claims about the relationship between pluralism and partic-ipation, and they invoke various qualifications to account for the exceptions that are brought to their attention. They have argued, for example, that religious con-flict can substitute for pluralism and competition as the energizing force behind religious vitality, and that decreasing conflict among religious groups has caused religious decline in the Netherlands and elsewhere (Stark & Iannaccone 1996). Leaving aside the issue of whether this substitute mechanism would apply to all the contrary historical cases, we note that a market explanation supplemented by qualifications of this sort is difficult to distinguish from more traditional explana-tions of religious change, which focus on the interaction between religious and political conflict, and cleavages of confession, class, and ideology (such as Martin 1978 and McLeod 1996).

What about the United States? Proponents of the market model have made much of the American case (Finke & Stark 1992, Finke 1990). They have argued that the opening of the religious market dramatically increased religious pluralism in the United States, and that pluralism dramatically increased religious involvement over time. The principal evidence for this claim is a long-term increase in church membership. But there is a problem with this indicator: Membership criteria have generally grown laxer over time. Today, formal membership levels are higher than attendance levels; in earlier periods, the opposite may have been true. That at least is the conclusion reached by one prominent historian of American religion who argues that "participation [as opposed to formal membership] in [US] congregations has probably remained relatively constant" since the seventeenth century (Holifield 1994, p. 24). Thus, an historic increase in formal church membership may not be a valid indicator of historic increase in religious participation. Whatever one decides about the specifics of the US historical case, however, it is of limited theoretical significance to debate about a general relationship between pluralism and participation. Even if we accept the claim that, in the United States, religious pluralism and participation are positively linked, that is an historical fact about a single case, not a basis for a theoretical claim about a general relationship between pluralism and participation.

Are there other times and places where the religious-economies propositions about pluralism, regulation, and participation fare better? At first blush, early modern Europe (ca. 1500–1750) might seem to fit the predictions of the supply-side approach quite well. The Protestant Reformation brought substantial increases in religious pluralism and religious competition. The Catholic monopoly was broken into three large multi-nationals (the Catholic, Lutheran, and Reformed Churches) and a host of smaller and more embattled religious suppliers, such as Baptists and Unitarians, which were all forced to battle for territory and people (Klueting 1989). Moreover, this increase in religious competition was accompanied by improvements in the quantity, quality, and availability of religious products—more priests and pastors, more cathedrals and churches, more schools and universities, more poor-houses and orphanages. Church-building and missionary campaigns of this period also brought religious services to many towns and villages that had been underserved or beyond the reach of the pre-Reformation Church. And, compared with their medieval predecessors, the post-Reformation clergy were better trained and probably more zealous as well.

Still, the fit between the religious-economies model and the early modern evidence is not as tight as it seems. While increased pluralism certainly brought increased competition, it did not create *market* competition in which local religious organizations competed to sell religious products to consumers. Outside a few privileged enclaves where a certain measure of religious toleration prevailed (a few German cities, most of the Netherlands, and, somewhat later, England), individuals were not really free to pick and choose the religious product that best matched their tastes (Grell & Scribner 1996, Monter 1984, Lecler 1955). The only religious product available to them, at least on the open market, was the one which their ruler(s) had chosen. Practically speaking, the only way to change religion, as a rule, was to change location—to move from Dresden to Munich, or from Paris to Edinburgh. Even in more tolerant areas, some religions were more privileged than others, and still others (such as Unitarianism) were banned altogether. With its complex intertwining of geopolitics, high ideology, and class struggle, the competition between Catholics, Lutherans, and Calvinists during the Confessional Era was more akin to the competition between communism and capitalism during the Cold War than to market competition between business firms.

Furthermore, we should be careful not to overestimate the actual increase in religious participation or vitality brought on by the increased religious competition of the Reformation era. The fact that medieval Christianity contained more pagan (that is, magical) elements than its post-Reformation counterparts indicates a change in the character of popular religiosity, but it does not necessarily imply an increase in the level of popular religiosity. And while an earlier generation of historical work (for example, Delumeau 1977, Thomas 1971, Dickens 1964) endorsed the view that a moribund medieval Christianity was revitalized by the Reformation—a view cited approvingly by advocates of the market approach (Stark & Iannaccone 1994, p. 214)—recent work on the late Middle Ages actually points to an upsurge in religious fervor in the decades preceding the Reformation (see, for example, Olin 1992, Oakley 1979, Duffy 1992). Thus, one could argue that religious vitality preceded pluralism during the Reformation, rather than the other way around.

Nor should we assume that increases in vitality during the Reformation era were produced entirely or even primarily by improvements in the quality or availability of the religious product, for there were many nonreligious incentives to participation and many nonreligious sanctions for nonparticipation. The churches were still the major providers of education and welfare during this period, and church membership was often a de facto or even de jure precondition for access to public office and public respectability. Conversely, failure to perform one's religious duties was often a public offense. These nonreligious incentives were strengthened during periods of confessional strife and warfare, when displaying irreligion—or displaying the wrong religion—could be seen as a sign of unreliability or even treason. Thus, religious participation might increase as a result of an intensified religio-political competition that bears little resemblance to market competition.

Like the large-N studies, the historical and comparative evidence fails to support the claim that there is a generally positive association between religious pluralism and religious participation. As with the evidence from the large-N studies, the historical and comparative evidence suggests only that there might be certain times and places, such as the nineteenth-century United States or, perhaps, post-War Japan (Iannaccone et al 1997, p. 357–58) where decreased religious regulation or increased religious pluralism was concomitant with increased religious participation. This evidence cannot be made to support the universalistic ambitions of market models of religion. For a theory with such ambitions, Stark et al (1995, p. 436) correctly note, "it is urgent that we test it in diverse times and places." Indeed, they say, "data for ninth-century China would be even better than data for nineteenth-century England." We have not found a study of ninth-century China, but the historical studies we have found clearly show that the theory does not travel well across historical time or cultural space.

We have not exhaustively reviewed all extant historical evidence, and perhaps there are additional settings—either in other parts of the Christian world (such as Latin America) or in parts of the world dominated by Islam or other non-Christian religions—in which increased religious pluralism seems to have produced increased religious vitality. Even in that event, however, the old wisdom that religious pluralism is negatively associated with religious vitality will be validly replaced only by the conclusion that "sometimes it is, sometimes it isn't," not by the conclusion that the relationship is generally positive. There are too many contexts in which the relationship appears to be nonpositive to justify a claim to the contrary.

CONCLUSION

We have done two things in this essay. First, we have weighed the evidence on religious pluralism contained in the relevant large-N studies. Second, we have used comparative and historical evidence drawn mainly from Western Europe and North America to assess the empirical and conceptual scope of the claim that religious diversity increases religious pluralism via market competition. Our conclusion is simple. The claim that religious pluralism and religious participation are generally and positively associated with one another—the core empirical hypothesis of the market approach to the study of religion—is not supported, and attempts to discredit countervailing evidence on methodological grounds must be rejected. A positive relationship between religious pluralism and religious participation can be found only in a limited number of contexts, while the concepts themselves translate poorly to nonmodern settings.

What does this conclusion imply about future research on religious pluralism, church-state relations, and religious competition?

First, the supply-side approach should be distinguished from a broader agenda that has been called a new paradigm in the sociology of religion. Although supply-side and rational choice approaches to religion are often equated with the new paradigm, it is important to note that the article that coined the term (Warner 1993) did not identify the new paradigm with an economic or rational-choice approach to religion, nor did it claim a positive association between pluralism and participation. Although Warner observed that organized religion in the United States has not experienced the kind of decline experienced in many European countries, and although he also observed that religious institutions in the United States operate in the context of an open religious market, he did not claim that there was any necessary connection between these two states of affairs, much less that open markets or pluralism are a sine qua non of religious vitality. Rather, he used the US case to argue that an older wisdom, developed on the basis of European experience and insisting that religious monopoly was a sine qua non of religious vitality, did not apply to the United States.

Our reading of the evidence suggests that Warner was right to question this older wisdom. The relationship between pluralism and vitality is not uniformly positive, but neither is it uniformly negative. One quarter of the published quantitative results on this relationship are null, and there are times and places where increased religious pluralism is accompanied by increased religious vitality. The original new paradigm analysis thus accurately identified a major weakness in the received wisdom, but it did not imply the stronger, unsupportable claim that pluralism and participation are positively related in any general way. Future scholarship should refrain from equating the analysis and agenda actually articulated in Warner (1993) with the religious economies or rational-choice approach to religion.

Second, future research might build on the literature reviewed here by investigating religious pluralism and its consequences in new ways. As we have emphasized throughout, there are some contexts in which pluralism and vitality are positively correlated, some in which they are negatively correlated, and some in which the correlation is null. One key task for future research will be to explain this variation by specifying the conditions under which one or another of these relationships obtains. Also, freed from the agenda of proving that either competition or plausibility is the primary mechanism by which pluralism might influence religious activity, future research on religious pluralism's consequences may yield interesting new results. Olson (1998b), for example, has investigated the possibility that pluralism affects religious participation by influencing individuals' social networks. Blau et al (1997) examine relationships between pluralism and growth for specific denominations, developing explanations for why pluralism might variously influence different religious groups. Smith et al (1998) have called attention to the cultural aspects of religious pluralism, emphasizing the connection between religious pluralism and the salience of religious identities. These are three examples of promising directions for future research on religious pluralism.

Another potential direction for research on pluralism is suggested by Finke & Stark's more recent proposal that pluralism increases religious participation only when pluralism crosses a rather low threshold. The "key distinction," they have written, "is between areas having no diversity and those having some degree of pluralism" (Finke et al 1996, p. 210, quoted in Finke & Stark 1998, p. 763). As Olson & Hadaway (1999, p. 504) point out, a hypothesis restricted to the difference between areas with some pluralism and areas with no pluralism will explain little of the world's cross-sectional and historical variation in religious vitality. In particular, this narrowed hypothesis will not help explain cross-sectional or historical variation in religious vitality in nineteenth- or twentieth-century United States, or in any other time or place where very few areas have so little religious pluralism that they fall below the posited theoretical threshold. Still, it seems plausible that religious participation is higher where individuals have some rather than no religious options, and this hypothesis might well indicate a properly narrowed scope for a market model of religious pluralism's effect on participation. Future research might productively be directed at establishing whether this more modest claim is true or false.

Third, there is more to learn about the connections between church-state institutional arrangements and religious activity in a society. As we have seen, the regulation hypothesis—that state intervention in the religious market leads to lower levels of religious pluralism and religious vitality—is at odds with much historical evidence. In the Reformation era, religious regulation, religious pluralism, and religious vitality all increased, a pattern inconsistent with supply-side arguments. In the modern era religious deregulation and religious pluralism have both increased throughout Europe and Canada, but religious participation has declined, the opposite of what the market model would predict. And even where deregulation is associated with increased pluralism (if not increased religious vitality), the causal order is not always clear. In at least some settings, institutional distancing between states and religion—deregulation—was actually a response to increased levels of pluralism, reversing the causal ordering assumed in market models (Beyer 1997). Dropping the market model assumption about causal order in favor of research aimed at discovering the proper causal order—or, more likely, discovering the balance of reciprocal causation between deregulation and pluralism—seems a fruitful agenda for future research.

Relatedly, our review of the historical and comparative evidence found both positive and negative associations between state regulation of religion and religious vitality. In some places, such as Russia and, perhaps, the United States, an increasingly open religious market seems to have produced higher levels of religious participation and vitality. But in much of Europe and Canada, the historical trajectory has been in the direction of an increasingly open religious market and *declining* participation. What explains this variation in the relationship between church-state changes and changes in religious participation? Future research might address this question.

Fourth, the absence of any general positive relationship between pluralism and participation does not bode well for the more general idea that market-like religious competition promotes religious vitality. One might, of course, try to protect claims about religious competition by arguing that pluralism is not an adequate measure of the competitive processes posited by market arguments, its common use to the contrary notwithstanding. This point has been made by proponents of market models, as when they write that "*competition* lies at the heart of our theory" and "religious *pluralism* is important *only* insofar as it increases choice and competition" (Stark & Iannaccone 1996, p. 266, emphasis in original). We agree that religious pluralism is not a good measure of religious competition, but it is important to recognize that, absent the pluralism literature, there is no other body of evidence on which to rest the claim that market-like religious competition generates higher overall levels of religious participation.

Beyond the pluralism literature, the much smaller literature on market share effects is the most likely place to look for support of a competition hypothesis. The argument here is that the amount of competition a religious group faces increases as that group becomes a smaller and smaller percentage of the population in a given area, and so finding that groups elicit more support and participation from their adherents when their market share is smaller shows that competition promotes religious participation. We argued above that a religious group's market share is not a valid measure of how much religious diversity it faces. For similar reasons it is not obvious why we should assume that a religious group constituting, say, 20% of the population faces more competition than a group constituting, say, 70% of the population. Among other considerations, the fact that minority religions are commonly associated with ethnic identities or language groups, and therefore are not competing with other religions for members, raises questions about the validity of a religious group's market share as a measure of how much competition that group faces for members. Moreover, whatever one thinks about this measurement issue, the empirical literature on market share effects provides only mixed support for the idea that religious groups with smaller market shares enjoy higher levels of participation (cf, for example, Stark & McCann 1993 and Perl & Olson 2000, on the one hand, with Phillips 1998, on the other hand).

Thus, given the absence of any support from the pluralism literature, the mixed support from the market share research, and the ambiguous relevance, anyway, of the market share research to claims about competition, it is difficult to discern any basis for the claim that a "large, rapidly growing, and remarkably diverse literature support[s] the thesis that competition strengthens religious organizations and increases the overall level of religious participation" (Finke & Stark 1998, p. 761). The general claim that religious competition generates religious vitality is no better supported by empirical evidence than is the narrower claim that religious pluralism generates religious vitality.

All that said, our fifth concluding point is that the empirical failure of the market model's core claim does not imply abandoning the agenda of investigating the consequences of religious competition. Advocates of market models of religion should be credited with bringing religious competition to the attention of the scholarly community, and we do not wish to discourage either additional work on this subject or the use of economic theory in analyses of religious competition. The weaknesses of extant research on religious competition are not endemic to the concept of religious competition or to the use of economic theory. Rather, the problems emerge from the inadequacies of the particular approach to the study of religious competition, and the particular application of economic theory, that have come to dominate the literature. New investigations of religious competition are likely to be valuable if they take more seriously the social and historical context in which competition occurs.

This is not the place to develop in full a more adequate conceptualization of religious competition to inform future research, but we can sketch some of its basic features. In settings in which religious congregations are voluntary associations dependent on donations from individuals, a more sociologically adequate framework for the study of religious competition would recognize, among other things, that there probably is more competition among congregations *within* denominations than there is *across* denominations; that religious markets are severely segmented along social class and ethnic lines; that religious groups and organizations compete for individuals' time and resources with secular as well as alternative religious voluntary associations and leisure activities; and that religious competition's consequences for religious identities is likely to be different than its consequences for religious participation.

As currently practiced, the empirical analysis of religious competition recognizes none of these realities. Instead, standard analyses using religious pluralism as a proxy for religious competition implicitly assume that all religious competition is between denominations, that all denominations within a geographically defined area compete equally with all other denominations in that area, that the only relevant kind of competition is competition among religious groups, and that the market mechanisms generating the percentage of a population identifying with any religious group will be the same market mechanisms generating the percentage of people who actively participate in religious groups.

Future research on religious competition in settings where religion is essentially voluntaristic should use a more conceptually adequate analytical framework. Improved conceptualization might preclude the use of some economic theories and models in the study of religious competition, but we see no reason that it should preclude the use, or lessen the value, of economic theories and models in general. Future research might follow Hull & Bold (1998) in exploring the possibility that economic theory other than that adopted by proponents of the supply-side model can be used to better understand religious phenomena.

Future research also should recognize that there are at least two qualitatively different types of religious competition. In settings where religious organizations depend on voluntary contributions from individuals, religious organizations will compete for individuals' time and resources, and they will compete both with each other and with mass entertainment, sports teams, political parties, and many other sorts of groups and activities. By contrast, in settings where religious membership is more like modern citizenship than like membership in a voluntary association, religion often becomes intertwined with political, social, and cultural conflict between states, classes, and national or ethnic groupings; religious allegiances become markers or signals of nonreligious allegiances; and religious competition means struggles over cultural, political, and territorial influence and power. As we argued above, the religious competition characterizing Reformation era Europe, and perhaps characterizing certain contemporary settings around the world, is of this second sort, and it is qualitatively different from the religious competition characterizing most of the contemporary West, which is of the first sort. One way for research to advance will be to discern when and where one rather than another type of religious competition occurs, and to develop explanations of the consequences of each type of religious competition.

Finally, let us state explicitly a conclusion that has been implied several times in the foregoing: The quest for a general law about the relationship between religious pluralism and religious participation should be abandoned. The evidence clearly shows that any such general law, to be accurate, would have to be formulated with so many exceptions and qualifications that its claim to generality or lawfullness would be empty. Rather than an either-or argument about whether religious pluralism is, in general, positively or negatively associated with religious participation, the most valuable future work on this subject is likely to include investigations into the social, cultural, and institutional arrangements that determine, in part, religious pluralism's consequences for religious vitality. This will be the route to a more adequate sociology of religion, one that moves toward a political economy of the religious sphere by placing religious markets in larger cultural and institutional contexts.

ACKNOWLEDGMENTS

Nancy Ammerman, Emily Barman, Penny Becker, Al Bergesen, Ronald Breiger, Lis Clemens, Karen Cook, Jay Demerath, John Evans, Claude Fischer, William Form, Ted Gerber, Helen Giesel, Michael Hout, Mary Ellen Konieczny, James Montgomery, Kate O'Neil, Chris Smith, Lynn Smith-Lovin, Sarah Soule, Steve Warner, Rhys Williams, and an anonymous reviewer offered helpful comments on earlier drafts of this essay. Special thanks to Helen Giesel for assistance in preparing the database of quantitative results.

Visit the Annual Reviews home page at www.AnnualReviews.org

LITERATURE CITED

Berger PL. 1969. *The Sacred Canopy: Elements of a Sociological Theory of Religion*. New York: Anchor

Beyer P. 1997. Religious vitality in Canada: the complementarity of religious market and secularization perspectives. *J. Sci. Study Relig.* 36:272–88

Blau JR, Land KC, Redding K. 1992. The expansion of religious affiliation. *Soc. Sci. Res.* 21:329–52

Blau JR, Redding K, Davis WR, Land KC. 1997. Spatial processes and the duality of church and faith: a Simmelian perspective on U.S. denominational growth, 1900–1930. *Sociol. Perspec.* 40:557–80

Blau JR, Redding K, Land KC. 1993. Ethnocultural cleavages and the growth of church membership in the United States. *Sociol. For.* 8:609–37

Breault KD. 1989a. New evidence on religious pluralism, urbanism, and religious participation. *Am. Sociol. Rev.* 54:1048–53

Breault KD. 1989b. A re-examination of the relationship between religious diversity and religious adherence: reply to Finke and Stark. *Am. Sociol. Rev.* 54:1056–59

Bruce S. 1992. Pluralism and religious vitality. In *Religion and Modernization: Sociologists and Historians Debate the Secularization Thesis*, ed. S Bruce, pp. 170–94. Oxford: Clarendon

Bruce S. 1999. *Choice and Religion: A Critique of Rational Choice Theory*. Oxford/New York: Oxford Univ. Press

Cesareo V, et al. 1995. *La Religiosità in Italia*. Milan: A. Mondadori. 2nd ed.

Chaves M, Cann DE. 1992. Regulation, pluralism, and religious market structure: explaining religion's vitality. *Ration. Soc.* 4:272–90

Christiano KJ. 1987. *Religious Diversity and Social Change: American Cities, 1890–1906*. New York: Cambridge Univ. Press.

Dekker G, de Hart J, Peters J. 1997. *God in Nederland 1966–1996*. Amsterdam: Anthos

Delumeau J. 1977. *Catholicism between Luther and Voltaire*. London/Philadelphia: Burnes & Oates/Westminster Press

Dickens AG. 1964. *The English Reformation*. London: B.T. Batsford

Duffy E. 1992. *The Stripping of the Altars.* New Haven: Yale Univ. Press

Duke JT, Johnson BL, Duke JB. 1993. Rates of religious conversion: a macrosociological study. *Res. Sociol. Rel.* 5:89–121

Finke R. 1990. Religious deregulation: origins and consequences. *J. Church State* 32:609–26

Finke R. 1992. An unsecular America. In *Religion and Modernization: Sociologists and Historians Debate the Secularization Thesis,* ed. S Bruce, pp. 145–69. Oxford: Clarendon

Finke R, Guest A, Stark R. 1996. Mobilizing local religious markets: religious pluralism in the empire state, 1855 to 1865. *Am. Sociol. Rev.* 61:203–18

Finke R, Stark R. 1988. Religious economies and sacred canopies: religious mobilization in American cities, 1906. *Am. Sociol. Rev.* 53:41–49

Finke R, Stark R. 1989. Evaluating the evidence: religious economies and sacred canopies. *Am. Sociol. Rev.* 54:1054–56

Finke R, Stark R. 1992. *The Churching of America, 1776–1990: Winners and Losers in our Religious Economy.* New Brunswick, NJ: Rutgers Univ. Press

Finke R, Stark R. 1998. Reply to Olson: religious choice and competition. *Am. Sociol. Rev.* 63:761–66

Gorski PS, Wilson FW. 1998. *The problem of unbelief in the nineteenth century: religious pluralism and religious vitality in the Netherlands, 1800–1996.* Presented at Annu. Meet. Social Sci. Hist. Assoc., Chicago

Greeley AM. 2000. *Religion in Europe at the End of the Second Millenium.* Book ms in review

Grell OP, Scribner B. 1996. *Tolerance and Intolerance in the European Reformation.* Cambridge/New York: Cambridge Univ. Press

Hamberg EM, Pettersson T. 1994. The religious market: denominational competition and religious participation in contemporary Sweden. *J. Sci. Study Relig.* 33:205–16

Hamberg EM, Pettersson T. 1997. Short-term changes in religious supply and church attendance in contemporary Sweden. *Res. Soc. Sci. Study Relig.* 8:35–51

Hechter M, Kanazawa S. 1997. Sociological rational choice theory. *Annu. Rev. Sociol.* 23:191–214

Helmreich EC. 1979. *Church and State in Europe, 1864–1914.* St. Louis: Forum

Höllinger F. 1996. *Volksreligion und Herrschaftskirche. Die Würzeln Religiösen Verhaltens in Westlichen Gesellschaften.* Opladen: Leske und Budrich

Holifield EB. 1994. Towards a history of American congregations. In *American Congregations,* Vol. 2: *New Perspectives in the Study of Congregations,* ed. JP Wind, JW Lewis, pp. 23–53. Chicago: Univ. Chicago Press

Hull BB, Bold F. 1998. Product variety in religious markets. *Rev. Soc. Econ.* 56:1-1-9

Inglehart R, Baker WE. 2000. Modernization, cultural change, and the persistance of traditional values. *Am. Sociol. Rev.* 65:19–51

Iannaccone LR. 1991. The consequences of religious market structure. *Ration. Soc.* 3:156–77

Iannaccone LR, Finke R, Stark R. 1997. Deregulating religion: the economics of church and state. *Econ. Inq.* 35:350–64

Johnson CD. 1995. Supply-side and demand-side revivalism? Evaluating the social influences on New York state evangelism in the 1830s. *Soc. Sci. Hist.* 19:1–30

Klueting H. 1989. *Das Konfessionelle Zeitalter, 1525–1648.* Stuttgart: Ulmer

Land KC, Deane G, Blau JR. 1991. Religious pluralism and church membership: a spatial diffusion model. *Am. Sociol. Rev.* 56:237–49

Lechner FJ. 1996. Secularization in the Netherlands? *J. Sci. Study Relig.* 35:252–64

Lecler J. 1955. *Histoire de la Tolérance au Siècle de la Réforme.* Paris: Aubier

Martin D. 1978. *A General Theory of Secularization.* Oxford: Blackwell

McLeod H. 1996. *Religion and Society in England, 1850–1914.* New York: St. Martin's

Michelat G, et al. 1991. *Les Français, Sont-ils Encore Catholiques?: Analyse d'un Sondage d'Opinion.* Paris: Editions du Cerf

Mola AA, ed. 1993. *Stato, Chiesa e Società: in Italia, Francia, Belgio e Spagna nei Secoli XIX-XX*. Foggia: Bastogi

Monter W. 1984. *Ritual, Myth, and Magic in Early Modern Europe*. Athens, OH: Ohio Univ. Press

Oakley F. 1979. *The Western Church in the Later Middle Ages*. Ithaca: Cornell Univ. Press

Olin JC. 1992. *The Catholic Reformation: Savonarola to Ignatius Loyola: Reform in the Church, 1495–1540*. New York: Fordham Univ. Press

Olson DVA. 1998a. Religious pluralism in contemporary U.S. counties. *Am. Sociol. Rev.* 63:759–61

Olson DVA. 1998b. *The influence of religious pluralism on close social ties and religious involvement*. Presented at Annu. Meet. Soc. Sci. Study Relig., Montreal

Olson DVA. 1999. Religious pluralism and U.S. church membership: a reassessment. *Sociol. Relig.* 60:149–73

Olson DVA, Hadaway CK. 1999. Religious pluralism and affiliation among Canadian counties and cities. *J. Sci. Study Relig.* 38:490–508

Perl P, Olson DVA. 2000. Religious market share and intensity of church involvement in five denominations. *J. Sci. Study Relig.* 39:12–31

Pettersson T, Hamberg EM. 1997. Denominational pluralism and church membership in contemporary Sweden: a longitudinal study of the period, 1974–1995. *J. Emp. Theol.* 10:61–78

Phillips R. 1998. Religious market share and Mormon church activity. *Sociol. Relig.* 59:117–30

Smith C, Emerson M, Gallagher S, Kennedy P, Sikkink D. 1998. *American Evangelicalism: Embattled and Thriving*. Chicago: Univ. Chicago Press

Stark R, Finke R, Iannaccone LR. 1995. Pluralism and piety: England and Wales, 1851. *J. Sci. Study Relig.* 36:431–44

Stark R, Iannaccone LR. 1994. A supply-side reinterpretation of the 'secularization' of Europe. *J. Sci. Study Relig.* 33:230–52

Stark R, Iannaccone LR. 1996. Response to Lechner: recent religious declines in Quebec, Poland, and the Netherlands: a theory vindicated. *J. Sci. Study Relig.* 35:265–71

Stark R, McCann JC. 1993. Market forces and Catholic commitment: exploring the new paradigm. *J. Sci. Study Relig.* 32:111–124

Thomas K. 1971. *Religion and the Decline of Magic*. London: Weidenfeld & Nicolson

Verweij J, Ester P, Nauta R. 1997. Secularization as an economic and cultural phenomenon: a cross-national analysis. *J. Sci. Study Relig.* 36:309–24

Warner RS. 1993. Work in progress toward a new paradigm for the sociological study of religion in the United States. *Am. J. Sociol.* 98:1044–93

Welch MR. 1993. Participation and commitment among American Catholic parishioners. In *Church and Denominational Growth*, ed. DA Roozen, CK Hadaway, pp. 324–45. Nashville: Abingdon

Zaleski PA, Zech CE. 1995. The effect of religious market competition on church giving. *Rev. Social Econ.* 53:350–67

Annu. Rev. Sociol. 2001. 27:283–305

COLLECTIVE IDENTITY AND SOCIAL MOVEMENTS

Francesca Polletta[1] and James M. Jasper[2]

[1]*Department of Sociology, Columbia University, 510 Fayerweather, New York, NY 10027; e-mail: Fap8@columbia.edu*
[2]*346 West 15ᵗʰ Street, New York, NY 10011; e-mail: jmjasper@juno.com*

Key Words   politics, protest, culture, group boundaries

■ **Abstract**   Sociologists have turned to collective identity to fill gaps in resource mobilization and political process accounts of the emergence, trajectories, and impacts of social movements. Collective identity has been treated as an alternative to structurally given interests in accounting for the claims on behalf of which people mobilize, an alternative to selective incentives in understanding why people participate, an alternative to instrumental rationality in explaining what tactical choices activists make, and an alternative to institutional reforms in assessing movements' impacts. Collective identity has been treated both too broadly and too narrowly, sometimes applied to too many dynamics, at other times made into a residual category within structuralist, state-centered, and rationalist accounts.

INTRODUCTION

Recent trends both inside and outside the academy have revived interest in collective identity. In the 1980s, battles over college curricula, multiculturalism, and affirmative action were both justified and attacked as "identity politics." Among gay and lesbian and feminist groups and movements for ethnic and racial justice, efforts to contest cultural representations and to celebrate alternative identities vied with more traditional strategies such as litigation and lobbying. Collective identity was hard to miss, and its prominence in contemporary movements encouraged sociologists to assess its role in all movements, new and old.

Sociologists of social movements have also been attracted to collective identity as a response to gaps in dominant resource mobilization and political process models. Those models sought to counter earlier collective behaviorist views of protesters as irrational individuals propelled into protest by crowd contagion or system strain. Mobilization and process theorists focused rather on the structural shifts that gave collective actors the resources to act collectively on longstanding grievances. But their emphasis on the how of mobilization over the why of it, their focus on the state as target of action, and their dependence on rationalistic images of individual action left important issues unexamined.

0360-0572/01/0811-0283$14.00

In response to these limitations, scholars turned to collective identity to answer four kinds of questions. One was why collective actors come into being when they do. Resource mobilization and political process theorists cut their teeth on the American civil rights movement, where the fact that insurgents had grievances was not particularly mysterious; the challenge was rather to explain how they secured the resources to do something collectively about those grievances. But in other movements, the very fact that a group formed around an issue demanded explanation. For example, why has abortion provoked such intense mobilization in this country and not in Europe? Focusing on identity seemed a way to explain how interests emerged rather than taking them as given. By examining the formation of collective identities, scholars would shed light on the macrohistorical context within which movements emerge.

A second challenging question had to do with people's motivations to act. Even with an acknowledged interest in an issue, of course, people often opt to free ride. But those who do participate usually do so in the absence of selective incentives or coercion, Olson's (1965) solutions to the free-rider dilemma. Collective identity seemed to capture better the pleasures and obligations that actually persuade people to mobilize. Identity was appealing, then, as an alternative to material incentives.

A third question neglected by mainstream models had to do with movements' strategic choices. If people choose to participate because doing so accords with who they are, the forms of protest they choose are also influenced by collective identities. Models of strategic choice that had movement leaders selecting among strategies, tactics, and organizational forms by instrumentally assessing environmental opportunities and constraints missed the fact that strategic options may also be intrinsically appealing. They reflect what we believe, what we are comfortable with, what we like, who we are. Collective identity thus responded to the inadequacies of instrumental rationality as an explanation for strategic choice. Finally, collective identity has been a way to get at the cultural effects of social movements. Dominant models of collective action have been better at measuring movement outcomes such as policy reform or expanded political representation than at gauging impacts outside the formal political sphere. But movements also transform cultural representations, social norms—how groups see themselves and are seen by others. Changes in collective identity captured movement impacts beyond institutional reform.

The questions that prompted social movement scholars to theorize about collective identity are important, and they have generated strong claims about the role of collective identity in movements' emergence, trajectories, and outcomes. Indeed we argue that collective identity has been forced to do too much analytically. The term has been used to describe many different dimensions and dynamics of social protest: the social categories predominating among activists (say "women" or "animal rights activists"), public representations of social categories (what Johnston et al 1994 refer to as "public identities"), activists' shared definition of their situation, the expressive character of all action, the affective bonds that motivate participation, the experience of solidarity within movements, and others. As a result of this definitional catholicity, key questions have been obscured. To what extent are collective identities constructed in and through protest rather than preceding it? Is the identity a group projects publicly the same one that its members experience? Are collective identities imposed on groups or invented by them? Do individuals choose collective identities to maximize their self-interest or do interests flow from identities? How is collective identity different from ideology? From interest? From solidarity?

To avoid overextension of the concept, we have defined collective identity as an individual's cognitive, moral, and emotional connection with a broader community, category, practice, or institution. It is a perception of a shared status or relation, which may be imagined rather than experienced directly, and it is distinct from personal identities, although it may form part of a personal identity. A collective identity may have been first constructed by outsiders (for example, as in the case of "Hispanics" in this country), who may still enforce it, but it depends on some acceptance by those to whom it is applied. Collective identities are expressed in cultural materials—names, narratives, symbols, verbal styles, rituals, clothing, and so on—but not all cultural materials express collective identities. Collective identity does not imply the rational calculus for evaluating choices that "interest" does. And unlike ideology, collective identity carries with it positive feelings for other members of the group.

There is another problem common in recent analyses. In relying on collective identity to fill the gaps in structuralist, rational-actor, and state-centered models, that is, to explain the processes those models miss, scholars have sometimes neglected the role collective identity plays in the processes those models foreground. They have turned identity into a kind of residual category, describing what happens outside structures, outside the state, outside rational action. We are not arguing for simply reversing the causal arrow, so that collective identities as cultural constructions determine interests, relations, and structures [a claim made by some post-structuralist analyses, for example, by Laclau & Mouffe (1985) and Joyce (1994)]. The best recent research, we believe, avoids a priori assumptions about causal mechanisms and allows for a number of different relationships between cultural and discursive practices on the one hand, and legal, political, economic, and social structures on the other. The analytical challenge is to identify the circumstances in which different relations between interest and identity, strategy and identity, and politics and identity operate, circumstances that include cultural processes as well as structural ones.

In the following, we examine the role of identity in four phases of protest: the creation of collective claims, recruitment into movements, strategic and tactical decision making, and movement outcomes. Because the scholarship that bears on collective identity and social movements is huge and spans numerous disciplines (sociology, political science, psychology, law, anthropology, women's studies, queer theory, and others), we concentrate on sociological treatments except where work in other disciplines promises to fill gaps in sociological models.

We omit discussions of class and national identities (for treatments of these, see Calhoun 1993, Cerulo 1997, Hanagan 1994, Krinsky 1999); as well as discussions of the relationship between personal and collective identities (see Goffman 1959, Holstein & Miller 1990, McCall & Simmons 1978, Jenkins 1996; for reviews of identity and social movements generally, see Johnston et al 1994, Hunt et al 1994, Krinsky 1999, Snow & McAdam 2000, Snow 2001). We try to address a range of movement dynamics in which identity may operate rather than covering every important work in the field.

MOVEMENT EMERGENCE: IDENTITY AND INTEREST

Why do movements emerge when they do? In the 1970s, resource mobilization and political process theorists stopped asking why people felt frustrated enough to engage in collective protest rather than organize through conventional political channels, and instead asked when and how they secured the resources to combat their exclusion from those channels. Collective actors' "interests" were implied by the very formulation; they lay in gaining access to the stable structure of political bargaining (Gamson 1975, Tilly 1978, McAdam 1982). Collective interests were taken to be longstanding: The model presumed an already-existing collective actor able to recognize the opening of political opportunities and to mobilize indigenous resources for political purposes.

That presumption was challenged by scholars of the "new social movements," the protests around peace, nuclear energy, local autonomy, homosexuality, and feminism that seemed to be displacing class-based political mobilization in Western Europe in the 1970s and 1980s (Touraine 1981, 1985, Melucci 1985, 1989, Offe 1985, Castells 1997, Laclau & Mouffe 1985, Cohen 1985, as well as Laraña et al's 1994 overview). New social movement theorists argued that participation in such movements could not be predicted by class location. Nor were participants seeking to gain political and economic concessions from institutional actors, to further their "interests" in conventional terms. Rather they sought recognition for new identities and lifestyles.

New social movement theorists saw a profoundly changed social formation behind these novel forms of collective action, variously dubbed "postindustrial," "programmed" (Touraine 1981), "information" (Melucci 1996), or "network" (Castells 1997) society. In Melucci's (1996) account, "modernization" has required that people be capable of processing the informational resources on which societies now depend, but expanded individual autonomy has been accompanied by strong pressures toward normative conformity. Social control has come to operate simultaneously through self-regulation and through the increasing penetration of standards of instrumental rationality into people's biological and emotional lives. As a result, protestors have been less likely to seek a redistribution of political power than to seek to change dominant normative and cultural codes by gaining recognition for new identities (see also Pizzorno 1978).

New social movement theories proved better at raising questions about the sources of movement identities than at answering them. Their explanations for how shifts in material production have affected social movements were not entirely clear and sometimes risked tautology, with new social movements taken as both evidence and consequence of a new social formation (see Touraine 1981 and Cohen's 1985 critique). Empirically, moreover, most new social movements have combined political goals with more culturally oriented efforts. However, new social movement theorists' arguments were provocative, and they did encourage sociologists to highlight identity-construction processes in older, class-based social movements—if only to rebut the claimed novelty of their successors (Calhoun 1995, Plotke 1990, Buechler 1990). Sociologists sympathetic to political process approaches also began to use collective identity to explain "how structural inequality gets translated into subjective discontent" (Taylor & Whittier 1992:104; see also Morris 1992, Mueller 1992).

Other scholars have agreed with new social movement theorists' claim that efforts to define, celebrate, enact, and deconstruct identity are more important in recent movements than they have been in the past, but have sought different explanations for that fact. Jasper (1997), for example, points to legal inclusion as a key distinction. Unlike the civil rights and early labor movements, which pursued full inclusion as citizens, post-citizenship movements are peopled by those who already enjoy most or all of the normal rights of citizens, including the ability to mobilize legally and to put pressure on political decision makers. Participants in these movements do not usually have an identity imposed on them by the political and legal systems; accordingly, they have more freedom to engage in creative reformulations of who they are.

New social movement theorists' determination to historicize a contemporary repertoire of protest has also encouraged efforts to account in macrohistorical terms for the construction of contentious identities. Some authors have looked to large-scale processes such as industrialization, urbanization, and state consolidation, as well as to the ascendance of new cognitive paradigms, to explain how particular identities become the basis for exclusion and/or discrimination but also for mobilization. For example, D'Emilio (1983) traces the emergence of a "homosexual" identity to the processes of urbanization and industrialization that made possible an autonomous personal life. Same-sex sex has always existed and, indeed, has often been severely punished, D'Emilio points out, but it was only at the beginning of this century that it became not just a deviant, immoral, illegal act but a deviant identity. A homosexual was a person whose nature—acts, feelings, personal traits, even body type—was sharply distinguishable from "normal" heterosexuals. That shift, aided by a new psychiatric model of homosexuality, made possible both heightened repression (one could now be fired or prosecuted as a homosexual whether or not one had engaged in sex), and the creation of a homosexual collective actor.

In a comparable dynamic, the legal institutionalization of racial privilege in the United States and South Africa generated severe and pervasive inequality *and* eventually provided the basis for demands by blacks for legal equality. By contrast, the absence of legalized racial categories, agencies, and statistics in Brazil impeded black mobilization (Marx 1998). Tilly (1998) attributes the rise of identity politics in nineteenth century Britain—the eclipse of local identities like spinner, neighbor, or tenant of a particular landlord by broader identities such as "citizen" and "worker"—to the increased salience of the national state in people's lives and the new patterns of claimsmaking that resulted. Rather than appealing to a powerful patron or unleashing their rage directly on the object of their dissatisfaction, claimsmakers increasingly made public demonstrations of their numbers and commitment to bid for participation in a national polity. "They declared 'We exist and have a right to exist. We have strength, coherence, and determination. National politics must take us into account'" (1998:14). Together, these analyses challenge views of race and homosexuality as transhistorical "natural" identities.

To explain the creation of mobilizing identities, several authors have turned to network analysis. They argue that such identities come not from fixed categories like race, class, gender, or nation, but from common positions in networks, whether networks of patronage (Gould 1998), urban residence (Gould 1995), or political affiliation (Mische 1996). For example, Gould (1998) argues that the leaders of the 1794 Whiskey Rebellion in Western Pennsylvania differed from other members of the political elite in only one respect: At a time when power was shifting to federal authorities and the eastern establishment, these power brokers sought to preserve their relationships with both western clients and eastern patrons. By leading an insurgency, even one likely to fail, they communicated to clients their willingness to champion their interests, even while suggesting to eastern elites that they were trying to stave off even greater civil war by assuming the leadership of a band of angry farmers. "Political identifications are not merely constrained by networks of social ties, in the sense that network position helps to determine which of a variety of exogenously available self-understandings an individual might embrace; in this instance, at least, the relevant identification was defined *in terms* of the network" (38).

Other authors have focused instead on the institutional contexts within which new identities are forged. Concepts of "submerged networks" (Melucci 1989, Mueller 1994), "halfway houses" (Morris 1984), "free spaces" (Evans & Boyte 1986), "havens" (Hirsch 1990a), "sequestered social sites" (Scott 1990), and "abeyance structures" (Rupp & Taylor 1987) describe institutions removed from the physical and ideological control of those in power, for example the black church before the civil rights movement (Morris 1984) and literary circles in communist Eastern Europe (Johnston 1998). Such institutions supply the solidary incentives that encourage movement participation, but they also represent a "free space" in which people can develop counterhegemonic ideas and oppositional identities. Why do such sites facilitate the development of oppositional identities? Some authors suggest that it is simply their distance from the physical coercion and ideological control of those in power (Hirsch 1990a). Others suggest that is rather the belief systems that are institutionalized in such sites that are important (Polletta 1999).

The latter dovetails with perspectives that give culture an independent role in constituting the collective identities around which people mobilize. In other words, what emerges from "free spaces" may not match up with "objective" categories of structurally derived interests. What "worker" or "citizen" or "African American" means, and what behavioral expectations it entails, are partly a function of the vocabularies, stories, and images available. Somers & Gibson (1994: 67) argue that people's experiences as workers, for instance, "were inextricably interconnected with the larger matrix of relations that shaped their lives—their regional location, the practical workings of the legal system, family patterns—as well as the particular stories (of honor, of ethnicity, of gender, of local community, of greed, etc.) used to account for the events happening to them." (See also Somers 1994, Steinberg 1996.) The categories that emerge from such processes make for diverse movements. For example, labels such as "worker" or the "working class" have promoted more pugnaciously anti-bourgeois labor movements than have labels like "citizen" or "the people," which encourage cross-class alliances (Sewell 1980).

Rather than reading off interests and identities from allegedly transparent structural positions, recent works have (*a*) revealed the historical construction of what seem "natural" identities such as "working class," "black," and "homosexual;" (*b*) advanced more sophisticated models of how the social, economic, and political relations in which people participate generate mobilizing identities; (*c*) recognized the independent role of culture in shaping the collective identities on behalf of which people make claims; and (*d*) identified the political conditions in which identity claims are likely to be prominent in movements.

Once movements have emerged, complete with organizations, organizers, and recruitment campaigns, strategic efforts to craft mobilizing identities become important. Even identities that are familiar, longstanding, and enforced by law and custom frequently need to be re-imagined by movement activists. At the very least, they must be integrated with a *movement* identity, i.e. a collective identity based on shared membership in a movement. We now turn to these efforts.

RECRUITMENT AND COMMITMENT: IDENTITY AND INCENTIVE

Why will people join collective efforts when they don't know whether their presence will do any good and they do know that they can ride free on the efforts of others? Sociologists have devoted a great deal of attention to this question, posed first by Olson (1965). He argued that shared interests are simply not enough to motivate individual effort in the absence of selective rewards that go only to participants. But as Fireman & Gamson (1979) and others have pointed out, individuals share prior bonds with others that make solidaristic behavior a reasonable expectation. "A person whose life is intertwined with the group [through friendship, kinship, organizational membership, informal support networks, or shared relations with outsiders] . . . has a big stake in the group's fate. When collective action is urgent, the person is likely to contribute his or her share even if the impact of that share is not noticeable" (22).

Activists are not the isolated, atomistic individuals sociologists once took them for. In many movements ranging from the French commune (Gould 1995) and the Russian revolution (Bonnell 1983) to Nichiren Shoshu Buddhism (Snow et al 1980) and the 1964 Mississippi Summer Project (McAdam & Paulsen 1993), recruitment has taken place primarily through preexisting solidarities (see also Marwell & Oliver 1993, Oberschall 1973, Tilly 1978). In these cases, prior ties motivated participation through norms of obligation and reciprocity. "Collective identity," for some authors, is shorthand for the affective connections one has to members of a group that oblige one to protest along with or on behalf of them.

However, this "loyalty" formulation raises a number of questions. First, what is the content of those ties? Does collective identity consist mainly of moral obligation, altruism, and personal loyalty, or can it be self-interested concern with the opinion of others? Instead of affective obligations, Chong (1991:50) argues that self-interested "reputational concerns" motivate participation. Since "people expect consistency from us, we tend to oblige by forging and living up to our reputations. And as Socrates advised, the easiest way to maintain a reputation is to become the person you want others to think you are." Participation is a rational bid to gain the benefits that accrue to those who share a collective identity. Friedman & McAdam (1992) similarly connect collective identity to self-oriented rational action. Highly regarded roles within communities may come to be linked with activism in a way that makes participation a requirement of that role. In the early civil rights movement, activism was linked with—normatively required of—churchgoers; in 1960, *student* became linked to activist, became a "prized social identity" which supplied the selective incentives to participate. But arguments like these, designed to show that cultural meanings and emotions are not logically incompatible with rational-actor models, yield convoluted causal pictures: We try to become an altruistic person because it is in our interest to seem one, yet it is hard to seem one without actually being one. Why not simply admit the emotional satisfactions of collective identity (Jasper 1997:23–29)?

Teske (1997:121) mediates between the loyalty and self-interest models, arguing that we err in seeing self-interested and moral action as opposed. Activism for many people is a way to construct a desirable self. They decide to participate "neither primarily on a quasi-quantitative calculating of costs and benefits, as in the rational choice approach to politics, nor on altruistic impulses .... Rather, identity construction points to the qualitative concerns and the desires activists have that certain qualities be instantiated in their actions and lives" (see also C. Taylor 1989). Lichterman (1996) makes a similar argument but historicizes it. Lacking the connection to unifying ideological traditions like the revolutionary left or religious radicalism, post-1960s activists turned instead to a "personalized politics" in which the individual self is the arbiter of moral choices. This isn't narcissism, Lichterman insists: a self-oriented politics can nurture rather than curb civic engagement. An activist collective identity, these models imply, can be a satisfying aspect of personal identity.

A second question for the loyalty model is whether collective identities necessarily precede mobilization. Some movements seem to attract participants even in the absence of prior identities and networks (Jasper & Poulsen 1995). "Moral shocks" produced, for example, by a photograph of a tortured animal or the disaster at Three Mile Island can mobilize people who do not know each other or the organizers (Jasper 1997). Participants may share demographic or economic traits—they tend to be middle class, say, or are mostly men—but these do not add up to a perception of the preexisting "groupness" of collective identity. Their political activity itself provides that kind of solidarity: We are student radicals, we are people who care about the environment, we are caring, critical citizens. These "movement identities" may come to serve much the same function as a preexisting collective identity [Jasper 1997; Klandermans's (1997:95) concept of "commitment," Hirsch's (1990b) of "solidarity;" and Buechler's (1990) social movement "community" seem functional equivalents of movement identity]. Minkoff (1997) argues that many collective actors such as women, the elderly, gays and lesbians, and the disabled have initially lacked the institutional infrastructures that have put members of other groups into regular day-to-day contact. In the absence of such infrastructures, movement organizations have generated the collective identities that then created network ties.

Since mobilization does not always require preexisting collective identities, activists' efforts to strategically "frame" identities are critical in recruiting participants. "Frames" are the interpretive packages that activists develop to mobilize potential adherents and constituents (Snow et al 1986, Gamson 1988, Snow & Benford 1988, Benford 1993, Tarrow 1998). When successful, frames make a compelling case for the "injustice" of the condition and the likely effectiveness of collective "agency" in changing that condition. They also make clear the "identities" of the contenders, distinguishing "us" from "them" and depicting antagonists as human decision makers rather than impersonal forces such as urbanization (Gamson 1988, 1992, also Hunt & Benford 1994, Hunt et al 1994, Klandermans 1997). Organizers often try to build a movement identity on another, independent collective identity [which may come from prior activism as well as from racial and other ascribed identities (Jasper 1997:ch. 8)]. ACT UP, for instance, sought to convince lesbians and gay men that protest around AIDS was an essential expression of their gay identity.

While organizers use considerable creativity in inventing new identities or attaching new behavioral requirements to old ones, such processes may also occur independently of organizers' strategic efforts. Polletta (1998a,b) found that the *stories* told by student protesters in the 1960 lunch counter sit-ins helped to forge an action-mobilizing collective identity. Students' accounts turned unfamiliar and potentially disturbing events into familiar epics of overcoming, with frightened students becoming triumphant heroes (see also Hirsch 1990b and Fantasia 1988 on how collective identities are developed in and through protest).

Beyond recruitment, identity work is crucial to sustaining solidarity and commitment. Taylor & Whittier (1992) show how boundary-setting rituals and institutions that separate challengers from those in power can strengthen internal solidarity; they call this solidarity "collective identity." But there are liabilities to strong and exclusive formulations of identity. Many groups are torn between asserting a clear identity and deconstructing it, revealing it to be unstable, fluid, and constructed (J. Gamson 1995; see also Epstein 1987, Seidman 1993, Phelan 1989, Fuss 1989). Where some members may see destabilizing a collective identity as an important goal in and of itself, with ramifications beyond the group, others may understandably see it as a threat to group unity or as confusing to the public (we return to this issue in our discussion of identity as a strategy of social protest).

If identities play a critical role in mobilizing and sustaining participation, they also help explain people's exodus from a movement. One of the chief causes of movement decline is that collective identity stops lining up with the movement. We stop believing that the movement "represents" us (the term suggests an expressive dimension as well as a strategic one). In some cases, cross-cutting identities come to the fore, just as the women's movement came to grief partly on the shoals of class and race [Echols 1989; Robnett (1997) shows, however, that cross-cutting identities are not inherently contradictory]. In other cases, people begin to see their identities as sufficiently represented in conventional political or nonpolitical arenas.

, In sum, any social movement group must continually manage its collective identities, and even identities predating movements are subjected to reconstruction. Organizers often concentrate on recasting constituents' identities to include participation as one of the responsibilities or benefits of group membership. Identities need to be integrated with injustice and agency frames so as to clearly distinguish "us" from opponents and bystanders. Finally, sustaining participants' commitment over time requires ritualized reassertions of collective identity and efforts to manage, without suppressing, difference. But in addition to identity management as an internally directed tactic, movement leaders use identity in a number of tactics oriented toward the world outside the movement, as we now examine.

TACTICAL CHOICE: IDENTITY AND STRATEGY

How do activists choose from among the strategies, tactics, targets, organizational forms, and deliberative styles available to them? Early resource mobilization and political process accounts tended to rely on a classically rational model of decision making to answer that question: activists adapt strategies to environmental constraints and opportunities on the basis of a cost-benefit calculus (Barkan 1979, Kitschelt 1986, McAdam et al 1988). Critics have pointed out, however, that activists also choose options that conform to "who we are," as pacifists, say, or women, or revolutionaries. Making decisions on the basis of collective identity has been treated accordingly as an alternative to relying on instrumental criteria; it reflects an expressive rather than a strategic logic. There are two other ways of relating strategy to identity, however. Rather than viewing it as at odds with strategy, making identity claims can be seen *as* a protest strategy. And rather than viewing an instrumental logic operating exclusive of identity concerns, we can see that instrumental calculation often depends on the collective identities that are widely associated with particular strategies, tactics, organizational forms, and even deliberative logics. We take up these three approaches in turn.

Collective identities can supply criteria for making decisions that compete with instrumentally rational ones. For example, members of the antinuclear Clamshell Alliance saw themselves both as an "opponent" of the atomic-industrial establishment, dedicated to stopping nuclear power, and its "opposite," seeking to eradicate domination within their own operation (Downey 1986, Epstein 1991). The latter identity was responsible for the Clamshell's distinctive strategies of consensus decision making and nonviolent civil disobedience, as well as for the organization's eventual demise as the increasingly heterogeneous group was paralyzed by the requirement of consensus. But to suspend the consensus requirement would have been, for many, to destroy the group's identity. For the "Green" environmental activists that Lichterman (1996) studied, sustaining the organizations that made up the movement was not of paramount concern. They would rather see an organization collapse than compromise their overriding commitments to democratic process. None of these activists abjure considerations of instrumental efficacy; they seek rather to balance them with the principled commitments that define who they are. Strategic choices are not simply neutral decisions about what will be most effective, in this view; they are statements about identity (see also Kleinman 1996).

People develop a "taste" for certain tactics, partly independently of their efficacy in attaining formal external goals (Jasper 1997). Some may enjoy staying within the bounds of legality, others stepping outside them. Some may pride themselves on their moderate demands and tactics, others on being avant-garde or radical. They may develop collective identities based on those tactical tastes. Tactical and organizational identities often coincide, as organizations embody forms of action. "Organizational forms may be a source of shared identity," says Clemens (1997:50). "The answer to 'who are we?' need not be a quality or noun; 'we are people who do these sorts of things in this particular way' can be equally compelling." Important to understanding tactical choice within movements is the operation of numerous identities, with varying salience. Activists may identify primarily with a movement organization, affinity group, style of protest, or degree of moderation or radicalism. Jasper (1997), for instance, distinguishes among "activist," "organizational," and "tactical" identities. The first involves a history of political activity that is usually broader than a specific movement. An organizational identity involves loyalty to a single organization and its fellow members, even something as small as an affinity group. Those with tactical identities may define themselves as on the cutting edge, or they may be proud of particular styles of action such as nonviolence or civil disobedience. Such identities may exist alongside both movement identities and preexisting collective identities, interweaving with them in complex ways. An individual might identify herself as a nonviolent feminist, ecological activist, and member of the affinity group "Matrix," each of these labels carrying an identification with some broader collectivity. In a similar scheme, Gamson (1991) distinguishes between solidary, movement, and organizational identities.

Tactical tastes may originate in collective identities that exist outside and prior to the movement (Ennis 1987) or within it. Whittier (1995) describes "micro-cohorts" in the women's movement of Columbus, Ohio: groups who entered radical feminist organizations together every year or two. Their experiences before they entered the movement and within it provided a collective identity and frame of reference for their understandings of feminism and politics, and a basis for their strategic preferences. Other accounts of the Clamshell Alliance have attributed its decline not so much to the "egalitarian/instrumental" tension that Downey describes as to an old guard/new guard conflict whereby newer members of the organization bid for status within the group by challenging veterans' commitment to fully democratic practices (Cohen 1988). In this case, as in Ross's (1983) description of battles in Students for a Democratic Society over organizational structure, tactical preferences and the collective identities they expressed originated not in newcomers' prior experiences but in and through a shared experience of marginality in the organization.

In a second approach, sociologists have shown how activists construct, deconstruct, celebrate, and enact collective identities as strategies of protest. For East German challengers to the Honecker regime in 1989, calling themselves "the people" not only inspired greater participation than if they had used some other label but prevented a regime that also associated itself with "the people" from attacking them as outsiders. It may also have discouraged police repression (Pfaff 1996). In this case, insurgents' public construction of their identity limited the actions that their opponents could take.

Activists may define their identities in different ways depending on the strategic situation. If they are representing their group to a public audience, they may cast themselves as more unified and more homogeneous than they would in a setting of fellow activists. Pulido (1996) found that nonwhite environmental-justice activists routinely invoked "people of color" as a primary identity when targeting the state or a polluter but narrower racial and ethnic identifications in their internal movement deliberations. Their identities, she concludes, were "situational" (see also Lichterman 1999). Another factor in determining how a group strategically constructs its identity may be the kind of opposition it confronts. Bernstein (1997) found that gay and lesbian activists campaigning for antidiscrimination statutes deployed strategies of "identity for critique," in which they castigated the homophobic practices of mainstream society, when they faced organized opposition and when they were led by exclusive organizations uninterested in coalition-building. By contrast, movements with strong organizational infrastructures or access to political decision makers tended to seek policy change and emphasize their similarities to the majority, using less controversial strategies of "identity for education," in which they suppressed rather than celebrated their differences from the mainstream.

As Bernstein's work indicates, movement leaders must strategize not only against single opponents, but within a "multiorganizational field" of allied, competing, and oppositional movement organizations, authorities, media, and funders (Hunt et al 1994, Gamson 1988, Klandermans 1997). What is the relationship between this organizational context and the identities that operate within it? Carroll & Ratner (1996) argue that certain broad identities, for example that of a victim of materially grounded injustice, are able to link diverse organizations. Does it work the other way? Are organizationally diverse movements better able to develop encompassing identities? Ferree & Roth's (1998) study of a failed strike by German day-care workers shows that the organizational insularity of potential coalition partners such as unions, women in the governing legislative coalition, and grassroots feminists led them to see day care workers as "difficult and different" (643) from their usual constituencies rather than as offering an opportunity to develop new allies. The predominance of "exclusionary" identities discouraging a coalition, in turn, resulted from the lack of organizational linkages to other movements (see also Gordon & Jasper 1996). The same kind of dynamic can operate within a movement group. Roth (1998) found that the existence of a feminist caucus within an ACT UP group effectively "compartmentalized" women's issues to the caucus because no one else would deal with them. Tarrow (1998:ch. 7) argues that movements at the end of protest cycles (presumably, any movement with dwindling appeal) often compensate for their lack of membership, allies, and broad appeal by defining their identities narrowly and rejecting alliances as "selling out" (see also Gitlin 1995). Such exclusiveness can help to sustain the commitment of the remaining stalwarts.

How successfully groups frame their identities for the public thus affects their ability to recruit members and supporters, gain a public hearing, make alliances with other groups, and defuse opposition. The studies we have cited indicate that how a group frames its identity (exclusive or inclusive, involuntary or chosen, challenging or conventional) depends on the setting and the audience to which it is speaking, the kind of opposition it confronts, and the organizational linkages it has to other groups and movements.

A third approach to the relations between identity and strategic choice breaks with a view of activists trying to juggle strategic imperatives and identity concerns by pointing to the ways that identity informs even the most self-consciously strategic calculation. Collective identities are already embedded in strategies, tactics, claims, organizational forms, and deliberative styles, and they influence how such options can be used. "Embedded in" can mean different things, though. For example, activists seeking legal change on behalf of women and minorities often struggle to decide whether to play up or down the differences on which their disadvantages rest. Discrimination cases brought by women have been limited by the implicitly male standard to which they must analogize their own situation. "Difference," whether it is the biological capacity to get pregnant (Scott 1988) or a dislike for high-pressure sales jobs (Scott 1988, Milkman 1986), is seen as "deviance," and activists must decide between the equally unacceptable alternatives of trying to be "like" men or to justify "special" treatment with its implications of inferiority. Groups' strategic efforts are thus constrained not only by their own perceived identities but by the definitions contained in not very objective but legally enforced definitions of equality: male, white, able-bodied, heterosexual, and so on (Minow 1990, Crenshaw 1990).

Clemens (1997) depicts a less formal process. Certain organizational forms have been widely seen as "appropriate for women" or "middle-class," in a way that influences who may legitimately use them. More broadly, our very conceptions of what is instrumental, strategic, efficacious, and political rest on the identities with which they are associated. For example, Bordt (1997) shows how collectivist styles of organization came to be seen in the 1970s as feminist in a way that made their adoption by new feminist groups a matter of common sense. Earlier, the same forms had come to be seen as white in the southern civil rights movement and, for that reason, had become increasingly unappealing to African Americans (Polletta 1997). This line of inquiry meshes with recent neo-institutionalist theorizing on organizations' propensity to mimic organizational forms that are widely seen as cutting edge (DiMaggio & Powell 1991). The question that neoinstitutionalists have not adequately answered, also relevant to strategic innovation in social movements, is whether such imitation benefits the organization strategically or whether the innovation is assumed to be strategic in the absence of any compelling evidence.

In sum, recent identity arguments reject the commonplace opposition between identity as expressive and strategy as instrumental in order to demonstrate that activists deploy identities strategically and that strategic options have meaning by reference to the groups with which they are identified.

MOVEMENT SUCCESS: IDENTITY AS OUTCOME

How successful are movements? And how do they affect individuals, groups, and broader structures? In accounting for movement outcomes, theorists have tended to treat identity under the heading of cultural impacts rather than institutional ones. Yet there are many kinds of movement impacts—institutional and extra-institutional—in which identity plays a role. In some cases, the impact is intended, in others, a byproduct of other aims.

First, changing identities is often a primary movement goal. This may be clearest in religious or self-help movements, but many movements have it as one goal alongside others. The development of group pride is a form of identity work. Identity talk within movements may be aimed not only at building solidarity but also at changing selves and relationships in ways that extend beyond the movement (Lichterman 1999, Breines 1989, Epstein 1991).

Second, participation usually transforms activists' subsequent biographies, marking their personal identities even after the movement ends, whether or not this is an explicit goal (McAdam 1988, Fendrich 1993, Rogers 1993, Andrews 1991, Whalen & Flacks 1989, Taylor & Raeburn 1995, Whittier 1995). This is not only true of people whose active participation was of long duration or high intensity, but also of many casual participants. Mansbridge (1995), for instance, argues that being a feminist does not require membership in a feminist organization, but only a sense of accountability to an ideal of feminism. Its behavioral requirements differ across social and historical contexts, but the core collective identity continues to shape an individual's sense of self.

Outside of public institutions, identity work within small circles of like-minded people is critical to sustaining "abeyance structures" during periods of limited political opportunities (Taylor 1989, Whittier 1995). Identities nurtured within these networks contribute to the spillover effect from one movement to another (McAdam 1994, Meyer & Whittier 1994, Tracy 1996). Broad identities such as radical pacifist or anarchist can also be preserved in popular cultural materials rather than organizations, thus becoming available for subsequent waves of protest (Eyerman & Jamison 1998).

Of special interest because it challenges the tendency to separate identity and power orientations (Rucht 1992), demanding recognition for a new or changed identity can both secure concessions and permanently change the terrain of political conflict. Putatively black, or women's or Green interests now have to be reckoned with by policymakers (Mueller 1987, Costain 1988). The formation of women's caucuses, centers, programs, and support groups within mainstream legal, medical, economic, religious, and military institutions has been an enduring outcome of the women's movement (Katzenstein 1998). Scientists in the 1960s who struggled to square their identities as activists and as nonpartisan truth seekers founded public science organizations like the Union for Concerned Scientists and the Center for Science in the Public Interest that continue today (Moore 1996). Collective identities developed within movements may have lasting impact on institutional political arenas and organizational forms.

In another kind of impact, a movement's association in the eyes of the public with a particular strategy, tactic, organizational form, or style can influence subsequent uses of it. When pro-life activists sing "We Shall Overcome," or sit-in at abortion clinics, they benefit from the popular identification of those tactics with the civil rights movement (Eyerman & Jamison 1998). No progressive group today would appropriate the goose step or the swastika. A feminist group that adopted a bureaucratic style of organization would be interpreted as signaling its departure from 1970s feminism—perhaps in its ideological commitments as well as its organizational form (Bordt 1997). Symbols and strategies resonate with the identities of prior users.

Finally, the creation of a strong movement identity usually leads to a backlash, as those portrayed as the enemy may be angered or frightened into counterorganization. Sometimes the countermobilization outstrips the original protest movement. For instance, several years of publicity and victories by the animal rights movement pushed the biomedical community into forging a new (and very effective) public identity for itself, emphasizing aid to sick individuals, especially children, rather than the abstractions of scientific progress (Jasper & Poulsen 1993). The American nuclear power industry, too, began fighting back once it realized it was under attack by a national movement (Jasper 1990:ch 7).

Rather than viewing collective identity exclusively as a kind of cultural movement impact, separated from the domain of institutional impacts like legal reform and policy change, these analyses point to the ways in which newly prominent or reformulated identities can transform the institutional political playing field.

CONCLUSION

What is collective identity? How do collective identities matter to social movements? And what don't we know yet? We conclude with one more cut at these questions.

Collective identity describes imagined as well as concrete communities, involves an act of perception and construction as well as the discovery of preexisting bonds, interests, and boundaries. It is fluid and relational, emerging out of interactions with a number of different audiences (bystanders, allies, opponents, news media, state authorities), rather than fixed. It channels words and actions, enabling some claims and deeds but delegitimating others. It provides categories by which individuals divide up and make sense of the social world.

What is *not* collective identity? Collective identities are in constant interplay with personal identities, but they are never simply the aggregate of individuals' identities. If collective identity describes what makes people occupying a category similar, personal identity is the bundle of traits that we believe make us unique. Nor is collective identity coextensive with culture; there are many cultural meanings that do not imply images of bounded groups. Collective identity is not the same as common ideological commitment. One can join a movement because one shares its goals without identifying much with fellow members (one can even, in some cases, despise them). Likewise, people can develop collective identity on the basis of their distinctive know-how or skills, but such know-how and skills can have influence even in the absence of collective identities around them. Those skilled in explosives may favor bombing as a protest tactic, but this does not necessarily give them a shared collective identity. Movements contain, symbolize, and ritualize all kinds of people and attributes; only some of them are collective actors. Collective identities are one particular form of culture, although they may be built on other forms.

How does collective identity matter to social movements? Paying attention to the causes and consequences of collective identity can move us beyond some theoretical impasses. The proliferation of work on the topic suggests that many sociologists realize as much. But too often collective identity has been invoked simply to fill gaps left by structuralist, state-centered, or rational choice models, in the process reproducing the very dichotomies the concept is supposed to challenge. Specifically, we should not assume that identity is the opposite of interest (with identity-oriented movements opposed to interest-based ones), that it is the opposite of incentives (with self-regarding action contrasted to altruistic action), that it is the opposite of strategy (with expressive criteria for choosing strategies contrasted with instrumental ones), or that it is the opposite of politics (with movement impacts on individual selves contrasted with those on institutional politics). Instead, the work we have highlighted here shows that structural interests are often recent in origin; that we may engage in moral protest to develop the kind of self we want; that what is considered a good strategy is often based on what groups it is symbolically associated with; and that movements promote new identities as a way to gain power as well as transform selves. The most interesting recent work on identity has inquired into the macrostructural processes by which new collective identities develop and into the micro-interactional processes by which people come to see themselves as obliged to protest. It has emphasized organizers' capacity to redefine old identities and create new ones, and the pressures on them to do so.

That said, there is still a lot that we do not know about collective identities. We have little evidence about how individuals sort out and combine different sources of identity, or about the psychological mechanisms behind collective identities. People have a range of groups, roles, and positions available to them, and we know little about how they juggle and choose among them; the relationship between personal and collective identities is a staple of social psychology that students of social movements have yet to incorporate (Tajfel 1981, Stryker 1980, Burke & Reitzes 1991). In addition, we know little about the emotions that accompany and shape collective identity. Collective identity is not simply the drawing of a cognitive boundary; it simultaneously involves a positive affect toward other group members (Jasper 1998).

Taken as a whole, the literature on collective identity still leaves fuzzy the relations between identity and an individual's calculus of self-interest. Is identity or interest the bedrock of individual choice? This question underpins several of the broader issues we have addressed, and scholars have answered it both ways. For some, individuals choose identities that will maximize their preferences. In Gould's (1998) account, for example, some Western Pennsylvanian elite brokers chose to identify with a cause that would gain them allies whether they won or lost. For Chong (1991), acting solidaristically is a way to improve one's reputation and the benefits that flow from it. For other authors, identities set the very terms of individual and strategic calculation. Pizzorno (1986) argues that the category of interest is meaningless without that of identity, in other words, without recognition of the self doing the rational choosing. "Circles of recognition" not only validate actions on behalf of already established interests, but help to constitute new identities and the interests that flow from them (see also Emirbayer 1997, Calhoun 1991). In a sense, the debate can be seen as a kind of sociological chicken and egg question akin to whether individual or society comes first. However, an alternative tack asks whether interest or identity is more salient in different contexts. Along these lines, Ringmar (1996) argues that actions driven by identity rather than calculations of interest are especially likely when political, economic, or social change has destabilized prior identities. During such formative moments, one acts—and "one" can be nations as well as persons—in order to reassert who one is.

We still know little about the cultural building blocks that are used to construct collective identities. Laws and political status have been studied as a source, but we should learn more about how intellectuals and group leaders use nostalgia and other elements of collective memory to construct a past for a group. What are other tools and raw materials of identity work? How important is place for example?

What about bodily differences and bodily needs? To what extent are metaphors and images created originally through nationalism central to other collective identities?

Finally, more attention to historical and non-Western movements would expose us to different understandings of the relationship between self and other, and to different dynamics of collective identity formation and contestation. Not least, they should help us move beyond simply asserting the constructedness of identities by showing the variety of forms that identities take and the very different behaviors they require. Like the other gaps we have noted, this one should spur us to better specify our concepts and questions, and to begin testing competing answers.

ACKNOWLEDGMENTS

Thanks to Mary Bernstein, John Krinsky, Kelly Moore, Verta Taylor, and Charles Tilly for comments on earlier drafts.

Visit the Annual Reviews home page at www.AnnualReviews.org

LITERATURE CITED

Andrews M. 1991. *Lifetimes of Commitment: Aging, Politics, Psychology.* New York: Cambridge Univ. Press

Barkan S. 1979. Strategic, tactical and organizational dilemmas in the protest movement against nuclear power. *Soc. Probl.* 27:19–37

Benford RD. 1993. 'You could be the hundredth monkey': collective action frames and vocabularies of motive within the nuclear disarmament movement. *Sociol. Q.* 34:195–216

Bernstein M. 1997. Celebration and suppression: the strategic uses of identity by the lesbian and gay movement. *Am. J. Sociol.* 103:531–65

Bonnell V. 1983. *Roots of Rebellion: Workers' Politics and Organization in St. Petersburg and Moscow, 1900–1914.* Berkeley: Univ. Calif. Press

Bordt RL. 1997. How alternative ideas become institutions: the case of feminist collectives. *Nonprofit Vol. Sect. Q.* 26:132–55

Breines W. 1989. *Community and Organization in the New Left 1962–68: The Great Refusal.* New Brunswick, NJ: Rutgers Univ. Press

Buechler S. 1990. *Women's Movements in the*

United States. New Brunswick, NJ: Rutgers Univ. Press

Burke P, Reitzes D. 1991. An identity theory approach to commitment. *Soc. Psychol. Q.* 54:239–51

Calhoun C. 1991. Indirect relationships and imagined communities: large-scale social integration and the transformation of everyday life. In *Social Theory for a Changing Society*, ed. P Bourdieu, J Coleman, pp. 95–121. New York: Russell Sage Found.

Calhoun C. 1993. Nationalism and identity. *Annu. Rev. Sociol.* 19:211–39

Calhoun C. 1995. 'New social movements' of the early nineteenth century. In *Repertoires and Cycles of Collective Action*, ed. M Traugott, pp. 173–215. Durham, NC: Duke Univ. Press

Carroll WK, Ratner RS. 1996. Master framing and cross-movement networking in contemporary social movements. *Sociol. Q.* 37:601–25

Castells M. 1997. *The Power of Identity.* Oxford, UK: Blackwell

Cerulo KA. 1997. Identity construction: new issues, new directions. *Annu. Rev. Sociol.* 23:385–409

Chong D. 1991. *Collective Action and the Civil Rights Movement*. Chicago, IL: Univ. Chicago Press

Clemens E. 1997. *The People's Lobby*. Chicago, IL: Univ. Chicago Press

Cohen E. 1988. *Ideology, Interest Group Formation, and the New Left*. New York: Garland

Cohen JL. 1985. Strategy or identity: new theoretical paradigms and contemporary social movements. *Soc. Res.* 52:663–716

Costain A. 1988. Representing women: the transition from social movement to interest group. In *Women, Power, and Policy*, ed. E Boneparth, E Stoper, pp. 26–47. New York: Pergamon. 2nd ed.

Crenshaw K. 1990. A Black feminist critique of antidiscrimination law and politics. In *The Politics of Law: A Progressive Critique*, ed. D Kairys, pp. 195–218. New York: Pantheon. 2nd ed.

D'Emilio J. 1983. *Sexual Politics, Sexual Communities*. Chicago, IL: Univ. Chicago Press

DiMaggio PJ, Powell WW. 1991. Introduction. In *The New Institutionalism in Organizational Analysis*, ed. WW Powell, PJ DiMaggio, pp. 1–38. Chicago, IL: Univ. Chicago Press

Downey G. 1986. Ideology and the clamshell identity: organizational dilemmas in the anti-nuclear power movement. *Soc. Probl.* 33:357–71

Echols A. 1989. *Daring to Be Bad*. Minneapolis: Univ. Minn. Press

Emirbayer M. 1997. A manifesto for a relational sociology. *Am. J. Sociol.* 103:281–317

Ennis J. 1987. Fields of action: structure in movements' tactical repertoires. *Soc. Forum* 2:520–33

Epstein B. 1991. *Political Protest and Cultural Revolution*. Berkeley: Univ. Calif. Press

Epstein S. 1987. Gay politics, ethnic identity: the limits of social constructionism. *Socialist Rev.* 17:9–54

Evans S, Boyte H. 1986. *Free Spaces: The Sources of Democratic Change in America*. New York: Harper & Row

Eyerman R, Jamison A. 1998. *Music and Social Movements*. Cambridge, UK: Cambridge Univ. Press

Fantasia R. 1988. *Cultures of Solidarity*. Berkeley: Univ. Calif. Press

Fendrich JM. 1993. *Ideal Citizens: The Legacy of the Civil Rights Movement*. Albany: State Univ. New York Press

Ferree MM, Roth S. 1998. Gender, class, and the interaction between social movements: a strike of West Berlin day care workers. *Gender Soc.* 12:626–48

Fireman B, Gamson WA. 1979. Utilitarian logic in the resource mobilization perspective. In *The Dynamics of Social Movements*, ed. M Zald, J McCarthy, pp. 8–44. Cambridge, MA: Winthrop

Friedman D, McAdam D. 1992. Collective identity and activism: networks choices and the life of a social movement. See Morris & Mueller 1992, pp. 156–73

Fuss D. 1989. *Essentially Speaking: Feminism, Nature, and Difference*. New York: Routledge

Gamson J. 1995. Must identity movements self-destruct? A queer dilemma. *Soc. Probl.* 42:390–407

Gamson WA. 1975. *The Strategy of Social Protest*. Homewood, IL: Dorsey

Gamson WA. 1988. Political discourse and collective action. *Int. Soc. Move. Res.* 1:219–44

Gamson WA. 1991. Commitment and agency in social movements. *Sociol. Forum* 6:27–50

Gamson WA. 1992. *Talking Politics*. Cambridge, UK: Cambridge Univ. Press

Gitlin T. 1995. *The Twilight of Common Dreams*. New York: Henry Holt

Goffman E. 1959. *The Presentation of Self in Everyday Life*. Garden City, NY: Doubleday

Gordon C, Jasper JM. 1996. Overcoming the 'NIMBY' label: rhetorical and organizational links for local protestors. *Res. Soc. Move. Confl. Change* 19:159–81

Gould RV. 1995. *Insurgent Identities: Class Community and Protest in Paris from 1848 to the Commune*. Chicago, IL: Univ. Chicago Press

Gould RV. 1998. Political networks and the

local/national boundary in the Whiskey Rebellion. See Hanagan et al 1998, pp. 36–53

Hanagan M. 1994. New perspectives on class formation: culture, reproduction, and agency. *Soc. Sci. Hist.* 18:77–94

Hanagan M, Moch LP, te Brake W, eds. 1998. *Challenging Authority.* Minneapolis: Univ. Minn. Press

Hirsch EL. 1990a. *Urban Revolt: Ethnic Politics in the Nineteenth-Century Chicago Labor Movement.* Berkeley: Univ. Calif. Press

Hirsch EL. 1990b. Sacrifice for the cause: group processes recruitment and commitment in a student social movement. *Am. Sociol. Rev.* 55:243–54

Holstein J, Miller G. 1990. Rethinking victimization. *Symb. Interact.* 13:103–22

Hunt SA, Benford RD. 1994. Identity talk in the peace and justice movement. *J. Contemp. Ethnog.* 22:488–517

Hunt SA, Benford RD, Snow DA. 1994. Identity fields: framing processes and the social construction of movement identities. See Laraña et al 1994, pp. 185–208

Jasper JM. 1990. *Nuclear Politics.* Princeton, NJ: Princeton Univ. Press

Jasper JM. 1997. *The Art of Moral Protest.* Chicago, IL: Univ. Chicago Press

Jasper JM. 1998. The emotions of protest: reactive and affective emotions in and around social movements. *Sociol. Forum* 13:397–424

Jasper JM, Poulsen J. 1993. Fighting back: vulnerabilities, blunders, and countermobilization by the targets in three animal rights campaigns. *Sociol. Forum* 8:639–57

Jasper JM, Poulsen JD. 1995. Recruiting strangers and friends: moral shocks and social networks in animal rights and antinuclear protest. *Soc. Probl.* 42:493–512

Jenkins R. 1996. *Social Identity.* New York: Routledge

Johnston H. 1998. Subcultures and the emergence of the Estonian nationalist opposition 1945–1990. *Sociol. Prospect.* 41:473–97

Johnston H, Laraña E, Gusfield JR. 1994. Identities, grievances, and the new social movements. See Laraña et al 1994, pp. 185–208

Joyce P. 1994. *Democratic Subjects.* Cambridge, UK.: Cambridge Univ. Press

Katzenstein M. 1998. Stepsisters: feminist movement activism in different institutional spheres. In *The Social Movement Society*, ed. D Meyer, S Tarrow, pp. 195–216. Lanham, MD: Rowman & Littlefield

Kitschelt H. 1986. Political opportunity structures and political protest. *Br. J. Polit. Sci.* 16:57–85

Klandermans B. 1997. *The Social Psychology of Protest.* Oxford, UK: Blackwell

Kleinman S. 1996. *Opposing Ambitions: Gender and Identity in an Alternative Organization.* Chicago, IL: Univ. Chicago Press

Krinsky. 1999. *Working classification: identity in social movements and class formation.* Available online from CIAO: Columbia Int. Affairs Online (www.columbia.edu/cu/libraries/indexes/ciao.html).

Laclau E, Mouffe C. 1985. *Hegemony and Socialist Strategy.* London: Verso

Laraña E, Johnston H, Gusfield JR, eds. 1994. *New Social Movements: From Ideology to Identity.* Philadelphia, PA: Temple Univ. Press

Lichterman P. 1996. *The Search for Political Community: American Activists Reinventing Commitment.* New York: Cambridge Univ. Press

Lichterman P. 1999. Talking identity in the public sphere: broad visions and small spaces in sexual identity politics. *Theory Soc.* 28:101–41

Mansbridge J. 1995. What is the feminist movement? In *Feminist Organizations*, ed. MM Ferree, PY Martin, pp. 27–34. Philadelphia, PA: Temple Univ. Press

Marwell G, Oliver P. 1993. *The Critical Mass in Collective Action: A Micro-Social Theory.* Cambridge, UK: Cambridge Univ. Press

Marx AW. 1998. *Making Race and Nation: A Comparison of the United States, South Africa, and Brazil.* New York: Cambridge Univ. Press

McAdam D. 1982. *Political Process and the Development of Black Insurgency, 1930–1970.* Chicago, IL: Univ. Chicago Press

McAdam D. 1988. *Freedom Summer*. New York: Oxford Univ. Press

McAdam D. 1994. Culture and social movements. See Laraña et al 1994, pp. 36–57

McAdam D, McCarthy JD, Zald MN. 1988. Social movements. In *Handbook of Sociology*, ed. N Smelser, pp. 695–737. Newbury Park, CA: Sage

McAdam D, Paulsen R. 1993. Specifying the relationship between social ties and activism. *Am. J. Sociol.* 99:640–67

McCall G, Simmons J. 1978. *Identities and Interactions*. New York: Free Press

Melucci A. 1985. The symbolic challenge of contemporary movements. *Soc. Res.* 52:789–816

Melucci A. 1989. *Nomads of the Present*. London: Hutchinson Radius

Melucci A. 1996. *Challenging Codes: Collective Action in the Information Age*. Cambridge, UK: Cambridge Univ. Press

Meyer D, Whittier N. 1994. Social movement spillover. *Soc. Probl.* 41:277–98

Milkman R. 1986. Women's history and the Sears case. *Feminist Stud.* 12:375–400

Minkoff D. 1997. Producing social capital: national social movements and civil society. *Am. Behav. Sci.* 40:606–19

Minow M. 1990. *Making All the Difference*. Ithaca, NY: Cornell Univ. Press

Mische A. 1996. Projecting democracy: the construction of citizenship across youth networks in Brazil. In *Citizenship, Identity, and Social History*, ed. C Tilly. Cambridge, UK: Cambridge Univ. Press

Moore K. 1996. Organizing integrity: American science and the creation of public interest organizations, 1955–1975. *Am. J. Sociol.* 101:1592–627

Morris A. 1984. *The Origins of the Civil Rights Movement*. New York: Free Press

Morris A. 1992. Political consciousness and collective action. See Morris & Mueller 1992, pp. 351–73

Morris A, Mueller CM, eds. 1992. *Frontiers in Social Movement Theory*. New Haven, CT: Yale Univ. Press

Mueller C. 1994. Conflict networks and the origins of women's liberation. See Laraña et al 1994, pp. 234–63

Mueller CM. 1987. Collective consciousness, identity transformation, and the rise of women in public office in the United States. In *The Women's Movements of the United States and Western Europe*, ed. M Katzenstein, C Mueller, pp. 89–108. Philadelphia, PA: Temple Univ. Press

Mueller CM. 1992. Building social movement theory. See Morris & Mueller 1992, pp. 3–25

Oberschall A. 1973. *Social Conflict and Social Movements*. Englewood Cliffs, NJ: Prentice-Hall

Offe C. 1985. New social movements: challenging the boundaries of institutional politics. *Soc. Res.* 52:817–68

Olson M. 1965. *The Logic of Collective Action*. Cambridge, MA: Harvard Univ. Press

Pfaff S. 1996. Collective identity and informal groups in revolutionary mobilization: East Germany in 1989. *Soc. Forces* 75:91–118

Phelan S. 1989. *Identity Politics*. Philadelphia, PA: Temple Univ. Press

Pizzorno A. 1978. Political exchange and collective identity in industrial conflict. In *The Resurgence of Class Conflict in Western Europe since 1968*, ed. C Crouch, A Pizzorno, pp. 277–98. London: Macmillan

Pizzorno A. 1986. Some other kinds of otherness: a critique of 'rational choice' theories. In *Development Democracy and the Art of Trespassing: Essays in Honor of Albert O. Hirschman*, ed. A Foxley, MS McPherson, G O'Donnell, pp. 355–72. Notre Dame, IN: Univ. Notre Dame Press

Plotke D. 1990. What's so new about the new social movements? *Socialist Rev.* 20:81–102

Polletta F. 1997. Culture and its discontents: recent theorizing on culture and protest. *Soc. Inq.* 67:431–50

Polletta F. 1998a. 'It was like a fever': narrative and identity in social protest. *Soc. Probl.* 45:137–59

Polletta F. 1998b. Contending stories: narrative in social movements. *Qual. Soc.* 21:419–46

Polletta F. 1999. 'Free spaces' in collective action. *Theory Soc.* 28:1–38

Pulido L. 1996. Development of the 'people of color' identity in the environmental justice movement of the Southwestern United States. *Socialist Rev.* 26:145–80

Ringmar E. 1996. *Identity, Interest, and Action: A Cultural Explanation of Sweden's Intervention in the Thirty Years War.* Cambridge, UK: Cambridge Univ. Press

Robnett B. 1997. *How Long? How Long? African-American Women in the Struggle for Civil Rights.* New York: Oxford Univ. Press

Rogers KL. 1993. *Righteous Lives: Narratives of the New Orleans Civil Rights Movement.* New York: New York Univ. Press

Ross R. 1983. Generational change and primary groups in a social movement. In *Social Movements of the Sixties and Seventies*, ed. J Freeman, pp. 177–88. New York: Longman

Roth B. 1998. Feminist boundaries in the feminist-friendly organization: the women's caucus of ACT UP/LA. *Gender Soc.* 12:129–45

Rucht D. 1992. The strategies and action repertoires of new movements. In *Challenging the Political Order*, ed. R Dalton, M Kuechler, pp. 156–75. New York: Oxford Univ. Press

Rupp L, Taylor V. 1987. *Survival in the Doldrums: The American Women's Rights Movement, 1945 to the 1960s.* New York: Oxford Univ. Press

Scott JW. 1988. Deconstructing equality versus difference. *Fem. Stud.* 14:33–50

Scott J. 1990. *Domination and the Arts of Resistance.* New Haven: Yale Univ. Press

Seidman S. 1993. Identity and politics in a 'postmodern' gay culture: some historical and conceptual notes. In *Fear of a Queer Planet: Queer Politics and Social Theory*, ed. M Warner, pp. 105–42. Minneapolis: Univ. Minn. Press

Sewell W. 1980. *Work and Revolution in France.* Cambridge, UK: Cambridge Univ. Press

Snow DA. 2001. Collective identity. In *International Encyclopedia of the Social and Behavioral Sciences*, ed NJ Smelser, PB Baltes. London: Elsevier Sci.

Snow DA, Benford RD. 1988. Ideology, frame resonance, and participant mobilization. *Int. Soc. Move. Res.* 1:197–217

Snow D, McAdam D. 2000. Identity work processes in the context of social movements. In *Self, Identity, and Social Movements*, ed. S Stryker, TJ Owens, R White. Minneapolis: Univ. Minn. Press

Snow DA, Rochford EB Jr, Worden SK, Benford RD. 1986. Frame alignment processes, micromobilization, and movement participation. *Am. Sociol. Rev.* 51:464–81

Snow DA, Zurcher LA, Ekland-Olson S. 1980. Social networks and social movements: a microstructural approach to differential recruitment. *Am. Sociol. Rev.* 45:787–801

Somers M. 1994. The narrative constitution of identity: a relational and network approach. *Theory Soc.* 23:605–49

Somers M, Gibson GD. 1994. Reclaiming the epistemological 'other': narrative and the social constitution of identity. In *Social Theory and the Politics of Identity*, ed. C Calhoun, pp. 37–99. Cambridge, MA: Blackwell

Steinberg MW. 1996. "The labour of the country is the wealth of the country": class identity, consciousness, and the role of discourse in the making of the English working class. *Int. Lab. Work.-Class Hist.* 49:1–25

Stryker S. 1980. *Symbolic Interactionism.* Menlo Park, CA: Benjamin-Cummings

Tajfel H. 1981. *Human Groups and Social Categories.* New York: Cambridge Univ. Press

Tarrow S. 1998. *Power in Movement: Social Movements, Collective Action, and Politics.* New York: Cambridge Univ. Press. 2nd ed.

Taylor C. 1989. *Sources of the Self: The Making of the Modern Identity.* Cambridge, MA: Harvard Univ. Press

Taylor V. 1989. Social movement continuity. *Am. Sociol. Rev.* 54:761–75

Taylor V, Raeburn NC. 1995. Identity politics as high-risk activism: career consequences for lesbian, gay, and bisexual sociologists. *Soc. Probl.* 42:252–73

Taylor V, Whittier NE. 1992. Collective identity in social movement communities: lesbian feminist mobilization. See Morris & Mueller 1992, pp. 104–29

Teske N. 1997. *Political Activists in America: The Identity Construction Model of Political Participation.* Cambridge, UK: Cambridge Univ. Press.

Tilly C. 1978. *From Mobilization to Revolution.* Reading, MA: Addison-Wesley

Tilly C. 1998. Political identities. See Hanagan et al 1998, pp. 3–16

Touraine A. 1981. *The Voice and the Eye.* Cambridge, UK: Cambridge Univ. Press

Touraine A. 1985. An introduction to the study of social movements. *Soc. Res.* 52:749–87

Tracy J. 1996. *Direct Action: Radical Pacifism from the Union Eight to the Chicago Seven.* Chicago, IL: Univ. Chicago Press

Whalen J, Flacks R. 1989. *Beyond the Barricades: The Sixties Generation Grows Up.* Philadelphia, PA: Temple Univ. Press

Whittier N. 1995. *Feminist Generations: The Persistence of the Radical Women's Movement.* Philadelphia, PA: Temple Univ. Press

Annu. Rev. Sociol. 2001. 27:307–36

SOCIAL IMPLICATIONS OF THE INTERNET

Paul DiMaggio[1], Eszter Hargittai[1], W. Russell Neuman[2], and John P. Robinson[3]

[1]Department of Sociology, Princeton University, Princeton, New Jersey 08540;
e-mail: dimaggio@princeton.edu, eszter@princeton.edu
[2]Annenberg School for Communication, University of Pennsylvania, Philadelphia,
Pennsylvania 19104; e-mail: rneuman@asc.upenn.edu
[3]Department of Sociology, University of Maryland, College Park, Maryland;
e-mail: robinson@bss1.umd.edu

Key Words   World Wide Web, communications, media, technology

■ **Abstract**   The Internet is a critically important research site for sociologists testing theories of technology diffusion and media effects, particularly because it is a
medium uniquely capable of integrating modes of communication and forms of content. Current research tends to focus on the Internet's implications in five domains:
1) inequality (the "digital divide"); 2) community and social capital; 3) political participation; 4) organizations and other economic institutions; and 5) cultural participation
and cultural diversity. A recurrent theme across domains is that the Internet tends to
complement rather than displace existing media and patterns of behavior. Thus in each
domain, utopian claims and dystopic warnings based on extrapolations from technical possibilities have given way to more nuanced and circumscribed understandings of
how Internet use adapts to existing patterns, permits certain innovations, and reinforces
particular kinds of change. Moreover, in each domain the ultimate social implications
of this new technology depend on economic, legal, and policy decisions that are shaping the Internet as it becomes institutionalized. Sociologists need to study the Internet
more actively and, particularly, to synthesize research findings on individual user behavior with macroscopic analyses of institutional and political-economic factors that
constrain that behavior.

INTRODUCTION

By "Internet" we refer to the electronic network of networks that links people
and information through computers and other digital devices allowing person-to-
person communication and information retrieval. Although the late 1960s saw the
inception of an ancestral network dedicated to scientific (and, after 1975, military)
communication, the Internet did not emerge until 1982; it began its rapid ascent
only in the early 1990s, when graphical interfaces became widely available and
commercial interests were allowed to participate (Abbate 1999, Castells 2001).

0360-0572/01/0811-0307$14.00   **307**

Access to and use of the medium diffused widely and swiftly. The number of Americans online grew from 25 million in 1995 (when only 3% of Americans had ever used the Internet) (Pew Research Center for People and the Press 1995) to 83 million in 1999 (Intelli-Quest 1999), with 55 million Americans going online on a typical day in mid-2000 (Howard et al, forthcoming). The amount of information available on the World Wide Web has also risen exponentially, from fewer than 20,000 Web sites in 1995 (Prettejohn 1996) to over 10 million in 2000 (Netcraft 2000), representing over two billion Web pages, with as many as two million pages added daily (Lake 2000).

Our focus in this chapter is on the Internet's implications for social change. The Internet presents researchers with a moving target: Agre (1998a) describes it as "a meta-medium: a set of layered services that make it easy to construct new media with almost any properties one likes." We use Internet to refer both to technical infrastructure (public TCP/IP networks, other large-scale networks like AOL, and foundational protocols), and to uses to which this infrastructure is put (World Wide Web, electronic mail, online multiperson interactive spaces). We focus primarily on general, public uses. Among the topics we do not address systematically are the use of digital technologies for communication *within* formal organizations, the technology's potential contribution to the conduct of social-science research and scholarly communication, or the much broader topic of social antecedents and consequences of computerization.

Many observers allege that the Internet is changing society. Perhaps not surprisingly, given the novelty of the new digital media, there is little agreement about what those changes are. Our purpose here is to summarize research by social scientists about the Internet and to encourage more sociologists to contribute actively to such research. We believe that it is important for sociologists to address these issues for three reasons. First, the medium's rapid growth offers a once-in-a-lifetime opportunity for scholars to test theories of technology diffusion and media effects *during the early stages of a new medium's diffusion and institutionalization*. Second, the Internet is unique because it integrates both different modalities of communication (reciprocal interaction, broadcasting, individual reference-searching, group discussion, person/machine interaction) and different kinds of content (text, video, visual images, audio) in a single medium. This versatility renders plausible claims that the technology will be implicated in many kinds of social change, perhaps more deeply than television or radio. Finally, choices are being made—systems developed, money invested, laws passed, regulations promulgated—that will shape the system's technical and normative structure for decades to come. Many of these choices are based on behavioral assumptions about how people and the Internet interact. We believe such assumptions should represent more than guesswork.

THEORETICAL CONTEXT

Sociology's major theoretical traditions emphasize different aspects of electronic media. For Durkheimians, point-to-point communications media like telephones reinforce organic solidarity, while broadcast media like radio or television yield powerful collective representations (Alexander 1988). Marxists focus upon exploitation of communications media to enhance elite control of both politics and production through cultural hegemony and enhanced surveillance (Schiller 1996, Davis et al 1997). Weberians attend to the ways in which point-to-point media advance rationalization by reducing limits of time and space, and broadcast media provide the elements of distinctive status cultures (Collins 1979).

Other traditions also offer perspectives on the digital media. Technological determinists suggest that structural features of new media induce social change by enabling new forms of communication and cultivating distinctive skills and sensibilities (McLuhan 1967, Eisenstein 1979). In the 1960s, students of social change suggested that in the face of new developments in communications technology, industrial society would yield to the "information society," with consequences in every institutional realm (Machlup 1962, Bell 1973). Critical theorists problematize the effects of technological change on political deliberation and the integrity of civil society (Habermas 1989, Calhoun 1998).

Daniel Bell (1977) appears to have been the first sociologist to write about the social impact of digital communications media themselves. Bell predicted that major social consequences would derive from two related developments: the invention of miniature electronic and optical circuits capable of speeding the flow of information through networks; and the impending integration of computer processing and telecommunications into what Harvard's Anthony Oettinger dubbed "compunications" technology. Anticipating the democratization of electronic mail and telefaxing, as well as digital transmission of newspapers and magazines, Bell explored the policy dilemmas these changes would raise, calling "the social organization of the new 'compunications' technology" the most central issue "for the postindustrial society" (1977:38).

More recently, Manuel Castells has argued that the world is entering an "information age" in which digital information technology "provides the material basis" for the "pervasive expansion" of what he calls "the networking form of organization" in every realm of social structure (1996:468). According to Castells, the Internet's integration of print, oral, and audiovisual modalities into a single system promises an impact on society comparable to that of the alphabet (p. 328), creating new forms of identity and inequality, submerging power in decentered flows, and establishing new forms of social organization.

The comprehensive visions of Bell and Castells, like the other theoretical traditions we have described, suggest a range of empirical questions one must answer to understand the Internet's influence upon society. From the Marxian and Weberian traditions come concerns about power and inequality in the access to the new technology. The Durkheimian perspective sensitizes us to the new media's impact on community and social capital. The work of Habermas and Calhoun leads us to ask how the Internet may alter the practice of politics. The Weberian tradition raises the question of the effect of Internet technology on bureaucracy and economic institutions. Critical theory raises important questions of how the Internet may affect the arts and entertainment media.

We address each of these five topics in turn, summarizing the results of research undertaken by social scientists and other investigators. In most of these areas, the research literature is limited, and many questions remain. But there is a pattern: Early writings projected utopian hopes onto the new technology, eliciting a dystopian response. Research on each topic yields two conclusions. First, the Internet's impact is more limited than either the utopian or dystopian visions suggest. Second, the nature of that impact will vary depending upon how economic actors, government regulation, and users collectively organize the evolving Internet technology.

MAJOR RESEARCH QUESTIONS

The Internet and Inequality: Opportunity or Reproduction?

Enthusiasts predicted that the Internet would reduce inequality by lowering the cost of information and thus enhancing the ability of low-income men and women to gain human capital, find and compete for good jobs, and otherwise enhance their life chances (Anderson et al 1995). By contrast, cyber-skeptics suggest that the greatest benefits will accrue to high-SES persons, who may use their resources to employ the Internet sooner and more productively than their less privileged peers, and that this tendency would be reinforced by better Internet connections and easier access to social support (DiMaggio & Hargittai 2001).

As in other areas, early research results suggest that the outcome is more complex than either of these predictions, and that the Internet's effects on inequality will depend on the social organization of its use. In this section, we examine research on individual-level inequality among users, as well as cross-national differences in Internet penetration and inequality in effective Internet access for content producers.

THE "DIGITAL DIVIDE" IN THE UNITED STATES   Anderson et al (1995) were among the first to highlight the potential of inequality in Internet access to limit people's opportunities to find jobs, obtain education, access government information, participate in political dialog, and build networks of social support. By "digital divide," we refer to inequalities in access to the Internet, extent of use, knowledge of search strategies, quality of technical connections and social support, ability to evaluate the quality of information, and diversity of uses. Although some speculate that current intergroup differences will evaporate as the Internet diffuses (Compaine 2000), Schement (1999) points out that inequalities in access to information services (e.g. telephone, cable) tend to persist in contrast to the rapid diffusion of information goods (e.g. radio, television, VCRs) that reach near saturation relatively quickly. This is because the former require ongoing expenditures, whereas the latter are based on one-time purchases. For example, although 94% of all American households have telephones, this figure drops below 80% for the low-income elderly and female-headed households below the poverty level (Schement 1996).

Because sociologists have conducted so little research on the digital divide, to chart the dimensions of inequality we must rely primarily on studies reporting bivariate statistics. Reports of the National Telecommunications and Information Administration (NTIA 1995, 1998, 1999, 2000) documented differences in Internet access favoring the college educated, the wealthy, whites, people under the age of 55 and, especially in earlier years, men and urban dwellers. (Moreover, less affluent and less well-educated users are more likely to become nonusers after trying it out [Katz & Aspden 1997].) Interestingly, despite the focus of early reports on income differences, the impact of educational attainment on Internet use is twice that of income after multivariate controls (Robinson et al 2000b). Research has also found that Internet non-users report as reasons for not going online that they are not computer users, they do not want their children to have Internet access, they lack time or interest, or they cannot afford it (Strover & Straubhaar 2000). There is some evidence that measures of access reflect resource control, whereas measures of intensity of use are driven more by demand. Thus teenagers are less likely to report Internet access than adults between the ages of 25 and 54 (NTIA 1998); but when homes have Internet access, teenagers are online much more than adults (Kraut et al 1996).

Patterns of inequality are likely to reflect such changing factors as public connection availability, private subscription price, services available, and the technology necessary to access them effectively, as well as the diffusion of knowledge and the evolution of informal technical-support networks. Therefore, it is crucial to examine change in inequality over time. Three surveys conducted between 1996 and 1998 found that the gap in access between whites and African Americans had increased over time (Hoffman et al 2000), but NTIA surveys (1998, 2000) found that divide diminishing between 1998 and 2000. Wilhelm (2000) reports that significant differences persist in Internet use among racial and ethnic groups, with socioeconomic status held constant, and he argues that access to telecommunications tools and lack of easy access to Spanish-language content explain lower usage rates among Hispanics. By contrast, broad evidence suggests that two gaps, the advantage of men over women and of the young over the old, have declined as the technology has diffused and become more user-friendly (Roper Starch 1998, Clemente 1998, Bimber 2000, NTIA 2000, Howard et al forthcoming). Other evidence suggests that late adopters have less formal education and lower incomes than earlier cohorts (Howard et al, forthcoming, Katz et al, forthcoming).

Several exemplary studies go beyond description to analysis. In a study notable for its use of multivariate analysis and multiple outcome measures, Bimber (2000) found that the gap between men and women in *access* to the Internet reflected male/female differences in income and other resources; but that women with access used the Internet less frequently than did otherwise similar men, a result he attributed to the fact that full-time employment had a significant effect on frequency of use for men, but not for women. In a study exemplary for tying individual-level inequality to institutional arrangements, Strover (1999) compared dial-up Internet connectivity in four rural US counties, concluding that low levels of commercial investment in telecommunications infrastructure in sparsely populated areas limits use by generating less choice among service providers and higher connection fees.

Other research has focused on public settings that provide Internet access for pesons unable to reach the Internet at home or work. A national survey of public libraries reported that urban libraries are almost three times as likely as rural libraries to offer high-speed Internet connections; and that because many urban libraries serve high-poverty areas, access to high-speed connections is relatively available to the urban poor (Bertot & McClure 1998). An evaluation of Internet access programs at two public libraries and two community centers indicated that effectiveness was a function of the extent to which staff were trained to assist Internet users and potential users found the atmosphere welcoming and nonthreatening (Lentz et al 2000). Research on schools, another key site for public access, indicates that the proportion of US public schools offering Internet access rose from 3% in 1994 to 63% in 1999 (US Department of Education 2000), but that training and support staffing necessary for teachers to incorporate the technology effectively in instructional plans has lagged behind (Bolt & Crawford 2000).

Much research and policy assumes that people can convert Internet access into other valued goods, services, and life outcomes. Researchers have not yet tested this premise for Internet access, but research on general computer use sustains its plausibility, while leaving much to be done. Krueger (1993) reported a substantial wage premium accruing to workers who use computers. Attewell & Battle (1999) found that home computer use was significantly related to students' test scores in mathematics and reading, with higher returns for boys, whites, and the well-to-do.

THE GLOBAL DIGITAL DIVIDE   The number of Internet users globally skyrocketed from 16 million in 1995 to almost 360 million by mid-2000 (NUA 2000a). Despite this rapid diffusion, this number represents just 5% of the world's population. As is the case with other communications devices, access across countries is very uneven, with 97% of Internet host computers located in developed countries (ITU 1998). With respect to content, US producers dominate the Web, creating and hosting a large percentage of the most visited Web sites (OECD 1997) and so establishing English as the Internet's dominant language.

Studies of cross-national variation in levels of Internet connectivity and use are few. Most reports on global Internet diffusion present little more than descriptive statistics, emphasizing correlations with national wealth and education (ITU 1997, 1999, Paltridge & Ypsilanti 1997). Cross-national differences reflect differences in the availability of local-language programming, but not that alone. Hargittai (1996) called attention to institutional factors, reporting that in 1995 three quarters of highly developed countries, but only 10% of LDCs, had commercial access providers (an indicator of private-sector involvement and thus additional impetus for diffusion). Although data quality constrains generalization, the divide between developed and less developed nations appears not to have lessened as the Internet has diffused.

Better data make it possible to analyze Internet diffusion in OECD countries in more detail. Using multivariate analyses of OECD nations, Hargittai (1999) demonstrated that national wealth and competition in the telecommunications sector (and regulatory environments fostering competition) were the strongest predictors of connectivity (see also Guillén & Suarez 2001).

Wilson (2000) distinguishes between "formal access" (physical availability) and "effective access" (affordable connectivity and diffusion of skills people need to benefit from the technology). In-depth case studies help develop this distinction. Rao et al (1999) suggest that lack of local content in native languages in South Asia discourages use. Based on a detailed review of statistics and case reports, Norris (2001) concludes that the Internet is reproducing cross-national inequalities in use of newspapers, telephones, radio, and television because diffusion largely depends on economic development and research and development investments that are unequally distributed across societies.

Yet a case study of Trinidad reports that by 1999 penetration was deep (approximately 30% of households had at least one regular user) and, while stratified by income, relatively broad. The authors attribute this both to Trinidad's comparatively strong communications infrastructure and healthy economy, and equally important, to the premium placed on email by residents of an island nation that exports its most successful young people abroad (Miller & Slater 2000). Technologies shape themselves to the contours of local priorities and ways of life: Just as some less developed countries were vanguard adopters of sound cassettes and cell phones, some may embrace the Internet relatively quickly, especially as wireless transmission creates convergence between Internet and cell phone technologies.

INEQUALITY IN CONTENT PROVIDERS' ACCESS TO ATTENTION   Sociologists should be concerned not only with inequality in access to the Internet, but with inequality in access to the attention of those who use the Internet. By dramatically reducing the cost of the replication and distribution of information, the Internet has the potential to create arenas for more voices than any other previous communication medium by putting product dissemination within the reach of the individual.

Information abundance creates a new problem, however: attention scarcity (Goldhaber 1997). Content creators can only reach large audiences if online gatekeepers—Web services that categorize online information and provide links and search facilities to other sites—channel users to them (Hargittai 2000b). Yet Internet traffic is highly concentrated: 80% of site visits are to just .5% of Web sites (Waxman 2000a). As was the case with broadcast media, the growth and commercialization of the Internet has been accompanied by a commodification of attention. A rapidly evolving mosaic of search engines and point-of-entry sites compete for dominance (NUA 2000a), playing a pivotal role in channeling users' attention toward some contents and away from others (Hargittai 2000b).

During the late 1990s, entrepreneurs developed comprehensive and strongly branded "portals"—Web sites containing search engines, category guides, and various shopping and information services—to match users and content. Such sites now account for one in four of the most visited destinations of the Web (Waxman 2000b). The search engines they feature are often biased in their identification and, especially, ranking of sites in response to user queries (Introna & Nissenbaum 2000). The effects of bias are compounded by the tendency of engine users to employ simple search terms and to satisfice by terminating searches at the first acceptable site. [A 1998 analysis of almost one billion queries on the Altavista search engine revealed that 77% of sessions included but one query and 85% of users viewed only the first screen of search results (Silverstein et al 1998)]. Thus, Web destinations that are displayed prominently on portal sites or ranked high by search engines are likely to monopolize the attention of all but the most sophisticated and committed Internet users. Understanding the processes by which such display opportunities and ranks are awarded is an important research tack.

Research on inequality in access to and use of the Internet—among individual users, groups, organizations, countries, and content creators—should be an important priority for sociologists. At the individual level, the priority should be on using multivariate methods to explore the determinants of different measures of inequality: not just whether or not one has "access," but inequality in location of access (home, work, public facilities); the quality of hardware, software, and connections; skill in using the technology; and access to social support networks. Because inequality reflects the technology's organization, not inherent qualities, special priority should be placed on studies of how inequality is affected by such factors as government programs, industry structure and pricing policies, and approaches to the provision and organization of content.

Impact on Time Use and Community: Social Isolation or Social Capital Formation

Initial enthusiasts anticipated that the Internet would boost efficiency, making people more productive and enabling them to avoid unnecessary transportation by accomplishing online tasks like banking, shopping, library research, even socializing online. The results (less stress, more time, new online contacts) would make individuals more fulfilled and build social capital for society at large. More recently, two studies have suggested that the Internet may induce anomie and erode social capital by enabling users to retreat into an artificial world (Kraut et al 1998, Nie & Erbring 2000). In this section, we explore research on what Internet users do with their time, how the Internet affects their well-being, and how the Internet influences communities, both real and virtual.

TIME DISPLACEMENT   Much of the debate over social capital is about whether the Internet attenuates users' human relationships, or whether it serves to reinforce them. Experience with earlier communications technologies suggests that Internet users may substitute time online for attention to functionally equivalent social and media activities (Weiss 1970). Thus, when television appeared in the United States, it had rapid impact on use of other media: Audiences abandoned their radio sets, movie theaters closed, and general-interest magazines stopped publishing fiction and eventually folded. Early studies documented reductions in time spent going to the movies, listening to radio, and reading fiction as television viewing time increased (Coffin 1954, Bogart 1956). Subsequent research replicated these results cross-nationally and also documented significant declines in out-of-home socializing, in-home conversation, housework, personal care activities, and even sleep (Robinson & Godby 1999).

If television, a unidirectional mass medium, displaced so many activities, then it stands to reason that the Internet, which permits interactive as well as one-way communication, might substitute for even more. Observers have expressed particular concern that Internet users may reduce the time devoted to off-line social interaction and spend less time with print media, as well as with television and other media (Nie & Erbring 2000).

The functional-equivalence model that described the effects of television thus far appears *not* to fit the experience of Internet users. Analyses of 1995 and 1998 national surveys by the Pew Center for the People and the Press, which asked respondents about activities "yesterday," have found Internet use to be unrelated or positively associated with social interaction (Robinson et al 1997, 2000a). Moreover, analysis of 1997 data from the federal Survey of Public Participation in the Arts indicates that Internet users (with appropriate controls) read more literature, attended more arts events, went to more movies, and watched *and* played more sports than comparable nonusers (Robinson & Kestnbaum 1999). A more recent study based on 1998 Pew Center data indicates intriguing changes associated with the Internet's diffusion: Among users who had been early adopters, Internet use was associated with *greater* use of print media. Among new Internet users, however, this relationship had disappeared (Robinson et al 2000b). No significant decline in TV viewing was found after demographic controls. Overall, then, these analyses provide scant support for time displacement due to functional equivalence with respect to other media. (See also Cole 2000, who found lower TV use among Internet users but slightly higher use of other media).

The situation with respect to social interaction is more complicated. Two well-publicized studies reported indications that Internet use substituted for other interactions. Kraut et al (1998), who used a rare longitudinal design to study 169 Pittsburgh-area families who were given computers and Internet connections over a two-year period, reported that higher levels of Internet use were "associated with declines in communication with family members, declines in social circles, and increased loneliness and depression." The authors inferred that heavy users substituted interactions with weak ties on the Internet for time spent with close friends and relatives. Yet as the researchers followed their sample they discovered that, except for increased stress, negative psychological effects decayed to statistical insignificance and some positive outcomes emerged. They attribute these changes to increases in experience and competence and, more speculatively, to the Internet's greater utility in the later period and to a change in sign of network externalities from negative to positive as more of these users' friends and family went online (Kraut et al forthcoming).

An innovative study that used special use-logging software to compare the online behavior of experienced and novice Web users reinforces the notion that the effect of Internet use may vary with user competence. Compared to experienced Internet users, the novices engaged in more aimless surfing, were less successful in finding information, and were more likely to report feeling a souring of affect over the course of their sessions. Their negative reactions reflected not the Internet experience per se but the frustration and sense of impotence of the inexperienced user without immediate access to social support (Neuman et al 1996).

Nie & Erbring (2000) surveyed four thousand Internet users online and asked how the Internet had changed their lives. Most reported no change, but heavier users reported declines in socializing, media use, shopping, and other activities. By contrast, analyses of national (off-line) sample surveys (from both 1995 and 1998) using more fine-grained activity measures indicate that Internet users are no less likely (with controls) to engage in social visiting or to call friends on the telephone. More recent surveys (online *and* off) have revealed that Internet users have *higher* levels of generalized trust and larger social networks than nonusers (Uslaner 1999, Robinson et al 2000b, Hampton & Wellman 2000, Cole 2000). Results from survey analyses also suggest that Internet use serves to complement rather than substitute for print media and offline socialization. Indeed, a detailed time diary study also found Internet users to be no less active media users or offline socializers than nonusers, though they did do less housework, devote less time to family care, and sleep less (Robinson et al 2000b).

COMMUNITY   Wellman (2001) argues that the Internet has contributed to a shift from a group-based to a network-based society that is decoupling community and geographic propinquity, and thus requiring new understandings and operational-izations of the former. Consistent with this insight, Katz et al (forthcoming) report that Internet users visit friends more and talk with them by telephone more fre-quently, but that they also travel more and have fewer friends in their immediate neighborhoods.

To some extent, whether one views the Internet as corrosive to or supportive of community depends in part on how one evaluates the things people do with it. For example, Nie & Erbring (2000, p. 4) view moderate to heavy-users' self-reported substitution of email for telephone contact as part of their loss of "contact with their social environment." By contrast, Lin (2001) regards online communication, including email, as markedly expanding the stock of social capital.

Indeed, an increasing body of literature suggests that the Internet enhances social ties defined in many ways, often by reinforcing existing behavior patterns. A report on a national survey of users (Howard et al forthcoming) revealed that the Internet puts users in more frequent contact with families and friends, with email being an important avenue of communication. This study also suggests that research on Internet use and social capital should distinguish among different types of Internet use: The Internet seems particularly unlikely to corrode the social capital of women, more of whom than men employ the medium as a complement to other channels of social interaction. Similarly, a longitudinal study by Kraut et al (forthcoming) found that Internet use increased interaction with family members and reported closeness to friends, especially for users whose perceived social-support networks were strong *before* they began using the Internet.

The Internet is unique among media in making it easy for people to assemble (at a distance) and communicate with many others at the same time in such settings as chat rooms or online discussion forums. "Online communities" come in very different shapes and sizes, ranging from virtual communities that connect geographically distant people with no prior acquaintance who share similar interests, to settings that facilitate interactions among friendship networks or family members, to community networks that focus on issues relevant to a geographically defined neighborhood (Smith & Kollock 1999, Wellman & Gulia 1999, Preece 2000). Research on "online community" should distinguish among these forms, lest results appear contradictory and confusing.

Early studies tended to focus on online role-playing games [e.g. multi-user dungeons or MUDs (Turkle 1995)] and newsgroups (Hauben & Hauben 1997). These were among the first online communities and are still popular research sites, in part because researchers can obtain full transcripts of discussions and events. Such "online ethnography" has provided useful insights into issues of identity formation (Paccagnella 1997) and the status and concerns of particular groups (e.g., Kolko et al 2000 on race in cyberspace). But as the technology matures, ever smaller percentages of Internet users participate in online games and newsgroups. Increasingly, researchers must follow users into newer kinds of online communities based on shared interests or (physical) community networks.

The number of case studies of online communities is large and growing. Participants value such online settings for making it easy (and inexpensive) to communicate across large distances, providing opportunities for participation by the homebound aged or infirm, and enabling people with minority interests or lifestyles to find companionship and counsel unavailable in their communities of residence (Etzioni & Etzioni 1997). Rheingold's (1993) classic study of an online community emphasized the capacity of online networks to provide their members with social support. And other researchers have noted that, compared to real-life social networks, online communities are more often based on participants' shared interests rather than shared demographic characteristics or mere propinquity (Wellman & Gulia 1999). Nonetheless, issues related to racial, gender, and sexual dynamics do permeate and complicate online interactions [e.g. requiring communities to establish norms for dealing with intimidating or offensive language (Lessig 1999, Silver 2000)].

Whereas some studies focus on "virtual" communities, others explore the impact of the Internet on geographic communities. An exemplary study of a highly wired residential community underscores the importance of examining online interactions in the context of offline everyday life (Hampton & Wellman 2000). It revealed that Internet users maintain community ties through both computer-mediated communication and face-to-face interaction. Although they maintain more long-distance relationships than do non-Internet users, they communicate even more with their neighbors—and are acquainted with three times as many of their neighbors as are their unwired peers. A study of a similar community revealed that residents make much use of the Internet for "social-capital building activities," but that individual-level community involvement and attachment increased only for residents who were already very active at the experiment's inception (Kavanaugh & Patterson forthcoming). Similarly, a study of scholarly networks found that although the Internet helps maintain contact over long distances, most email contacts are between people who also interact face-to-face (Koku et al 2001). In other words, research suggests that the Internet sustains the bonds of community by complementing, not replacing, other channels of interaction.

SOCIAL CAPITAL   Many scholars believe that the Internet facilitates the creation of social capital and other public goods by making information flow more efficiently through residential or professional communities (Lin 2001, Wellman 2001). Yet Putnam (2000) reports that, after demographic controls, Internet users are no different than non-users on measures of civic engagement. He notes, however, that it is premature to project this result onto future user cohorts, and he is agnostic about the Internet's contribution to social capital at the community level. Putnam calls attention to the need to understand qualitative differences between mediated and face-to-face interaction and to explore a tension between the technology's potential and the dangers of unequal access and "cyberbalkanization" (Putnam 2000:177; for an operationalization, see Van Alstyne & Brynjolfsson 1997).

Other studies indicate that, under some circumstances at least, Internet use may enhance social capital. In a longitudinal study of Pittsburgh residents, Kraut et al (forthcoming) found Internet use associated with greater participation in community activities and more trust (though less commitment to remaining in their community), with the positive effects greater for more extroverted participants. An analysis of online survey respondents from the United States, United Kingdom, Canada, and Australia found that increased Internet use tended to have a direct positive effect on social capital (operationalized as participation in community networks and activities) and a positive indirect effect (through social capital) on political participation (Gibson et al 2000).

There is much anecdotal evidence that the Internet provides significant benefits to people with unusual identities or concerns (e.g., rare medical conditions). But there is some evidence that "social capital" produced by less focused networks is rather thin. For example, a survey of users of Amsterdam's "Digital City," a multi-use space created to encourage Internet access and public-spirited interaction, found that, despite soaring membership figures, most users participated relatively infrequently and for recreational purposes (Van den Besselaar & Beckers 1998).

It has also been argued that the Internet builds social capital by enhancing the effectiveness of community-level voluntary associations, but little research evaluates this claim. The Internet has also been described as an inexpensive and effective means of organizing oppositional social movement. Lin (2001) describes the fascinating case of China's Falun Gong organization, which used the Internet to establish a powerful, hierarchical religious movement under the noses of an authoritarian regime. Whether similar movements will follow suit will depend on the success of states in monitoring and controlling such activities.

We draw five morals from the research to date. First, the Internet has no intrinsic effect on social interaction and civic participation. This nonfinding should challenge scholars to understand the circumstances under which different effects are produced, which will doubtless lead them to distinguish different profiles of Web use and different orientations of users. Second, Internet use tends to intensify already existing inclinations toward sociability or community involvement, rather than creating them ab initio. Third, we need to know more than we do about the qualitative character of online relationships. Fourth, we know that virtual communities exist in large number, but we know relatively little about their performance. Research on how virtual communities address problems of commitment and trust (like Kollock's [1999] innovative study of institutionalized reputation on E-Bay and Usenet barter sites) is necessary to understand the limits and possibilities of community online. Fifth, we need more systematic studies of how civic associations and social movements use the Internet, so that we can move beyond single cases to understanding the institutional conditions that encourage or discourage successful exploitation of this technology for collective ends.

Impact on Politics: Renewed Public Sphere or Electronic Battleground?

In the political domain we again find utopians and doomsayers at odds. Enthusiasts find early evidence of a re-engaged, more deliberative, more equitable political community (Browning 1996, Hill & Hughes 1998, Negroponte 1995). Skeptics foresee the re-emergence of an unresponsive commercial sphere dominated by the usual corporate players—but with an increased capacity to invade the privacy of individual citizens (Beniger 1996, Lessig 1999). Most research suggests that effects thus far have been mixed and modest.

Drawing conclusions at such early stages of technology diffusion before the emergence of stable norms is risky because it is difficult to disentangle: 1) the unique characteristics of early adopters from the characteristics of the medium in question; 2) the primitive limitations of the early Web from the technology's mature characteristics; and 3) the Web's explosive growth from other political trends (Rogers 1995, Bimber 1999). As with other topics, the literature about politics on the Internet has progressed through three stages: unjustifiable euphoria, abrupt and equally unjustifiable skepticism, and gradual realization that Web-based human interaction really does have unique and politically significant properties.

AN INFORMED PUBLIC   Empirical research on mass political knowledge in industrial democracies, and particularly in the United States, has drawn heavily on the 'information cost' perspective of Downs (1957) and Schumpeter (1947) to explain why the public is so poorly informed. Because it takes time and energy to seek out, interpret, and remember political information, it may be rational to free-ride on the civic attentiveness of others. The political promise of the Internet is that it significantly lowers the behavioral costs of finding, storing, and communicating specific and personally relevant political information at convenient, timely intervals.

The literature reveals, however, that after controlling for education and political interest, there is little evidence of an effect of Internet use on political knowledge. Those who seek political information online are generally well informed to begin with, politically oriented, and heavy users of other media (Bimber 2000, Johnson & Kaye 1998). At present, the Internet supplements and complements rather than replaces traditional sources of political information (Pew 1998, 1999, Robinson et al 2000b). A June 2000 survey revealed that 33% of US adults (and 46% of those under thirty) go online for news at least once a week, compared to 20% in 1998, and 15% they say do so every day. About half say they seek out political news, fewer than report that they look for weather, technology, business, and sports news (Howard et al forthcoming). In some cases they access news not readily available through print or broadcast media, but often the Web is a supplementary medium through which conventional news organizations distribute information available through other means.

AN ENGAGED PUBLIC   The economic and psychological dynamics of Web-based human communication, however, are potentially distinct enough from those of traditional print and broadcast news media that in time we may see evidence of an Internet effect. For example, news sites often provide interactive links that encourage users to "send a copy of this article to a friend or colleague." The capacity for horizontal interpersonal communication, to rebroadcast a news article with personal commentary, enhances the capacity for discussion, engagement, and the two-step flow that serves as the critical antidote to anomic mass communication (Kornhauser 1968). Evolving third-voice technologies would permit users to unilaterally convert every mass-medium Web site into an open public discussion (Dibbell 1999). Discussion groups on the Web at present lack the selective, highly edited character of letters to the editor and citizen op-eds. But though they may not achieve the ideal of deliberative discourse envisioned by Habermas (1981, Elster 1998), they would appear to be a step in that direction.

There is great concern about the political malaise and disengagement presumably reflected in low voter turnouts in US national elections. Will reduced costs of gathering political information produce higher voting rates? Probably not, due to the complex and tangled influences of multiple historical, cultural and economic trends, which render bivariate analyses of relationships between media use and electoral participation ill advised. Schudson (1998) points out that US electoral participation rates were highest in the second half of the nineteenth century, when citizens were generally uninformed and uneducated, the media were limited and sensationalistic, and quality of public debate was largely undistinguished. Bimber (2000) argues that political impact derives less from the character of the medium than from the character of information and the day-to-day culture of its use. The successful Jesse Ventura candidacy in Minnesota is widely cited as an example of grass-roots Internet populism; but in that case the Net was primarily used to organize the already engaged, not to mobilize disaffected or uninterested voters (Stromer-Galley 2000). Online financial contributions and voting online by the already politically active may prove more significant in the long run (Mintz 2000).

POLITICAL POLARIZATION   Perhaps the most central question for sociological analysis of changing technical structures of interpersonal and mass communication is the tension between forces of social integration and polarization (Neuman 2000). Many fear that the Internet will weaken the cultural center and "political commons" that network television and metropolitan newspapers provided (Neuman 1991, Hirsch 1978). Negroponte, for example, predicts that an artificially intelligent Web-based Daily Me will select news and information based on the predilections and prejudices of the individual cybercitizen and further displace the cultural commons (Negroponte 1995).

Research on earlier media, however, indicates that individuals tend to be aware of the most popular cultural artifacts and to monitor the latest hot programs and motion pictures (Neuman 1991). Ideologically inclined individuals do choose to attend to media that reinforce their prejudices (e.g., conservatives listen to conservatively oriented radio talk shows), but expose themselves as well to opposing views (Freedman & Sears 1965, Frey 1986). The Net's capacity for anonymous communication may heighten the level of extremist and hate speech in the early stages of diffusion. But institutions of self-regulation may emerge to constrain such expression in cyberspace, as they have in nonelectronic public forums (Lessig 1999).

DELIBERATIVE DEMOCRACY   Web proponents may concede that historically apolitical social strata are unlikely to be mobilized overnight by Internet political content, and agree that there are few signs thus far that the Internet has increased political fragmentation and polarization. But they insist that the Internet will enhance the quality of political discussion and the viability, meaningfulness, and diversity of the public sphere by lowering the access barrier to meaningful public speech. No longer is it necessary to own a newspaper or television station to participate: The Web is a two-way medium, and every Internet receiver can be a publisher as well (Compaine & Gomery 2000, Todreas 1999). Such claims provide critics of commercial (and especially American) dominance of the mass media and the international flow of news and culture with a new focal point for inquiry (Bennett 1995, Bourdieu 1999, Garnham 1990, McChesney 1996, Schiller 1989).

Can the Web make a real difference? It is clear that the Internet significantly lowers entry barriers and other Downsian cost factors for participation in the electronic public sphere. Bimber finds that many of the distortions of group discussion resulting from dominant personalities and group dynamics are reproduced in cyberspace, but he concludes that virtual political space (notably Usenet-style threaded discussion groups) has its place as a significant supplement to, if not replacement for, the face-to-face discussions of Habermas' idealized nineteenth-century salon (Bimber 2000, Hill & Hughes 1998, Schneider 1996). Lowering the economic costs to initiate and sustain an accessible political voice—compare a teenager's bedroom-based Web site to the cost of sustaining a printed magazine or broadcasting facility—can lower access barriers for minority voices, as well.

Skeptics argue that the commercial incentives of advertising-based media may lead ultimately to an Internet culturally indistinguishable from modern commercial television (Davis 1998, Margolis & Resnick 1999, Rheingold 1993). This debate is particularly interesting in the case of Web-based political campaigning in the United States, where by 2000, most candidates had their own Web sites, many with detailed issue and policy information unavailable through traditional media (Schneider 2000b). Will such diverse sites attract sufficient traffic to sustain themselves? Or will dominant commercial portals like AOL or specialized startups like *voter.com* dominate attention, paying for access to the public sphere through political advertising? As of this writing the jury is out, but researchers are actively studying elite and mass behavior (Schneider 2000a).

THE POLITICS OF THE INTERNET   A final note: It may be that the battle for control of the Net and for dominance in the electronic marketplace of ideas will prove to be the most fruitful arena for sociological inquiry. The tension between political ideals of openness and the strong economic incentives to sustain and protect scarcity and its corresponding economic return should sustain significant scholarship in this domain for years to come (Lessig 1999, Neuman et al 1998, Shapiro 1999).

Impact on Organizations: Flexible Networks or Panopticons?

Some management writers depict information technology as transforming organizations: replacing hierarchical bureaucracy with flat, networked structures in which local initiative supplants authoritative command; and replacing formal organizations themselves with "network organizations" in which agency is interstitial and strategy constantly renegotiated (Tapscott 1999). Others suggest that digital telecommunications may increase management control by permitting unprecedented degrees of surveillance (Zuboff 1989). In this section, we focus primarily on organizations' use of the public Internet, rather than on communications networks internal to the firm (the use of which is reviewed in Sproull & Kiesler 1991, Wellman et al 1996, and O'Mahoney & Barley 1999).

LIMITS ON INTERNET IMPACT   Little research bears directly on these claims, and what there is finds limited effects for three reasons. First, authors who make the strongest claims often conflate different types of digital technology, including workplace applications, local area networks, and the Internet. The Internet is less central to some notable organizational trends (e.g., the shrinkage of middle management) than computerization of internal functions (Board on Science, Technology & Economic Policy 1999).

Second, many structural changes associated with the "networked firm" predate the rise of information technologies alleged to have caused them (Powell 2001, Castells 1996). Although some argue that the Internet causes large firms to devolve into loosely integrated production networks by reducing information and transaction costs (Brynjolfsson et al 1994), the move toward network organizations was under way before the Internet became popular. (The Internet, though not determinant, is important. Although network forms emerged in response to competitive environments, new information technologies contributed to their rapid development [Castells 1996].)

Third, technology's effects reflect *not* its inherent potential, as futurists assume, but active choices that are shaped by technology owners' perceived interests, existing organizational structures and routines, and by cultural norms (O'Mahoney & Barley 1999, Orlikowski & Iacono 2000). Many traditional firms heavily constrain use of email and the Internet, especially by clerical and service employees, and such firms often implement systems that facilitate surveillance rather than enabling flexible, decentralized interaction (Zuboff 1989, Wellman et al 1996, Frenkel et al 1999).

Telecommuting, once predicted to rise exponentially, is a good example. Of a national sample of 1050 workers interviewed in late 1999, 41% believed they could work effectively from home, but only 10% reported their employers provided that option (and 9% reported doing so at least once a week) (Heldritch Center 2000). Other evidence suggests that most employees use home Internet connections to supplement hours at the workplace, not to substitute for them (O'Mahony & Barley: 131).

WORK GROUP EFFECTS   Research on work groups (much of it in laboratory settings) suggests that electronic communications influence interaction style and work flow. Use of electronic mail compared to telephones, for example, enables workers to control the pace of their response and thus facilitates multitasking. Digital conferencing may make employees less risk-averse and render group decision-making less predictable, more time-consuming, and more egalitarian (Sproull & Kiesler 1991, Wellman et al 1996). Whether such effects enhance organizational performance or will persist as the technologies evolve is uncertain, in part because they depend on details of system design and implementation (Sproull & Kiesler 1991, O'Mahony & Barley 1999). In vivo research suggests that formally egalitarian "network" structures may coexist with substantial hierarchy and centralization in patterns of communication (Ahuja & Carley 1998).

FIRM STRUCTURE EFFECTS   There is little evidence that the Internet is reshaping organizational structures. O'Mahoney & Barley report that "whether information technologies further centralization or decentralization" varies depending on how managements uses them. The few empirical studies of the relationships between digital technology and organizational size, buy-or-sell decisions, and organizational boundaries are anecdotal or inconclusive (O'Mahoney & Barley 1999: 143–45). The Internet may induce change, but we will not know until researchers undertake large-sample studies that specify changes precisely, treat separately different kinds of information technology, and distinguish effects on different kinds of workers and different business functions.

Take, for example, technology's impact on interfirm networks. Most electronic networks complement, rather than substitute for, more intimate media. For many "network organizations" propinquity is crucial in breeding trust and rapport among participants, for example enabling companies in small-firm networks to share information and exchange specialized assets (Harrison 1994). Spatial agglomeration is also central to the success of biotechnology firms (and to venture capitalists who sustain them) (Powell 2001). The most thorough review of technology-transfer research emphasizes the role of "the mobility and activity of technically trained people" over that of impersonal networks (Board on Science, Technology & Economic Policy 1999). Digital telecommunications seem most important for routine transactions (e.g., inventory systems in which multiple firms share a data base) and for communication among knowledge workers accustomed to scientific norms of exchange (e.g., R&D), and least sufficient when interactions entail risk and require interpersonal judgment.

INDUSTRY SPECIFIC EFFECTS   Studies of specific industries indicate that digital telecommunications can facilitate transformative change when market pressures require it and organizational resources and structures render it possible. For example, when fierce competition and deregulation provoked change and rising demand made it profitable, trucking firms used the Internet (with such other technologies as global positioning) to develop logistics capacity and reposition themselves as transportation-services companies (Nagarajan Bander & White 2000). Hospitals and medical practices have used the Internet to pool information across entities, enabling the emergence of the "integrated healthcare systems" that are transforming many regional healthcare markets (Scott et al 2000, Starr 1997). Other industries that have used Internet technology to effect significant change are banking and financial services (Rochlin 1997) and, with distance learning, higher education (Brown & Duguid 2000:25). In each case, firms adapted the technology to specific strategies, rather than yielding to general technological imperatives.

Thus, the Internet is implicated in profound changes in organizational structures, practices, and strategies. But the extent and nature of these changes— which business functions they restructure, which employees they affect—vary markedly by industry. And rather than causing change, digital technologies are ordinarily pressed into the service of developments to which managers are already committed. The area is ripe for both organizational case studies that focus on the Internet's use in particular industries and organizational surveys that permit confident generalization.

The Internet is also implicated in organizational change in the public sector, where enthusiasts have hailed its potential for saving tax dollars, reducing red tape, and making government more responsive. In an empirically detailed and theoretically sophisticated study, Fountain (2001a,b) has demonstrated both the potential and impediments to its realization. Implementing digital technology saves governments money, but how much depends on network externalities. It reduces some aspects of bureaucratic rigidity but strengthens others by embedding them in code. It enhances the flow of information to citizens and enables government workers to cut through red tape, but in expanding the latter's discretion, it risks imposing new forms of inequality among citizens in their relations with the state (Fountain 2001a,b).

Impact on Culture: Bountiful Diversity, Hypersegmentation, or Massification?

Many sociologists feared that the original mass media (general-interest magazines, radio, and television) would inexorably "massify" taste, as profit-seeking firms produced only those homogeneous and banal programs or texts with the greatest audience appeal (Shils 1963). Since 1980, changes in consumer demand have combined with new media technologies to segment markets and differentiate cultural goods, enabling individuals and groups to individualize their media habits. As an "interconnected network of audio, video, and electronic text communication that will blur the distinction between interpersonal and mass communications and between public and private communications" (Neuman 1991, p. 12), the Internet seems designed to take these trends to their logical conclusion.

Not surprisingly, early observers viewed the new technology as profoundly liberating, opening up outlets for the creative energies of people of every taste and persuasion (Barlow 1996). Because posting information on the Web is so inexpensive, the technology's enthusiasts believed it would virtually eliminate barriers to entry in fields like music recording, book publishing, and even film-making. In this view, the Internet would democratize the flow of information, supplanting top-down dependence on traditional news and media organizations with bottom-up sharing among consumers themselves.

Such optimistic scenarios assume that the Internet's only impact is a direct one on costs (of cultural goods to consumers and of publication to producers). But a second, perhaps more important, effect of the Internet may be to induce the re-structuring of the culture industries themselves. When goods are distributed on the Internet, they can be repackaged in many ways: newspapers, for example, can be disassembled, their parts distributed separately; recorded music can come with more textual documentation than will fit in a CD jewel box. New distribu-tion systems may also alter the size distribution of firms within industries, the relative power of gatekeepers and artists, and the nature of competitive strategies. The Web's earliest cultural impact has been in the music industry, where it has reinforced existing trends toward deconcentration, product differentiation, and the multiplication of market channels (Dowd 2000, Caves 2000).

Some observers suggest that economic imperatives will keep the Internet from realizing its technical potential as a font of cultural abundance (Neuman 1991, Castells 1996). True, barriers to entry are formally lower; but savage competition for users' limited attention may erect new barriers based on investments in marketing and production. The major media producers are developing the Internet commercially after the model of earlier media (albeit with more interactivity), with the expectation that Internet content, broadcast entertainment, and news will soon enter homes through a single system (Castells 1996, but see Owen 1999).

A third position holds that corporate power will overwhelm the Web's liberating potential by radically accelerating long-term trends toward narrower market segmentation and more fine-grained product customization. In this view, Web sites' ability to use "cookies" to track users' browsing habits provides an unprecedented opportunity for targeting appeals. Marketers will divide the public into countless market segments and bombard them with messages that reinforce dispositions and tastes their previous browsing-and-buying patterns have revealed, engendering isolation and myopia (Turow 1997.)

We have little purchase on which perspective is right for two reasons. First, aside from industry reports that many users have robust appetites for free music and sexual images, we know little about cultural practice on the Web. To be sure, the Web offers a remarkable smorgasbord of free cultural products and services. But we know little about who uses them, due to the lack of scholarly research on the extent to which, and ways in which, Internet users listen to music, visit museum sites, or read literature online. Nor do social scientists know to what extent culture consumers use the Web to cultivate existing tastes or, instead, to explore unfamiliar genres.

Second, we cannot yet tell to what extent (and how) media firms will be able to wring profits from Web-based entertainment. They will develop the Web as mass medium only if consumer demand for entertainment suffices to justify large investments (Castells 1996:365). Tendencies toward cultural fragmentation may be repelled by cultural omnivores: well-educated consumers with eclectic tastes for many (finely differentiated) genres (Peterson & Kern 1996). Government will influence the outcome through legislation and court rulings (e.g., the Napster injuncion) that define intellectual property rights.

The Internet's cultural effects may vary among user groups. Because marketers are most interested in reaching people who consume the most, their "fragmenting" efforts may focus on the well-to-do; but such users, especially when they are highly schooled, are the ones most likely to use sophisticated search strategies, so their online behavior may be less easily affected. Castells (1996:371) predicts a Web "populated by two essentially distinct populations, the *interacting and the interacted,*" the first using the medium's full capacity, the latter limited to a "restricted number of prepackaged choices."

THE EVOLVING INTERNET

Research on technological change teaches us that the relationship between technology and society is never unidirectional. Rather technologies are often developed in response to the agendas of powerful social actors. Initially, they shape themselves to the contours of custom; ultimately, they follow paths selected through struggles among groups seeking to turn technologies to their own interests (McGuire & Granovetter 1998).

We see this malleability in the history of the telephone, which was created as a business tool (and even a broadcasting device), but which became an instrument of sociable interaction (Fischer 1992). We see it especially in the history of radio, which emerged as an interactive medium tailored to the needs of military communication, grew into a point-to-point communications device linking amateur enthusiasts, developed into a commercial broadcast system beaming a standardized mass culture across national societies, and finally, under the impact of television's competition, transformed itself into a finely differentiated medium specializing in broadcasting musical genres to narrowly defined subcultural market segments (Douglas 1988, Hargittai 2000a, Owen 1999).

If anything, the Internet is even more pliant because it combines point-to-point and broadcast capability within a single network (Robinson et al 2000b, Wellman 2001). It can be a telephone: literally, or through email, chat rooms, and other forms of real-time communication between individuals. It can serve as a library: specialized Web sites "narrowcast" information to users interested enough to use search engines to find them. It can act as a soapbox for individuals expressing themselves to e-lists and discussion forums. Or it can operate as a conventional mass medium: Internet Service Providers like AOL and services like RealMedia let providers broadcast information to huge user publics simultaneously. Precisely because *it can be all of these things at once*—because it affords users choices among multiple *modes of appropriation* that coexist at any given time—the Internet is unprecedentedly malleable. This malleability raises the stakes for actors who wish to shape its evolution (Hargittai 2000b).

The findings of individual-level research on Internet use reflect the technology as it has emerged, not patterns intrinsic to the medium itself. Economic competition and public policies will shape the extent to which the Internet develops as point-to-point communicator, library, or mass medium; and this, in turn, will alter the incentives and opportunities for different kinds of individuals to use it. Thus, the social impact of the Internet depends on the impact of society on what the Internet becomes. It follows that sociologists should be studying carefully the organization of the Internet field, as well as the manner in which different ways of organizing content shape patterns of use, because such research holds the key to anticipating and understanding the Internet's effects.

Sociologists have been largely remiss in meeting this challenge. A useful exception is Aldrich's (1999:312) analysis of the Web from the standpoint of community, in which he distinguishes among governance structures (regulators and informal consortia), commercial users, service providers to those users, browser developers, and other "infrastructural populations" (hardware and software firms, ISPs, search engines, and portal sites) that occupy niches in the Web's ecology. Owen (1999: ch. 11) presents a useful overview of the Internet industry from an economics perspective, with a particularly thorough treatment of the underlying technology and of the firms that maintain the network and offer connection services. A small but interesting literature explores the Internet's emergent structure through analysis of the network created by the hyperlinks that Web sites send to one another (Zook forthcoming). Early studies using huge data sets were able to map sites onto coherent topical clusters (Larson 1996) and also reported high levels of integration, with most sites reachable from most others at a path distance of four or less (Jackson 1997).

The Internet's future, and thus its social impact, will be influenced by the resolution of three crucial policy issues. The first, establishing equality in Internet access, is necessary to ensure that less well-to-do or technically sophisticated citizens are not excluded from the political, economic, and social opportunities that the Internet increasingly provides. As our discussion of empirical work on this issue demonstrates, a sociological perspective calls attention to the need to go beyond the conventional focus on access per se to explore inequality in the combination of technical and social resources required for effective participation (DiMaggio & Hargittai 2001).

The second, establishing meaningful and enforceable norms of privacy for Internet users, involves the quest for balance between the functionality that people and businesses seek from the Internet and the sacrifice of access to personal information that the technology currently requires people to offer in exchange (Lessig 1999). Sociological research on the beliefs and practices of Internet users, online vendors, and service providers is necessary to inform policy deliberations in this area.

The third, defining rules governing intellectual property for a world in which copying and transmitting cultural works is essentially costless, entails the search for a balance between incentives necessary to motivate creative workers and the interest of society in maximizing access to works of the mind (Computer Science and Telecommunications Board 2000). Currently the pendulum has swung far in the direction of the companies that control rights to intellectual property, with implications not just for music-loving teenagers but for social scientists eager to access formerly public data bases as well (Lessig 1999). Sociologists can contribute to this debate by testing behavioral assumptions about motivations of creative workers and the requirements of markets sufficient to sustain production of intellectual goods.

Lessig (1999) makes a valuable distinction among three ways that states and private interests can regulate communications media: law, norms, and code. The Internet, he argues, is distinctive in that code—the details of the programs that facilitate the exchange of messages and information—is a particularly powerful source of social control, with direct regulation relatively less effective. His work calls attention to the importance of studying aspects of the technology that remain invisible to most observers (and of the need for sociologists studying the Web to acquire sufficient technical expertise to address these questions.).

CONCLUSION

Sociology has been slow to take advantage of the unique opportunity to study the emergence of a potentially transformative technology in situ. Too much of the basic research has been undertaken by nonacademic survey organizations, yielding theoretically unmotivated description at best, and technically flawed and/or proprietarily-held data at worst. (Fortunately, this is changing with such new data-collection efforts as the 2000 General Social Survey's topical module on Internet use, and with increased accessibility of data, much of which is now available on the statistically interactive web site *www.webuse.umd.edu.*) The relatively few sociologists who study the Internet have focused disproportionately on virtual communities, a worthy topic, but not the only one. And in that area, as well as in research on the Internet's impact on inequality, politics, organizations, and culture, we need to develop explanatory models that distinguish between different modes of Internet use and that tie behavior directly to social and institutional context.

Research has suffered, as well, from a disproportionate emphasis on individuals, implicitly treating the nature of the Internet itself as fixed. This is regrettable because this protean technology's character and effects will reflect the outcome of ongoing struggles among powerful economic and political actors. Yet few sociologists have examined the Internet's institutional structure, industrial organization, or political economy. Some sociologists *are* doing important work; but unless their numbers grow, a magnificent opportunity to build and test theories of social and technical change may go unexploited.

If sociology needs the Internet as a laboratory, policy makers need sociology to illuminate the collective choices that will shape the Internet's future. As Philip Agre (1998b:19) has written, discussions of the Internet are often informed less by positive knowledge than by "the cultural system of myths and ideas that our society projects onto the technology." Social science remains the best hope for substituting knowledge for myth and informing public discourse about current conditions and policy alternatives.

ACKNOWLEDGMENTS

We are grateful to Phil Agre, Philip Howard, and Barry Wellman for wise and helpful comments on earlier drafts, and we take full responsibility for persistent defects and limitations. Research support to the authors from the National Science Foundation (grants SBR9710662, SES9819907, and IIS0086143), the Russell Sage Foundation, the Markle Foundation, and the Pew Charitable Trusts is gratefully acknowledged.

Visit the Annual Reviews home page at www.AnnualReviews.org

LITERATURE CITED

Abbate J. 1999. *Inventing the Internet.* Cambridge, MA: MIT Press

Agre P. 1998a. *The Internet and public discourse. First Monday 3.* http://www.firstmondaydk/issues/issue3_3/agre/index.html.

Agre P. 1998b. Presentation in *Proceeding of a Congressional Breakfast Seminar on Information Technology and Social Change*, pp. 14–19. Washington, DC: Consortium of Soc. Sci. Assoc.

Ahuja MK, Carley KM. 1998. Network structure in virtual organizations. *J. Computer-Mediated Commun.* http://www.ascusc.org/jcmc/vol3/issue4/ahuja.html

Aldrich H. 1999. *Organizations Evolving.* Beverly Hills, CA: Sage

Alexander JC, ed. 1988. *Durkheimian Sociology: Cultural Studies.* New York: Columbia Univ. Press

Anderson RH, Bikson TK, Law SA, Mitchell BM. 1995. *Universal Access to E-Mail—Feasability and Societal Implications.* Santa Monica, CA: RAND

Attewell P, Battle J. 1999. Home computers and school performance. *Info. Soc.* 15:1–10

Barlow JP. 1996. *A Declaration of the Independence of Cyberspace.* http://www.eff.org/~barlow/Declaration-Final.html

Bell D. 1973. *The Coming of Post-Industrial Society: A Venture in Social Forecasting.* New York: Basic

Bell D. 1977 [1980]. Teletext and technology: new networks of knowledge and information in postindustrial society. In *The Winding Passage: Essays and Sociological Journeys, 1960-1980*, ed. D Bell, pp. 34–65. New York: Basic

Beniger JR. 1996. Who shall control cyberspace? In *Communication and Cyberspace: Social Interaction in an Electronic Environment*, ed. L Srate, R Jacobson, SB Gibson, pp. 49–58. Cresskill, NJ: Hampton

Bennett WL. 1995. *News: The Politics of Illusion.* New York: Longman. 3rd ed.

Bertot JC, McClure CR. 1998. *The 1998 National Survey of U.S. Public Library Outlet Internet Connectivity: Final Report.* Washington, DC: Am. Library Assoc. Natl. Com. on Libraries & Info. Sci.

Bimber B. 1998. The Internet and political transformation: populism, community and accelerated pluralism. *Polity* 31:133–60

Bimber B. 1999. The Internet and citizen communication with government: Does the medium matter. *Polit. Commun.* 16:409–28

Bimber B. 2000a. The gender gap on the Internet. *Soc. Sci. Q.* 81:868–76

Bimber B. 2000b. The study of information technology and civic engagement. *Polit. Commun.* 17: In press

Bimber B. 2001. Information and civic engagement in America: The search for political effects of the Internet. *Polit. Res. Q.*

Board on Science, Technology and Economic Policy. National Research Council. 1999. *Securing America's Industrial Strength.* Washington, DC: Natl. Acad. Press

Bogart L. 1956. *The Age of Television: A Study of Viewing Habits and the Impact of Television on American Life.* New York: Ungar

Bolt D, Crawford R. 2000. *Digital Divide: Computers and Our Children's Future.* New York: TV Books

Bourdieu P. 1999. *On Television.* New York: New Press

Brown JS, Duguid P. 2000. *The Social Life of Information.* Boston: Harvard Bus. School Press

Browning G. 1996. *Electronic Democracy: Using the Internet to Influence American Politics.* Wilton CT: Pemberton

Brynjolfsson E, Malone T, Gurbaxani V, Kambil A. 1994. Does information technology lead to smaller firms? *Mgmt. Sci.* 40:1628–44

Calhoun C. 1998. Community without propinquity revisited: communication technology and the transformation of the urban public sphere. *Soc. Inquiry* 68:373–97

Castells M. 1996. *The Rise of the Network Society.* Vol. 1 of *The Information Age: Economy, Society and Culture.* Oxford, UK: Blackwell's

Castells M. 2001. *Internet Galaxy: Reflections on the Internet, Business and Society.* New York: Oxford Univ. Press. Forthcoming

Caves R. 2000. *Creative Industries: Contracts Between Art and Commerce.* Cambridge: Harvard Univ. Press

Clemente PC. 1998. *State of the Net: The New Frontier.* New York: McGraw Hill

Coffin T. 1955. Television's impact on society. *Am. Psychol.* 10:630–41

Cole J. 2000. *Surveying the Digital Future.* Los Angeles: UCLA Ctr. Telecommun. Policy (www.ccp.ucla.edu)

Collins R. 1979. *The Credential Society.* New York: Academic

Compaine B. 2000. *Re-examining the digital divide.* Pap. pres. 28th Annual Telecommun. Policy Res. Conf., Arlington, VA

Compaine B, Gomery D, eds. 2000. *Who Owns the Media? Competition and Concentration in the Mass Media Industry.* Mahwah, NJ: Erlbaum

Computer Science and Telecommunications Board, National Research Council. 2000. *The Digital Dilemma: Intellectual Property in the Information Age.* Washington, DC: Natl. Acad. Press

Davis J, Hirschl T, Stack M, eds. 1997. *Cutting Edge: Technology, Information Capitalism, and Social Revolution.* New York: Verso

Davis R. 1998. *The Web of Politics : The Internet's Impact on the American Political System.* New York: Oxford Univ. Press

Dibbell J. 1999. Let third voice be heard. *Intellectual Capital* (August 19). http://www.intellectualcapital.com/issues/issue282/item-6125.asp

DiMaggio P, Hargittai E. 2001. From the 'Digital Divide' to digital inequality: studying Internet use as penetration increases. Work. Pap, Ctr. for Arts Cult. Policy Stud., Princeton Univ.

Douglas S. 1987. *Inventing American Broadcasting, 1899–1922.* Baltimore: Johns Hopkins Univ. Press

Dowd T. 2001. Musical diversity and the mainstream recording market, 1955–1990. *Rassegna Italiana di Sociol.* Forthcoming

Downs A. 1957. *An Economic Theory of Democracy.* New York: Harper & Row

Eisenstein EL. 1979. *The Printing Press as an Agent of Change.* Cambridge Univ. Press

Elster J. ed. 1998. *Deliberative Democracy.* New York: Cambridge Univ. Press

Etzioni A, Etzioni O. 1997. Communities: virtual vs. real. *Science* 277:295

Fischer C. 1992. *America Calling: A Social History of the Telephone to 1940.* Berkeley: Univ. Calif. Press

Fountain JE. 2001a. The economic impact of the Internet on the government sector. In *The Economic Payoff from the Internet Revolution*, Rep. Brookings Task Force on the Internet. Washington, DC: Brookings Inst.

Fountain JE. 2001b. *Building the Virtual State: Information Technology and Institutional Change.* Washington, DC: Brookings Inst.

Freedman JL, Sears D. 1965. Selective exposure. In *Advances in Experimental Social Psychology*, ed. L Berkowitz, 2:58–98. Orlando: Academic Press

Frenkel SJ, Korczynski M, Shire KA, Tam M. 1999. *On the Front Line: Organization of Work in the Information Economy.* Ithaca, NY: Cornell Univ. Press

Frey D. 1986. Recent research on selective exposure to information. *Adv. Exp. Soc. Psychol.* 19:41–80

Garnham N. 1990. *Capitalism and Communication: Global Culture and the Economics of Information.* Newbury Park, CA: Sage

Gibson RK, Howard PEN, Ward S. 2000. Social capital, Internet connectedness and political participation: A four-country study. Pap. pres. 2000 Int. Polit. Sci. Assoc. Meet., Quebecé, Canada

Guillén M, Suarez S. 2001. Developing the Internet: entrepreneurship and public policy in Ireland, Singapore, Argentina and Spain. *Telecommun. Policy* 25

Goldhaber MH. 1997. The attention economy and the Net. *First Monday*

Habermas J. 1981. *The Theory of Communicative Action*, Vol. 1. *Reason and the Rationalization of Society.* Boston: Beacon

Habermas J. 1989. *The Structural Transformation of the Public Sphere.* Cambridge MA: MIT Press

Hampton K, Wellman B. 2000. Examining community in the digital neighborhood: early results from Canada's wired suburb. In *Digital Cities: Experiences, Technologies and Future Perspectives*, ed. T Ishida, K Isbister, pp. 475–92. Heidelberg, Germany: Springer-Verlag

Hargittai E. 1996. *Holes in the Net: The Internet and International Stratification.* Senior Honors Thesis. Smith College. (http://cs.smith.edu/~hargitta/Thesis)

Hargittai E. 1999. Weaving the Western Web: Explaining difference in Internet connectivity among OECD countries. *Telecommun. Policy* 23:701–18

Hargittai E. 2000a. Radio's lessons for the Internet. *Commun. ACM* 43:50–57

Hargittai E. 2000b. Open portals or closed gates? Channeling content on the World Wide Web. *Poetics.* 27:233–53

Harrison B. 1994. *Lean and Mean: The Changing Landscape of Corporate Power in the Age of Flexibility.* New York: Basic

Hauben M, Hauben R. 1997. *Netizens: On the History and Impact of Usenet and the Internet.* Los Alamitos, CA: IEEE Computer Soc. Press

Heldritch Center for Workforce Development (Rutgers Univ.) and Center for Survey Research and Analysis (Univ. Conn.). 2000. *Nothing but Net: American Workers and the Information Economy.* New Brunswick NJ: Heldritch Ctr.

Hill KA, Hughes JE. 1998. *Cyberpolitics: Citizen Activism in the Age of the Internet.* Lanham, MD: Rowman & Littlefield

Hirsch PM. 1978. Television as a national medium: Its cultural and political role in American society. In *Handbook of Urban Life*, ed. David Street, pp. 389–427. San Francisco: Jossey-Bass

Hoffman DL, Novak TP, Schlosser A. 2000. The evolution of the Digital Divide: How gaps in Internet access may impact electronic commerce. *J. Computer-Mediated Commun.* 5 March.

Howard PEN, Rainie L, Jones S. 2001. Days and nights on the Internet: the impact of a diffusing technology. Special issue of *Am. Behav. Sci.* ed. B Wellman, C Haythornthwaite. Forthcoming

Intelli-Quest. 1999. Intelliquest study shows 83 million U.S. Internet users and 56 million online shoppers. Press release, April 19. http://www.intelliquest.com/press/release78.asp

ITU (International Telecommunications Union) 1997. *Challenges to the Network: Telecoms and the Internet.* Geneva: ITU Press

ITU. 1998. *World Telecommunication Development Report.* Geneva: ITU Press

ITU. 1999. *Challenges to the Network: Internet for Development 1999.* Geneva: ITU Press

Introna L, Nissenbaum H. 2000. Shaping the Web: Why the politics of search engines matters. *Info. Soc.* 16

Jackson M. 1997. Assessing the communication structure of the World Wide Web. *J. Computer-Mediated Commun.* 3. http://www.ascusc.org/jcmc/vol3/issue1/jackson.html

Johnson TJ, Kaye BK. 1998. A vehicle for engagement or a haven for the disaffected?

Internet use, political alienation and voter participation, In *Engaging the Public: How Government and the Media Can Reinvigorate American Democracy*, ed. TJ Johnson, CE Hays, SP Hays. New York: Rowman & Littlefield

Katz JE, Aspden P. 1997. Motives, hurdles and dropouts. *Commun. ACM* 40:97–102

Katz JE, Rice R, Aspden P. 2001. The Internet, 1995–2000: Access, civic involvement and social interaction. Special issue of *Am. Behav. Sci.* ed. B Wellman, C Haythorn-Waite.

Kavanaugh AL, Patterson SJ. 2001. The impact of community computer networks on social capital and community. involvement. Special issue of *Am. Behav. Sci.*, ed. B Wellman, C Haythornthwaite. Forthcoming

Koku E, Nazer N, Wellman B. 2001. International scholarly networks. *Am. Behav. Sci.* Forthcoming.

Kolko BE, Nakamura L, Rodman GB. 2000. *Race in Cyberspace*. New York: Routledge

Kollock P. 1999. The production of trust in online markets. *Adv. Group Processes* 16:99–123

Kornhauser W. 1968. Mass society. In *The Encyclopedia of the Social Sciences*, ed. D. Sills. New York: Free Press/Macmillan

Kraut R, Scherlis W, Mukhopadhyay T, Manning J, Kiesler S. 1996. The HomeNet field trial of residential Internet services. *Commun. ACM* 39:55–63

Kraut R, Patterson M, Lundmark V, Kiesler S, Mukophadhyay T, Scherlis W. 1998. Internet paradox: A social technology that reduces social involvement and psychological well-being? *Am. Psychol.* 53:1011–31

Kraut R, Kiesler S, Boneva B, Cummings J, Helgeson V. 2001. Internet paradox revisited. *J. Soc. Issues.* Forthcoming

Krueger AB. 1993. How computers have changed the wage structure: evidence from micro data. *Q. J. Econ.* 108:33–60

Lake D. 2000. The Web: growing by 2 million pages a day. *Indust. Standard* Feb 28

Larson R. 1996. Bibliometrics of the World Wide Web: an exploratory analysis of the intellectual structure of Cyberspace. Ray R. Larson. In *ASIS '96 Proceedings of the 59th ASIS Annu. Mtg.*, ed. S Hardin. Baltimore, MD, Oct 21–24, 1996. Medford, NJ: Info. Today. http://sherlock.berkeley.edu/asis96/asis96.html

Lentz B, Straubhaar J, LaPastina A, Main S, Taylor J. 2000. *Structuring access: the role of public access centers in the "Digital Divide."* Pap. pres. Annu. Meet. Int. Commun. Assoc., Acapulco, June.

Lessig L. 1999. *Code and Other Laws of Cyberspace*. New York: Basic

Lin N. 2001. *Social Capital: A Theory of Social Structure and Action*. New York: Cambridge Univ. Press

Machlup F. 1962. *The Production and Distribution of Knowledge in the United States*. Princeton, NJ: Princeton Univ. Press

Margolis M, Resnick D. 1999. *Taming the Cyber-Revolution: How Money and Politics Domsticate the Web*. Thousand Oaks, Calif: Sage

McChesney RW. 1996. The Internet and U.S. communication policy-making in historical and critical perspective. *J. Commun.* 46:98–124

McGuire P, Granovetter M. 1998. *Business and bias in public policy formation: the National Civic Federation and the social construction of electric utility regulation, 1905–1907*. Pap. pres. meet. Am. Sociol. Assoc., San Francisco

McLuhan M. 1967. *Understanding Media: The Extensions of Man*. New York: McGraw Hill

Miller D, Slater D. 2000. *The Internet: An Ethnographic Approach*. New York: Berg

Mintz J. 2000. McCain camp enjoys a big Net advantage. *Washington Post*. Feb 9

Nagarajan A, Bander JL, White CC. 2000. Trucking. In *U.S. Industry in 2000: Studies in Competitive Performance*, ed. Board on Sci., Technol. Econ. Policy, Natl. Res. Coun., pp. 123–53. Washington, DC: Natl. Acad. Press

NTIA (National Telecommunications and Information Administration). 1995. *Falling Through the Net: A Survey of the 'Have Nots' in Rural and Urban America.* Washington, DC: US Dep. Commerce

NTIA. 1998. *Falling Through the Net II: New Data on the Digital Divide.* Washington, DC: US Dep. Commerce

NTIA. 1999. *Falling Through the Net III: Defining the Digital Divide.* Washington, DC: US Dep. Commerce

NTIA. 2000. *Falling through the Net: Toward Digital Inclusion.* Washington, DC: US Dep. Commerce

Negroponte N. 1995. *Being Digital.* New York: Knopf

Netcraft. 2000. *The Netcraft Web Server Survey.* Online document available at http://www.netcraft.com/survey/ (last accessed Aug. 25, 2000)

Neuman WR. 1991. *The Future of the Mass Audience.* New York: Cambridge Univ. Press

Neuman WR. 2000. The impact of the new media: fragmentation, stratification and political evolution. In *Mediated Politics: Communication in the Future of Democracy,* ed. WL Bennett, RM Entman. New York: Cambridge Univ. Press

Neuman WR, McKnight LW, Solomon RJ. 1998. *The Gordian Knot: Political Gridlock on the Information Highway.* Cambridge: MIT Press

Neuman WR, O'Donnell SR, Schneider SM. 1996. The Web's next wave: a field study of Internet diffusion and use patterns. Ms., MIT Media Lab.

Nie NH, Ebring L. 2000. *Internet and Society: A Preliminary Report.* Stanford, CA; Inst. for Quant. Stud. Soc.

Norris P. 2001. *Digital Divide? Civic Engagement, Information Poverty and the Internet in Democratic Societies.* New York: Cambridge Univ. Press

NUA. 2000a. How many online? *NUA Internet Surveys.* Online document available at http://www.nua.ie/surveys/how_many_online/world.html

NUA. 2000b. February 14. Portals draw lion's share of audiences. *NUA Internet Surveys.* http://www.nua.ie/surveys/?f = VS&art_id = 905355592&rel = true

O'Mahony S, Barley SR. 1999. Do digital telecommunications affect work and organization? The state of our knowledge. *Res. Org. Behav.* 21:125–61

OECD. 1997. *Webcasting and Convergence: Policy Implications.* Paris: OECD. (http://www.oecd.org/dsti/sti/it/cm/prod/e_97-221.htm)

Orlikowski WJ, Iacono CS. 2000. The truth is not out there: an enacted view of the 'digital economy.' In *Understanding the Digital Economy: Data, Tools, and Research,* ed. E Brynjolfsson, B Kahin, pp. 352–80. Cambridge, MA: MIT Press

Owen BM. 1999. *The Internet Challenge to Television.* Cambridge: Harvard Univ. Press

Paccagnella L. 1997. Getting the seats of your pants dirty: strategies for ethnographic research on virtual communities. *J. Computer-Mediated Commun.* http://www.ascusc.org/jcmc/vol3/issue1/paccagnella.html

Paltridge S, Ypsilanti D. 1997. A bright outlook for communications. *OECD Observer.* 205:19–22

Peterson RA, Kern RM. 1996. Changing highbrow taste: from snob to omnivore. *Am. Sociol. Rev.* 61:900–7

Pew Center for the People and the Press. 1995. *Technology in the American household.* Washington, DC http://www.people-press.org/tech.htm

Pew Center for the People and the Press. 1998. *Internet news takes off.* http://www. people-press.org/med98rpt.htm.

Pew Center for the People and the Press. 1999. *The Internet news audience goes ordinary.* January. Washington DC, Pew Res. Ctr. for People & Press

Powell WW. 2001. The capitalist firm in the 21st century: emerging patterns. In *The 21st Century Firm: Changing Economic Organization in International Perspective,* ed. P. DiMaggio. Princeton, NJ: Princeton Univ. Press

Preece J. 2000. *On-line Communities:Designing Usability and Supporting Sociability.* New York: Wiley

Prettejohn M. 1996. *The first year: August*

1995–August 1996. Netcraft. http://www.net-craft.com/survey/year1.html

Putnam RD. 2000. *Bowling Alone: The Collapse and Revival of American Community.* New York: Simon & Schuster

Rao M, Rashid I, Rizvi H, Subba R. 2000. *Online content in South Asia.* South Asia Networks Organisation. Online document http://www.sasianet.org/onlinecont.html last accessed August 26

Rheingold H. 1993. *The Virtual Community: Homesteading on the Electronic Frontier.* Reading, MA: Addison-Wesley

Robinson JP, Barth K, Kohut A. 1997. Personal computers, mass media, and use of time. *Soc. Sci. Computer Rev.* 15:65–82

Robinson JP, Kestnbaum M. 1999. The personal computer, culture and other uses of free time. *Soc. Sci. Computer Rev.* Summer: 209–216

Robinson JP, Godbey G. 1999. *Time for Life.* State College, PA: Penn State Univ. Press. 2nd ed.

Robinson JP, Kestnbaum M, Neustadtl A, Alvarez A. 2000. *IT, the Internet, and time displacement.* Pap. pres. Annu. Meet. Am. Assoc. Pub. Opin. Res, Portland, OR, May 2000

Rochlin GI. 1997. *Trapped in the Net: The Unanticipated Consequences of Computerization.* Princeton: Princeton Univ. Press

Rogers EM. 1995. *Diffusion of Innovations,* New York: Free Press. 4th ed.

Roper Starch Worldwide Inc. 1998. *America Online Roper Starch Cyberstudy 1998.* New York

Sandvig C. 2000. *The information apologue: play and Internet access in the children's library.* Pap. pres. Int. Commun. Assoc. Annu. Meet., Acapulco, Mexico. June 1–5

Schement J. 1996. *Beyond Universal Service: Characteristics of Americans without Telephones, 1980–1993.* Commun. Policy Work. Pap. No. 1. Washington, DC: Benton Found.

Schement J. 1999. Of gaps by which democracy we measure. *Info. Impacts.* Dec.

Schiller HI. 1989. *Culture, Inc.: The Corporate Takeover of Public Expression.* New York: Oxford Univ. Press

Schiller H. 1996. *Information Inequality: The Deepening Social Crisis in America.* New York: Routledge

Schneider SM. 1996. Creating a democratic public sphere through political discussion: a case study of abortion conversation on the Internet. *Soc. Sci. Computer Rev.* 14:373–93

Schneider SM. 2000a. *Political portals and democracy: threats and promises.* May.netelection.org/commentary/2000015. php3

Schneider SM. 2000b. *The dot-not candidates.* July. netelection.org/commentary/2000023.php3

Schudson M. 1998. *The Good Citizen: A History of American Civic Life.* New York: Free Press

Schumpeter JA. 1947. *Capitalism, Socialism and Democracy.* New York: Harper & Row

Scott WR, Ruef M, Mendel P, Caronna CA. 2000. *Institutional Change and Organizations: Transformation of a Healthcare Field.* Chicago: Univ. Chicago Press.

Shapiro AL. 1999. *The Control Revolution: How the Internet is Putting Individuals in Charge and Changing the World We Know.* New York: Century Found.

Shils E. 1963. The theory of mass society. In *American as a Mass Society,* ed. P Olson, pp. 30–50. Glencoe, IL: Free Press

Silver D. 2000. Margins in the wires: looking for race, gender and sexuality in the Blacksburg Electronic Village. In *Race in Cyberspace,* ed. BE Kolko, L Nakamura, GB Rodman. New York: Routledge

Silverstein C, Henzinger M, Marais H, Moricz M. 1998. Analysis of a very large AltaVista query log. *SRC Tech. Note* 1998-014. Oct 26

Smith M, Kollock P, eds. 1999. *Communities in Cyberspace.* London: Routledge

Sproull LS, Kiesler SB. 1991. *Connections: New Ways of Working in the Networked Organization.* Boston: MIT Press

Starr P. 1997. Smart technology, stunted policy: developing health information networks. *Health Affairs* 15:91–105

Stoll C. 1995. *Silicon Snake Oil: Second Thoughts on the Information Highway.* New York: Doubleday

Stromer-Galley J. 2000. Online interaction and why candidates avoid it. *J. Commun.* 50. In press

Strover S. 1999. *Rural Internet Connectivity.* Rural Policy Res. Inst. Rep. P99-13. http://www.rupri.org/pubs/archive/reports/P99-13/

Strover S, Straubhaar J. 2000. *E-Government Services and Computer and Internet Use in Texas. A Report from the Telecommunications and Information Policy Institute.* Austin, TX. http://www.utexas.edu/research/tipi/reports/dir_final2.htm

Tapscott D. 1999. Introduction. *Creating Value in the Network Economy,* ed. D. Tapscott, pp. vii-xxvi. Boston: Harvard Bus. School Press

Todreas TM. 1999. *Value Creation and Branding in Television's Digital Age.* Westport CT: Quorum

Turkle S. 1995. *Life on the Screen: Identity in the Age of the Internet.* New York: Simon & Schuster

Turow J. 1997. *Breaking Up America: Advertisers and the New Media World.* Chicago: Univ. Chicago Press

US Dep. Education. 2000. Internet access in U.S. public schools and classrooms: 1994-1999. Stats in Brief. Nat. Ctr. Educ. Stat. Feb

Uslaner E. 2001. The Internet and social capital. *Proc. ACM.* Forthcoming

Van Alstyne M, Brynjolfsson E. 1997. *Global village or cyberbalkans.* http://web.mit.edu/marshall/www/papers/CyberBalkans.pdf.

Van den Besselaar P, Beckers D. 1998. Demographics and sociographics of the "Digital City." In *Community Computing and Support Systems Social Interaction in Networked Communities,* ed. T Ishida. Heidelberg: Springer. http://www.swi.psy.uva.nl/usr/beckers/publications/kyoto.html

Waxman J. 2000a. *The Old 80/20 Rule Take One on the Jaw. Internet Trends Report 1999 Review.* San Francisco: Alexa Res.

Waxman J. 2000b. *Leading the Pack...Internet Trends Report 1999 Review.* San Francisco: Alexa Res.

Weber M. 1968 [1924]. *Economy and Society,* ed. G Roth, C Wittich. New York: Bedminster

Weiss R. 1970. Effects of mass media of communication. In *Handbook of Social Psychology,* ed. G Lindzey, E Aronson, 5:77–195. Reading, MA: Addison-Wesley.

Wellman B. 2001. Physical place and cyberplace: Changing portals and the rise of networked individualism. *Int. J. Urban Regional Res.* Forthcoming

Wellman B, Salaff J, Dimitrova D, Garton L, Gulia M, Haythornwaite C. 1996. Computer networks as social networks: collaborative work, telework, and virtual community. *Annu. Rev. Sociol.* 22:213–38

Wellman B, Gulia M. 1999. Net surfers don't ride alone: virtual community as community. In *Networks in the Global Village,* ed. Barry Wellman, pp. 331–67. Boulder, CO: Westview

Wilhelm A. 2000. *Democracy in the Digital Age.* New York: Routledge

Wilson EJ. 2000. *Closing the Digital Divide: An Initial Review. Briefing the President.* Washington, DC: Internet Policy Inst. May. http://www.internet policy. org/briefing/ErnestWilson0700.html

Zook M. 2001. Old hierarchies or new networks of centrality? The global geography of the Internet content market. *Am. Behav. Sci.* 44: Forthcoming

Zuboff S. 1988. *In the Age of the Smart Machine: The Future of Work and Power.* New York: Basic

Annu. Rev. Sociol. 2001. 27:337–62

THE SCALE OF JUSTICE: Observations on the Transformation of Urban Law Practice

John P. Heinz[1], Robert L. Nelson[2], and Edward O. Laumann[3]

[1]*American Bar Foundation, Chicago, Illinois 60611 and Northwestern University Law School, Chicago, Illinois 60611; e-mail: j-heinz@northwestern.edu*
[2]*American Bar Foundation, Chicago, Illinois 60611 and Department of Sociology, Northwestern University, Evanston, Illinois 60201; e-mail: rnelson@abfn.org*
[3]*Department of Sociology, University of Chicago, Chicago, Illinois 60637; e-mail: ob01@midway.uchicago.edu*

Key Words   lawyers, law firms, professions, lawyer/client relations, legal profession

■ **Abstract**   In the last quarter of the twentieth century, urban law practice changed markedly. Using data from two surveys of Chicago lawyers, the first in 1975 and the second in 1995, the article argues that the most consequential development was the sheer increase in the size of firms. The organization of the delivery of legal services was restructured, and the relationships between lawyers and clients changed. Growth in the power and prestige of corporate inside counsel, greater competition among law firms, and the move by those firms into broader geographic markets precipitated changes in firm management. The recent movement into the international market for legal services of large accounting firms, financial services firms, and consulting firms (creating "multidisciplinary" partnerships) suggests the possibility of more far reaching changes in the next decade or two.

INTRODUCTION

In the last quarter of the twentieth century, the social organization of the practicing bar changed in several important ways.

- Women began to enter the bar in large numbers in the mid-1970s.

- New specialties came into prominence, such as sports law and entertainment law (these are primarily specializations in a particular clientele) and cyber law and health law (these are more substantive).

- Lawyers employed within corporations (sometimes referred to as house counsel) enjoyed an increase in power and prestige; formerly, they had been denigrated (Slovak 1980:32) (as their prestige increased, the term corporate inside counsel was often substituted for the earlier label).

0360-0572/01/0811-0337$14.00

- Ties between corporations and the law firms that represent them became less stable, less intimate, and more varied.

- Partners in major law firms, formerly treated as having life tenure, were now sometimes to be expelled from the partnership; to replace them, partners were recruited from competing firms, a practice once regarded as unprofessional (Smigel 1969:57).

- The incomes of partners and associates in major firms increased greatly, while the earnings of solo practitioners and lawyers in small firms declined (Sander & Williams 1989; R. L. Sandefur, E. O. Laumann, unpublished data).

- While almost all law firms were once locally based, by the 1980s and 1990s it had become commonplace for law firms to have offices in several major cities in the United States and abroad (C. Silver, 2000).[1]

- Many tasks traditionally performed by lawyers were assigned to unlicensed paraprofessionals (Abel 1989:197–98).

But the most consequential change in the profession over these decades is probably the increase in sheer scale. Scale increased both in the profession overall—i.e., in the number of lawyers and in the volume of legal work—and within the several types of organizations in which law is practiced.

The most extensive changes took place in large corporate law firms. These changes made those firms the subject of complaints about a host of maladies, including alienation and overwork (Schiltz 1999; but see Heinz et al, 1999), the elevation of economic interest over professional values (especially, values concerning community service and independence from clients) (Kronman 1993), and the decline of civility and ethicality in practice (Burger 1995:953; Glendon 1994; Linowitz 1994). In this article, using data drawn from a study of Chicago lawyers, we offer several observations on the changing nature of large law firms and the relationships of those changes to broader developments in the economy and society.

SIZE

The number of US lawyers increased from 355,242 in 1971 (one per 572 residents) to 857,931 in 1995 (one per 303 residents) (Sikes et al, 1972; Carson 1999). According to the Census of Service Industries, total US expenditures on legal services grew from $32 billion in 1972 to $101 billion in 1992 in constant (1992)

---

[1]In the late 1950s, there was considerable controversy within the bar over the prospect that Adlai Stevenson's newly merged firm would have offices in three cities—Chicago, Washington, DC, and New York. A 1961 book noted that "[t]he bar was startled recently by the announcement of the formation of a nation-wide firm with offices interlocking in Illinois, Washington, DC, and New York.... The setup was so unusual that it had to be approved in advance by the Bar Association; and it occasioned considerable comment among local lawyers (Levy 1961:20; see also Galanter & Palay 1991:23).

dollars (Bureau of the Census 1976, 1996). This rate of increase was twice that of the gross national product during the same period, and it exceeded the percentage increase in spending for health services (R. E. Litan & S. Salop, unpublished data).

The "large" New York law firms that Smigel (1969) studied in the late 1950s had an average of 22 partners each. In 1957, only 20 New York firms had as many as 50 lawyers, counting both partners and associates (Smigel 1969:358). In 1969, however, Smigel observed that "[l]aw firms have, in fact, grown to such proportions that when reference is made in Wall Street to 'large firms' it is beginning to mean offices of 100 or more attorneys" (Smigel 1969:359). By 1995, according to one count, there were 124 law firms in New York State with more than 100 lawyers.[2] The largest firms in New York (and elsewhere, since the big firms are now national and international) have 1000 or more lawyers. In two American Bar Foundation surveys of Chicago lawyers, respondents were asked the number of lawyers in their firms—in 1975, the average was 27; in 1995, it was 141 (Heinz et al 1998:768).[3] The largest firm represented in the 1995 sample employed 1800 partners and associates.

This increase in the scale of law practice organizations is not confined to private firms. Between the 1975 and 1995 surveys of the Chicago bar, the size of corporate inside-counsel offices represented in the Chicago samples increased from an average of 17 lawyers each in 1975 to 55 lawyers in 1995, and government law offices (national, state, and local) grew on average from 64 lawyers each to 399. The office of the Cook County State's Attorney (called the district attorney in many places) employed 850 lawyers in 1995.

DEMAND

When increases in scale of this order of magnitude occur, significant consequences are likely to follow—and they have. But we should attend not only to the consequences, but also to what is driving the increase in scale and to whether the growth has been uniform across the full range and variety of the profession. The ABF's Chicago surveys estimate that the percentage of lawyers' efforts devoted to the

---

[2]This information was compiled by Clara Carson of the American Bar Foundation, using data from the Martindale-Hubbell Lawyers Directory.

[3]In both ABF surveys, random samples were drawn from the full population of licensed lawyers having offices within Chicago, including all areas of practice, lawyers engaged in other occupations, and retired and unemployed lawyers. There were 777 respondents in 1975 and 788 in 1994–1995, and the response rate was over 82% in both surveys. Interviews were conducted face to face and averaged more than an hour in length. Note that, because the ABF surveys used random samples of lawyers, not firms, the probability that any given firm will be represented in the samples is directly proportional to the number of lawyers in the firm. Thus, the average number of lawyers per firm will be smaller than the numbers given here, which are instead a measure of the nature of the contexts in which the lawyers practice.

corporate sector increased from 53% in 1975 to 64% in 1995, while effort devoted to individual clients and small businesses declined from 40% in 1975 to 29% in 1995 (Heinz et al, 1998:765, Table 3). But although the market for legal services to individuals and small businesses has declined relative to legal work for corporations and government, both have grown in absolute terms. That is, the total number of lawyers in Chicago was roughly twice as great in 1995 as in 1975 (approximately 15,000 in 1975, 30,000 in 1995). Thus, while the individual and small business sector of the market consumed 40% of the total effort of Chicago lawyers in 1975 and 29% in 1995, our estimate is that the absolute amount of lawyers' time devoted to that market sector actually increased—but not nearly as substantially as the time devoted to corporations and government. These findings are generally consistent with data reported by the Census of Service Industries for many (but not all) major US cities.[4]

---

[4]It is possible that some of the change is attributable to a decline in demand for personal legal services because of changes in law (e.g., an increase in the size of estates that are exempt from taxation, or the change to "no-fault" divorce). But note that the best estimate is that overall demand for such services has increased. One might also speculate that some or all of the shift from personal client work toward corporate work between 1975 and 1995 is attributable to a movement of middle class population from the city to the suburbs. Thus, so the thesis goes, lawyers are likely to have followed the clientele, given "white flight" to the suburbs. This would explain, for example, the decline in trusts and estates practice in the city. But there are reasons to doubt the validity of this thesis.

The Census of Service Industries data indicate that the percentage of lawyers' income received from individual clients (persons) has declined, nationally, while the percentage received from businesses has increased substantially. Receipts from individuals decreased from 52.2% of total U.S. lawyer receipts in 1972 to 39.6% in 1992, while receipts from businesses increased from 42.0% to 50.9% (and receipts from government increased from 2.9% to 3.8%) (Bureau of the Census 1976, 1996). The distribution of Chicago lawyers' receipts is similar to that in several other major cities, though not in all. According to the Census of Service Industries, in Sacramento receipts from individuals decreased from 50.4% of total receipts in 1982 to 46.3% in 1992, while receipts from businesses increased from 38.8% to 45.2%. In Los Angeles, receipts from individuals fell from 46.2% in 1982 to 31.0% in 1992, while receipts from businesses increased from 49.5% to 56.6%. In Philadelphia, however, the percentages of receipts from the two categories of clients were virtually unchanged from 1982 to 1992 (varying only from 45% to 47% for each), and in Phoenix the changes were modest (individuals fell from 43.3% to 38.3%, while businesses rose only from 51.7% to 53.7%) (Bureau of the Census 1986, 1996). Thus, the largest city in this set, Los Angeles, displays the pattern that is most similar to that of Chicago.

Moreover, available data do not appear to indicate a great shift of lawyer population from the city to the suburbs. The first year that "official" counts of lawyers became available from the Illinois Attorney Registration and Disciplinary Commission (ARDC) was 1976. According to those reports, the number of lawyers in Cook County increased from 19,072 in 1976 to 36,158 in 1995, while the lawyer population in the five surrounding "collar" counties in the metropolitan area increased from 2,156 to 7,008 (ARDC 1977, 1996). Thus, the collar counties had a larger percentage increase on a much smaller base, but they grew by less than 5,000 lawyers while Cook increased by more than 17,000.

The relatively modest increase in demand for legal services to individuals and small businesses is probably largely a function of simple growth in the size of the population. In spite of considerable public discussion of a "litigation explosion" and the correlative demand for "tort reform"—some of it stimulated by an advertising and public relations campaign by the insurance companies (Daniels & Martin 1995; Glaberson 1999)—there is little evidence of a major change in community norms concerning disputing behavior or resort to litigation (Galanter 1993). With the exception of mass tort suits (such as the asbestos cases), often brought as class actions on behalf of large categories of individuals, much of the increase in litigation is attributable to suits brought by businesses against other businesses (Dunworth & Rogers 1996). The Chicago surveys found that the percentage of effort devoted to personal injury work for plaintiffs, 6%, was unchanged from 1975 to 1995 (Heinz et al, 1998:765, Table 3). Changes in law that affect individuals (e.g., increasing use of the condominium form of ownership) have not generally increased the rate at which people use lawyers [indeed lawyers now appear to be involved in sales of residences less often: In the two Chicago surveys, the estimated percentage of effort devoted to personal real estate transactions declined from 6% in 1975 to 3% in 1995 (Heinz et al, 1998:765, Table 3)]. Some new laws have created novel rights and remedies (regarding employment discrimination, for example), but most of the regulatory legislation of recent decades (for example, that concerning occupational safety and health) has primarily given rise to government enforcement proceedings rather than to private law suits.

The relative stability in the nature of the legal work done for individuals and in the rate at which claims are brought on their behalf has meant that there has been less impetus to alter the form and character of organizations providing such services. Thus, legal work for individuals and small businesses is still ordinarily done by small firms and solo practitioners. Seron (1996:87, 168) finds evidence that some small firms are adopting an entrepreneurial approach to this market segment, but that traditionalists still far outnumber innovators. Although a few

---

Now, Cook County includes some suburbs as well as the City of Chicago. Unfortunately, the ARDC data are not disaggregated below the county level—i.e., they do not give a separate count for the city. To examine the division between Chicago and suburban Cook County, therefore, we must use the Martindale-Hubbell Lawyers Directory compilation, which is less inclusive than the ARDC register. According to Martindale-Hubbell, the 1995 breakdown was 24,021 lawyers in the city and 5,065 lawyers in the Cook suburbs (Martindale-Hubbell 1995–96). Since earlier Martindale-Hubbell compilations are not available in a form that permits sorting by computer, we now turn to yet another source. The Lawyer Statistical Report estimated that there were 19,476 lawyers in Chicago in 1980 (Curran et al, 1985:320). Comparing that figure to 22,310 lawyers in Cook County registered with the ARDC in 1980, we arrive at an estimate of 2,834 lawyers in the Cook suburbs in 1980. This would mean that the lawyer population in suburban Cook increased by 2,231 from 1980 to 1995, while the Chicago lawyer population increased by 4,545. Again, then, although the suburbs show a larger percentage increase (on a relatively small base), the city has a far larger increase in the absolute number of lawyers.

firms operating nationally or regionally have attempted to use advertising to acquire a "brand name" identity in the market for routine wills, divorces, and residential real estate sales, and then to exploit that asset by selling franchises to use the name or by contracting with lawyers to provide services in the name of the firm (Van Hoy 1997), these companies have not succeeded in capturing a large share of the market. Some "group legal service plans" provide services to members of unions or other organizations, often using lawyers employed on a contractual basis, but again these plans have not acquired much of the market for personal legal services.

The manner in which legal service is provided to corporations and other large organizations (e.g., not-for-profit organizations and government entities), however, has changed dramatically. That is where the great increase in the scale of law firms has occurred, and that is where the relationships among lawyers and between lawyers and their clients have been significantly altered (Michelson et al, 2000).

A part of the increase in law firm size in the corporate sector is the result of mergers of preexisting firms, but most is accounted for by overall growth in the number of lawyers doing corporate legal work, in response to a great increase in demand for such services. Some of this demand is cyclical. When the economy slowed in the early 1990s, after the rapid growth of the 1980s, corporate law firms reduced their hiring of new lawyers [and many of them discharged excess lawyers, both associates and partners; Kirkland & Ellis, a Chicago-based firm, reportedly dismissed 55 associates and nonequity partners (Hall 2000)]. When the economy accelerated again in the mid- and late 1990s, those firms resumed their expansion. Thus, much of the demand for corporate legal services is attributable simply to the rate of business activity—if more business transactions take place, more lawyers' time will be needed. But changes in law or in government enforcement strategy may also affect demand. In the 1980s, the Reagan administration took a newly permissive view of the antitrust laws. As a result, corporations had greater freedom to pursue mergers and the acquisition of other companies, and large law firms created M&A (mergers and acquisitions) departments. New employment discrimination laws, occupational safety regulations, and tax reporting requirements also created new legal problems for corporations, much more than they did for individuals.

Changes in the character of American business enterprise, however, had even more impact on the demand for corporate legal services. When the largest sectors of the American economy were agriculture and heavy industry, those enterprises probably generated fewer demands for legal services, per dollar of product, than does the service economy (Nelson 1994). In a survey of companies headquartered in the Chicago area, Bell (1999:22–24) found that "companies dealing with financial services and insurance and those in the transportation industry are the most intensive consumers of legal services" and that "manufacturers in heavily science-dependent fields are considerably more likely than others to make extensive use of lawyers."

Service businesses typically create a larger number of transactions, with personal contact among a larger number of players, than do manufacturing or agribusiness. Businesses that create a relatively small number of transactions, and where there is greater concentration in a smaller number of companies, generate fewer points of contact that may give rise to disputes. Moreover, where the number of suppliers of a product is small, the consumers will be more highly dependent on continuing relations with their suppliers, and therefore less disposed to initiate legal action against them, than will purchasers who may choose from many potential suppliers. Thus, where ease of entry into a business is greater, litigation will be more likely—purchasers of computer services may be more willing than automobile dealers to sue their suppliers (Macaulay 1963). Changes in the mix of types of businesses represented in the economy, then, may alter (*a*) the volume of transactions, (*b*) the likelihood that those transactions will be conducted with the participation of lawyers, and (*c*) the likelihood that the transactions will result in formal disputes.

REASONS FOR GROWTH

Why does the larger demand for corporate legal services result in larger law firms? The workgroups within the firms, handling each of the particular cases or issues, may be no larger than they were when demand was lower and law firms were smaller. Where are the economies of scale? Although access to electronic communication technology is now probably essential to an efficient and effective law practice—and clients expect it—that technology is not so expensive that large numbers of lawyers must share it in order to make it a sensible investment. Computers, fax machines, and copy machines, once costly items, are now in the offices of even the smallest law firms. The 1995 Chicago survey found that 89% of solo practitioners and 98% of respondents in firms with two to four lawyers had access to computers, while 97% of the solos and 100% of the lawyers in very small firms had access to fax machines. But such computerized legal research tools as Lexis and Westlaw were available to only about half of those lawyers—52% of the solos and 48% of those in small firms lacked these search tools. A firm does not need to be very large, however, to be able to afford Lexis or Westlaw and thus eliminate that competitive disadvantage. But personnel costs for receptionists, secretaries, paralegals, messengers, and an around-the-clock wordprocessing staff (not to mention accounting, information technology, and marketing departments) are substantial, and such staff costs are probably more efficiently borne by larger operations. In 1997, the six Chicago firms that had 300 or more lawyers within the State of Illinois employed from 435 to 613 nonlawyers each. The average for these big firms was about 1.5 support staff persons per lawyer (*Illinois Legal Times* 1997:20). Smaller firms might need greater staff-to-lawyer ratios in order to provide comparable levels of service. Similar economies of scale in personnel costs may well occur in government law offices and in the legal departments maintained within corporations.

One explanation for the growth of private law firms is provided by "portfolio theory" (Gilson & Mnookin 1985). That is, providing services to a larger number of clients, in a larger number of fields of law, helps to spread economic risk. It makes the firm less dependent on any one client or any one area of practice. If a big client goes out of business or takes its legal work elsewhere, the larger, more diversified firm is more likely to have work from other clients to fill the void. If there is a downturn in the economy, so that the amount of corporate transaction work declines, it will be advantageous for the firm to have a bankruptcy department to handle work arising from business failures. Thus, firms may add clients and specialty areas in order to diversify and spread risk.

Another reason for the growth of large law firms is that the firms have incentives to provide their clients with "one-stop shopping." That is, many firms appear to believe that their corporate clients will find it advantageous to be able to have all their legal problems—taxes, transactions, securities issues, labor and employment matters, or litigation—dealt with by the same law firm. This will spare the client the trouble of shopping around to find several firms to handle the several types of work and the expense of educating additional lawyers about the nature of their business and will permit the client and the firm to develop a relationship of trust and confidence to an extent that might be difficult to achieve if the client were dealing with multiple law firms. It will also, not incidentally, maximize the amount of the client's business that the firm is able to obtain and retain. If a firm sends a client to another firm, for example for litigation, the client will be thrust into the arms of the firm's competitors and may decide to stay there. The client may find the lawyers in the second firm preferable, so much so that they get not only litigation but transactional business as well. When a law firm finds it necessary to refer out some piece of work it lacks the expertise to handle (an environmental pollution problem or a patent law issue, for example), the firm will seek to send the matter to a "boutique" specialty firm that handles only that subject and thus will not be a competitor for the other work of the client. Thus, a firm may well prefer to create a broad range of competencies under its own roof, having its own lawyers do as much of the client's work as possible. This will probably require the firm to add lawyers.

Galanter & Palay (1991) have suggested that law firms must grow in order to satisfy the imperatives of their own internal labor markets: Whenever a new partner is admitted to the firm, new associates will be hired to support and feed the work of the partner (to exploit the assets or "human capital" of the partner fully), and eventually some of these associates must be made partners so that the firm will be able to recruit and motivate new associates (Galanter & Palay 1991). This process then creates a growth pyramid—indeed, Galanter & Palay argue that it typically results in a geometric rate of growth in the number of lawyers per firm (Galanter & Palay 1991:87–91). But we are skeptical about this thesis. In fact, large law firms appear to grow at widely varying rates—some grow rapidly, some slowly, and some persist while growing not at all (Nelson 1988:49). Galanter & Palay argue that, because it is difficult or costly for law firms to monitor the work of their associates and then adjust salaries to reflect individual productivity, the firms motivate the associates to use their best efforts by offering the prospect of a future prize—at the end of a period of years (now, usually, 7 to 10 years), a percentage of the associates (the percentage being within an understood, relatively stable range) will be rewarded with partnership in the firm. Galanter & Palay refer to this as the "promotion-to-partner tournament." But Kordana argues that associates are not, in fact, difficult to monitor, and that the firms do so routinely (Kordana 1995:1914–17). Kordana observes that promotion-to-partner rates at large law firms vary widely from year to year, which is inconsistent with the existence of an implicit contract with each cohort of associates to promote a stable percentage (Kordana 1995:1921–22). Moreover, there appears to have been an abrupt increase in the growth rate of the firms in 1970 (Galanter & Palay 1991:78), which is not explained by the "tournament" theory. The rate change is not fatal to the theory, but it is not accounted for by the logic of the tournament. This is especially important because about half of all growth after 1970 is attributable not to the hypothesized geometric rate of increase but to the sudden change in that rate (Galanter & Palay 1991:88; Heinz 1992:9).[5] Indeed, the amount of growth attributable to the unexplained 1970 change is so great that the fit to the observed data of a geometric growth function (i.e., growth by X percent per year) is not significantly better than the fit of a simple linear function (i.e., growth by X lawyers per year) if each takes into account the 1970 increase (Nelson 1992:742). Since geometric growth is a necessary consequence of the hypothesized tournament, this is of considerable importance.

If there was a sudden change in the trend of the growth rates in 1970, there must have been either (*a*) a change in the level of demand for corporate legal services across the board, or (*b*) mimetic tendencies in the management of large law firms, causing several firms to follow the growth strategy of some industry leader (DiMaggio & Powell 1983). For the latter to persist, the increase in firm size would at least need to be supported by a sufficient augmentation of demand (and, thus, of firm revenues) to permit the firms to cover the costs of the additional lawyers and support staff. Thus, we believe that the primary explanation for the increasing size of law firms is that the volume of corporate financial transactions, and of the litigation that sometimes is occasioned by those transactions, increased substantially,[6] and that firms already present in the market for corporate legal services had a substantial competitive advantage in capturing the resulting demand. The competitive advantage might flow from the established relationships existing firms possessed with corporate clients (a considerable "marketing" advantage) and, perhaps more important, from the investment the clients had already made in their old lawyers' acquisition of detailed knowledge about their business. Thus, unless a new firm included lawyers who had previously done work for the client,

---

[5]As Sander & Williams (1992:406) point out, however, the growth rates of several of the firms examined by Galanter & Palay did not increase in 1970; in fact, some decreased.

[6]The pace of certain types of corporate transactions (notably, mergers, acquisitions, and securities work generally) has also increased markedly, thus requiring additional staff to process the matters quickly. One Chicago lawyer told us that "a deal that might have taken a month or two in 1975 may take a week or less today."

either the client would need to pay those "start-up costs" once again or the law firm would have to absorb the costs. Obviously, this creates a disincentive to switching. Nonetheless, corporations do in fact establish relationships with new suppliers of legal services, not infrequently.

LAWYER/CLIENT RELATIONSHIPS

As the demand for corporate legal services increased and law firms grew in response to that demand, the nature of the relationships among corporate clients and the leading partners of the firms began to change. Three factors contributed to a weakening of the ties. First, long-term personal relationships became less common as players on both sides moved. Increasing turnover of personnel, both in the law firms and in corporate management, made it more difficult for the officers of the corporations to maintain close relationships with their lawyers. Second, the growth stimulated a further division of labor—as the volume of legal work grew, law firms found it efficient to disaggregate the client's business and to assign particular pieces of the work to specialized groups within the firms. Third, the sheer number of lawyers in the firm and the resulting complexity of firm management made it more difficult for clients to penetrate the layers of responsibility within the firm. When a law firm expands from 30 lawyers to 50, then to 100, then to 300 or 800, the officer of the corporation can no longer count on access to the personal advice of the firm's senior partner on all legal issues. Tax matters will be sent to the tax department and litigation to the litigation department, while the senior partner may be tied up with staffing decisions for the firm's new office in Prague. The firm will, of course, continue to cultivate personal relationships with corporate officers who are in a position to bring in substantial business. But as the size of the law firm increases and the number of clients grows, it becomes more and more difficult for the firm's leaders to give personal attention to every CEO or General Counsel. Some will get their telephone calls answered much more quickly than others.

The great increases in size of firms and volume of business meant that the organization of work within firms was increasingly rationalized, especially through specialization of function. The particular form of departmentalization of the law firm often reflects the character and organization of its dominant clients. Thus, if the firm represents a large bank, it may well have a banking law department. Law firms are shaped by their clients, as well as motivated by the dynamics of their own production system and their internal labor markets. But the client organizations realize that if law firms are able to disaggregate the tasks, clients can do it as well. This, in turn, means that the corporations can parcel the tasks out to separate firms if they think that doing so will be more effective, efficient, or inexpensive than bundling all those tasks at one firm. Thus, although law firms have incentives to encourage one-stop shopping, corporate clients may have incentives to shop around. Long-term personal relationships with particular lawyers once helped to tie the clients to particular firms, but when such relationships dwindled, the ties were loosened.

We should note, however, that durable relations among law firms and corporate clients remain important. Between the 1975 and 1995 Chicago surveys, the percentage of clients represented by large law firms for three years or more decreased, but not greatly. In 1975, lawyers in firms with 30 or more lawyers reported continuing relationships of that duration with 56.4% of their clients, while in 1995 lawyers in firms of 150 or more reported that 51.9% had been represented for three years or more and respondents in firms of 300 or more lawyers reported that only 45% of their clients were of that duration.[7] Now, because an individual case, government investigation, or legal transaction may well require three or more years to come to fruition (especially in major corporate matters), these statistics do not provide an ideal measure of the stability of client relationships. Nonetheless, available data are consistent with the proposition that many large corporations follow a hybrid strategy in retaining firms: They maintain long-term relationships for some of their work and distribute another portion adventitiously. Baker found that corporations followed a similar strategy with investment banks—they maintained a relationship with a lead bank to conserve on information costs and gain volume discounts while they placed some business at many other banks to gain additional information on innovations in the field and to keep the lead bank competitive (Baker 1990).

A key factor in the weakening of the ties between law firms and their clients was the changing role of corporate inside counsel. To manage their growing inventory of legal issues, corporations hired more lawyers for their internal legal staffs, and they also sought to enhance the level of sophistication and experience of those lawyers—some top partners in prominent law firms agreed to take leaves of absence from their firms, or to spend part of their time working within corporations, in order to reorganize and strengthen the corporations' legal departments.[8] The inside counsel make decisions about how to divide and allocate the corporation's legal work: about which work should be done inside and which should be sent to outside law firms, and about which outside firms should receive the business. This role obviously gives inside counsel great power vis-a-vis the outside law firms. If the inside lawyer (the chief one is often called the vice-president for law) knows, respects, and likes the lawyers in an outside firm, that firm will clearly have an

---

[7]In the 1975 data, there is no clear relationship between size of firm and the percentage of stable clients—i.e., larger firms did not consistently have a greater or lesser percentage of clients represented for 3 years or more. In 1995, however, the percentage of stable clients increased steadily from 41% for solo practitioners to a high of 60% in firms of 100–299 lawyers, but then dropped to 45% in firms with 300 or more lawyers. This may indicate that firms in the 100–299 category are still relatively likely to be locally based—i.e., they are likely to represent companies headquartered in Chicago. Client mobility appears to be greater in the largest law firms, which operate in several cities and which represent national or multinational corporations.

[8]Examples include Elmer Johnson from Kirkland & Ellis at General Motors, Howard Trienens from Sidley & Austin at AT&T, and Ted Tetzleff from Jenner & Block at Tenneco. From the point of view of the law firms, of course, these arrangements also served to solidify the relationships between the firms and their corporate clients.

advantage in securing some of the corporation's legal work. If those conditions are not present, the law firm will have a difficult time making its attributes known to corporate management. The networks of relationships among inside and outside counsel are thus a principal determinant of the distribution of legal work (Nelson 1988:68).

Inside counsel also monitor and evaluate the performance of outside lawyers. They review the billings from the law firms, and they exercise judgment about whether the charges are excessive (D. S. Ruder, unpublished data). They establish rules or standards for outside counsel concerning the number and kinds of personnel used by the firms for certain purposes, such as discovery or depositions (Nelson 1998:782). In many cases, inside counsel consult with the outside lawyers about the strategy to be used in handling cases. Thus, inside counsel now stand between outside lawyers and corporate management and mediate those relationships. In the 1970s and earlier, corporate house counsel were regarded as second-class citizens of the legal profession—they were sometimes lawyers who had failed to make partner in a major law firm and were sent by the law firm to the corporation in order to cement the ties between the two (Slovak 1980; D. S. Ruder, unpublished data). As the power of inside counsel has increased, their status within the profession has increased as well.

In selecting outside lawyers, house counsel seek competition on both price and quality of service. In a marked departure from the earlier model of firm/client relations, many corporations now require law firms to bid on their work. Earlier, firms customarily devoted as many hours to the work as they thought it required, and they billed for those hours at more-or-less standard rates. Discounts were possible but relatively uncommon. In the 1995 Chicago survey, however, 61% of the respondents in firms with 100 or more lawyers reported that their firms bid for work.[9] (In 1975, this was so infrequent that the survey did not inquire about it.) Some potential clients invite competing firms to make presentations regarding the character and quality of their services. The presentations are referred to as "dog and pony shows" or "beauty contests." Corporate clients do not confine this competition to firms in one locale, and large firm practice has thus become more national in character. In the two Chicago surveys, we found that, in firms of 30 or more lawyers, the percentage of clients located outside the Chicago metropolitan area doubled from 1975 to 1995—from 20% to 40%.

There is a relationship between the growth of the power of corporate inside counsel and the emergence of the trend toward multi-city law firms. Until about the 1970s, law firms usually exercised control over the referral of cases (or pieces

---

[9]There is a clear relationship between size of firm and the likelihood of bidding for work. The percentage of respondents who reported in 1995 that they had not obtained clients by competitive bidding within the past 3 years was 97% for solo practitioners, 74% for firms with two to nine lawyers, 64% for firms of 10–30 lawyers, 53% for firms of 31–99 lawyers, 48% for firms of 100–299 lawyers, and only 31% for firms with 300 or more lawyers ($x^2 = 106.7, P < 0.001$).

of cases) to other firms. Thus, if a Wall Streeet firm decided that it would be helpful to have a Chicago firm handle a problem involving Midwest interests, the New York lawyers would send the work to Chicago counsel in whom they had confidence (and with whom, quite probably, they had a personal relationship). So long as that was the practice, the Chicago firm had reason to stay out of New York—if it had opened a New York office, it would have become a direct competitor of the New York firm and thus a less likely referral partner. Once control of the allocation of legal work shifted from the outside firm to corporate inside counsel, however, the client made its own decision about the choice of Chicago lawyers. Since Chicago firms were then no longer dependent upon the goodwill of New York firms for referral (and vice versa), there was less reason to refrain from direct competition.

CHANGES IN FIRM STRUCTURE AND MANAGEMENT

When the demand for corporate legal services was growing most rapidly, large law firms found it difficult to recruit enough lawyers to supply the demand. Some firms were hiring 70 or more new lawyers per year (Stracher 1998:29),[10] and the need for bodies led the big firms to hire from a broader range of law schools than had previously been the case. The 1975 Chicago survey found that, although 45% of the respondents had attended one of four "local" law schools (De Paul, Chicago Kent, Loyola, and John Marshall), only 15% of the respondents in firms with 31–99 lawyers and only 7% of those in firms of 100 or more came from those four schools. In the 1995 survey, about the same percentage of all Chicago lawyers were produced by those schools (44%), but their share of lawyers in large firms had increased substantially—26% of respondents in firms with 100–299 lawyers and 17% of those in firms with 300 or more had attended the local schools. Thus, while graduates of the local schools were still underrepresented in the largest firms in 1995, their presence in such firms had increased substantially.

One of the consequences of this broader recruitment and the general demand for personnel was that the firms opened their doors to categories of lawyers not previously represented in large numbers. The most conspicuous of these changes was the entry of substantial numbers of women. Abel (1989:91) observed that "because the absolute number of male law students has not increased since 1973, *all* subsequent growth of law school enrollments is attributable to the entry of women" (emphasis in original). A considerable number of the new women lawyers were hired by law firms, although disproportionate numbers practice in the legal departments of corporations or government agencies (Hull & Nelson 2000, Hagan & Kay 1995). Another area of change was the ethnic composition of the large firms. The 1975 Chicago survey found evidence of pronounced ethnoreligious

---

[10]In 1999, the Skadden Arps firm reportedly hired 143 entering associates (Parsa 1999:31). This does not take into account growth through mergers with other firms.

stratification within the bar. Protestants were more likely to be found in large firms, and Catholics and Jews were more likely to be in solo practice and local government (Heinz & Laumann 1982:Ch. 6), as had been found in previous studies (Carlin 1962; Ladinsky 1963; *Yale Law Journal* 1964), but there were also large differences among particular fields of practice. Catholic respondents were three times more likely to be prosecutors than were Protestants and Jews. Catholics were also overrepresented in personal injury work, on both the plaintiff and defense sides, and underrepresented in banking, securities, and labor union work. Jews were significantly overrepresented in divorce and commercial law and underrepresented in antitrust defense, patents, probate, and business litigation. The more socially elite Protestant denominations (Episcopalians, Presbyterians, Congregationalists) were very heavily overrepresented in securities work, overrepresented in patents, banking, and tax work, and underrepresented in divorce and personal injury work (Heinz & Laumann 1982:446–49, Table B.5). Earlier in the century, leaders of the organized bar had expressed strong opposition to permitting immigrants from southern and eastern Europe, or their children, to enter the legal profession (Auerbach 1976; Abel 1989:85). In the mid-1970s, the social structure of the profession still displayed the effects of these exclusionary attitudes and practices. But the great demand for corporate lawyers in the 1980s did much to break down the barriers. In addition to hiring women and recruiting the high-ranking graduates of less prestigious law schools, the large law firms now began to hire substantial numbers of Catholics and Jews. In the 1995 Chicago survey, ethnoreligious differentiation across fields and practice settings is greatly diminished. In 1975, the percentage of lawyers in any given field of practice who were Jewish was significantly correlated with the percentage of all practitioners in that field who were in large firms, the percentage in solo practice, the percentage who served clients who were blue collar workers, and the volume of clients served. Thus, the overall characteristics of the fields, including client type, were correlated with the percentages of Jewish lawyers in the fields. In 1995, none of these correlations was significant. Similarly, the overrepresentation of high-status Protestant denominations among securities lawyers, for example, had disappeared by 1995. While 36.4% of the securities lawyers were high-status Protestants (compared with only 13% of the bar overall) in 1975, by 1995 the representation of those denominations had declined to 11.1% of securities practitioners (compared with 11.7% of the full random sample of Chicago lawyers).

When outside lawyers were in direct and frequent contact with the top levels of corporate management, the law firms asserted that corporate officers preferred to deal with lawyers who resembled themselves—i.e., white males, usually Anglo-Saxon Protestants (Baltzell 1964, 1966, 1976). This was alleged to make the clients feel more comfortable and thus facilitate a close relationship. Whether these assertions ever had a sound empirical foundation or were merely a convenient excuse is beside the point. In either case, when inside counsel began to select the outside firms, to move business from one firm to another, and to mediate the relationships between outside lawyers and corporate executives, and when corporate legal departments themselves became more diverse, these arguments for social homogeneity lost much of their force. Besides, the law firms needed bodies—there were not enough WASPs to go around.

Law firms, of course, still seek to employ lawyers who are especially widely acquainted or notably influential in the hope that they may be useful in recruiting and retaining clients. (These lawyers are called "rainmakers.") Indeed, there is now much more lateral mobility among the firms than there was a few decades ago. Until the 1970s, a partnership in a major law firm was generally assumed to be a lifetime job—lawyers stayed in those positions for their entire careers. Information about the earnings of partners in other firms (and, generally, whether the grass was greener) was scarce and hard to come by. Firms did not discuss such matters with outsiders, and even within the firms compensation information was frequently kept secret. This has changed. With the advent of newspapers specializing in coverage of the legal profession, information about salaries has become much less closely held. The *National Law Journal* now publishes an annual survey of lawyers' compensation (*National Law Journal* 1999). Income data are also available on the Internet at a web site maintained by the Altman & Weil consulting firm (www.altmanweil.com). Lawyers who want to maximize their earnings will have more information about possibilities, and they will have opportunities to pursue them. Law firms actively recruit both partners and associates from other firms, especially if they are likely to bring with them the business of a client or group of clients (referred to in the trade as "a book of business"). If enough business is to be gained, firms will even recruit whole "practice groups"—i.e., the group of lawyers serving a particular client at another firm, or a group with special expertise in an area of law where the acquiring firm perceives an opportunity for new business (e.g., government contracts). For example, the Greenberg Traurig firm, based in Florida, grew from 120 lawyers in 1990 to 401 in 1998 by acquiring practice groups in New York, Washington, D.C., and other major cities (Goldhaber 1999). The *National Law Journal* (1999:A8) reports the following:

> In Washington, DC, the firm started with international partner Howard Vine and one associate. Soon, the firm started an info-tech cluster in Tysons Corner, Va. In recent weeks, it has added a telecom team from Fleischman and Walsh and the big-league litigation group of Joe Reeder, from Patton Boggs L.L.P. Its presence in greater Washington has grown from the two attorneys in 1993 to 46 lawyers and consultants today.

> The hallmarks of Greenberg's expansions are patience and opportunism. It looked on and off in Atlanta, Tampa, Fla., and London for years but refused to overpay or settle for a bad fit. Ultimately, it acquired an entertainment boutique in Atlanta; in Tampa and London, it's still looking. Philadelphia is an unpopular place for branches, but when Michael Lehr came along, Greenberg snapped him up along with his eight-lawyer group at Ballard, Spahr, Andrews & Ingersoll L.L.P.

In his study of Wall Street lawyers, based on research done in the late 1950s, Smigel (1969:57–58) observed: "Competition for lawyers among the large firms in New York City is limited in two major ways: the firms will not pirate an employee from another law office, and they maintain a gentleman's agreement to pay the same beginning salary, commonly called the going rate." No longer.

As the demand for corporate legal services grew and law firms perceived the opportunity for rapid growth, competition among firms both for new clients and for new lawyers became intense. "Grow or die" and "bigger is better" were articles of faith. Although it was in fact the case that some firms managed to survive while growing slowly or very little, and others failed because they had expanded too rapidly (Nelson 1988:49), these facts appeared to give most law firms only a little pause. The clients had legal problems to be solved, and the firms feared, perhaps quite reasonably, that if they did not provide the solutions the clients would take their business elsewhere. But many clients were, at the same time, disaggregating their legal work and spreading it around among several firms, which might well have led firms (and did lead some) to attempt to retain only a portion of the client's business. The firms with slow rates of growth were often highly prestigious ones [Nelson (1988:49) cites Sullivan & Cromwell, Dewey Ballantine, White & Case, Covington & Burling, and Hogan & Hartson as examples] that may have been especially concerned to maintain the quality of their personnel and especially confident of their ability to retain clients.Thus, many law firms perceived these prominent examples to be exceptional cases.

The competition for personnel drove the firms to pay higher salaries, and the higher compensation then created a need for ever greater levels of earnings. In the ABF surveys of Chicago lawyers, the median income of associates in the largest firms, in constant (1995) dollars, increased from $70,828 in 1975 to $85,000 in 1995. The median real income of partners in such firms increased from $198,318 to $225,000 over the same interval. In small firms and solo practice, however, the pattern was quite different. For partners in small firms, median income decreased from $127,490 in 1975 to $112,500 in 1995, and for solo practitioners it decreased from $99,159 to $55,000, in constant dollars. Thus, the income gap between lawyers in large firms and those in small firms and solo practice widened considerably.

At the end of the 1990s, the salaries of lawyers in the largest firms increased even more dramatically. The stock market was booming, and American companies—especially, internet-based businesses (the dot-com companies)—were expanding rapidly and needed skilled personnel. Earnings in such companies, with opportunities to acquire stock options, became more attractive than law firm salaries. Law firms thus came to be regarded as talent depositories that could be raided (Skertic 2000:1). The *New York Times* reported that at Brobeck, Phleger & Harrison, a San Francisco-based firm, "turnover among associates rose to 25 percent last year [1999], from 12 percent in 1998, as lawyers jumped ship for both legal and executive jobs at eBay, E*trade and an array of Web start-ups" (Leonhardt 2000a:C14).

Law firms in Silicon Valley and the San Francisco Bay area responded to these pressures first, but firms in New York and other major cities quickly followed. At the most prestigious firms, salaries of first-year associates (i.e., entering lawyers) jumped from the $95,000/$105,000 range to the $125,000/$140,000 range, plus bonuses (Leonhardt 2000a,b; Skertic 2000). Fourth-year associates at these firms were given raises to $200,000 or more (Leonhardt 2000a:C14). Some of the firms also began to take a portion of their fees in stock or stock options in client companies, and the firms then created "equity pools" in which associates were permitted to invest, in order to provide their lawyers with opportunities for capital appreciation. The value of the shares held in 1999 by the largest Silicon Valley firm, Wilson Sonsini, "on a per-partner basis was more than the average profits per partner, which reached about $700,000" (Orenstein 2000:154). The founder of a firm called the Venture Law Group described his organization as "a hybrid of a startup law firm, a venture capital firm, a consulting firm and an investment bank" (Orenstein 2000:144).

The increasingly vigorous competition among large law firms, as client corporations became more likely to shop around and to move from firm to firm, pushed the firms to cut costs so that they could price their services attractively and thus maintain or increase market share. If they were to be able to recruit and retain the lawyers they needed to handle the work, however, they could not reduce costs by reducing compensation. The firms, therefore, sought to achieve economies through "rationalization" of their production systems. The goal, of course, was to achieve greater output per employee or other unit of cost.

One way to do this is to devote fewer resources to training new personnel. Newly recruited associates, therefore, were increasingly expected to become productive immediately—or, at least, very soon. In an earlier day, firms had rotated new associates among the various departments or practice groups so that the associates could try out various kinds of work and decide what they liked best, and so that the firm could evaluate the associates' particular abilities. But most types of lawyers become more productive when they specialize, and pressure for productivity thus becomes pressure for the associate to specialize early. In most large law firms today, in fact, lawyers are hired for a specific department or area of practice within the firm. When Smigel did his research on Wall Street lawyers, firms were committed to training their recruits—the firm's role in socializing and "molding" their lawyers was an accepted part of the professional ideology (Smigel 1960:63). Now the firms demand that law schools produce graduates who are able to "hit the ground running."[11] (This is a popular phrase used by the firms.)

---

[11]The 1998 "strategic plan" of the Northwestern University School of Law notes: "Legal employers demand graduates who are able to enter practice with the judgment and the maturity to assume responsibility quickly. Even in large law firms, a new lawyer has little time to develop these traits on the job."

There have also been changes in the management of the firms that are designed to promote efficiency. In the older, smaller firm model, a relatively small set of powerful senior partners presided over separate hierarchies within the firm (Nelson 1988). These workgroups, consisting of associates and junior partners working under the supervision of one or more seniors, typically served the needs of a particular, limited group of clients. The law firm's relationships with these clients were tended and nurtured by the seniors, and the workgroup often dealt with the full range of the clients' problems—commercial transactions, antitrust, securities regulation, real estate acquisition, and so on. In the newer, larger firm model, specialized departments replace the personal hierarchies. Instead of being built around dominant seniors, these departments are defined by substantive expertise or skill types—e.g., tax, litigation, real estate, mergers and acquisitions. Typically, the allocation of work within each department is managed by a chairman, assisted by a second level of supervisors.

When most law firms were simple partnerships of 10 or 20 lawyers, they were governed informally. The partners saw each other often or daily, and important decisions could be made over lunch or in the hallways. But now that many lawyers practice in complex organizations with hundreds of lawyers and even larger numbers of support staff, management of the firms has become a major concern. Many of the firms employ professional managers,[12] and most are governed by a committee of partners operating within detailed rules set forth in the partnership agreement.[13] As the size of the organization increases, formal votes tend to replace informal consensus as the typical governing mode, and the freedom of action of individual lawyers becomes limited by rules and procedures.

Traditional hierarchies tend to be relatively inefficient because the importance of personal relationships in the maintenance of such hierarchies may make the decisionmakers more tolerant of waste. Thus, a partner in a major Chicago law firm observed that firms were formerly willing to accommodate lawyers who had become unproductive, who had "retired in place." Now, even if they are partners, such lawyers will be sent away.

The increase in scale of law firms and other law practice organizations has thus led to changes in the personnel management practices within those organizations. In the older model, lawyers in private firms were divided simply into partners and associates. The associates were almost always more junior lawyers who hoped to become partners in due course. In rare cases, lawyers were employed by firms for longer terms as "permanent associates," but these were the

---

[12]In the 1995 Chicago survey, we found that 65% of the respondents in firms with 30 or more lawyers reported that their firms had an executive "responsible primarily for administrative policy, rather than doing legal work."

[13]In the 1950s, many of the most prestigious firms did not even have written partnership agreements. Smigel (1969:199) quotes a New York lawyer: "We do not have a partnership agreement. Mr. De Gersdorff of Cravath used to say, 'We don't want people for partners with whom we need written agreements.'"

exceptions. To be a "partner," in this older model, meant that the lawyer was one of the owners of the firm—the partners shared in the profits. Now, however, many large law firms have two classes of partners. Some lawyers called "partners" are not owners of the firm. Thus, although they enjoy the title, they are not partners in the traditional sense. The partners who do have an ownership interest are referred to as "equity partners." In our 1995 Chicago survey, we found that 68% of the respondents in firms of 30 or more lawyers reported that their firms had adopted this three-tiered system—associates, nominal partners, and equity partners. A variety of other terms, such as "of counsel" and "senior attorney," are sometimes used to refer to lawyers who have nonstandard roles in the firm. These terms can mean whatever the firms and the lawyers choose to have them mean. Some law firms now also use the services of temporary or "contract" lawyers (Cherovsky 1991; Scheffey 1995; Frederick 1995; Hackney 1996). This permits the firm to add or subtract personnel as demand may dictate. If the firm gets a big case, it buys the services of several additional lawyers for the duration of that case, with no intention of retaining them for the long term. We are told that in some firms these independent contractors may amount to as much as 10 or 15 percent of the total number of lawyers at times of peak workload. Thus, the law firms are behaving more like corporations and less like traditional, collegial partnerships.

THE FUTURE (?)

What is the future of large law firms? Will they simply continue to grow—from 300 lawyers to 500 to 1000 or 2000 (as some already have), and then to 5000? If so, will this growth occur primarily through mergers or through continuing expansion in the size of the overall market? In 1992, the eight largest accounting firms earned 28.1% of the total national receipts for accounting services, while the eight largest law firms received only 2.4% of the spending for legal services; the 50 largest law firms had only a 9% market share (Bureau of the Census 1996). Concentration in the markets for architecture and advertising services has also been much greater than that in law (Bureau of the Census 1996).

There is probably nothing inherent in the character of legal services that would prevent a substantially greater concentration of the business in larger firms. At present, however, rules concerning conflicts of interest are a significant impediment to the acquisition of new clients by major firms—i.e., a firm may not take on a new client if it represents another whose interests are or may be materially adverse to those of the potential client. This is based in the lawyer's ethical obligation of loyalty to the client and the duty of confidentiality in communication with the client. The principal difference between law firms and accounting firms in this respect is that the ethical rules of the legal profession impute the knowledge and loyalties of each lawyer to every other lawyer in the firm, even in its offices in other cities, while the rules of the accounting profession permit the firms to erect "screens" or "walls" within the firm, separating the knowledge, roles, and decisions of accountants working for one client from those working for others. Therefore, conflicts of interest pose fewer problems for accounting firms than for law firms.[14] Indeed, even with several hundred lawyers, much less thousands, a law firm has great difficulty managing and avoiding conflicts. But the legal profession's ethical rules are subject to change, and they probably respond to market forces to one degree or another.

What would happen if consulting firms, accounting firms, and financial services companies moved into the market for legal services to an extent that threatened the livelihood of law firms? The judges who ultimately set the ethical rules for the legal profession are, of course, lawyers—they came from the practicing bar, and some of them will return to it. If the survival of law firms were seriously threatened, would the judges then modify the rules so as to permit the law firms to compete more effectively?

Some would argue that accounting firms are already making substantial inroads into corporate law practice (Van Duch 1997). The major accounting firms are far more wealthy than any law firm. They have the deep pockets. Law firms are undercapitalized; they live on annual earnings and cannot sustain years with net losses. Phillip L. Mann, former chair of the American Bar Association's tax section, has said: "[It] isn't so much the issue of who has the smarter or the harder-working lawyers on their staffs. . . . The real footsteps we're hearing is the scale of competition. . . . the vast amount of money and capital that the Big Six [accounting firms] can spend on marketing. . . . They apparently have become convinced that the existing parochial jurisdiction-by-jurisdiction approach to the licensing of the legal profession will be considered just another barrier to international trade and, like tariffs, will one day come down" (Van Duch 1997: A13).

---

[14]In recent years, however, as they have added a portfolio of consulting services to their auditing work, accounting firms have increasingly encountered conflicts problems. Auditors of public companies have a duty to disclose problems of which they become aware, so that investors and potential investors can assess the risks, but clients who go to expert consultants for business, tax, and financial advice have an expectation of confidentiality. The Securities and Exchange Commission (SEC) has criticized the accounting firms for compromising the independence of their auditing function through the provision of consulting services to the same clients and has threatened to take remedial action (Gibeaut 2000). Responding in part to pressure from the SEC, several of the largest accounting firms have recently moved to separate the auditing division from the part of the company that provides consulting services. In most cases, the consulting practice would become a separate corporation (Michaels & Peel 2000; Tagliabue 2000). In making these moves, the firms have also been motivated by the need to raise capital to finance the expansion of the consulting practice (MacDonald 2000; Michaels & Peel 2000:18). By separating the consulting entity from the auditors, it would become possible for the consulting company to raise capital through a public offering or from a private investor.

As Mann's comment indicates, the globalization of law practice[15] is one of the factors that is making it more difficult to maintain the traditional lines of distinction among the professions (Abbott 1988). While the ethical rules in all US jurisdictions except the District of Columbia prohibit nonlawyers from having an ownership interest in law firms, the rules in many other nations do not. Accounting firms have bought law firms abroad and have hired lawyers to handle litigation as well as transactional work. Many American lawyers would no doubt prefer to retain their separate professional identity and to work within contexts controlled by their own profession (NY State Bar Assoc. 2000). But others are quite ready to defect: one, commenting on his decision to leave his law firm and join an accounting firm, was quoted as saying "I didn't want to be the last one off the boat" (Van Duch 1997:A13). In 1997, Deloitte & Touche reported that it employed 1104 tax lawyers and another 384 non–tax lawyers worldwide (Van Duch 1997). As of January 2000, Arthur Andersen employed 2,734 lawyers in 35 countries (Campo-Flores 2000). Lawyers who do not want to work for accounting firms certainly still have the option not to, but if the accounting firms possess vastly greater resources (including marketing resources), then it may become increasingly difficult for firms composed exclusively of lawyers to remain competitive. In the foreseeable future, however, it seems unlikely that consulting firms and financial services firms will threaten the livelihood of the elite of the bar. The most sophisticated work done in the top Wall Street firms and in their counterparts in other major cities requires a level of experience and expertise that is difficult to duplicate. Corporations are probably likely, therefore, to continue to take their most complex and consequential work to such law firms. But this is, after all, a relatively small market niche, important though it may be. The corporate work done by mid-range and lesser law firms—and, perhaps, the more routine work done by large firms—is likely to be squeezed by competition from consulting firms, banks, and other financial services firms (*The Economist* 2000:81; Gibeaut 2000:18). The clients will make their choices; the market is more likely to determine the outcome than are the regulators of the bar.

As law firms become international in scope, American firms will find that their options are limited if they are prohibited from sharing fees with entities in which accountants, management consultants, investment bankers, or other non-lawyers have an ownership interest. Mergers of law firms with such entities [creating so-called multidisciplinary practices (MDPs)] have been taking place abroad for several years (Dezalay 1992). The European Union has already eroded the formerly exclusive licensing rules of the legal professions in its member countries. If lawyers practice across national boundaries (as is increasingly the case),

---

[15]Silver (2000) analyzes the move of U.S. law firms into foreign markets. She reports that of the firms on the *American Lawyer* list of the 100 largest U.S. law firms, 71 now have offices abroad. New York firms opened 204 foreign offices between 1925 and 1999 and subsequently closed 63 of these, while firms from other U.S. cities opened 245 foreign offices and subsequently closed 64 (Silver (2000:37; see also *Economist* 2000)).

then it will be difficult for local licensing authorities to restrict entry into those markets.

Large law firms now devote great care and substantial resources to the effort to avoid conflicts of interest. They do so not only because of ethical rules but because of the expressed preferences of some of their clients (Shapiro 2001). The firms are understandably wary of giving offense to important clients by taking on the representation of the clients' adversaries (Heinz & Laumann 1982:371–73). But it is not at all clear that corporations value exclusivity of representation as much or as often as the official ideology of the legal profession may suggest—clients, in fact, commonly waive their right to object to conflicts of interest, and the alternative approach to conflicts that is used in accounting firms does not appear to have stemmed the flow of legal work to multidisciplinary practices in Europe (Campo-Flores 2000). It is not apparent why the preferences of American businesses should be markedly different in this regard [the *Wall Street Journal* reports that "European corporate clients who have used the Big Five's legal services praise the efficiency and cost savings" (Jacobs 2000)]. Indeed, some of the work sent to MDPs in Europe has come from US-based firms. And consulting firms are hiring more and more lawyers in the United States as well as abroad—presumably these lawyers are kept fully occupied.[16] Perhaps some clients flex their muscles when dealing with law firms on conflicts issues because they know they can get away with it. Big corporate clients are many times larger and more powerful than their law firms, and those clients know that lawyers will be attentive to their wishes. In dealing with accounting firms, however, corporations have less room for choice—the degree of concentration in that market means that fewer options are available. In the early 1990s, the "Big Six" accounting firms (now further consolidated as the Big Five) audited 98% of the Fortune 500 industrial corporations (Cook et al, 1992).

It is possible, however, that some substantial segment of the market for legal services deals with matters in which the client has a preference for stringent conflict-of-interest rules. Some work may be of especially great sensitivity, so that a stronger assurance of confidentiality is desired, or may be especially vulnerable to adversarial interests, as in the planned acquisition of a real estate tract or the assemblage of a block of stock. In such matters, the client might prefer to consult an American law firm rather than a MDP that could also advise an adversary. Indeed, a rational choice model might suggest that the greater attention given by law firms in recent years to the monitoring and avoidance of

---

[16]According to the *American Lawyer*, the fiscal 1998 revenue of Andersen Legal, the global law network of Arthur Andersen, was $482 million, which "would place it in the top five of the Am Law 100"—i.e., among the five American law firms with the largest gross earnings. But the article also notes that revenue per lawyer was "an unspectacular $176,000," well below that of the most profitable U.S. law firms (Campo-Flores 2000). The cost of living and average wages in many other countries, however, are substantially less than in the United States.

conflicts helped the law firms to differentiate their services from those offered by accounting firms. Thus, by adopting rules and practices that distinguish them from consultants in situations where conflicts of interest may be especially worrisome, law firms may have created a market niche that is relatively secure from incursion. But the question is, how large is that niche? Is it big enough to employ most of the existing corporate bar?

Some lawyers doubt that the current conflicts rules of their profession truly serve the interests of clients (Fischel 2000). The system designed to prevent conflicts is expensive, it causes delay, and it probably sharpens conflict by requiring lawyers to serve as champions rather than as mediators (Shapiro 2001). Sophisticated clients, therefore, may choose to place their work within that system only when they believe that the work is especially sensitive. The example of the European model is now available for all to see—lawyers and clients alike. As the globalization of business transactions and corporate law practice proceeds, it is unlikely that multidisciplinary practice could be a success in Europe, South America, and Asia, and a failure in the United States. The large American law firm has been a distinctive form, which has had considerable success and has been copied abroad, notably by the British solicitors firms. It remains to be seen whether the form will endure.

ACKNOWLEDGMENTS

We acknowledge, with gratitude, the comments, criticism, and advice of Ken Gaines, Bryant Garth, Gillian Hadfield, Don Hilliker, Roman Hoyos, Gary Johnson, Harris Kim, Robert MacCrate, Heather MacIndoe, Tom Morsch, Milton C. Regan, David Ruder, Rebecca Sandefur, Susan Shapiro, Carole Silver, and David Van Zandt.

Visit the Annual Reviews home page at www.AnnualReviews.org

LITERATURE CITED

Abbott A. 1988. *The System of Professions.* Chicago: Univ. Chicago Press

Abel RL. 1989. *American Lawyers.* New York: Oxford Univ. Press

Atty. Regist. Discipl. Comm. 1977. *Annual Report.* Chicago: Supreme Court Illinois

Atty. Regist. Discipl. Comm. 1996. *Annual Report.* Chicago: Supreme Court Illinois

Auerbach JS. 1976. *Unequal Justice: Lawyers and Social Change in Modern America.* New York: Oxford Univ. Press

Baker WE. 1990. Market networks and corporate behavior. *Am. J. Sociol.* 96:589–625

Baltzell ED. 1964. *The Protestant Establishment: Aristocracy and Caste in America.* New York: Random House

Baltzell ED. 1966. *Philadelphia Gentlemen: The Making of a National Upper Class.* New York: Free Press

Baltzell ED. 1976. The Protestant establishment revisited. *Am. Sch.* 45:499–518

Bell R. 1999. *Some determinants of Corporate use of Attorneys.* Am. Bar Found. Work. Pap. Ser., Chicago

Burger WE. 1995. The decline of professionalism. *Fordham Law Rev.* 63:949–58

Bureau of the Census. 1976. *1972 Census of Selected Service Industries*, Vol. 1. Washington, DC: US Dep. Commer.

Bureau of the Census. 1986. *1982 Census of Service Industries*. Washington, DC: US Dep. Commer.

Bureau of the Census. 1996. *1992 Census of Service Industries*. Washington, DC: US Dep. Commer.

Campo-Flores A. 2000. Bar talk: King Arthur. *Am. Lawyer* 22:17

Carlin JE. 1962. *Lawyers on Their Own: A Study of Individual Practitioners in Chicago*. New Brunswick, NJ: Rutgers Univ. Press

Carson CN. 1999. *The Lawyer Statistical Report: The U.S. Legal Profession in 1995*. Chicago: Am. Bar Found.

Cherovsky E. 1991. The use of temporary lawyers is on the rise in many firms. *NY Law J*. Mar 4, 1991, p. 44

Cook JM, Freedman EM, Groves RJ, Madonna JC, O'Malley SF, Weinbach LA. 1992. The liability crisis in the United States: impact on the accounting profession. *J. Account*. 174(5):18–23, Nov. 1992

Curran BA, Rosich KJ, Carson CN, Puccetti MC. 1985. *The Lawyer Statistical Report: A Statistical Profile of the U.S. Legal Profession in the 1980s*. Chicago: Am. Bar Found.

Daniels S, Martin J. 1995. *Civil Juries and the Politics of Reform*. Evanston, IL: Northwest. Univ. Press

Dezalay Y. 1992. *Marchands de Droit: La Restructuration de L'Ordre Juridique International par les Multinationales du Droit*. Paris: Lib. Artheme Fayard

DiMaggio P, Powell W. 1983. The iron cage revisited: institutional isomorphism and collective rationality in organizational fields. *Am. Sociol. Rev.* 48:147–60

Dunworth T, Rogers J. 1996. Corporations in court: big business litigation in U.S. Federal Courts, 1971–91. *Law Soc. Inq.* 21:497–592

Economist. 2000. Lawyers go global: the battle of the Atlantic. Economist. Feb. 26, p. 79

Fischel DR. 2000. Multidisciplinary practice. *Bus. Lawyer* 55:951–74

Frederick SA. 1995. Teaming up with temporary lawyers. *Am. Lawyer*. May 1995 (Suppl.), p. S58

Galanter M. 1993. News from nowhere: the debased debate on civil justice. *Denver Univ. Law Rev.* 71:77–113

Galanter M, Palay T. 1991. *Tournament of Lawyers: The Transformation of the Big Law Firm*. Chicago/London: Univ. Chicago Press

Gibeaut J. 2000. MDP in SEC crosshairs. *Am. Bar Assoc. J.* 86:16

Gilson R, Mnookin R. 1985. Sharing among the human capitalists: an economic inquiry into the corporate law firm and how partners split profits. *Stanford Law Rev.* 37:313–92

Glaberson W. 1999. When the verdict is just a fantasy. *NY Times*. June 6, p. 1

Glendon MA. 1994. *A Nation Under Lawyers: How the Crisis in the Legal Profession is Transforming American Society*. New York: Farrar, Straus & Giroux

Goldhaber MD. 1999. How Greenberg got so big. *Natl. Law J*. Apr. 26, p. A1

Hackney MM. 1996. Some large Philadelphia firms embrace contract lawyers; degree of acceptance varies from somewhat reluctant to not at all. *Legal Intell*. Apr. 15, p. 3

Hagan J, Kay F. 1995. *Gender in Practice: A Study of Lawyers' Lives*. New York: Oxford Univ. Press

Hall K. 2000. That was then . . . *Am. Lawyer*. Mar 2000, p. 24

Heinz JP. 1992. Review of *Tournament of Lawyers*. *Law Polit. Book Rev.* 2:6–10

Heinz JP, Hull KE, Harter AA. 1999. Lawyers and their discontents: findings from a survey of the Chicago Bar. *Indiana Law J*. 74:735–58

Heinz JP, Laumann EO. 1982. *Chicago Lawyers: The Social Structure of the Bar*. New York/Chicago: Russell Sage Found., Am. Bar Found.

Heinz JP, Nelson RL, Laumann EO, Michelson E. 1998. The changing character of lawyers' work: Chicago in 1975 and 1995. *Law Soc. Rev.* 32:751

Hull KE, Nelson RL. 2000. Assimilation, choice or constraint? Testing three theories of gender differences in the careers of lawyers. *Soc. Forces* 79:1–36

Illinois Legal Times. 1997. 100 largest law firms in Illinois. Ill. *Legal Times (Suppl.)* 11(123):01

Jacobs MA. 2000. Accounting firms covet forbidden fruit: piece of U.S. legal market. *Wall Str. J.* May 31, p. B1

Kordana KA. 1995. Law firms and associate careers: tournament theory versus the production-imperative model. *Yale Law J.* 104:1907–34

Kronman AT. 1993. *The Lost Lawyer: Failing Ideals of the Legal Profession.* Cambridge, MA: Belknap

Ladinsky J. 1963. The impact of social backgrounds of lawyers on law practice and the law. *J. Legal Educ.* 16:127–44

Leonhardt D. 2000a. Law firms' pay soars to stem dot-com defections. *NY Times.* Feb. 2, p. 1

Leonhardt D. 2000b. And let the lawyers sing: "Glory to the salary king." *NY Times.* Feb. 4, p. C8

Levy BH. 1961. *Corporation Lawyer: Saint or Sinner?* Philadelphia: Chilton

Linowitz SM. 1994. *The Betrayed Profession: Lawyering at the End of the Twentieth Century.* New York: Scribner's

Macaulay S. 1963. Non-contractual relations in business. *Am. Sociol. Rev.* 28:55–67

MacDonald E. 2000. Grant Thornton set to restructure consulting division. *Wall Str. J.* Feb. 25, p. C16

Martindale Hubbell. 1995–96. *Martindale-Hubbell Law Directory.* Reed Ref. CD-ROM.

Michaels A, Michael P. 2000. PwC plans ground-breaking split. *Finan. Times.* Feb. 18, p. 1

Michelson E, Laumann E, John H. 2000. The changing character of the lawyer-client relationship: evidence from two Chicago surveys. In *The Management of Durable Relations,* ed. R Werner, J Wessie, pp. 106–7. Amsterdam: Thela/Thesis

Natl. Law J. 1999. What lawyers earn. *Natl. Law J.* X:B7–15

Nelson RL. 1988. *Partners with Power: The Social Transformation of the Large Law Firm.* Berkeley: Univ. Califor. Press

Nelson RL. 1992. Of tournaments and transformations: explaining the growth of large law firms. *Wisc. Law Rev.* 1992:733

Nelson RL. 1994. The futures of American lawyers: a demographic profile of a changing profession in a changing society. *Case West. Reserve Law Rev.* 44:345–406

Nelson RL. 1998. The discovery process as a circle of blame: institutional, professional, and socio-economic factors that contribute to unreasonable, inefficient, and amoral behavior in corporate litigation. *Fordham Law Rev.* 67:773–808

NY State Bar Assoc. 2000. *Preserving the Core Values of the American Legal Profession: The Place of Multidisciplinary Practice in the Law Governing Lawyers. Rep. NYSBA Spec. Comm. Law Governing Firm Struct. and Operation.* Albany, NY: NY State Bar Assoc.

Orenstein S. 2000. Lawyers need equity, too. *Ind. Stand.* April 10, p. 142

Parsa TZ. 1999. The Drudge report. *NY Times.* June 21, p. 24

Sander R, Williams ED. 1992. A little theorizing about the big law firm: Galanter, Palay, and the economics of growth. *Law Soc. Inq.* 17:391–414

Sander RH, Williams ED. 1989. Why are there so many lawyers? Perspectives on a turbulent market. *Law Soc. Inq.* 14:431–79

Scheffey T. 1995. Turning lawyers' hourly services into a commodity. *Legal Times.* May 22, p. 529

Schiltz PJ. 1999. On being a happy, healthy, and ethical member of an unhappy, unhealthy, and unethical profession. *Vanderbilt Law Rev.* 52:871–951

Seron C. 1996. *The Business of Practicing Law: The Work Lives of Solo and Small-Firm Attorneys.* Philadelphia: Temple Univ. Press

Shapiro S. 2001. *Tangled Loyalties.* Ann Arbor: Univ. Mich. Press. In press

Sikes BH, Carson CN, Gorai P. 1972. *The 1971*

Lawyer Statistical Report. Chicago: Am. Bar Found

Silver C. 2000. Globalization and the U.S. market in legal services. Shifting identities. *Law Policy Int. Bus.* 31:1093–1150

Skertic M. 2000. Dot-coms lure lawyers. *Chicago Sun-Times*. Feb. 14, p. 1

Slovak JS. 1980. Giving and getting respect: prestige and stratification in a legal elite. *Am. Bar Found. Res. J.* 1980:31–68

Smigel E. 1960. The impact of recruitment on the organization of the large law firm. *Am. Sociol. Rev.* 25:56–66

Smigel E. 1969. *The Wall Street Lawyer: Professional Organization Man?* Bloomington: Indiana Univ. Press

Stracher C. 1998. *Double Billing: A Young Lawyer's Tale of Greed, Sex, Lies, and the Pursuit of a Swivel Chair*. New York: Morrow

Tagliabue J. 2000. Cap gemini to acquire Ernst & Young's consulting business. *NY Times.* Mar. 1, p. C1

Van Duch D. 1997. Big six in hot pursuit of legal biz: major law firms lose stars, market share to accountants. *Natl. Law Rev. Aug.* 18, p. A1

Van Hoy J. 1997. *Franchise Law Firms and the Transformation of Personal Legal Services.* Westport, CT: Quorum Books

Yale Law J. 1964. The Jewish law student and New York jobs—discriminatory effects in law firm hiring practice. *Yale Law J.* 73:625–60

Annu. Rev. Sociol. 2001. 27:363–85

CONCEPTUALIZING STIGMA

Bruce G. Link[1] and Jo C. Phelan[2]

[1]Columbia University and New York State Psychiatric Institute, New York, NY 10032;
e-mail: BGL1@Columbia.edu
[2]Department of Sociology, Columbia University, New York, NY 10021;
e-mail: JCP13@Columbia.edu

Key Words   labeling, stereotype, discrimination, exclusion, deviance

■ **Abstract**   Social science research on stigma has grown dramatically over the past two decades, particularly in social psychology, where researchers have elucidated the ways in which people construct cognitive categories and link those categories to stereotyped beliefs. In the midst of this growth, the stigma concept has been criticized as being too vaguely defined and individually focused. In response to these criticisms, we define stigma as the co-occurrence of its components–labeling, stereotyping, separation, status loss, and discrimination–and further indicate that for stigmatization to occur, power must be exercised. The stigma concept we construct has implications for understanding several core issues in stigma research, ranging from the definition of the concept to the reasons stigma sometimes represents a very persistent predicament in the lives of persons affected by it. Finally, because there are so many stigmatized circumstances and because stigmatizing processes can affect multiple domains of people's lives, stigmatization probably has a dramatic bearing on the distribution of life chances in such areas as earnings, housing, criminal involvement, health, and life itself. It follows that social scientists who are interested in understanding the distribution of such life chances should also be interested in stigma.

INTRODUCTION

Erving Goffman's (1963) book *Stigma: Notes on the Management of Spoiled Identity* inspired a profusion of research on the nature, sources, and consequences of stigma. Both PsychInfo and Medline show dramatic increases in the number of articles mentioning the word stigma in their titles or abstracts from 1980 (PsychInfo 14, Medline 19) to 1990 (PsychInfo 81, Medline 48) to 1999 (PsychInfo 161, Medline 114).

Research since Goffman's seminal essay has been incredibly productive, leading to elaborations, conceptual refinements, and repeated demonstrations of the negative impact of stigma on the lives of the stigmatized. The stigma concept is applied to literally scores of circumstances ranging from urinary incontinence (Sheldon & Caldwell 1994) to exotic dancing (Lewis 1998) to leprosy (Opala &

0360-0572/01/0811-0363$14.00

Boillot 1996), cancer (Fife & Wright 2000), and mental illness (Angermeyer & Matschinger 1994, Corrigan & Penn 1999, Phelan et al 2000). It is used to explain some of the social vagaries of being unemployed (Walsgrove 1987), to show how welfare stigma can lead to the perpetuation of welfare use (Page 1984), and to provide an understanding of situations faced by wheelchair users (Cahill & Eggleston 1995), stepparents (Coleman et al 1996), debtors (Davis 1998), and mothers who are lesbian (Causey & Duran-Aydintug 1997).

A substantial portion of the productive research on stigma has been contributed by social psychologists who have used the insights of the social cognitive approach to understand how people construct categories and link these categories to stereotyped beliefs. This line of research represents a major advance in the understanding of stigma processes, and sociologists would do well to attend to it thoroughly (for a comprehensive review, see Crocker et al 1998). Given these advances in the social psychology of stigma and given the accumulated scientific impact of research on stigma more generally, we propose a return to the stigma concept from a distinctly sociological perspective. We engage our sociological perspective by attending to several core criticisms of the stigma concept and its application. The first of these criticisms is directed toward the clarity of the concept and follows from the observation that stigma is defined in different ways by different investigators. The second is a set of criticisms regarding the way in which the stigma concept has been applied by some researchers. We use these criticisms both as a stimulus to return to the stigma concept and as a critical analytic lens in constructing a revised conceptualization. We follow our explication of the stigma concept with a more detailed discussion of each of its component parts. We end by applying our conceptualization to several core issues in the stigma literature with an eye to assessing whether our conceptualization is helpful in understanding those issues. In doing so, we attend more to the nature and consequences of stigma than to its sources. (For a review of some ideas about the origins of stigma see Crocker & Lutsky 1986.)

VARIATIONS IN THE DEFINITION OF STIGMA

One of the curious features of literature concerning stigma is the variability that exists in the definition of the concept (Stafford & Scott 1986). In many circumstances investigators provide no explicit definition and seem to refer to something like the dictionary definition ("a mark of disgrace") or to some related aspect like stereotyping or rejection (e.g., a social distance scale). When stigma is explicitly defined, many authors quote Goffman's definition of stigma as an "attribute that is deeply discrediting" and that reduces the bearer "from a whole and usual person to a tainted, discounted one" (Goffman 1963, p. 3).

Since Goffman, alternative or elaborated definitions have varied considerably. For example, Stafford & Scott (1986, p. 80) propose that stigma "is a characteristic of persons that is contrary to a norm of a social unit" where a "norm" is defined as a "shared belief that a person ought to behave in a certain way at a certain time" (p. 81). Crocker et al (1998, p. 505) indicate that "stigmatized individuals possess (or are believed to possess) some attribute, or characteristic, that conveys a social identity that is devalued in a particular social context." An especially influential definition is that of Jones et al (1984), who use Goffman's (1963, p. 4) observation that stigma can be seen as a relationship between an "attribute and a stereotype" to produce a definition of stigma as a "mark" (attribute) that links a person to undesirable characteristics (stereotypes). In our own reviews of stigma and mental illness (e.g., Link & Phelan 1999), we have added the component of discrimination to the Jones et al (1984) definition.

Of the many reasons that definitions of stigma vary, two seem particularly prominent. First, as indicated above, the stigma concept has been applied to an enormous array of circumstances. Each one of these is unique, and each one is likely to lead investigators to conceptualize stigma in a somewhat different way. Second, research on stigma is clearly multidisciplinary, including contributions by psychologists, sociologists, anthropologists, political scientists, and social geographers. Although there is a great deal of overlap in interests across these disciplines, there are nevertheless some differences in emphasis. Even within disciplines, people approach the stigma concept from different theoretical orientations that produce somewhat different visions of what should be included in the concept. Thus, different frames of reference have led to different conceptualizations.

Because of the complexity of the stigma phenomenon, it seems wise to continue to allow variation in definition so long as investigators are clear as to what is meant by stigma when the term is used. Having said this, we shall also attempt to move matters ahead by specifying a conceptualization of stigma that includes many of the concerns that people working in this area of research share. Before proceeding, however, it is important to note that the use of the stigma concept has been challenged by some social scientists who have focused on the perspective of persons who are stigmatized (Schneider 1988, Fine & Asch 1988, Sayce 1998; Kleinman et al 1995). Understanding these challenges is important for the further development of research on stigma, particularly from a sociological perspective.

CHALLENGES TO THE STIGMA CONCEPT

There are two main challenges to the stigma concept. The first is that many social scientists who do not belong to stigmatized groups, and who study stigma, do so from the vantage point of theories that are uninformed by the lived experience of the people they study (Kleinman et al 1995, Schneider 1988). For example, in writing about the experience of disability, Schneider (1988) asserts that "most able-bodied experts" give priority "to their scientific theories and research techniques rather than to the words and perceptions of the people they study." The result is a misunderstanding of the experience of the people who are stigmatized and the perpetuation of unsubstantiated assumptions. Writing about disability, Fine & Asch

(1988) identify five assumptions: (*a*) that disability is located solely in biology, (*b*) that the problems of the disabled are due to disability-produced impairment, (*c*) that the disabled person is a "victim," (*d*) that disability is central to the disabled person's self-concept, self-definition, social comparisons, and reference groups, and (*e*) that having a disability is synonymous with needing help and social support.

The second challenge is that research on stigma has had a decidedly individualistic focus. For example, according to Oliver (1992), the central thrust of stigma research has been focused on the perceptions of individuals and the consequences of such perceptions for micro-level interactions. According to Oliver (1992), research examining the sources and consequences of pervasive, socially shaped exclusion from social and economic life are far less common. Interestingly, this criticism is echoed by at least one renowned student of stereotyping, prejudice, and discrimination. In her review of these topics, Susan Fiske (1998) concludes that (at least within social psychology) the literature on discrimination is far less extensive than that on stereotyping and that more attention needs to be addressed to structural issues. In another vein, even though Goffman (1963, p. 3) initially advised that we really needed "a language of relationships, not attributes," subsequent practice has often transformed stigmas or marks into attributes of persons (Fine & Asch 1988). The stigma or mark is seen as something *in the person* rather than a designation or tag that others affix to the person. In this respect the term stigma directs our attention differently than a term like "discrimination." In contrast to "stigma," "discrimination" focuses the attention of research on the producers of rejection and exclusion—those who do the discriminating—rather than on the people who are the recipients of these behaviors (Sayce 1998). Thus, the terms we use could lead to "different understandings of where responsibility lies for the 'problem' and as a consequence to different prescriptions for action" (Sayce 1998).

Researchers on stigma could respond to these challenges by disputing their validity or pointing to exceptions in the now voluminous literature on stigma. We find these critiques to provide a useful stimulus for a reassessment of the conceptualization of stigma and related concepts. One way in which some of the issues raised by the critiques can be addressed is to propose that stigma be described with reference to the relationships between a set of interrelated concepts.

DEFINING STIGMA IN THE RELATIONSHIP OF INTERRELATED COMPONENTS

An important precedent to locating the meaning of stigma in the relation between concepts is available in Goffman's observation that stigma can be seen as the relationship between an "attribute and a stereotype." We expand the nexus of relationships somewhat with the intent of capturing a fuller set of meanings for the term by doing so. We state our conceptualization as concisely as we can and then elaborate the components it contains.

In our conceptualization, stigma exists when the following interrelated components converge. In the first component, people distinguish and label human differences. In the second, dominant cultural beliefs link labeled persons to undesirable characteristics—to negative stereotypes. In the third, labeled persons are placed in distinct categories so as to accomplish some degree of separation of "us" from "them." In the fourth, labeled persons experience status loss and discrimination that lead to unequal outcomes. Finally, stigmatization is entirely contingent on access to social, economic, and political power that allows the identification of differentness, the construction of stereotypes, the separation of labeled persons into distinct categories, and the full execution of disapproval, rejection, exclusion, and discrimination. Thus, we apply the term stigma when elements of labeling, stereotyping, separation, status loss, and discrimination co-occur in a power situation that allows the components of stigma to unfold. With this brief explication of the stigma concept as background, we turn to a more detailed examination of each component we identified.

COMPONENT 1—ON DISTINGUISHING AND LABELING DIFFERENCES

The vast majority of human differences are ignored and are therefore socially irrelevant. Some of these—such as the color of one's car, the last three digits of one's social security number, or whether one has hairy ears—are routinely (but not always) overlooked. Many others such as one's food preferences or eye color are relevant in relatively few situations and are therefore typically inconsequential in the large scheme of things. But other differences, such as one's skin color, IQ, sexual preferences, or gender are highly salient in the United States at this time. The point is that there is a social selection of human differences when it comes to identifying differences that will matter socially.

The full weight of this observation is often overlooked because once differences are identified and labeled, they are typically taken for granted as being just the way things are—there are black people and white people, blind people and sighted people, people who are handicapped and people who are not. The taken-for-granted nature of these categorizations is one of the reasons that designations like these carry such weight. There are, however, some observations we can make that bring to light just how social this social selection of human differences is.

First, substantial oversimplification is required to create groups. One example is the assignment of individuals to categories of "black" or "white" when there is enormous variability within the resulting categories and no clear demarcation between categories on almost any criterion one can think of, even attributes like skin color, parentage, or facial characteristics that are believed to define the categories

(Fullilove 1998). The same can be said for other categorizations like gay or straight, blind or sighted, handicapped or not.

Second, the central role of the social selection of human differences is revealed by noting that the attributes deemed salient differ dramatically according to time and place. For example, in the late nineteenth century, human physical characteristics such as small foreheads and large faces were particularly salient—these characteristics were thought to be ape-like—and were believed to reveal the criminal nature of the people possessing them (Gould 1981). And, of course, cultures vary extensively in characteristics deemed socially significant. For example, ancient Mayan culture gave unusual significance to being cross-eyed and sought to create this desirable characteristic in children through devices that encouraged babies to focus on objects in ways that forced their eyes to cross. Sociological studies of social construction and medicalization are also good examples (Conrad 1992). Hyperactivity is much more salient now, as an indicator of a disorder, than it used to be, and the medical term ADHD (attention deficit hyperactivity disorder) is part of common parlance.

Because human differences are socially selected for salience, we have chosen to use the word "label" rather than "attribute," "condition" or "mark." Each of these latter terms locates the thing that is being referred to in the stigmatized person and risks obscuring that its identification and election for social significance is the product of social processes. In contrast, a label is something that is affixed. Moreover in the absence of qualifications, terms like "attribute," "condition," or "mark" imply that the designation has validity. In contrast the word "label" leaves the validity of the designation an open question—an option that has great utility as, for example, when one wishes to discuss the stigma some women experienced as a consequence of being labeled witches.

With regard to this aspect of the stigma process, the critical sociological issue is to determine how culturally created categories arise and how they are sustained. Why is it that some human differences are singled out and deemed salient by human groups while others are ignored? What are the social, economic, and cultural forces that maintain the focus on a particular human difference?

COMPONENT 2—ON ASSOCIATING HUMAN DIFFERENCES WITH NEGATIVE ATTRIBUTES

The second component of stigma occurs when labeled differences are linked to stereotypes. This aspect of stigma was highlighted in Goffman's (1963) work and has been central to the conceptualization of stigma ever since. It is the aspect of stigma that has been most salient in the psychological literature about stigma, perhaps because it poses critical questions of a psychological nature about the thought processes that facilitate connections between labels and stereotypes. Consistent with this emphasis in psychology is the centrality of this dimension in psychologists' definitions of stigma. For example, Crocker and colleagues (1998) define stigma, as noted above, as an "attribute or characteristic that conveys a social identity that is devalued in a particular context."

In our terms, this aspect of stigma involves a label and a stereotype, with the label linking a person to a set of undesirable characteristics that form the stereotype. An example of this component is evident in a vignette experiment conducted by Link et al (1987). The study experimentally manipulated labeling, tagging a random half of the vignettes "former mental patients" and the other half "former back-pain patients." It also included a measure of the extent to which respondents believed that mental patients *in general* were "dangerous." When the vignette described a former back-pain patient, beliefs about the dangerousness of people with mental illness played no part in rejecting responses toward the vignette subject. When the vignette described a former mental patient, however, these beliefs were potent predictors of rejecting responses: Respondents who believed mental patients were dangerous reacted negatively to the person described as a former mental patient in the vignette. Apparently, for many people, the "mental patient" label linked the described person to stereotyped beliefs about the dangerousness of people with mental illness, which in turn led them to desire for social distance from the person.

As indicated above, this connection between labels and stereotypes has been a major aspect of the psychological study of stigma in recent years, following the social cognitive approach (Fiske 1998). This intriguing and very fruitful body of research seeks to elucidate the cognitive processes underlying the use of categories and the linking of those categories to stereotypes (Crocker et al 1998). We focus briefly on some selected aspects of this extensive body of research.

According to this literature, categories and stereotypes are often "automatic" and facilitate "cognitive efficiency." The automatic nature is revealed in experiments that indicate that categories and stereotypes are used in making split-second judgments and thus appear to be operating preconsciously. For example, Gaertner & McLaughlin (1983) conducted an experiment in which one group of white subjects was primed by the word "whites" and another by the word "blacks," and then both groups were tested as to the speed with which they were able to identify whether two strings of letters were both words. Both high- and low-prejudiced subjects responded more rapidly to positive words like "smart," "ambitious," and "clean" when primed by the word "whites" than when primed by the word "blacks." In addition to operating in a preconcious, automatic way, some studies suggest that category use preserves cognitive resources. Thus, for example, if subjects are provided with labels like doctor, artist, skinhead, or real estate agent when asked to form an impression of a vignette, they are better able to simultaneously perform another task like turning off a beeping computer than are subjects who are not provided these labels (Macrae et al 1994). Thus, from a psychological standpoint, culturally given categories are present even at a preconcious level and provide people with a means of making shorthand decisions that free them to attend to other matters. At the same time, other research in social psychology reveals considerable latitude in the cognitive processes that transpire such that very different outcomes may occur depending on the nature of the cognitions people employ and the contexts in which people are embedded (Crocker et al 1998).

COMPONENT 3—ON SEPARATING "US" FROM "THEM"

A third feature of the stigma process occurs when social labels connote a separation of "us" from "them" (Morone 1997, Devine et al 1999). United States history and politics offer many examples as established old-order Americans defined African-American slaves, American Indians, and successive waves of immigrants as outgroups—the "them" who were very different from "us." Few groups were entirely spared. For example, Morone (1997) provides quotes from Benjamin Franklin's observations of the impact of Dutch immigrants ("them") on the English colonists ("us"). "Already the English begin to quit particular neighborhoods, surrounded by the Dutch, being made uneasy by the disagreeableness of dissonant manners . . . Besides, the Dutch under-live, and are thereby enabled to under-work and under-sell the English who are thereby extremely incommoded and consequently disgusted" (Franklin 1752). And of course, while the groups representing "us" and "them" have changed, this separation is still prominent today. "They" are a menace to "us" because they are immoral, lazy, and predatory (Morone 1997). Thus, other components of the stigma process—the linking of labels to undesirable attributes—become the rationale for believing that negatively labeled persons are fundamentally different from those who don't share the label–different types of people. At the same time, when labeled persons are believed to be distinctly different, stereotyping can be smoothly accomplished because there is little harm in attributing all manner of bad characteristics to "them." In the extreme, the stigmatized person is thought to be so different from "us" as to be not really human. And again, in the extreme, all manner of horrific treatment of "them" becomes possible.

Evidence of efforts to separate us from them are sometimes directly available in the very nature of the labels conferred. Incumbents are thought to "be" the thing they are labeled (Estroff 1989). For example, some people speak of persons as being "epileptics" or "schizophrenics" rather than describing them as having epilepsy or schizophrenia. This practice is revealing regarding this component of stigma because it is different for other diseases. A person *has* cancer, heart disease, or the flu—such a person is one of "us," a person who just happens to be beset by a serious illness. But a person *is* a "schizophrenic."

COMPONENT 4—STATUS LOSS AND DISCRIMINATION

In this component of the stigma process, the labeled person experiences status loss and discrimination. Most definitions of stigma do not include this component, but as we shall see, the term stigma cannot hold the meaning we commonly assign to it when this aspect is left out. In our reasoning, when people are labeled, set apart, and linked to undesirable characteristics, a rationale is constructed for devaluing, rejecting, and excluding them. Thus, people are stigmatized when the fact that they are labeled, set apart, and linked to undesirable characteristics leads them to experience status loss and discrimination.

Consistent with this, stigmatized groups are disadvantaged when it comes to a general profile of life chances like income, education, psychological well-being, housing status, medical treatment, and health (e.g. Druss et al 2000, Link 1987). While some groups escape the experience of some disadvantaged outcomes sometimes (e.g., African Americans regarding self-esteem—see Crocker 1999), when one considers the profile of all possible outcomes, the general principle clearly holds for most stigmatized groups. How does this happen?

Status Loss

An almost immediate consequence of successful negative labeling and stereotyping is a general downward placement of a person in a status hierarchy. The person is connected to undesirable characteristics that reduce his or her status in the eyes of the stigmatizer. The fact that human beings create hierarchies is, of course, evident in organizational charts, who sits where in meetings, who defers to whom in conversational turn-taking, and so on. One strand of sociological research on social hierarchies, the so-called expectation-states tradition, is particularly relevant to the study of stigma and status loss (Cohen 1982, Driskell & Mullen 1990). Based on finding a reliable tendency of even unacquainted indivdiuals to form fairly stable status hierarchies when placed in group situations, researchers set out to understand the processes that produced this state of affairs. What they have found is relevant to research on stigma in many ways, two of which we shall emphasize here. First, this research shows that external statuses, like race and gender, shape status hierarchies within small groups of unacquainted persons even though the external status has no bearing on proficiency at a task the group is asked to perform. Men and whites are more likely than women and blacks to attain positions of power and prestige—they talk more frequently, have their ideas more readily accepted by others, and are more likely to be voted group leader (Mullen et al 1989). These findings are important to research on stigma because they show how having a status that is devalued in the wider society can lead to very concrete forms of inequality in the context of social interactions within small groups. Second, although inequalities in status-related outcomes definitely occur in the groups, they do not result from forms of discrimination that would be readily apparent to a casual observer. Instead group members use external statuses (like race and gender) to create performance expectations that then lead to a labyrinth of details that involve taking the floor, keeping the floor, referring to the contributions of others, head nodding, interrupting, and the like. This is important to research on stigma because it shows that substantial differences in outcome can occur even when it is difficult for participants to specify a single event that produced the unequal outcome.

Discrimination

INDIVIDUAL DISCRIMINATION   The standard way of conceptualizing the connection between labeling, stereotyping, and discrimination in the stigma literature follows a relatively simplistic formulation. In this approach, the importance of attitudes and beliefs are thought to lie in whether person A's labeling and stereotyping of person B leads person A to engage in some obvious forms of overt discrimination directed at person B, such as rejecting a job application, refusing to rent an apartment, and so on. There is no doubt that this rather straightforward process occurs with considerable regularity, although some social psychologists with interests in stigma have recently bemoaned the fact that documenting discriminatory behavior has not been their strong suit (Fiske 1998). Connecting attitudes to behaviors is, therefore, conceptualized as something the area of research on stigma and stereotyping needs (Fiske 1998). In this regard Ajzen & Fishbein's (1980) "theory of reasoned action" has been successfully applied to the prediction of many behaviors and might also be useful in predicting discriminatory behaviors. The approach they propose is effective because it asks us to narrow our focus to a very specific behavior and to be attentive to the intricacies of the beliefs and attitudes toward performing the specific act in question. But the area of stigma research needs to expand its conception of the processes through which labeling and stereotyping lead to social inequalities in life circumstances. By itself the standard model that asks "what-makes-person-A-discriminate-against-person-B" is inadequate for explaining the full consequences of stigma processes. In fact, getting tangled up in the narrow intricacies of explaining a specific act from knowledge of a specific set of attitudes and beliefs could cloud rather than illuminate our understanding of why stigmatized groups experience so many disadvantages.

STRUCTURAL DISCRIMINATION   The concept of institutional racism sensitizes us to the fact that all manner of disadvantage can result outside of a model in which one person does something bad to another. Institutional racism refers to accumulated institutional practices that work to the disadvantage of racial minority groups even in the absence of individual prejudice or discrimination (Hamilton & Carmichael 1967). For example, employers (more often white) rely on the personal recommendations of colleagues or acquaintances (more often white and more likely to know and recommend white job candidates) for hiring decisions. The same kind of structural discrimination is, of course, present for other stigmatized groups. For example, disabled persons may be limited in their ability to work not so much because of their inherent limitations but because they are exposed to what Hahn (1983) calls "a disabling environment" created by the barriers to participation that reside in architecture we humans have constructed (Fine & Asch 1988). Consider some possible examples of structural discrimination for a mental illness like schizophrenia. Suppose that because the illness is stigmatized, less funding is dedicated to research about it than for other illnesses and less money is allocated to adequate care and management. Moreover, consider that, because of historical processes influenced by stigma, treatment facilities tend to be either isolated in settings away from other people (Rothman 1971) or confined to some of the most disadvantaged neighborhoods in urban settings in communities that do not have enough clout to exclude this stigmatized group from their midst (Dear & Lewis 1986). At the same time, the most successful and accomplished mental health personnel tend to accrue more status and money by treating less serious illnesses in private offices in affluent areas, leaving the care of people with schizophrenia to a generally less accomplished group (Link 1983). To the extent that the stigma of schizophrenia has created such a situation, a person who develops this disorder will be the recipient of structural discrimination whether or not anyone happens to treat him or her in a discriminatory way because of some stereotype about schizophrenia. Stigma has affected the structure around the person, leading the person to be exposed to a host of untoward circumstances.

STATUS LOSS AS A SOURCE OF DISCRIMINATION   In keeping with observations about the role of stigma in the loss of status, it is important to note that lower placement in a status hierarchy can begin to have effects of its own on a person's life chances. It is not necessary to revisit the labeling and stereotyping that initially led to the lower status, because the lower status itself becomes the basis of discrimination. For example, low status might make a person less attractive to socialize with, to involve in community activities, or to include in a business venture that requires partners who have political influence with local politicians. In this way, a lower position in the status hierarchy can have a cascade of negative effects on all manner of opportunities. Because the discrimination that occurs is one step removed from the labeling and stereotyping, it is easy to miss the more distal effects of these factors in any accounting of the effects of these stigma components.

SOCIAL PSYCHOLOGICAL PROCESSES OPERATING THROUGH THE STIGMATIZED PERSON   Once the cultural stereotype is in place, it can affect labeled persons in important ways that do not involve obvious forms of discriminatory behavior on the part of people in the immediate presence of the stigmatized person. For example , according to a modified labeling theory about the effects of stigma on people with mental illnesses (Link 1982, Link et al 1989), people develop conceptions of mental illness early in life as part of socialization into our culture (Angermeyer & Matschinger 1996, Scheff 1966, Wahl 1995). Once in place, people's conceptions become a lay theory about what it means to have a mental illness (Angermeyer & Matschinger 1994, Furnham & Bower 1992). People form expectations as to whether most people will reject an individual with mental illness as a friend, employee, neighbor, or intimate partner and whether most people will devalue a person with mental illness as less trustworthy, intelligent, and competent. These beliefs have an especially poignant relevance for a person who develops a serious mental illness, because the possibility of devaluation and discrimination becomes personally relevant. If one believes that others will devalue and reject people with mental illnesses, one must now fear that this rejection applies personally. The person may wonder, "Will others look down on me, reject me, simply because I have been identified as having a mental illness?" Then to the extent that it becomes a part of a person's world view, that perception can have serious negative consequences. Expecting and fearing rejection, people who have been hospitalized for mental illnesses may act less confidently and more defensively, or they may simply avoid a potentially threatening contact altogether. The result may be strained and uncomfortable social interactions with potential stigmatizers (Farina et al 1968), more constricted social networks (Link et al 1989), a compromised quality of life (Rosenfield 1997), low self-esteem (Wright et al 2000), depressive symptoms (Link et al 1997), unemployment and income loss (Link 1982, 1987). While this theory has been most thoroughly examined with respect to mental illnesses, the process is probably much more general. In keeping with this possibility, Pinel (1999) has recently called the expectation of stereotyping "stigma consciousness" and has proposed its application to other stigmatized statuses.

A related but slightly different approach to understanding the effect of stereotypes is Steele & Aronson's (1995) concept of "stereotype threat." According to this idea, people know about the stereotypes that might be applied to them—African Americans know they are tagged with attributes of violence and intellectual inferiority, gay men know they are seen as flamboyant and promiscuous, and people with mental illnesses know that they are believed to be unpredictable and dangerous. The insight that Steele & Aronson provide is that the stereotype becomes a threat or challenge either because one might be evaluated in accordance with the stereotype or because one might confirm the stereotype through one's behavior. In keeping with this idea, Steele & Aronson have shown that, controlling for initial differences on SAT scores, African-American students perform worse than white students on a test when study participants are led to believe that the test measures intellectual ability. In contrast, when the same test is not labeled as being diagnostic of ability, African Americans score as well as whites. This research tells us that the existence of a stereotype and the administration of a test of "ability" can lead to an invalid assessment of the academic potential of African-American students and thereby to discrimination against such students on the basis of a seemingly "objective" test.

Note that in both the modified labeling theory and theory about stereotype threat, no one in the immediate context of the person needs to have engaged in obvious forms of discrimination. Rather, the discrimination lies anterior to the immediate situation and rests instead in the formation and sustenance of stereotypes and lay theories. Still the consequences are sometimes severe and undoubtedly contribute greatly to differences in the life chances of people in stigmatized groups.

INTERCHANGEABLE MECHANISMS   The problem of stigma has been described as a predicament or a dilemma by Goffman and others (Ainlay et al 1986, Crocker et al 1998). One reason for this is brought to light by the sociological observation that mechanisms like the ones we have described are both interchangeable and mutually reinforcing in achieving ends that discrimnate against stigmatized groups (Lieberson 1985). If powerful groups are motivated to discriminate against a stigmatized "them," there are many ways in which such discrimination can be achieved. If stigmatized persons cannot be persuaded to voluntarily accept their lower status and inferior rewards, direct discrimination can be used to accomplish the same outcome. If direct discrimination becomes ideologically difficult, sophisticated forms of structural discrimination—such as tests that induce stereotype threat—can achieve some of the same ends. The mechanisms are mutually reinforcing as well. To the extent that stigmatized groups accept the dominant view of their lower status, they are less likely to challenge structural forms of discrimination that block opportunities they desire. Further, direct discrimination reinforces the belief among stigmatized groups that they will be treated in accordance with stereotypes and therefore reinforces processes like those explicated in the context of modified labeling theory and the stereotype-threat concept. From this vantage point, stigma is a predicament in the following sense—as long as dominant groups sustain their view of stigmatized persons, decreasing the use of one mechanism through which disadvantage can be accomplished simultaneously creates the impetus to increase the use of another. This latter observation brings us to the final aspect of our stigma concept—its dependence on power differences.

THE DEPENDENCE OF STIGMA ON POWER

Stigma is entirely dependent on social, economic, and political power—it takes power to stigmatize. In some instances the role of power is obvious. However, the role of power in stigma is frequently overlooked because in many instances power differences are so taken for granted as to seem unproblematic. When people think of mental illness, obesity, deafness, and having one leg instead of two, there is a tendency to focus on the attributes associated with these conditions rather than on power differences between people who have them and people who do not. But power, even in these circumstances, is essential to the social production of stigma.

In order to reason about the role of power in stigma, first consider instances in which it is clear that social power is important. To begin, take the example provided earlier in which eighteenth century English colonists tagged the Dutch with attributes of disagreeableness and low-living. Along the same lines, people of Irish background were stereotyped as "temperamental, dangerous, quarrelsome, idle and reckless" by old-order Americans in the nineteenth century. The Irish at the time were likened to apes and were portrayed as such in cartoons of the day (Feagin & Feagin 1996). In the light of current circumstances, it is clear that English colonists of the eighteenth century and the old-order Americans of the nineteenth century were able to stigmatize the Dutch and Irish because of their positions of power over these groups at the time. And, of course, it was the power of the Nazis that allowed their thorough and devastating stigmatization of Jewish people.

But how can we think of the role of power in circumstances like mental illness, obesity, deafness, and one leggedness? One way is to recognize that stigmatized groups often engage in the same kinds of stigma-related processes in their thinking about individuals who are not in their stigmatized group. Consider for example patients in a treatment program for people with serious mental illness. Patients in such a setting are likely to identify and label human differences in staff members. For instance, they might tag some clinicians with the label "pill pusher" and apply stereotypes connected with the labels they create such as that pill pushers are cold, paternalistic, and arrogant. Finally they might treat the people they identify as pill pushers differently in accordance with the conclusions they have drawn about them by avoiding or minimizing communication with them, exchanging derogatory comments and jokes about them, and so on. Thus although the patients might engage in every component of stigma we identified, the staff would not end up being a stigmatized group. The patients simply do not possess the social, cultural, economic, and political power to imbue their cognitions about staff with serious discriminatory consequences.

Consider further that scenarios similar to the one just described exist for all sorts of other circumstances in which relatively powerless groups create labels and stereotypes about more powerful groups and treat members of the more powerful group in accordance with those stereotypes. Such a realization clarifies why the definition of stigma must involve reference to power differences. Without such a reference, stigma becomes a very different and much broader concept that might be applied to lawyers, politicians, Wall Street investors, and white people. Stigma is dependent on power.

Because of the importance of power in stigmatization, it is critical to ask the following set of questions: Do the people who might stigmatize have the power to ensure that the human difference they recognize and label is broadly identified in the culture? Do the people who might confer stigma have the power to ensure that the culture recognizes and deeply accepts the stereotypes they connect to the labeled differences? Do the people who might stigmatize have the power to separate "us" from "them" and to have the designation stick? And do those who might confer stigma control access to major life domains like educational institutions, jobs, housing, and health care in order to put really consequential teeth into the distinctions they draw? To the extent that we can answer yes to these questions, we can expect stigma to result. To the extent that we answer no, some of the cognitive components of stigma might be in place, but what we generally mean by stigma would not exist.

IMPLICATIONS OF THE STIGMA CONCEPT

The stigma concept we have articulated has implications for how one might reason about several persistent questions including: (*a*) the definition of stigma, (*b*) stigma as a matter of degree, (*c*) the origins of stigma, (*d*) the image of the stigmatized person as a passive victim versus an active challenger, (*e*) the consequences of stigma, (*f*) stigma as a persistent dilemma, (*g*) what we should do to change stigma processes, and (*h*) the importance of stigma in understanding the distribution of life chances.

The Definition of Stigma

Our explication of the stigma concept is revealing with regard to why so many definitions of stigma are extant in the literature—there are several components, each one of which has been described as stigma. We chose to define stigma in the convergence of interrelated components. Thus, stigma exists when elements of labeling, stereotyping, separation, status loss, and discrimination occur together in a power situation that allows them. This is a definition that we derived, not one that exists in some independent existential way. As such, its value rests in its utility. One reason it is helpful is that the term stigma is in very wide use, and some degree of clarity will help us communicate about the concept. Second, there are words that aptly describe each of the components like label (or mark or status), stereotyping, exclusion, status loss, and discrimination so that the use of the word stigma to describe any particular aspect is not necessary. Third, the definition coheres with the current usage of the term as it is applied to groups that are commonly referred to as stigmatized groups. Recall that if we only used the cognitive components of labeling and stereotyping to define stigma, groups like lawyers, politicians, and white people would have to be considered stigmatized groups. Our incorporation of power, status loss, and discrimination allows the formal definition we derived to cohere with current understandings of what a stigmatized group is. Fourth, we believe that the definition helps us envision and thereby more fully understand several important issues in the stigma literature as described below.

Stigma as a Matter of Degree

Our conceptualization leads to the conclusion that stigma exists as a matter of degree. The labeling of human differences can be more or less prominent. A label can connect a person to many stereotypes, to just a few or to none at all. Moreover, the strength of the connection between labels and undesirable attributes can be relatively strong or relatively weak. The degree of separation into groups of "us" and "them" can be more or less complete, and finally the extent of status loss and discrimination can vary. This means that some groups are more stigmatized than others and that some of the components we have described can be used analytically to think about why differences in the extent of stigma experienced vary from group to group.

The Origins of Stigma

Our paper has been focused on the nature and consequences of stigma rather than its sources. Nevertheless our conceptualization provides some ideas about how to think about the origins of stigma. As we indicated at the outset of this paper, a great deal of attention in the literature on stigma has been directed toward the cognitive processing of stigma-relevant information. As crucial as the knowledge gained from this literature is, it is not a sufficient basis for understanding the origins of stigma. As we have pointed out, groups both with and without power label and form stereotypes about the other group—members of each group engage in the kinds of cognitive processes that are studied in the now voluminous social psychological literature. But what matters is whose cognitions prevail—whose cognitions carry sufficient clout in social, cultural, economic, and political spheres to lead to important consequences for the group that has been labeled as different. Here is where the sociological study of stigma is badly needed—for while cognitive processes may be necessary causes for the production of stigma, they are not sufficient causes. We need to further understand the social processes that allow one group's views to dominate so as to produce real and important consequences for the other group.

Passive Victim Versus Active Challenger

One of the most troublesome issues in the study of stigma emerges when social scientists seek to articulate the real constraints that stigma creates in people's lives, and in doing so they end up portraying members of the stigmatized group as helpless victims (Fine & Asch 1988). Ironically, this produces more lines in the list of undesirable attributes that form the stereotype about the stigmatized group—they are additionally "passive," "helpless," or "acquiescent." Because of this, there are from time to time articles that remind us that people artfully dodge or constructively challenge stigmatizing processes (e.g. Reissman 2000). These are very important reminders, and the message they deliver needs to be incorporated into our understanding of stigma. At the same time, the simple fact that these forms of resistance exist suggests there *is* something out there to avoid and that there *are* powerful constraining forces at work. How can we reason about these contrasting images and portray constraint and resistance in research about stigma? Here, our emphasis on the importance of power differences in stigma and our observation that stigma is a matter of degree are helpful. Specifically, these allow us to see issues of constraint and resistance in the context of a power struggle. We can see that people in stigmatized groups actively use available resources to resist the stigmatizing tendencies of the more powerful group and that, to the extent that they do, it is inappropriate to portray them as passive recipients of stigma. At the same time, to the extent that power differences exist, resistence cannot fully overcome constraint. The amount of stigma that people experience will be profoundly shaped by the relative power of the stigmatized and the stigmatizer.

The Outcomes of Stigma

Our conceptualization of stigma demands the assessment of multiple outcomes, not just one or two. We cannot assess the extent of stigmatization when we assess just one outcome, whether that single outcome be self-esteem, housing status, or access to medical care. From one vantage point, this is an odd stricture to impose on the study of stigma. If we adopt a narrow conceptualization of stigma, for example as a label linked to a stereotype, we might expect specificity in the outcomes. We might identify the elements of the stereotype and then, based on what the stereotype entails, predict which outcomes might be affected. If the stereotype is math incompetence, then we might expect the person to be excluded from endeavors where math competence is required. As important as this kind of theorizing might be for understanding some aspects of stigma, it will cloud our vision of the full consequences if it is the only approach we employ.

Among the reasons our conceptualization of stigma calls for the scrutiny of many outcomes are three we consider here. First, stigma involves status loss—a downward placement in the status hierarchy. To the extent that this occurs, we can expect members of stigmatized groups to accrue all manner of untoward outcomes associated with lower placement in a status hierarchy, ranging from the selection of sexual partners to longevity. Second, structural discrimination can produce negative outcomes that have little to do with the stereotyped beliefs that initially motivated the structural discrimination. For example, the Not In My Back Yard (NIMBY) phenomenon resulted in treatment facilities for people with mental illness being located in relatively poor and powerless areas of the city that were also crime ridden and dangerous (Dear & Lewis 1986). As a consequence, people with mental illness are much more likely to be victimized than other people. Third, people's efforts to cope with stigma may have untoward consequences that are seemingly unrelated to the stereotype (James et al 1984, Smart & Wegner 1999). For example, social epidemiologist Sherman James puts forward the concept of what he calls "John Henryism"—the tendency for some African Americans to work extremely hard and with great pressure to disprove the stereotype of laziness and inability. According to James et al (1984), under some conditions this coping effort bears costs in the form of hypertension. In short, a comprehensive exploration of the stigma concept makes it clear that stigma can involve many outcomes and that any full assessment must look to a broad range of such outcomes.

Stigma as a Persistent Predicament

As previously mentioned, the literature makes reference to stigma as a predicament or dilemma. Our conceptualization draws attention to one way in which stigma is a persistent predicament—why the negative consequences of stigma are so difficult to eradicate. When powerful groups forcefully label and extensively stereotype a less powerful group, the range of mechanisms for achieving discriminatory outcomes is both flexible and extensive. We mentioned three generic types of mechanisms—individual discrimination, structural discrimination, and discrimination that operates through the stigmatized person's beliefs and behaviors. But lying below these broad-band designations are a whole multitude of specific mechanisms—there are many ways to achieve structural discrimination, many ways to directly discriminate, and many ways in which stigmatized persons can be encouraged to believe that they should not enjoy full and equal participation in social and economic life. Moreover, if the mechanisms that are currently in place are blocked or become embarrassing to use, new ones can always be created. This is the main reason that stigma is such a persistent predicament. When people in a stigmatized group take action to avoid a negative consequence, they frequently do so by counteracting (e.g. confronting or avoiding) the specific mechanism that leads to the undesirable outcome they seek to escape. But when the range of possible mechanisms is broad, the benefit is only temporary because the mechanism that has been blocked or avoided can be easily replaced by another.

A second and related reason that stigma is a persistent predicament is that there are a multitude of associated outcomes. One can exert great effort to avoid one stigma-related outcome, like discrimination in medical insurance or injury to self-esteem, but doing so can carry costs. For instance, the coping effort can be stressful, as in the case of John Henryism and hypertension levels among African Americans (James et al 1984). In that example, the effort to eliminate one bad outcome ironically produces strain that leads to another. Also, focusing particular attention on one outcome means that less attention is available to deal with other aspects of life. As a result, while benefits may accrue in one domain, concomitant harms may result in others. It is the existence of multiple stigma mechanisms and multiple stigma outcomes that helps explain why stigma is a persistent predicament—why, on average, members of stigmatized groups are disadvantaged in a broad range of life domains (e.g. employment, social relationships, housing, and psychological well-being).

We end our discussion of stigma as a persistent predicament with a point of clarification. First, to say that stigma is a persistent predicament is not to say that every individual in a group suffers the same outcome. Individual differences in personal, social, and economic resources also shape the life circumstances of persons in stigmatized groups, thereby producing substantial variation within stigmatized groups in any outcome one might consider. Thus, no one is fully trapped in a uniform disadvantaged position. All of the other characteristics of persons influence an outcome in the same way they influence outcomes for persons who are not members of the stigmatized group in question. The persistent predicament refers to a general pattern of disadvantage that is connected to stigma processes of labeling, stereotyping, status loss, and discrimination.

Changing Stigma

If stigma is a persistent predicament, how can it be changed? One approach is to focus on a particular behavior in a particular group. For example, one might target hiring practices with the aim of increasing the employment chances for a stigmatized group such as people with mental illnesses. One could then try to change employers' beliefs about and attitudes toward hiring persons with such illnesses. This approach is very appealing because it breaks down the morass of interconnecting stigma-facets into a more tractable problem. If one were to develop an intervention, one could target the intervention to the specific beliefs, attitudes, and behaviors of employers, thereby increasing the likelihood of an apparently successful outcome for the intervention research study. But what is appealing about this approach is also what makes it such an inadequate response to the broader problem of stigma. The intense focus on one specific behavior in one specific group leaves the broader context untouched and as a consequence even the very positive outcomes of an unusually successful program will erode with time. This will occur for reasons we have stated: There exists a flexible package of mutually reinforcing mechanisms linking the attitudes and beliefs of dominant groups to an array of untoward outcomes for stigmatized persons.

Our conceptualization leads us to focus on two principles in considering how to really change stigma. The first is that any approach must be multifaceted and multilevel. It needs to be multifaceted to address the many mechanisms that can lead to disadvantaged outcomes, and it needs to be multilevel to address issues of both individual and structural discrimination. But second, and most important, an approach to change must ultimately address the fundamental cause of stigma—it must either change the deeply held attitudes and beliefs of powerful groups that lead to labeling, stereotyping, setting apart, devaluing, and discriminating, or it must change circumstances so as to limit the power of such groups to make their cognitions the dominant ones. In the absence of fundamental changes, interventions targeted at only one mechanism at a time will ultimately fail, because their effectiveness will be undermined by contextual factors that are left untouched by such a narrowly conceived intervention. Thus, in considering a multifaceted multilevel response to stigma, one should choose interventions that either produce fundamental changes in attitudes and beliefs or change the power relations that underlie the ability of dominant groups to act on their attitudes and beliefs.

Understanding the Influence of Stigma Processes on the Distribution of Life Chances

A core concern of sociology is to understand the distribution of life chances, whether those refer to careers, earnings, social ties, housing, criminal involvement, health, or life itself. We believe that stigma processes have a dramatic and probably a highly underestimated impact on such life chances. Most research proceeds by examining the stigma associated with one circumstance at a time (e.g. AIDS, obesity, mental illness, minority racial status, female gender, homosexuality, etc), and most also assesses only one outcome at a time (e.g. earnings, self-esteem, housing, social interactions, etc.). When this occurs, researchers often find some level of effect for a particular stigmatized group on a particular outcome. However, it is also usually true that many factors other than the stigma processes in question influence the outcome, leaving stigma as just one factor among many. This can lead to the conclusion that stigma matters but that its effect is relatively modest compared to other factors. This accounting is misguided for two reasons. First, in seeking to understand the impact of stigma for a particular circumstance, one must keep in mind that it can affect many life chances, not just one. Thus, a full accounting must consider the overall effect on a multitude of outcomes. Second, there are a host of stigmatizing circumstances that need to be considered in studying a particular outcome. A full assessment of the impact of stigma on such an outcome must recognize that many stigmatizing circumstances contribute to that outcome and not just the one selected for the particular study in question. When viewed broadly, stigma processes likely play a major role in life chances and deserve scrutiny not just by investigators who happen to be interested in stigma but by a variety of social scientists who are interested in the distribution of life chances more generally.

CONCLUSION

Almost forty years after the publication of Goffman's book on stigma, we revisited the concept in light of research that has been undertaken in the interim. Attending to criticisms of the concept and its application by researchers from Goffman to the present, we constructed a revised conceptualization of the term. In our definition, stigma exists when elements of labeling, stereotyping, separating, status loss, and discrimination co-occur in a power situation that allows these processes to unfold. After developing this definition and explicating its component parts, we found it useful in providing a substantially different perspective on several crucial issues in the literature on stigma. Moreover, our conceptualization suggests that stigma is likely to be a key determinant of many of the life chances that sociologists study, from psychological well-being to employment, housing, and life itself. A propitious avenue for future research would involve the incorporation of stigma concepts and measures in community-based survey research that seeks to understand the social determinants of a broad array of life chances. Such an undertaking would greatly advance research on stigma because it would assess the linkage between stigma and outcomes that clearly matter in people's lives, thereby overcoming the criticism we alluded to earlier regarding the overemphasis on microlevel interactions in stigma research. At the same time, the incorporation of stigma concepts and measures in research focused on life chances would provide investigators in many areas of sociological research with additional possibilities for understanding the social distributions of the particular outcomes that are the focus of their attention. Most importantly, however, such an endeavor would tell us much more than we already know about the conditions under which stigma is related to untoward outcomes in real life situations. Knowledge of this sort should form the basis for the kinds of multifaceted multilevel interventions that represent our best hope for producing real change in stigma-related processes.

ACKNOWLEDGMENTS

We thank Patrick Corrigan, Bruce Dohrenwend, David Penn, and Elmer Struening for valuable comments on an earlier version of this paper.

Visit the Annual Reviews home page at www.AnnualReviews.org

LITERATURE CITED

Ainlay SC, Becker G, Colman LM. 1986. *The Dilemma of Difference: A Multidisciplinary View of Stigma.* New York: Plenum

Ajzen I, Fishbein M. 1980. *Understanding Attitudes and Predicting Social Behavior.* Englewood Cliffs, NJ: Prentice Hall

Angermeyer M, Matschinger H. 1994. Lay beliefs about schizophrenic disorder: the results of a population study in Germany. *Acta Psychiatr. Scand.* 89:39–45

Angermeyer MC, Matschinger H. 1996. The effect of violent attacks by schizophrenia persons on the attitude of the public towards the mentally ill. *Soc. Sci. Med.* 43:1721–28

Cahill S, Eggleston R. 1995. Reconsidering the stigma of physical disability. *Sociol. Q.* 36:681–98

Causey KA, Duran-Aydintug C. 1997. Tendency to stigmatize lesbian mothers in custody cases. *J. Divorce Remarriage* 28:171–82

Cohen EG. 1982. Expectations states and interracial interaction in school settings. *Annu. Rev. Sociol.* 8:209–235

Coleman M, Ganong L, Cable S. 1996. Perceptions of stepparents: an examination of the incomplete institutionalization and social stigma hypotheses. *J. Divorce Remarriage* 26:25–48

Conrad P. 1992. *Deviance and Medicalization: From Badness to Sickness.* Philadelphia: Temple Univ. Press

Corrigan PW, Penn Dl. 1999. Lessons from social psychology on discrediting psychiatric stigma. *Am. Psychol.* 54:765–76

Crocker J, Lutskey N. 1986. Stigma and the dynamics of social cognition. In *The Dilemma of Difference*, ed. SC Ainlay, G. Becker, LM Coleman. New York: Plenum

Crocker J. 1999. Social stigma and self-esteem: situational construction of self-worth. *J. Exp. Soc. Psychol.* 35:89–107

Crocker J, Major B, Steele C. 1998. Social stigma. In *The Handbook of Social Psychol-* ogy, ed. DT Gilbert, ST Fiske, 2:504–53. Boston, MA: McGraw-Hill

Davis KR. 1998. Bankruptcy: a moral dilemma for women debtors. *Law Psychol. Rev.* 22:235–49

Dear ML, Lewis G. 1986. Anatomy of a decision: recent land use zoning appeals and their effect on group home locations in Ontario. *Can. J. Commun. Mental Health* 5:5–17

Devine PG, Plant EA, Harrison K. 1999. The problem of us versus them and aids stigma. *Am. Behav. Sci.* 42:1212–28

Driskell JE, Mullen B. 1990. Status, expectations, and behavior: a meta-analytic review and test of the theory. *Personality Soc. Psychol. Bull.* 16:541–53

Druss BG, Bradford DW, Rosenheck RA, Radford MJ, Krumholz HM. 2000. Mental disorders and the use of cardiovascular procedures after myocardial infarction. *J. Am. Med. Assoc.* 283:506–11

Estroff SE. 1989. Self, identity and subjective experiences of schizophrenia: in search of the subject. *Schizophrenia Bull.* 15:189–96

Farina A, Allen JG, Saul B. 1968. The role of the stigmatized in affecting social relationships. *J. Personality* 36:169–82

Feagin JR, Feagin CB. 1996. *Racial and Ethic Relations.* Upper Saddle River, NJ: Prentice Hall

Fife BL, Wright ER. 2000. The demensionality of stigma: a comparison of its impact on the self of persons with HIV/AIDS and cancer. *J. Health Soc. Behav.* 41:50–67

Fine M, Asch A. 1988. Disability beyond stigma: social interaction, discrimination, and activism. *J. Soc. Issues* 44:3–22

Fiske ST. 1998. Stereotyping, prejudice, and discrimination. In *The Handbook of Social Psychology*, ed. DT Gilbert, ST Fiske, 2:357–411. Boston, MA: McGraw Hill

Franklin B. 1752. Letter to James Parker. In *The Importance of Gaining and Preserving the*

Friendship of the Indians to the British Interest Considered, ed. A Kennedy. London: E Cave

Fullilove MT. 1998. Abandoning race as a variable in public health research: an idea whose time has come. *Am. J. Pub. Health* 88:1297–98

Furnham A, Bower P. 1992. A comparison of academic and lay theories of schizophrenia. *Br. J. Psychiatr.* 161:201–10

Gaertner SL, McLaughlin JP. 1983. Racial stereotypes: associations and ascriptions of positive and negative characteristics. *Soc. Psychol. Q.* 46:23–30

Goffman E. 1963. *Stigma: Notes on the Management of Spoiled Identity.* Englewood Cliffs, NJ: Prentice Hall

Gould SJ. 1981. *The Mismeasure of Man.* New York: Norton

Hahn H. 1983. Paternalism and public policy. *Society* XX:36–46

Hamilton C, Carmichael S. 1967. *Black Power.* New York: Random House

James SA, LaCroix AZ, Kleinbaum DG, Strogatz DS. 1984. John Henryism and blood pressure differences among black men: II. The role of occupational stressors. *J. Behav. Med.* 7:259–75

Jones E, Farina A, Hastorf A, Markus H, Miller DT, Scott R. 1984. *Social Stigma: The Psychology of Marked Relationships.* New York: Freeman

Kleinman A, Wang W-Z, Li S-C, Cheng X-M, Dai X-Y, Li K-T, Kleinman J. 1995. The social course of epilepsy: chronic illness as social experience in interior China. *Soc. Sci. Med.* 40:1319–30

Lewis J. 1998. Learning to strip; the socialization experiences of exotic dancers. *Can. J. Hum. Sexuality* 7:51–66

Lieberson S. 1985. *Making It Count: The Improvement of Social Research and Theory.* Berkeley: Univ. Calif. Press

Link B. 1982. Mental patient status, work, and income: an examination of the effects of a psychiatric label. *Am. Sociol. Rev.* 47:202–15

Link B. 1987. Understanding labeling effects in the area of mental disorders: an assessment of the effects of expectations of rejection. *Am. Sociol. Rev.* 52:96–112

Link BG. 1983. Reward system of psychotherapy: implications for inequities in service delivery. *J. Health Soc. Behav.* 24:61–69

Link BG, Cullen FT, Frank J, Wozniak J. 1987. The social rejection of ex-mental patients: understanding why labels matter. *Am. J. Sociol.* 92:1461–1500

Link BG, Cullen FT, Struening E, Shrout P, Dohrenwend BP. 1989. A modified labeling theory approach in the area of mental disorders: an empirical assessment. *Am. Sociol. Rev.* 54:100–23

Link BG, Phelan JC. 1999. Labeling and stigma. In *The Handbook of the Sociology of Mental Health,* ed. CS Aneshensel, JC Phelan. New York: Plenum

Link BG, Struening EL, Rahav M, Phelan JC, Nuttbrock L. 1997. On stigma and its consequences: evidence from a longitudinal study of men with dual diagnoses of mental illness and substance abuse. *J. Health Soc. Behav.* 38:177–90

Macrae CN, Milne AB, Bodenhausen GV. 1994. Stereotypes as energy saving devices: a peek inside the cognitive toolbox. *J. Personality Soc. Psychol.* 66:37–47

Morone JA. 1997. Enemies of the people: the moral dimension to public health. *J. Health Polit., Policy Law* 22:993–1020

Mullen B, Salas E, Driskell JE. 1989. Salience, motivation, and artifact as contributions to the relation between participation rate and leadership. *J. Exp. Soc. Psychol.* 25:545–59

Oliver M. 1992. *The Politics of Disablement.* Basingstoke: Macmillan

Opala J, Boillot F. 1996. Leprosy among the limba: illness and healing in the context of world view. *Soc. Sci. Med.* 42:3–19

Page RM. 1984. *Stigma.* London: Routledge & Keegan Paul

Phelan JC, Link BG, Stueve A, Pescosolido B. 2000. Public conceptions of mental illness in 1950 and 1996: What is mental illness and is it to be feared. *J. Health Soc. Behav.* 41:188–207

Pinel EC. 1999. Stigma consciousness: the psychological legacy of social stereotypes. *J. Personality Soc. Psychol.* 76:114–128

Reissman CK. 2000. Stigma and everyday resistance: childless women in South India. *Gender Soc.* 14:111–35

Rosenfield S. 1997. Labeling mental illness: the effects of received services and perceived stigma on life satisfaction. *Am. Sociol. Rev.* 62:660–72

Rothman D. 1971. *The Discovery of the Asylum.* Boston: Little Brown & Coompany

Sayce L. 1998. Stigma, discrimination and social exclusion: what's in a word *J. Mental Health* 7:331–43

Scheff TJ. 1966. *Being Mentally Ill: A Sociological Theory.* Chicago, IL: Aldine de Gruyter

Schneider JW. 1988. Disability as moral experience: epilepsy and self in routine relationships. *J. Soc. Issues* 44:63–78

Sheldon K, Caldwell L. 1994. Urinary incontinence in women: implications for therapeutic recreation. *Ther. Recreation J.* 28:203–12

Smart L, Wegner DM. 1999. Covering up what can't be seen: concealable stigma and mental control. *J. Personality Soc. Psychol.* 77:474–86

Stafford MC, Scott RR. 1986. Stigma deviance and social control: some conceptual issues. In *The Dilemma of Difference*, ed. SC Ainlay, G Becker, LM Coleman. New York: Plenum

Steele CM, Aronson J. 1995. Stereotype vulnerability and the intellectual test performance of African Americans. *J. Personality Soc. Psychol.* 69:797–811

Wahl OF. 1995. *Media Madness: Public Images of Mental Illness.* New Brunswick N J: Rutgers Univ. Press

Walsgrove D. 1987. Policing yourself: social closure and the internalization of stigma. In *The Manufacture of Disadvantage*, ed. G Lee, R Loveridge. Philadelphia: Open Univ. Press

Wright ER, Gonfrein WP, Owens TJ. 2000. Deinstitutionalization, social rejection, and the self-esteem of former mental patients. *J. Health Soc. Behav.* 41:68–90

Annu. Rev. Sociol. 2001. 27:387–413

SOCIOLOGICAL MINIATURISM: Seeing the Big Through the Small in Social Psychology

John F. Stolte,[1] Gary Alan Fine,[2] and Karen S. Cook[3]

[1]Department of Sociology, Northern Illinois University, DeKalb, Illinois 60115;
e-mail: soci@sun.soci.niu.edu
[2]Department of Sociology, Northwestern University, Evanston, Illinois 60208;
e-mail: G-Fine@northwestern.edu
[3]Department of Sociology, Stanford University, Stanford, California 94305;
e-mail: kcook@stanford.edu

Key Words   negotiated order, social exchange, power, collective identity, symbolic interaction

■ **Abstract**   The distinctive contribution of sociological social psychology can be referred to as sociological miniaturism, a way of interpreting social processes and institutions that is microsociological more than it is psychological. We argue that social psychology of this variety permits the examination of large-scale social issues by means of investigation of small-scale social situations. The power of this approach to social life is that it permits recognition of the dense texture of everyday life, permits sociologists to understand more fully a substantive domain, and permits interpretive control. In the chapter we provide examples of this approach from two quite distinct theoretical orientations: symbolic interactionism and social exchange theory. We discuss the ways in which the study of two substantive topics, social power and collective identity, using these perspectives can be informed by closer collaboration between theorists within sociological social psychology. In the end it is our hope that pursuing such integrative theoretical and methodological efforts will produce a more complete understanding of important social phenomena. We offer sociological miniaturism as a promising vehicle for advancing the earlier call for greater mutual appreciation of and rapprochement between diverse lines of social psychological work in sociology.

INTRODUCTION

The social psychological perspective in sociology has had a long, if uncertain, history. Sociological social psychology has a longevity equal to its history in psychology, although its growth has been in spurts and starts, and its theoretical development has been, until recently, less continuous. In 1908 two textbooks of social psychology were published in the United States: one by William McDougall in psychology, one by Edward A. Ross in sociology. Within a few decades, after flirting with introspectionism, psychological social psychology claimed the

0360-0572/01/0811-0387$14.00

laboratory experiment as its standard methodology (Fine & Elsbach 2000). The agenda of social psychology in psychology was to demonstrate how the behaviors of individuals were influenced by the existence of a social world and how individuals developed cognitive strategies to take their social surroundings into account. The primary thrust of this approach was to comprehend individual behaviors and attitudes as a function of an external reality.

In both methodological and theoretical terms, sociological social psychology has been less self-assured, perhaps bracingly more diverse. Our goal in this chapter is to present a model that helps explain the development of a distinctively sociological social psychology, interprets the current state of social psychology, and points to future developments. In making this claim we impose a single, if broad, model of social psychology, and in so doing we recognize that we miss significant developments that a more nuanced treatment would examine.

We argue that the distinctive contribution of sociological social psychology is not a singular methodological or theoretical perspective, but, in contrast, a way of interpreting social processes and institutions. Specifically sociologists attempt to use the investigation of interpersonal situations as a lens through which broader social forces, properties, and processes can be understood. Microsituations are used to simulate the dynamics of larger social units. This chapter represents a collaboration between social psychologists whose orientations are widely divergent—from symbolic interactionism to social exchange theory—suggesting that the approach taken here is not narrowly partisan, but disciplinarily robust.

The distinctive contribution of this approach is what we label *sociological miniaturism*. We assert that sociological social psychology is not fundamentally social *psychological*, but, in contrast, is a form of *microsociology*. Specifically we claim that social psychology permits the examination of large-scale social issues by means of the investigation of small-scale social situations. A sociological social psychology will be linked inexorably to concerns of macrosociology. Macrosociology and microsociology recursively provide the foundations for each other's existence. In making this claim, we contend that a miniaturist approach posits three fundamental claims about the nature of reality: transcendence, representation, and generalizability.

Miniaturism assumes that processes transcend levels. The phenomena that apply to one level of analysis (e.g. the interpersonal) can also be observed on other levels (e.g. the institutional or interorganizational) (Harrington & Fine 2000). Second, this model assumes that the behavior of individuals can be treated, on certain occasions, as representing larger social entities. The individual sometimes stands in for the group, and, more important, is taken as standing for that group. The individual is treated as the larger entity, so that individual action becomes recognizable as, and treated as, the action of a collective actor. Thus, the behavior of a clerk represents the store or the government. The behavioral choices and motivations of individual actors have recognizable parallels in the behavior of groups, organizations, and other collective units. Although individuals need not always represent their organizations, nor need they always be taken as representing their organizations, this behavioral synecdoche is routine and is grounded in common-sense interpretations. Finally, we assume that situations can be meaningfully generalized. This assumption is important for legitimating and justifying the value of both laboratory experiments and ethnographic investigations. For the sociologist the experiment that did not apply to phenomena outside of the laboratory would be of marginal utility for the development of theoretical understanding. Similarly, most ethnographic studies are based in a particular setting in which the characteristics of that setting are idiosyncratic and relevant to the description of the research. However, it is assumed that the findings apply to a world beyond the setting. The data from one case study stand for the results of others (Burawoy 1979). Admittedly the extent of generalizability must be specified by the researcher.

In attempting to justify sociological miniaturism, we rely on two different but complementary perspectives, negotiated order and social exchange, to address two substantive topics, (*a*) social power and (*b*) collective identity. We do not attempt an exhaustive literature review of these areas but hope to demonstrate the relevance of a social psychology that addresses these concerns in such a way as to provide a basis for macrosociological analysis. There are several interrelated reasons to choose a focus on power and collective identity. These phenomena are of central importance across the microsocial to macrosocial continuum, from families, through work organizations, to nation-states. At each level, power and collective identity are counterpoints in a fundamental social dialectic (Blau 1964), involving complex forces of conflict and division, on the one hand, and consensus and solidarity, on the other hand. Whether the social actors at issue are the members of a street-corner gang, the Chief Executive Officers of a loosely coupled corporate network, or the officially appointed representatives of a United Nations body, crucial social psychological questions tend to emerge around the tension and interplay between power and collective identity. Further, sociological social psychologists have made important research contributions to our understanding of power and collective identity, both those in the group process/experimental research tradition and those in the symbolic interactionist/ethnographic research tradition. As research in both traditions has shown, the experiment or the ethnographic setting becomes a miniature arena in which social actors enact larger themes of power and/or collective identity.

JUSTIFYING MINIATURISM

We believe that an approach that recognizes the power of sociological miniaturism has several distinct advantages for developing theory and exploring substantive constructs. Central among these virtues are that it permits the recognition of the dense texture of everyday life, permits sociologists to understand a substantive domain, and permits a measure of interpretive control.

Texture

In contrast with purely macrosociological approaches, social psychological approaches are densely textured. More so than in macroanalyses, the details of the processes being examined can be known in their behavioral particulars. The process of boiling down information to its essence or core—a process that introduces bias into the analysis by virtue of the choices of what is left out—is less evident when the details of interaction are examined. By examining the particulars of a situation or a specific social process, we are better able to determine the conditions under which effects occur and to specify them theoretically. A study of individual action or of actors engaged in interaction reveals details that the study of organizational or societal change can only suggest in faint outline form.

Knowability

A second virtue is the increased knowability of a domain. Because of the relatively limited scope of social psychological topics, it becomes possible for the researcher to gain a handle on the dynamics of what is being examined. The whole of the situation or the social process is potentially graspable, at least more so than would be true for a more elaborate or complex scenario. Thus a researcher creates access to a wider range of causal factors that produce a phenomenon.

Control

A third virtue of miniaturism is that it provides more opportunities for researchers to manipulate and control a small situation than would be the case with respect to a larger, more complex domain. This recognition is, of course, central to the justification for experimental methodology. One or two dimensions can be manipulated as independent variables to examine the effects on dependent variables. While the effects of such change are measured, the rest of the situation (the constants) remain unchanged. Changes in the dependent variable can thus be reasonably attributed to variation in the independent variable(s). While control is especially central in experimental studies, it also applies in some measure to ethnographic research. Part of the control aspect of ethnography is the ability of the researcher to define the problem and to select the research site. These choices, while not explicitly constraining informants, determine the kinds of processes that they are likely to observe and sensitize them to ways that observations should be interpreted. These choices–being intentional and self-conscious–control the observational field in ways that are similar to experimental strategies. Further, while in the field setting, the researcher can vary his or her behavior to examine the resulting variations in the responses of the group. Since the researcher is a part of the behavioral context of the group, choices of action have something of the same quality as independent variables in the laboratory. Given that the impacts of the ethnographer are small and easily controllable, the range of effects and outcomes produced may be significantly expanded, increasing our capacity to specify theoretically the key features of the social process(es) involved.

Limitations of Miniaturism

Despite its virtues, miniaturism is insufficient to create a fully adequate sociology. Moving from the small group, whether a laboratory experimental group or ethnographic group, to the macrosocial world of organizations and institutions is fraught with challenges. Central to these challenges is the fact that generalization from experimental or ethnographic data is, first and foremost, a theoretical endeavor. Often this endeavor encounters substantial obstacles connected to the complexity of social life and to variations among social phenomena at different levels along the micro-to-macro continuum.

Zelditch's (1969) provocative question, "Can you really study an army in a laboratory?" together with subsequent discussions (Berger et al 1972, Berger et al 1976, Walker & Cohen 1985), has clarified the generalizing strategy of theory-building as a rationale for designing laboratory experiments to test theories of group process. But an argument—similar in certain fundamental respects—also applies to the symbolic interactionist tradition with its ethnographies in which the goal is to have the results of one case study represent other interactional domains. Here, generalization is also undertaken as a theoretical enterprise.

Among both kinds of social psychologists, group-process-experimenters and negotiated-order-ethnographers, a distinctive *strategy* of theory construction is central. This strategy aims expressly at creating knowledge that is "abstract-generalizing," not "particular-historical." For example, a group process researcher might wish to account in a general way for social change in a power-imbalanced exchange network through coalition formation as a power-balancing process. If so, s/he does not limit attention to the localized particulars of a laboratory group of undergraduates at a given university at a given time. Rather, s/he demonstrates a lawful power-balancing process concretely in a laboratory, assuming that the process will operate inexorably *whenever* certain scope conditions obtain—whether they occur in a university laboratory, in a factory, in an urban community, or in a network of nation-states.

For another example, a symbolic interactionist ethnographer might wish to account for the tendency of friendship cliques to undergo significant changes with the arrival of a new member. If so, s/he does not limit attention to the local particulars obtaining to a natural neighborhood clique composed of preadolescent baseball players. Instead, s/he constructs a theoretical interpretation, albeit one that is grounded in the real-life neighborhood clique, rather than one deliberately operationalized in a university laboratory, that applies to friendship cliques wherever and whenever they exist—whether in a neighborhood, an automobile factory, or a large-scale political body such as the World Trade Organization.[1] The inductive model, often linked to "grounded theory" that is postulated in many (although not all) ethnographic investigations, will stand in contrast to the deductive emphasis in experimental research. Yet, even here, it is well to recall that the grounded and inductive theoretical insights characteristic of ethnographic research are always "tested" in later observations, just as the hypotheses of experimental research are sparked by some observation of the empirical world. The differences, though real in practice, often shade into each other.

As suggested above, however, sociological miniaturists, whether negotiated order ethnographers or group process experimenters, face significant obstacles or constraints when they implement a generalizing strategy of theory building. The key constraints are: differences in content, differences in population, and differences in process that arise across the micro-to-macro span.

Content

When extrapolating from a group attempting to divide up a minimal reward in a social psychological experiment to societal systems of reward distribution, much will be missed if we assume that the former can simply be overlaid on the latter. The issues that arise around units of differing size are significant. While the scale of the division is relevant to our understanding, often what is to be distributed differs as well. In a laboratory study, the money that is distributed may be seen as a benefit, but it is unlikely to be defined as a matter deserving a great commitment of time and effort. In organizations, the content of what is being divided (power, responsibility, salaries) can often lead to heated battles. In other words, the differing meaning of the divisions to the actors involved contributes to variations in the responses of the parties. Many differences derived from variations in scale require careful theoretical investigation.[2]

Population

The traditional social psychological research study examines the attitudes and behaviors of individuals. This focus stands in sharp contrast to issues

---

[1]Clearly there are important differences in how the generalizing theory strategy is implemented by ethnographers, on the one hand, and experimenters, on the other. Among the core differences is the *level of theoretical formalization* sought. Negotiated order/ethnographic researchers typically tend toward the relatively more informal end of the theorizing continuum. They usually frame and communicate theoretical concepts and principles discursively. In contrast, group process/experimental researchers typically tend toward the relatively more formal end of the theorizing continuum. They often use conceptual and logical (often mathematical) tools, deliberately aiming to organize and communicate the elements of theory more explicitly. It seems reasonable to believe that the two kinds of theorizing might, under certain conditions, supplement one another, expanding sociological understanding in interesting new directions.

[2]This constraint of content is closely related to issues of "scope" definition, as discussed by Walker & Cohen (1985).

found in macrosociological investigations in which organizations and institutions are the focus of analytical concern. When individuals are brought into macrosociological investigations, these persons serve as representatives of the organization that stands behind them. They are representatives of organizations, as we noted above, but simultaneously they have agency as actors in their own right. The interpretations of their organizational role are legitimate but so is their recognition of their personal abilities and choices. Thus, an examination of board linkages or networks of organizations views the individuals who serve on boards only as representatives or agents of their primary organization with a transparent connection to the organization. Such is not the case, however much we and they may see that representation as central to their action. The implications of acting for oneself in contrast to acting on behalf of others are sufficiently distinct that simple generalizations from individuals to collective actors are not adequate (Cook & Whitmeyer 1992). We are compelled to ask: To what extent do the perspective and the range of actions of individuals overlap with those of organizational and collective actors? While there is congruence, we should not assume that the overlap is complete. In the relevant literatures in political science and economics, this general class of concerns is analyzed as the "principal-agent" problem (e.g. Jensen & Meckling 1976, Mitnick 1975, Miller 2001). Congruence of the interests of both parties is presumed to be a central issue in analyses of principal-agent relations.

Process

At the heart of microanalyses of social life is the exploration and delineation of process. The symbolic interactionist approach to social life, for instance, often enshrines the examination of process, while simultaneously downgrading both the structure and the content of the scene being examined. The interactionist approach of grounded theory, developed by Glaser & Strauss (1967), uses the constant comparative method explicitly as a means to look beyond the immediate case to understand general processes. Even the group process approach emphasizes the process through which outcomes develop. Yet, the question of whether we are examining the same process when we can propound a metaphor that seems to operate on several levels is difficult to answer. What appears to be the same process may have distinctly different dynamics in interpersonal interaction as opposed to interorganizational relations. While the outcomes might be similar metaphorically, exchanging a collective actor for an individual may shift the dynamics of the relevant process.

Although extrapolating large-scale social processes by examining microlevel phenomena can provide great insight, we must proceed with care. Organizations and individuals are both similar in some respects and vastly different in many ways. Sociological miniaturism does not provide a snapshot of the social world in which explanations are transparent. Rather, there is an insistent need for translation: a process that is theoretical and interpretive.

ILLUSTRATING SOCIOLOGICAL MINIATURISM: THE NEGOTIATED ORDER AND SOCIAL EXCHANGE PERSPECTIVES

We now turn to a brief, selective review of two literatures. One is focused on negotiated order (Strauss 1978, Fine 1984) and the other on social exchange (Emerson 1962, 1972, Cook 1987, Molm & Cook 1995). Specifically, we explore how these literatures have illuminated two important sociological phenomena: social power and collective identity.[3] We shall demonstrate sociological miniaturism by showing how this model operates in two distinct, but complementary, lines of social psychological research.

Social Power

NEGOTIATED ORDER AND SOCIAL POWER   Drawing from earlier work by Strauss (1978), Fine (1984:241) argues that "the structure of the organization and the micropolitics of the negotiated order are closely connected," even though not all negotiations are feasible. A recurring theme in the writings of negotiated order theorists is that an obdurate social reality circumscribes and constrains negotiations. Such an objectively factual reality is evident, for example, in the unequal power enjoyed by some actors relative to other actors in their ability to define the social situation. For example, a psychiatrist or a lawyer will have considerably more power to shape the definition of the situation than a client. Similarly, a police officer can unilaterally impose a definition of "proper" conduct upon an ordinary citizen through his or her formal authority. However, one friend, a peer to a second friend, must negotiate a consensual definition of proper conduct. "When an individual has a need that must be satisfied (e.g., treatment, pay, protection), he or she is severely constrained by the wishes of those who can satisfy it" (Fine 1984:251, Strauss 1978). It is emblematic of the negotiated order perspective, deriving as it does from symbolic

---

[3]We do not suggest that these two lines of research are the **only** ones that might be used to illustrate the promise of sociological miniaturism. From the symbolic interactionist tradition, the topics of social coordination (Couch 1987), emotion work (Hochschild 1983), the social construction of deviance (Becker 1963), and identity-formation (Stryker 1980) among others might have been used. From the group processes tradition, theoretical research programs focused on status (Berger et al 1977, Ridgeway & Walker 1995), legitimacy (Walker et al 1988), bargaining (Lawler & Ford 1995), justice (Hegtvedt & Markovsky 1995), or other issues, might have been used instead. Each of these lines of work is miniaturist in basic thrust. We have selected the negotiated order and social exchange approaches for emphasis here, however, because these two perspectives offer exciting opportunities for cross-fertilization and points of synthesis, beyond and above the value each has as a separate example of miniaturism. Paranthetically, it needs to be noted that we do not have space in this paper to discuss the ways in which the social structure and personality tradition, represented by House's work and its derivatives (see, for example, Kessler et al 1995), exhibit elements of the miniaturist perspective.

interaction theory, that the power of agents such as psychiatrists, lawyers, or police officers is a power to define a social situation. Such power is anchored directly in the surrounding macro-to-micro web of shared cultural meanings. Social exchange theory, to be discussed later, emphasizes the structural source of such power differences.

Another facet of power from a negotiated-order point of view is that the interpretations different actors have of the negotiation situation conflict. That is, disagreements may exist concerning who properly should engage in negotiation and how those individuals ought to act (Kleinman 1996). The procedures and rules to be followed in negotiation may also be in dispute. Resolving disputes about meanings, rules, and procedures through the give-and-take of interpersonal communication is a process that demonstrates the anchorage of the negotiated order perspective in symbolic interaction theory.

Social power, considered from this perspective, also entails organizational segmentation. Subgroups of individuals form and, through symbolic interaction, construct subcultures. Even though one subgroup (e.g., management) may have greater formal power than another subgroup (e.g., labor), the dominant group's power may be resisted by those subject to it. Indeed, each subgroup may generate stories and jokes reflecting harshly on the other group. Often, within obdurate structural limits, workers negotiate the conditions of their work so as to secure a measure of autonomy, moderating the stifling effects of bureaucratic authority and tedious written regulations.

Further, certain forms of group action or collective behavior in organizations are viewed as important facets of the power process by the negotiated order approach. Social power tactics such as strikes, lockouts, and boycotts are especially likely to be employed when an organizational crisis has been precipitated; that is, when a serious breakdown of communication patterns has occurred. An organizational crisis demands a more intense, more specific communication of meaning than is needed under normal, routine circumstances.

Besides organizations, social movements provide an alternative context for a negotiated order analysis of the operation of power processes. Central to such analysis are the dynamics of culture. "From a 'macro' perspective . . . sociologists recognize that a social movement is not only politically and socially situated, but culturally situated as well" (Fine 1995:127). Ideological elements of the macroculture are used to define, frame, and legitimate the movement. Fine's focus, however, is on the microsocial processes of culture, examining how interactants engage one another in discourse to construct a "bundle of narratives" ("stories") regarding their social movement. The cache of such narratives along with "a system of knowledge, beliefs, behaviors, and customs shared by members of an interacting group to which members can refer and which they can employ as the basis of further interaction" constitute the "idioculture" of the social movement.

At the core of the negotiated order approach to power within social movements is the notion that a movement constitutes a staging area for social action and resource mobilization. It is a place in which individuals tell one another stories and otherwise talk, publicly performing elements of culture for one another. As Fine

(1995:130–32) puts it: "Through the public sharing of talk and behavior, culture becomes a resource. . . . The group serves as a place of cultural enactment, where values take form and are invested with shared meaning. . . . Culture both is a product of a resource base and contributes to the likelihood of gaining additional resources."

Following the lead of Zurcher & Snow (1981), Fine (1995:132) draws attention to the intimate and crucial link between "symbolic" and "material" resources, asserting that: ". . . the analysis of resources should focus not only on the material utility of resources, but also on the centrality of resources as symbolic goods . . . [S]logans and patterns of rhetoric are vital resources—manipulated consciously or emergent spontaneously . . . to symbolize the causes of discontent for movement actors and serve to energize and justify their actions." In other words, members of the social movement interact to construct and implement a shared, socially motivated focus for collective action. The emotionally energized and socially justified collective aim is to oppose and vanquish a set of actors outside the boundaries of the movement, who are constituted as sources of injustice and exploitation. In this account of a social movement as a power process "public support, communications, authority and social control, and material resources [are combined to] facilitate cultural expression" (Fine 1995:132).

The above account emphasizes some of the central theoretical ideas about power considered from a negotiated order standpoint. Along with these ideas, relevant ethnographic data have also been collected and reported. An example is Fine's (1995) brief ethnography of individuals who had been accused of child abuse and had organized to fight the charge and the system that produced it, focusing on the powerful influence of social workers. These individuals, typically parents or day-care providers, were members of a social movement organized to counter the rhetorical claims and political power of those state agents, who, due to the cultural climate of the times, were in a position to inflict dramatic and severe reputational damage (i.e., could impose serious stigma) by merely mounting charges of child abuse.

Qualitative data were collected via observation and interviews at a national convention of Victims of Child Abuse Laws (VOCAL) and at local movement meetings. Telephone interviews of the participants were also conducted. Many of the specific theoretical patterns discussed above were found to operate in the behavior of the members of VOCAL. Narrative accounts ("horror stories," "war stories," and "happy endings") were framed in the movement's idioculture and were shared to mobilize resources among members of the movement.

A second ethnography addressing alternative facets of power examined cooks in four Twin City (Minneapolis-St. Paul) restaurants. As Fine (1992) suggests, cooking is an art form, a form of aesthetic production. Like other work, culinary work, under certain conditions, provides a cook an opportunity to display aesthetic skill. And when conditions permit, a cook is motivated to exercise her/his artistic talent to produce a beautiful meal, a meal that evokes a pleasing "sensory response in an audience" (a restaurant customer), one that looks good and tastes good. Effectively doing so is a significant source of pride, a source of "craftsmanship," a source of experiential "flow" (Csikszentmihalyi 1990). Further, a competent cook knows what is necessary to create a culinary success, that is, s/he has a personal set of artistic standards for judging excellence in cooking. However, frequent tension or conflict existed between the sentiment toward aesthetic production, on the one hand, and toward practical, efficient, economic production, on the other. Such tension or conflict necessitates a negotiated compromise. A balance must be struck between striving for the artistic ideal and accommodating the obdurate reality of external power. Cooks must shape their cooking to meet "client demands," "organizational efficiency," and the material (economic) "resource base" (Fine 1992:1279). Regardless of ideal standards, a cook must prepare what clients wish, must spend no more time cooking than allotted by the management, and must balance considerations of quality against considerations of price. In short, a cook's aesthetic sensibilities are pitted against the power of various intractable external agents and economic constraints.

While symbolic interactionists primarily emphasize the cultural aspects of power, exchange theorists focus on the more structural sources of power. That actors are typically embedded in social situations that exert profound influence over their behavior, however, is a key assumption shared by both interactionists and exchange theorists.

SOCIAL EXCHANGE AND SOCIAL POWER   Anchored in both operant psychology and microeconomics, social exchange is a broad perspective that has been used to explore many important facets of social interactive behavior and the social structures it generates. One of the most significant features of exchange theory is its attention to power and related topics. This fact is reflected in the works of Homans (1958, 1961, 1974), Blau (1964), and Emerson (1972, 1976) as well as in the more current formulations often referred to as network exchange theories (developed by Cook, Emerson, Yamagishi, Anderson & Willer, Markovsky, Skvoretz, Lovaglia, and Friedkin). For reviews of some of this work see Cook (1987), Stolte (1987), Molm & Cook (1995)[4] and Walker, Thye, Simpson, Lovaglia, Willer & Markovsky (2000). These reviews cover the basic concepts and core assumptions of the various theoretical formulations of social exchange as well as the history of this tradition and the significant intellectual controversies that have surrounded the development of this perspective in the social sciences over the past four decades. Rather than produce another review, we provide a brief overview and comment on the exchange approach to the analysis of power relations. This sets the stage for a discussion of the intersection between the exchange perspective and the approaches to the role of power in social settings adopted by symbolic interactionists.

Power is perhaps the most fundamental concept in social exchange theory. Not only was it central to the foundation of exchange theory, it has remained the key focus of most of the empirical research conducted both inside and outside of the

---

[4]Molm & Cook (1995) discuss in more detail some of these theoretical formulations and the various strains of contemporary research. In addition, they include a discussion of the standardized laboratory settings for the experimental study of both negotiated and non-negotiated (reciprocal) exchange.

laboratory since the early 1970s. Emerson (1972) developed an exchange theoretic conception of power-dependence relations that formed the basis for much of the early work on exchange networks and the structural determinants of power. In Emerson's formulation an exchange relation was defined as a "longitudinal sequence of opportunities, initiations, and transactions" (Emerson 1972; see also Stolte 1987:775). The focus on longitudinal sequences of transactions and the relations actors form over time through exchange was an important distinction because it separated the distinctly sociological view of exchange from the spot-market or one-shot transaction focus of economists. (Economists were more concerned with topics like supply, demand, pricing mechanisms, and market clearing than they were with social structures.) Actors involved in exchange relations provide each other with resources of value either through direct negotiated transactions with one another or through reciprocal acts of giving and receiving (Molm 1997). These resources can be economically valued as in the exchange of goods between two parties such as wheat and rice or money and services, or they can be things like time, effort, and affection. Some resources have purely symbolic value and can be exchanged simply for symbolic reasons (e.g. to consummate a friendship or partnership).

In the typical dyadic encounter each actor has a resource valued by the other. Thus, each actor depends upon the other as a source of that valued resource in what can be termed a power-dependence relation. Central to the analysis is the *mutual dependence* of the two actors; that is, they need each other in order to engage in a rewarding exchange. The existence of mutual dependence accounts for the initiation of exchange and its continuation over time. In Emerson's formulation, the power of actor A over actor B is determined by the dependence of B upon A for resources of value (Emerson 1962, 1972, Molm & Cook 1995). Theoretically, two variables, resource value and resource availability, determine the dependence (and thus the relative power) of the actors in the exchange relation. The higher the value of the resource B wants to obtain from A, the greater A's power over B. And, the greater the availability of that resource to B from alternative sources, the lower A's power over B. With alternatives, B can simply go elsewhere. Social interaction in such a setting is often characterized by explicit bargaining as actors engage in negotiations to settle the terms of trade.[5]

In exchange relations actors are assumed to "behave in ways that increase outcomes they positively value and decrease outcomes they negatively value . . . an assumption that includes both 'rational action' and 'operant behavior'" (see Molm & Cook 1995:210). Thus, the dyadic exchange relation can be viewed as a "mixed-motive" relationship (Schelling 1960) in that each actor simultaneously has an interest in cooperating up to a level sufficient to consummate a transaction,

---

[5]As Molm & Cook (1995:219) note, not all exchange is negotiated. See Molm (1988) for one study in her program of research on non-negotiated reciprocal exchange framed within the power-dependence tradition. For a more complete description of her ongoing research, see Molm (1997) and Molm et al (1999).

but also has an interest in competing at a level sufficient to maximize net value from the transaction or set of transactions. While the exchange can often take the form of explicit bargaining, in many cases the interaction may proceed without explicit negotiation. Actors may initiate rewarding actions and anticipate rewarding reactions from others in return as an implicit form of bargaining (Lawler & Ford 1995) or as a form of reciprocal exchange (also referred to by Molm 1997, as non-negotiated exchange).

Exchange theory makes predictions about changes in the exchange ratios attained by the actors within an exchange relationship. If actors A and B are equally dependent upon one another and thus have an equal power relationship, the theory predicts that their exchange ratios will stabilize at a point of equality across a series of transactions or at the point of equidependence (see also Yamagishi & Cook 1993). Such an exchange relationship is considered power-balanced. If, in contrast, one of the actors is more dependent upon the other, then there is a discrepancy in power within the relationship, and the less dependent actor holds a power advantage. In this case, the more dependent actor is said to be at a power disadvantage. Exchange theory predicts that a power advantage, if it exists, will tend to be used across a series of transactions. The exchange ratios will reflect this use of power.

Stolte (1987:776) argues, "Of the two determinants of power-dependence, availability of resources has greater sociological significance than value because it channels attention toward structural units of exchange that are larger and more complex than the dyadic exchange relation." Dyadic relations are components of larger exchange network structures in Emerson's (1972) theoretical formulation. By virtue of a network position one actor can have more access to valued (and substitutable) sources of a resource. The network position thus provides a structurally based power advantage. In the special case in which only one actor has access to alternative sources of substitutable valued resources, the network is negatively connected and is referred to as a "unilateral monopoly" (Emerson 1972). Various power-balancing mechanisms (see Molm & Cook 1995:221–23) are discussed by Emerson, including coalition formation, network extension, status-giving, and withdrawal from the exchange relation or network. For example, in the case of the unilateral monopoly, the suppliers may form a coalition or engage in collective action in order to gain power and diminish the power advantage of the monopolist in the network. Coalition formation among the exploited actors in the network is one of the power-gaining strategies that can be adopted in power-imbalanced network structures (or in what Markovsky et al 1988 refer to as strong power networks).

One example of the potential for combining insights from both the exchange and symbolic interaction traditions is Stolte's (1987:777–78) analysis of the role of symbolic interaction among potential coalition members in a power-balancing coalition. Similarly power-disadvantaged actors, who have contact with one another in a network, he argues, might well symbolically interact in ways that enable them to come to share a common definition of their structural situation. The form of the interaction involves the mutual construction and exchange of definitions of the situation. That is, they might form an agreement that they face a common plight, recognizing the structural power advantage of the actor from whom they must obtain resources of value. (This analysis assumes no alternative sources outside the network.) Power-disadvantaged actors might also devise a joint plan aimed at solving their collective problem. Such a plan could entail an agreement to set a clear ceiling on the price they are willing to offer to and accept from the power-advantaged actor. This agreement amounts to a jointly constructed norm. Consistent conformity with the norm would have the objective effect of reducing the power inequality in the network of exchange between the more powerful actor and the coalition of power-disadvantaged actors.[6] Other mechanisms for altering the balance of power in a network include withdrawal from the network and the search for new sources of valued resources. Either process results in changes in the size (and density) of the network in which the exchange relations are embedded. Economic history is full of examples of this type of alteration in exchange structures as a result of the collusion and collective action of actors who stand to gain from it.

Empirical research on exchange networks over the past three decades (Cook & Emerson 1978, Cook et al 1984, Markovsky et al 1988, Skvoretz & Willer 1993) examined the specific structural determinants of the distribution of power in different types of networks (i.e. positively and negatively connected networks, strong and weak power networks, etc.) and the factors that mitigate the exercise of structural power such as commitment, affect, emotions, and fairness concerns (see the recent work of Molm, Lawler & Yoon, and Yamagishi, Cook & Watabe). Current research on the role of status in the production of power in exchange relations (e.g. Lovaglia 1995, Thye 2000) and on the role of trust in exchange settings (Molm et al 2000) open relatively new topics of research with the potential for integrating insights from symbolic interactionism within the exchange perspective. Clearly, one area of potential interchange is in the conception of the actor and the motivations involved. Others include the process of interaction and the nature of the resources at stake. For example, as researchers search for the connections between status dynamics and power processes in exchange networks and relations, consideration of the role of symbolic resources as indicators of status becomes important in the analysis. Also, the process of interaction may be layered. The exchange of the more economically valued resources and services may be embedded

---

[6]Note that this illustration of coalition formation is based on simple, distributive exchange. Emerson (1972) and Molm & Cook (1995:217–18) also discuss an alternative form of social exchange known as "productive exchange," in which two or more actors pool resources to create a joint product of value. For example, one child brings sugar, another brings water, and a third brings lemons. Together the children combine their respective resources to create lemonade for sale on a streetcorner. Here groups/organizations, as systems of differentiated behavioral roles, in contrast to the distributive exchange network, described above, emerge from the productive exchange process.

within the symbolic exchange of meaning and resources of purely symbolic value that signify important aspects of the relation.

Lawler & Yoon (1993, 1996, 1998) have produced a variant of exchange theory that treats the formation of the exchange relation as a theoretical and empirical focus. Their relational theory of exchange presents a process model of the formation of exchange relations involving the commitment of actors to the relation itself (referred to as relational cohesion), not just for instrumental purposes of exchange. They treat as intervening processes the outcomes of prior exchanges within the dyad and the positive or negative emotions that emerge as a result. Frequent positive exchanges are considered to lead to positive emotions that in turn lead to commitment to the exchange relation. In contrast, negative exchange does not lead to positive emotions and thus fails to result in commitment of the actors to the relation itself. While other researchers have examined commitment in exchange relations and networks (e.g. Cook & Emerson 1978, 1984, Kollock 1994, Yamagishi et al 1998), the focus has been upon commitment as a mechanism to reduce uncertainty in the exchange situation, rather than as a direct result of the positive outcomes of exchange and the consequent emotions. Shifting the focus to the relation and the commitment of actors to one another opens the door even more to the study of such social relations and their meaning to the actors involved, a task that symbolic interactionists are best equipped to address. We address this topic in our subsequent discussion of collective identity.

One example of the potential for theoretical synthesis is provided in the work of Brines (1994), which is significant because it addresses the link between exchange theory and symbolic interactionism in research conducted outside the laboratory. In her study of the division of housework (1994), she finds that when men are the primary breadwinners, women do most of the housework. When women are the primary breadwinners, women do most of the housework. The inequality in resources obtained in employment outside the home seems to translate differentially for men and women into responsibilities for work inside the home. Men maintain their power advantage; women do not. When the man is economically dependent upon the woman (and thus less powerful), he does less housework on average than the man who is not economically disadvantaged. Brines argues that a symbolic exchange is superimposed on the more economic exchange to balance out the inequality. In this way she believes men and women are enacting traditional gender roles in the home, despite their nontraditional roles in the workplace. In this research the symbolic exchange and the economic exchange are both significant factors in the effort to predict the division of labor in the home. Without considering both types of exchange, predictions based on exchange theory or on the symbolic reproduction of gender alone would be insufficient. Brines' research also indicates the importance of considering issues both of power and of identity (in this case gender identity) in working out theoretical explanations of inequality in exchange relations (see Hollander & Howard 2000 for a more complete discussion).

The study of power includes analysis of the ways in which individuals and groups act to achieve and maintain their power. As indicated in some of the examples we have given, collective identity is an important element in the study of power relations. Studying the formation of collective identities based on structural forces and how these identities are used to alter the shape of the social world in which the actors are embedded is an important topic for collaboration between exchange theorists and symbolic interactionists.

Collective Identity

NEGOTIATED ORDER AND COLLECTIVE IDENTITY   Just as the examination of power relations is informed by the negotiated order perspective, so is collective identity. Identity is not something that is given or taken, but something that is made or constructed. Social actors must engage in identity work (Snow & Anderson 1987) to create a public self. Consider the Minnesota Mycological Society, a voluntary group of people pursuing the leisure activity of collecting mushrooms (Fine & Holyfield 1996). A voluntary group such as this, which cannot compel membership, requires substantial social cohesion ("we-ness," "belongingness," "solidarity") to exist, persist, and function.

Fine & Holyfield find a balance among two opposing forces within such a group. On the one hand, group members compete for scarce resources (mushrooms). The self-interested pursuit of such resources is certainly part of the attraction of such a leisure time activity. Member A will enjoy the personal pleasure of a relatively higher status than member B if A has been more successful than B in locating mushrooms that are rare and exotic. Separating oneself from other mushroomers through the pursuit of personal status requires some level of secrecy to ensure that one's own successes in locating rare mushrooms are kept to oneself. Yet, on the other hand, within such a potentially dangerous form of leisure, where mistakes in mushroom collecting and consumption could produce severe illness or death, trust in one's fellow members is essential. For example, if a novice mushroom hunter lacks knowledge about whether a given kind of mushroom is edible or poisonous, s/he must trust the other, more knowledgeable group members to provide truthful information for her/his safety. Thus, the need to cultivate trust counterbalances the self-interested striving for personal distinction and status. As Fine & Holyfield (1996:8) note:

> The establishment of trust locates attachment in rapport and identification, not merely in common interest or spatial co-presence. Trust, which originates in confidence in information provided by groups and individuals, and builds on personal commitment to the group . . . is translated into a "pure" relationship. This relationship, when generalized to the collectivity, produces organizational loyalty . . . Trust is a fundamental anchoring dimension of cohesion.

The nature and importance of collective identity is further clarified in Fine's (1995) negotiated order-based ethnography of the social movement, VOCAL

(Victims of Child Abuse Laws). Sharing narratives in the context of the movement's idioculture builds committed cooperation toward the pursuit of collective goals.

Every social movement organization (and, by extension, the broader social movement as a whole) develops through interaction, and, like all interaction, depends on members' recognition of a set of shared, repeated, and meaningful references that together lead to collective identity.... Culture is a tool through which a group cements members to itself, legitimating requests for commitment and practical assistance. Moral and social discourse helps groups counteract the free rider problem.... (T)he movement itself becomes valued to members, separate and apart from any material rewards that might be provided, mitigating economic and psychological costs.... Beliefs can become (behaviorally) ritualized through the 'meaning' of a secret handshake or blood brotherhood—one throws one's body into the breach, embodying one's commitment (Fine 1995:128, 131).

Another facet of collective identity, considered from the negotiated order perspective, is seen in work organizations. Ethnographers of work have documented the various ways through which workers avoid an unremittingly grim and personally stifling life on the job, by finding ways to have fun. Workers invent clever ways to have fun. They might, for example, engage in ritual banter. Workers transform instrumental work into aesthetic enterprise. Added up, such forms of social behavior transpire within work organizations, using desires for creativity and autonomy to build organizational commitment, that is, collective identity among workers with their work. "Such commitment is a consequence of the meaning that work and belonging have for the worker, and, in turn, affects the quality of life within that organization" (Fine 1984:246).

Exchange theorists also examine the emergence of commitments among actors. Commitment formation can derive from uncertainty (Kollock 1994, Yamagishi et al 1998) as it does to some extent among mushroom collectors. It can also derive from the positive emotions generated by successful exchange (Lawler & Yoon 1996, 1998). When commitment exists, it can serve as the foundation for cohesion and solidarity. In the next section we discuss some of the more recent developments in exchange theory that have taken a turn toward Blau's (1964) original concerns with the dialectic between forces of conflict and cohesion. An important element is role of collective identity.

SOCIAL EXCHANGE AND COLLECTIVE IDENTITY   As Molm & Cook note (1995:225), the research on social exchange over the past fifteen years has focused primarily on the implications of exchange structure, as illustrated, for example, by a concern with position-based power in exchange networks, or structural change through power-balancing. "Increasingly, however, researchers are bringing other variables into the theory . . . [including] commitments to partners [and] normative constraints" (Molm & Cook 1995:226). It is in such developments that we can see how social exchange theory has begun to deal with issues closely linked to collective identity such as commitment, cohesion, solidarity, and trust. Some of these topics have already been the focus of efforts to integrate into exchange theory insights based on symbolic interactionism.

For example, Stolte (1987) introduced principles from symbolic interaction theory into Emerson's structural exchange formulation of power, as a means of accounting for the formation of several specific norms of distributive justice (i.e. equality, equity, need, and status). He argues that subjective meanings are transformed through symbolic interaction into socially negotiated, socially shared meaning agreements. A given meaning agreement will define the boundaries of a given kind of collective actor (social coalition) and will reflect the objective, factual pattern of power-dependence and exchange that underlies the coalition. When a collective actor has formed and confronts any individual actor, imposing its meaning agreement, there is a symbolic transformation of the "is" (what collective power makes possible factually) into the "ought" (what collective power defines as just, fair, proper, and legitimate in light of its collective interest). Under certain conditions, all actors might willingly accept and abide by the emergent justice norm, in which case, there emerges a high level of collective identity.

As another illustration of issues of collective identity from a social exchange theory standpoint, we consider the study reported by Cook & Emerson (1978). These authors note that strictly economic exchange, based on assumptions of perfect competition and complete rationality, "carries with it the implicit assumption that exchange partners develop no loyalties or longitudinal commitments to one another" (Cook & Emerson 1978:728). Another implicit assumption is that there would be no normative constraints (e.g., "equity concerns") operating to curb the self-interested use of a structural power advantage to achieve an exchange ratio of maximum personal benefit. These researchers, however, clearly show how social exchange theory differs from traditional economic exchange theory. They argue (and show experimentally) that actors will, under certain conditions, ignore "better alternatives in favor of staying with old partners," and they predict and find support for the operation of equity norms as brakes on the use of position-based power advantage. Such principles and results attest to the operation of elementary forms of "collective identity," as considered from an exchange theory perspective.

More recently, Yamagishi & Cook (1993) have examined the interplay between generalized exchange and social dilemmas, shedding light on some complex issues pertaining to collective identity. These authors distinguish two forms of generalized exchange. One form is designated "network-generalized exchange": "In this structure, each participant provides benefits to an actor in the network who does not return benefits directly to that participant. Instead the provider receives benefits from some other actor in the network" (Yamagishi & Cook 1993:237). Person A might stop to help person B who is stranded on a mountain road and get no benefit in return. However, at some later time, when A is stranded on a similar road, person C might help A, with A providing no direct benefit to C. And so on. A second form of generalized exchange "involves resource pooling and public goods. For example, villagers pool their labor to dig an irrigation ditch, build a school, or construct a bridge, and then collectively enjoy the benefits" (Yamagishi & Cook 1993: 236). The two kinds of generalized exchange are vulnerable to underlying social dilemma incentives to "free ride," that is, enjoy the benefits without making a contribution. Free riding implies a low level of collective identity. The authors argue and show experimentally that the "network-generalized exchange structure promotes a higher level of participation (or cooperation) than the group-generalized exchange structure" (Yamagishi & Cook 1993:245).

A key element in the formation of collective identity is the emergence of interpersonal commitments among actors involved in exchange. Such commitments need not be simply dyadic in focus, but can entail larger sets of actors linked through exchange either in groups or networks. Theorists are now working out the nature of the social processes involved in commitment formation within exchange networks. As noted earlier, Lawler & Yoon (1996, 1998), for example, argue that frequent positive exchanges generate positive emotions about the exchange relation itself and form the basis for commitment to the relationship or the group members engaged in the exchanges.

Earlier theorizing formulated uncertainty as the primary source of the pressure to form commitments within particular exchange relations. Cook & Emerson (1978) argue that commitments can emerge over time as actors engage in continued, repeated exchange with specific partners ignoring potentially more rewarding alternatives. This process, they argue (Cook & Emerson 1983), is exacerbated by uncertainty. While there was some early evidence in support of this argument, the hypothesis was not fully tested until an experiment was conducted by Kollock (1994) and, subsequently, replicated and extended by Yamagishi et al (1998). Research on commitment also implies that solidarity and cohesion may be emergent processes, deriving in part from the initial conditions of exchange. Positive, rewarding exchanges lead to emotional responses (Lawler & Yoon 1996) that foster further exchange with the same actors and thus the formation of committed relations. Kollock's (1994) experiment suggests that such commitments can lead to trust between the partners as they prove themselves trustworthy over time. Continued exchange with the same partners also increases the mutual dependence of the actors on the exchange relation that reinforces the commitment, reduces availability of alternatives, and increases cohesion. If we obtain separate measures of dependence and cohesion, such expected effects can be examined empirically. Emerson's treatment of average total mutual dependence on the relation as a measure of cohesion makes the hypothesis linking an increase in mutual dependence with an increase in cohesion tautological, unless independent measures of these constructs are obtained.

Molm's work with Takahaski & Petersen (1999; Molm et al 2000) raises other interesting questions about the nature of the relationship between social exchange conditions, commitment, and trust. She argues that commitment and trust are likely to be higher when the exchange is non-negotiated rather than when it is directly negotiated. Her reasoning is that explicit bargaining (setting the terms of trade) reduces uncertainty and often takes the place of trust relations since trust is not required. The actors need not consummate a trade that they do not view as mutually beneficial. In contrast, in non-negotiated exchange relations in which there is no explicit bargaining, each actor must trust that in the future the actor who received rewarding actions or resources will reciprocate. The key factor in understanding differences between these forms of exchange is the nature of the uncertainty involved. The risk and uncertainty surrounding non-negotiated (reciprocal) transactions allow the actors in the situation to demonstrate more convincingly their trustworthiness that leads to stronger trust and affective commitment to the relation. Commitment to the relation forms the basis for collective identification and the potential for cohesion. The extent to which collective identities form under various exchange structural conditions is an important avenue for future research. Understanding the meanings attached to these collective identities will require further efforts to integrate exchange and symbolic interactionist perspectives. While the negotiated order and social exchange perspectives have much in common, they offer distinctly different angles of vision on matters of relevance to the development of what we have called sociological miniaturism.

NEGOTIATED ORDER AND SOCIAL EXCHANGE: DIVERGENCE, CONVERGENCE, AND THE PROMISE OF SOCIOLOGICAL MINIATURISM

Divergence

The negotiated order and social exchange perspectives differ in a number of ways, due to the distinctive intellectual traditions from which the two perspectives derive. As noted, the negotiated order perspective is anchored in symbolic interaction theory, while social exchange theory has been influenced by microeconomics and operant psychology (Fine 1984, Molm & Cook 1995). Stemming from these alternative intellectual traditions, the two perspectives have taken different paths.

To reiterate, the negotiated order viewpoint is committed to grounded theory (Glaser & Strauss 1967, Fine 1984), an inductive strategy for developing sensitizing concepts and principles within real life contexts. (In addition to generating new theoretical insights inductively, however, negotiated order ethnographers also aspire to formulate theoretical concepts and principles of general significance transcending a particular ethnographic setting, as noted above.) In contrast, social exchange theory (and other group process research) is dedicated from the outset to the pursuit of a generalizing theoretical strategy (Berger et al 1972, 1977). This strategy entails a more formal, deductive, and programmatic approach in which explicit scope conditions, abstract concepts, and deterministic principles are formulated from which testable hypotheses can be derived.

The negotiated order approach tends to use ethnography as its chief means of gathering empirical data. An ethnographer enters a natural field setting, equipped with a well-prepared sociological imagination, collects qualitative data through observations and/or in-depth interview, and assembles a meaningful picture of social life in that setting. By contrast, the social exchange approach (and the group process approach more generally) relies on the pre-designed laboratory experiment as its primary means of data collection. An experimenter, guided by explicit theoretical predictions, develops a structured, standardized protocol, in which cases are randomly assigned to varying conditions, independent variables are manipulated, and dependent variables are precisely measured. Cumulative theoretical research is conducted under standardized experimental conditions.

The main substantive focus of the negotiated order approach is culture, examined through the meanings that social actors—as active, creative agents—construct through symbolic interaction. Individuals establish "idiocultures" or group cultures—"the knowledge, beliefs, behaviors, and customs shared by members of an interacting group to which members can refer and which they can employ as the basis for further interaction" (Fine 1995:128–29). By contrast, the primary substantive focus of the social exchange approach is the underlying, obdurate social behavioral structure. Primacy of interest centers on the objective exigencies of dependence, as determined by the configuration of control over valued resources in exchange relations, networks, and groups.

Convergence

As the literature review undertaken above demonstrates, the negotiated order and social exchange frameworks both address power and collective identity. Both frameworks also direct attention to negotiation as a major way of depicting the process of social interaction. Further, and most important, the negotiated order and social exchange perspectives represent the key strengths of sociological miniaturism, permitting sociologists to examine larger social concerns through the examination of small, interaction scenes.

As shown above, social power has been a focus for both the negotiated order and social exchange approaches. The frameworks provide alternative means of capturing how conflicts of interest and power constraints surround and shape individual behavior and social interaction. Negotiated order clarifies the rise and resolution of interpersonal disagreements, especially disagreements over the meanings of various issues. Social exchange explains how structural inequality benefits some actors at the expense of others. Both perspectives thus share a concern with a complicated set of social centrifugal forces of microsocial life, conditions that push actors apart and create interpersonal divisions.

On the other hand, both frameworks simultaneously deal with a complementary set of social centripetal forces, the forces that pull actors together in interactive bonds of solidarity. Negotiated order theory clarifies the sources and functions of social cohesion, belonging, trust, and loyalty among the members of a group. Similarly, social exchange theory stresses equity constraints on the use of power, self-sacrificial commitments to old exchange partners regardless of immediate short-term profit, and network-generalized exchange where an actor, under certain conditions, will provide a benefit without expecting an immediately reciprocated return.

Further, the negotiated order and social exchange perspectives both address the central role of social negotiation in social interaction. Although not everything is negotiable or negotiated, much of social interaction is portrayed as a dynamic give-and-take process. The negotiated order approach dwells mainly on the construction and communication of meanings in this process, with such meanings tending toward tacit bargaining (Schelling 1960, Lawler & Ford 1995). Such negotiation involves imaginative ploys, strategies, and tactics that frequently implicate a person's identity or self. The social exchange framework typically gives primacy to "explicit bargaining" (Lawler & Ford 1995), highlighting the frequent (but not always evident) tendency of actors to focus squarely on the crucial issue underlying the relationship: how to arrange the terms of exchange, how to decide on an exchange outcome regarding the quantity of resource x and quantity of resource y to be mutually transferred. Despite the primacy given in much of exchange theory to explicit negotiation (e.g. Cook & Emerson, as well as Willer, Markovsky and their collaborators), Molm (1997) examines non-negotiated exchanges in which there is greater uncertainty over the terms of trade since each actor must decide how much to offer an exchange partner without the benefit of negotiating on each transaction. The uncertainty surrounding exchange in this type of setting permits the effects of a variety of tactics and strategies.

Most importantly, the negotiated order and social exchange frameworks share the quality of being excellent instances of sociological miniaturism. They join other lines of contemporary social psychology (see footnote 3) to represent strong, growing, vibrant versions of microsociology. Both frameworks aim ardently to illuminate the big through the small, focusing on limited cases to examine societal processes. Negotiated order, although focusing on group culture and interaction, is inspired by issues of interest to students of societal culture as well as issues of concern to students of large-scale organizations, institutions, and movements. Social exchange, although originally focused on the two-actor power-dependence dyad, is similarly committed to explaining the rise and change of larger, more complex configurations of social structure conceptualized as networks and groups, many of which are composed of collective actors.

Returning to the three advantages of sociological miniaturism (texture, knowability, and control), it is clear that both the negotiated order and social exchange approaches permit densely textured research. For example, in the ethnography described above, Fine (1995) not only documented the importance of narratives in organizing a social movement, but he also identified detailed symbolic functions of particular narrative genres ("horror stories," "war stories," and "happy endings"). Details such as these probably would not have been noted in a more macrocultural analysis. As another illustration, Yamagishi & Cook's (1993) contrast between group-generalized and network-generalized exchange is a deeply textured analysis identifying complex facets of the structural conditions shaping social dilemma incentives that make free riding more or less likely. A more macroeconomic analysis probably would have not clarified such finely textured features of exchange.

Both approaches also permit realization of enhanced knowability. For instance, Fine & Holyfield's (1996) ethnographic data on the Minnesota Mycological

Society provide a comprehensive sociological picture of how secrecy and trust function in significant ways to enhance cohesiveness throughout not only the leisure group they studied, but generally in similar voluntary groups. Or, for example, Stolte's (1987) fictional depiction of an ecological setting made up of a group of island peoples engaged in economic trade, by virtue of the general theory of power-dependence/exchange, provides a comprehensive view of such a setting that uses events at the level of the two-party relationship to create an understanding of the multi-actor exchange network and collective actor.

Further, both the negotiated order and social exchange frameworks allow for enhanced control. For example, in conducting his ethnography of Twin City cooks, Fine (1992) could vary his own behavior or ask pointed questions of his informants in ways that allowed him to control the research issues he wanted to address. Interpretive control, guided by the emerging pattern of data and ideas, allowed him to isolate and identify important facets of the interplay between aesthetic and economic production. Also, Cook & Emerson (1978), using their standardized laboratory protocol, were able to conduct a highly controlled laboratory study of the interplay of positional power-dependence, knowledge, equity concerns, and commitment in social exchange networks. This type of protocol formed the basis for a wide range of subsequent controlled studies of social exchange processes.

The Promise of Sociological Miniaturism

Nearly a quarter of a century ago, there was a prominent, widely applauded call for a "mutual appreciation" of the different "faces of social psychology" (Stryker 1977, House 1977). Basically, this was a plea for increased integrative efforts and the sharing of concepts and ideas. It was a call encouraging researchers to read one another's work more carefully, to build bridges among findings, thereby seeking innovative and significant insights about individuals, interaction processes, groups, organizations, and institutions. While that clarion call struck a resonant note for many social psychologists at the time, one cannot escape the sense that substantial division, fragmentation, and factionalism still abound in sociological social psychology today. What was seen as an excellent idea in principle has not led to enough bridge-building in fact. We offer sociological miniaturism as a promising vehicle for recapturing and advancing that earlier call for greater mutual appreciation of and rapprochement between diverse, often competitive, lines of social psychological work. In making this argument, we wish to underline the three claims about sociological miniaturism that we proposed earlier in the paper: that it provides for seeing social reality in terms of the core concepts of transcendence, representation, and generalizability. By emphasizing the bridges between levels of analysis, we can engage social psychology within the sociological enterprise. First, we argue that the processes that have been taken as characteristic of the microbehavioral level of analysis transcend that level of analysis and apply on macrolevels of analysis as well. Second, we recognize that individuals not only stand for themselves, but also represent organizations, institutions, and social categories to which they are perceived as being linked. Finally, we emphasize that the processes linked to particular situations can be generalized beyond those local settings to other social settings sharing relevant characteristics.

To conclude this paper, we direct attention briefly to three specific recent research issues that provide promising hints of how the miniaturist model might be used to spur new, exciting developments in sociological social psychology.

The first issue is methodological in nature. Fine & Elsbach (1998) have recently suggested that ethnographers and experimentalists in social psychology can and should collaborate. Instead of viewing one another as irrelevant or mutually hostile, they should seek to learn from one another. It might even be useful for both kinds of researchers to work together explicitly on common theoretical projects. Both data-gathering techniques can provide complementary insights for the investigation of social psychological questions. The strengths of each technique can offset the limitations of the other. Mutually appreciating and bridging the ethnographic and experimental strategies might well provide the best of both worlds.

The second issue is theoretical, and it involves three questions. What is culture? What is social structure? How do culture and social structure intersect to affect a person's thoughts, feelings, and actions? House (1995) has been especially concerned with these vital social psychological questions. He has suggested that social structure and culture are distinct but interrelated parts of any organized social environment (e.g., work, education, law, medicine, class, gender, race, ethnicity, and politics). House suggests that "social structure refers descriptively to persisting and bounded patterns of behavior and interaction among people or positions and dynamically to the tangible or material forces that tend to maintain such patterns (e.g., physical, biological, or social resources and power deriving there from). . . . Culture (is) cognitive and evaluative beliefs shared among members of a social system and generally developed and maintained through processes of socialization" (House 1995:390). In light of the foregoing discussion, we believe that the negotiated order approach offers important insights into the operation of culture, while social exchange theory offers significant insights about the nature and operation of social structure. Sociological miniaturism, by revealing parallels and convergences between these two perspectives, and by encouraging further bridge building, promises new insights into the links among culture, social structure, and the person.

The third issue is also theoretical. In an analysis inspired by Emerson's (1987) value theory, Stolte (2000) distinguishes two basic sociocultural value domains. One domain is "socially intrinsic." In this domain, "an actor can usually obtain outcomes from other people whose value is inseparable from those other people. In a basic way, the people are the valued outcomes" (Stolte 2000:194). Being "particularistic" in nature, socially intrinsic outcomes are likely to be the main focus of social exchange within family and friendship situations. The other domain is "socially extrinsic." In this domain, "an actor can usually obtain outcomes from other people whose value is separable from those other people . . . (and such outcomes) . . . can be rationally assessed against objective, impersonal . . . standards of worth" (Stolte 2000:195). Being "universalistic" in nature, socially extrinsic outcomes are likely to be the primary focus of social exchange within political and economic situations. Again, in the spirit of sociological miniaturism, the search for possible links between the negotiated order and social exchange frameworks might expand the significance of this distinction between basic domains of value and provide a foundation for further theoretical development and empirical research. Perhaps socially intrinsic resources are very close to what Fine (1995) identifies as "symbolic resources," while socially extrinsic resources are very close to what he describes as "material resources." Clearly, the negotiated order approach seems especially well suited for understanding the dynamics of symbolic/intrinsic resource exchange, while social exchange theory seems well-suited for grasping material/extrinsic exchange. By encouraging the construction of a bridge between the two perspectives, sociological miniaturism spurs the development of a more comprehensive, more integrated and complete understanding of the interface of both types of resource exchange.

Visit the Annual Reviews home page at www.AnnualReviews.org

LITERATURE CITED

Becker HS. 1963. *Outsiders*. New York: Free Press

Berger J, Zelditch M Jr, Anderson B, Cohen B, eds. 1972. *Sociological Theories in Progress*, Vol. 2. Boston: Houghton Mifflin

Berger J, Fisek H, Norman RZ, Zelditch M Jr. 1977. *Status Characteristics in Social Interaction: An Expectation States Approach*. New York: Elsevier

Blau P. 1964. *Exchange and Power in Social Life*. New York: Wiley

Brines J. 1994. Economic dependency, gender, and the division of labor at home. *Am. J. Sociol.* 100:652–88

Burawoy M. 1979. *Manufacturing Consent*. Chicago: Univ. Chicago Press

Cook KS, ed. 1987. *Social Exchange Theory*. Newbury Park, CA: Sage

Cook KS, Emerson RM. 1978. Power, equity and commitment in exchange networks. *Am. Sociol. Rev.* 43:721–39

Cook KS, Emerson RM. 1984. Exchange networks and the analysis of complex organizations. In *Research in the Sociology of Organizations*, vol 3, ed. SB Bacharach, EJ Lawler, pp. 1–30. Greenwich, CT:JAI

Cook KS, Emerson RM, Gillmore MR, Yamagishi T. 1983. The Distribution of power in exchange networks: theory and experimental results. *Am. J. Sociol.* 89:275–305

Cook KS, Whitmeyer JM. 1992. Two approaches to social structure: exchange theory and network analysis. *Annu. Rev. Sociol.* 18: 109–27

Cook KS, Fine GA, House J, eds. 1995. *Sociological Perspectives on Social Psychology*. Boston: Allyn & Bacon

Couch C. 1987. *Researching Social Processes in the Laboratory*. Greenwich, CT: JAI

Csikszentmihalyi M. 1990. *Flow: The Psychology of Optimal Experience*. New York: Harper & Row

Emerson RM. 1962. Power-dependence relations. *Am. Sociol. Rev.* 27:31–41

Emerson RM. 1972. Exchange theory. Part II: Exchange relations and networks. In *Sociological Theories in Progress*, ed. J Berger, M Zelditch Jr, B Anderson, 2:58–87. Boston: Houghton Mifflin

Emerson RM. 1976. Social exchange theory. *Annu. Rev. Sociol.* 2:335–62

Emerson RM. 1981. Social exchange theory. See Rosenberg & Turner, pp. 30–65

Emerson R. 1987. Toward a theory of value in social exchange. See Cook 1987, pp. 11–46

Fine GA. 1984. Negotiated orders and organizational cultures. *Annu. Rev. Sociol.* 10:239–62

Fine GA. 1992. The culture of production: Aesthetic choices and constraints in culinary work. *Am. J. Sociol.* 97:1268–94

Fine GA. 1995. Public narration and group culture: discerning discourse in social movements. In *Social Movements and Culture*, ed. H Johnston, B Klandermans, pp. 127–43. Minneapolis: Univ. Minn. Press

Fine GA, Elsbach KD. 1998. Ethnography and experiment in social psychological theory building: tactics for integrating qualitative field data with quantitative lab data. *J. Exp. Soc. Psychol.* 36:51–76

Fine GA, Holyfield L. 1996. Secrecy, trust, and dangerous leisure: generating group cohesion in voluntary organizations. *Soc. Psychol. Q.* 59:22–58

Friedkin NE. 1995. The incidence of exchange networks. *Soc. Psychol. Q.* 58:213–22

Glazer B, Strauss A. 1967. *The Discovery of Grounded Theory.* Chicago: Aldine

Harrington B, Fine GA. 2000. Opening the black box: small groups and twenty-first century sociology. *Soc. Psychol. Q.* 63:312–23

Hegtvedt K, Markovsky B. 1995. Justice and injustice. See Cook et al 1995, pp. 257–80

Hochschild A. 1983. *The Managed Heart: Commercialization of Human Feeling.* Berkeley: Univ. Calif. Press

Hollander JA, Howard JA. 2000. Social psychological theories on social inequalities. *Soc. Psychol. Q.* 65:338–51

Homans G. 1958. Social behavior as exchange. *Am. J. Sociol.* 62:597–606

Homans G. [1961] 1974. *Social Behavior: Its Elementary Forms.* New York: Warcourt, Brace & World

House JS. 1977. The three faces of social psychology. *Sociometry* 40:161–77

House JS. 1995. Social structure, relationships, and the individual. *Sociological Perspectives on Social Psychology*, ed. KS Cook, GA Fine, JS. House. pp. 387–395. In Boston: Allyn & Bacon.

Jensen MC, Meckling WH. 1976. Theory of the firm: managerial behavior, agency costs and ownership structure. *J Finan. Econ.* 3:305–60

Kessler RC, House JS, Anspach R, Williams DR. 1995. Social psychology and health. See Cook et al 1995, pp. 548–70

Kleinman S. 1996. *Opposing Ambitions.* Chicago: Univ. Chicago Press

Kollock P. 1994. The emergence of exchange structures: an experimental study of uncertainty, commitment and trust. *Am. J. Sociol.* 100:313–45

Lawler EJ, Ford R. 1995. Bargaining and influence in conflict situations. See Cook et al 1995, pp. 236–56

Lawler EJ, Yoon J. 1993. Power and the emergence of commitment behavior in negotiated exchange. *Am. Sociol. Rev.* 58:465–81

Lawler EJ, Yoon J. 1996. Commitment in exchange relations: test of a theory of relational cohesion. *Am. Sociol. Rev.* 61:89–108

Lawler EJ, Yoon J. 1998. Network structure and emotion in exchange relations. *Am. Sociol. Rev.* 63:871–94

Lovaglia MJ. 1995. Power and status: exchange, attribution, and expectation states. *Small Group Res.* 26:400–26

Markovsky B, Willer D, Patton T. 1988. Power relations in exchange networks. *Am. Sociol. Rev.* 53:220–36

Miller G. 2001. Why is trust necessary in organizations? In *Trust in Society*, ed. KS Cook. New York: Russell Sage Found. Forthcoming

Mitnick BM. 1975. The theory of agency: a framework. *Sch. Public Admin. Ohio State Univ. Work. Pap. Ser.* 75–17

Molm L. 1997. Risk and power use: constraints on the use of coercion in exchange. *Am. Sociol. Rev.* 62:113–33

Molm L, Cook KS. 1995. Social exchange and exchange networks. See Cook et al 1995, pp. 209–35

Molm L, Petersen G, Takahashi N. 1999. Power in negotiated and reciprocal exchange. *Am. Sociol. Rev.* 64

Molm L, Takahashi N, Petersen G. 2000. Risk

and trust in social exchange: an experimental test of a classic proposition. *Am. J. Sociol.* 105:1396–1427

Molm LD. 1997. *Coercive Power in Social Exchange*. Cambridge, UK: Cambridge Univ. Press

Ridgeway C, Walker H. 1995. Status structures. See Cook et al 1995, pp. 311–32

Rosenberg M, Turner R, eds. 1981. *Social Psychology: Sociological Perspectives*. New York: Basic

Schelling T. 1960. *The Strategy of Conflict*. New York: Oxford Univ. Press

Snow D, Anderson L. 1987. Identity work among the homeless: the verbal construction and avowal of personal identities. *Am. J. Sociol.* 92:1336–71

Skvoretz J, Willer D. 1993. Exclusion and power: a test of four theories of power in exchange networks. *Am. Sociol. Rev.* 58:801–18

Stolte JF. 1987. The formation of justice norms. *Am. Sociol. Rev.* 52:774–84

Stolte JF. 2000a. Beyond the concept of value in power-dependence theory: expanding a model of the "whole actor." *Adv. Group Processes* 17:179–202

Stolte JF. 2000b. Stratification, religious commitment, and self reported health: probing the empirical and theoretical distinction between social structure and culture. Pap. pres. Miniconf. Soc. Psychol. Section, Am. Sociol. Assoc. Mtgs, Chicago, 1999

Strauss A. 1978. *Negotiations*. San Francisco: Jossey-Bass

Stryker S. 1977. Developments in two social psychologies: toward an appreciation of mutual relevance. *Sociometry* 40:145–60

Stryker S. 1980. *Symbolic Interactionism: A Social Structural Version*. Menlo Park, CA: Benjamin Cummings

Thye SR. 2000. A status value theory of power in exchange relations. *Am. Sociol. Rev.* 65:407–32

Walker HA, Thye SR, Simpson B, Lovaglia MJ, Willer D, Markovsky B. 2000. Network exchange theory: recent developments and new directions. *Soc. Psychol. Q.* 63:324–37

Walker H, Rogers L, Zelditch M Jr. 1988. Legitimacy and collective action: a research note. *Soc. Forces* 67:216–28

Walker H, Cohen B. 1985. Scope statements: imperatives for evaluating theory. *Am. Sociol. Rev.* 50:288–301

Willer D, Anderson B. 1981. *Networks, Exchange, and Coercion*. New York: Elsevier

Yamagishi T, Cook KS. 1993. Generalized exchange and social dilemmas. *Soc. Psychol. Q.* 56:235–48

Yamagishi T, Cook KS, Watabe M. 1998. Uncertainty, trust, and commitment formation in the United States and Japan. *Am. J. Sociol.* 104:165–94

Yamagishi T, Gillmore MR, Cook KS. 1988. Network connections and the distribution of power in exchange networks. *Am. J. Sociol.* 93:833–51

Zelditch M Jr. 1969. Can you really study an army in the laboratory? In *A Sociological Reader On Complex Organizations* ed. A Etzioni, pp. 528–39. New York: Holt

Zurcher LA, Snow DA. 1981. Collective behavior: social movements. See Rosenberg & Turner, pp. 447–82

Annu. Rev. Sociol. 2001. 27:415–44

BIRDS OF A FEATHER: Homophily in Social Networks

Miller McPherson[1], Lynn Smith-Lovin[1], and James M Cook[2]

[1]*Department of Sociology, University of Arizona, Tucson, Arizona 85721;*
e-mail: mcpherson@u.arizona.edu; smithlov@u.arizona.edu
[2]*Department of Sociology, Duke University, Durham, North Carolina 27708;*
e-mail: jcook@soc.duke.edu

Key Words   human ecology, voluntary associations, organizations

■ **Abstract**   Similarity breeds connection. This principle—the homophily principle—structures network ties of every type, including marriage, friendship, work, advice, support, information transfer, exchange, comembership, and other types of relationship. The result is that people's personal networks are homogeneous with regard to many sociodemographic, behavioral, and intrapersonal characteristics. Homophily limits people's social worlds in a way that has powerful implications for the information they receive, the attitudes they form, and the interactions they experience. Homophily in race and ethnicity creates the strongest divides in our personal environments, with age, religion, education, occupation, and gender following in roughly that order. Geographic propinquity, families, organizations, and isomorphic positions in social systems all create contexts in which homophilous relations form. Ties between nonsimilar individuals also dissolve at a higher rate, which sets the stage for the formation of niches (localized positions) within social space. We argue for more research on: (*a*) the basic ecological processes that link organizations, associations, cultural communities, social movements, and many other social forms; (*b*) the impact of multiplex ties on the patterns of homophily; and (*c*) the dynamics of network change over time through which networks and other social entities co-evolve.

INTRODUCTION

People with different characteristics—genders, races, ethnicities, ages, class backgrounds, educational attainment, etc.—appear to have very different qualities. We often attribute these qualities to some essential aspect of their category membership. For example, women are emotional, educated people are tolerant, and gang members are violent. These essentialist attributions ignore the vast differences in the social worlds that these people occupy. Since people generally only have significant contact with others like themselves, any quality tends to become localized in sociodemographic space. By interacting only with others who are like ourselves,

0360-0572/01/0811-0415$14.00   **415**

anything that we experience as a result of our position gets reinforced. It comes to typify "people like us."

Homophily is the principle that a contact between similar people occurs at a higher rate than among dissimilar people. The pervasive fact of homophily means that cultural, behavioral, genetic, or material information that flows through networks will tend to be localized. Homophily implies that distance in terms of social characteristics translates into network distance, the number of relationships through which a piece of information must travel to connect two individuals. It also implies that any social entity that depends to a substantial degree on networks for its transmission will tend to be localized in social space and will obey certain fundamental dynamics as it interacts with other social entities in an ecology of social forms.

The literature on these ecological phenomena is spread through the studies of social networks, voluntary associations, social capital (at the individual and community levels), social movements, culture, organizations, and a variety of substantive topics that are affected by network processes. Because the principle of homophily is so key to the operation of these systems, we use it as our organizing concept. We first review the classic uses of the concept, then briefly summarize the voluminous evidence for this empirical pattern. In particular, we focus on the many *types* of network relationships that researchers have found to be homophilous, and on the wide range of *dimensions* on which similarity induces homophily. We then examine the sources of homophily, focusing on the social structures that induce propinquity among similar others and the cognitive processes that make communication between similar others more likely. Finally, we end with implications for future research.

HOMOPHILY: A BASIC ORGANIZING PRINCIPLE

A pattern as powerful and pervasive as the relationship between association and similarity did not go unnoticed in classical Western thought. In Aristotle's *Rhetoric* and *Nichomachean Ethics*, he noted that people "love those who are like themselves" (Aristotle 1934, p. 1371). Plato observed in *Phaedrus* that "similarity begets friendship" (Plato 1968, p. 837).[1] The positive relationship between the similarity of two nodes[2] in a network and the probability of a tie between them was one of the first features noted by early structural analysts (see a historical review in Freeman 1996). Social scientists who began systematic observations of group formation and network ties in the 1920s and 1930s (e.g., Bott 1928,

---

[1]Both Aristotle and Plato stated in other locations (Aristotle 1934:1155; Plato 1968:837) that opposites might attract, so it would be inappropriate to think of them as unambiguously anticipating later social scientific observations.

[2]A "node" is any element (person, organization or other entity) that can be connected (or not) to other nodes through relational ties in a network.

Wellman 1929, Hubbard 1929) noted that school children formed friendships and play groups at higher rates if they were similar on demographic characteristics.

The classic citation in the sociological literature seems to be Lazarsfeld & Merton's (1954) study of friendship process in Hilltown and Craftown. Lazarsfeld & Merton drew on the theoretical work of Simmel (1971) and Park & Burgess (1921). Their use of the term "homophily" coalesced the observations of the early network researchers and linked it to classic anthropological studies of homogamy (homophily in marriage formation). They also quoted the proverbial expression of homophily, "birds of a feather flock together," which as has been used to summarize the empirical pattern ever since.[3]

Studies of Homophily Across the Century: Methodological and Substantive Progressions

The earliest studies of homophily concentrated on small social groups, in which an ethnographic observer could easily ascertain all of the ties between members (whether those ties were behavioral, like sitting together at a cafeteria table, or reported, as when an informant tells about his or her close friends). Therefore, our first systematic evidence of homophily in informal network ties came from school children, college students, and small urban neighborhoods. The initial network studies showed substantial homophily by demographic characteristics such as age, sex, race/ethnicity, and education (e.g., Bott 1929, Loomis 1946), and by psychological characteristics like intelligence, attitudes, and aspirations (e.g., Almack 1922, Richardson 1940).

By mid-century a vigorous research tradition had grown, with two main themes. As issues of race and school desegregation dominated the US political arena, many researchers focused on the extent of informal segregation in newly desegregated schools, buses, and other public places (see review in Schofeld 1995). While observation of relationships eventually lagged behind the study of prejudice and other attitudinal measures, researchers found strongly homophilous association patterns by race and ethnicity (although these behavioral patterns were sometimes weaker than the attitudinal prejudice). A second tradition began with the strong assumption that peer groups were an important source of influence on people's behavior (especially among adolescents). Whether the focus was positive influence (e.g., of college aspirations) or negative influence (e.g., of deviant subcultures), cross-sectional association between some individual characteristic and the corresponding characteristics of that individual's friends were used as evidence for the potency of peer context.

---

[3]Lazarsfeld & Merton attributed the proverb to Robert Burton (1927[1651]:622). Like Lazarsfeld & Merton, Burton acknowledged his own conceptual predecessors in classic Western thought. The closest to the modern proverb is Diogeniasnus' observation that "Jackdaw percheth beside Jackdaw" (quoted in Burton 1927[1651]:622).

The 1970s and 1980s produced a change in scale of the evidence on homophily, as researchers applied the technology of modern sample surveys to the study of social networks for the first time (see a brief review in Marsden 1987, pp. 122–24). Whether in large-scale studies of schools (Duncan et al 1972, Shrum et al 1988), communities (Laumann 1966, 1973, Verbrugge 1977, Fischer 1982), or the US population as a whole (Burt 1985, Marsden 1987), we now had information about the networks in large systems with the ability to generalize to a known population. These large-scale studies also allowed us to measure homophily simultaneously on multiple characteristics, just as theoretical developments about cross-cutting social circles (P Blau 1977) made us aware of the importance of a multidimensional view for the integration of society.

Recent work has concentrated on the organizational contexts of networks (and, to a lesser extent, on networks connecting social entities above the level of the individual—organizations, movements, web pages, and the like). An interest in the effects of networks on both individual careers and organization success fostered many studies of connections in work organizations (Ibarra 1997, Burt 1992, 2000), in the work force more generally (Campbell 1988, Lin et al 1981a,b, Ibarra & Smith-Lovin 1997), or on the interconnected resources necessary to accomplish tasks in the business world (e.g., Aldrich et al 1989, 1996, Burt 1998). As studies moved back to the context of social organizations, longitudinal data occasionally became available to sort out the effects of selection, socialization, and attrition (Hallinan & Smith 1985, Matsueda & Heimer 1987, Podolny & Baron 1997; see review in Burt 2000).

Types of Relationships

Researchers have studied homophily in relationships that range from the closest ties of marriage (see review in Kalmijn 1998) and the strong relationships of "discussing important matters" (Marsden 1987, 1988) and friendship (Verbrugge 1977, 1983) to the more circumscribed relationships of career support at work (Ibarra 1992, 1995) to mere contact (Wellman 1996), "knowing about" someone (Hampton & Wellman 2001) or appearing with them in a public place (Mayhew et al 1995). There are some subtle differences that we mention below, but in general the patterns of homophily are remarkably robust over these widely varying types of relations. The few studies that measured multiple forms of relationship (notably Fischer 1982 and others who have analyzed his data) show that the patterns of homophily tend to get stronger as more types of relationships exist between two people, indicating that homophily on each type of relation cumulates to generate greater homophily for multiplex than simplex ties.

The analytic strategies for analyzing homophily have varied almost as widely as the types of ties. Some researchers, guided by Blau's (1977) theoretical ideas, have concentrated on the relative frequency of in-category and out-category ties (Blau et al 1982, McPherson & Smith-Lovin 1987). The fact that these patterns are powerfully affected by the relative size of groups in the pool of potential contacts is one of the central insights of the approach. Others discuss homophily as a deviation from what a baseline model of random assortment would predict. Here, the concept represents a bias that leads similar people to associate more often than they would be expected to, *given* their relative numbers in the opportunity pool (Coleman 1958, Marsden 1988, Mayhew et al 1995).[4] Many other researchers simply use the homogeneity of a network or the similarity of a dyad, measured on some characteristic, as a source or outcome of social processes, without being clear whether this homogeneity is created by demographic opportunity or selection within that opportunity framework (e.g., Fischer 1982). Perhaps surprisingly, full network measures of heterogeneity and measures of dyad similarity often are not strongly related; Marsden (1990: footnote 7) finds the correlations of diversity-based and difference-based personal network measures range between .47 and .63.

We review all of these variants in the work below, attempting to distinguish between homophily effects that are created by the demography of the potential tie pool as *baseline homophily* and homophily measured as explicitly over and above the opportunity set as *inbreeding homophily*.[5] In addition, we occasionally introduce related research on range, density, embeddedness, and other concepts closely related to homophily but not equivalent. See Campbell et al (1986) for a discussion of how different measures of density, diversity, and multiplexity coalesce as indicators of network range.

Evidence about Homophily: Salient Dimensions

Lazarsfeld & Merton (1954) distinguished two types of homophily: *status homophily*, in which similarity is based on informal, formal, or ascribed status, and *value homophily*, which is based on values, attitudes, and beliefs. Status homophily includes the major sociodemographic dimensions that stratify society—ascribed characteristics like race, ethnicity, sex, or age, and acquired characteristics like religion, education, occupation, or behavior patterns. Value homophily includes the wide variety of internal states presumed to shape our orientation toward future behavior. We begin with the former, then move to the latter because they often prove to be derivative of social positions themselves.

---

[4]Fararo & Skvoretz (1987) called this feature *tau bias* in their theoretical formulation, while Marsden (1988) called it *inbreeding* or *social distance*, depending on whether the dimension was two category, ordered category, or continuous in nature.

[5]While one might be tempted to think of inbreeding homophily as equivalent to choice homophily [a concept used in McPherson & Smith-Lovin (1987) to refer to selections within voluntary organizations[5]], notice that we use 'inbreeding' here to refer both to homophily induced by social structures below the population level (e.g., voluntary organizations and other foci of activity), to homophily induced by other dimensions with which the focal dimension is correlated (which Blau 1977 called consolidation), and to homophily induced by personal preferences. Therefore, it does not in any sense indicate choice or agency purified of structural factors.

RACE AND ETHNICITY   Race and ethnicity are clearly the biggest divide in social networks today in the United States, and they play a major part in structuring the networks in other ethnically diverse societies as well. In this domain, the baseline homophily created by groups of different sizes is combined with the differences in racial/ethnic groups' positions on other dimensions (e.g., education, occupation, income, religion) and the personal prejudices that often result from the latter to create a highly visible, oft studied network divide. We find strong homophily on race and ethnicity in a wide array of relationships, ranging from the most intimate bonds of marriage (Kalmijn 1998) and confiding (Marsden 1987, 1988), to the more limited ties of schoolmate friendship (Shrum et al 1988) and work relations (Lincoln & Miller 1979, Ibarra 1995), to the limited networks of discussion about a particular topic (Schneider et al 1997), to the mere fact of appearing in public together (Mayhew et al 1995) or "knowing about" someone else (Lawrence 2000). Even the negative ties of crime victimization and rape follow the pattern (South & Felson 1990, South & Messner 1986).

In a national probability sample, only 8% of adults with networks of size two or more mention having a person of another race with whom they "discuss important matters" less than one seventh the heterogeneity that we would observe if people chose randomly from that population (Marsden 1987). People also are much more likely to report that their confidants are connected to one another if these confidants are same race (Louch 2000). Of course, people often mention spouses and other kin as confidants, so the powerful marital homogamy on race increases the homophily of confiding relations. But the degree of the racial heterogeneity is still only one fourth the potential, even if we look only at people who mention no kin in their discussion network (Marsden 1987).[6]

This summary picture includes powerful elements of both baseline homophily and inbreeding homophily. Baseline homophily within most opportunity structures—the national population, SMSAs, workplaces, and other foci of activity—leads Anglos to have much more racially homogeneous networks than any other racial or ethnic group. African Americans and Hispanics fall at moderate levels of homophily, while smaller racial and ethnic groups have networks that are dominated by the majority group (see Marsden 1987 for the clearest example of this ordering; Laumann 1973, p. 45, provides an excellent early treatment). Blau and his colleagues (Blau et al 1982a,b, 1984, 1991, Blum 1984) have demonstrated that many facets of ethnicity (e.g., mother tongue, national origins, ethnic group, and region of birth) also display this characteristic. Interestingly, African-American/Anglo contacts are the occasional exception to the pattern, in that their intermarriage rates are not well explained by their population distributions (Blau

---

[6]Other ways of measuring interracial friendships have produced higher estimates of cross-race contact, but there is good evidence that these other measures underestimate homophily (Smith 2000). Asking people if they have a friend or confidant who is of another race leads people to search their memory more broadly for any cross-race tie, oversampling cross-race ties relative to same-race ties in memory and possibly creating interviewer demand effects.

et al 1982). This rare failure to support Blau's structural predictions about baseline homophily is a result of the fact that areas where African Americans are a larger part of the population also show larger African-American/Anglo differences in education, income and other social class variables. Once the extent of these group differences (which Blau calls *consolidation*) is controlled, the effect of population distributions again predicts the homogeneity of ties. Blau's structural ideas have remarkable power in explaining both positive (intermarriage, friendship) and negative (crime) contacts (e.g. South & Messner 1986, Sampson 1984).

The baseline phenomenon is important not just in large populations, but also in more limited settings like classrooms and work organizations. Reskin et al (1999) report that almost one in four business establishments employ no minorities, while slightly more than one quarter employ fewer than 10% minority. Similarly, the National Organization Study found that 34% of all establishments are all white; the median establishment is 80% white (Kalleberg et al 1996, p. 53–55). Ibarra (1995) found that racial/ethnic minorities in such a skewed workplace have much more heterogenous advice and support networks than their majority counterparts. Instrumental networks of mentoring and advice show this pattern more strongly than social support networks, because minorities reach beyond the bounds of their local organization and occupational level to achieve some same-race friends (Ibarra 1995, Lincoln & Miller 1979). In classrooms, where children have fewer options for moving outside the organizational bounds, being in a numerically small racial category makes cross-race friendships more likely to grow close over the course of a school year (Hallinan & Smith 1985), probably because there are fewer same-race alternatives in the setting.

The extraordinary level of racial/ethnic homophily is due not just to baseline phenomena, however. This sociodemographic feature also leads to the highest level of inbreeding homophily (in-group deviations from a random assortment model) of all the characteristics that researchers have studied. Racial homophily occurs in friendship networks by the early grades (at least in the Southern towns and urban neighborhoods where researchers have tracked it). In the third grade, for example, Shrum et al (1988) observed only two thirds of the cross-race friendships expected by chance. Racial homophily increases steadily until only 10% of expected cross-race friendships are observed in middle school, then levels out for the rest of the high school years. Boys are less homophilous in their racial choices than girls, probably because of the nature of boys' play in larger, less intimate groups (Maccoby 1998).

In both schoolchild and adult studies, African Americans display more inbreeding homophily than do Anglos (and, in the school studies, show it earlier) (Shrum et al 1988, Marsden 1988). Since this pattern of inbreeding homophily works against the pattern of baseline homophily (which would lead African Americans to have networks of mostly majority members), it suggests that (*a*) foci of activity are more segregated for smaller racial/ethnic categories or that (*b*) minorities actively counteract the markedly cross-race patterns generated by the opportunity structure to generate some same-category contacts.[7] Laumann (1973), in his classic analysis of the Detroit Area Study, provided an unusually detailed analysis of ethnic and religious friendship. He found a rank order correlation of $-.821$ between an ethnic group's size and its tendency to select friends from within the group (Laumann 1973, p. 45). These choices were structured to a substantial degree by the overlap between ethnic, religious, and socio-economic characteristics (Laumann 1973, p. 67–68). In an unusual study of five different ethnic groups in Toronto, Ooka & Wellman (2001) found that more recently arrived groups had more homophilous job search networks. The pattern was accentuated among less educated, first generation respondents, reinforcing the idea that other domains of segregation (residential, voluntary association, occupation, language, etc.) and hidden value homophily (information, attitudes, tastes, etc.) may drive the inbreeding process (see also Kalmijn 1998, p. 410, Marsden & Gorman 2001).

SEX AND GENDER   The homophily of networks with regard to sex and gender poses a remarkable contrast to that of race and ethnicity. Race and ethnic homophily are dominated by the strong structural effects of category size and by category differences on many socially important features (education, income, residence, etc.). In contrast, men and women are roughly equal in number and are linked together in households and kinship networks that induce considerable similarities in residence, social class, and other characteristics. Until men and women enter the sex segregated voluntary association structure and labor force, most sex homophily is created by inbreeding rather than baseline phenomena.

By the time children enter school, they have learned that gender is a permanent personal characteristic. At about the same developmental stage, researchers first observe homophily in play patterns and a tendency for girls to play in smaller groups than boys (see reviews in Smith-Lovin & McPherson 1993, Maccoby 1998).

Hallinan and her colleagues have done the most comprehensive studies of gender in young children's network relationships. Eder & Hallinan (1978) found that girls are more likely to resolve intransitivity by deleting friendship choices, while boys are more likely to add them. For example, if A likes B and B likes C, a young boy would be more likely to add an A–C relation to resolve the intransitivity, while a young girl would be more likely to drop B as a friend. The Hallinan results are important primarily because of their implications for the emergence of cliques and larger network structures. Her data demonstrate how sex barriers to youthful friendships and these patterns in the resolution of relationship intransitivity influence the development of social networks. Children are significantly more likely to resolve intransitivity by deleting a cross-sex friendship than by adding another cross-sex friendship. In fact, most youths are more likely to delete a same-sex choice than to resolve the intransitivity by adding a cross-sex one (Tuma &

---

[7]Marsden (1988) found no significant social distance effect for race, after taking baseline and inbreeding into account. The key distinction appears to be same-different, not any more elaborated form of stratification.

Hallinan 1979). These simple, small tendencies toward homophily and sex differences in resolving problems in the structure of relationships mean that boys and girls will move toward very different social circles. Their worlds become gender segregated, with boys in larger, more heterogeneous cliques and girls in smaller, more homogeneous groups. This tendency is especially marked in the early grades and abates as adolescents move into the romantic ties of puberty (Shrum et al 1988).

By the time that they are adults, people have friendship and confidant networks that are relatively sex-integrated (at least when compared to other dimensions like race, age, and education). People "discuss important matters with" a group of confidants that are roughly 70% as sex heterogenous as the general population (Marsden 1987). While 22% of people have no cross-sex confidants, 37% have networks that are almost perfectly mixed by sex. This pattern is a bit misleading, however, since close ties contain many kin, and kinship links one to confidants of the other sex. When Marsden (1987) controlled for kin, he found that among kin the heterogeneity of networks was very close to the population value, while for nonkin there was considerable gender homophily. Still, the inbreeding homophily for sex in confiding networks is considerably less than that for race, education, and other social dimensions (Marsden 1988).[8] In contrast, Huckfeldt & Sprague (1995, p. 195–201) found considerable homophily in political discussion networks, with men showing much higher levels of segregation than women; 84% of men reported discussing politics only with other men.[9] There may be a tendency for less intimate, more content-bound relationships to be more gendered than close, strong ties.

Gender homophily is lower among the young, the highly educated, and Anglos (as compared with African Americans and Hispanics) (Marsden 1987). This structuring of gender homophily is mirrored in other societies (Blau et al 1991, Verbrugge 1977) and in more ephemeral relations (Mayhew et al 1995).

Interestingly, the pattern of connections *among* respondents' confidants is quite different for sex than for race/ethnicity. Alters of the same sex are significantly *less* likely to be connected than alters that aren't matched on sex (Louch 2000). This patterns appears because spouses are quite unlikely to know other-sex friends. This is especially true for men, whose wives are especially unlikely to know their female friends from other foci like work or voluntary organization membership.

While the general population is almost perfectly sex heterogeneous (with men and women being almost equal-sized groups), most environments where networks have been studied are not. Work establishments, for example, are highly sex

---

[8]Verbrugge (1977) found that sex homophily was stronger than education and religion, especially among closest friends, where 90% of all men and 68% of all women mentioned a same-sex person. Verbrugge did not study race in her Altneustadt, German, data.

[9]Part of the gender difference is evidently a reporting difference between men and women. When Huckfedlt & Sprague (1995:197–99) looked at political discussion between spouses, they found that wives were much more likely to report discussing politics with their husbands than husbands were to report discussing politics with their wives.

segregated (Bielby & Baron 1986, Kalleberg et al 1996 pp. 53–55) as are voluntary associations (McPherson & Smith-Lovin 1982, 1986, 1987, Popielarz 1999). Therefore, it is not surprising that the networks formed in these settings display a significant amount of baseline homophily on gender. The sex composition of the establishment, group, and occupational level creates powerful sex differences in homophily of networks, with the minority sex having much more heterophilous networks than the majority category members (South et al 1982, 1983, McPherson & Smith-Lovin 1986, 1987). Researchers have studied this baseline phenomenon most intensively among upper-level managers and entrepreneurs. Here, the findings are very consistent. Men tend to have more sex homophilous networks than do women, especially in establishments where they are a strong majority (Ibarra 1992, 1997, Brass 1985). This pattern is especially strong when we consider instrumental or status-loaded ties of advice, respect, and mentoring; socio-emotional ties of friendship and support are much more sex homophilous, in spite of skewed environments (Ibarra 1992, 1997, Lincoln & Miller 1979, Greenberger & Sorenson 1971). Across many cultures and work settings, both men and women use men as network routes to accomplish tasks and to connect to information in more distant domains (Aldrich et al 1989, Bernard et al 1988).

AGE   The degree of age homophily in networks varies a great deal, depending on the type of tie studied. Homogamy on age in marriage is so taken for granted that it is seldom even studied (see the lack of discussion in Kalmijn 1998). In studies of close friendship, homophily on age can be stronger than any other dimension (excepting perhaps race, which is seldom even studied in these contexts) (Verbrugge 1977, Fischer 1977, pp. 93–98). Fischer (1977) found that 38% of all Detroit men's close friends were within two years of their age; 72% were within eight years. Similarly, when the ties studied are relatively superficial (like talking about hobbies or work, or general sociability and support around the neighborhood), age homophily is high (Feld 1982). When ties are close confiding relations or involve emergency help with money or other services, ties are less age homophilous because significant numbers of kin are mentioned (Feld 1984, Marsden 1987, Blau et al 1991). Marsden (1987, p. 127) found that age heterogeneity in confiding networks was about 60% of what would be expected by random assortment in the population; eliminating kin confidants reduces age heterogeneity to less than half of expected. Fischer (1982) found that nonkin friends were separated by only six years of age, compared to 24 years for nonsibling kin alters.

Age homophily includes a powerful baseline component. The fact that schools group ages together into classrooms induces strong homophily, although this tendency weakens as children move from early to later grades (Shrum et al 1988). Age homogeneity of contexts like neighborhoods, work environments, and voluntary organizations induces considerable age homophily in both positive ties like friendship and negative ones like crime (Feld 1982, Sampson 1984).

Age homophilous ties tend to be more close, longer lived (often reflecting the perseverence of ties formed in childhood), to involve a larger number of exchanges, and to be more personal (Fischer 1982). The probability that two nonkin confidants will themselves be connected decreases with their absolute age difference (Louch 2000).[10] Age-similar dyads are slightly *less* likely to have multiplex relations, however (Fischer 1977).[11] Evidently this is because people tend to keep in close touch with same-age childhood friends with whom they share no other current ties.

Marsden (1988) found an interesting patterning of age homophily for different age categories. In confiding relations, there was both a strong tendency to confide in someone of one's own age (especially for the four youngest age categories) and a social distance effect: The further away someone was in age, the less likely that they were someone with whom one "discussed important matters." There was more distance between the 60+ age group and other age groups than there was between other age categories, perhaps indicating the social importance of retirement and other institutional processes associated with aging. The over-60 category was the only age group for which there was significant outbreeding. Older people often connect with younger confidants, especially their children (see also Blau et al 1991, Burt 1990, 1991).

RELIGION   Marriage, friendship, and confiding relations show religious homophily in all societies with religious diversity, although the pattern is not as typically strong as it is for race and ethnicity (Laumann 1973, Verbrugge 1977, Fischer 1977, 1982, Marsden 1988, Louch 2000). Kalmijn (1998) argues that it appears to be decreasing during the past few decades.[12] As with the other forms of homophily, there is a combination of baseline and inbreeding occurring here. Protestants are likely to marry and be friends with other Protestants in the United States, because they are such a large group (Kalmijn 1998, Fischer 1977). Residents of small towns risk falling away from their religious roots, presumably because suitable coreligionists are less likely to be available, while residents of larger cities are more likely to be enveloped in a religious subculture (Fischer 1982). If we look at departures from these group size effects, however, Protestants show the lowest levels of inbreeding homophily, while Catholics, those with no religion and "other" religions, and Jews show higher levels of homophily (in that order) (Fischer 1982, Marsden 1988, Kalmijn 1998). As with race/ethnicity, we see a tendency for inbreeding homophily to counteract the likelihood that members of smaller categories will have almost totally outgroup relationships by chance. The Jewish men in Fischer's (1977) Detroit sample, for example, have 80% of their friendships with other Jews, while few would be predicted by random assortment. And 80% of all Jewish marriages are to Jews in this group that makes up less than 2% of the population (Kalmijn 1998).

Ties between people with the same religion are more likely to be close ties of giving emergency help, loaning money, giving trusted advice or even therapeutic

[10]This pattern weakens as the age difference gets very large, probably because of large age differences in relations among in-laws, mentor-protégés, etc.

[11]In another departure from the general pattern, Verbrugge (1984) also found that age dissimilarity of best friends actually increased their frequency of contact.

[12]Conservative fundamentalist Protestant groups are the exceptions to this decline.

counseling, while the less intense ties of hobby and work talk often show less religious homophily (Feld 1984, Marx & Spray 1972). This relationship between religious similarity and closeness extends even within the family: Men are more likely to name their spouses as someone with whom they discuss important matters (and to name them first, if they name them at all), if their spouse shares their religion (Liao & Stevens 1994). In relationships of less closeness, religion may not matter much at all. Bainbridge & Stark (1981) found that among West Coast college students, religious attitudes and beliefs were salient only when they were activated by a social movement or formal organization. Again, fundamentalist students were more likely to make this dimension a keystone of their friendships. Iannaccone (1988) reviewed literature differentiating churches and sects, indicating that sects (which tend to be more conservative, evangelical, and fundamentalist) are a more total social environment for their members, spawning a larger proportion of their friendships and social support networks while taking up more of their time. Parents also show greater religious homophily in their network ties than nonparents, supporting the idea that religious institutions are sought out for children's benefit (Fischer 1982). (An alternative hypothesis, of course, is that religious people both have more same-religion friends and are more likely to have children.)

EDUCATION, OCCUPATION, AND SOCIAL CLASS   The dimensions of homophily that we have discussed up to this point are largely ascribed or strongly inherited from one's family of origin. Here, we address dimensions that, in modern industrial societies, are to a large extent achieved (although still shaped by family origins, of course). Social class of origin often determines neighborhood residence; education locates people in school settings; and occupation affects both workplace and voluntary association activity. Therefore, it is not surprising that we find significant homophily on these achieved characteristics as well. Marsden (1987) found that about 30% of personal networks were highly homophilous on education, with a standard deviation of less than one year. On average, respondents' confiding networks showed about half the educational diversity of the general population. This parallels Verbrugge's (1977) results a decade earlier, showing that education, occupation, and occupational prestige all showed roughly the same levels of homophily as religion and sex. Louch (2000) found that interconnections among alters were more likely when they had had the same education too, although this effect was less strong than for race and religion. Yamaguchi (1990) found that homophily in education extended to inbreeding bias among the statuses of the friends themselves, with one choice predisposing other choices of the same educational level. Laumann (1973, p. 81–82) found that the occupational structure of Detroit men's friendships had at least two dimensions: One was the dominant action of social status, education, and income, while the other represented a contrast between more bureaucratic and more entrepreneurial work activities (see also Laumann & Pappi 1976, p. 57–64). Wright (1997, p. 208–22) explored the class structuring of friendships in more detail, finding significant boundaries to friendship across property, skill, and authority boundaries. The property boundary is the most impermeable to friendships in most societies (with the notable exception of Sweden).

Kinship ties tend to introduce educational and class hetergeneity into confiding and support networks, for while marriages are quite homophilous on these characteristics (Kalmijn 1998) the cohort differences in educational achievement mean that many cross-generational links are dissimilar (Marsden 1987). Higher education and being male also lead people to have more diverse networks, since these groups have both homophilous high-status relationships *and* ties that extend lower into the educational/occupational status hierarchy (Marsden 1987, Campbell et al 1986, Campbell 1988, Fischer 1982). All educational groups show inbreeding tendencies, as well as a social distance effect: People are both more likely to confide in others who share their same educational level and become less and less likely to form such a tie as their difference from others' achievement increases (Marsden 1988). The edge categories of extremely high and low education show the biggest inbreeding tendency (Marsden 1988, Kalmijn 1998), with a socially significant divide between the college-educated and those without college experience and another major distinction between the white collar and blue collar occupations (Kalmijn 1998, Hout 1982, Hauser 1982).

Researchers have found educational and occupational homophily in a large number of societies, but there is some indication that its level varies somewhat from country to country (Wright 1997, p. 203–22). Blau et al (1991) found roughly the same level of homophily in a Chinese city as in the United States, but Verbrugge (1977) found that Altneustadt (German) friendship ties were more structured by occupation than those in Detroit. Educational homogamy in marriage has been increasing strongly in the United States, but most countries show no trend and some show a decrease (Kalmijn 1998). Indications are that it is the operation of US colleges as a locus of marriage formation and the cultural aspects of educational and occupational homophily, rather than the economic ones, that drive the structure.

In spite of the fact that we see strong educational, occupational, and class homophily in strong ties like marriage and confiding relations, there is some indication that such similarity is perhaps more important in the less intimate ties of one's network. Occupational homophily is one of the few factors that Verbrugge (1977) found was weaker for best friends than for second and third friends. Louch (2000) found that education was less likely to create links between confidants than most other characteristics (religion, race, etc.). Galaskiewicz & Shatin (1981) show that cooperative ties between community organizations are most likely to be activated between those with educationally similar backgrounds in turbulent, problematic times. Schneider et al 1997 find strong educational homophily in information flows about education choices in voucher systems.

NETWORK POSITIONS   When networks within organizations or small communities are studied, they often display a core-periphery pattern, with a central group of closely interconnected people and a larger group of people who are less densely connected to the core and to each other (e.g., Brass 1985). Festinger's (1950) classic theory of social comparison posited that people would use as a reference group those who are similar to them in various ways, including structural position. More modern network research (Burt 1982, Friedkin 1993) has confirmed this hypothesis. People who are more structurally similar to one another are more likely to have issue-related interpersonal communication and to attend to each other's issue positions, which, in turn, leads them to have more influence over one another. There are powerful homophily effects in who we consider to be the relevant others in our organizational environment: those to whom we compare ourselves, those whose opinions we attend to, and simply those whom we are aware of and watch for signals about what is happening in our environment (Lawrence 2000). While homophily on structural similarity has focused almost exclusively on influence and comparison processes, the core-periphery pattern that networks often show may indicate that other types of advice, friendship, and association respond to this basis of homophily as well.

BEHAVIOR   A long tradition in the literature on adolescence demonstrates the tendency of teenagers to associate with others who share their behavior patterns, either of achievement or delinquence. Traditionally, these patterns were interpreted as evidence of peer influence. As your mother always told you, hanging out with the wrong crowd could get you into trouble. Longitudinal data first became available in the 1970s, and this led to a rather decisive shift in the interpretation of behavioral homophily. Cohen (1977) and Kandel (1978) demonstrated that both positive behaviors of school achievement and negative behaviors like smoking marijuana were homophilous more because of selection into relationships with similar others than because of behavioral influence within friendship cliques. There also was a slight tendency for relationships to disband when behavioral similarity did not support them. Later, Billy et al (1984) showed the same patterns for adolescent sexual behavior.

Among adults, behavioral homophily has been studied along two dimensions. Verbrugge (1977) noted a mover-stayer pattern in Altneustadt (German) friendships, with residential stability predicting friendship formation about as strongly as did sex, nationality, or religion. Knoke (1990) found homophily of political behavior and practice, with stronger shared political orientations predicting more behavioral involvement, especially within the context of voluntary associations.

ATTITUDES, ABILITIES, BELIEFS, AND ASPIRATIONS   Having established that homophily exists on a wide array of sociodemographic and behavioral dimensions, we finally turn to the arena where most people spontaneously recognize that similarity breeds fellowship: value homophily. An extensive experimental literature in social psychology established that attitude, belief, and value similarity lead to attraction and interaction (see review in Huston & Levinger 1978). Homophily on traits like intelligence was one of the first phenomena studied in the early network literature (Almack 1922). The classic status attainment literature picked up this assortative pattern and used it to argue that aspirations for higher educational attainment were shaped by peer groups (Duncan et al 1968). As with behaviors, however, the selection into relationships with similar others appears to be a much more powerful force than interpersonal influence within the friendship network (Kandel 1978, Cohen 1977). Much of what appears to be value homophily or influence also comes from the misperception of friends' beliefs and attitudes (Jussim & Osgood 1989, Huckfedlt & Sprague 1995); people tend to assume that their friends are like them, when in fact areas of disagreement simply are not discussed. There is considerable tendency for adults to associate with those of their own political orientations (Verbrugge 1977, 1983, Knoke 1990, Huckfedlt & Sprague 1995), but it unclear whether this homophily is due to actual political similarity or similarity on other social characteristics that are correlated with political beliefs. At any rate, selection almost certainly trumps influence or attrition in this domain as well.

SUMMARY   The literature is remarkably consistent across many different relationships and many different dimensions of similarity: Homophily characterizes network systems, and homogeneity characterizes personal networks. In diverse societies, race, and race-like ethnicity create the most stark divides. Sex, age, religion, and education also strongly structure our relations with others. Occupation, network position, behaviors, and intrapersonal values also show considerable homophily, but they seem to be more specific to certain types of networks and/or derived from the basic facts of sociodemographic homophily. Baseline patterns strongly shape networks by influencing the opportunity structure for contacts, both within large populations and within smaller social settings. Inbreeding homophily often complements baseline, such that smaller categories of individuals who would otherwise have networks dominated by the majority group actually have associates that are much more similar to them than we would predict from the opportunity structure. We now move on to the sources of this remarkably consistent structural feature.

CAUSES OF HOMOPHILY: FOCI OF FORMATION, PROCESSES OF TIE DISSOLUTION

Geography

Perhaps the most basic source of homophily is space: We are more likely to have contact with those who are closer to us in geographic location than those who are distant. Zipf (1949) stated the principle as a matter of effort: It takes more energy to connect to those who are far away than those who are readily available. The classic community studies illustrated this fact (e.g., Gans 1968; see review in Campbell 1990), although purely local networks are a source more of contacts than close ties (Wellman 1996) and tend to become less important over time as other types of homophily trump mere propinquity (Gans 1968, Michaelson 1976). Even factors so seemingly trivial as the arrangement of streets (Hampton & Wellman 2000, Sudman 1988), dorm halls (Festinger et al 1950), and legislative seating (Calderia &

Patterson 1987) can influence the formation of relatively weak ties (and the potential for stronger friendship formation).[13] Women are more likely than men to form close ties with neighbors (Moore 1990, p. 729) because they are less likely to be tied to extralocal foci of tie formation like work and their voluntary associations are more likely to be geographically local (Fischer & Oliker 1983, McPherson & Smith-Lovin 1986). Older people also are more constrained by their immediate geographic environment and have networks that are more reflective of it (Fischer 1982, p. 184).

The advent of new technologies like print, the telegraph, the telephone, and e-mail may have loosened the bounds of geography by lowering the effort involved in contact (Kaufer & Carley 1993), but these new modes have certainly not eliminated the old pattern; Verbrugge (1983) still finds that residential proximity is the single best predictor of how often friends get together to socialize. Since most high-tech contacts still reflect contacts that are originally made and sustained through face-to-face encounters, even ties measured through this mechanism usually show geographic patterning (Wellman 1996). However, the new technologies may have allowed people greater latitude to create ties that are homophilous on other dimensions (Hampton & Wellman 2000; see review in Wellman et al 1996). In fact, these technologies seem to have introduced something of a curvilinear relationship between physical space and network association, with very close proximity no longer being so privileged over intermediate distances but both being considerably more likely than distant relations. Geographic space also seems more important in determining the "thickness" of a relationship (its multiplexity and the frequency of actual contact) than it does in determining the presence of a tie.

The homogeneity of neighborhoods on characteristics that are transmitted by parents—ethnicity, race, religion, and family background (Lieberson 1980)—clearly influences the homophily of ties that are formed in this arena as opposed to organizational foci like schools and workplace, which are organized along different dimensions. Urban areas, with their greater diversity within a moderate geographic distance, produce networks with higher levels of racial and ethnic heterogeneity (Marsden 1987, pp. 128–29). Geographic effects evidently influence the tendency for people with a farm background to marry others like themselves (Kalmijn 1998, p. 409). Similarly, the regional distribution of religions (with Baptists and Methodists concentrated in the South and Catholics in the Northeast) contributes to the religious endogamy observed in marriages (Kalmijn 1998, p. 408). Blau et al (1984) demonstrated systematically that the composition of an area with regard to its occupational structure, income structure, industry mix, and educational distribution all influenced the level of homophily in marriages formed there.

---

[13]Sudman (1988) found a large interaction effect between geographic proximity and the type of dwelling, with large apartment buildings creating little geographic distance effect and single family dwellings creating the most. Clearly, architecture and other sociocultural factors affect the use and influence of space.

Family Ties

While geography is the physical substrate on which homophily is built, family connections are the biosocial web that connect us to those who are simultaneously similar and different. The prevalence of heterosexual coupling and the roughly equal likelihood of having male and female children ensures that family connections will produce high heterogeneity on sex. Generational ties of exchange and affection also produce much greater age heterophily in the family than occurs in any other foci of tie formation. In a mobile society where generations often move to follow educational or occupational opportunities, kin ties often produce relatively close, frequent contacts among those who are at great geographic distance. Similarly, cohort shifts in the base rate of educational or occupational opportunities create substantial kin-based contacts with different educational and class levels.

On the other hand, the importance of the marriage bond within families and in larger society, creates rather dramatic structuring of kinship ties on other dimensions. Family-based ties are much more likely to be same race, same ethnicity, and same religion. In fact, the tendency to marry within group is so revealing of the underlying importance of dimensions for structuring our society that tracking the rise or decline of homogamy on a characteristic is an interesting, complex sociological question (see the debates in Raymo & Xie 2000 and Smits et al 2000).

While the fact that family ties have a somewhat different structure than the more voluntary, less intense social ties of co-employment, co-membership, or friendship is interesting, it should not hide the fundamental similarity: (*a*) family ties are homophilous on most characteristics, and (*b*) strong, homophilous ties on one characteristic may act to induce heterophily on other characteristics. Family ties, because of their strong affective bonds and slow decay, often allow for much greater value, attitudinal, and behavioral heterophily than would be common in more voluntary, easier to dissolve ties formed in the foci discussed below.

Organizational Foci

School, work, and voluntary organizational foci provide the great majority of ties that are not kin (Louch 2000, p. 53), supporting Feld's (1981, 1982, 1984) argument that focused activity puts people into contact with one another to foster the formation of personal relationships. After the propinquity created by neighborhood play groups, schools are the next major focus of tie formation across the life course. Shrum et al (1988) found that 88% of all third graders' friendship ties are formed in their own grade at school. Tracking within schools assures that children of similar backgrounds, abilities, and achievement levels are grouped into the same classes, where homophilous ties can form (Kubitschek & Hallinan 1998, Hartup & Stevens 1997). Indeed, Neckerman (1996) found that children's friendships are quite unstable without organizational support. School organizations help not only to breed ties, but also to maintain them. Some of the homophily in age and behavioral characteristics induced by school structures survives into adulthood, as childhood friendships occasionally are maintained in spite of few other connections. Fischer (1977) found that 20% of Detroit men's (nonkin) friendships were formed in childhood.

After school, most people move into a work environment that also segregates their opportunities for tie formation. The general literature on organizational demography has been reviewed elsewhere (Pfeffer 1983, Reskin et al 1999). Here, we simply note that a large number of both strong and weak ties are formed at work [809 out of 4423 close confiding relationships in the General Social Survey, roughly half of the nonkin ties (Marks 1994)], and that the composition of these ties is strongly influenced by the composition of the work establishment (Ibarra 1992, 1995, Brass 1985, Feld 1982, see review in Reskin et al 1999). In general, ties formed among co-workers tend to be more heterogeneous in race and religion than ties formed elsewhere, and more homogeneous on sex and education because of the highly segregated character of the workplace on these two dimensions (Marsden 1990, pp. 402–3).

Recent research has concentrated attention on the role of voluntary associations in creating interpersonal ties (McPherson & Smith-Lovin 1986, 1987, McPherson et al 1992). While voluntary groups are probably less important sources of ties than school or work, they are important because they operate over the entire life course, from childhood to death, and because they represent a unique arena for watching the strong interplay of structurally induced and choice-produced homophily. Since voluntary groups are, by definition, less constrained than family, school, or work (which may be biologically or legally mandated), they represent an excellent opportunity to examine the co-evolution of groups, ties, and memberships.

There is a structural duality of persons and groups: The fact that groups are made up of people means that every group creates a set of co-membership ties among its members (Breiger 1974), and these connections can be used to sample groups by sampling from their members in a population of individuals (McPherson 1982). Larger organizations create proportionally more co-membership ties than smaller ones, of course, because the number of potential interpersonal relationships is $(n(n-1)/2)$, where n is the number of members in the group (McPherson 1983a, McPherson & Smith-Lovin 1982). Since higher SES people join more groups and leave them less frequently, they experience more voluntary organizations over their life course and have more co-memberships (McPherson 1981, pp. 718–20). Men also gain more ties from their voluntary organization memberships than women because they belong to larger groups, on average (McPherson & Smith-Lovin 1982). The extreme gender segregation of the voluntary system leads most co-membership ties to be sex-homogeneous (McPherson & Smith-Lovin 1986); the average male membership generates 37 co-membership ties, eight of which are female, whereas the average female membership generates 29 ties, only 4 of which are male. All-female groups, in particular, lead women into relationships that are highly homophilous on age, education, religion, marital status, and work status (Popielarz 1999a).

When we look at ties closer than mere co-membership, we find that many friendships, confiding relations, and social support ties are formed within voluntary groups. Close confiding relations are about as likely to be embedded in voluntary groups as they are to be found at work (Marsden 1990, p. 403).[14] Feld (1982) found that 68% of the relationships in Fischer's (1982) Northern California Community Study were formed in some type of foci of activity, with roughly a third of those formed in work and voluntary organizations.

The social homogeneity of most organizational foci creates a strong baseline homophily in networks that are formed there. Feld (1982) found that organizational foci produced ties that were twice as homogeneous as would be expected by chance. More specifically, Marsden (1990) found that co-membership sources reduced age, race, and especially religious diversity of confiding relations. McPherson & Smith-Lovin (1987) showed that the composition of voluntary groups induces strong homophily in the ties that are formed there, with group size, consolidation of dimensions, and social diversity within organizations all affecting the extent to which ties were formed with similar others. In particular, the voluntary groups induced strong homophily in sex, age, and occupational prestige; Peoples' choices of close associates *within* the groups (inbreeding, in our classification here) were more important in creating educational homophily. McPherson (1983b) noted that different types of voluntary groups have specialized demographic structures, with church, youth, and elderly groups tending to specialize in the age dimension (and therefore inducing age homophilous co-membership ties), while professional groups induce educational homophily. Civic groups integrate different age groups, and groups serving the elderly integrate those with different educational backgrounds. Hobby groups are the most generalist overall, integrating a wide array of characteristics (especially occupational statuses).

Researchers have also examined the impact of organizational foci within more specific institutional domains. Caldeira & Patterson (1987) found that joint committee memberships had powerful effects inducing friendship, shared attitudes and information, shared understandings of the legislative role, and behavioral homophily (voting together) in a state legislature. Cook (2000) found that the same key variable—shared committee membership—was the most important predictor of bill co-sponsorship in the United States Congress, even when controlling for a large number of individual and district characteristics.

Voluntary organizations can also be important in reinforcing the effects of other types of ties. Galazkiewicz (1985) found that nonprofit officers that belonged to the same professional organizations ended up more proximate in personal networks and more similar in their evaluation of prospective donors (attitudinal homophily). Knoke (1990) found that discussing politics with at least one other member of a voluntary organization strongly boosted a person's political mobilization both inside the organization and in the larger community. Davis & Aldrich (2000) found

---

[14]These co-membership confidants are more likely to be kin than co-worker confidants, however.

that co-membership in instrumental organizations (especially when coupled with intensive organization activity) increased entrepreneur's odds of gaining access to resources like expert advice. This was especially true for women entrepreneurs. The fact that the effect operated more strongly for women may be created by the fact that women often were seeking help from men with greater experience. Beggs & Hurlbert (1997) found that female seeker/male contact ties were less effective than same sex ties in providing support during a job search, *unless* the sex heterogeneous tie was reinforced by a shared voluntary organization membership. If reinforced by the organizational context, the nonhomophilous ties were as effective as same-sex contacts in providing support. Therefore, it appears that organizational co-membership is capable of reinforcing nonhomophilous ties, to allow them to operate as homophilous ones would.

Isomorphic Sources: Occupational, Family, and Informal Roles

Early in the modern era of social network analysis, Burt (1982) made the point that people who occupy similar positions (i.e., have the same role relationships to similar others) often influence each other in the adoption of innovations. Such equivalent actors are often linked by direct ties, of course, although Burt argued that the influence could occur even when they were not. If we accept the proposition that role occupants are more likely to be similar than randomly chosen people, the connections between people who occupy equivalent roles will induce homophily in the system of network ties. Studies illustrating this point have concentrated in three domains. The most common, by far, are the detailed studies of connections within the workplace. There also has been some attention to the effect of family roles and the more intricate study of structurally equivalent actors within informal networks.

Many studies of the workplace, for example, find that the advice, respect, and support networks formed there are shaped not just by the composition of the work establishment as a whole, but even more strongly by the organizational demography at a person's own level or job title (Ibarra 1992, 1995, Brass 1985). Employees are especially likely to have ties to others who occupy their same job, and occupational sex segregation induces strong baseline homophily. Lazega & Van Duijin (1997) found that position in the formal structure of a workplace (including status, seniority, and the functional division of work) influenced the choice of advisors. Several studies have examined detailed networks of communications among scientists (perhaps because we know more about the dimensions of their work). Fuchs (1995) found that status organizes gossip among scientists into a core-periphery pattern. Judith Blau (1974) found that local contacts among high energy physicists were strongly structured by whether or not they shared a similar role within the academy (teaching versus other research roles). Such contacts also were structured by research accomplishments and specialty even within this small, elite subfield. Because we know that such stratification in the academy has demographic parallels, structuring of ties by any of these positional factors will induce demographic homophily as well.

In the world of family life, Fischer & Oliker (1983) found that friendship contacts are likely to be created as a result of one's role as spouse. Women's networks, in particular, were formed with the other wives that they met through their husbands. Given significant homogamy in marriage, and the tendency of men's friendships to form at work (Marks (1994), friendships formed through this spousal role are likely to induce considerable levels of homophily. Munch-Rotolo (2000) showed that the onset of parenthood induced considerable similarity in the networks of men and women, as they both became more tied to female kin and other parents with children in their immediate geographic area. Given the tendency of kin and neighborhoods to stratify contacts in terms of a variety of social dimensions (see above), this increasing concentration on the two sources of ties will create substantial racial, ethnic, religious, and class homophily.

A smaller number of researchers have examined the extent to which structural equivalence in more informal networks induces behavioral or attitudinal homophily. Calderia & Patterson (1987) found that political leadership roles and friendship patterns in a state legislature induced considerable homophily of attitudes and beliefs. Galaskiewicz (1985) found that similar network positions induced considerable levels of agreement about potential donors to nonprofits that he studied.

Cognitive Processes

We have focused overwhelmingly on the structural sources of homophily in our discussion above because the literature routinely shows the potency of such forces when compared directly with some type of personal choice or selection (e.g., McPherson & Smith-Lovin 1987). Here, we briefly note the processes that have historically dominated the research on homophily: the tendency of people to choose to interact with similar others. The psychology literature has demonstrated experimentally that attraction is affected by perceived similarity (Huston & Levinger 1978). Carley (1991) has developed a sociological approach called *constructuralism* that has at its core the assumption that people who share knowledge with one another are more likely to interact (and, we might extrapolate, form ties). If demographic similarity tends to indicate shared knowledge (see this argument developed in Mayhew et al 1995), we would expect people to associate with similar others for ease of communication, shared cultural tastes (Mark 1999), and other features that smooth the coordination of activity and communication. Researchers often have studied this process within adolescent subcultures, where selection of association among similar others is found to be a much more potent force than socialization within the group (Cohen 1977, Kaplan et al 1987, Billy et al 1984).

Selective Tie Dissolution

Most of the review above on sources of homophily has implicitly concentrated on the creation of ties. Clearly, social ties are usually created in segregated foci of activity, which induces homogeneous personal networks. Researchers less often study the process of tie dissolution, since this requires data on associations over time (see review in Burt 2000).

Hallinan and her colleagues have assembled one of the most impressive sets of dynamic data, on schoolchildren's friendship ties over the course of school years. They find consistently that ties that are cross-sex or cross-race are more likely to be dropped than ties among demographically similar friends (Hallinan & Williams 1989, Tuma & Hallinan 1979). These nonhomophilous ties are especially likely to be dropped when they are involved in intransitive friendship patterns. Basically, homophilous relations help friendships survive other structural challenges. This pattern parallels the findings among adults that homophily becomes more important to tie activation during times of crisis or trouble (Galaskiewicz & Shatin 1981, Hurlbert et al 2000).

McPherson and his colleagues have studied how ties of co-membership are affected by similarity to other members of a group. Both strong and weak ties to others in the group, which are likely to be among similar others, tend to increase the duration of memberships (McPherson et al 1992). More direct evidence comes from Popielarz & McPherson (1995), which showed that the closer a member is to the edge of a group's niche (i.e., the more s/he is unlike the other members of the group), the more likely s/he is to leave the group.

Burt (2000) has done a detailed study of tie decay across four years in the investment banking division of a large financial organization; In this case, a tie was being involved in regular business dealings with another. He finds that ties among bankers survive much longer than ties between bankers and those outside the banker role. There is also a clear core-periphery pattern, such that ties with the people who are highly ranked in both the formal and informal hierarchy last longer than those with and among those lower in the hierarchies. Age homophily also decreased the probability that a tie would dissolve, with this effect being especially strong for those who are either unusually young or unusually old within their occupational structures.[15]

In general, we find that the patterns of tie dissolution mimic those of tie formation, but perhaps in a somewhat weaker manner. While there is much less evidence here, homophily seems to affect the probability that a tie will dissolve or decay, net of other factors (like the liability of newness, embeddedness, structural supports, etc.). The relative strength of homophily in tie formation and tie dissolution may be a function of the preeminent importance of structural foci in the tie formation process. Once ties have been formed in highly segregated organizational and role foci, their dissolution may be shaped primarily by changes in these supportive structures or by cognitive/communication processes. These may be somewhat

---

[15]Burt did not find similar gender homophily effects. Instead, women seemed to dissolve contacts with both men and women at a very high rate. This pattern probably has more to do with the position of women within this fairly male occupational environment than of homophily, per se.

more idiosyncratic than the highly structured world of tie formation. But, given the paucity of evidence on tie dissolution, this conclusion may be premature. We therefore turn now to our recommendations for future research on homophily in networks.

IMPLICATIONS FOR FUTURE RESEARCH

Need for Studies of Multiplexity

It is striking that 20 years after Fischer's (1982) classic study of networks in North California communities, so few large-scale studies investigate the multiple, overlapping networks of different types of relationships that his research so admirably chronicled. If different types of relations are structured by different levels of homophily on different dimensions, then multiplex relations among individuals may create systematic, important patterns of cross-cutting social circles. Attention to this complexity may produce findings as important for the larger issue of the integration of society as did Peter Blau's (1977) groundbreaking insights about the impact of consolidated (correlated) dimensions.

An analogous concern is the operation of overlapping, cross-cutting foci that may shape tie formation. Since we find that geographic, organizational and role foci are powerful structural forces inducing homophily, it makes sense that studying how these foci interrelate would be important for examining community structure more generally. Popielarz (1999b), for example, has developed a propositional theory of how memberships in multiple voluntary organizations can influence the homophily of networks formed in this domain. The attempts of McPherson and his colleagues to trace the flow of co-membership ties within a community of competing voluntary organizations has developed a similar theme at the organizational level (McPherson 1983a, McPherson et al 1992, McPherson & Rotolo 1996). If foci are where homophilous ties form, it is important to understand in more specific terms how the organizational structure relates to the personal networks of the individuals that make up those organizations.

Need for Dynamic Data

Burt (2000) has pointed to the very limited evidence that we have on the dynamics of networks over time. As with the multiplexity issue above, collecting measures of even *one* type of network tie at *one* point in time for a large, loosely bounded system is an onerous task;[16] this fact limits our ability to study networks over time. Still, cross-sectional data on networks can never answer the important questions about the extent to which network patterns, including homophily, are created by

---

[16]The social network module of the General Social Survey took approximately 15 minutes of survey time to elicit information on up to five network alters with one network relation, with minimal information about the context in which the relationships were formed.

selective tie formation or selective tie dissolution. While we have evidence that both processes are important, we have little comprehensive information of how the two processes interrelate[17] or about their relative strength of the two processes are highly tentative.

Several studies have shown that the effects of organizational composition can last far beyond the actual embeddedness of the individual (Sorenson 2000, Sparrowe & Popielarz 1995). Only by tracking both the organizational and role history of the individual along with their personal networks can we see the full impact of such factors. Analyses of cross-sectional data often leave such long-term effects of organizational environments misclassified as individual choice or (more appropriately) as unexplained variance, when in fact they are the systematic residues of past foci.

Need for Study of the Co-evolution of Foci and Networks

Our final suggestion is, in actuality, a combination of the two themes that we discuss above' the need for expanded consideration of multiplexity of both networks and foci, and the need for dynamic data on changes over time in networks. Carley (1999) recently has called for an ecology of how social networks evolve, a "socio-cognitive physics." While the powerful law-like pattern of homophily in networks encourages such a call, we argue that the structural sources of homophily will most likely require a consideration of the co-evolution of social entities like voluntary organizations, employment establishments, and other social entities that breed ties along with the study of network change. Focusing more on the organizational levels, researchers have used network homophily in combination with an ecological model to predict changes over time in the composition of voluntary organizations and occupations (McPherson & Ranger-Moore 1991, McPherson & Rotolo 1996, Rotolo & McPherson 2001). We now argue for attention to the analogous problem on the network side: The ways in which networks evolve over time through cumulative processes of tie creation and dissolution as they are embedded in a changing community of multiplex relations spawned by multiple organizational affiliations. While the need to layer multiple relations over time in connection with a system of organizations and other foci is a tall order, we have a much more solid base of empirical knowledge and theory in this domain than in most substantive areas. Further, we have ample evidence that the network phenomena that we hope to explain are more systematic and orderly than some other areas of social life. Therefore, Carley's call for a sociophysics of network ecology may not be farfetched.

---

[17]Even the path-breaking studies that examine dynamic data often look at only one direction of influence. For example, van Duijn et al (1999) found if homogeneity of friends in terms of age, marital status or work rose over time, the stability of the relationship rose as well. They don't examine whether relationships have a corresponding influence on changes in work or marital status.

ACKNOWLEDGMENTS

The authors would like to thank Peter V. Marsden and Claude S. Fischer for helpful comments on earllier drafts of this chapter.

Visit the Annual Reviews home page at www.AnnualReviews.org

LITERATURE CITED

Aldrich H. 1989. Networking among women entrepreneurs. In *Women-Owned Businesses*, ed. O Hagan, C Rivchun, D Sexton, pp. 103–132. New York: Praeger

Aldrich HE, Elam A, Reese PR. 1996. Strong ties, weak ties and strangers: Do women business owners differ from men in their use of networking to obtain assistance? In *Entreprenuership in a Global Context*. ed. S Birley, I MacMillan, pp. 1–25. London: Rutledge

Aldrich H, Reese PR, Dubini P. 1989. Women on the verge of a breakthrough': Networking among entrepreneurs in the United States and Italy. *J. Entrepreneur. Region. Dev.* 1:339–56

Almack JC. 1922. The influence of intelligence on the selection of associates. *Sch. Soc.* 16:529–30

Aristotle. 1934. *Rhetoric. Nichomachean ethics*. In *Aristotle in 23 volumes*. Rackman transl. Cambridge: Harvard Univ. Press

Bainbridge WS, Stark R. 1981. Friendship, religion and the occult: a network study. *Rev. Relig. Res.* 22:313–27

Beggs JJ, Hurlbert JS. 1997. The social context of men's and women's job search ties: membership in voluntary organizations, social resources and job search outcomes. *Sociol. Perspect.* 40:601–22

Bernard HR, Killworth PD, Evans MJ, McCarty C, Shelley GA. 1988. Studying social relations cross-culturally. *Ethnology* 27:155–79

Bielby WT, Baron JN. 1986. Men and women at work: sex segregation and statistical discrimination. *Am. J. Sociol.* 91:759–99

Billy JOG, Rodgers JL, Udry JR. 1984. Adolescent sexual behavior and friendship choice. *Soc. Forces* 62:653–78

Blau J. 1974. Patterns of communication among theoretical high energy physicists. *Sociometry* 37:391–406

Blau PM. 1977 *Inequality and Heterogeneity: A Primitive Theory of Social Structure*. New York: Free Press

Blau PM, Beeker C, Fitzpatrick KM. 1984. Intersecting social affiliations and intermarriage. *Soc. Forces* 62:585–606

Blau PM, Blum TC, Schwartz JE. 1982. Heterogeneity and intermarriage. *Am. Sociol. Rev.* 47:45–62

Blau PM, Ruan D, Ardelt M. 1991. Interpersonal choice and networks in China. *Soc. Forces* 69:1037–62

Blau PM, Schwartz JE. 1984. *Crosscutting Social Circles*. Orlando, FL: Academic Press

Blum TC. 1984. Racial inequality and dalience: an examination of Blau's theory of social structure. *Soc. Forces* 62:607–17

Bott H. 1928. Observation of play activities in a nursery school. *Genet. Psychol. Monogr.* 4:44–88

Brass DJ. 1985. Men's and women's networks: a study of interaction patterns and influence in an organization. *Acad. Mgmt. J.* 28:327–43

Breiger RL. 1974. The duality of persons and groups. *Soc. Forces* 53:181–89

Burt RS. 1982. *Toward a Structural Theory of Action*. New York: Academic

Burt RS. 1985. General social survey network items. *Connections* 8:119–23

Burt RS. 1990. Kinds of relations in American discussion networks. In *Structures of Power and Constraint*, ed. C Calhoun, MW Meyer, WR Scott, pp. 411–51. New York: Cambridge

Burt RS. 1991. Measuring age as a structural concept. *Soc. Networks* 13:1–34

Burt RS. 1992. *Structural Holes*. Cambridge, MA: Harvard Univ. Press

Burt RS. 1998. The gender of social capital. *Rationality Soc.* 10:5–47

Burt RS. 2000. Decay functions. *Soc. Networks* 22:1–28

Burton R. 1927 [1651]. *The Anatomy of Melancholy*. New York: Farrar & Rinehart

Caldeira GA, Patterson SC. 1987. Political friendship in the legislature. *J. Politics* 4: 953–75

Campbell KE. 1988. Gender differences in job-related networks. *Work Occup.* 15:179–200

Campbell KE. 1990. Networks past: a 1939 Bloomington neighborhood. *Soc. Forces* 69:139–55

Campbell KE, Marsden PV, Hurlbert JS. 1986 Social resources and socioeconomic status. *Soc. Networks* 8:97–117

Carley KM. 1991. A theory of group stability. *Am. Sociol. Rev.* 56:331–54

Carley KM. 1999. On the evolution of social organizational networks. *Res. Sociol. Org.* 16:3–30

Cohen J. 1977. Sources of peer group homogeneity. *Sociol. Educ.* 50:227–41

Coleman J. 1958. Relational analysis: the study of social organizations with survey methods. *Human Org.* 17:28–36

Cook M. 2000. The social structure of political behavior: action, interaction and Congressional cosponsorship. Unpubl. doctoral diss., Univ. Ariz., Tucson, AZ

Davis AB, Aldrich HE. 2000. The organizational advantage? Social capital, gender and small business owners' access to resources. Pap. pres. Am. Sociol. Assoc. mtg., Washington, DC

Duncan OD, Featherman DL, Duncan B. 1972. *Sociometric Background and Achievement*. New York: Seminar

Duncan OD, Haller AO, Portes A. 1968. Peer influences on aspirations: a reinterpretation. *Am. J. Sociol.* 74:119–37

Eder D, Hallinan MT. 1978. Sex differences in children's friendships. *Am. Sociol. Rev.* 43:237–50

Fararo TJ, Skvoretz JV. 1987. Unification research programs: integrating two structural theories. *Am. J. Sociol.* 92:1183–1209

Feld S. 1981. The focused organization of organizational ties. *Am. J. Sociol.* 86:1015–35

Feld S. 1982. Structural determinants of similarity among associates. *Am. Sociol. Rev.* 47:797–801

Feld S. 1984. The structured use of personal associates. *Soc. Forces* 62:640–52

Festinger L. 1950. Informal social communication. *Psychol. Rev.* 57:271–82

Festinger L, Schachter S, Back K. 1950. *Social Processes in Informal Groups*. Stanford, CA: Stanford Univ. Press

Fischer CS. 1977. *Networks and Places: Social Relations in the Urban Setting*. New York: Free Press

Fischer CS. 1982. *To Dwell among Friends*. Chicago: Univ. Chicago Press

Fischer CS, Oliker SJ. 1983. A research note on friendship, gender and the life cycle. *Soc. Forces* 62:124–33

Freeman L. 1996. Some antecedents of social network analysis. *Connections* 19:39–42

Friedkin NE. 1993. Structural bases of interpersonal influence in groups. *Am. Sociol. Rev.* 58:861–72

Fuchs S. 1995. The stratified order of gossip: informal communication in organizations and science. *Sociale Systeme* 1:47–72

Galaskiewicz J. 1985. Professional networks and the institutionalization of a single mind set. *Am. Sociol. Rev.* 50:639–58

Galaskiewicz J, Shatin D. 1981. Leadership and netowrking among neighborhood human service organizations. *Admin. Sci. Q.* 26:434–48

Gans H. 1968. People and plans: essays on urban problems and solutions. New York: Basic

Greenberger E, Sorenson A. 1971. Interpersonal choices among a junior high school faculty. *Sociol. Educ.* 44:198–216

Hallinan MT, Smith SS. 1985. The effects of classroom racial composition on students' interracial friendliness. *Soc. Psychol. Q.* 48:3–16

Hallinan MT, Williams R. 1989. Interracial friendship choice in secondary schools. *Am. Sociol. Rev.* 54:67–78

Hampton KN, Wellman B. 2000. Examining community in the digital neighborhood: Early results from Canada's wired suburb. In *Digital Cities: Technologies, Experiences and Future Perspectives*, ed. T Ishida, K Isbister, pp. 194–208. Heidelberg: Springer-Verlag

Hartup W, Stevens N. 1997. Friendships and adaptation in the life course. *Psychol. Bull.* 121:355–70

Hauser RM. 1982. The structure of social relationships: cross-classifications of mobility, kinship and friendship. In *Social Structure and Behavior: Essays in Honor of William Hamilton Sewell*, ed. RM Hauser, D Mechanic, AO Haller, TS Hauser, pp. 205–68. New York: Academic

Hout M. 1982. Association between husband's and wive's occupations in two-earner families. *Am. J. Sociol.* 88:397–409

Hubbard RM. 1929. A method of studying spontaneous group formation. In *Some New Techniques for Studying Social Behavior*, ed. DS Thomas, pp. 76–85. Child Dev. Monogr.

Huckfeldt R, Sprague J. 1995. *Citizens, Politics and Social Communication: Information and Influence in an Election Campaign*. New York: Cambridge Univ. Press

Hurlbert JS, Haines VA, Beggs JJ. 2000. Core networks and tie activation: what kinds of routine networks allocate resources in nonroutine situations. *Am. Sociol. Rev.* 65:598–618

Huston TL, Levinger G. 1978. Interpersonal attraction and relationships. *Annu. Rev. Psychol.* 29:115–56

Iannaccone LR. 1988. A formal model of church and sect. *Am. J. Sociol.* 94S:S241–68

Ibarra H. 1992. Homophily and differential returns: sex differences in network structure and access in an advertising firm. *Admin. Sci. Q.* 37:422–47

Ibarra H. 1995. Race, opportunity and diversity of social circles in managerial networks. *Acad. Mgmt. Rev.* 38:673–703

Ibarra H. 1997. Paving an alternative route: gender differences in managerial networks. *Soc. Psychol. Q.* 60:91–102

Ibarra H, Smith-Lovin L. 1997. Alternative routes: a social network perspective on gender and careers. *Creating Tomorrow's Organizations*, ed. C Cooper, S Jackson, pp. 359–84. New York: Wiley

Jussim L, Osgood DW. 1989. Influence and similiarity among friends: an intergative model applied to incarcerated adolescents. *Soc. Psychol. Q.* 52:98–112

Kalleberg AL, Knoke D, Marsden PV, Spaeth JL. 1996. *Organizations in America: Analyzing Their Structures and Human Resource Practices*. Thousand Oaks CA: Sage

Kalmijn M. 1998. Intermarriage and homogamy: causes, patterns and trends. *Annu. Rev. Sociol.* 24:395–421

Kandel DB. 1978. Homophily, selection and socialization in adolescent friendships. *Am. J. Sociol.* 84:427–36

Kaplan HB, Johnson RJ, Bailey BA. 1987. Deviant peers and deviant behavior: further elaboration of a model. *Soc. Psychol. Q.* 50:277–84

Kaufer DS, Carley KM. 1993. *Communication at a Distance: The Effect of Print on Socio-Cultural Organization and Change*. Hillsdale, NJ: Lawrence Erlbaum

Knoke D. 1990. Networks of political action: toward theory construction. *Soc. Forces* 68:1041–63

Kubitschek W, Hallinan M. 1998. Tracking and students' friendships. *Soc. Psychol. Q.* 61:1–15

Laumann EO. 1966. *Prestige and Association in an Urban Community*. Indianapolis, IN: Bobbs-Merrill

Laumann EO. 1973. *Bonds of Pluralism: The Form and Substance of Urban Social Networks*. New York: Wiley

Laumann EO, Pappi FU. 1976. *Networks of Collective Action: A Perspective on Community Influence Systems*. New York: Academic

Lawrence BS. 2000. Organizational reference

groups: how people constitute the human component of their work environment. Anderson Grad. Sch. Mgmt., Univ. Calif. Los Angeles, Work. Pap.

Lazarsfeld PF, Merton RK. 1954. Friendship as a social process: a substantive and methodological analysis. In *Freedom and Control in Modern Society*, ed. M Berger, pp. 18–66. New York: Van Nostrand

Lazega E, Van Dujin M. 1997. Position in formal structure, personal characteristics and choices of advisors in a law firm: a logistic regression model for dyadic network data. *Soc. Networks* 19:375–97

Liao TF, Stevens G. 1994. Spouses, homogamy and social networks. *Soc. Forces* 73:693–707

Lieberson S. 1980. *A Piece of the Pie: Blacks and White Immigrants Since 1880.* Berkeley: Univ. Calif. Press

Lin N, Ensel N, Vaughn JC. 1981a. Social resources and strength of ties: structural factors in occupational status attainment. *Am. Sociol. Rev.* 46:393–405

Lin N, Ensel WM, Vaughn JC. 1981b. Social resources and occupational status attainment. *Soc. Forces* 59:1163–81

Lincoln JR, Miller J. 1979. Work and friendship ties in organizations: a comparative analysis of relational networks. *Admin. Sci. Q.* 24:181–99

Loomis CP. 1946. Political and occupational cleavages in a Hanoverian village. *Sociometry* 9:316–33

Louch H. 2000. Personal network integration: transitivity and homophily in strong-tie relations. *Soc. Networks* 22:45–64

Maccoby E. 1998. *The Two Sexes: Growing Up Apart, Coming Together.* Cambridge MA: Belknap/Harvard Univ. Press

Marks SR. 1994. Intimacy in the public realm: the case of co-workers. *Soc. Forces* 72:843–58

Marsden PV. 1987. Core discussion networks of Americans. *Am. Sociol. Rev.* 52:122–313

Marsden PV. 1988. Homogeneity in confiding relations. *Soc. Networks* 10:57–76

Marsden PV. 1990. Network diversity, substructures and opportunities for contact. In *Structures of Power and Constraint: Papers in Honor of Peter Blau*, ed. C Calhoun, M Meyer, RS Scott, pp. 397–410. New York: Cambridge

Marsden PV, Gorman EH. 2001. Social networks, job changes and recruitment. In *Sourcebook on Labor Markets: Evolving Structures and Processes*, ed. I Berg, AL Kalleberg. New York: Kluwer Academic/Plenum

Marx JH, Spray SL. 1972. Psychotherapeutic "birds of a feather": social class status and religio-cultural value homophily in the mental health field. *J. Health Soc. Behav.* 13:413–28

Matsueda R, Heimer K. 1987. Race, family structure and delinquency: a test of differential association and social control theories. *Am. Sociol. Rev.* 52:826–40

Mayhew BH, McPherson M, Rotolo T, Smith-Lovin L. 1995. Sex and ethnic heterogeneity in face-to-face groups in public places: an ecological perspective on social interaction. *Soc. Forces* 74:15–52

McPherson JM. 1981. Voluntary affiliation: a structural approach. In *Continuities in Structural Inquiry*, ed. PM Blau, RK Merton, pp. 325–52. London: Sage

McPherson JM. 1981. A dynamic model of voluntary affiliation. *Soc. Forces* 59:705–21

McPherson JM. 1982. Hypernetwork sampling: duality and differentiation among voluntary associations. *Soc. Networks* 3:225–49

McPherson JM. 1983a. The size of voluntary associations. *Soc. Forces* 64:1044–64

McPherson JM. 1983b. An ecology of affiliation. *Am. Sociol. Rev.* 48:519–32

McPherson JM, Popielarz P, Drobnic S. 1992. Social networks and organizational dynamics. *Am. Sociol. Rev.* 57:153–70

McPherson JM, Ranger-Moore J. 1991. Evolution on a dancing landscape: organizations and networks in dynamic Blau space. *Soc. Forces* 70:19–42

McPherson JM, Rotolo T. 1996. Diversity and change: modelling the social composition of voluntary groups. *Am. Sociol. Rev.* 61:179–202

McPherson JM, Smith-Lovin L. 1982. Women and weak ties: sex differences in the size of voluntary associations. *Am. J. Sociol.* 87:883–904

McPherson JM, Smith-Lovin L. 1986. Sex segregation in voluntary associations. *Am. Sociol. Rev.* 51:61–79

McPherson JM, Smith-Lovin L. 1987. Homophily in voluntary organizations: status distance and the composition of face-to-face groups. *Am. Sociol. Rev.* 52:370–79

Michaelson W. 1976. *Man and His Urban Environment: A Sociological Approach.* Reading, MA: Addison-Wesley

Moore G. 1990. Structural determinants of men's and women's personal networks. *Am. Sociol. Rev.* 55:726–35

Munch-Rotolo AC. 2000. *Childbearing, social contact, and depression: a structural analysis of the transition to parenthood.* PhD Diss., Univ. Ariz., Tucson, AZ

Neckerman H. 1996. The stability of social groups in childhood and adolescence: the role of the classroom social environment. *Soc. Dev.* 5:131–45

Ooka E, Wellman B. 2001. Does social capital pay off more within or between ethnic groups? Analyzing job searchers in five Toronto ethnic groups. In *Inside the Mosaic*, ed. E Fong.

Park RE, Burgess EW. 1921. *Introduction to the Science of Sociology.* Chicago: Univ. Chicago Press

Pfeffer J. 1983. Organizational demography. In *Research in Organizational Behavior*, Vol. 5, ed. LL Cummings, BM Staw. Greenwich CT: JAI

Plato. 1968. Laws. *Plato in Twelve Volumes, Vol. 11.* Bury translator. Cambridge: Harvard Univ. Press

Podolny JM, Baron JN. 1997. Resources and relationships: social networks and mobility in the workplace. *Am. Sociol. Rev.* 62:673–93

Popielarz PA. 1999a. (In)voluntary association: a multilevel anaysis of gender segregation in voluntary organizations. *Gender Soc.* 13:234–50

Popielarz PA. 1999b. Organizational constraints on personal network formation. *Res. Sociol. Org.* 16:263–82

Popielarz P, McPherson JM. 1995. On the edge or in between: niche position, niche overlap, and the duration of voluntary memberships. *Am. J. Sociol.* 101:698–720

Raymo JM, Xie Y. 2000. Temporal and regional variation in the strength of educational homogamy. *Am. Sociol. Rev.* 65:773–80

Reskin BF, McBrier DB, Kmec JA. 1999. The determinants and consequences of workplace sex and race composition. *Annu. Rev. Sociol.* 25:335–61

Richardson HM. 1940. Community of values as a factor in friendships of college and adult women. *J. Soc. Psychol.* 11:303–12

Rotolo T, McPherson JM. 2001. The system of occupations: modeling occupations in sociodemographic space. *Soc. Forces* 79:1095–1130

Sampson RJ. 1984. Group size, heterogeneity and intergroup conflict: A test of Blau's *Inequality and Heterogeneity. Soc. Forces* 62:618–39

Schneider M, Teske P, Roch C, Marschall C. 1997. Networks to nowhere: segregation and stratification in networks of information about schools. *Am. Polit. Sci. Rev.* 41:1201–23

Schofeld JW. 1995. Review of research on school desegregation's impact on elementary and secondary school students. In *Handbook of Research on Multicultural Education*, ed. JA Banks, CA McGee, pp. 597–616. New York: Macmillan

Shrum W, Cheek NH Jr., Hunter SM. 1988. Friendship in school: gender and racial homophily. *Soc. Educ.* 61:227–39

Smith TW. 2000. Measuring inter-racial friendships: experimental comparisons. *Public Opin. Q.* 64:

Smith-Lovin L, McPherson JM. 1993. You are who you know: a network perspective on gender. In *Theory on Gender/ Feminism on Theory*, ed. P England, pp. 223–51. New York: Aldine

Smits J, Ultee W, Lammers J. 2000. More or less educational homogamy? A test of different versions of modernization theory using cross-temporal evidence for 60 countries. *Am. Sociol. Rev.* 65:781–88

Sorenson JB. 2000. The longitudinal effects of group tenure composition on turnover. *Am. Sociol. Rev.* 65:298–310

South SJ, Bonjean CM, Markham WT, Corder J. 1982. Social structure and group interaction: men and women of the federal bureaucracy. *Am. Sociol. Rev.* 47:587–99

South SJ, Bonjean CM, Markham WT, Corder J. 1983. Female labor force participation and the organizational experiences of men and women. *Sociol. Q.* 24:367–80

South SJ, Felson RB. 1990. The racial patterning of rape. *Soc. Forces* 69:71–93

South SJ, Messner SF. 1986. Structural determinants of intergroup association: interracial marriage and crime. *Am. J. Sociol.* 91:1409–30

Sparrowe RT, Popielarz PA. 1995. Weak ties and structural holes: the effects of network structure on careers. Unpublished paper, Dep. Mgmt, Univ. Ill., Chicago

Sudman S. 1988. Experiments in measuring neighbor and relative social networks. *Soc. Networks* 10:93–108

Tuma NB, Hallinan MZ. 1979. The effects of sex, race and achievement on schoolchildren's friendships. *Soc. Forces* 57:1265–85

van Duijn MAJ, van Busschbach JT, Snijders TAB. 1999. Multilevel analysis of personal networks as dependent variables. *Soc. Networks* 21:187–209

Verbrugge LM. 1977. The structure of adult friendship choices. *Soc. Forces* 56:576–97

Verbrugge LM. 1983. A research note on adult friendship contact: a dyadic perspective. *Soc. Forces* 62:78–83

Wellman B. 1929. The school child's choice of companions. *J.Educ. Res.* 14:126–32

Wellman B. 1996. Are personal communities local? A Dumptarian reconsideration. *Soc. Networks* 18:347–54

Wellman B, Salaff J, Dimitrova D, Garton L, Gulia M, Haythronwaite C. 1996. Computer networks as social networks: collaborative work, telework and virtual community. *Annu. Rev. Sociol.* 22:213–38

Wright EO. 1997. *Class counts: Comparative studies in class analysis.* New York: Cambridge Univ. Press

Yamaguchi K. 1990. Homophily and social distance in the choice of multiple friends: an analysis based on conditional symmetric log-bilinear association models. *J. Am. Stat. Assoc.* 85:356–66

Zipf GK. 1949. *Human Behavior and the Principle of Least Effort.* Menlo Park, CA: Addison-Wesley

Annu. Rev. Sociol. 2001. 27:445–77

EARLY TRADITIONS OF AFRICAN-AMERICAN SOCIOLOGICAL THOUGHT

Alford A. Young, Jr. and Donald R. Deskins, Jr.

Department of Sociology and Center for Afroamerican and African Studies, University of Michigan, Ann Arbor, Michigan 48109; e-mail: ayoun@umich.edu, ddeskins@umich.edu

Key Words   theory, culture, social organization, methods

■ **Abstract**   This article documents the empirical, methodological, and theoretical contributions of African-American sociologists from the late 1800s until 1945, an era that constitutes the early tradition of African-American sociological thought. African-American sociologists came to the discipline with the desire to assess the stake of African Americans in modernity, which centered on their transition to the urban sphere and the industrial socio-economic order in American society. Despite the connections between the sociological project writ-large and the quest of African-American sociologists in particular, the latter remained little regarded in the profession for years to come. While providing an overview of the contributions of African-American sociologists and the assessments made by other scholars about those contributions, this essay focuses upon the ways by which African-American sociologists have depicted the social character of black Americans. This essay also accounts for the ways that such scholars have introduced or enriched the standard paradigms and methodologies employed in American sociology, and documents the legacy that these efforts had on later sociological depictions of African Americans.

INTRODUCTION

This article documents the empirical, methodological, and theoretical contributions of African-American sociologists prior to 1945, an era that constitutes the early tradition of African-American sociological thought. This early tradition, which began in the 1890s, is also considered by historians of African-American sociology to be the "golden age in the sociology of blacks in America (Bracey et al 1971)." It is bounded by the publications of W.E.B. DuBois' *The Philadelphia Negro* (1996 [1899]) and St. Claire Drake and Horace Cayton's *Black Metropolis* (1993 [1945]). While these are two of the most well-known publications of the era, dozens more were produced that framed this early tradition along three dimensions: empirical, theoretical, and methodological. The latter half of this era—post 1930—has received considerably more attention than the earlier. This is due, in no small measure, to the training of African-American sociologists in formal departments of sociology, who then went on to canonize modes of inquiry into African-American social life (McKee 1993, Bracey et al 1971, Janowitz 1977). The first half of this essay, then, is an effort to counter the dearth of scholarly investigations of the beginning of this tradition.

Sociology emerged across Europe and the United States with the project of interpreting and critically assessing modernity, the preeminent social preoccupation of the twentieth century (Hinkle 1954, Martindale 1988, Ross 1991, Schwendinger & Schwendinger 1974). Modernity is a concept that has been applied to a wide range of social conditions and circumstances, all of which began to unfold in post-Enlightenment society. Sociology's considerations of modernity most often centered on exploring the proliferation of bureaucracy and formal institutions designed to help regulate social life, urbanization, capitalism, industrialization, and other social developments associated with these occurrences and transformations. African-American sociologists came to the discipline with the desire to assess the stake of African Americans in modernity, which centered on their transition to the urban sphere and the industrial socioeconomic order in American society. Despite the connections between the sociological project writ-large and the quest of African-American sociologists in particular, the latter remained little regarded in the profession for years.

This essay is motivated by a desire to increase sociologists' awareness of that connection. Our objective is to do more than produce a history of African-Americans' sociological contributions during the golden age. That effort implicitly supports a ghettoized vision of the involvement of African Americans in sociology. Moreover, a complete history of African-American sociological contributions, however that might be construed, is beyond the scope of this work.

Instead, this essay offers another approach toward the recovery of African-American sociological thought. While providing an overview of the contributions of African-American sociologists, and the assessments made by other scholars about those contributions, this essay focuses upon the ways by which African-American sociologists have depicted the social character of black Americans. In addition to exploring the ways by which the character of African Americans was framed in the scholarship of African-American sociologists, this essay will also account for the ways that such scholars have introduced or enriched the standard paradigms and methodologies employed in American sociology, and we will document the legacy that these efforts had on later depictions of the state of the African-American populace.

The Calling of Early African-American Sociologists: Social and Intellectual Conditions

African-American sociologists of the first part of the early tradition were barely visible in many of the mainstream sociological publications (Jones 1974). The fact that many of the figures discussed in this essay provided provocative and insightful commentary on the situation of African Americans conveys the extent to which sociology suffered as a consequence of this lack of attention. Moreover, the traditionally acknowledged early tradition of African-American sociological thought is limited to far fewer figures than were actually involved in the American sociological enterprise because most black Americans were not located in institutions that supported or maintained a strong research environment (Jones 1974). Instead, these individuals most often were located at historically black colleges and universities or in government and public sector agencies that emphasized advocacy more than research.

Throughout the early part of the twentieth century, historically black colleges and universities produced legions of African-American sociologists. These institutions were rarely able to sustain any large-scale research agenda, nor become highly prominent research centers for the sociological study of African Americans. Most of the historically black institutions were under-funded for research purposes, and federal government and public sector organizations emphasized programmatic initiatives or policy oriented research more than general scholarship (Jones 1974). Consequently, this examination of three phases of the early tradition of African-American sociological thought only considers the few sociologists who produced research during that time, and not the legacy of scholars who served as educators and mentors to successive generations of African-American sociologists.[1] The pioneer African-American sociologists came of age in the midst of a broader intellectual current in black America near the turn of the century (Fullinwider 1969, Gaines 1996, Meier 1966, Postock 1998). A major current was the emergence of the modern black intellectual stratum in the mid-nineteenth century. The creation of the early black Church, the abolitionist movement, and the post–Civil War black convention movement each provided a milieu for the growth of a black intellectual community. Most of the early African-American scholars who were a part of those milieux were polemical in their writing and public commentary. They sought not simply to investigate and interpret social life, but to redress the conditions affecting the lives of African Americans.

Efforts to form a collective of black intellectuals who foregrounded scholarship culminated in the founding of the American Negro Academy on March 5, 1897 in Washington DC (Moss 1981). Two of the leading figures of the first generation of African-American sociologists, W.E.B. DuBois and Kelly Miller, participated in the organization. The objective of the Academy was to organize black scholars, artists, and "those distinguished in other walks of life, for the promotion of Letters,

---

[1]One notable exception to this pattern was Atlanta University. There, under the guidance of W.E.B. DuBois, a Laboratory of Sociology was founded after the turn of the century that served as a headquarters for a series, the "Atlanta University Studies." While there DuBois also founded two academic journals, *Crisis* and *Phylon*, (Lewis 1993). The other exception was Fisk University in Nashville, Tennessee. From the late 1930s to the end of 1940s sociologist Charles S. Johnson managed to secure funding for a series of studies that provided graduate training for a some African-American sociologists (Blackwell and Janowitz 1974; KcKee 1993; Smith 1974, Stanfield 1982b, 1987). He did so in his capacity as Chair of the Department of Social Science and as President of Fisk University, a position he assumed in 1946.

Science, and Art" (Moss 1981, p. 1). The group published 22 Occasional Papers between 1897 and 1924 on subjects related to the culture, history, religion, social rights, and social institutions of African-American people. While its members were principally committed to intellectual exchange, they believed that their work would inform and direct public action on behalf of black America.

With the Academy serving as a model for scholarly engagement, the first black sociologists entered the field with passionate concern about the African-American condition. These scholars also had their own distinct objectives for the socio-logical endeavor, which directly spoke to the conditions of the newly emancipated freedmen and women and the public mindset on the connections between race and cultural attributes. For the early black sociologists the objective for scholarly inves-tigation was quite clear; "Is the Negro to demand full integration and risk losing his racial attributes through assimilation, or is he to accept segregation as the means to develop his particular genius, safely protected from the contaminating mores of American civilization?" (Fullinwider 1969, p. 98). These social conditions and strands of thought circumscribed the contributions of the first African-American sociologists.

Empirically, much of the research of the earliest period focused on the social organization and behavioral traits of black Americans, with a special emphasis on class differences in the African-American community and the experiences of urbanization. Another part of the empirical agenda was defining and providing solutions to the social problems of black Americans. This objective drew upon and developed certain theoretical perspectives on the social character of African Americans. There was much overlap in the two leading perspectives, but clear dis-tinctions as well. One was explicitly moralistic. It emphasized profligate behaviors and patterns of cultural adaption as much as structural conditions in discussions of the problematic aspects of the African-American confrontation with modernity. The other perspective involved a racialist discourse that in some ways reflected, and in others rejected, the racialist logic of turn-of-the-century America. This was evident in how some sociologists commented on the so-called inherent qualities or capacities of African Americans to function in, or contribute to, societal advance. Methodologically, most of the research in this era was comprised of comprehensive community-study approaches that entailed participant-observational techniques. Later this effort often was coupled with the analysis of census or other aggregate data garnered from surveys. There were some divergences from these approaches, and they receive appropriate attention in this essay.

The Progenitors of the Early Tradition: Anna Julia Cooper, Ida Wells Barnett, and W.E.B. DuBois

Anna Julia Cooper occupies an extremely unsettled place in the early tradition of African-American sociological thought. This is because she has only recently been more widely acknowledged as a contributor to that arena of ideas. Although a focus of substantive discussion in the past two decades in literary studies and

African-American intellectual history (Carby, 1987, Gaines 1996, Giddings 1984, hooks 1981), Cooper has only recently been more thoroughly recognized as a pioneer contributor to sociology. This was due, in large part, to her being included in Patricia Hill Collins's discussion of the legacy of African-American female social thinkers in *Black Feminist Thought* (1991) and the republication of Cooper's major work, *A Voice From the South* (originally published in 1892), together with a collection of her essays and correspondences (Lemert & Bhan 1998). Cooper produced most of this work prior to receiving a PhD in Sociology (from the Sorbonne in Paris in 1925).

The lack of that degree did not prevent her from scribing some ideas that are now being recognized as precursors to much of the contemporary sociological debates on African-American womanhood. Rather than engage in any consistent form of data collection, Cooper wrote critical essays that explored the situation of African-American women in the public domain and on the homefront. She argued that these women had particular roles and duties to fulfill in each sphere, each of which were especially suited for women. Moreover, Cooper tied the sociopolitical circumstances concerning and affecting African-American women to those of the country more generally. The increasingly more complex industrial order in American society, she argued, would reach its fullest potential only by including African-American men and women into the citizenry and allowing them to participate fully in social, political, and economic realms of life.

A Voice from the South included discussion of sexual exploitation (a phenomenon that at the time of her writing was still decades away from achieving mainstream legitimacy in debates about gender relations and social justice), class differences, gender-specific education, and other issues that remain at the forefront of debates on the social status and prospects for African-American women today. In advancing her claims, Cooper left an impression that she was conservative on some matters (such as emphasizing the homefront as a particularly legitimate space for women in general, not only black women), but progressive on others (such as claiming that women should have a role in the political arena and as formal agitators for social progress). Her life experiences, including the rearing of seven children (five of whom were adopted) as a single parent, the founding and management of a school in Washington, DC, and the constant interchange with Booker T. Washington and other African-American civic leaders and spokespeople, was the best empirical example of the social philosophy that she espoused.

Whereas Cooper's scholarship took the form of critical essays and commentaries, Ida Wells Barnett introduced empirical approaches toward uncovering certain problems and concerns for African Americans. She was born in 1862 and wrote extensively in the late 1800s for the newspaper, *The Memphis Free Speech*. As a journalist, Barnett was even farther removed professionally and socially from academia than was Cooper. Yet, her efforts resulted in the first substantive account of how social analysis could inform public understanding of important social issues and events. More specifically, Barnett provided a keen analysis of the sociological foundations for the lynchings of African Americans (1991). In the course of her career as a journalist, she prepared statistical accounts of the phenomena (which, as one should imagine, were extremely hard to document). Those accounts, together with data that she amassed while studying the involvement of white women in civic and social organizations that served the African-American community, helped her challenge the public notion that lynchings were a justifiable response to sexual assaults suffered by white women at the hands of African-American men. Not only did Barnett show that occurrences of such assaults were not as common as had been believed, but she also showed that the argument itself was a technique used by whites to sanitize the practice of lynching (1987[1892]).

Barnett also argued against the exclusion of African-American women from the analytical debate on womanhood that was a part of the chivalrous culture of the nineteenth century South. Altogether, her work resulted in a strong theoretical association between racism, sexism, and classism as it existed in southern social relations in the post bellum era. Both Barnett and Cooper precede the the scholarship usually regarded as the beginning of an African-American sociological tradition. Yet, each actually introduced the two ends of the continuum, critical commentary on the one hand and empirical investigation on the other, that shape modern sociological inquiry. As African-American women with no formal place in the academy, Cooper and Barnett were left on the margins of an already marginal constituency in American sociological thought.

Most of the theoretical, empirical, and methodological points of origin for many African-American sociological pursuits—indeed for African-American pursuits in social science overall—are found in the works of W.E.B. DuBois, particularly those produced by 1910 (including DuBois 1896, 1987a,b, 1898a,b, 1899a,b, 1900, 1901a,b,c,d, 1902, 1903, 1903a,b, 1904a,b,c, 1906, and 1910, among which are studies that he directed, and material that he authored, co-authored, or edited). Educated at Fisk University, the University of Berlin, and Harvard University (where he became the first African American to receive a PhD in the social sciences, taking one in History in 1895), DuBois is the subject of literature, the sheer amount of which is an affirmation that DuBois was the seminal figure in turn-of-the-century studies of African Americans and race relations. Scholars have assessed his contribution to racial theory (Appiah 1986, Brodwin 1972, Gilman 1972, Holt 1990, Moses 1993, Mostern 1996, Posnock 1998, Rampersad 1976, Schrager 1996, Zamir 1995), his place in the emerging discipline of sociology (Baltzell 1967, Lewis 1993, Rudwick 1974, Segrue & Katz 1997), his academic training and vision of scholarship in public affairs (Broderick 1958a,b, De Marco 1983, Lange 1983, Rudwick 1957, 1969), and his place in American social thought (La Rue 1971, Meier 1966, Reed 1997, West 1990). All of this has been in addition to the comprehensive biographies of him (Broderick 1974, Green & Driver 1976, Hamilton 1972, Lacy 1972, Lewis 1993, Marable 1986, Moore 1981) and anthologies on varied aspects of his life and work (Bracey et al 1971, Freedomways 1965, Logan 1971).

It would be inadequate to describe DuBois's scholarship as strictly sociology, history, or political science. Prior to 1910 (after which he became more an activist),

DuBois's early scholarly mission was to transcend the still-developing formal academic disciplines in order to create a supradisciplinary understanding of the social character, cultural status, and policy needs of African Americans (1898a, Lewis 1993, Fullinwider 1969). However, DuBois did attribute to sociology a particular role in this process, which for him was the discipline's orientation to interpreting, defining, and measuring social problems (1897, 1898a, 1903, 1904, 1940). In a comment published in the *American Journal of Sociology* (1908)—the only publication of his to appear in that journal, DuBois argued that the American Sociological Society (the precursor to the American Sociological Association) and other scholarly organizations should encourage "a most thorough and unbiased scientific study of the race problem in America" (p. 836).

In its early years, sociology had a strong emphasis on social reform, if not by designing reform strategies, then by supplying analyses and arguments about aspects of social life perceived to be in need of reform (Lyman 1972, McKee 1993, Schwendinger & Schwendinger 1974). This makes it all the more disturbing that DuBois's scholarship, which was empirically centered on a reform agenda, was rarely considered by the flagship journal, *American Journal of Sociology* (Bracey et al 1971). In discussing his early ambitions concerning sociology, DuBois said:

> I determined to put science into sociology through a study of the conditions and problems of my own group. I was going to study the facts, any and all facts, concerning the American Negro and his plight, and by measurement and comparison and research, work up any valid generalization which I could (1940).[2]

After receiving his PhD (completed while he was teaching at Wilberforce College), DuBois began an academic career that took him to Philadelphia in the mid-1890s [where he conducted his classic study *The Philadelphia Negro* (1899)] and then to Atlanta University from 1897 until 1910. Over the course of his academic career, DuBois aimed to design and implement a series of systematic studies on African-American social organization and culture. Although this never unfolded due to a lack of financial and social support, DuBois intended to create an "Atlanta Laboratory" at Atlanta University that would be a "centre of sociological research"

---

[2]Some of this agenda was revisited when DuBois returned to Atlanta University in 1933 to become the first Chairman of the Graduate Department of Sociology. This return occurred after years of working with the N.A.A.C.P., and editing its journal, *Crisis*. Upon his return to Atlanta University DuBois founded *Phylon*, an interdisciplinary journal committed to the explorations of race and race relations. Taking all of this into account, making a comprehensive assessment of his still insufficiently recognized contributions to the not yet mature social science disciplines in American higher education would take space beyond that which is granted for this essay. Indeed, an appropriate review of the works that address his contributions to sociology alone would comprise an essay lengthier than the present one. However, the depth and significance of DuBois' contributions to the discipline locate him as the point of origin of any effort to document the early methodological, empirical, and theoretical traditions of African-American sociological thought.

(1898b). While at Atlanta he supervised the preparation of sixteen monographs on topics ranging from the black family, Negro church, Negro education, to Negro economic and business development. This was to be part of his ultimate goal of a 100-year-long study of black Americans, which would entail an exploration of a single theme or topic each year for an initial ten year period, followed by a revisitation of each topic every ten years or so thereafter (Lewis 1993). Following *The Philadelphia Negro*, the studies that initiated this objective constituted DuBois's major empirical contributions prior to 1910. It was through this body of work that DuBois offered a substantive multi-method platform for sociological inquiry that incorporated survey research, ethnography, census reports, and community surveys.

In terms of theoretical, empirical, and methodological dimensions, the scholarly career of DuBois can be categorized as an effort to ascertain the meaningfulness of race as a social category (the theoretical dimension, cf. 1978[1897a], 1986 [1903a],), to document the barriers and obstacles inhibiting the social advancement of African Americans, and to define some strategies and ideas for resolving them (the empirical dimension, cf. 1897b, 1898a,b, 1996 [1899a], 1899b, 1901, 1904a,b, 1906, 1910), and to illustrate how historical analysis, demographic data, field work, and survey research can be employed to further prior objectives (the methodological dimension, cf. 1896, 1996 [1899a], 1898b, 1900, 1969 [1901b], 1901c, 1903b).

Taking theory first, extensive debate has illuminated the changing nature of DuBois's writings on the importance of race in social life. One writer argues that DuBois's personal tribulations with race throughout his life correspond with the changes in his writing on the topic, which are three-fold (Mostern 1996). The first is an individualist orientation, where DuBois maintained that race was an identity construct foisted upon the individual by the external social world, thus circumscribing how the public read and reacted to individuals. The second is an essentialist orientation that causes beings ascribed to a particular race to function in thought and action in ways similar to others of the same race (thus recreating a sense of racial culture and racial collectives). The third involves fostering a claim that the problematics of race must be overcome until race is no longer socially meaningful. DuBois's contributions to sociology appeared as he emerged from the first of these orientations and continued through his immersion into the second.

Early in his scholarly career DuBois became a major voice in the debates in the early black intellectual community on the issue of innate cultural or physiological qualities of African Americans. It is with respect to this matter that DuBois's theoretical contributions to African-American sociology loom large. It is also in this arena that the work of DuBois has been more systematically reviewed after a period of earlier misreadings. The work that most fully reflected DuBois's theoretical approach to race around the turn of the century is *The Souls of Black Folk* (1903). This work was celebrated as a literary work at least as much as a contribution to social science. In *Souls* DuBois uncovered the complexities involved in being an African American, including the struggle to affirm identity, to articulate a meaningful and viable approach to social uplift, and to ascertain the meaning of social equality in American society. Part poetry, part polemic, and part political commentary, this book exemplified DuBois's ability to transcend disciplinary foci on the conditions of African Americans decades before interdisciplinarity gained legitimacy in the American academic enterprise.

In *Souls* and other work (1987a), DuBois argued that racial differences extended beyond the merely physical to spiritual and psychical differences. This did not mean, as some readings suggest (see Fullinwider 1969) that DuBois argued for the existence of any innate qualities or traits in the African-American community that were racially constituted. Instead, it illustrated DuBois's long-standing struggle with the significance of race as a social force—not just in terms of micro-level social interaction, but also in terms of how people apprehend and evaluate aspects of the social world as these are affected by their location in a racial category. The subtleties in DuBois's writings often appear to convey an essentialism that he actually did not intend to advance (Lewis 1993, Mostern 1996, Posnock 1998). DuBois argued that among other things, race profoundly affects how people perceive and conceive reality (perhaps more than any other social force). He did not claim that racial classification determined the inherent agentic capacities of people. Yet casual readings of his work often make it appear that he was a strong essentialist.

The essentialist claims were not the only critical takes on DuBois's scholarship. In his discussions of African Americans and cultural advance (1897, 1897b, 1899, 1901a,b, 1903), he has been read as elitist and as favoring a "whitening" of the race as a means of social uplift (Zamir 1995). For DuBois, cultural advance was the turn away from vice, criminal activity, and folk mores and toward the staples of American modernity. Wage labor in an emerging industrial sphere and community-level organizing for social betterment on the homefront were two such objectives. Others have argued that DuBois did not equate whiteness per se with being culturally advanced (Posnock 1998). Instead, it has been argued that DuBois asserted that without having suffered the burdens of being African Americans, white Americans generally achieved a level of cultural advance that most black Americans had yet to acquire. DuBois's high regard for cultural advance together with his finding that the most socio-economically disadvantaged African Americans lacked his sense of cultural sophistication is what has lead some observers to consider him a cultural elitist. DuBois's rigorous pursuit of the social significance of race coupled with his equally adamant stress on cultural advance is the basis for the divergence of opinions on his racial theories.

The strength of DuBois's empirical contributions is best found in his most regarded study, *The Philadelphia Negro* (1899). DuBois's approach to this work was influenced by his reading of Charles Booth's *Life and Labour of the People of London* (1891–1897) and the *Hull House Maps* and *Papers* (1895), authored by the Residents of Hull House. In this work, DuBois observed and documented the life experiences and social conditions affecting African Americans in the city's Seventh Ward, which housed one fifth of the city's African-American population. He set out to document and interpret a range of social issues pertinent to the black experience in Philadelphia, including northern migration, social conditioning, the social institutions and life styles of the black community, and the enduring effects of slavery. DuBois employed a questionnaire on family structure, income and wealth, and qualities of residential life. He also observed public interaction in the community. Finally he acquired or created diagrams and blueprints of the physical structures throughout the seventh ward in order to offer a comprehensive account of unemployment, family decay, and social hierarchies in the ward.

DuBois's commitment to empirical research emerged during his studies in Germany, where under Gustav von Schmoller he was exposed to empiricism (Broderick 1958a,b, Lewis 1993). His work preceded American sociological forays into empiricism. The multiple method approach to data collection, unparalleled in social research for years afterward, blended structural analysis with microlevel depictions of public interaction and behavior in private settings. In *The Philadelphia Negro*, DuBois provided a masterful weaving of class and racial effects in documenting the conditions of the Seventh Ward in Philadelphia. Through such an effort, he was able to argue that the urban slum was a symptom, and not a cause, of the economic, social, cultural, and political condition of African-American urban life. In the chapters where he presented his agenda for whites and blacks, he divided his discussion of what black Americans must do for racial advance into specific charges for the different class segments of the African-American community. This effort reflected DuBois's reformist inclinations. He aimed to produce not only a scholarly contribution, but an illustration of how scholarship connects to a policy platform for redressing problems, as in Philadelphia's Seventh Ward.

His efforts here helped him to argue that slavery, prejudice, and environmental factors were the three principal causal factors affecting African-American life in Philadelphia. Moreover, he promoted a nonhomogenous depiction of African Americans by elucidating the class distinctions along the behavioral and organizational dimensions of social life. *The Philadelphia Negro* was the first comprehensive community study in American sociology. Indeed, one commentator (Watts 1983) has argued that although DuBois was not acknowledged by his contemporaries as having introduced this kind of approach to sociological research, *The Philadelphia Negro* reflects precisely the kind of community-centered sociology that appeared on the American landscape in the following two decades (in large part because its proponent, and one of the early leaders of the University of Chicago school of sociology, Robert Ezra Park, also studied under the empiricists in Germany). In any case, *The Philadelphia Negro* remains a pathbreaking community study that helped establish a vernacular for writing about the social conditions of black Americans, despite its moralistic claims and an elitist disposition taken toward lower-income black Americans.

Another of DuBois' works, similar in scope and interpretation to *The Philadelphia Negro*, was "The Negroes of Farmville, Virginia: A Social Study" (1898). This work, which actually preceded and thus informed the logic of the Philadelphia study, was the first contribution in a project intended to produce studies of "well-defined" Negro groups throughout the United States. That study, as well as "The Negro in the Black Belt: Some Social Sketches (1899)," "Negroes of Dougherty County, Georgia (1901)", and "The Black North in 1901: New York

(1901)" were commissioned by the US Bureau of Labor Statistics. Each argued the importance of emerging class differentiation in the social relations within African-American communities.

Yet another area of empirical and methodological contributions is reflected in DuBois's dissertation (1896), "The Suppression of the African Slave-Trade to the United States of America, 1638–1870," which was published under the same title as the first installment in Harvard University's Historical Series. In this work, DuBois offered an analysis in the scope of what much later became comparative-historical sociology. He explored the legislative efforts in several states to restrict and suppress the slave trade. He analyzed and compared the outcomes of these initiative to formulate a thesis about how and why the slave trade was conducted in the manner that it was prior to the Emancipation. DuBois argued that moral, political, and economic factors converged at the domestic and international levels to hinder, and then cause the eventual abandonment, of slavery in the United States. A blaring methodological weakness in this work is one that DuBois, himself, acknowledged later in his life (Lewis 1993). In an "Apologia" that appeared in a 1954 edition of the book, DuBois stated that he neglected including the contributions of Karl Marx and Sigmund Freud in his analysis, as their efforts would have better informed his discussion of the moral and structural dimensions of the trans-Atlantic slave trade (Lewis 1993). This matter aside, this publication was one of a number of his analyses that could be categorized as comparative-historical sociology (1935, 1939).

Shortly prior to 1910, as historian David Levering Lewis (1993) argued, DuBois came to the realization that "fourteen years of preparation, research, and writing suddenly seemed mockingly irrelevant" in the face of the terroristic oppression that black Americans confronted. This was brought home to DuBois while he was working at Atlanta University and took note of the lynching of an African-American farmer from Georgia, Sam Hose. That was the moment when W.E.B. DuBois began to abandon his disposition as "a calm, cool, and detached scientist while Negroes were being lynched, murdered, and starved" (quoted in Lewis 1993, p. 226).

Determining to move on to more activist involvements, DuBois left behind a pioneering legacy for African-American sociological pursuits. He pioneered the sociological investigation of the black community in two areas. First, he espoused a credible, scientific approach for investigating the social processes of the black community. Secondly, he fostered the idea that racial difference was socially significant beyond mere biological or physiological perspectives. Such was the sociological world that other African-American sociologists became a part of in contributing to a framework for black social identity and cultural status.

Contributions to the Early Tradition: Methodological, Empirical, and Theoretical

As evidenced by Cooper, Wells, and DuBois, the early tradition of African-American sociology was initiated by scholars who were not trained as sociologists, but who found the emerging discipline an appropriate site for the kinds of inquiry and commentary that they desired to offer on the situation of African Americans at the turn of the century. The rest of the early African-American sociologists produced most of their work from the turn of the century until the early 1920s. The other prolific figures of the tradition include Kelly Miller and George Edmund Haynes, who founded the Departments of Sociology at Howard and Fisk University, respectively.

Some other early scholars produced little work in comparison to these men. For example, James R. Diggs is credited as being the first African American to receive a PhD in sociology as an area of specialization, but not a formal academic discipline (Greene 1946). He earned his PhD from Illinois Wesleyan University in 1906 with a dissertation entitled "The Dynamics of Social Progress," but he did nothing else that endured in any legacy of research.

The first PhD awarded to an African American in the discipline of sociology went to Richard Robert Wright, who earned his degree from the University of Pennsylvania in 1911. His dissertation, "History of the Pennsylvania Negro," was published as *The Negro in Pennsylvania* (1911). The work, which addressed the problems emerging from the migration of African Americans to that state, became his most noted publication. Wright was educated at the University of Chicago and the Student Universities of Berlin and Leipzig; he thus acquired much of the same exposure to empiricism that W.E.B. DuBois received a few years before him (Greene 1946). While a significantly less noted figure than the other African-American sociologists of his era, Wright's approach to research fit in with that of his African-American peers in the discipline. In some earlier work he researched the turbulent transition of black Americans to urban life (1905, 1906). Thereafter, while in the midst of becoming a minister in the African Methodist Episcopal Church, Wright moved into an area of research and writing on African Americans that can be described as a precursor to liberation theology (Fullinwider 1969).

As for the more prominent of DuBois's peers, Kelly Miller was educated at Howard University (he received a BA in mathematics in 1886) and Johns Hopkins University, where he studied mathematics from 1887 until 1889. In 1890 he returned to Howard to teach mathematics. It was during his return to Howard that Miller gradually became interested in the emerging new discipline of sociology. He became the Dean of Social Sciences at Howard in 1907 and starting teaching sociology courses in 1912. Miller committed himself solely to the field of sociology by 1918, after ending his service as a Dean. He founded Howard University's Department of Sociology in 1918 and led it from then until 1934 (when E. Franklin Frazier assumed the chair). Despite his early study of mathematics, his prominent work derived from the sociological thought and social theory of the turn-of-the-century era.

The other major early figure, George Edmund Haynes, did graduate work at Yale University and the University of Chicago, and received his PhD in Social Economy (the precursor to the Department of Sociology) from Columbia University in 1912. He was that institution's first African-American doctorate. Unlike Miller,

George Edmund Haynes spent most of his intellectual energy conducting empirical research. His formal training, in Columbia University's Department of Social Economy, provided him with the capacity to do so, whereas Miller's training in mathematics left him without a formal background in social research. Haynes also maintained a strong commitment to reformist scholarship, and in fact he worked for social service agencies as much as in the university setting throughout his life. He taught at Fisk University from 1910 until 1921, and between 1908 and 1941 worked for or with agencies such as the Young Men's Christian Association, the National Urban League (known in the early 1900s as the National League on Urban Conditions Among Negroes), the New York Bureau of Social Research, and the Federal Council of Churches of Christ in America. The differences in approach to sociology between Miller and Haynes are striking, yet they found common ground promoting a certain kind of cultural framing of black Americans.

Miller generally was not an empiricist, and his work reflects more argument and abstract commentary than researched findings or carefully analyzed data (similar, in fact, to the approach taken by Anna Julia Cooper). However, his training in mathematics did provide him with the capacity to make some empirical contributions to the discipline. One was an article that contained a series of corrections to the Census Bureau's undercount of the African-American population in the 1920 census (1922). Another was an assessment of the schooling of African-American children in the south, which became a report to the United States Bureau of Education (1900–1901). Otherwise, much of Miller's work involved polemical contributions and essays in social thought (cf. 1918, 1921, 1924). Such pursuits allowed him to connect with the theoretical dimension of DuBois's contribution to the tradition, which, in large part, rested in arguing that black Americans were less culturally equipped for modernity than were white Americans.

Miller's contribution to the black sociological canon was a brand of racialism similar to that of DuBois. As did many black social thinkers of his era, Miller defined the state of the black community during the late nineteenth and early twentiethth century in terms of its comparative status with white America. He considered African Americans to be less culturally advanced for success in an emerging industrial society than were white Americans (1908). In other work he located them as more culturally sophisticated than Africans, but not yet on par with white Americans (1900). Indeed much of his scholarship included vociferous arguments about how much black Americans had much to do in order to achieve the degree of social and cultural advancement that had been attained by white Americans (1899, 1900, 1908, 1933, 1936, 1980).

Miller did argue that black Americans possessed some degree of complex culture and modern civilization. Much of this discussion centered on documenting what he felt were some inherent racial qualities of the black Americans. In such commentary, Miller adapted the logic of racialist humanism in making his arguments, which included references to a "smothered mental, moral, and spiritual power" (1899). Such views were reflected in some of his other works as well (1899, 1980).

Despite these character traits, Miller maintained that black Americans necessitated something of a conversion process in order to further enrich those attributes. He went as far as to spell out the stages of development that he believed all social groups underwent in the course of experiencing contact with other groups (1908). In doing so he also relied on much of the racialist discourse of his time to ascertain and frame the potential of African Americans. This was exemplified in his scholarship by his constant references to the role that a Higher Being would play in affecting the destiny of all races and to a cosmic plan of human progress that would incorporate the particular fruits and riches that each racial group could offer toward that end.

Altogether, this commentary reflected both the social Darwinist logic that permeated turn-of-the-century discussions of social progress in American life and the utopian sentiment that flourished during the late nineteenth century (Hofstadter 1955). While vehemently asserting that black Americans were capable of competing in and contributing to America, Miller still accepted the general contours of the social Darwinist logic. He stressed almost as much as the Darwinists, that cultural hierarchies indicated where people stood in terms of their capacity to function in a complex society. Miller did so by speaking of the social problems and social circumstances affecting black Americans, not simply in terms of structural constraints on opportunity, but as indicators of cultural lag (especially in his assessment of the emerging great African-American migration to cities).

The tenets of Miller's cultural thesis also were made evident in his agenda for African-American social uplift. For example, he stressed that the Negro college was the principal institution in which blacks could begin to develop their culture to the level of the stronger (white) race (1933, 1936). In particular, he felt that black commitment to these schools would, (*a*) provide blacks with the moral stamina and fortitude to face and change an increasingly more complex world, and (*b*) allow blacks the opportunity to identify and cultivate the particular qualities and endowments of the black race that were superior to those of other races (1908). Miller also believed that such educational opportunities would help blacks to abandon their "boisterousness of manner and extravagant forms of taste" (1908).

Although he promoted a racialist humanism in his discussions of the potential of black Americans, when discussing the actual conditions of African-American urban life, especially in the urban context, Miller was somewhat more inclined to stress social conditioning as the causal force for their troubles in trying to adjust that life there (1908). The challenge for black Americans to overcome, therefore, came from the fact that "the weaker race has been brought into the territory of the stronger as a servant," and that blacks must somehow move forward from that predicament (Miller 1980).

In contrast to Miller, George Edmund Haynes made his objective the translation of empirical findings into a more practical policy agenda (similar to the approach taken by Ida Wells Barnett). Theoretically, his work more forcefully stressed the effects of social conditioning on African Americans. Empirically, it centered on the African-American presence in the urban landscape. Methodologically, Haynes favored something of an interdisciplinary approach because he saw it as the most fruitful way of discerning the complex condition of African Americans still within a few generations of slavery.[3] Haynes's most regarded work was *The Negro at Work in New York City: A Study in Economic Progress* (1912). With this and subsequent works, including "The Negro Newcomer to Detroit" (1917), and "Negroes and Work During the World War and Reconstruction" (1921), Haynes established himself as the voice of scientific inquiry, in contrast to Miller's more polemical disposition.

Following a trail established by DuBois, Haynes became a pioneer African-American sociologist of the African-American urban transition and its effect on their social and economic status. His emphasis on work and its relationship to mobility contributed a more structural foundation for assessing the social situation and prospects for black Americans. The relationship between these two arenas of life would go on to have a central place in sociological studies of African Americans.

While there were clear differences in the sociological contributions of Miller and Haynes, there were points of overlap as well. Some of this had to do with how each depicted the social position and social character of black Americans. For instance, Kelly Miller maintained that in the post–Civil War environment, the relations of black and white Americans changed from one of informal super-ordinate–subordinate interaction, laden with paternalistic intimate relations, to one of formal business-like interaction between freely functioning human beings (1899). Hence, he argued that it was imperative that black Americans be prepared to navigate the new modes of interaction in modern life. Haynes's work provided empirical evidence about how black Americans stood with respect to this transformation.

Moreover, in other work, Haynes offered a brand of cultural analysis and commentary similar to the work of both Miller and DuBois. This is evident in his *The Trend of the Races* (1922), where he put forth an argument about the cultural traits of black Americans that was couched in the language of inherent and innate capacities. Here, Haynes argued that the marginality that black Americans faced situated them as critical observers of the emerging American industrial order, and made them people who, if encouraged and given the opportunity to do so, could contribute to the humanization of the country as it immersed itself to greater commercialism and economic competition. One commentator argued that Haynes's strong religiosity was the source of his explicit moral voice in this work (Fullinwider 1969). Whatever the case, *The Trend of the Races* sounded much like Kelly Miller's argument that black Americans strive to serve as appraisers of the conscience of the nation in the same way that women function as the "conservators of moral stamina" in American life, despite their being the "weaker" sex (1908). The comments of Haynes and Miller show how much both shared forms of the

---

[3]As Fisk University maintained a Department of Social Science rather than departments in specific disciplines, Haynes worked within an institutional arrangement that promoted interdisciplinary considerations of African Americans.

racialist thinking of their times despite their different approaches to sociological inquiry.

Cooper, Barnett, DuBois, Miller, and Haynes fought against certain prevailing notions about the potential for blacks to participate fully in early twentieth century American society. Yet each engaged this effort by using many of the same paradigms, language, and logic employed by the creators of not just racialist, but racist American social thought. As pioneer contributors to an African-American sociological discourse, they had no tradition behind them with which to provoke a more critical response to the paradigm of race dialogue that existed at that time. Consequently, their scholarly contributions make more sense when viewed as efforts to address, with the intellectual tools available at the time, issues of civilization for a people who had recently been liberated from the status of chattel and who had traditionally not been thought of by many Americans as competent and capable human beings. These sociologists' sensibilities about modernity were shaped by an environment that defined white American civilization as the standard. Therefore, any effort to defend the humanity of black people would have to be born out of ideological frameworks used to suppress African Americans. Thus, this early phase of the African-American sociological tradition reflected the modernist impulse of turn-of-the-century American social thought.

The Second Wave of the Early Tradition: Incorporation into American Sociology

Sociology was a two-decade old and fully formed academic discipline by the beginning of the second phase of the early tradition. Consequently, the milieu within which the members of this wave produced their scholarship was different in many ways, yet similar in others, to that of the first wave. The similarity is found in the explicit attention to social conditioning as a primary causal force for the dilemmas confronting African Americans (the major exception, as examined later, is found in the work of Oliver Cox). Furthermore, the second wave scholars also adapted a strong social reform logic in their work, which was directly in line with W.E.B. DuBois's initial calling for the discipline. However, the depth of the second wave's emphasis (as well as its different depiction of the social character of black Americans) displaced the earlier, more intense preoccupation with moral and cultural advance as essential for racial uplift.

It was still the case that some argued that this reform agenda often relied too heavily upon a vision of white America as a measuring rod for the possibilities of African Americans in the twentieth century (Watts 1983) and thus fostered a pathological conception of the cultural and social dimension of African-American life (Szwed 1972, Valentine 1968). This claim is found especially in the critical commentary about E. Franklin Frazier, as one commentator argued, because he was far more theoretically committed than were his contemporaries in the second wave, and in doing so Frazier was more assertive in forwarding a theoretical logic that centered on pathology and social disorganization as prominent features of

African-American urban life (Watts 1983). Others claim that Frazier's attention to social disorganization and pathology was aimed at defining neither inherent cultural traits of African-American life nor some long-standing effects of social conditioning. Instead, it was argued that these depictions captured and defined the position African Americans were in during their adjustment to more northern-based, urban patterns of living, as opposed to the southern-based, rural contexts that they had been accustomed (McKee 1993). This debate makes clear that some of the criticism about how the first wave positioned white Americans relative to black Americans continued to be applicable through the second wave. However, the differences in scholarly tone and argument were quite significant.

Some of the conditions particular to the second generation of African-American sociologists rather than the first were; less concern with the need to refute the racist arguments of the late nineteenth and early twentieth century; more specific concern with the conditions and effects of urbanism, integration, rural poverty, and segregation on the individual and community psyche of African Americans; more complete adaptation of standard sociological methods and paradigms; more prone to stress the contemporary notion of scientific inquiry rather than abstract theorizing; somewhat less involved in direct action protest or politics; and slightly greater acceptance into the formal sociological community (Key 1978). In large part, the emergence of these factors was due to the connection of many of these scholars to Robert Ezra Park and the early Chicago School of Sociology.

Many commentators have argued that Park's contributions to sociology did not serve to agitate the racial order of his time, nor did he intend to do so (Lyman 1972, Matthews 1977, McKee 1993, Persons 1987, Raushenbush 1979, Stanfield 1982b). Instead, Park assumed the position of the detached observer of social life. Although he brought into sociology the largest number and most renowned African-American sociologists of the early and middle part of the twentieth century, and this was a radical act of some magnitude, his scholarly legacy and that of his African-American students as well, lacked a critical disposition toward the racial attitudes of white Americans and the structural foundations of racism in American life.

Furthermore, the absence of a more critical disposition was also due in part to the increasing role of philanthropic entities in the study of African-American life, particularly the southern-rural to northern-urban migration (Stanfield 1982b). From 1900 until 1940, the evolution of foundation support for research on African Americans moved from a narrow focus on manual training for the freedmen and women of the late nineteenth century to detailed data collection and observation of the urban migration process in the early twentieth century (Stanfield 1982a,b). This transition was mirrored by a shift in the funding of the study of African Americans from white to African-American scholars. However, very narrow parameters circumscribed the kind of issues that could be studied and the kinds of interpretations that could be offered about the findings (Stanfield 1982a,b). Hence, the research of the latter half of the early tradition generally was less critical of the American cultural and social order than would be the case in years to come. In an extension of the modernist orientation of early American sociology, the second wave promoted an assimilationist paradigm that reflected the first wave's emphasis on cultural advance and improved social organization. However, the principal difference was the absence of an explicit naturalist theme in discussions of culture and social organization.

Much of the work of the second wave evolved from Robert Park's (1950a,b) conception of the race relations cycle, his evolutionary model of racial and ethnic contact and social change.[4] This framework endorsed the Melting Pot vision of American social life, with Anglo-Saxon cultural underpinnings as somewhat predominant. Additionally, Park's approach to urban sociology also informed the work of the second wave. He and his colleagues at the University of Chicago asserted that the city should serve as a natural laboratory for examining the social organization of heterogeneous people in an emerging industrial, financial, commercial, administrative, and cultural sphere, including the negative and positive aspects of such a transformation (Park & Burgess 1921, Wirth 1928). His race relations cycle was a heuristic for exploring cultural transmission in the urban sphere. Park argued that, as black Americans became acclimated to the city, they would gradually abandon the ideas, memories, and norms from prior patterns of social existence, while assuming the dominant (white) culture.

Another major foundational contributor to the scholarship of the second wave was the University of Chicago-based anthropologist, W. Lloyd Warner, who promoted a caste framework for assessing social hierarchies and social inequality (Warner 1936, Warner & Davis 1939). Warner, his students, and his students' students formalized an approach to community studies in rural and urban settings (Davis & Dollard 1940, Davis et al 1941, Dollard 1937). He emphasized the importance of life style and modes of public interaction at the individual and group level as key indicators of the social adjustment of people to geographic and social spaces (Warner et al 1941, Warner & Lunt 1942, Warner & Srole 1945). He also paid careful attention to the movement of African Americans to the northern urban sector, which for him was the source of the formation of the contemporary system of caste and class-based oppression for black Americans. Warner's guidance of St. Claire Drake and Allison Davis was his direct tie to the African-American sociologists in the second wave. Warner's ideas, however, influenced the African-American sociologists who studied under Park at the University of Chicago and

---

[4]Here Park argued that racial and ethnic groups, upon coming into contact with each other, would engage a process of competition, conflict, accommodation, and assimilation, occurring in that order. Park argued that this process took place in each of four dimensions of social life; ecological, political, economic, and cultural (Park and Burgess 1921). Changes in any dimension affected what would occur in the others. Empirical study would illustrate exactly how that affect would occur at different points in time and with respect to different ethnic groups. However, Park asserted that irrespective of the different patterns of evolution, the groups entering social relations with the most social power, or control of societal resources, would emerge as dominant.

who engaged in scholarly interaction with anthropologists who were interested in race and the urban sphere.[5]

These and other contributions helped to establish a sociological enterprise that defused an older, more explicitly moralizing emphasis in research and privileging a pragmatic analytical perspective. It also moved sociology away from a sociobiologically to a culturally grounded perspective for exploring racial matters. Unlike Warner, Park did little empirical application of his concepts and framework. However, his African-American students, especially E. Franklin Frazier and Charles S. Johnson, applied the concepts and framework, as well as the ideology underlining them, to help constitute the second wave of the early tradition

Empirical, Methodological, and Theoretical Contributions of the Second Wave

The second wave of African-American sociologists sought to investigate the black American rural to urban transition and its consequences for the cultural and organizational disposition of African Americans. The empirical emphases of the second wave included the African-American family (Frazier 1931, 1932, 1940), the transition to urban living (Drake & Cayton 1945, Frazier 1925, 1928, Johnson 1925, Reid 1927, 1939), that status of black Americans in urban employment sectors (Cayton & Mitchell 1939, Reid 1969 [1930], 1936) the etiquette of race relations (Doyle 1937, Johnson 1934a, 1936a), the social organization of southern rural life (Davis & Dollard 1940; Davis et al 1941, Johnson 1934a,b,c, 1941), and the views and orientations of African Americans toward future opportunity (Davis & Dollard 1940, Frazier 1940, Johnson 1941, Reid 1940).

Much of this work concerned the social processes, circumstances, and dilemmas of African-American adjustment to industrial society. Theoretically, this wave moved away from either combating or supporting purist racialist arguments that centered on innate racial abilities or character traits. Instead, these scholars asserted notions of culture that focused on shared patterns of adaptation to social contexts rather than on classification according to any grand schema of cultural capacities and potential. Additionally, they argued that black American culture was an American phenomenon, and that social progress for black Americans could be ensured by increasing their opportunities for acculturating and assimilating further into American society. Methodologically, these scholars employed the range of research techniques that had become by their time standard approaches for

---

[5]The best evidence of this is *Black Metropolis* [1993(1945)] which was co-authored by St. Claire Drake, a student of Warner's, and Horace Cayton, a student of Robert Park. Moreover, Allison Davis, soon to become a prominent African-American anthropologist, also shared in scholarly exchanges with these and other African-American sociologists, beginning with his tenure as a graduate student at Chicago. The interaction between anthropologists and sociologists was first engineered by the fact that anthropology and sociology became independent departments at Chicago in the early 1930s. Prior to then they constituted a single department.

sociological inquiry (census data analysis, field observations, archival research, interviewing, etc.). These approaches were reflected in community studies (Drake & Cayton 1945, Davis & Dollard 1940, Davis et al 1941, Frazier 1940, Johnson 1934a,c, Reid 1927), participant observation (Doyle 1937), interviewing (Johnson 1934a,c), and analysis of survey and census data (Cayton & Mitchell 1939, Frazier 1932, 1934, Reid 1937).

Much of the empirical agenda had to do with the urban sphere. As much as these scholars affirmed that northern migration was a ticket to a better future, they also acknowledged that the transition to the urban sphere was fraught with problems and difficulties. A major part of their empirical agenda was the exploration of these difficulties. The guiding concept for African-American sociological investigations of the transition to the urban sphere was social disorganization (Frazier 1925, 1931, Johnson 1932, 1934b). This concept was a catch-all phrase for vice, disease, and other social ills that have been associated with the formation of ethnic ghettoes. However, unlike some of the earlier scholars who were preoccupied with exploring the racial character of black Americans, the second wave confronted this issue by focusing on how social conditions affected and oppressed and disenfranchised people.

E. Franklin Frazier focused more specifically on the social organizational patterns of African-American life and the stake they had in the urban arena. Having published until the late 1950s, his work spans a number of eras of black scholarly productivity (Platt 1991). However, prior to 1945, Frazier paid much attention to the urban transition and the sedimentation of African Americans into urban communities. He argued that disorganization (crime, vice, illegitimacy, and delinquency) ensued as black Americans began the tumultuous process of adjusting to what was for them a new urban environment (Frazier 1931). He stressed that the social organization of black communities would be enriched by the immersion of black Americans into the industrial infrastructure of the city (1925, 1968).

For Frazier, the city represented an opportunity for social and cultural renewal, and he believed that race consciousness would be cultivated by the proximity of residents in urban enclaves (1932). The significance of migration to the city, in Frazier's mind, was what it meant for the black American family—the unit of observation for most of his empirical work (1931, 1932). He believed that a pattern of social disorganization, followed by a turbulent effort at reorganization, encapsulated the situation of the African-American family's attempt to cohere in city life. Accordingly, Frazier explained profligate behavior in terms of what it indicated about the gradual adjustment process of black Americans to urban life (1932). Here Frazier implied that black Americans began the transition to urban life at the early phase of the race relations cycle. He also alluded to the end-stage of the race relations cycle as the ultimate point of social evolution for black migrants to American cities.

The capacity of African Americans to adjust to the urban context and create their own social world within it was best captured by St. Claire Drake and Horace

Cayton's study *Black Metropolis* (1945). Working mostly in the Warner tradition of the community study approach, these scholars illustrated how interactive and socialization processes in an all-black urban sector (Chicago's south side) maintained status differentials and social hierarchies resembling that of the larger American social landscape. Drake & Cayton's work elucidated how black Americans had adapted to city life, and what social problems remained or were created by pervasive racial discrimination in the midst of the migration effort. Their work depicted a virtual city within a city, where black Americans constructed an institutional ghetto that was self-sustaining in many ways by virtue of local business development, the establishment of churches and civic groups, and the creation of a local newspaper.

Charles Johnson, who assumed the chair of the Department of Social Science at Fisk University in 1927, following George Edmund Haynes, found that the transition to the urban arena meant the release of African Americans from the effects of systemic control in the south. This, to be sure, was a positive outcome in his mind. He believed that black Americans could reorganize their "personalit(ies) upon new basis of greater (self) control" in the city (1934a, p. 457).[6] Whereas Frazier attended to social disorganization, Johnson looked more carefully at the social psychological consequences and effects of black American life, particularly the effect of social structure on the human condition.

Johnson's work on racial conciousness, defensive psychology, and inferiority complexes (1934f, 1934g) was a precursor to social psychological inquiries on black Americans and race relations. The goal here was to fight against the internalization of inferiority that he felt preoccupied so much of black life in the early twentieth century (Fullinwider 1969). He believed that culture was a product of one's position in the social structure. Therefore, a reconstitution of that structure would affect the life styles, social codes, and social attitudes of those who toiled at the bottom (1934a). Johnson also spoke of white Americans as psychologically affected by race relations as well that they cultivated attitudes that legitimated the

---

[6]The immense talent of Charles S. Johnson is indicated in the fact that he also carved out his own distinct path away from the Park tradition. His last published work, *Bitter Canaan*, reflected his ability to transcend academic boundaries in order to explore more precisely the social phenomena of his interest. *Bitter Canaan* was a literary work that relied upon the techniques of social scientific investigation to explore the African-American domination of Liberian society in the early 1930s. The uniqueness of this work indicates that Johnson was neither not hindered by the limitations of disciplinary structures or the objectives of the philanthropic entities that he was so heavily involved with in his career. The irony for Johnson was that he considered *Bitter Canaan* his best work, but he could not get it published because of the specific negative reaction that was emitted from reviewers of the manuscript (see Stanfield's "Introductory Essay" in *Bitter Canaan* for more commentary on this aspect of Johnson's life). Here, Johnson was ahead of his time. He had written a book that was critical of oppressive African-American capitalistic exploits at a time when advancement within the cultural parameters of America was considered the ideal for blacks. *Bitter Canaan* was eventually published in 1987, 21 years after Johnson's death.

oppression of African Americans (1934c). However, his comments on that topic were considerably less extensive and less well developed.

Whether the empirical lens was on the urban or rural landscape, much of the theoretical emphasis of the second wave rested in discussions of culture in the African-American community. There was little racial theory from this era of scholars that argued for a distinct and autonomous African-American culture. Instead, the theoretical aims of this generation were to discover and delineate the means by which cultural adaption could take place such that black Americans could gain parity with white Americans (cf. Johnson 1928). In essence, these scholars believed that African Americans brought unique and important contributions to the American cultural scene, but that these contributions were distinctly American, not artifacts of an African cultural retention. E. Franklin Frazier typified this sentiment most clearly in his denial of African cultural retention. Frazier considered blacks to be culturally and socially bounded within the American experience. He assumed, however, that blacks could distance themselves from the mainstream American panorama. Similar to Park's description of the status of the marginal man, Frazier (1924) believed that the social distance that blacks were subjected to provided them with a means by which to consider ways more conducive for adapting to American society than had immigrants before them.

Frazier (1928, 1934) argued that African cultural elements did not survive the Middle Passage and the multigenerational enslavement of blacks. He asserted that African cultural elements in no way survived the Middle Passage to become a part of the Afro-American cultural system (Frazier 1928, 1934). Frazier defined African-American culture as distinctively American in all but skin color. He considered black religious expression—at that time considered one of the most authentic cultural practices of African Americans—to be a distinctively American tradition. He also stressed that the objectives of black education should be to bind the black American to the American experience (Frazier 1928). Frazier's logic in arguing that black Americans were foremost products of the American experience was that he considered the history of blacks in America as a series of social shocks. The order of shocks was, first, the enslavement of blacks on the coast of Africa, followed by the Middle Passage, then the slave experience itself, and lastly, a profound social disorganization following emancipation. In Frazier's mind, the residue from all of this was a folk culture in the South that exemplified the expression of a people attempting to reconcile their awkward status in American society (Fullinwider 1969:105).

Charles Johnson's confrontation with the issue of a cultural link between Africans, American slaves, and the black American community of the twentieth century was done in a much milder form than that of black social thinkers before him. Johnson had extensive scholarly exposure to African-American life in both the South and the North, which allowed him to regard the black American community as an amalgamation of different kinds of experiences each shaped by different patterns of social adjustment to a particular ecological structure. He stressed that different living arrangements, and access to resources and social networks, create a foundation for gauging the level of cultural sophistication of any subgroup of black Americans (1934b). In doing so, Johnson dismissed the views of scholars like Kelly Miller who regarded vice, disease, crime, and unsanitary living as phenomena effecting blacks because of their lack of a civilizing experience (1934b). Instead, he embedded these phenomena in the context of the lack of economic and social resources for better adaptation to city life.

Furthermore, Johnson (1936a,b) stated that although cultural differences existed between Europeans and Africans, this did not imply European cultural superiority. While he did not deny that some cultural elements in African-American life may have derived from Africa, Johnson shared with many of his contemporaries the view that black cultural expression, including religious expression, music, and general attitudes, was distinctly American in its manifestations (Johnson 1934b,d). Moreover, Johnson endorsed Park's view that black Americans had as their only viable option acculturation to dominant American cultural patterns (1934e).

For many of these scholars, the transition to the northern urban sphere of living meant the destruction of a backward folk culture that they believed African Americans maintained while living in the South (Drake & Cayton 1945, Frazier 1928, 1932). This transformation would enhance a developmental process toward social and cultural sophistication that blacks had been undergoing, so argued these scholars, since the end of slavery (Frazier 1968, Johnson 1934c).

These perspectives contrasted with their considerations of southern, rural experiences. The rural context was considered by most of these scholars as the site for the preservation of a folk culture that, while helping to build community cohesiveness, inhibited the capacity of black Americans to respond to modernity (Frazier 1925, 1931, 1934, 1940, Johnson 1934a,b,c). A major statement about the response of African Americans in this social milieu was Bertram Doyle's *Etiquette of Race Relations in the South* (1937), a University of Chicago dissertation that became his most respected publication. His work offered a mild critique of racial inequality in American life, without moving toward a systemic critique of American society. Although not intending to, according to historians of race research in sociology (McKee 1993, Persons 1987), Doyle presented what was taken to be an account of the inertia working against change in race relations in the south. By applying William Graham Sumner's framework of social group adaptation to southern race relations, black Americans were depicted in this work as emotionally committed to traditional forms of racial interaction that could not be radically altered by purposive intervention. With the promotion of such an argument, Doyle's work was similar to most other African-American sociologists of his era (Oliver Cox being the principal exception) who did not incorporate profound cultural criticism of the dominant social order in their work.

E. Franklin Frazier was one of the more critical commentators on any notion of an enduring folk culture of African Americans. He considered the folk culture of the South to be fatalistic as it inhibited African-American adjustment to the urban industrial order. In his dissertation, which was later published as *The Negro Family In Chicago* (1932), Frazier pointed out that slavery-era and post-emancipation black folk culture was an expression of "surrender" to the white man in terms of attitude and acceptance of life.

On the other hand, Johnson provided a slightly different take on the notion of an African-American folk culture. He deemed it an essential arena for social scientific inquiry into the black experience without retreating into the position that such a manifestation was inherently flawed and problematic for African Americans in their struggle to thrive in modern times (Wacker 1983, Stanfield 1987). Johnson believed that the kind of overt, public expressivity displayed by black Americans, a trait strongly associated with African-American folk culture, first emerged as a way to express social criticism of American slavery (1936). Some critics of his view on folk culture asserted that he never clarified whether this phenomenon was an attempt by blacks to create some form of normative culture from what was in the nineteenth century a socially disorganized one, or if this culture was itself a reflection of social disorganization (Stanfield 1985). Regardless of his possible shortcomings in addressing the emergence of black folk culture, a persistent point in Johnson's thought was that folk culture was a substantive phenomenon that had a clear, instrumental role in the southern rural black community in terms of how black southerners responded to the social conditions affecting their lives.

The dark side of folk culture remained in Johnson's extension of the ideas expressed by Bertram Doyle about the effects of race relations on the collective psyche of African Americans (Johnson 1934c, 1936). Johnson argued that the effect of social conditioning in this case was a pervasive feeling of inferiority on the part of black Americans. Johnson argued that blacks suffer an "enforced self-consciousness (that) has developed strange distortions of conduct: it has increased sensitiveness of many Negroes to slights, and prompted the fabrication of compensations for their inferior station" (Johnson 1934f, p. 233).

The debate concerning culture was central to the approaches taken toward policy by the scholars in the second phase. Essentially, these scholars argued that ameliorating the social condition of black Americans necessitated their adaptation to what contemporary scholars would consider American mainstream values and norms. There was some caution about how the adaptation process should evolve. For instance, E. Franklin Frazier's (1928) most persistent concern was that the most capable element of the black community strive for equal footing with whites by way of "temperamental" development rather than focusing on status quests and crass consumption. He hoped that the unique social position of black people would allow them to identify and adopt the best values and mores in American life while disregarding the worst. In making this claim it is evident that Frazier's nationalistic tendencies—a prominent part of the scholarly activities of his later years—were exemplified as early as the mid-1920s.

On the other hand, Charles Johnson affirmed that as victims of the American experience, black Americans required educational opportunities that would allow them to take into account their history and historical condition in order to develop proper perspective (1934h). Johnson, like many of his scholarly peers, claimed that slave culture caused great difficulty in black adjustment to society following emancipation (1936). However, unlike the tradition encouraged by Kelly Miller,

Johnson (1934h) felt that blacks needed to realize, through education, the insignif-icance of racial essentialist claims in matters concerning African-American social advancement. Instead, he felt that the emphasis should be placed on defeating the effects of social conditioning. A "character education," Johnson believed, would combat the sentiment of black social inadequacy that was prevalent in his view of black life (1934h, p. 381). Hence, Johnson stressed that black Americans who were more secure socioeconomically and better adapted to the urban, industrial order take the lead in encouraging the sociocultural advancment of other black Americans (1936).

A more radical, and subsequently much less recognized prescription for the condition of African Americans during this period in time was offered by Oliver C. Cox. Having completed his PhD in 1938 from the Department of Sociology at the University of Chicago, Oliver C. Cox stands at the tail end of the early tradition of African-American sociological thought. With the exception of a few essays that laid the foundation of his thinking (1942, 1943, 1944), all of his major work (1948, 1959, 1962, 1964, 1976) was published after 1945. However, Cox developed his sociological vision during the time of the second wave, and it pro-posed an alternative framework to that construed by the members of the early tradition. Cox opposed pluralistic and nationalistic approaches to race relations; instead he promoted a world systems approach that was predicated on Marxism, yet critical of some aspects of marxist thought. He argued that the capitalist sys-tem grounds the patterns and processes of race relations in American society, and that remaining empirically committed to examining only those relations missed the mark in understanding their manifestation in the larger socio-economic world order. Consequently, Cox's work stood as a precursor to split labor market theories that inspired marxian sociological and economic thought in the years to come, and as a robust critique of the caste arguments forwarded by University of Chicago anthropologist W. Lloyd Warner.

Cox was marginalized within the already marginal African-American sociolog-ical tradition. Some attempts have been made to revisit his work (Hunter 1983a,b, Hunter & Abraham 1987, Robinson 1990) and to situate it within both the world systems brand of marxist sociology and race relations studies. Yet, as the golden age of African-American sociological thought had reached its end, Cox remained on the margins largely because of the ingenuity of his contributions at a time when marxist thought held minimal capital in American sociology. The fact that he was an Afro-Caribbean scholar striving to promote such a framework intensified his marginality (Meier 1977).

The second wave of early African-American sociologists helped to further race studies by enhancing methodological and conceptual approaches to the study of black Americans that delegitimated the racialist paradigm preceding their work. The methodologies included case histories, survey research, census data analysis, the construction of social interaction models, and ethnographic analysis. The re-sult of such applications in the research on black Americans revealed that these subjects were a rich and complex group of people who did not possess an in-herent lack of civilizing qualities based on their race. By rescuing a sense of the humanity of black Americans in an era following one in which their humanity was fervently challenged, these scholars helped to facilitate the twentieth century vision of black Americans as a functional, but troubled, constituency. This resultant image comprised the notion of the Negro Problem that social science became preoccupied with when examining the case of black Americans and American race relations.

CONCLUSION

Throughout the span of the "golden age," African-American sociological thought moved from a defense of the humanity of black Americans to assessments of their social functioning by applying standard conceptual, theoretical, and methdological frameworks. However, the contemporary notion of the Negro Problem was, perhaps, the primary negative consequence of the legacy of these scholars. Some of their work helped to constitute a research tradition that objectified black Americans as a marginal community that was, in critical ways, out of step with mainstream American society. Because they were grounded in white American research traditions and paradigms, the negative consequences of the historical path of these scholars were that black American scholars are left today still struggling to identify the most appropriate devices and concepts to extrapolate about the black American situation.

The early tradition of African-American sociological thought was a period in which African Americans were not considered normative referents in social research. The standard for assessing their cultural and social organizational capacities was the cultural and organizational apparatus of mainstream American society. Clearly, African-American sociologists of that period considered racism to be a pathological response of white Americans toward the black presence in American society. Yet, they did little to critically examine other cultural artifacts of white America in order to explicate what linkages might have existed between them and the social phenomena extant in black life. For instance, the framing of much of African-American culture as underdeveloped and in need of social reform indicates how white America was legitimated as normative in the evaluation of American cultural and social life. Yet a more intensive examination of folk culture in the black community might have brought about a vision of how resistance to oppressive sites, scenes, and conditions, and how reconstitution of meaning for black Americans might have been facilitated through such cultural forms. The suppression of this vision left sociological considerations of the black American narrowly and solely focused on how to make black Americans achieve parity with mainstream America. The issue of how and why their subordination in American society in some ways facilitated their creative capacities both culturally and socially became a marginal issue in sociological inquiry until the late twentieth century. Consequently, there remains much left to explore about African-American sociologists and sociological thought.

The past three decades of American sociology have been an era of increasing recognition and deliberation of the century-long contributions of African-American sociologists (Blackwell & Janowitz 1974, Bowser 1981, Bracey et al 1971, Platt 1991, Watts 1983, Stanfield 1982a,b, 1985, Young 1993). Along with this scholarship has come efforts to document the history of American sociological inquiry on race and race relations (Lyman 1972, McKee 1993), and the republication of a series of classic studies by black American sociologists, including *The Philadelphia Negro* by W.E.B. DuBois (1996 [1899]) and *Black Metropolis* by St. Claire Drake and Horace Cayton (1993 [1945]).

By creating a space for other scholars to recognize the breadth of sociological thought on racial theory, race relations, and social power and subordination, these occurrences have rescued significant sociologists and sociological work from obscurity. The possibilities for reconsidering the development of the sociological cannon now stand before American sociology. Success in this pursuit can only be ensured if those that attend to it do more than celebrate the achievement of African-American scholars who produced in eras of extreme racial oppression. Moreover, such efforts must go beyond the project here of documenting the methodological approaches or findings advanced by these scholars. It must be supplemented by critical discussions of the interplay between the contributions of these scholars and the intellectual resources available at the time. Most importantly, this project must include inquiry into the ontological claims about black and white Americans that such research has either affirmed or implied. Pursuit of the latter task will allow African-American sociological thought to become better connected to the epistemological foundations of the discipline, thereby more fully informing the sociological enterprise.

Visit the Annual Reviews home page at www.AnnualReviews.org

LITERATURE CITED

Appiah A. 1986. The uncompleted argument: DuBois and the illusions of race. In *Race, Writing, and Difference*, ed. HL Gates, Jr. Chicago: Univ. Chicago Press

Baltzell D. 1967 [1899]. Introduction. In *The Philadelphia Negro*, WEB DuBois, pp. ix–xliv. New York: Schoken

Barnett IW. 1987[1892]. *On Lynchings*. Salem, NH: Ayer

Barnett IW. 1991. *Selected Works of Ida B. Wells-Barnett*, ed. T Harris. New York: Oxford Univ. Press

Blackwell J, Janowitz M, eds. 1974. *Black Sociologists: Historical and Contemporary Perspectives*. Chicago: Univ. Chicago Press

Booth C. 1891–1897. *Life and Labour of the People of London*. London/New York: Macmillan

Bowser B. 1981. The contribution of Blacks to sociological knowledge: a problem of theory and role to 1950. *Phylon* XLII(2):180–93

Bracey J, Meier A, Rudwick E. 1971. *The Black Sociologist: The First Half Century*. Belmont, CA: Wadsworth

Broderick FL. 1958a. The academic training of W.E.B. DuBois. *J. Negro Educ.* Winter (27): 10–16

Broderick FL. 1958b. German influences on the scholarship of W.E.B. DuBois. *Phylon* Winter (19):367–71

Broderick FL. 1974. W.E.B. DuBois: history of an intellectual. In *Black Sociologists: Historical and Contemporary Perspectives*, ed. JE Blackwell, M Janowitz, pp. 3–24. Chicago: Univ. Chicago Press

Brodwin S. 1972. The veil transcended: form and meaning in W.E.B. DuBois' *The Souls of Black Folk. J. Black Stud.* March (2):303–21

Bureau of the Census. 1935. *Negroes In The United States*. Washington, DC: US Dep. Commerce

Carby HV. 1987. *Reconstructing Womanhood: The Emergence of the Afro-American Woman Novelist*. New York : Oxford Univ. Press

Cayton H, Mitchell G. 1939. *Black Workers and the New Unions*. Chapel Hill: Univ. N Carolina Press

Collins PH. 1991. *Black Feminist Thought: Knowledge, Consciousness, and the Politics of Empowerment*. New York: Routledge

Cooper AJ. 1892. *A Voice From the South; By A Black Woman of the South*. Xenia, OH: Aldine

Cox OC. 1942. The modern caste school of race relations. *Social Forces* 21(Dec):218–26

Cox OC. 1943. Race relations. *J. Negro Educ.* 12(Spring):14–153

Cox OC. 1944. Racial theories of Robert E. Park, et al. *J. Negro Educ.* 13(Fall):452–63

Cox OC. 1948. *Caste, Class, and Race: A Study in Social Dynamics*. New York: Monthly Reader Paperbacks

Cox OC. 1959. *The Foundations of Capitalism*. New York: Philosophical Library

Cox OC. 1962. *Capitalism and American Leadership*. New York: Philosophical Library

Cox OC. 1964. *Capitalism as a System*. New York: Monthly Rev.

Cox OC. 1976. *Race Relations: Elements and Dynamics*. Detroit: Wayne State Press

Davis A, Dollard J. 1940. *Children of Bondage: The Personality Development of Negro Youth in the Urban South*. Washington, DC: Am. Council Educ.

Davis A, Gardner BR, Gardner MR. 1941. *Deep South: A Social Anthropological Study of Caste and Class*. Chicago: Univ. Chicago Press

De Marco JP. 1983. *The Social Thought of W.E.B. DuBois*. Lanhma, MD: Univ. Press Am.

Dollard J. 1937. *Caste and Class in a Southern Town*. New Haven: Yale Univ. Press

Doyle BW. 1937. *The Etiquette of Race Relations in the South: A Study in Social Control*. Chicago: Univ. Chicago Press

Drake St. C, Cayton H. 1993 [1945]. *Black Metropolis*. Chicago: Univ. Chicago Press

DuBois WEB. 1896. *The Suppression of the African Slave Trade to the United States of America, 1683–1870*. Cambridge, MA: Harvard Hist. Stud. I

DuBois WEB. 1978 [1897a]. The conservation of the races. In *W.E.B. DuBois On Sociology and the Black Community*, ed. DS Green, ED Driver, pp. 238–49. Chicago: Univ. Chicago Press

DuBois WEB. 1897b. The striving of the Negro people. *Atlantic Monthly* 80(Aug):194–98

DuBois WEB. 1898a. The study of Negro problems. *Ann. Am. Acad. Polit. Soc. Sci.*, 11(Jan):1–23

DuBois WEB. 1898b. The Negroes of Farmville, Virginia: a Social Study. *Bull. Dep. Labor*, 14(Jan):1–38. Also in *W.E.B. DuBois On Sociology and the Black Community*, ed. DS Green, ED Driver, pp. 165–96. Chicago: Univ. Chicago Press

DuBois WEB. 1996 [1899a]. *The Philadelphia Negro: A Social Study*. Philadelphia: Univ. Penn. Press

DuBois WEB. 1899b. The Negro in the black belt: some social sketches. *Bull. Dep. Labor*, 4(May):401–17

DuBois WEB. 1900. The twelfth census and the Negro problems. *Southern Workman* 29(Jan):305–9

DuBois WEB. 1901a. The Negro landholder of Georgia. *Bull. Dep. Labor* 6(July):6471–77

DuBois WEB. 1969 [1901b]. *The Black North in 1901: A Social Study*. Reprint New York: Arno Press

DuBois WEB. 1901c. The problem of housing the Negro. *Southern Workman* 30(July–Dec

1901):390–95, 486–93, 535–42, 601–4, 688–93; 31 (Feb 1902):65–72

DuBois WEB. 1901d. The relation of the Negroes to whites in the South. *Ann. Am. Acad. Polit. Soc. Sci.* 18(July):121–40

DuBois WEB. 1902. Of the training of black men. *Atlantic Monthly* 90(Sept):289–97

DuBois WEB. 1986 [1903a]. *The Souls of Black Folk.* New York: Vintage Books

DuBois WEB. 1903b. The laboratory in sociology at Atlanta Univ. *Ann. Am. Acad. Polit. Soc. Sci.* 21(May):160–63

DuBois WEB. 1904a. The talented tenth. In *The Negro Problem: A Series of Articles by Representative American Negroes of Today,* ed. BT Washington. New York: James Pott

DuBois WEB. 1904b. The future of the Negro race in America. *East and West* 2(Jan):4–19

DuBois WEB. 1904c. The Negro farmer. *Bull. Bur. Census, No. 8* Washington, DC: US Govt. Print. Off. (USGPO)

DuBois WEB. 1906. The economic future of the Negro. *Publ. Am. Econ. Assoc.* 7(Feb):219–42

DuBois WEB. 1910. Reconstruction and its benefits. *Am. Hist. Rev.* 15(July):781–99

DuBois WEB. 1969 [1935]. *Black Reconstruction in America, 1860–1880.* New York: Athenium Press.

DuBois WEB. 1970 [1939]. *Black Folk Then and Now: An Essay in the History and Sociology of the Negro Race.* Reprint New York: Octogon

DuBois WEB. 1968 [1940]. *Dusk of Dawn: An Essay Toward An Autobiography of a Concept.* New York: Schoken Books

Frazier EF. 1924. A note on Negro education. *Opportunity* Mar:75–77

Frazier EF. 1925. Social equality and the Negro. *Opportunity* June:165–68

Frazier EF. 1928. The mind of the American Negro. *Opportunity* April:263–66, 284

Frazier EF. 1931. Family disorganization among Negroes. *Oppportunity* July:204–7

Frazier EF. 1932. *The Negro Family In Chicago.* Chicago: Univ. Chicago Press

Frazier EF. 1934. Traditions and patterns of Negro family life in the United States. In *Race and Culture Contacts,* ed. BT Washington. New York: McGraw-Hill

Frazier EF. 1940. *Negro Youth at the Crossways: Their Personality Development in the Middle States.* Washington, DC: Am. Council Educ.

Frazier EF. 1968. Durham: capital of the Black middle class. In *The New Negro,* ed. A Locke. New York: Antheneum

Freedomways. 1965. *W.E.B. DuBois Memorial Issue,* 1

Fullinwider SP. 1969. *The Mind and Mood of Black America.* Homewood, IL: Dorsey

Gaines KK. 1996. *Uplifting The Race: Black Leadership. Politics, and Culture in the Twentieth Century.* Princeton, NJ: Princeton Univ. Press

Giddings P. 1984. *When and Where I Enter: The Impact of Black Women on Race and Sex in America.* New York : Morrow

Gilman SC. 1972. The color line and humanism: an ethical study of W.E.B. DuBois. *J. Hum. Relat.* 20:397–415

Green DS, ED Driver, eds. 1978. Introduction. *W.E.B. DuBois: On Sociology and the Black Community.* Chicago: Univ. Chicago Press

Greene HW. 1946. *Holders of Doctorates Among American Negroes.* Boston: Meador

Hamilton V. 1972. *W.E.B. DuBois: A Biography.* New York: Crowell

Haynes GE. 1912. *The Negro at Work in New York City: A Study in Economic Progress.* New York: Columbia Univ. Press

Haynes GE. 1917. *The Negro Newcomer to Detroit.* Natl. Urban League

Haynes GE. 1921. *Negroes and Work During the World War and Reconstruction.* Washington, DC: Dep. Labor

Haynes GE. 1922. *The Trend of the Races.* New York: Missionary Educ. Movement United States & Canada

Hinkle RC. 1954. *The Development of Modern Sociology, its Nature and Growth in the United States.* New York: Random House

Hofstadter R. 1955. *Social Darwinism in American Thought.* Philadelphia: Univ. Penn. Press

Holt T. 1990. The political uses of alienation:

W.E.B. DuBois on politics, race, and culture. *Am. Q.* 42 (2):

Hooks B. 1981. *Ain't I a Woman : Black Women and Feminism*. Boston: South End

Hunter HM. 1983a. Oliver C. Cox: biographical sketch of his life and work. *Phylon* XLIV (4):249–61

Hunter HM. 1983b. Oliver C. Cox: marxist or intellectual radical? *J. Hist. Sociol.* V(1):1–27

Hunter HM, Abraham S. 1987. Introduction. *Race, Class, and World System: The Sociology of Oliver C. Cox*, ed. HM Hunter, S Abraham. New York: Monthly Review

Janowitz. 1977. See Meier 1977

Johnson CS. 1925. The new frontage on American Life. In *The New Negro*, ed. A Locke. New York: Anthenem

Johnson CS. 1928. The social philosophy of Booker T. Washington. *Opportunity* (April):102–5, 115

Johnson CS. 1934a. Negro personality and changes in a Southern community. In *Race and Contacts*, ed. A Locke. New York: McGraw-Hill

Johnson CS. 1934b. The cultural development of the Negro. See Weatherford & Johnson 1934

Johnson CS. 1934c. *Shadow of the Plantation*. Chicago: Univ. Chicago Press

Johnson CS. 1934d. The African background of the American Negro. In *Race Relations*, ed. WD Weatherford, CS Johnson. Boston: DC Heath

Johnson CS. 1934e. Can there be a separate Negro culture? See Weatherford & Johnson 1934

Johnson CS. 1934f. Social dogmas in race relations. See Weatherford & Johnson 1934

Johnson CS. 1934g. The changing attitude of the Negro. See Weatherford & Johnson 1934

Johnson CS. 1934h. On the need of realism in Negro education. See Weatherford & Johnson 1934

Johnson CS. 1935. Incidents upon the Negroes. *Am. J. Sociol.* XL(6):737–45

Johnson CS. 1936a. *A Preface To Racial Understanding*. New York: Friendship

Johnson CS. 1936b. The conflict of caste and class in an American industry. *Am. J. Sociol.* XLII(2):55–65

Johnson CS. 1941. *Growing Up in the Black Belt: Negro Youth in the Rural South*. Washington, DC: Am. Council on Educ.

Johnson CS. 1943. *Patterns of Negro Segregation*. New York: Harper

Johnson CS. 1970 [1925]. The new frontage on American Life. In *The New Negro*, ed. A Locke. New York: Anthenem

Johnson CS. 1987. *Bitter Canaan*. New Brunswick, NJ: Transaction Books

Johnson CS, Embree ER, Alexander WW. 1935. *The Collapse of Cotton Tenancy*. Chapel Hill: Univ. N Carolina Press

Jones B. 1974. The tradition of sociology teaching in Black colleges: the unheralded profesionals. In *Black Sociologists: Historical and Contemporary Perspectives*, ed. JE Blackwell, M Janowitz, pp. 121–63. Chicago: Univ. Chicago Press

Key C. 1978. Society and sociology: the dynamics of Black sociological negation. *Phylon* 39 (1):35–48

Lacy LA. 1972. *Cheer the Lonesome Traveler: The Life of W.E.B. DuBois*. New York: Dell

Lange WJ. 1983. W.E.B. DuBois and the first scientific study of Afro-America. *Phylon* XLIV

La Rue HC. 1971. W.E.B. DuBois and the pragmatic method of truth. *J. Hum. Relat.* 19:82–96

Lemert C, Esme B. 1998. *The Voice of Anna Julia Cooper: Including A Voice From The South and Other Important Essays, Papers, and Letters*. Lanham SMD: Rowan & Littlefield

Lewis DL. 1993. *W.E.B. DuBois: Biography of a Race*. New York: Henry Holt

Logan RW, ed. 1971. *W.E.B. DuBois: A Profile*. New York: Hill & Wang

Lyman S. 1972. *The Black American in Sociological Thought*. New York: G.P. Putnam

Marable M. 1986. *W.E.B. DuBois: Black Radical Democrat*. Boston: Twayne

Martindale D. 1988. *The Nature and Types of*

Sociological Theory. Prospect Heights, IL: Waveland. 2nd ed.

Matthews FH. 1977. *Quest for an American Sociology: Robert Park*. Montreal: McGill-Queen's Univ. Press

McKee J. 1993. *Sociology and the Race Problem: The Failure of a Perspective*. Champaigne, IL: Univ. Illinois Press

Meier A. 1960. The racial and educational thought of Kelly Miller 1895–1915. *J. Negro Educ*. Spring 121–27

Meier A. 1966. *Negro Thought in America, 1880–1915*. Ann Arbor: Univ. Mich. Press

Meier A. 1977. Review of *Black Sociologists in White America. Social Forces*. 56 (1):259–70

Miller K. 1899. *Primary Needs of the Negro Race*. Washington, DC: Howard Univ.

Miller K. 1900–1901. The Education of the Negro. *US Bur. Educ. Rep*. Washington, DC: USGPO

Miller K. 1900 (circa). *The Negro In The New Reconstruction*. Washington DC: Howard Univ.

Miller K. 1908. *Race Adjustment*. New York: Neale

Miller K. 1918. Appeal to the Conscience: America's Code of Caste—A Disgrace to Democracy. New York: Macmillan

Miller K. 1921. Booker T. Washington: Five Years After. Washington, DC: [Perhaps self-published]

Miller K. 1922. Enumeration errors in the Negro population. *Sci. Monthly* 14(2):168–77

Miller K. 1924. *Everlasting Stain*. Washington, DC: Assoc. Publ.

Miller K. 1933. The past, present, and future of the Negro college. *J. Negro Educ*. July:411–22

Miller K. 1936. The reorganization of the higher education of the Negro in light of changing conditions. *J. Negro Educ*. July:

Miller K. 1980. *An Appeal To Conscience*. New York: Mnemosyne

Moore JB. 1981. *W.E.B. DuBois*. Boston: Twayne

Moses W. 1993. W.E.B. DuBois' The Conser-

vation of race' and its context: idealism, conservatism, and hero worship. *Mass. Rev*. 34 (2):275–94

Moss AA Jr. 1981. *The American Negro Academy*. Baton Rouge: Louisiana State Univ. Press

Mostern K. 1996. Three theories of the race of W.E.B. DuBois. *Cultural Critique*. Fall:27–63

Park RE. 1950a. An autobiographical note. See Wirth et al 1950

Park RE. 1950b. Education in its relation to the conflict of fusion of cultures. See Wirth et al 1950

Park RE. 1950c. The nature of human relations. See Wirth et al 1950

Park RE, Burgess E. 1921. *An Introduction to the Science of Sociology*. Chicago: Univ. Chicago Press

Persons S. 1987. *Ethnic Studies at Chicago*. Urbana, IL: Univ. Ill. Press

Platt AM. 1991. *E. Franklin Frazier Reconsidered*. New Brunswick, NJ: Rutgers Univ. Press

Postock R. 1998. *Color and Culture: Black Writiers and the Making of the Modern Intellectual*. Cambridge: Harvard Univ. Press

President's Conference on Home Building and Home Ownership. 1932. *Report of The Committee On Negro Housing*. Washington, DC

Rampersad A. 1976. *The Art and Imagination of W.E.B. DuBois*. New York: Schoken

Raper AF, Reid I de A. 1941. *Sharecroppers All*. Chapel Hill, NC: Univ. N Carolina Press

Raushenbush W. 1979. *Robert E. Park: Biography of a Sociologist*. Durham, NC: Duke Univ. Press

Reed A. 1997. *W.E.B. DuBois and American Political Thought: Fabianism and the Color Line*. New York: Oxford Univ. Press

Reid I de A. 1927. Mirrors of Harlem: investigations and problems of America's largest colored community. *Soc. Forces* 5(Jun):634

Reid I de A. 1969 [1930]. *Negro Membership in American Labor*. New York: Negro Univ. Press

Reid I de A. 1938. *The Urban Negro Worker in*

the United States, 1925–1936. Washington, DC: USGPO

Reid I de A. 1939. *The Negro Immigrant: His Background Characteristics and Social Adjustment, 1899–1937.* New York: Columbia Univ. Press

Reid I de A. 1940. *In a Minor Key: Negro Youth in Story and Fact.* Washington, DC: Am. Council on Educ.

Residents of Hull House. 1895. *Hull House Maps and Papers.* New York: Crowell

Robinson C. 1990. Oliver Cromwell Cox and the historiography of the West. *Cultural Critique* Winter: 5–19

Ross D. 1991. *The Origins of American Social Science.* Cambridge/New York: Cambridge Univ. Press

Rudwick E. 1957. W.E.B. DuBois and the Atlanta Univ. sudies of the Negro. *J. Negro Educ.* XXVI:466

Rudwick E. 1969. *W.E.B. DuBois: Propagandist of the Negro Protest.* New York: Antheneum

Rudwick E. 1974. W.E.B. DuBois as sociologist. In *Black Sociologists: Historical and Contemporary Perspectives,* ed. JE Blackwell, M Janowitz, pp. 25–55. Chicago: Univ. Chicago Press

Schrager CD. 1996. Both sides of the veil: race, science, and mysticism in W.E.B. DuBois. *Am. Q.* 48(4):551–86

Schwendinger J, Schwendinger H. 1974. *Sociologists of the Chair: A Radical Analysis of the Formative Years of North American Sociology (1883–1922).* New York: Basic

Segrue TJ, Katz MB, eds. 1997. *W.E.B. DuBois, Race, and the City: The Philadelphia Negro and Its Legacy.* Philadelphia: Univ. Penn. Press

Smith SH. 1974. Sociological research and Fisk Univ.: a case study. In *Black Sociologists: Historical and Contemporary Perspectives,* ed. JE Blackwell, M Janowitz, pp. 164–90. Chicago: Univ. Chicago Press

Stanfield JH II. 1982a. The 'Negro Problem' within and beyond the institutional nexus of pre–World War I sociology. *Phylon* XLIII (3):187–201

Stanfield JH II. 1982b. The cracked back door: foundations and Black social scientists between the World Wars. *Am. Sociol.* 17(Nov):193–204

Stanfield JH II. 1985. *Philosophy and Jim Crow in American Social Science.* Westport, CT: Greenwood Press

Stanfield JH II. 1987. Introduction. *Bitter Canaan.* New Brunswick, NJ: Transaction

Szwed J. 1972. An American anthropological dilemma: the politics of Afro-American culture. In *Reinventing Anthropology,* ed. D Hymes. New York

US Bureau of Education. 1900–1901. *The Education of the Negro. United States Bureau of Education Report.* Washington DC: USGPO

Valentine CA. 1968. *Culture and Poverty: Critique and Counter-Proposals.* Chicago: Univ. Chicago Press

Wacker RF. 1983. *Ethnicity, Pluralism, and Race: Race Theory in America Before Myrdal.* Westport, CT: Greenwood

Wallace WL. 1974. Some elements of sociological theory in studies of Black Americans. In *Black Sociologists: Historical and Contemporary Perspectives,* ed. J Blackwell, M Janowitz. Chicago: Univ. Chicago Press

Warner WL. 1936. American caste and class. *Am. J. Sociol.* 42(Sept):234–37

Warner WL, Davis A. 1939. A comparative study of American caste. In *Race Relations and the Race Problem,* ed. ET Thompson. Durham, NC: Duke Univ. Press

Warner WL, Srole L. 1945. *The Social Systems of American Ethnic Groups.* New Haven, CT: Yale Univ. Press

Warner WL, Yunt PS. 1942. *The Status System of a Modern Community.* Yankee City, Vol. II, New Haven: Yale Univ. Press

Warner WL, Lloyd WW, Junker BJ, Adams WA. 1941. *Color and Human Nature: Negro Personality Development in a Northern City.* Washington, DC: Am. Council Educ.

Watts JG. 1983. On Reconsidering Park, Johnson, DuBois, Frazier, and Reid: Reply to

Benjamin Bowser's 'The Contribution of Blacks to Sociological Knowledge'. *Phylon* XLIV(4):273–91

Weatherford WD, Johnson CS, eds. 1934. *Race Relations*. Boston: DC Heath

West C. 1990. *The American Evasion of Philosophy: A Genealogy of Pragmatism*. Madison: Univ. Wisc. Press

Wirth L. 1928. *The Ghetto*. Chicago: Univ. Chicago Press

Wirth L, Hughes EC, et al. 1950. *Race and Culture: The Collective Papers of Robert Ezra Park*. Glencoe, IL: Free Press

Wright RR. 1905. The Negro in times of industrial unrest. *Charities* 15(Oct):7

Wright RR. 1912. *The Negro in Pennsylvania: A Study in Economic History*. Philadelphia: A.M.E. Book Concern Printers

Young AA Jr. 1993. The 'Negro Problem' and the Social Character of the Black Community: Charles S. Johnson, E. Franklin Frazier, and the Constitution of a Black Sociological Tradition, 1920–1935. *Natl. J. Sociol.* 7(1):95–133

Zamir S. 1995. *Dark Voices*. Chicago: Univ. Chicago Press

Annu. Rev. Sociol. 2001. 27:479–504

HATE CRIME: An Emergent Research Agenda

Donald P. Green[1], Laurence H. McFalls[2], and
Jennifer K. Smith[1]

[1]Department of Political Science, Yale University, New Haven, Connecticut 06520-8301;
e-mail: Donald.Green@yale.edu, Jennifer.Smith@yale.edu
[2]Département de Science Politique, Université de Montréal, Montréal, Québec H3C 3J7,
Canada; e-mail: Laurence.McFalls@umontreal.ca

Key Words bias crime, prejudice, discrimination, racial violence

■ **Abstract**   Hate crime is difficult to define, measure, and explain. After summarizing some of the leading conceptual issues and theoretical perspectives, we discuss the practical difficulties associated with data collection. Although the research literature remains small and largely descriptive, recent studies have begun to relate hate crime patterns to economic cycles, population flows, and changes in the political environment. The task ahead is to extend these analyses to other settings and levels of aggregation.

INTRODUCTION

Those seeking to understand the nature and origins of bigoted violence are likely to be disappointed by extant scholarship on prejudice, racism, and discrimination. Although many scholars aspire to explain behavioral manifestations of intergroup hostility, this literature is dominated by the investigation of attitudes and beliefs. Study after study examines how adults regard minority groups and policies designed to advance minority interests (for a recent overview, see Sears et al., 2000), typically relying on surveys to gauge what is variously termed prejudice, intolerance, racism, or xenophobia. Although survey researchers assess prejudice in increasingly sophisticated ways (see Fazio et al., 1995; Hurwitz & Peffley 1998), they devote relatively little attention to the study of prejudiced conduct, apart from voting behavior. Behavioral manifestations of prejudice figure more prominently in the work of social psychologists, but the laboratory experiments that dominate this literature are often contrived and rely almost entirely on undergraduate subjects. A small number of field experiments or unobtrusive studies of bigotry (Crosby et al., 1980; Kremer et al., 1986; Fix & Struyk 1993) focus on behavioral data to assess the pervasiveness of prejudice, but these studies tend not to link patterns of behavior to contextual factors such as economic conditions, levels of residential segregation, and the like. It might take the better part of a lifetime to read the prodigious research literature on prejudice, particularly if one were to include studies that investigate the manner in which institutions, organizations, and social groups have introduced, perpetuated, or dismantled discriminatory practices and policies throughout the world. Yet, scarcely any of this research examines directly and systematically the question of why prejudice erupts into violence.

This lacuna has grown increasingly apparent in recent years as scholars have turned their attention to the subject of hate crime. The term hate crime is commonly used to refer to unlawful, violent, destructive, or threatening conduct in which the perpetrator is motivated by prejudice toward the victim's putative social group. Although hate crime can scarcely be called a new phenomenon, the term came into currency in the United States during the 1980s, following a series of well-publicized incidents directed at Jews, Asians, and blacks. The topic of hate crime, and the term itself, gained prominence internationally as a wave of what was otherwise termed racist or antiforeigner violence swept Northern Europe during the 1990s. These incidents and the publicity surrounding them attracted unprecedented attention from both journalists and policy makers. For the first time, public agencies and community organizations made a concerted effort to document incidents and track patterns. Although data gathering proved to be fraught with problems, it helped foster a nascent research literature, particularly in the United States and Germany.

This article attempts to describe the principal research questions in this literature, assemble important empirical results, and suggest directions for future investigation. We begin by explicating the concept of hate crime, distinguishing it from ordinary crime, bigoted attitudes, bigoted but lawful conduct, state-sanctioned discrimination, and ethnic warfare. Next, we summarize leading theories of why hate crimes occur, drawing out, where possible, their testable empirical implications. Turning to the research literature, we provide an overview of the empirical studies that have examined the social, political, and economic contexts in which hate crimes are more likely to occur. To complement these ecological studies, we also consider ethnographic and survey evidence concerning the psychological characteristics of hate crime perpetrators and the social milieux in which they operate. Finally, we discuss what extant theory and evidence imply about ways of reducing the incidence and severity of hate crime.

DEFINITIONS

The terms hate crime and bias crime were coined in the United States during the 1980s, as journalists and policy advocates groped for new terminology to describe bigoted violence directed against Jews, blacks, and homosexuals.[1]

---

[1]Germany's Basic Law and federal statutes forbid racist, Nazi-inspired, and other extremist behavior and organizations. As a result, legislation in Germany tends to skew the definition and measurement of hate crime toward its ideological and organized forms (cf. Aronowitz 1994).

Unlike other neologisms, such as ethnoviolence (Pincus & Ehrlich 1994), racially motivated crime (Green et al., 1998b), antiforeigner violence (Krell et al., 1996), or heterosexist violence (Herek 1992), hate crime encompasses unlawful conduct directed at a wide array of different target groups. Moreover, the term refers not simply to acts of violence, but also to crimes involving destruction of property, harassment, or trespassing. Thus, such disparate phenomena as cross burnings in front of homes owned by blacks, vandalism directed against Jewish cemeteries, and assaults against men leaving putatively gay bars are brought together under a common heading. Existing definitions specify various (*a*) applicable target groups, (*b*) forms of illegal conduct, and (*c*) types of motivation as characteristics of hate crime. Before offering our own views, let us first summarize the range of existing definitions.

Applicable Target Groups

To proponents of hate crime legislation, the breadth of conduct that can be encompassed within the definition of hate crime is one of its main virtues. Still, there is little agreement across jurisdictions on the list of protected groups. Fewer than half of all states with hate crime laws specify sexual orientation as a protected category (Wang 1994) because, ironically, legislators are frequently unsympathetic to laws designed to help gay men and lesbians or in any way legitimate their "lifestyles" (Berrill & Herek 1992, pp. 291–93; Jenness & Broad 1997, p. 42; Haider-Markel & Meier 1996). Social scientists tend to be more inclusive in their definition of hate crime, but the boundaries differ from one scholar to the next. For example, Boyd et al (1996, p. 819) define hate-motivated crimes as "crimes committed against persons or property that are motivated by the perpetrator's hatred or prejudice against the racial, ethnic, religious, or sexual identity of the victim." Craig (1999, p. 139) and Barnes & Ephross (1994, p. 247) broaden this definition somewhat to include physical disability, while Craig & Waldo (1996, p. 113) offer the most expansive definition: "Crimes that are motivated by hate include words or actions intended to harm or intimidate an individual because of his or her perceived membership in or association with a particular group." In the latter definition, all groups become protected categories.

Formulating a principled defense of any particular list of protected groups is complicated further by the two-sided quality of each category. To specify, for example, that hate crime encompasses violence motivated by racial hatred means that both white-on-black and black-on-white attacks are lumped into the same classification. Whatever its merits as public policy or as a vehicle for consensus building, an evenhanded definition that makes no distinction between attacks committed by dominant as opposed to subordinate groups poses a challenge to those who seek to explain why hate crime occurs. Should one expect that the same factors that propel straight-on-gay attacks also produce gay-on-straight attacks? Scholars such as Craig (1999, p. 139) sidestep this problem by defining hate crime to be "an illegal act involving intentional selection of a victim based on a perpetrator's bias or prejudice that relates to either the actual or perceived status of the victim" but stipulating that "[v]ictims of hate crimes include members of racial, ethnic, and religious minority groups, gays, lesbians, and bisexuals, as well as the physically challenged." By this definition, hate crime is restricted to unlawful conduct directed at subordinate groups.

Forms of Conduct

What kinds of unlawful activity constitute hate crime? The expansive definition by Craig & Waldo given above encompasses activities ranging from violence to "words . . . intended to harm." More restrictive definitions confine hate crime to violence against persons or property, a category that usually includes criminal threats but rules out behaviors such as illegal housing discrimination. Most US statutes conform to the latter definition and enhance the punishment for conventional forms of crime when they are committed by someone motivated by bigotry.[2]

In addition, a number of states also have specific prohibitions against cross burnings and institutional vandalism, acts that involve criminal mischief and trespassing. Unlike Germany, which forbids the display of Nazi flags and dissemination of racist literature, the United States allows individuals and political groups to advocate racial hatred and even genocide. Thus, while right-wing political activity is often discussed in conjunction with hate crime (Hamm 1994a, Kleg 1993), the two are conceptually distinct.

Motivation

A common ingredient in the aforementioned definitions is bigoted motivation. The perpetrator attacks out of contempt or disdain for the perceived social characteristics of the victim. Motivation presents a range of conceptual and epistemological problems (Berk 1990). Must this motivation be the exclusive reason for the hate crime in question, or is it sufficient for prejudice to be one of several motives? When hate crime is defined to encompass only those acts entirely motivated by animus, crimes such as robbery and rape are presumably excluded from the definition. When animus need be just one of several motives, however, the definition becomes porous. Any trace of hate motivation in the selection of targets or the manner in which a crime is carried out would then warrant its classification as a

---

[2]Lawrence (1999) points out that hate crime statutes in the United States vary in the kinds of motivations they ascribe to the perpetrator. Regulations promulgated by the Federal Bureau of Investigation in the wake of the Hate Crime Statistics Act define bias crime as criminal conduct motivated in whole or in part by negative attitudes toward the victim's group, whereas other statutes, including the statute upheld by the Supreme Court in *Wisconsin v. Mitchell*, require only that the perpetrator select the victim because of his or her putative group membership. The latter standard potentially encompasses crimes such as purse snatching, which may not arise from misogyny but may involve the discriminatory selection of female targets. For further discussion of the nature and diffusion of hate crime law, see Jenness (1999) and Grattet et al (1998).

hate crime. As a practical matter, this definition generates a presumption that intergroup crime is hate crime. This presumption has special relevance to hate crime statutes that include gender as a protected category, since rape may be regarded as an expression of misogyny.

One interesting but apparently incidental feature of definitions that require hate motivation is that, under ordinary circumstances, only individuals can commit hate crimes. Motives per se are generally not attributable to states, political parties, or other corporate entities that authorize violence against a particular group. In our view, the exclusion of institutions from the purview of these definitions is fortuitous. The study of spontaneous or loosely coordinated actions by individuals and small groups has a very different feel from systematic persecution carried out by a state. Granted, the two can be causally related, as when a state encourages (or does nothing to discourage) acts of violence against particular groups. But a theory of why actors within states and other organizations authorize and pursue certain courses of action will doubtless look very different from a theory that seeks to explain why street-level actors behave as they do. Somewhere in between are ethnic riots (Horowitz 1985, 2001) and acts of bigoted violence carried out by members of right-wing groups, which range from spontaneous acts of pell-mell violence to carefully orchestrated acts of terrorism.

If we accept that motivation is an essential ingredient in hate crime, what kind of motivations suffice? One is the desire to terrorize a broader social group, as when a person scrawls anti-Semitic threats on a synagogue or singles out a victim who will be "made an example of." A second motivation is more elemental: The perpetrator lashes out against targets because he fears or despises the group to which they belong. In both cases, specific targets are selected based on their putative group characteristics. A different form of motivation is a desire to elevate one's esteem in the eyes of others or oneself. The gang member who believes that his attacks against other racial groups will command greater status in the eyes of his peers may single out victims on account of their race, even if he harbors no special racial hatred (Levin & McDevitt 1993). Whether this kind of other-directed hate crime satisfies the definition has direct bearing on the classification of many incidents involving juveniles, who often protest that their conduct was a prank rather than a manifestation of hatred toward the target group.

These practical concerns loom large when considering the issue of motive. Even under ideal circumstances motivation is often difficult to discern. While it is tempting to rely on extrinsic evidence of bigoted motivation—e.g., the perpetrator hurled racial epithets during the attack or has a history of bigoted statements and conduct—one can never pin down motivation with certainty. Racial epithets might be exchanged during an altercation not because an assault was racially motivated but because name-calling is simply the parlance of violent struggle. A perpetrator's history of racial hatred is relevant but nonetheless circumstantial evidence. In sum, the task of establishing empirical criteria for discerning motivation is as complex and difficult as that of formulating persuasive definitions.

Synthesis

Faced with so much conceptual uncertainty, it is tempting for scholars to regard the very notion of hate crime as specious—an outgrowth of "identity politics" rather than a serious object of inquiry (cf. Jacobs & Potter 1998). To be sure, it is difficult, if not impossible, to adjudicate among the competing definitions on purely conceptual grounds without imposing a series of rather arbitrary stipulations. Still, a great many conceptual issues can be reexpressed as empirical questions. Imagine, for example, that researchers develop a statistical model describing the causes of hate crime. To what extent are the quantitative results affected when they expand or contract the definition's scope? That is, how do the results change when cases of hate crime are admitted or dropped depending on different criteria concerning motivation, unlawful conduct, or target groups? If results are consistent across different definitions (cf. Krueger & Pischke 1997; Green & Rich 1998), one may conclude that definitional issues do not bear directly on the question of how hate crime covaries with other variables. On the contrary, if results do vary with definition, then a further empirical question is whether these patterns of change are interpretable theoretically. Finding that "ordinary" white-on-black murders have different predictors than corresponding racially motivated homicides suggests that hate crime has its own special characteristics. By the same token, finding that black-on-white hate crime has different correlates from white-on-black hate crime suggests the importance of distinguishing between majority and minority perpetrators. This inductive approach does not resolve questions of definition but transforms them into issues that themselves become part of the research process.

THEORETICAL EXPLANATIONS OF HATE CRIME

General Typology

The ambiguities and debates surrounding the definition of hate crime are reflected in the competing theoretical explanations of this phenomenon. Varying explanations for hate-motivated crime reflect different elements of the possible definitions, alternatively emphasizing, for example, the circumstances of criminal acts, the sources and translation of motivations, or the sociocultural construction of hate targets. Any typology of hate crime theories must distinguish between two broad levels of analysis: individual and societal.

Individual-level analyses seek to understand the psychological causes that impel people to commit hate crimes. Sometimes these causes are sought in enduring psychological orientations or propensities; in other cases, hate crime is said to arise because individuals with certain kinds of beliefs and aversions find themselves in situations where these psychological attributes are brought to the fore. In contrast to individual-level analyses, macrosociological theories focus attention on broad social forces, such as modernization, integration, or economic downturn, that may lead to a surge in aggregate rates of hate crime. Just as Durkheim (1951) proffered an etiological analysis of suicide by constructing suicide as a "social fact" and looked for the sociostructural correlates of suicide rates without regard for the circumstances and personal profiles of individual suicides (i.e., their morphology), the second, sociological approach to hate crime seeks to establish the social, economic, and political conditions favorable to the proliferation of individual hate crimes. Not surprisingly, given the extreme difficulty of studying hate crime (or suicide) by tracking individuals over time and recording their behavior, most theoretical accounts of hate crime adopt this societal level of analysis.

Although researchers do not always state their theoretical premises explicitly and often combine perspectives into multicausal narrative accounts, it is possible to identify at least six general types of explanation for hate crime: (*a*) psychological, (*b*) social-psychological, (*c*) historical-cultural, (*d*) sociological, (*e*) economic, and (*f*) political. Our classification of different researchers and explanations within this rather coarse typology is meant to indicate the variety of approaches and competing potential hypotheses for continuing hate crime research. We briefly delineate the theoretical approaches subsumed within these six types before considering some theoretical syntheses.

Psychological Traits

Most theoretical accounts of hate crime assume a necessary psychological cause, since leading definitions of hate crime presuppose individual hostility toward the victim's social group. Individual-level psychological accounts of hate crime, however, limit themselves to the analysis of the cognitive and affective processes by which perpetrators identify their victims, generate hostility, and become disposed to aggression and violence. This approach both defines and explains hate crime as an extreme or disproportionate form of prejudice (Kleg 1993; Roberts 1995) and usually draws on Allport (1954), according to which the common cognitive shorthand of stereotyping coupled with affective disorders, ranging from frustration to guilt avoidance, projection, and paranoia, pushes individuals to acts of discrimination, ranging from avoidance to insults, assault, and extermination. Theories of authoritarian personalities (Adorno et al., 1950; Altmeyer 1981) elaborate this model of hate crime by characterizing the psychological attributes and formative experiences of individuals most liable to resort to prejudiced violence (Maaz 1991; Heitmeyer 1992; Hopf et al., 1995; Modena 1998; see also the discussion of Pfeiffer in Sharma 1999). Although the idea that a particular personality profile can identify hate crime perpetrators appeals to journalists as well as educators, social workers, and police, individual psychological accounts do not suffice, for as attitudinal surveys confirm (Green et al., 1999), hate criminals may have authoritarian tendencies, but only a small subset of authoritarians are hate criminals.

Social-Psychological Explanations

To get at the sufficient causes of hate crime, social-psychological theories seek to identify not only the source of potentially violent prejudicial orientations but also the circumstances under which they will express themselves. Models of small group dynamics suggest how contagion, conformism, extremification of attitudes, disinhibition, and yearning for group acceptance can all conspire to push a person to acts of hate crime (Böhnisch & Winter 1993; Erb 1993; Willems et al., 1993; Watts 1996; Rieker 1997; Wahl 1997). Accounts of hate crime committed by members of white supremacist groups, in particular, tend to attribute this behavior to peer-group pressure (Kleg 1993, p. 182) or group norms (Hamm 1994b). Ethnographic studies emphasize the power of community norms (e.g. Rieder 1985; Suttles 1972) or racist youth subcultures (e.g. Sichrovsky 1993; Frindte et al., 1996) as forces that legitimate and encourage attacks against out-groups.

Other social-psychological approaches focus on the interplay between psychological orientations and broader societal influences. European scholars in particular attribute a significant causal role to the electronic and print media. Not only does media coverage of hate crime, particularly sensationalist coverage of spectacular events, allegedly have a demonstration effect that can produce a hate crime contagion (Esser & Brosius 1995, 1996), the media can also instigate hate crime by formulating, propagating, and legitimating stereotypes about potential target populations. Linguistic, semiotic, and communications analysts stress the role of the media in creating meaning and hence the motives for hate crime (Weiss 1993; Scheffer 1997; Jäger & Kretschmer 1998). Political scientists emphasize the media's dissemination of hate-mongering political discourse produced by elites, parties, and other organized groups (Leenen 1995; Karapin 1996; Koopmans 1996). The media, it is argued, make possible politicians' cynical manipulation and exacerbation of existing racist or homophobic sentiments for electoral ends (Thränhardt 1995; von Trotha 1995).

Historical-Cultural Accounts

An emphasis on political discourse also characterizes historical-cultural explanations of hate crime, although from the latter perspective discourse is not subject to short-term manipulation. Instead, political discourse and political culture as well as propensities for hate crime are rooted in longstanding, if not immutable, cultural traditions and patterns of behavior. Thus, for example, one Canadian scholar suggests that the lower rate of violent hate crime in his country relative to the structurally similar United States is attributable to Canada's history as a "peaceable kingdom" with a tradition of deference to authority (Ross 1992, p. 94). Indeed, the very manner in which societies define and debate hate crime depends on their political-cultural traditions, so that a similar occurrence might be termed a racial incident in Britain, an attack on republican values in France, and a problem with refugee policy in Germany. Although historical-cultural explanations seldom, if ever, succeed in demonstrating causality, they nonetheless gain plausibility in light of striking and consistent differences in rates of hate crime between similar societies (cf. Koopmans 1996), assuming of course that these differences are not artifacts of reporting criteria and data collection.

In the wake of Germany's hate crime wave in the 1990s, historical and cultural arguments predictably dominated both journalistic and academic explanations. Although serious scholarship discounted the claim that outbreaks of racist violence and the resurgence of the far right marked the simple revival of Nazism (Merkl & Weinberg 1997; Prowe 1997), social scientists and social critics did link contemporary right-wing extremism and xenophobic violence to the Nazi past by way of an on-going national identity crisis exacerbated by reunification in 1990 (Tuttle 1994; von Trotha 1995; McFalls 1997).

Sociological Accounts

Similar to broad historical-cultural explanations in their abstraction away from individual incidents of hate crime are sociological explanations that draw on classic Durkheimian modernization theory. These accounts treat hate crime as a variant of youth violence and delinquency, phenomena attributable to the ravages of rapid social change. Hate crime results alternatively from an anomic outburst of socially disintegrated individuals or from the solidaristic reaction of a threatened community or group. In either case, hate crime is the work of collective or individual losers of modernization. This model enjoyed prominence in Germany before unification (Heitmeyer 1987) and seemed to win confirmation with the outburst of racist violence in eastern Germany after 1990. Indeed, modernization theory dominated postcommunist transformation studies of the former German Democratic Republic (Habermas 1990) in part because it offered a parsimonious and plausible explanation for antiforeigner hostility: Economic dislocation, the breakdown of social norms and authority, and unprecedented social and spatial mobility coincided with an upsurge in racist hate crime (Heitmeyer 1992; Boers et al., 1994; Hagan et al., 1995; Willems 1995; Watts 1996).

While the radical and rapid changes of postcommunist transformation suggest a temporally and spatially unique explanation for hate crime, another variant of modernization theory aspires to universal validity. "Globalization," or an unprecedented international circulation of goods, services, people, and ideas, allegedly represents a qualitative leap in modernization, the consequences of which in developed societies include the social and economic exclusion of the unskilled and undereducated as well as their easy identification as scapegoats in the growing migrant population. Such a theoretical perspective at least implicitly underpins much of the empirical research linking antiforeigner violence to immigration and unemployment rates (Alber 1994; Krell et al., 1996; Chapin 1997; McLaren 1999).

Economic Accounts

Although an emphasis on social change links the two, sociological theories of hate crime stress the anomie engendered by social disintegration, whereas economic theories see the roots of hate crime in displaced frustration and competition for material resources. Raper's (1933) observation that antiblack lynchings and cotton prices were inversely correlated was interpreted by Hovland & Sears (1940) to mean that Southern whites displaced the frustrations caused by economic down-turns onto vulnerable racial targets. The theme of frustration and unmet economic needs figures prominently in Pinderhughes's (1993) ethnographic study of hate crime perpetrators in New York City and remains a prominent explanation for hate crime in general (Hamm 1994b).

The link between macroeconomic downturn and hate crime has also been inter-preted as an outgrowth of intergroup competition for scarce economic resources. In their investigation of lynching patterns over time, Tolnay & Beck (1995) con-tend that "whites attacked when they believed that blacks were threatening their privileged access to . . . society's scarce resources" (1995, p. 59). Realistic group conflict theory (LeVine & Campbell 1972), which argues that hostilities arise from power differentials among groups, has prompted several recent attempts to gauge the connection between economic hardship in postunification Eastern Germany and the proliferation of racist attitudes and acts there (Legge 1996; Krueger & Pischke 1997; McLaren 1999). Although realistic group conflict theory instructs researchers to look for connections between sources of economic contention and hate crime, it leaves open a variety of core empirical questions. Which dimensions of economic competition (jobs, housing, education) matter? Should one expect an established group to attack preemptively when a challenging group is small and weak, or when the dominant group is on the verge of losing its numerical or power advantage (cf. Green et al., 1998b, p. 373–78)? The subjective perception of "realistic" conflict may well depend on whether frustrations are made salient and mobilized by political elites and interest groups (Olzak 1989; Green et al., 1998a).

Political Accounts

Political theories of hate crime seek to explain the mobilization of grievances—whether rooted in frustration, fear, or disdain. One political explanation of hate crime draws on social movement theory to argue that beyond the strength of their particular real or imagined grievances toward their victims, hate criminals are moved to act on the basis of the "political opportunity structure," i.e., the availability of channels to express grievances, the legitimacy of grievances within public and political discourse, and the likelihood of prevention or punishment of hate-motivated crimes (Karapin 1996; Koopmans 1996).[3]

---

[3]Another political theory of hate crime considers it not a social phenomenon that may be facilitated by political circumstances but rather a political movement per se. This conception of hate crime, however, derives from definitional confusion. Outside the United States in particular, the term hate crime is practically synonymous with extreme right-wing violence, and (as a glance at the titles in the bibliography below illustrates) an assimilation of the two phenomena often occurs. Thus, many researchers implicitly posit that hate crime arises from the prevalence and strength of racist attitudes and ideology in the population at large (Heitmeyer 1992; Frindte et al., 1996; Watts 1996; Esses et al., 1998), and some simply assume, contrary to empirical evidence, that racist violence is necessarily the work of

These arguments lead to divergent explanations of the wave of antiforeigner violence in postreunification Germany. One account attributes xenophobic violence to the absence of a legitimate electoral outlet, that is, an organized right-wing political party akin to the French National Front (Koopmans 1996, p. 207). Other researchers ascribe the surge in xenophobic violence to inflammatory statements by politicians who appeared to condone racist violence (Leenen 1995; Karapin 1996) and to the timidity, incompetence, or racist complicity of the police and courts (Weitekamp et al., 1996; Hess 1997; Ireland 1997; Müller-Münch 1998). A more synoptic account of how politics engenders hate crime must therefore distinguish the cathartic effects of opportunity from the amplifying effects of elite encouragement.

Theoretical Syntheses

Recurrent among the aforementioned theories are the themes of competition-bred grievance, the salience of group-related discord, and normalization of violence against out-groups. Synthesizing these perspectives means integrating structural and social-psychological approaches. While structural perspectives suggest potential sources of intergroup friction, social-psychological investigation illuminates the manner in which macrosociological phenomena are apprehended and transformed into behavioral proclivities. Surprisingly few researchers, however, have drawn on both objective conditions and subjective interpretation in constructing theories specific to hate crime. One exception is Hamm (1994b), who integrates psychological, communicational, sociological, and political variables in his "modified deterrent vicarious social control theory," but at the cost of excluding most hate crimes, which are not the work of organized ideological groups. Similarly, Koopmans' (1996) and Karapin's (1996) applications of social movement theory to the rise of racist and right-wing violence in Western Europe in the early 1990s combine real and perceived grievances with objectively as well as subjectively constructed opportunity structures. These models, though, seem inapplicable to the day-to-day hate crimes that occur in times or places outside the purview of any identifiable social movement.

A more broadly applicable theoretical synthesis is offered by Green et al (1998b), whose multicausal "defended-neighborhoods" model endeavors to explain both spectacular hate crime waves, such as the one that appeared to follow the massive influx of refugees into Germany in the early 1990s (Aronowitz

---

organized and ideologically informed Skinhead gangs or neo-Nazi thugs. Although he distinguishes between hate crime in general and the particular forms of it associated with groups such as Skinheads, neo-Nazis, or the Ku Klux Klan, Hamm (1993, 1994b,c) proposes a theoretical model of hate crime that applies only to its organized, ideological form. Hamm defends his narrow conceptualization of hate crime on the grounds that "neo-Nazi skinheads are responsible for the most egregious acts of violence in the world today" (1994c, p. 175), but in doing so he leaves the overwhelming majority of hate crimes beyond the purview of his theory.

1994), and the consequences of the movement of Asians into London's East End (Bowling 1994) and similar population flows in American cities. Like realistic group conflict theory, the defended neighborhood hypothesis postulates that interracial violence results from demographic movement in which the arrival of members of a different group prompts the violent response of the homogenous, locally dominant group. This "defensive" or exclusionary action does not, however, follow mechanistically from the power differential between the dominant and challenging groups but from the belief anchored in the collective identity of the established group that the in-migrating group threatens its status, well-being, or way of life. Since it incorporates subjective motives, the defended-neighborhood model predicts that hate crime against members of the arriving group will be greatest at the beginning of a sudden influx, not because the newcomers' greater numbers later on alter the local balance of power in their favor but because social learning changes the "host" group's collective identity and values. In other words, as familiarity defuses contempt and communities redefine their identity to include new members, the hostility that greeted the first significant group of newcomers gives way to acceptance or indifference, and those prone to violence lose the active encouragement or passive acceptance of their community.

As presented by Green et al (1998b), the defended-neighborhoods perspective incorporates many, but not all, of the central perspectives described here. Notably absent is a discussion of politics. A more general model could incorporate the role of elites in defining which boundaries must be defended, which outsiders must be excluded, and what forms of exclusion are permissible. When viewed in historical perspective, the form and frequency of hate crime seems closely connected to elite behavior; one cannot understand the advent and decline of lynching, for example, without reference to the tacit (and sometimes active) support of public officials (Finkelman 1992).

EMPIRICAL RESEARCH FINDINGS

The empirical investigation of the causes of hate crime remains a science in its infancy. Although a relatively large literature exists on the jurisprudence of hate crime legislation (e.g. Greenspan & Levitt 1993; Ross 1994; Jacobs & Potter 1998; Lawrence 1999), on law enforcement (e.g. Taylor 1991; Roberts 1995), and on patterns, rates, and effects of victimization (e.g. D'Augelli 1992; Barnes & Ephross 1994; Herek et al., 1997; Craig 1999), little rigorous empirical work on the causes of hate crime in North America and Western Europe has been published. To be sure, the outburst of xenophobic violence in Germany in the 1990s gave impetus to the international and occasionally comparative investigation of hate crime, yet, as we see below, not much conclusive evidence has emerged, in part due to the persistent absence of reliable, consistent, and disaggregated statistical data. Most published work consists of speculative historical narratives that adduce evidence for a particular explanation of hate crime on the basis of journalistic accounts and aggregated statistics provided by government agencies or victims' advocacy groups. We mentioned and cited much of this literature in the previous section. The remaining empirical studies can be classified as either (*a*) descriptive studies, (*b*) morphological investigations, (*c*) attitudinal surveys, (*d*) media analyses, or (*e*) ecological or etiological studies.

Data Quality

Antecedent to any causal explanation of hate crime must be its documentation. In addition to the publications of organizations such as the Anti-Defamation League, Klanwatch, and the National Gay and Lesbian Task Force, many scholarly and journalistic accounts describe and denounce incidents of hate crime, occasionally with language that betrays a greater concern with normative than with methodological issues. The sometimes lurid and sensationalist quality of this work has invited skeptics to criticize unsubstantiated claims about trends and epidemics (Jacobs & Heney 1996), but both the reports and the criticism surrounding them have contributed to scholarship on hate crime by impelling public authorities to devote resources to data collection.

In Germany, for example, the federal government did not provide a monthly report on xenophobic crimes by type and state until pressured by the parliamentary questions of a civil rights activist legislator and her publication of journalistic chronologies of hate crime (Jelpke 1993). Journalistic reports have also served as the basis for attempts to construct statistical descriptions of hate crime patterns where official statistics do not exist, are unreliable, or have only recently been collected (Ross 1992; Karapin 1996; Krueger & Pischke 1997). The latter conditions unfortunately apply virtually everywhere. In the United States, federal law requires the Federal Bureau of Investigation to collect hate crime statistics on an annual basis, but the Bureau is reliant on the voluntary compliance of state and local jurisdictions, each of which has different reporting standards. Many US states supply no information. In Germany, where federal statistics appear to be consistent and complete, the definition of antiforeigner crimes has changed over the 1990s, and nothing guarantees consistent reporting standards across jurisdictions (Boyd et al., 1996). As a result, hate crime researchers are at a loss to make trustworthy comparisons of hate crime rates across jurisdiction. The same argument applies as well to comparisons across victim groups, since different types of victims may have different propensities to report incidents to police (Comstock 1991).

Somewhat more reliable, though hardly unproblematic, are comparisons within a single jurisdiction (Bowling 1993). If the jurisdiction is studied longitudinally, one must assume that the rate at which incidents are reported remains constant over time. This requirement rules out the use of data from newly created data collection agencies. For example, the Los Angeles County Commission on Human Relations reported 4 racially motivated and 26 religiously motivated hate crimes when its data gathering efforts began in 1981; by 1989, with both increasing public awareness of hate crime and improved police reporting procedures, these numbers had risen to 167 and 125 (Los Angeles County Comm. Hum. Relat. 1990, p. 2). An implication of this pattern is that the institutional development of monitoring agencies may give rise to spurious trends.

Several recent studies have employed cross-sectional and longitudinal comparison within jurisdiction for specific target groups. Green et al. (1998b) examined racially motivated hate crime in 51 communities of New York City, using data gathered by the New York Police Department (NYPD) for the period 1987–1995. Green & Rich (1998) studied cross burnings at the county level in North Carolina for the period 1987–1993, using data gathered by two different hate crime monitoring organizations. The most ambitious attempt to measure cross-sectional variation in hate crime is Green et al (2001), who use a multi-method, multi-trait design. Hate crime against gay men and lesbians is measured using both NYPD data and reports gathered by the Anti-Violence Project, while both census and market research data are used to assess gay and lesbian population density. Heartening to those who lament the problems of obtaining reliable hate crime reports is the central finding of this study: Despite the fact that the Anti-Violence Project and the NYPD have different reporting procedures, apply different definitions of hate crime, and report total numbers of incidents directed against gay men that differ by a factor of six, the correlation between their respective accounts of hate crime by zip code ($n = 161$) is a remarkable 0.97. When citywide hate crime figures are analyzed on a monthly basis for the period January 1994–December 1995, the correlation between the two measures is 0.62 (Green et al., 2001).

The fact that different data sources paint a similar picture of cross-sectional and longitudinal variation within jurisdiction is grounds for more optimism than hate crime researchers are accustomed to showing. Before summarizing the descriptive literature, however, we hasten to point out that many forms of comparison remain problematic. One cannot, for example, compare victimization rates across target groups unless one is prepared to make the strong assumption that victims in both groups are equally likely to make their experiences known to reporting agencies, and that these agencies are equally assiduous about recording these events. Similarly, we must be skeptical when drawing inferences from the reported frequency with which hate crime takes the form of assault, vandalism, or threats, because different types of crime may have different likelihoods of being reported. Only in those rare cases where hate crime statistics are gathered using substantially different methodologies (e.g., police reports and probability surveys) can we begin to relax some of these concerns.

Descriptive Studies

Much of the hate crime literature centers on the frequency with which hate crime occurs. Many studies of gay and lesbian populations, for example, seek to describe the nature, frequency, and psychological repercussions of victimization. These researchers generally agree that criminal victimization and non-criminal harassment of gay men and lesbians are both widespread and underreported to authorities, and that the psychological correlates of victimization (including anger, anxiety, depression, and fear) are more severe and longer-lasting among victims of hate crime than among victims of non–bias-related incidents (Barnes & Ephross 1994; D'Augelli 1992; Herek et al., 1997, 1999; Hershberger & D'Augelli 1994; Otis & Skinner 1996).

As critics of this research note (Jacobs & Potter 1998), such studies rarely make use of probability samples, and to the extent that the data are gathered as part of a community event or by dissemination of the survey instrument through personal networks (D'Augelli 1992; Herek et al., 1997, 1999), respondents who have victimization experiences to report may be disproportionately likely to participate. Probability samples, however, suffer from measurement uncertainties of their own. In a few instances, random samples of the public have been asked whether they have been victimized or whether hate crimes have occurred in their county (*Los Angeles Times* Poll 1993a,b, Institute for Social Research 1995). The problem with these studies is that respondents are as likely to recall an event occurring during the past year as during the past five years, and younger respondents are significantly more likely than older respondents to report having been victimized at some time during their lives. A more effective measurement strategy may be to ask respondents to recall specific experiences with crime and then ask whether these crimes might have been motivated by bigotry (Bowling 1994; but see Herek et al., 1997).

In general, it is difficult to draw rigorous comparisons between hate crimes and corresponding conventional crimes. One of the rare efforts to compare the two systematically is Garofalo's (1991) study of police reports in New York City. Matching racially motivated hate crimes to conventional crimes of similar description committed on the same day, Garofalo found that hate crimes were more likely to involve multiple offenders and victims and to occur between strangers and in public places, and that both victims and perpetrators of racially motivated crimes were more often young and male than those in the matched set of non–bias-related crimes.

Broad comparisons between hate crime and conventional crime are complicated by the fact that different types of victims tend to report different types of crime to police (McDevitt et al., 2000). One of the more interesting and consistent patterns to emerge from official reports is illustrated by Illinois' summary of its hate crimes for 1997–1998. The state reports that 42% of the 368 antiblack hate crimes were assaults, compared with 32% of the anti-Jewish ($n = 38$) and 63% of the antigay/antilesbian incidents ($n = 117$) (Illinois State Police 1997, 1998). Whether hate crimes directed against gay/lesbian victims indeed are more likely to involve violence or whether factors that inhibit reporting in general (Comstock 1991; Herek et al., 1999) also censor reporting of nonviolent incidents remains an open research question.

Studies of Perpetrators

Biographies of individual criminals and ethnographies of racist groups and subcultures offer a reconstruction of the motives and circumstances, or morphology, of hate crimes. In the United States, urban ethnographers have described incidents of racial violence and tension in the context of local identity and status issues, thus lending credence to the defended-neighborhoods hypothesis (Rieder 1985; De Sena 1990). In a test of his domestic terrorism theory of hate crime, Hamm (1993, 1994b) conducted an original and daring ethnography of the nationwide neo-Nazi skinhead subculture by tracking down and securing interviews with 36 violent skinheads. For Germany, a large corpus of published interviews and in-depth biographical and social milieu studies exists (Erb 1993; Sichrovsky 1993; Engel & Menke 1995; Hopf et al., 1995; Ross 1996; Bitzan 1997; Müller 1997; Müller-Münch 1998). These studies tend to stress the arbitrary or accidental nature of involvement with a racist milieu; the importance of family dynamics, youth rebellion, and peergroup pressure; the absence of strong ideological commitment; and a resistance to formal organization. They thus echo the more compelling findings of a quantitative analysis of perpetrators of xenophobic crimes and violence, commissioned by the German Federal Ministry for Women and Youth (Willems et al., 1993). Based on 1398 police reports and 53 court decisions involving 148 suspects, this report concluded that the overwhelming majority of perpetrators were teenaged boys with relatively low scholastic achievement but not unemployed or from broken families or marginalized social milieux; that they had little ideological or political consciousness; that their criminal acts were collective but unplanned, arising from a group dynamic of drinking, listening to racist music, and discussing sensational media reports; and that they felt justified in their behavior by prevailing community and national attitudes toward foreigners. While neither representative of all the cases of German hate crime where no arrest was made (i.e., the overwhelming majority) nor specific enough to predict when and where more antiforeigner violence could erupt, these findings did cast doubt on arguments based on modernization and deprivation theories.

Similar conclusions emerge from other surveys of hate crime perpetrators. Green et al (1999) conducted a probability survey of North Carolina adults, with an oversample of names that had appeared in newspapers in connection with hate crimes. The 14 alleged perpetrators interviewed resembled other whites under age 40 in terms of their economic outlook and opinions on matters such as health care. The contrast between the two groups surfaced on questions involving intergroup mixing and cultural encroachment. Hate crime perpetrators were much more likely to endorse a ban on interracial marriage, express discomfort with rap music, and favor restrictions on immigration. Like Franklin (2000), who finds a connection between antipathy toward homosexuality and self-reports of violence directed against gay men in her survey of community college students, Green et al (1999) demonstrate a correlation between bigoted attitudes and behavior. These findings also suggest the importance of situational factors that go unobserved in surveys. Although their statistical analysis successfully distinguishes most hate crime perpetrators from ordinary citizens, based on attitudes, one sixth of their North Carolina sample fits the attitudinal profile of a hate crime perpetrator.

Attitudinal Studies

Lacking reliable data on hate crime, some scholars have chosen to study attitudes that strike them as correlates of bigoted conduct (Craig 1999; Craig & Waldo 1996). In Germany, a great deal of survey research has been conducted with young people, who are most prone to acts of xenophobic violence. The best known of these studies is the so-called Bielefeld study (Heitmeyer et al., 1992; see also Heitmeyer 1987, 1992) based on a panel study of over 1000 western German youths between 1985 and 1990. It debunks simplistic economic deprivation and competition explanations for extreme right-wing and violence-prone attitudes and instead attributes them to the dynamics of youth identity construction in a context of social disintegration. A nonrandom survey of 1177 eastern German youths in 18 schools in Thuringia arrived at a similar conclusion, though its authors note that the social profile of youths with extreme right-wing attitudes does not correspond to that of perpetrators of right-wing violence (Frindte et al., 1996; see also Hagan et al., 1995; Watts 1996).

Since negative stereotypes and feelings of out-group hostility are more wide-spread than criminal conduct expressing these thoughts and feelings, a large number of studies that purportedly explain hate crime at best supply a partial explanation for individual behavior. At the collective level, the climate of public opinion seems to be weakly associated with the overall rate of hate crime. According to Eurobarometer polling data, for example, Germany did indeed have a relatively high level of xenophobia in the early 1990s, but so did France (Halman 1994), with a rate of xenophobic violence four times lower by one estimate (Koopmans 1996, p. 193). Similarly, while Eastern Germans voice xenophobic opinions marginally more often than do Western Germans (Leenen 1995; Stöss & Niedermayer 1998), rates of xenophobic violence in the early 1990s in the East were easily double or triple those in the West (Sur 1993, Krueger & Pischke 1997). No studies of the United States have looked closely at the aggregate-level correlation between public opinion and hate crime. It is noteworthy that few opinion surveys find a correlation between respondents' tolerance and the racial composition of their cities, counties, and states (Sears et al., 1979; but see Taylor 2000; Fetzer 2000; Oliver & Wong 2000). The absence of a relationship runs counter to the findings of Green et al (1998b), which suggest a strong correlation between racial composition and hate crime. It may be that the units of analysis in these opinion studies are too large to detect this correlation, or it may turn out that the connection between hate crime and public opinion is undercut by the fact that frequently victimized groups tend to gravitate toward more tolerant settings in which to live and work.

Media Analyses

Precisely because it attracted such spectacular media attention, the German hate crime wave of the 1990s prompted the application of media content analysis to the empirical explanation of hate crime. Temporal peaks and troughs in hate crime incidents and the clustering of peaks around (and shortly after) spectacular events, such as the pogrom-like attacks on refugee hostels in Hoyerswerda (September 1991) and Rostock (August 1992), or the incendiary murders of Mölln (November 1992) and Solingen (May 1993), suggest that media coverage created a contagion of xenophobic violence if not a climate favorable to its initial outburst. Initial media coverage also influenced the number of subsequently reported incidents. On the basis of a content analysis of the two German national newspapers of reference, Brosius & Eps (1995) show that coverage of the four aforementioned events did shape and distort the media reporting of subsequent events, and several other quantitative time-series analyses demonstrate that both officially and journalistically reported incidents of xenophobic violence soared after key events and with a noticeable replication of types of violence (Quinkert & Jäger 1991; Leenen 1995; Esser & Brosius 1995, 1996; Koopmans 1996; Karapin 1998, 1999). Of these studies, Karapin (1996) comes closest to establishing a statistical link between politicians' hostile statements toward asylum seekers (as reported in the popular, conservative populistic *Bild Zeitung*) and subsequent upsurges in racist violence. The very complexity of the causal processes that these media content analyses purport to describe, however, means that they can at best establish some media responsibility for the propagation of xenophobic violence. They cannot isolate the causal weight of factors as divergent as the cultural meanings encoded in mediated messages and the social and psychological conditions of those who receive them and translate them into action.

Etiological Studies

Given the distortions associated with journalistic coverage, newspaper accounts may provide an inadequate database from which to construct longitudinal or cross-sectional measures of hate crime. Yet, if the alternative to faulty newspaper data is government data of arguably lesser quality, it seems sensible to see what journalistic reports suggest about the correlates of hate crime. For example, in the absence of official statistics disaggregated below the state level, Krueger & Pischke (1997) compiled a data set of 1056 antiforeigner incidents of varying types for 543 counties in Eastern and Western Germany, on the basis of reports in over 15 regional and national daily and weekly (but exclusively western) newspapers during the period from January 1991 to June 1993. Krueger & Pischke (1997, p. 206) report that "the incidence of anti-foreigner crime is unrelated to the unemployment rate in an area." If anything, their statistical results suggest that a significant negative association between unemployment rates and hate crime existed in Eastern Germany (1997, p. 201). With respect to demographic composition, Krueger & Pischke find a strong positive relationship between hate crime and size of the foreign proportion of the population in the East but not in the West. This regional contrast is suggestive given the political circumstances in which foreigners settled in the two regions. In December 1990, the newly unified German government initiated a policy whereby new applicants for asylum were settled in the East in proportion to the Eastern states' share of the total German population. Prior to that point, immigration patterns in East and West Germany had differed considerably, with foreign residents concentrated in the immigrant communities of the West. For the period covered by the Krueger & Pischke study, therefore, the settlement of foreigners in the East resembled something of a natural experiment, in which foreigners were settled exogenously by the government. It is telling that the sudden introduction of foreigners into the East was followed by an explosion of hate crime, particularly in areas where in-migration was most pronounced. Equally interesting, but beyond the scope of the Krueger & Pischke study, is the fact that hate crime declined, after asylum policy was made significantly more restrictive in 1993.

In-migration of outsiders plays a prominent role as well in the study by Green et al (1998b) of communities in New York City. Using the number of hate crimes reported to the police, census reports on demographic change, and unemployment statistics, Green et al report that crimes against Asians, Latinos, and blacks were most frequent in predominantly white areas that had experienced an in-migration of minorities. Consistent with the results of Krueger & Pischke, unemployment rates and other indicators of economic hardship did not correlate with hate crime, nor were there any apparent interactions between unemployment rates and other variables [see also Green & Rich (1998), which shows faint links between unemployment rates and cross burnings].

Evidence of macroeconomic effects becomes more mixed as we turn our attention to time-series analyses. The classic Hovland & Sears (1940) study, which discerned a correlation between lynching and both cotton prices and national economic conditions for the period 1883–1930, has been rejuvenated by scholarship that revisits this data. Using a more precise accounting of lynchings in the deep south, Tolnay & Beck (1995) find a statistical link between cotton prices and lynching, while Hepworth & West (1988), using more sophisticated econometric techniques, detect a link between lynchings and national economic conditions. These findings, however, have come under criticism by Green et al (1998a), who contend that these relationships are sensitive to seemingly innocuous modeling and sampling decisions. For example, when the data set is extended into the early years of the Depression, the relationship between lynching and economic conditions largely disappears.

Time-series analyses using contemporary data also show mixed evidence of economic effects. McLaren (1999) constructs a time-series analysis of official annual statistics on antiforeigner crime in Germany for the period 1971–1995. Using annual national unemployment and foreign population as predictors, she finds that unemployment correlated with hate crime only in interaction with an increase in foreign population. These findings contrast with the results reported by Green et al (1998a), who analyze the monthly unemployment rates and hate crime reports in New York City over a 9-year period. Green et al find no apparent link between macroeconomic fluctuations and hate crimes directed at Asians, Latinos, blacks, whites, gays/lesbians, or Jews. It remains unclear whether these contrasting findings arise from differences in setting, data quality, levels of aggregation, or the time period under consideration.

CONCLUSION

The dearth of hate crime research reflects both the newness of the topic and the difficulty of assembling reliable information. To a degree unusual in behavioral science, researchers are highly dependent on statistics compiled by government and watchdog organizations. The ambiguous and contested nature of hate crime means that these groups paint different pictures of who is victimized and with what frequency. In most jurisdictions, the effort expended to gather hate crime data is at best perfunctory. Thus, unlike the sociological investigation of conventional crime, the study of hate crime is not propelled by a steady stream of new data. Moreover, the absence of a data-gathering infrastructure means that when new developments occur, such as the surge in German hate crime in 1992, researchers are unable to track spatial and cross-temporal patterns. Ideally, hate crime data collection would be a continuous process that relies on multiple data sources, such as official reports, victimization surveys, and ethnographic investigation.

The study of hate crime would also profit from a clearer distinction between incidence and risk. Presently, research focuses almost entirely on incidence (the number of attacks of a given type that are directed against a certain type of victim). The literature pays relatively little attention to risk (the probability that a given behavior by a certain category of victim will result in a hate crime). For example, gay men are frequently attacked in relatively tolerant "gay neighborhoods" rather than in neighborhoods known to be hostile to them. Yet, the risk to men who hold hands in a hostile neighborhood is much greater. Following the lead of unobtrusive investigations of discrimination, studies of hate crime should endeavor to map the propensity for bigoted violence. As this is difficult and dangerous work, a useful starting point would be to examine reactions to undercover officers who, as part of their police work, pose as members of various victim groups. This behavior simulates a natural experiment in which potential hate crime perpetrators are confronted with exogenous intrusions into their environment.

Suggestions such as these may seem a bit outlandish, but it is difficult to imagine how the study of hate crime will progress without creative new approaches to data collection and research design. To date, research has largely been descriptive and exploratory. The challenge is to use the emergent hypotheses about encroachment, political discourse, and economic dislocation to guide the manner in which cases are sampled and studied. To what extent, and under what political conditions, did the severe economic downturn in Asia during the 1990s precipitate hate crime? How will the election of a right-wing government in Austria affect rates of hate crime in that country? How does immigration from the Caribbean, North Africa, and Southern Europe into a racially homogeneous and newly prosperous country such as Ireland affect its rates of hate crime? Only by capitalizing on these and other natural experiments can researchers hope to accumulate knowledge of wide applicability.

Finally, students of hate crime need to attend to the potential linkages to cognate topics, such as genocide, ethnic conflict, and discrimination. These topics overlap with hate crime. Genocide and ethnic civil war, for example, may be interpreted as extreme instances of hate crime. The topics coincide insofar as the orchestrated violence of genocide and ethnic warfare are accompanied by uncoordinated hate crime. The challenge before hate crime researchers is to demonstrate both conceptually and empirically how hate crimes differ from other manifestations of conflict. In what way are the causal forces that precipitate hate crime different from those that lead to other forms of bigoted conduct?

ACKNOWLEDGMENTS

The authors are grateful to the Institution for Social and Policy Studies at Yale University, which supported this reasearch.

Visit the Annual Reviews home page at www.AnnualReviews.org

LITERATURE CITED

Adorno TW, Frenkel-Brunswik E, Levinson DJ, Sanford RN. 1950. *The Authoritarian Personality*. New York: Harper & Row

Alber J. 1994. *Towards explaining anti-foreign violence in Germany. Work. Pap. No. 4.8.* Cambridge, MA: Minda de Gunzburg Ctr. Eur. Stud, Harvard Univ.

Allport GW. 1954. *The Nature of Prejudice.* Reading, MA: Addison-Wesley

Altmeyer B. 1981. *Right Wing Authoritarianism*. Winnipeg: Univ. Manitoba Press

Aronowitz A. 1994. A comparative study of hate crime: legislative, judicial, and social responses in Germany and the United States. *Eur. J. Crim. Policy Res.* 2/3:39–63

Barnes A, Ephross PH. 1994. The impact of hate violence on victims: emotional and behavioral responses to attacks. *Soc. Work* 39(3):247–51

Berk RA. 1990. Thinking about hate-motivated crimes. *J. Interpers. Violence* 5(3):334–49

Berrill KT, Herek GM. 1992. Primary and secondary victimization in anti-gay hate crimes: official response and public policy. See Herek & Berrill 1992, pp. 289–305

Bitzan R. 1997. *Rechte Frauen: Skingirls, Walküren und feine Damen.* Berlin: Elefanten

Boers K, Ewald U, Kerner HJ, Lautsch E,

Sessar K, eds. 1994. *Sozialer Umbruch und Kriminalität.* Bonn: Forum Verlag Godesberg

Böhnisch L, Winter R. 1993. *Männliche Sozialisation: Bewältigungsprobleme männlicher Geschlechtsidentität in Lebenslauf.* Munich: Juventa

Bowling B. 1993. Racial harassment and the process of victimization: conceptual and methodological implications for the local crime survey. *Br. J. Criminol.* 33(2): 231–50

Bowling B. 1994. Racial harassment in East London. See Hamm 1994a, pp. 1–36

Boyd EA, Berk RA, Hamner KM. 1996. "Motivated by hatred or prejudice": categorization of hate-motivated crimes in two police divisions. *Law Soc. Rev.* 30(4):819–50

Brosius HB, Eps P. 1995. Prototyping through key events: news selection in the case of violence against aliens and asylum seekers in Germany. *Eur. J. Commun.* 10(3):391–412

Chapin WD. 1997. Ausländer raus? The empirical relationship between immigration and crime in Germany. *Soc. Sci. Q.* 78(2):543–58

Comstock GD. 1991. *Violence Against Lesbians and Gay Men.* New York: Columbia Univ. Press

Craig KM. 1999. Retaliation, fear, or rage: an

investigation of African-American and white reactions to racist hate crimes. *J. Interpers. Violence* 14(2):138–51

Craig KM, Waldo CR. 1996. "So, what's a hate crime anyway?": Young adults' perceptions of hate crimes, victims, and perpetrators. *Law Hum. Behav.* 20(2):113–29

Crosby F, Bromley S, Saxe L. 1980. Recent unobtrusive studies of black and white discrimination and prejudice: a literature review. *Psychol. Bull.* 87(3):546–63

D'Augelli AR. 1992. Lesbian and gay male undergraduates' experiences of harassment and fear on campus. *J. Interpers. Violence* 7(3):383–95

De Sena JN. 1990. *Protecting One's Turf: Social Strategies for Maintaining Urban Neighborhoods.* Lanham, MD: Univ. Press Am.

Durkheim É. 1951 (1897). *Suicide.* Transl. JA Spaulding, G Simpson. New York: Free Press

Engel M, Menke B. 1995. *Weibliche Lebenswelten, gewaltlos?* Münster: Agenda Verlag

Erb R. 1993. Ausländerfeindschaft und Jugend(gruppen)gewalt in den neuen Bundesländern. *Int. Schulb.forsch.* 15:105–20

Esser F, Brosius HB. 1995. *Eskalation durch Berichterstattung? Massenmedien und fremdenfeindliche Gewalt.* Wiesbaden: Westdeutscher

Esser F, Brosius HB. 1996. Television as arsonist? The spread of right-wing violence in Germany. *Eur. J. Commun.* 11(2):235–60

Esses VM, Jackson LM, Armstrong TL. 1998. Intergroup competition and attitudes toward immigrants and immigration: an instrumental model of group conflict. *J. Soc. Issue* 54(4):699–724

Fazio RH, Jackson JR, Dunton BC, Williams CJ. 1995. Variability in automatic activation as an unobtrusive measure of racial attitudes: a bona fide pipeline. *J. Pers. Soc. Psychol.* 69(6):1013–27

Fetzer JS. 2000. *Public Attitudes Toward Immigration in the United States, France, and Germany.* Cambridge, UK: Cambridge Univ. Press

Finkelman P, ed. 1992. *Lynching, Racial Violence, and Law.* New York: Garland

Fix M, Struyk RJ, eds. 1993. *Clear and Convincing Evidence: Measurement of Discrimination in America.* Washington, DC: Urban Inst. Press

Franklin K. 2000. Antigay behaviors among young adults: prevalence, patterns, and motivators in a noncriminal population. *J. Interpers. Violence* 15(4):339–62

Frindte W, Funke F, Waldzus S. 1996. Xenophobia and right-wing extremism in German youth groups: some evidence against unidimensional misinterpretations. *Int. J. Intercult. Relat.* 20(3/4):463–78

Garofalo J. 1991. Racially motivated crimes in New York City. In *Race and Criminal Justice*, ed. MJ Lynch, EB Patterson, pp. 161–73. New York: Harrow & Heston

Grattet R, Jenness V, Curry TR. 1998. The homogenization and differentiation of hate crime law in the United States, 1978 to 1995: innovation and diffusion in the criminalization of bigotry. *Am. Sociol. Rev.* 63(2):286–307

Green DP, Abelson RP, Garnett M. 1999. The distinctive political views of hate-crime perpetrators and white supremacists. In *Cultural Divides: Understanding and Overcoming Group Conflict*, ed. DA Prentice, DT Miller, pp. 429–64. New York: Russell Sage Found.

Green DP, Glaser J, Rich A. 1998a. From lynching to gay bashing: the elusive connection between economic conditions and hate crime. *J. Pers. Soc. Psychol.* 75(1):82–92

Green DP, Rich A. 1998. White supremacist activity and crossburnings in North Carolina. *J. Quant. Criminol.* 14(3):263–82

Green DP, Strolovitch DZ, Wong JS. 1998b. Defended neighborhoods, integration, and racially motivated crime. *Am. J. Sociol.* 104(2):372–403

Green DP, Strolovitch DZ, Wong JS, Bailey R. 2001. Measuring gay population density and the incidence of anti-gay hate crime. *Soc. Sci. Q.* 82(2) In press

Greenspan L, Levitt C, eds. 1993. *Under the Shadow of Weimar: Democracy, Law, and*

Racial Incitement in Six Countries. Westport: Preager

Habermas J. 1990. *Die nachholende Revolution.* Frankfurt: Suhrkamp

Hagan J, Merkens H, Boehnke K. 1995. Delinquency and disdain: social capital and the control of right-wing extremism among East and West Berlin youth. *Am. J. Sociol.* 100(4):1028–52

Haider-Markel DP, Meier KJ. 1996. The politics of gay and lesbian rights: expanding the scope of the conflict. *J. Polit.* 58(2):332–49

Halman L. 1994. Variation in tolerance levels in Europe: evidence from the Eurobarometers and European Values Study. *Eur. J. Crim. Policy Res.* 2/3:15–38

Hamm MS. 1993. *American Skinheads: The Criminology and Control of Hate Crime.* Westport: Praeger

Hamm MS, ed. 1994a. *Hate Crime: International Perspectives on Causes and Control.* Cincinnati, OH: Anderson

Hamm MS. 1994b. A modified social control theory of terrorism: an empirical and ethnographic assessment of the American neo-Nazi skinheads. See Hamm 1994a, pp. 105–49

Hamm MS. 1994c. Conceptualizing hate crime in a global context. See Hamm 1994a, pp. 173–94

Heitmeyer W. 1987. *Rechtsextremistische Orientierungen bei Jugendlichen: Empirische Ergebnisse und Erklärungsmuster einer Untersuchung zur politischen Sozialisation.* Weinheim: Juventa

Heitmeyer W. 1992. *Rechtsextremistische Orientierungen bei Jungendlichen: Empirische Ergebnisse und Erklärungsmuster einer Untersuchung zur politischen Sozialisation.* Weinheim: Juventa. 2nd ed.

Heitmeyer W, Buhse H, Liebe-Freund J. 1992. *Die Bielefelder Rechtsextremismus- Studie: Erste Langzeituntersuchung zur politischen Sozialisation männlicher Jugendlicher.* Weinheim: Juventa

Hepworth JT, West SG. 1988. Lynchings and the economy: a time-series reanalysis of Hovland and Sears (1940). *J. Pers. Soc. Psychol.* 55(2):239–47

Herek GM. 1992. Psychological heterosexism and anti-gay violence: the social psychology of bigotry and bashing. See Herek & Berrill 1992, pp. 149–69

Herek GM, Berrill KT, eds. 1992. *Hate Crimes: Confronting Violence Against Lesbians and Gay Men.* Newbury Park, CA: Sage

Herek GM, Gillis JR, Cogan JC. 1999. Psychological sequelae of hate-crime victimization among lesbian, gay, and bisexual adults. *J. Consult. Clin. Psychol.* 67(6):945–51

Herek GM, Gillis JR, Cogan JC, Glunt EK. 1997. Hate crime victimization among lesbian, gay, and bisexual adults. *J. Interpers. Violence* 12(2):195–215

Hershberger SL, D'Augelli AR. 1994. The impact of victimization on the mental health and suicidality of lesbian, gay, and bisexual youths. *Dev. Psychol.* 31(1):65–74

Hess H. 1997. Skins, Stigmata und Strafrecht. *Kriminol. J.* 29:38–51

Hopf C, Rieker P, Sanden-Marcus M, Schmidt C. 1995. *Familie und Rechtsextremismus: Familiale Sozialisation und rechtsextreme Orientierungen junger Männer.* Weinheim: Juventa

Horowitz DL. 1985. *Ethnic Groups in Conflict.* Berkeley: Univ. Calif. Press

Horowitz DL. 2001. *The Deadly Ethnic Riot.* Berkeley: Univ. Calif. Press

Hovland CI, Sears RR. 1940. Minor studies of aggression: VI. Correlation of lynchings with economic indices. *J. Psychol.* 9:301–10

Hurwitz J, Peffley M, eds. 1998. *Perception and Prejudice: Race and Politics in the United States.* New Haven, CT: Yale Univ. Press

Illinois State Police. 1997. *Crime in Illinois 1997.* Springfield, IL: Illinois State Police, Div. Admin., Crime Stud. Sect

Illinois State Police. 1998. *Crime in Illinois 1998.* Springfield, IL: Illinois State Police, Div. Admin., Crime Stud. Sect

Institute for Social Research. 1995. *The Carolina Poll of the School of Journalism and the Institute for Research in the Social Sciences, Fall 1995.* Chapel Hill: Univ. NC Press

Ireland PR. 1997. Socialism, unification policy and the rise of racism in eastern Germany. *Int. Migr. Rev.* 31(3):541–68

Jacobs JB, Heney JS. 1996. The social construction of a hate crime epidemic. *J. Crim. Law* 86(2):366–91

Jacobs JB, Potter KA. 1998. *Hate Crimes: Criminal Law and Identity Politics*. New York: Cambridge Univ. Press

Jäger S, Kretschmer D. 1998. Die Medien als Anstifter der Brandstifter? Völkischer Nationalismus in den Medien. In *Der Spuk ist nicht vorbei: Völkisch-nationalistische Ideologeme im öffentlichen Diskurs der Gegenwart*, ed. S Jäger, pp. 120–213. Duisburg, Ger.: Duisburger Inst. Sprach- & Sozialforschung

Jelpke U. 1993. *Über den schonenden Umgang der Bundesregierung mit dem Rechtsextremismus*. Bonn: Partei Demokrat. Sozial.

Jenness V. 1999. Managing differences and making legislation: social movements and the racialization, sexualization, and gendering of federal hate crime law in the US, 1985–1998. *Soc. Probl.* 46(4):548–71

Jenness V, Broad K. 1997. *Hate Crimes: New Social Movements and the Politics of Violence*. New York: Gruyter

Karapin R. 1996. *Explaining the surge in rightwing violence by German youth*. Manuscript. New York: Hunter College. Unpubl. ms

Karapin R. 1998. Radical right-wing populism in Western Europe. *Compar. Polit.* 30(2):213–34

Karapin R. 1999. The politics of immigration control in Britain and Germany: subnational politicians and social movements. *Compar. Polit.* 31(4):423–44

Kleg M. 1993. *Hate Prejudice and Racism*. Albany: State Univ. NY Press

Koopmans R. 1996. Explaining the rise of racist and extreme right violence in Western Europe: grievances or opportunities? *Eur. J. Polit. Res.* 30:185–216

Krell G, Nicklas H, Ostermann Ä. 1996. Immigration, asylum, and anti-foreigner violence in Germany. *J. Peace Res.* 33(2):153–70

Kremer J, Barry R, McNally A. 1986. The mis-directed letter and the quasi-questionnaire: unobtrusive measures of prejudice in Northern Ireland. *J. Appl. Soc. Psychol.* 16(4):303–9

Krueger AB, Pischke J. 1997. A statistical analysis of crime against foreigners in Germany. *J. Hum. Resour.* 32:182–209

Lawrence F. 1999. *Punishing Hate: Bias Crimes under American Law*. Cambridge, MA: Harvard Univ. Press

Leenen WR. 1995. Ausländerfeindlichkeit und politische Öffentlichkeit. *Deutsch. Arch.* 28(6):603–24

Legge JS. 1996. An economic theory of Antisemitism? Exploring attitudes in the new German state. *Polit. Res. Q.* 49(3):617–30

Levin J, McDevitt J. 1993. *Hate Crime: The Rising Tide of Bigotry and Bloodshed*. New York: Plenum

LeVine RA, Campbell DT. 1972. *Ethnocentrism: Theories of Conflict, Ethnic Attitudes, and Group Behavior*. New York: Wiley

Los Angeles County Comm. Hum. Relat. 1990. *Hate Crime in the 1980s: A Decade of Bigotry. Rep. LA County Board Supervisors*. Los Angeles: LA County Comm. Hum. Relat.

Los Angeles Times Poll. 1993a. Asians in Southern California. No. 318, conducted Aug 7–10. At http://www.latimes.com/news/timespoll/stats/pdfs/318ss.pdf

Los Angeles Times Poll. 1993b. Orange County immigration and race relations. No. 319, conducted Aug. 12–15. At http://www.latimes.com/news/timespoll/stats/pdfs/319ss.pdf

Maaz HJ. 1991. *Der Gefühlsstau: Ein Psychogramm der DDR*. Berlin: Argon

McDevitt J, Balboni JM, Bennett S, Weiss JC, Orchowsky S, Walbolt L. 2000. *Improving the Quality and Accuracy of Bias Crime Statistics Nationally: An Assessment of the First Ten Years of Bias Crime Data Collection*. Washington, DC: Bur. Just. Stat.

McFalls LH. 1997. Living with which past? Postwall, postwar German national identity. In *A User's Guide to German Cultural Studies*, ed. S Denham, I Kacandes, J Petropoulos, pp. 297–308. Ann Arbor: Univ. Mich. Press

McLaren LM. 1999. Explaining right-wing violence in Germany: a time series analysis. *Soc. Sci. Q.* 80(1):166–80

Merkl P, Weinberg L, eds. 1997. *The Revival of Right-Wing Extremism in the 1990s*. London: Cass

Modena E. 1998. *Das Faschismus-Syndrom. Zur Psychoanalyse der neuen Rechten*. Giessen, Ger.: Psychosozial-Verlag

Müller J. 1997. *Täterprofile. Hintergründe rechtsextremistisch motivierter Gewalt*. Vienna: Deutscher Univ.verlag

Müller-Münch I. 1998. *Biedermänner und Brandstifter*. Bonn: Dietz

Oliver E, Wong J. 2000. *Racial context and inter-group prejudice in a multi-ethnic setting*. Princeton, NJ : Princeton Univ. Unpubl. ms

Olzak S. 1989. Labor unrest, immigration, and ethnic conflict in urban America, 1880–1914. *Am. J. Sociol.* 94:1303–33

Otis MD, Skinner WF. 1996. The prevalence of victimization and its effect on mental wellbeing among lesbian and gay people. *J. Homosex.* 30(3):93–121

Pincus FL, Ehrlich HJ, eds. 1994. *Race and Ethnic Conflict: Contending Views on Prejudice, Discrimination and Ethnoviolence*. Boulder, CO: Westview

Pinderhughes H. 1993. The anatomy of racially motivated violence in New York City: a case study of youth in Southern Brooklyn. *Soc. Probl.* 40:478–92

Prowe D. 1997. National identity and racial nationalism in the new Germany: Nazism versus the contemporary radical right. *Ger. Polit. Soc.* 15(1):1–21

Quinkert A, Jäger S. 1991. *Warum dieser Hass in Hoyerswerda? Die rassistische Hetze von BILD gegen Flüchtlinge im Herbst '91. DISS-Skript, No. 4*. Duisburg, Ger.: Duisburger Inst. Sprach- & Sozialforschung

Raper A. 1933. *The Tragedy of Lynching*. Chapel Hill: Univ. NC Press

Rieder J. 1985. *Canarsie: The Jews and Italians of Brooklyn Against Liberalism*. Cambridge, MA: Harvard Univ. Press

Rieker P. 1997. *Ethnozentrismus bei jungen Männern*. Weinheim: Juventa

Roberts J. 1995. *Les Crimes Motivés par la Haine au Canada. Dep. Just. Work. Doc. WD1995-11f*. Ottawa: Gov. Canada

Ross C. 1996. *Mordskameradschaft: Tim, unter Skinheads geraten*. Munich: Bertelsmann

Ross JI. 1992. Contemporary radical right-wing violence in Canada: a quantitative analysis. *Terrorism Polit. Violence* 4(3):72–101

Ross JI. 1994. Hate crime in Canada: growing pains with new legislation. See Hamm 1994a, pp. 151–72

Scheffer B. 1997. *Medien und Fremdenfeindlichkeit*. Opladen: Leske & Budrich

Sears DO, Hensler CP, Speer LK. 1979. Whites' opposition to "busing": self-interest or symbolic politics? *Am. Polit. Sci. Rev.* 73:369–84

Sears DO, Sidanius J, Bobo L, eds. 2000. *Racialized Politics: The Debate about Racism in America*. Chicago: Univ. Chicago Press

Sharma Y. 1999. "East made racists" claim. *Times Educ. Suppl.* 4319:16

Sichrovsky P. 1993. *Unheilbar deutsch. Rechte Schicksale und Lebensläufe*. Cologne: Kiepenheuer & Witsch

Stöss R, Niedermayer O. 1998. *Rechtsextremismus, politische Unzufriedenheit und das Wählerpotential rechtsextremer Parteien in der Bundesrepublik im Frühsommer 1998. Work. Pap. No. 1*. Berlin: Otto-Stammer-Zentrum, Freie Univ.

Sur É. 1993. A propos de l'extréme-droite en Allemagne. *Hérodote* 68:18–40

Suttles GD. 1972. *The Social Construction of Communities*. Chicago: Univ. Chicago Press

Taylor MC. 2000. The significance of racial context. See Sears et al 2000, pp. 118–36

Taylor N, ed. 1991. *Bias Crime: The Law Enforcement Response to Bias-Motivated Crimes*. Chicago: Off. Int. Crim. Just.

Thränhardt D. 1995. The political uses of xenophobia in England, France and Germany. *Party Polit.* 1(3):323–45

Tolnay SE, Beck EM. 1995. *A Festival of*

Violence: An Analysis of Southern Lynchings, 1882–1930. Urbana: Univ. Ill. Press

Tuttle D. 1994. The assimilation of East Germany and the rise of identity-based violence against foreigners in the unified German state. *Ger. Polit. Soc.* 31:63–83

von Trotha T. 1995. Political culture, xenophobia and the development of the violence of the radical right in the Federal Republic of Germany. *Crime Law Soc. Change* 24:37–47

Wahl P. 1997. "Wenn die Jungs mal loslegen": Anmerkungen zur Cliquen-Dynamik. In *Jahrbuch für Rechts- und Kriminalsoziologie '96*, ed. J Kersten, H Steinert, pp. 77–84. Baden-Baden: Nomos Verl. ges.

Wang L. 1994. *Hate Crime Laws*. New York: Clark, Boardman, Callaghan

Watts M. 1996. Political xenophobia in the transition from socialism: threat, racism and ideology among East German youth. *Polit. Psychol.* 17(1):97–126

Weiss HJ. 1993. *Gewalt von Rechts, (k)ein Fernsehthema*. Opladen, Ger.: Leske & Budrich

Weitekamp EGM, Kerner HJ, Herberger SM. 1996. *Right-wing violence, xenophobia, and attitudes towards violence in Germany*. Presented at Int. Study Group on Youth Violence and Control Conference, Minerva Cent. for Youth Policy, Haifa, Israel.

Willems H. 1995. Development, patterns and causes of violence against foreigners in Germany. *Terrorism Polit. Violence* 7(1):162–81

Willems H, Würtz S, Eckert R. 1993. *Fremdenfeindliche Gewalt: Eine Analyse von Täterstrukturen und Eskalationsprozessen. Res. Rep. Fed. Minist. Women and Youth*. Bonn: Gov. Fed. Rep. Ger.

Subject Index

A

"Abeyance structures"
during periods of limited
political opportunities,
297
ABF
See American Bar
Foundation
Ability-based homophily,
428–29
Access
to the evolving Internet,
equalizing, 328
Activists
identity in tactical choices
made by, 292–96
Adolescence
risk of victimization
peaking in, 4–5
Advertising
portrayal of athletes, by
race, 195–96
African-American
sociological thought
early traditions of, 445–77
incorporation into
American sociology,
460–63
African-American
sociologists
Barnett, Ida Wells, 449–50
calling of, 446–48
Cayton, Horace, 464–65
contributors to the early
tradition, 455–60
Cooper, Anna Julia,
448–49
Cox, Oliver C., 469
Doyle, Bertram, 467–68
Drake, St. Claire, 464–65
DuBois, W.E.B., 450–55

empirical, methodological,
and theoretical
contributions of second-
wave, 463–70
Frazier, E. Franklin, 464
Johnson, Charles, 465–69
progenitors of the early
tradition, 448–55
second wave of the early
tradition, 455–60
African Census Analysis
Project, 182
Africans
being granted religions,
128
Age-based homophily,
424–25
Agency
and authenticity, 69–70
implications of
victimization for an
individual's sense of,
11–12
Agribusiness
Jeffersonian populism in
views of, 112–13
Agricultural development
Marxian theory of, 107
Agricultural transition
conceptual explanations
for, 110–13
and households, 115–18
and its effects on
communities, 113–15
in twentieth century US,
103–24
Alcohol dependence
increased in victims of
violence, 7–8
Alexander, Jeffrey, 131–32,
142

theory of civil society, 126,
146–49
Algeria
Islamic Salvation Front,
134
Alliances
See Limitation of political
alliances model
Ambiguous concepts and
measures
literature on child health
and fertility using, 166–67
of SES and class, 163
America-centered theory and
research, 222–26
capitalists and the
development of social
policy, 223–24
democratic polities and
practices, 226–27
patronage-oriented
political parties, 225–26
race and U.S. social policy,
222–23
role of public opinion,
224–25
social movements and
interest groups, 223
American Bar Foundation
(ABF), 339
American civil rights
movement, 284
American fundamentalist
religion, 134
American Revolution
and "the Great
Awakening," 129–30
Animal husbandry
totalitarianism in, 60
Animals
constructing

505

CUMULATIVE INDEXES

CONTRIBUTING AUTHORS, VOLUMES 1–27

CHAPTER TITLES, VOLUMES 1–27

Prefatory

Theory and Methods

Social Processes

Institutions and Culture

Formal Organizations

Political and Economic Sociology

Differentiation and Stratification

Individual and Society

Demography

Urban and Rural Community Sociology

Policy

Historical Sociology

Sociology of World Regions

Bicentennial Articles

Special Supplement: Reflections on Sociology in the 21st Century